KU-621-990

EPISTLE DEDICATORY

**To my wife, Loraine, and
my son, Joey -**

On account.

David Kent

THE NEWSPAPERS

In order to obtain wide, balanced coverage of the Borden murders, the editor's research utilizes clippings from the following newspapers, many now extinct. This preservation of the writings and drawings of their unknown reporters and artists can be the only thanks to these papers:

The Baltimore Sun
The Boston Advertiser
The Boston Enterprise
The Boston Globe
The Boston Herald
The Boston Post
The Boston Record
The Brockton Enterprise
The Concord Patriot
The Dover Democrat
The Fall River Globe
The Fall River Herald
The Holyoke Democrat
The Lewiston Journal
The Lowell Times
The Milton News
The New Bedford Journal
The New Bedford Mercury
The New London Day
The New London Telegraph
The New York Herald
The New York Journal
The New York Press
The New York Recorder
The New York Telegram
The New York Times
The New York Tribune
The New York World
The Newport Herald
The Newport News
The Newport Observer
The Pawtucket Times
The Philadelphia Record
The Portland Express
The Providence Journal
The Providence News
The San Francisco Examiner
The Springfield Union
The Taunton News
The Taunton Gazette
The Woonsocket Call
The Worcester Spy
The Worcester Telegram

THE PARTICULARS

PREFACE

The Borden murders are to the United States what the Jack the Ripper murders are to England. They are the two most celebrated, investigated and unsolved mysteries in the annals of crime. Millions of words have been written by scores of authors about each case, yet we are no nearer to deciphering either than we were a century ago.

Theories have been advanced that "Jack" was a member of the royal household, or that he was a prominent London physician, or that he was a famous actor, or even that he was a member of the police contingent relentlessly tracking him, or a butcher by trade with a foreign accent or a number of others. One may be correct or all may be wrong.

There is one pivotal difference between the Ripper murders and the Borden tragedy. There is no question that Jack, whoever he was, was the murderer stalking London's East End slums. In the Borden misadventure, even after a hundred years of microscopic examination, there is no agreement among the masters of crime as to who it was who wielded the hatchet that dispatched Andrew and Abby Borden to premature graves. Popular conception is guided by the ancient doggerel that says Lizzie Borden, youngest daughter of Andrew, took an axe to them, but just as every shred of evidence indicates this to be true, those same shreds prove she did not; could not.

The Borden mystery is thus pristinely unique in the archives of mayhem, set apart from all other murders wherein the question is only whether X did it, or was it Y or Z. The contradictions in the evidence have nagged aficionados since the fourth day of August in 1892.

Just as virtually all authors who have written about the Ripper have had a theory to sell, so has it been with the Borden enigma. So much has been written about the "Fall River Tragedy", so much have the facts been tortured to conform to the preconceived notions of the authors, that the simple truths of both the investigation and the subsequent trial of Lizzie are obscured under layers of myths and legends.

One reason Lizzie was despised, legend has it, was because she was so disdainful of the double tragedy she did not even wear mourning black to the funeral. The truth is that she **did** wear black and, in this book is a detailed description of her attire written by a female reporter who stood within touching distance from her that day.

Any one at all familiar with the story will tell you Lizzie was a stocky, broad-shouldered hulk of a woman, obese and odious in appearance. Read herein the descriptions written by reporters who knew her to be five-feet three-inches and 130 pounds.

If you are familiar with the legend that she never displayed an emotion from the time the bodies of her father and stepmother were found until the jury pronounced her innocent, you will be enlightened by the eye-witness accounts of tears, times of prostration and anguish.

It is common lore that Lizzie nursed a murderous hatred of her stepmother. The evidence, sworn to in court by the two people sure to be aware of it, tells of the true relationship.

It is clear that each of the passing hundred years has added yet another layer of legend upon the old. The truth lies, not in today, but in the years 1892 and 1893, before ambitious writers and gossipers reshaped the simple story of a complex event.

In the main, the newspaper reporters assigned to cover the news of the murders, the hasty week of investigation, the preliminary hearing and the resulting trial of Lizzie, reflected the opinion of their editors much as they do today. Reporters with a liberal bent do not work for conservative newspapers, nor is the opposite true. Some newspapers, notably the Fall River Globe, were virulent in their opinion Lizzie was guilty of the ghastly murder of her father and stepmother. Others, notably the New York Times, from a distance, and the Boston Advertiser, closer to the scene, reported without pronounced bias. The Boston Globe was reserved in its coverage, with the exception of the irresponsible "Trickey Affair" explored later in this book.

It being vital to establish a balance of reporting, each of the consequential developments is chronicled here by more than one report. Many of these reproduced clippings contain inaccuracies which have not been corrrected. They were occasioned usually by speculation; sometimes by carelessness on the part of the reporter. No attempt has been made to point them out.

Most of the news clippings and photographs, particularly those delineating the trial, come from a scrapbook compiled by William Emery, who reported for the New Bedford Evening Journal. This essential journal of more than 150 scrapbook-pages miraculously survived the century and is now the crown jewel in the collection of Lizzie memorabilia owned by Robert A. Flynn of Flynn Books, Portland, Maine, generally acknowledged the Chairman of the Board of Lizzie buffs. I am indebted to him for unrestricted use of that cornucopia of material and for his diligence in compiling the bibliography. Those clippings covering the murder, the investigation, preliminary hearing and the events up to the date of the trial are from the editior's personal collection compiled in an equal-size scrapbook. The archives of the Fall River Historical Society provided the remainder and it is to the Society that the editor owes the most substantial thanks.

Reproducing these clippings, brown and brittle from age, presented formidable obstacles and the results are not always perfect. Some had to be computer enhanced;

most required retouching with an artist's brush. In some instances where restoration was not possible and when neither microfilm nor original issues were satisfactory, stories have been re-typed. Only in rare instances have any been edited, but when their sometimes extraordinary length necessitated it, it was done with caution and with an eye toward preserving the writer's intent.

Photographs were virtually unknown in newspapers of 1892. The only illustrations expected by the readers were line drawings and those accompanying only the major stories. They are reproduced here not only because of their worth in depicting the story but because they add a 19th century flavor essential to the unvarnished recreation of the atmosphere.

Particular Two contains the unabridged text of Lizzie's testimony given at the so-called inquest following the murders. Because the Superior court ruled it inadmissable at her trial, it did not, therefore, become a part of that record. It is, however, part of the legend. Many maintain that, had it been admissable, the outcome of the trial would have been different. Prosecutor Knowlton even referred to it as "her confession". It is left to the reader to determine what, if anything, her testimony revealed that indicated her guilt, other than insignificant instances when her remembrance of events varied from the recollections of Bridget, the servant girl. Significantly, it provides the only extant study of Lizzie Borden through her own words and is a fascinating glimpse of her complete competence under stress.

The entire justification of this book rests upon an unbiased presentation of the Borden murder story and in the following pages there will be no attempt to persuade you of Lizzie's innocence or guilt.

For the first time, you will be able to study this eternally mystifying case as it unfolded day by day in Victorian New England. It is doubtful that you will be able to solve the tormenting puzzle, but when you have turned the last page, you will, at least, be one of the select group of Lizzie buffs able to spot the four inacuracies in the ageless bit of doggerel which tormented her while she was alive and is still heard today wherever innocent children skip rope while chanting:

Lizzie Borden took an axe
and gave her mother forty whacks.
And when she saw what she had done...
She gave her father forty-one!

David Kent

Shreveport, Louisiana - 1992

PARTICULAR ONE

THE MURDERS AND THE INVESTIGATION

The Fall River Herald

SHOCKING CRIME.

A Venerable Citizen and His Aged Wife

HACKED TO PIECES AT THEIR HOME.

Mr. and Mrs. Andrew Borden Lose Their Lives

AT THE HANDS OF A DRUNKEN FARM HAND.

Police Searching Actively for the Fiendish Murderer.

The community was terribly shocked this morning to hear that an aged man and his wife had fallen victims to the thirst of a murderer, and that an atrocious deed had been committed. The news spread like wildfire and hundreds poured into Second street. The deed was committed at No. 62 Second street, where for years Andrew J. Borden and his wife had lived in happiness.

It is supposed that an axe was the instrument used, as the bodies of the victims are hacked almost beyond recognition. Since the discovery of the deed the street in front of the house has been blocked by an anxious throng, eagerly waiting for the news of the awful tragedy and vowing vengeance on the assassin.

"FATHER IS STABBED."

The first intimation the neighbors had of the awful crime was a groaning followed by a cry of "murder!" Mrs. Adelaide Churchill, who lives next door to the Bordens, ran over and heard Miss Borden cry: "Father is stabbed; run for the police!"

Mrs. Churchill hurried across the way to the livery stable to get the people there to summon the police John Cunningham, who was passing, learned of the murder and telephoned to police headquarters, and Officer Allen was sent to investigate the case.

Meanwhile the story spread rapidly and a crowd gathered quickly. A HERALD reporter entered the house, and a terrible sight met his view. On the lounge in the cosy sitting room on the first floor of the building lay Andrew J. Borden, dead. His face presented a sickening sight. Over the left temple a wound six by four had been made as if the head had been pounded with the dull edge of an axe. The left eye had been dug out and a cut extended the length of the nose. The face was hacked to pieces and the blood had covered the man's shirt and soaked into his clothing. Everything about the room was in order, and there were no signs of a scuffle of any kind.

SEVEN WOUNDS.

Upstairs, in a neat chamber in the northwest corner of the house, another terrible sight met the view. On the floor between the bed and the dressing case lay Mrs. Borden, stretched full length, one arm extended and her face resting upon it. Over the left temple the skull was fractured and no less than seven wounds were found about the head. She had died, evidently where she had been struck, for her life blood formed a ghastly clot on the carpet.

Dr. Bowen was the first physician to arrive, but life was extinct, and from the nature of the wounds it is probable that the suffering of both victims was very short. The police were promptly on hand and strangers were kept at a distance. Miss Borden was so overcome by the awful circumstances that she could not be seen, and kind friends led her away and cared for her.

A squad of police who had arrived conducted a careful hunt over the premises for trace of the assailant. No weapon was found and there was nothing about the house to indicate who the murderer might have been. A clue was obtained, however. A Portuguese whose name nobody around the house seemed to know, has been employed on one of the Swansey farms owned by Mr. Borden. About 9 o'clock this man went to the house and asked to see Mr. Borden. He had a talk with his employer and asked for the wages due him. Mr. Borden told the man he had no money with him, to call later. If anything more passed between the men it cannot be learned. At length the Portuguese departed and Mr. Borden soon afterward started down town. His first call was to Peter Leduc's barber shop, where he was shaved about 9:30 o'clock. He then dropped into the Union bank to transact some business and talked with Mr. Hart, treasurer of the savings bank, of which Mr. Borden was president. As nearly as can be learned after that he went straight home. He took off his coat and composed himself comfortably on the lounge to sleep. It is presumed, from the easy attitude in which his body lay, that he was asleep when the deadly blow was struck. It is thought that Mrs. Borden was in the room at the time, but was so overcome by the assault that she had no strength to make an outcry. In her bewilderment, she rushed upstairs and went into her room. She must have been followed up the stairs by the murderer, and as she was retreating into the furthest corner of the room, she was felled by the deadly axe.

MISS BORDEN ATTRACTED.

The heavy fall and a subdued groaning attracted Miss Borden into the house. There the terrible sight which has been described met her gaze. She rushed to the staircase and called the servant, who was washing a window in her room on the third floor. So noislessly had the deed been done that neither of them was aware of the bloody work going on so near them.

To a police officer, Miss Borden said she was at work in the barn about 10 o'clock. On her return she found her father in the sitting room with a horrible gash in the side of his head. He appeared at the time as though he had been bit while in a sitting posture. Giving the alarm, she rushed up stairs to find her mother, only to be more horrified to find that person lying between the dressing case and the bed

THE CROWD GATHERED AT 92 SECOND STREET

sweltering in a pool of blood. It appeared as though Mrs. Borden had seen the man enter, and the man, knowing that his dastardly crime would be discovered, had followed her upstairs and finished his fiendish work. It was a well known fact that Mrs. Borden always left the room when her husband was talking business with anyone. A person knowing this fact could easily spring upon his victim without giving her a chance to make an outcry. Miss Borden had seen no person enter or leave the place. The man who had charge of her father's farm was held in the highest respect by Mr. Borden. His name was Alfred Johnson, and he trusted his employer so much that he left his bank book at Mr. Borden's house for safe keeping. The young lady had not the slightest suspicion of his being connected with the crime. As far as the Portuguese suspected of the crime was concerned, she knew nothing of him, as he might have been a man who was employed by the day in the busy season. What his motive could have been it is hard to tell, as Mr. Borden had always been kind to his help.

Another statement made by the police, and which, though apparently light, would bear investigation, is the following: Some two weeks ago a man applied to Mr. Borden for the lease of a store on South Main street that was vacant. After a short time as Miss Borden was passing the room loud words were heard, her father making the remark. "I will not let it for that purpose." Quietness was restored in a short while, and when the man departed her father said: "When you come to town next time I will let you know." This was two weeks ago, but in the meantime the store has been let to another party, but why a person would commit such a brutal affair because of being refused the rental of a store is hard to see. Miss Borden thinks that the party wanted the store for the sale of liquor and her father refused. It was dark at the time of his calling and she did not recognize his features.

WENT TO SWANSEY.

At 12:45 o'clock Marshal Hilliard and Officers Doherty and Connors procured a carriage and drove over to the farm, hoping that the suspected man would return there in order to prove an alibi. The officers will arrive at the place some time before the man, as the distance is some ten miles, though it is hardly probable that he will return there. What makes it rather improbable that the man suspected is a Portuguese laborer is the statement of Charles Gifford of Swansey. Mr. Gifford says that the only Portuguese employed on the upper farm is Mr. Johnson, and he is confined to his bed by illness. Another man might be employed by Mr. Borden on the lower farm for a few days, but he does not believe it. An attempt was made to reach Swansey by telephone, but no answer was received.

A SIGNIFICANT INCIDENT.

Among the significant incidents revealed in the search through the premises was brought to light by John Donnelly, who with others searched through the barn to see if any trace of the fugitive could be found there. In the hay was seen the perfect outline of a man as if one had slept there over night. Besides this, it was evident that the sleeper was either restless or had been there before, because an imprint was found in another part of the hay that corresponded with the outlines of the first impression. Somebody may have been in the habit of going there for a nap, but the imprint was that of a person of about five feet six inches tall, and was shorter than Mr. Borden. This has given rise to the suspicion that the murderer may have slept about the place and waited for an opportunity to accomplish his deed.

ANOTHER STORY.

Another sensational story is being told in connection with the murder. It ap-

ANDREW JACKSON BORDEN

pears that the members of the family have been ill for some days and the symptoms were very similar to those of poison. In the light of subsequent events this sickness has been recalled. It has been the custom of the family to receive its supply of milk from the Swansey farm every morning, and the can was left out of doors until the servant opened the house in the morning. Ample opportunity wae afforded, therefore, for anybody who had a foul design to tamper with the milk, and this circumstance will be carefully investigated by the police.

Medical Examiner Dolan, who promptly responded to the call for his presence, made a careful examination of the victims and reached the conclusion that the wounds were inflicted by a heavy, sharp weapon like an axe or hatchet. He found the skull fractured in both instances and concluded that death was instantaneous. As to the blow which killed Mrs. Borden he thought that it had been delivered by a tall man, who struck the woman from behind.

A BOGUS LETTER.

It is reported that Mrs. Borden received a letter this morning announcing the illness of a very dear friend and was preparing to go to see her. This letter has turned out to be a bogus one, evidently intended to draw her away from home. In this case it would look as if the assault had been carefully planned. A suspicious character was seen on Second street this morning who seemed to be on the lookout for somebody, and the police have a description of the man.

Marshal Hilliard, Officers Dowty and Connors went to Swansey this afternoon, but found the men at work on the upper farm who had been employed there of late. The lower farm will be visited at once. William Eddy has charge of this one.

At 2:15 o'clock a sturdy Portuguese named Antonio Auriel was arrested in a saloon on Columbia street and brought into the police station. The man protested his innocence and sent after Joseph Chaves, clerk for Talbot & Co., who recognized the man, and he was immediately released.

SKETCH OF MR. BORDEN.

Andrew J. Borden was born in this city 69 years ago. By perseverance and industry he accumulated a fortune. A short time since he boasted that he had yet to spend his first foolish dollar. Mr. Borden was married twice. His second wife was the daughter of Oliver Gray and was born on Rodman street. He had two children by his first wife, Emma and Elizabeth. The former is out of town on a visit and has not yet learned of the tragedy.

Mr. Borden was at the time of his death president of the Union saving's bank and director in the Durfee bank, Globe yarn, Merchants and Troy mill. He was interested in several big real estate deals, and was a very wealthy man.

ABBY DURFEE GRAY BORDEN

The Fall River Herald

SENSATIONS in this city always move in cycles. It has been so for fully a dozen years. It will be a fortunate thing if the Borden murder is not followed by another tale of bloodshed.

The Boston Advertiser

MURDER MOST FOUL.

ANDREW BORDEN AND HIS WIFE KILLED

BY AN ASSASSIN WHO LEAVES NO CLEW TO THE AWFUL DEED.

Fall River Excited by a Crime Which Has No Equal in its History—Police Baffled by the Lack of a Definite Clew, Though Members of the Family Are Suspected—The House Now Guarded by Officers.

FALL RIVER, Aug. 4.—An aged man and his aged wife were killed today, their heads chopped to pieces by repeated and fiendish blows with an axe, the murderer and the implement of slaughter both disappeared, and now, 12 hours after the bloody deed, the police and the people are in just as utter ignorance as they were when it was first noised abroad this noon.

For 27 years A. J. Borden and Abbie D. Borden had lived together as man and wife in peace and comfort. Two daughters of Mr. Borden by a previous marriage grew up around them. The family, united and harmonious as far as the townspeople knew or suspected, lived in a plain, unpretentious story and a half house on Second st., not a pistol shot from the City Hall, not a stone's throw from the heart of the city. In this quiet homestead Andrew Borden and his wife were foully and mysteriously murdered this morning, so mysteriously that the police are not only without the criminal, but without the least clew to his person or his motive. The very weapon with which the deed was done has not been found.

Last night the family consisted of Mr. and Mrs. Borden; Miss Elizabeth Borden, the daughter of the murdered man; the servant girl, Bridget Sullivan, and John Morse. the brother of Mr. Borden's first wife, who wa paying a visit to his brother in law. After breakfast this morning the family separated. Morse proceeded to another part of the town to make a call, from which he did not return till after the tragedy. Mrs. Rorden went out to visit a sick neighbor and Mr. Borden went down town on business. He spent some time at the Union Savings Bank, of which he was president, got home about 10:30, and was never seen again alive except by his wife, daughter and murderer. Mrs. Borden had also returned. At 11:30 both were dead.

Mr. Borden, when he came in, took off his coat, put on a jacket, and lay down on a lounge with his coat for a pillow, complaining of not feeling well. When found he lay in an easy position, showing that he had not moved and had been instantly killed, without warning or struggle. His face was so mutilated as to be unrecognizable. One great gash extended from the face around on the side of the head to the nose. The cuts, all made with an axe or hatchet, numbered seven. all on the head. Back on the top of the head was a great fracture of the skull evidently made with the back of the instrument. There was not a drop of blood on the walls or floor anywhere in the room.

In the guest chamber occupied by Mr. Morse lay Mrs. Borden, face down upon the floor. She, too, lay as if she had died instantly. Her wounds were mostly on the top and back of the head.

The first known of the murder was when the daughter, Lizzie, alarmed the next door neighbors and begged them to call Dr. Bowen, the family physician, who lived directly opposite. Dr. Bowen was on hand in a few minutes, and was the first one outside the family to see the murdered bodies. He found all traces of life extinct He was about to notify the police, when Lizzie Borden and the Sullivan girl swooned, and he had to turn his attention to them. Finally Officer Allen arrived, and became so excited that he ran at once with an incoherent story to the police station. Today was the dace of the policemen's excursion, and half of the force was at Rocky Point when the murder occurred. A small posse of police surrounded the house, and in a short time they were busy in keeping back the host of business men and curiosity seekers who thronged Second st., attracted by the tragedy.

Medical Examiner Dolan was summoned and was on the scene within half an hour. When Mrs. Borden was first seen it was supposed that she had died from heart disease, to which she had been subject. A reporter first noticed blood in her hair, but when the bed near which she was lying had been drawn away, it was seen that she, too, had been frightfully battered about the face and skull.

The first thing which confronted the police was the utter absence of a clew,even the slightest. The murderer had disappeared as completely as if the earth had swallowed him up and taken the weapon along. No one outside the family had been seen to enter the house. No suspicious person had been seen to pass on the street. The murder was done with such deadly suddenness, the fatal work accomplished so quickly, and the murderer had vanished so completely, that it was clear the assassin had planned the deed and chosen the moment with wonderful exactness. The daughter declared that she was attracted to the house by her father's dying groans. It was clear that he was killed instantly. Therefore the time for the murderer's escape was as brief as that escape was complete. Undoubtedly the murderer had been lying in wait for the victims, and it was in the house that he had been lying. After the murder the back door was found to be hasped on the inside, and the front door was locked, showing that no one could have got in after Mr. Borden's return.

The motive of the crime is another mystery. It was not robbery, as Mr. Borden's watch and money were untouched. There is no one to whom a motive of revenge could be attributed. So far as known, the dead couple had no enemies. There were several stories got up and sent out during the day of discharged workmen, one, a Portuguese, being seen at Mr. Borden's house early in the morning. There was nothing in them. He had not been employing Portuguese, and had not discharged anyone. So on the whole, the police believe that the deed was done in the interests of some one who would benefit by the death of the old couple.

At this hour police suspicions rest on persons who were in the family circle, particularly on Morse and on the daughter Lizzie, who first discovered the body of her father. J. W. Morse is 55 years of age, and came here from Hastings, Iowa, two years ago. He became very intimate with Mr. Borden and the latter's daughter, and spent a great portion of his time with them. He came from New Bedford at noon yesterday and spent the night at the Borden homestead. He left there this morning at 9 o'clock, and was next seen on the premises about 20 minutes after the bodies were discovered. After the most careful searching it has been decided that neither of the victims engaged in a struggle, both being struck down instantly and hacked to pieces afterward. The police say the only motive for murder was gain, else one of the victims would have been spared. The fact that so little ado was made by those who were most directly interested and so little attempt was made at first to discover the possible murderer, is strengthening the police in the opinions they now hold. At one time the police threatened to place Morse in custody, but it has been decided to keep him under close surveillance until further developments. The murder has caused the greatest sensation known here since the Granite Mill fire. Tonight, great throngs of people hang around the family residence.

An element in the case is a mysterious sickness that has been troubling several members of the family for two or three days. Yesterday nearly every one of the household was attacked with vomiting just after breakfast. Dr. Bowen was called in, and prescribed some simple remedies for digestive trouble, together with recommendations as to diet. The cause of the trouble was a mystery, as no one had indulged in any indiscretion in eating, and they are inclined to attribute it to the milk. This morning the servant girl was similarly attacked, and since the murder suspicions of poison are rife. At the autopsy Medical Examiner Dolan removed the stomachs of both victims without opening them, and will today send the stomachs together with samples of the milk to Prof. Wood of Harvard Medical School, for analysis.

The daughter Lizzie's story of the crime is as follows: She arose late and walked down stairs, seeing and speaking to her father as she passed through the room. She supposed her mother was out. She went into the yard and stepped into the barn. While there she heard a cry of distress, coming apparently from the house, and she ran in. She went directly to a sitting-room leading from the main hallway in the house, and there saw her father on the sofa, bloody and lifeless. She ran out shrieking, and her cries attracted the servant and a neighbor. They made a hasty search for the mother and found her lifeless body upstairs. The woman ran downstairs, terrified, and summoned Dr Bowen.

Several arrests have been made during the day, none of them of any account, and none of them suspected, but merely of suspicious persons. Two were Russian Jews travelling through town and the third a Portuguese, and they were locked up simply by way of precaution. No one believes that they had anything to do with the crime. More arrests, and more important ones, are promised for tomorrow. Miss Emma Borden, the elder daughter, arrived home at night from Fairhaven, where she had been on a visit. She was greatly prostrated by the awful news that greeted her.

BORDEN'S FATHER'S MONEY.

Suspicions Felt Concerning Morse's Connection With the Matter.

TAUNTON, Aug. 4.—It being learned that the Fall River police are watching John Morse, the brother of the late A. J. Borden's first wife, an effort has been made to obtain information relative to the condition of the property left by A. B. Borden, father of A. J. It appears that Morse has been at Borden's house for the last two days, and that a settlement of the estate is in progress. It was thought that the will of Abraham Borden might have left the property in such manner as to revert to Morse, in case of the death of Andrew Borden, but a search of the probate office shows that no will was left by Abraham, and that A. J. was appointed administrator of the estate. A. J.'s mother left a will, but her property amounted to less than $3000, and that was all willed to her brothers and nieces.

Mr. Borden's Life.

FALL RIVER, Aug. 4.—A. J. Borden was born in this city in 1822. He was in the furniture business 33 years with William Almy, under the firm nsme of Borden & Almy, and accumulated a large amount of real estate, valued at $350,000. He owns two farms in Swansea. He was a pattern of the old New England type of industry, thrift and conservatism, and was outspoken in his advocacy of temperance and moral issues. He was president of the Union Savings Bank, a director of the B. M. C. Durfee Safe Deposit and Trust Co., a director in the Troy and Merchants mills, and a director of the Globe Street Railway Co. He was twice married, his second wife being Miss Abbie D. Gray. Mr. Borden was 70 years of age and Mrs. Borden 67 years. He was worth probably $500,000, and during his whole business career never gave a note nor borrowed a cent of money. He was what is called close fisted, but square and just in his dealings.

The New York Herald

HUSBAND AND WIFE MURDERED IN DAYLIGHT.

President Borden, a Wealthy Mill Owner of Fall River, Cut Down by an Assassin, Who Afterward Kills Mrs. Borden.

DISCOVERED BY THEIR DAUGHTER.

Although Three Persons Were Within Call No One Heard an Outcry or Knew of the Crime Until the Bodies Were Found.

SUSPECTING THE DAUGHTER LIZZIE.

[BY TELEGRAPH TO THE HERALD.]

FALL RIVER, Mass., August 4, 1892.—Andrew J. Borden, a wealthy real estate and mill owner and president of the Union Savings Bank, and his wife were murdered here this morning almost in the face and eyes of the public. At least two persons were within conversational distance of the tragedy and a third within easy calling, and yet the assassin came and did his work and departed without leaving a trace of any kind which might lead to his identification. Neither are there any attendant incidents which serve to throw light upon the affair or to explain it in the least.

Mr. Borden's agent yesterday paid him a large sum of money collected from tenants, and at half-past nine this morning he started from home to deposit it at his bank. He returned at about twenty minutes past eleven and went into the sitting room at once to lie down on the lounge. Mrs. Borden went up stairs to the front chamber at the same time. Bridget Sullivan, the servant, was up in the third story, cleaning windows. Miss Elizabeth, or Lizzie, as she was called, the daughter, was assisting in this, and at the time Mr. Borden was lying down to read his paper she passed through his room to the barn in search of an iron window scraper.

HOW THE MURDERER ENTERED.

Adjoining the apartments in which Mr. Borden was, was the dining room, opening into the kitchen. A back entry leads from it to the yard on the north side of the house. To the left of this back entry, coming out, are the stairs, and to the right the panty. Directly under these stairs is the door leading to the cellar. It is now the presumption that the assassin was concealed in this cellarway directly under the staircase as Miss Lizzie passed out to go to the barn.

It is the theory of the police, and it seems well substantiated by all the evidence, that as soon as the murderer found the coast clear he stole through the kitchen, Bridget Sullivan being up stairs, and passed into the sitting room, where he found Mr. Borden. Whether there were any words or not no witness is left to say. No sound was heard by anybody outside or by Bridget Sullivan up in the top of the house.

KILLED WITH ONE BLOW.

In the opinion of Medical Examiner Dolan Mr. Borden was killed with one blow, and the police are at a loss to discover the instrument. It was apparently a cleaver. There was a horrible gash, cleaving the skull and penetrating to the brain. This cut passed directly across the right eye, cutting through the cheek, as well as the frontal bone. There were one or two detached cuts higher up on the head, but it is believed they were made by this same blow. Mr. Borden was struck dead instantly, and must have expired without a groan. Certainly he made no outcry.

It would seem, however, that Mrs. Borden's attention was aroused and probably she started to come down the front stairs from the parlor chamber. The assassin, hearing her movements and knowing he must leave no witness, rushed up the flight, and she, with the instinct of self-preservation, ran back to the chamber she had just left. In this room are two windows opening directly upon the street. There she was struck by the assassin, who was too quick for her. Her skull was cloven in twain at one blow, just as her husband's had been, by the cleaver. There was no shriek, no groan that anybody heard until Miss Lizzie Borden's horrorfraught cry came ringing up the back stairs to Bridget Sullivan, the servant girl, in the attic, "Come down here quick, father's dead."

NO CLEW TO THE MURDERER.

The alarm was given at once and the police began to search for clews. The peculiarity of the cuts and the neatness with which the heads of both victims were cleft gave every evidence that the weapon was a cleaver, but no such article was to be found; neither were any bloody tracks or finger-marks about the house.

The only blood there was was a little pool under the lounge on which Mr. Borden's body lay and some spots under his arms when his body was raised. There was very little blood up stairs in the bedroom, and that was in close proximity to Mrs. Borden's body.

The lack of evidence of the presence of the murderer beyond the terribly mutilated bodies of his victims was baffling. There was not the slightest thing to indicate that any man had been in the house. Three arrests have been made during the afternoon, one of John Joseph Maher, who was found under a car intoxicated, and the others two pedlers, but there is nothing more than suspicion attached to them. No motive can be suggested for the crime.

TWELVE CUTS IN HIS HEAD.

Medical Examiner Dolan, assisted by other physicians, held an autopsy this afternoon on the bodies of the victims of the tragedy. It was found that Borden sustained twelve cuts in the face and skull, varying in length from four to eight inches, and also suffered a fracture of the skull, two by four inches and three inches deep. His wife's head and face were battered all out of shape. There was no doubt in the minds of the physicians that the victims met death at the hands of a murderer. The stomachs of both was removed and placed in alcohol to be sent to Boston to-morrow for analysis with a view of determining whether or not milk poisoning was attempted.

LIZZIE IS SUSPECTED.

At this hour police suspicions rest upon persons who were in the family circle, particularly on John W. Morse, brother-in-law of Mr. Borden by his first marriage, also on the daughter, Lizzie, who first discovered the body of the father. John W. Morse is fifty-five years of age, and came here from Hastings, Iowa, two years ago. He became very intimate with Mr. Borden and the latter's daughter, and spent a great portion of his time with them. He came from New Bedford at noon yesterday and spent the night at the Borden homestead. He left there this morning at nine o'clock and was next seen on the premises about twenty minutes after the bodies were discovered. After the most careful searching it has been decided that neither of the victims engaged in a struggle, both being struck down instantly and hacked to pieces afterward. The police say the only motive for murder was gain, else one of the victims would have been spared.

The Fall River Herald

THURSDAY'S AFFRAY

No Clue as Yet to its Perpetrator.

POLICE WORKING HARD TO REMOVE THE VEIL

Of Mystery That Envelops the Awful Tragedy.

A POSTAL CARD THAT WOULD SERVE AS A LINK.

Further investigation into the circumstances of the Borden murder shroud it with an impenetrable mystery. Nothing that has ever occurred in Fall River or vicinity has created such intense excitement. From the moment the story of the crime was first told to long after midnight Second street was crowded with curious people anxious to hear some particulars that had not been told before.

ANDREW J. BORDEN.

Theories were advanced, some of them plausible enough, but not one could be formed against which some objection could not be offered from the circumstances surrounding the case. Everybody agreed that money was at the bottom of the foul murder, but in what measure and concerning what person could not be conceived. That a bloody deed such as that perpetrated in broad daylight, in a house on one of the busiest streets could have been so quickly and noiselessly accomplished and the murderer escape from the house without attracting attention is wonderful to a degree. Nobody was seen to enter the house by any of the occupantf, although all of them except Mr. Borden were busy about the rooms or in the yard.

WAS HE CONCEALED?

Could it be that the murderer was concealed inside the dwelling and had awaited a favorable moment to carry out his nefarious plans? The more the circumstances are considered, the more probable becomes this view of the case. People who have carefully examined the ground believe that Mr. Borden was the first victim, and that the killing of Mrs. Borden was by no means unpremeditated. Having accomplished the bloody work downstairs, the murderer slipped stealthily into the rooms above in search of the wife and, finding her in the northwest chamber walking across the floor to the dressing case, had crept up behind her without attracting her attention and delivered the fatal blow.

The plausibility of this view lies in the fact that the fall of Mrs. Borden, who weighed very nearly 200 pounds, would certainly have jarred the building and awakened her husband, who could only have been sleeping lightly on the lounge, as it was but a few moments after his daughter had seen him quietly reading there that the deed was done. Further investigation confirms the belief that Mrs. Borden was not chased upstairs by the murderer because she was so near the end of the room that she would have been forced to turn and face her pursuer, and the cuts on the head would have been of a different nature.

Twenty minutes were all the time the murderer had to finish his terrible work; conceal the weapon with which he accomplished his crime, and conceal it in such a way as to leave no traces of blood on the carpet or through the house that would reveal how he escaped; to pass out of the house by the side door within 15 feet of the barn where the daughter was engaged and a like distance from the Buffinton house on the north; pass the length of the house and disappear up or down Second street. John Cunningham was going down the street about that time, and he saw nobody pass him, and people who live below saw nobody.

TALKS WITH INMATES.

There are no new developments in the case to be gathered from the people in the house. Regarding the servant, Bridget Sullivan, a woman of about 25, it is pretty well established that at the time that Mr. Borden was assaulted she was in the attic of the house. Her statement to the police is as follows: "I was washing windows most all of the morning and passed in and out of the house continually. At the time Miss Lizzie came down stairs I went to one of the upper rooms to finish the window washing. I remained there until Lizzie's cries attracted my attention; then I came down and went for Dr. Bowen; I never saw any one enter or leave the house."

Miss Borden made the following statement to Officer Harrington as soon as she was sufficiently composed to talk coherently of the affair. It differs in only one particular from the one she told Dr. Bowen, namely, the time in which she was out of the house and in the barn. She said that she was absent 20 minutes, and, upon being requested to be particular, insisted that it was not more than 20 minutes or less than that time. She said that her father enjoyed the most perfect confidence and friendship of his workmen across the river, and that she was in a position to know this, unless something unusual had happened within a few days. She told the story of the angry tenant, saying that the man came to her father twice about the matter, and that he persistently refused to let the store which he wanted for the purpose desired. The only vacant property of Mr. Borden was the room recently vacated by Baker Gadsby, and it is thought that this is the place the man wanted to use. Mr. Borden told the man at the first visit to call again and he would let him know about the rental. It is supposed to be an out-of-town man and that he called and found that Jonathan Clegg had occupied the store. It is also thought that the tenant wanted to use the place as a rum shop; this Mr. Borden would not allow. It may be added that the police attach little importance to this latter matter.

MR. MORSE TALKS.

Visiting at the house on the day of the murder was John W. Morse, a brother of Mr. Borden's first wife. He is fully six feet in height with gray beard and hair. He was not averse to talking, and said in response to questions:

"My sister, Sarah A. Morse, married Andrew Borden in the city of Fall River when both were, as I remember, in their 22d year. That was 47 years ago. At that time Mr. Borden was in reduced circumstances and was just beginning to enter business. They lived for years on Ferry street. They had three children, one of whom died when he was but three or four years old. The others, both girls, grew to womanhood and are now living; they are Emma L., aged 37, and Lizzie A., aged 32.

"Mr. Borden first went into the furniture business on Anawan street, where he remained for 30 years or more. My sister died 28 years ago. At that time Mr. Borden was worth fully $150,000, which amount he had invested largely in mill stocks, which were highly paying securities. He told me on one occasion that he had $78,000 in mill stocks alone. He afterwards invested heavily in a horsecar line, but now I am ahead of my story.

"About 20 years ago I went out west, and settled at Hastings Mills, Ia. On the 14th of of April two years ago I returned home, and since last February I have been staying with a butcher by the name of Davis, in the little town of South Dartmouth, which is near New Bedford. Yes, I am a bachelor. I have a sister living in this city. She married Joseph Morse, a second cousin. I have also one brother whose name is William, who lives at Excelsior, Minn. He is 65 years of age.

"Wednesday I came here from New Bedford early in the afternoon. I left that city on the 12:35 train, which arrived here about 1:30 o'clock. I walked from the station up to the house and rang the front door bell. Mrs. Borden opened it. She welcomed me and I went in. Andrew was then reclining on the sofa in about the position he was found murdered. He looked up and laughed saying, 'Hullo, John, is that you? Have you been to dinner?' I replied in the negative. Mrs. Borden interrupted Mr. Borden, saying: 'Sit right down, we are just through and everything is hot on the stove. It won't cost us a mite of trouble.' They sat by my side through dinner, and then I told them I was going over to Kirby's stable and get a team to drive over to Luther's. I invited Andrew to go, but he declined, saying he didn't feel well enough. He asked me to bring him over some eggs from his farm which is there located. I returned from the ride about 8:30 o'clock and we sat up until about 10 o'clock. Then Mr. Borden showed me to my room, his wife having previously retired, and bade me good night. That was the last I saw of him until Thursday morning.

"It was about 6 o'clock when I got up, and had breakfast about an hour later. Then Andrew and I read the papers, and we chatted until about 9 o'clock. I am not positive as to the exact time, and it may have been only 8:45 o'clock. While at the table I asked Andrew why he did not buy Gould's yacht for $200,000, at which price it was advertised, and he laughed, saying what little good it would do him if he really did have it. We also talked about business. I had come to Fall River, for one reason, to buy a pair of oxen for Butcher Davis, with whom I lived. He had wanted them, and I had agreed to take them on a certain day, but had not done so. Andrew told me when I was ready to go after them to write him at the farm, which would save him bothering in the matter. When I left the house I started for the postoffice. I walked down Second street, and, stopping in, got a postal card and wrote to William Vinnicum of South Swansey. I dropped it in the office and then went out of the north door of the building to Bedford street, and thence on to Third street, to Pleasant, to Weybosset street. I stopped there at the house of my cousin, Daniel Emery, No. 4; I went there to see my nephew and niece, the former of whom I found away. There I remained until 11:30 or 11:45 and then I started back to Borden's, as I had been asked there to dinner. I hailed a car going by and rode to Second street and thence I walked to the house.

"When I entered the premises I did not go by the front door. On the contrary, I walked around behind the house and picked some pears. Then I went in the back door. Bridget then told me that Mr. and Mrs. Borden had been murdered. I opened the sitting-room door and found a number of people, including the doctors. I entered, but only glanced once at the body. No, I did not look closely enough to be able to describe it. Then I went upstairs and took a similar hasty view of the dead woman. Everything is confusion, however, and I recall very little of what took place."

THE MEDICAL EXAMINER.

Dr. Dolan was called upon after the autopsy, but he had no further facts to disclose. He described the wounds and said that death must have been almost instantaneous in both cases after the first blow. Acting upon the rumor about the poisoned milk, the doctor took samples of it and saved the soft parts of the body for further analysis. He was of the opinion that the wounds were inflicted by a hatchet or a cleaver, and by a person who could strike a blow heavy enough to crush in the skull. In the autopsy, Drs. Coughlin, Dedrick, Leary, Gunning, Dutra, Tourtellot, Peckham and Bowen assisted.

NOTES.

John J. Maher was on a street car on New Boston road Thursday afternoon rather under the influence of liquor. He was telling that when a reward was offered for the man he could find him in 15 minutes. When questioned by an officer as to what he really knew, Maher said that a boy had seen a small man with a dark moustache come out of the house at the time of the murder and, going down Second street, had turned up Pleasant. Maher was locked up on a charge of drunkenness.

Officers Doherty and Harrington have been on continuous duty since the case was reported.

It was rather warm for the officers who were detailed to hunt for the murderer's weapon in the loft of the barn, but they thoroughly examined every corner for the article.

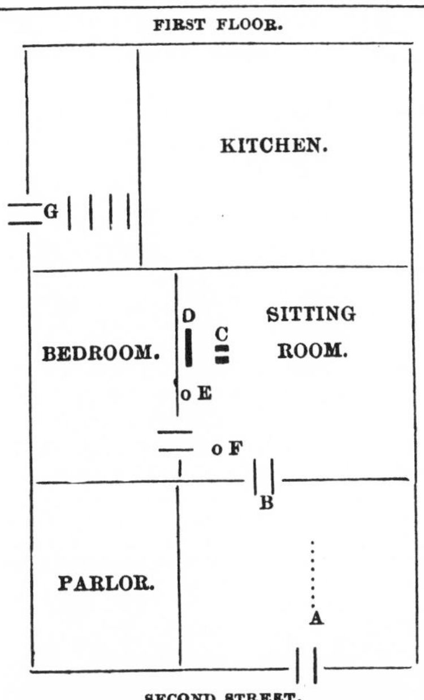

A—front door. B—door to room where murder was committed. C—where the body was found. D—the lounge where Mr. Borden was lying. E and F—blood spots. G—back stairs and door.

ROOM WHERE BODY OF MR. BORDEN WAS FOUND.

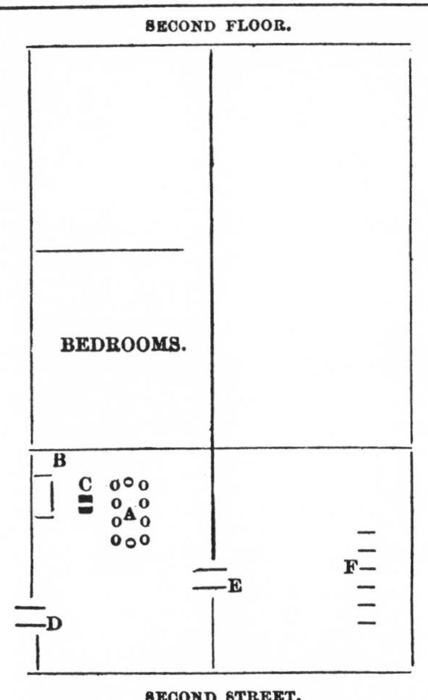

A—the bed. B—dressing case. C—where body of Mrs. Borden was found. D—window. E—door to room. F—staircase.

WHERE BODY OF MRS. BORDEN WAS FOUND.

Officer Medley was one of the busiest men about town Wednesday night, and every remark or idea connected with the tragedy was thoroughly sifted by him.

When the news of the murder reached the people on the excursion it seemed too incredible, and a great many would not be convinced untill they reached home.

If interest and hard work in the case were to land the perpetrator of the crime into custody Assistant Marshal Fleet would have the man behind the bars long before now.

Every morning paper in Boston had a representative in this city Thursday night, and as a result the telegraph operators were kept busy into the small hours of the morning.

The excitement attending the tragedy continued at blood heat throughout the night, and it required a number of officers to keep the street clear in front of the house up to midnight.

Among the many articles secured on the premises is a crowbar over three feet long and weighing about nine pounds. It was found in the shed by one of the officers. It appeared, at first that there was blood on it, and a hasty investigation by two or three policemen convinced the finder that the substance with which it was spotted was blood. It was consequently brought to the police station, where it was found that the spots were nothing else than a few drops of paint and rust.

MORSE'S NIECE.

Mrs. Emery, upon whom Mr. Morse called, was disposed to talk freely to Officer Medley, who interviewed her Thursday night. She said in reply to questions that she had several callers during the day, and that one of them was John Morse.

"Was Morse the name we heard?" asked the officer of a companion.

"Yes," retorted Mrs. Emery quickly, "Morse was the man. He left here at 11:30 o'clock this morning."

"Then you noticed the time?" observed the officer.

"Oh, yes," was the reply, "I noticed the time.

"How did you fix it?" was the next question.

After some little hesitation, Mrs. Emery said that one of her family was sick, and that Dr. Bowen was her physician. "Dr. Bowen came in just as Mr. Morse left."

"Did they meet?" queried the officers.

"No, they did not," said Mrs. Emery.

At this point the niece in question entered the room and corroborated Mrs. Emery's statements, though both women finally fixed upon 11:20 as the exact time of Mr. Morse's departure.

Mrs. Emery volunteered information that Mr. Morse was well-to-do, at least she supposed he was comfortably off and that he had come east to spend his money. She was not positive on this point, however. Morse's niece was asked if she had ever seen her uncle before, and replied that she had. She had met him when she was five years old, and three weeks ago he had taken her from the cars at Warren to the Borden farm, Swansey.

THE OLDEST DAUGHTER.

Miss Emma Borden, who had been visiting in Fairhaven, returned home Thursday evening, having been summoned by the news of the crime. The details of the murder had not been told to her, and she was overcome by the recital. She is the oldest daughter of Andrew Borden by his first wife. All through the early hours of the evening the street was crowded with people, none of whom was admitted to the premises until they had disclosed the nature of their business.

A watch surrounded the house all night, and officers were on guard inside. No further developments were reported. The family retired soon after 10 o'clock and all was in darkness. Undertaker Winward had taken charge of the remains at the request of Miss Borden, and will prepare them for burial.

THE THEORIES DISCUSSED.

Today nothing but the murder was talked about on the streets, and the interest continues to be intense. The announcement that the family had offered a reward of $5000 for the detection of the murderers was the only new item to be discussed.

The theories which were advanced by those who have been closely connected with the case agree in one thing, and that is that the murderer knew his ground and carried out his bloodthirsty plan with a speed and surety that indicated a well matured plot. How quickly the report that was gathered about the premises five minutes after the deed was discovered that a Portuguese had done it was scattered abroad after the murder is looked on with suspicion.

Detective Seaver and other members of the state police force are assisting the local department in its work, and the office of the city marshal is the busiest place in town. New clues are being reported every hour and officers are busy tracking the stories to earth.

Mr. Morse, the guest of the Bordens, is well known in this city where he was born and lived many years. People recall that he went west quite early in life and engaged in raising horses in Iowa. He was said to have had considerable success with his stock and to have gathered together considerable property. Nothing definite about his affairs was known other than that he had told friends that he had brought a train load of horses with him from Iowa to sell, and they were now at Fairhaven.

SIGNIFICANT DISAPPEARANCE.

That letter of which mention was made Thursday as having been sent to Mrs. Borden, announcing that a friend was sick, has since disappeared. The explanation that was given out was that after reading its contents, Mrs. Borden tore it up and threw the pieces in the fire. Bits of charred paper were found in the grate, but not enough to give any idea of the nature of the note. Nobody about the house seems to know where the letter could have come from, and since publicity has been given and considerable importance attached to it, it is considered probable that the writer will inform the family of the circumstances and thus remove suspicions.

Various rumors have been started, one of which was that Miss Borden had assured a friend last winter after a mysterious robbery at the house that her father had an enemy somewhere. A HERALD reporter interviewed a lady to whom it was said this story had been told, but she denied any knowledge of it. Another was that the axe had been found in the yard, but the police have not heard of it.

A TENANT THEORY.

Causes for the murder are arising so fast at the present time that it is nearly impossible to investigate them. Hardly any of them are of sufficient weight to put a person under the ban of suspicion, but all are being thoroughly investigated. The latest story is about a former tenant named Ryan. According to the informant Ryan occupied the upper floor of a house belonging to Mr. Borden, and was so abnoxious that he ordered him to move. While notifying the people he was compelled to seek the lower floor to escape the torrent of abuse that was heaped on him, and when the family moved the remark was made that they would like to see him dead. There is nothing more than this in the matter, but as all acts or words in connection with Mr. Borden in the past are being looked into the affair was looked into and found to amount to nothing.

A MAN WITH A CLEAVER.

Griffiths Bros., the carpenters on Anawan street, tell a story which may have an important bearing upon the terrible tragedy. They were driving up Pleasant street about 10 o'clock Thursday morning, when their attention was drawn to a man who was proceeding rapidly along the sidewalk in front of Flint's building. Under his arm, with the handle down, he carried a cleaver entirely unlike anything they had ever seen. It was the size of the instrument that caused them to take more than a passing glance at it. To them it looked like a tool sometimes used by fish dealers. It had a rusty appearance, as if it had not been used for some time.

The man was dressed very poorly. He had no beard and was short in stature. As the weapon with which the deed was committed has not been found, the carpenters venture the opinion that the cleaver they saw was the means by which Mr. Borden and his wife were killed.

SOUTHARD H. MILLER,

one of the city's most venerable citizens, and Mr. Borden's intimate friends, was spoken to on the matter. He replied that as far as motive was concerned for the deed he could not answer. He had known Mr. Borden for over half a century, and his dealings were such that nobody could take offence with him. Having learned the cabinet making business, Mr. Borden applied to him in 1844, when the city hall was building, for a situation as carpenter, work at cabinet making being dull. Mr. Borden continued in Mr. Miller's employ for about two years. He was a generous, plain and simple man. The reason he went into the bank business was so that he could more handily manage the property of Thomas Borden, his uncle.

The building in which Mr. Borden was killed had been erected by Mr. Miller, and throughout all their transactions he had found him to be a man of his word. As far as Mr. Morse was concerned, Mr. Miller had known him but for about a year, and in that time he had seen nothing that would prejudice him against the man. Mr. Borden's daughters were ladies who had always conducted themselves so that the breath of scandal could never reach them.

As the reporter was leaving Mr. Miller's parlor, Mrs. Miller who was present during the interview, said that she had lost, in Mrs. Borden, the best and most intimate neighbor she had ever met.

CONTEMPORARY EMPLOYMENT OPPORTUNITY

Wanted.

GIRL who understands mending loom harness. Steady work; weekly pay from $7 to $9 per week. H. J. Langley, Reed and Harness Manufacturers, 14 and 16 County street. 246

The Boston Daily Globe

DISCOVERY!

A Woman Inquired for Poison.

Said That Drug Clerk Identified Her.

Strange Story Told by Lizzie Borden.

Members of the Family Are Shadowed.

Stepmother the Cause of Trouble.

Reward of $5000 Has Been Offered.

[Associated Press.]

FALL RIVER, Mass., Aug. 5.—The Globe will publish the following tonight:

"At police headquarters, Thursday night at 7 o'clock, Capt. Desmond was posting himself on the murder by reading the papers and receiving reports.

"Marshal Hilliard was busy with his men, and inquiry for assistant Fleet revealed the fact that he had gone to supper. In a few minutes Mr. Fleet returned, and then a conversation took place between him and the marshal. Officers Harrington and Doherty were given instructions and passed out.

"Within 30 minutes after that the most important clue yet discovered was in their possession.

"The two officers made their discovery on Main st.

"At D. R. Smith's drug store they got the first important evidence.

"They approached the clerk, Eli Bence, and from him learned that Miss Borden had been in the store within 36 hours past and had inquired for a certain poison.

"The clerk was asked to accompany the officers and closely questioned as to the exact facts relative to the time, the girl's condition mentally, the amount and quality of the poison she had bought, or called for.

"The officers then led the drug clerk to a residence on 2d st. where Miss Lizzie was stopping for the time being. The young man was not previously well acquainted with the young woman, but he told them that he could identify her at sight.

"He did identify her, and in the presence of the police officers informed them that she was in his place of business and made inquiry for a bottle of poison.

"Miss Borden's reply to this accusation, as well as the exact language which was used at the time, is known only to the two policemen and herself.

"The statement above made is absolutely correct, and was verified in every particular by a GLOBE reporter last night within 10 minutes after it happened."

POLICE AT THE DOORS.

Shadowing Everybody Who Comes and Goes at House.

FALL RIVER, Mass., Aug. 5.—In the closely shuttered dining-room of the Borden residence on 2d st. are the bodies of the victims of yesterday's tragedy, which will tomorrow with brief burial services be consigned to the grave.

At the front door is a police officer whose instructions are to pass no one into the

ROOM WHERE A.J. BORDEN WAS MURDERED
At left is the sofa where he laid. The door next to that leads to the yard, and the right-hand door leads to the kitchen.

---

house, unless in authority, without the consent of the family.

A second officer stands in a sheltered nook at the rear of the premises, for what purpose cannot he said. The rear fence is fully 25 feet high, and it could scarcely be scaled with the aid of a ladder.

Still a third sentinel is at the outer gate, his duty is to keep the sidewalk clear and open for travel.

A crowd of men, women and children are braving a severe shower this forenoon for the privilege of lingering on the street and watching the scene of the tragedy.

Among them are officers in citizens' clothes, who are instructed to shadow and follow closely any member of the household who may go out.

Very little of importance has transpired around the house this morning. The family were astir at 6.30 o'clock, and about an hour later breakfast was served. There were the Misses Borden, Mr. Morse and a lady friend of the daughters present, and from the statements of the servant girl, Bridget Sullivan, they ate but little and talked less.

Miss Emma Borden, who was absent from home at the time of the tragedy, returned late yesterday afternoon. She appears very calm and self-possessed, and was seen this morning and interviewed by officers in the case. Miss Lizzie has not yet decided to speak for publication, and has denied all press visitors an interview. The city marshal will call on her today and take her statement, together with that of the servant.

The details of the funeral have not been arranged as yet, but will be before the day ends.

It is becoming well settled that there was

Not Perfect Harmony

in the Borden household.

It is said Lizzie and her stepmother never got along together peacefully, and that for a considerable time back they have not spoken.

When seen this morning, however, Mr. Morse denied the story, saying Lizzie and Mrs. Borden were always friendly.

Mr. Morse made his first appearance about 8 o'clock. He had a basket in his hand, and was evidently on his way to a store. He walked down 2d st. with a policeman at his heels, and soon after returned and went indoors.

He came out later on another errand, and again was trailed by the sleuth-hound of the law.

Then he stayed indoors until noon.

The writer has the assurance of the chief of police that no move will be made by his department until after the funeral tomorrow. Then the procedure will depend upon a combination of circumstances that are now being investigated.

The New York Times

A LARGE REWARD OFFERED

STEADY SEARCH INTO THE MYSTERIOUS BORDEN MURDER

POLICE KEEP THE CLOSEST WATCH ON THE HOUSE AND ON SUSPECTED RELATIVES-MR. BORDEN'S WEALTH-PUBLIC EXCITEMENT IS STILL ON THE INCREASE.

FALL RIVER, Mass., Aug 5.-After a most thorough and persistent search no trace has been found of the murderer of Mr. and Mrs. Andrew J. Borden, who were killed yesterday at their home. Four policemen are on guard at the house and have been patrolling the neighborhood since the affair was made public. A few very near relatives are allowed to enter. Those who went in today were a Mr. Morse of New Bedford, a cousin of the suspected man and another close friend who gave his name as Fish. These men can give no reason why Morse should be under suspicion other than the fact he happened to be in this neighborhood at the time. He would not benefit by the death of either of the parties unless a will was made, and none has been found.

Emma, the daughter who was visiting in the vicinity of New Bedford when the murders took place, is at home today and has charge of the house. Her sister Lizzie is in no better condition than she was yesterday when she discovered her father dead.

This morning State Detective Seaver and City Marshal Hilliard held a long consultation and later on visited and interrogated Miss Lizzie at the house. The result of their investigation will not be known until an arrest of some kind has been made, and that is not likely to take place until after the funeral unless they find reason to change their suspicions.

The funeral will take place to-morrow morning at 11 o'clock and will be strictly private. The services will be conducted by City Missionary Buck, who is a close friend of the family, and the interment will take place at Oak Grove Cemetery. At the present time both bodies are lying in the dining room, the windows of which the servant girl was washing shortly before the tragedy became known.

The following advertisement will appear in to-night's local papers:

$5,000 REWARD

The above reward will be paid to any one who may secure the arrest and conviction of the person or persons who occasioned the death of Andrew J. Borden and his wife.

EMMA J. BORDEN
LIZZIE J. BORDEN

To-day the business men of the city have been discussing Mr. Borden's wealth and business methods, and the discussion serves to add to the general astonishment that a crime of such a nature should be perpetrated within a stone's throw of the City Hall.

The Assesor's books show that he was taxed for $173,650 worth of real estate, most of which is situated on South Main Street, in the very centre of the city. His latest purchase was the Birch property, for which he paid $23,000.

He rarely, if ever, owed anybody. Whenever he made a purchase he paid for it in cash or checks, never caring to handle notes of any kind. One of the largest financiers here said this morning that he doubted if a summary of his debts would show more than $1,000 due. His personal estate is variously estimated at between $175,000 and $250,000. Most of it is invested in mill stocks, bank stocks, and Government bonds.

The Evening Globe says this evening that a nost important clue is in posssession of the police. From Clerk Eli Bence, at D.R. Smith's drug store, they learned last night that Miss Borden had been in the store within the past two days and had inquired for a certain poison.

The clerk was asked to accompany the officers, who closely questioned him as to the facts relative to the time, the girl's condition mentally and the amount and quantity of the poison she had bought. The officers then took the drug clerk to a residence on Second Street, where Miss Lizzie was stopping for the time being. The young man was not previously well acquainted with the young woman, but he had told them that he could identify her at sight. He did identify her and told the police officers that she was in his place of business and made inquiry for a bottle of poison.

The Boston Herald

LIZZIE BORDEN

Her School and Later Life - A Noble Woman, Though Retiring.

FALL RIVER, Aug 6.-It is the men who have, since the murder, been accorded the space to talk to Lizzie A. Borden, the younger daughter, during the past few days.

It is the gentlemen with whom she was acquainted who have given her character and her personality to the world since the public cared to know about her.

None of her lady friends, the women who knew her, with whom she grew up, those with whom she has been associated day by day and year after year, have yet presented their Lizzie Borden.

A woman's opinion of a woman is a consideration Lizzie Borden has not yet been allowed.

Desiring to present this young woman as her friends have known her, to picture her as she daily appeared among women, the writer spent the greater part of the afternoon and evening in conversation with Lizzie's friends.

They talked of her life, of her inclinations, her interest in church work, her modesty of manner, unswerving sincerity, gentle forbearance and aspirations to be and to do all that is best and right in life.

From the consensus of opinion it can well be said: In Lizzie Borden's life there is not one unmaidenly nor a single deliberately unkind act.

Lizzie Borden's life is full of good works, kindly offices in the church and in the society of her friends.

As Lizzie Borden appeared today, as she was stepping into the carriage to follow her parents remains to the cemetery, to the writer, who had never seen her before, it seemed as if she was well-deserving of the ecomiums of her friends and of the kind words which follow.

She makes an exceedingly favorable impression and her dignity and her reserve are at once impressed.

It was a trying ordeal to pass before the eyes of a crowd of 1500 morbidly curious spectators.

She wore a tight fitting black lace dress with a plain skirt and waist of equally modest cut and finish, while a dark hat, trimmed with similar material, rested upon her head.

Of medium height, she is possessed of a symmetrical figure with a retiring manner and a carriage which would dignifiedly repel the attention

Her Personal Charms

might attract.

A wealth of black hair is revealed under the hat which, arranged on top of her head, is trained about her forehead in short curls, parted in the centre and thrown over to the sides.

Her dark, lustrous eyes, ordinarily flashing, were dimmed, and her pale face was evidence of the physical suffering she was undergoing and had experienced.

To sum up, Miss Lizzie Borden, without a word from herself in her own defence, is a strong argument in her own favor.

Although over 30 years old, it cannot be said that she looks it.

In contradistinction from her sister, she looks as much as six years younger than she is as Emma L. Borden looks as many years older than she is.

Lizzie was born in the old family homestead on Ferry st., in which her father has lived and his father before him.

It is the same estate which the dead Andrew J. Borden deeded to the two girls in 1887.

As a child she was of a very sensitive nature, inclined to be non-communicative with new acquaintances, and this characteristic has tenaciously clung to her all through life, and has been erroneously interpreted.

Her sister, being older, was a constant guide and an idolized companion.

An unusual circumstance is that of her practically having no choice of friends until she attained womanhood.

At the usual age she was sent to the Morgan street school, embracing primary and grammar grades.

Her school days were perhaps unlike most girls in this lack of affiliation with her fellow pupils.

As a scholar she was not remarkable for brilliancy, but she was conscientious in her studies and with application always held a good rank in her class.

She entered the high school when about 15 or 16 years old. It was then held in a wooden building on the corner of June and Locust sts., which was removed when the present mammoth structure was presented to the city.

Her life was uneventful during the few years following her leaving school. She abandoned her piano music lessons because, although making encouraging progress, she conceived the idea that she was not destined to become a good musician,

If she could not excel in this accomplishment she did not wish to pursue the study, and so her friends heard her play thereafter but little.

Her father and mother were religious and regular church attendants, and she has been surrounded by

Christian Home Influences.

When a young girl, she accompanied her parents to Chicago and was there a member of the Sunday school class and punctual in attendance.

She was, however, a girl with anything but an enthusiastic idea of her own personal attainments.

She thought people were not favorably disposed toward her and that she made a poor impression.

This conduced to the acceptance of this very opinion among church people, and consequently the young woman was to some extent avoided by the young women of the church.

There was a remarkable change in her some five years ago and at that time she first began to fraternize with church people.

Then, of course, when she was thoroughly understood, when the obnoxiously retiring manner was dissipated and the responsive nature of the girl came to view, she became at once popular and then came the acquisition of the friends who today sound her praises.

THE MISSION CHAPEL OF THE CENTRAL CONGREGATIONAL CHURCH

The chapel, located on Pleasant Street, where Lizzie taught a Sunday School class.

The New York Times

THE FALL RIVER MYSTERY

LOOKING FOR THE ASSASSIN OF MR. AND MRS. BORDEN.

FALL RIVER, Mass., Aug.6.-Some interesting clues were worked out by the police to-day relative to two mysterious visitors at the Borden homestead prior to the assassination of old Mr. and Mrs. Borden. No positive light was thrown on the mystery of the murders, however.

Last Monday morning, about 9 o'clock, a horse and buggy turned into Second Street out of Spring, and stopped in front of the Borden residence. A man who is employed nearby sat in his buggy almost opposite and facing south. He had ample opportunity and time to take a careful look at the vehicle, and the circumstances of the two strange men calling at the Borden house made an impression on his mind which he remembers distinctly. One of the men got out of the buggy and rang the doorbell. As he stood there the observer saw him plainly, and remembers that his description was that of a man about twenty-five years of age, with sallow complexion, soft hat, dark trousers, with a wide strip of dark material running down the leg, and russet, or baseball, shoes. He was about 5 feet 9 inches high. The shoes in particular attracted his attention, as they were of peculiar make and color and were laced. Mr. Borden opened the door and the man spoke a few words and was admitted. The man who remained in the buggy was not as closely scrutinized, and his description is not so well remembered. The man who entered remained about ten minutes and then came out with his hat in his hand. The team was driven off in the direction of Pleasant Street.

The circumstance is considered of importance when the fact is known that the police have in their possession knowledge of the only person who tells of having seen a strange man at the Borden house at the time of the murders.

The bodies of the murdered couple were buried today. As early as 9 o'clock the house was surrounded by a great crowd of curiosity seekers. Reporters, artists, photographers, and policemen were active among them. Mr. Morse came from the house and talked freely with a group of reporters. He said it was a terrble thing to be suspected and shadowed as he has been, but he courts the fullest investigation and is anxious and willing to do all that he can to trace the perpetrators of the great crime. He said that Miss Lizzie Borden's health was in about the same condition as it was last Thursday afternoon. She did not mingle with the family to any great extent. When Mr. Fish of Hartford, a nephew of her stepmother, appeared she gave him a very cool reception. About 11 o'clock preparations were commenced for the funerals. People numbering between 3,000and 4,000 assembled in front of the house and about twenty policemen maintained a clear passageway.

The Rev. Dr. Adams of the First Congregational Church and City Missionary Buck soon arrived. The bodies were laid in two plain black, cloth-covered caskets in the sitting room where Mr. Borden was killed. An ivy wreath was placed on Mr. Borden's bier and a bouquet of white roses and fern leaves, tied with a white satin ribbon, was placed beside Mrs. Borden. There were about seventy-five persons present at the services in the house, which consisted of reading from the Scriptures and prayer. There was no singing and no remaarks. The mourners were Mrs. Oliver Gray, stepmother of the dead woman; G. H. Fish and wife of Hartford, the latter a sister of Mrs. Borden; Dr. Bowen and wife, Southard H. Miller, and a few of the neighbors. The burial was private, that is, only a few of the immediate friends were asked to accompany the remains to the cemetery.

The pall bearers for Mr. Borden were Abram C. Hart, cashier of the Union Savings Bank; George W. Dean, a retired capitalist; Jerome C. Borden, a relative of the deceased; Richard B. Borden, Treasurer of the Troy Mills; in which Mr. Borden was a Director; James M. Osborn, an associate of the deceased in several mills; Andrew J. Borden, Treasurer of the Merchants' Mill, in which Mr. Borden was a large owner. The pall bearers for Mrs. Borden were James C. Eddy, Henry C. Buffington, Frank L. Almy, J. Henry Wells, Simeon B. Chase, and John H. Boone.

As the procession wended its way along North Main Street many old associates of Mr. Borden were seen to raise their hats. Miss Lizzie C. Borden and Miss Emma Borden were, of course, the principal mourners. Miss Lizzie went out of the house first, leaning on the undertaker's arm. Her nerves were completely unstrung, as was shown by the trembling of her body and the manner in which she bore down on her supporter. When she reached her carriage she fell back exhausted on the cushions.

The New York Herald

NO MOTIVE YET FOUND FOR THE BORDEN MURDER.

Lizzie and Emma, the Daughters, and Morse, the Brother-in-Law, Are Suspected and Kept Under Close Surveillance.

THOROUGHLY SEARCHED THE HOUSE.

While the People Are at the Cemetery the Police Push Their Investigations, but Decline to Say with What Results.

ARRESTS MAY SOON BE MADE.

Active Movements Among the Authorities Which May Presage Action—Theorizing on the Tragedy.

[BY TELEGRAPH TO THE HERALD.]

FALL RIVER, Mass., August 6, 1892.—**Fifty hours after the killing of Mr. and Mrs. A. J. Borden, which goes on record as the most remarkable murder New England has ever known, the suspected persons are still free.**

Though the day brought no arrest, it was one of intense excitement. At this hour the unusual activity in police circles seems significant. It follows closely upon the detailed search of the Borden house, made to-day while its inmates were at Oak Grove Cemetery, the destination of that strangest of funerals which walked down Second street precisely forty-eight hours after the murderer found his victims.

The chief mourners were John V. Morse, the dead man's brother-in-law; Emma Borden and Lizzie Borden.

These people were practically under arrest, particularly Lizzie Borden. The orders given the police who guard the Borden house, that none of the inmates shall move without having an officer in close company, held good at the funeral.

Before the mourners had gone half a block from the house the police were at work. It was their first chance to work undisturbed by the presence of the Borden girls or the servant. They ransacked the house from attic to cellar. Lizzie's room, which she refused to allow the police to enter on the day of the murder, was minutely searched.

LOOKED LIKE AN ARREST.

Then the police went away. A little later Police Captain Desmond returned and instituted a second inspection of the premises. Then the Captain hurried away after Marshal Hilliard. Those who saw his haste and evident excitement thought an arrest was to follow. It did not come, however.

Clew after clew has been followed. At this hour the searchers are as ignorant of the facts as they were when Officer Allen, in breathless horror, rushed to Police Headquarters on Thursday and gasped, "Mr. and Mrs. Borden have been murdered."

MRS. BORDEN, THE MURDERED WOMAN.
[From the last picture taken of her, fifteen years ago, at the age of fifty-two.]

Suspicion undoubtedly centres about Lizzie Borden, the prepossessing daughter of the murdered man. The reasons for this are various. She it was who gave the alarm; she, according to her own statement, left her father alive and well at a quarter to eleven in the sitting room; she went to the barn after a piece of lead, to return in twenty minutes and discover the crime.

The fact that she tried to buy hydrocianic acid at D. R. Smith's drug store on Wednesday and has since been identified by Eli Bence, has done much to direct suspicion toward her. But the motive is not there, or at least it is not yet apparent. While it might have been possible for Lizzie to have hacked the heads of her father and mother to pieces, no good reason why she should have done so has been advanced.

If the woman is sane, and her family physician tells me he has no reason to think her deranged, it is inconcievable that she could have despatched the old people, gone to the barn for the purpose of concealing the weapon, according to a preconceived plan, and then returned to play the part of a bereaved daughter so well.

WORE THE SAME DRESS.

The statement of the servant girl that Lizzie Borden wore the same dress all the morning and that upon that garment there was no spot of blood has been verified. So terrible were the wounds and so violent the hemorrhage from them that the murderer must have carried some mark of the deed upon him.

The police have found no fitting motive for the crime. Cause for hard feeling against Borden there undoubtedly was, but its source was not such as would give rise to the fiendish hatred so evident in the work of Thursday.

As some one has aptly said, had Lizzie and John Morse been so anxious to have the old people out of the way that they decided upon murder they would have killed their victims genteelly, instead of lending to the scene that Jack the Ripper aspect which marked it. Morse has practically proven an alibi.

Hypolyte Martel, a clerk for Philias Martel, a druggist, on Pleasant street, relates the following story:—Last Monday he was approached in the store by a young lady who wanted to buy arsenic from him and was willing to give any price for it. The clerk told her that as the druggist was not present he could not possibly comply with her wishes, whereupon she went out much disappointed. She returned twenty minutes later and asked for prussic acid. The article was again refused her with the advice to return when the druggist would be back from dinner.

Mr. Martel describes the caller as being about twenty-six years and weighing about 150 pounds. He says he could recognize her if he should see her.

Lawyer Jennings, who handled Borden's legal affairs, says the crime will benefit no one financially. His statement of the case shows how light is the evidence yet collected.

"Who," I asked him, "would profit by Borden's death?"

"I don't know that there is a will. No one would profit further than the natural distribution of the estate. There was nothing in the distribution of it to offer a motive. Nothing at all."

"Have you any theory of the crime?"

"I have not. I have read many cases in the books, the newspapers and in fiction, in novels, and I never heard of a case like this. A most outrageous, brutal crime, perpetrated in midday in an open house on a prominent thoroughfare and absolutely motiveless.

"The theories advanced about quarrels over wages and about the possession of stores and that sort of thing are simply ridiculous. They do not offer a motive. If it was shown that the thing was done during even such a quarrel in the heat of passion it would be different. But to suppose that for such a matter a man will lie in wait or steal upon his victim while asleep and hack him to death is preposterous. Even with revenge in his heart the sight of his victim would disarm any man."

"Then to consider the almost miracle necessary for a man to enter, commit the deed and escape without being discovered," I suggested.

"It would be a remarkable combination of circumstances, but not a miracle," said Mr. Jennings. "I have recalled how frequently I have entered and gone through my mother's house and out again without meeting a soul, and how I could at such times have carried off most anything without being discovered."

"What is your notion about it being done by some member of the household?"

"Well, there are but two women of the household and this man Morse, whose name is connected with it. He accounts satisfactorily for every hour of that morning. Further than that he appeared on the scene almost immediately after the discovery from the outside and in the same clothes that he had worn in the morning. Now it is almost impossible that this frightful work could have been done without the clothes of the person who did it being bespattered with blood.

"Then came Lizzie Borden, dressed to-day in the same clothes she wore yesterday. She has not changed her clothes since. This, together with the improbability that any woman could do such a piece of work, makes the suspicion seem altogether irrational."

To-day it has been given out that the hatchet or axe with which the murder was done has been found and that it was slightly marked by blood, and had a few hairs clinging to it.

The story was groundless. no weapon has been found since Thursday when the police carried away two axes and two hatchets, neither of which were of suspicious appearance.

The latest story is that Borden, who had nearly $500,000 to dispose of, was taking stock of his assets during the week previous to the crime, with a view to making a will. It is thought that this might have given some one a motive for killing the old man previous to the completion of the will, but it is difficult to see why the daughter had any cause to fear that she was to be disinherited.

Attempts have been made to-day to connect John V. Morse with the crime in the rôle of accessory, by the story that a stranger seen on the steps of the Borden house on Monday, tallies in description with the chief of a band of itinerant horse traders whose headquarters are at Westport. This is near South Dartmouth, where Morse had been staying previous to the murder. He had done some business in horses and from that theorists jump to connecting him with the gang.

A Frenchman picked up a suspicious stranger a few miles out of New Bedford on Thursday, and says the man hastily thrust money into his hands and asked to be driven to Westport in haste. The Frenchman went only as far as his own house. His wife utterly refused to let him go further with the stranger, as she did not like his appearance and manner. The Frenchman

THE BORDEN HOMESTEAD AT 92 SECOND STREET IN FALL RIVER

gave the stranger his dollar back again and declined to aid him in any way.

Important as these clews may be if nothing tangible to back them up can be found there are many circumstances which render them of doubtful value. A man such as the Frenchman's stranger would have been noticed by some one in Fall River if his actions were so suspicious. As a matter of fact, no one in the town or about the Borden home saw any suspicious stranger on the day of the murder, though it would have been seemingly impossible for him to have left the house or entered it without having been seen. No stranger had a motive for killing old man Borden unless there is some awful skeleton in the Borden closet which does not yet appear, or unless the work was that of an assassin hired to do the job.

In the latter case it would naturally be supposed that the method would have been very different and the mutilation omitted.

Late to-night John V. Morse left the Borden House and walked rapidly down Second street and toward the business portion of the town. There was an officer at his heels. He wandered around for nearly an hour and then returned to the house, the detective never leaving him for an instant. Whether he wished to get the air or merely to test the closeness of the espionage to which he is subject is not certain.

The fact that a physician was hurriedly summoned to the Borden house to-night gave rise to the story that Lizzie had attempted to take poison. The guards at the house deny all knowledge of any such attempt. Mayor Coughlin and Marshal Hilliard spent an hour at the house to-night. The Mayor, himself a surgeon, can suggest no good theory of the crime.

THEY WERE NOT POOR.

The Borden girls were not poor. If their father had died without a cent to his credit they would have been in no danger of starving. About town they are reported to be worth $10,000 each, perhaps more, but not less. Both girls have been given property by their father. He did not spend money unnecessarily and would buy as closely as he could, but he was good to his family and didn't propose to see the girls suffer. He gave them different properties at different times, until in the aggregate the united possessions amounted to a considerable sum.

It is related that when there was trouble about the collection of the rents of two tenement houses which the girls owned he traded with them and gave them a block of stock in return for the houses, as the girls much preferred collecting dividends to dunning for rents. This fact shows that the old gentleman had no disposition to treat his own kin unfairly or too closely.

The talk about the girls having feelings against their stepmother is not regarded as in any way pertinent to the case at present. Their mother died at Lizzie's birth and their father married a second time when the younger girl was three years old. Lizzie has known no other mother.

Rumor after rumor of the most sensational character is being set on foot to-night. The latest is the worst of all. It is now said that the police in their examination of Lizzie Borden's bedroom found some spots of blood on some of her discarded clothing.

When asked to-night if he had found the weapon with which he thought the crime was committed, Marshal Hilliard said:—"We have discovered four—two axes and two hatchets," replied the Chief, smiling, "and they are now locked up in my private office."

"Have you found any traces of blood on them or is there any evidence that they have been cleaned recently?"

"Not that I have noticed, and I should say that not one of the four was ever used in the commission of the crime. They are ordinary axes and hatchets and were found in the cellar of the house by my officers. Two of them looked as though they had been considerably used and are somewhat rusty, but so far as we can see there is no evidence of either having been recently sharpened or cleaned."

"Did you find any hair, presumably human, on one of the hatchets?"

"I did not, and I do not know that any of the officers did. I am inclined to question any statement that a weapon bearing evidence of having been used in this murder has been found. I certainly do not know of any."

"Did the officers find any hatchet in the barn?"

"No, sir; the two axes and two hatchets were in the cellar. They were found in places similar to those where any man keeps like tools in his cellar."

There may be civil as well as criminal complication in the Borden tragedy. They would come in reaching a decision as to whether Mr. and Mrs. Borden met death first. There is a diversity of opinion in this phase of the case and there is little to show which side has taken the correct stand.

The police at present are working on the theory that Mrs. Borden was killed first, and with that opinion is involved the only motive which can now be assigned for the crime—that of gain. Quite a tidy sum is the issue in the case. On the basis that Mr. Borden was worth in the vicinity of $400,000 it represents one-third of an estate termed the widow's dower.

If the wife was killed first this would not be taken into consideration. But if the murderer struck down the old gentleman in the beginning, the one-third share goes to the heirs of Mrs. Borden, even if she was a widow but five seconds.

In the latter case the Misses Borden, who are not the heirs of Mrs. Borden, will be entitled in the division of the property to only two-thirds of the estate, and the one-third will go to the nearest kin of Mrs. Borden. If, however, it is decided the other way, that the wife died first, the entire estate will be divided between the two daughters.

LIZZIE J. BORDEN, DAUGHTER OF THE VICTIMS.

WHO WAS KILLED FIRST?

The police are working on the latter theory. With witnesses to the murder as scarce as they are at present, the circumstantial evidence as incomplete as it is, it will be a hard matter to show five minutes between the deaths. It may however, be less difficult to prove that there was an hour or so between the time of the murder of Mrs. Borden and that of her husband. Her movements are not accounted for after nine o'clock in the morning, at which time she went up stairs to arrange the apartment in which Mr. Morse slept the night before.

How much time was required in this work cannot be estimated. It certainly was completed when the murder was committed, whether fifteen minutes, an hour or two hours after she went upstairs.

It is believed by the police that in those two hours she could have more than completed the work and gone to another part of the house, or in any event to her own room, if alive, when really it is evident that she had not left the room she first entered.

The analysis of the stomachs will probably show by the amount of food digested whether there was any material difference in the time of the fatal attacks. Of course, if the second murder was committed only a few minutes after the first the digestive organs will fail to show the difference, but if an hour or more elapsed it can be shown, provided breakfast was eaten by the couple at the same time.

There is one fact which, more than anything else, leads the police to believe that when Mr. Borden returned to his home from his trip down town to deposit the money and checks received Wednesday, his wife's body rested in a room above, brutally hacked.

It is this:—When the medical examiner reached the scene the remains of Mr. Borden were still warm, while the body of the wife was cold. If both had been killed at the same time it is reasonable to suppose that Mrs. Borden's body would have retained heat much longer than her husband, because she was large and fleshy and several years younger than he was, and naturally her vitality was greater.

WHERE MR. BORDEN WAS MURDERED

Therefore this fact is almost conclusive that the murderer's work was first done in the parlor chamber, where John V. Morse slept last Wednesday night.

At the present time few question the alibi which Morse has attempted to establish. The fact has been established that Mr. Borden was murdered between ten minutes to eleven and three minutes past eleven o'clock Thursday forenoon. His wife probably met death a short time before that. But at the time mentioned John V. Morse was visiting his niece and nephew from Minnesota. They are reasonably positive about the time he left the house, and the time is established beyond a doubt by the horse car conductor who had charge of the vehicle in which Mr. Morse rode that day, and by another conductor whose car passed the one in which he rode.

The New York Times

THE BORDEN MURDER CASE

NO PROGRESS HAS BEEN MADE TOWARD SOLVING ITS MYSTERY

FALL RIVER, Mass., Aug 7-City Marshal Hilliard was interviewed to-night regarding the Borden double murder. Speaking of the spots of blood said to have been found on the axe in the custody of the police last night, he said:

"I don't know whether these spots were blood or iron rust. They might be taken for either, but until the Boston chemists pass an opinion it would be folly for me to speak. At this moment I can say there is nothing to connect any members of the family with the murder. We can reach a certain point, but thenceforward things will not match, and we can't make them. A great deal has been said about the fact that no arrests have been made up to this time. Those persons in the house have practically been under arrest the past few days. It would be folly for us to place this family behind bars when so many outside clues are yet to be looked up."

There is much faultfinding in town at the lack of progress in the case. Most persons think the family should have been made to talk long before this time; also, that a thorough search should have been initiated at once. At present persons who were near the family are under the protection and direction of ex-Inspector Hanscom and Lawyer Jennings, with instructions to refer to them all inquiries even when asked by their most intimate friends.

The Fall River Herald

VISITED THE TOMB.

Medical Examiner Dolan Examines Borden's Body.

AXE FAILS TO FIT SOME OF THE WOUNDS.

The Absence of Blood Continues a Puzzle.

Mrs. Borden's Letter as Yet Unaccounted For.

Minister Jubb Speaks About the Murder.

Four days have now past since the terrible Borden murder was perpetrated, and the murderer is still at large. For four days the police authorities have bent their best energies to the discovery of the perpetrator of the crime or his motive, and have reached one conclusion only. Still they hesitate, because their chain of evidence is purely circumstantial at best,and there are important missing links in it at that.

Andrew J. Jennings, who has followed the evidence carefully in behalf of the Borden estate, declares that he does not believe the police have evidence enough upon which to make an arrest. For the want of a better clue, public opinion has accepted the theory that the deed must have been done by somebody inside the Borden house. Accordingly a persistent clamor has been made for the arrest of the suspects. It may be reassuring to such people to know that from an hour after the murder every person who was in the Borden house has been practically under arrest. Night and day the police have stood guard there and have closely watched all the goings and comings, and there has been no chance for anybody to escape even if there was any desire to do so.

A SEARCH OF THE HOUSE.

Saturday and Sunday were devoid of startling revelations in the case, but during that time the best efforts of the police were made. While the bodies lay in the house no attempt was made to search the premises thoroughly. Faith was lodged in the officers to prevent the removal of any article from the house, and while the various clues were being run down by the detectives of the police force, the hunt for a concealed weapon inside of the house was deferred until after the funeral.

About 4 o'clock Marshal Hilliard, Assistant Marshal Fleet, Captain Desmond, Detective Seaver, Medical Examiner Dolan and Andrew J. Jennings,Esq., entered the house and proceeded to make a thorough hunt of the premises. Every facility was offered to them to carry on their search, and the members of the family volunteered any assistance in their power. This is in direct opposition to the story printed Saturday that Lizzie Borden had declined to admit the police into her room to make a search. The attic to which the visitors ascended was spacious. It contained four rooms and an open area, into which the stairway extends. The two rooms in the rear were found to be scantily furnished. One of them was occupied by the servant, Bridget Sullivan, whose personal effects were about all contained in a small trunk. The lid was quickly raised and the contents inspected. It contained only clothing and a few mementoes treasured by the owner, as might be judged by the careful manner in which they were preserved. The bed was carefully inspected, the mattress shaken up and pounded and the adjoining closet searched in vain. All that met the searchers' gaze were packages and boxes of heavy clothing stored for the summer, comforters for the beds and similar articles.

The search then extended to the second furnished room, which contained a painted set. The bed had the appearance of not having been used for some time. Every corner and every crevice in which an article might be secreted was examined, but nothing bearing on the murder was discovered. Nearly an hour was spent in the attic alone.

Then the party went downstairs. The ladies heard them coming and went further downstairs, leaving the searchers in full possession of their rooms. To illustrate the officers' movements, a description of the house is necessary. On the front, facing Second street, at the northern corner, is the guest chamber, which leads out of a spacious hall to the right. It was here the murder of Mrs. Borden took place, positively some time in advance of the husband's death, and there it was that Mr. Morse slept on the night preceding the tragedy. The room is large, with windows on two sides, and is handsomely papered. The windows are adorned with lace draperies. The furniture is a heavy set of black walnut. In one corner was the stain where the ill-fated victim fell, and where he life-blood colored the floor a deep crimson.

A long time was consumed in a minute inspection of the parlor, library, sitting-room, dining-room and kitchen, which availed nothing. In the cellar the wood pile was overturned and every crevice and crack looked into. There was nothing that could shed any light upon the crime. About 6:30 o'clock Marshal Hilliard concluded that the search had been carried far enough.

THOSE AXES.

After the search of the house, Mayor Coughlin visited the police station to have a conference with Marshal Hilliard. Throughout this entire affair he has been a close adviser with the police. He was among the first at the house after the murder and was present at the autopsy. Since then, night and day, the mayor has devoted himself to the case, urging the police to do their utmost in their hunt for the murderer and assisting by his medical knowledge the workings of the clues which had their origin in the physical condition of the victims.

Two axes and a hatchet were picked up in the cellar on the day of the murder and carried to the police station. Mayor Coughlin closely examined these, and on one of them detected spots that looked like blood. It was a long handled axe, and there were three suspicious stains upon it. The microscope gave evidence of blood, and the axe will be saved for further examination. The mayor is determined to allow no clue to be left unworked, but he admits that he does not place great confidence in the importance of his find. These axes lay on the cellar floor just after the murder and were seen by a great many people who ranged through the cellar. Several persons picked them up and looked them over with curiosity. This was within ten minutes of the announcement of the murder. In order to remove the blood from the axe it would have been necessary to have dipped it into water, and the amateur detectives would have found the blade and handle wet when they made their inspection. It was reported that a spot of blood had been discovered on one of Lizzie Borden's garments, but little importance has been ascribed to that.

AN UNSATISFACTORY INTERVIEW.

After consulting for a long time, Mayor Coughlin and Marshal Hilliard got into the mayor's carriage and drove to the Borden house Saturday evening to have a conversation with the family. Mayor Coughlin assured the members that every means would be taken by the authorities to discover the murderer and to clear up the mystery. The police would be on hand to keep the crowd in the street from becoming annoying. An attempt was then made to elicit information from the Bordens or Morse, who were present during the conversation, which would be of advantage to the police. Mayor Coughlin first went into particulars concerning the whereabouts of the mother, Mrs. Borden.

"When did you last see your mother, Lizzie?" inquired the mayor.

"I don't think I saw mother after 9 o'clock. She went up stairs to put shams on the pillows."

The question was repeated several times, but Miss Borden seemed positive that she could not be mistaken as to the time.

She was then examined as to the door which leads from one of the lower rooms to the staircase in the front hall, which connects the first floor with the upper entry. As nearly as the young woman could recall, that door was closed. She had seen nobody open or close it, of course, but her impression was that it was closed and had remained closed during the morning, until Dr. Bowen ascended in search of her mother.

It would naturally be surmised that if the murderer passed through the house while Miss Lizzie was in the barn and before Mr. Borden returned from his trip down town, he would have left this door open. He found the coast clear when he descended the stairs, and a man as clever as he would have arranged to command as much of a view after the foul deed had been accomplished as possible. If, when he attempted to make his escape, he noticed that the rooms leading to the rear or side door were occupied, he could have sneaked back and waited for a more favorable opportunity. If he were concealed upstairs and had been in hiding for some time, he would have had to take his chances on doors, of course, and as has been demonstrated, his chances from beginning to end were good fairies so far as his precious skin was concerned.

It appears then that nobody saw Mrs. Borden for two hours, unless the servant, who has not been questioned, can give some information of her whereabouts. It is plain, too, that nobody knows what she was doing. She could not have been busy in the spare chamber for that length of time, for there was absolutely nothing to do there. The bed was made, the shams were arranged on the pillows, the towels laid scrupulously clean on a rack, and the room was in perfect order when Dr. Bowen entered, all but that heavy form with the mangled head, which was stretched motionless on the floor. Mrs. Borden had not gone out during the morning, at least the gown indicated that she had not left the house, because she wore an old calico dress, much worn, and not her street gown.

RUMORS OF ALL SORTS.

Saturday night all sorts of strange rumors were rife upon the street, and crowds of people made their way into Second street to stare at the windows of the house and to speculate concerning the secret which it contained. Police officers guarded front and rear, and a squad kept the crowds from congregating in the roadway. Early in the night there was considerable commotion at police headquarters and rumors were thick to the effect that a fresh trail had been struck. The marshal hurried up to his office from the supper table and in company with a couple of officers drove off hastily. They refused to make known their errand, however, and the announcement was made to the press representatives that there would be no important developments before Sunday. That did not fit into a story which leaked out from another quarter, however, and the reporters concluded to sit up a while. Nothing of an alarming nature happened, however.

Sunday was a quiet day around the house. Emma Borden appeared at the door at 8 o'clock to take in the milk. The servant girl, Bridget Sullivan, could stand the strain no longer and left the house Saturday night to join her friends. She will be on hand when the police want her to testify in the case. None of the family ventured out to church, and there was nobody visible at the windows.

EVENT OF SUNDAY.

The event of the day was the arrival at the house of Supt. Hanscom of the Boston Pinkerton agency, who entered with Lawyer Jennings during the forenoon. Hanscom arrived at the Mellen house late Saturday night, and there was a big stir when it became known that he had been hired by the Borden's to look after their interests. This was intensified somewhat Sunday when it was learned that he chose to work on lines independent of the police, and had had little conversation with the local authorities.

Detective Hanscom talked at length to the reporters in the Mellen house, and his ideas do not correspond with the government theory. He reviewed the case at length, but admitted that he had been at work on it too short a time to form a definite opinion. He had questioned Lizzie, but found her too exhausted physically for a searching examination. The reaction had come and he did not want to weary her. He was favorably impressed with her appearance, and stated that she, like her sister, Miss E., appeared to be sincere and truthful. He questioned particularly the time that she spent in the barn, and she was positive that she was there 20 minutes or possibly half an hour. The murder looked like the work of a lunatic, while Lizzie appeared to be a level-headed, self-possessed woman. If she was in the barn half an hour, a man might have entered the house, committed both murders, and escaped by the way of the basement through the door leading to the back yard. That door was found open after the murders, though it was usually closed. Detective Hanscom admitted that he had a varied experience, and usually began by looking for the cause of death and the motive. Here the cause was apparent, but he had as yet found no motive. He had attempted to discover if Mr. Borden had any enemy capable of the deed.

At last account Lizzie Borden had given way under the great strain and excitement of the last four days and Dr. Bowen had been summoned twice last evening to attend her. It was expected that morbid curiosity would fill Oak Grove cemetery with crowds of pedestrians yesterday, but for some reason or other there were fewer visitors than usual. A friend of the Borden family called during the day and two of John Morse's acquaintances from South Dartmouth paid him a visit.

DR. DOLAN AT A LOSS.

There was no special excitement at police headquarters. Medical Examiner Dolan held a long interview with Marshal Hilliard in the latter's office, and Detective Hanscom had a talk with Andrew Jennings. The medical examiner states that the only discovery of importance made during the thorough search of the Borden house Saturday afternoon was in the spare bed room, where Mrs. Borden's body was found. Out near the window drops of blood were found, which indicated that the murdered woman had moved after the first blow was delivered. It is thought that that blow was the glancing one which has been described. The supposition is that the axe fell on the right side of the head, taking off the flesh and hair, and that the woman turned and reeled to the space between the dressing case and bureau where the mortal wound was delivered. After that, the blows fell thick and fast. It is believed that when she was approached, Mrs. Borden stood looking out of the window in this room, and her blood which stained it at this point bears out that view. Dr. Dolan says that the more he reflects on the small quantity of blood that was spilled, the more at a loss he is to account for it. To him it seems utterly inexplicable. Ordinarily, no matter how sharp the weapon used, the rooms would have been stained crimson had such a tragedy taken place in them. Even if no arterial blood made its appearance, and though the wounds were inflicted after death, the veins and brain would have discharged enough fluid and gray matter to have left their mark on the furniture. But with the exception of the stains near the window and the thick pool about the head of the unfortunate woman, the chamber was as clean as though it had been freshly washed and swept. Every time the axe fell it cut deeply, but there was no gush of blood from the frightful gashes. The same condition prevails in the sitting room below where Mr. Borden was butchered, and there was nothing to raise the suspicion that the murderer had cleaned anything, except the dripping axe.

That letter which it is alleged Mrs. Borden received on the morning of the tragedy continues to excite interest, and on this head Dr. Dolan likewise had a little information to give. He says that both Lizzie Borden and the servant told him that Mrs. Borden had received such a letter, and when he asked Lizzie what had become of it, she told him that she had been unable to find it; she feared that it had been burned in the kitchen stove. Nobody in the household seems to be able to give anything more than a general idea of the contents of the letter or note. It was from a friend who was ill, but if Mrs. Borden made this much known, it is curious that she did not state who the friend was or that the person with whom she was conversing did not have the curiosity to inquire.

It is certain that, so far as the public is

SIDE VIEW OF THE BORDEN HOUSE AND BARN

concerned, the time of all the occupants of the Borden homestead has not been satisfactorily accounted for. If Mrs. Borden disappeared at 9 o'clock to put shams on the pillows, and did not appear again, it is presumed that her stepdaughter remained downstairs while she was occupied on the second floor. At some time before Mr. Borden was killed, Bridget Sullivan went upstairs, and she may have seen her mistress on the floor. If the latter were in the habit of attending to household duties on the second floor for two hours at a time, her absence would have attracted attention, but if she visited all parts of the house like women do, it is a little singular that nobody missed her. At all events, no harm could come from ascertaining just what Miss Lizzie and the servant did with their time from the hour of rising until the murders were discovered.

EMPLOYED A MASON.

Another thorough research was made this morning. Among those present at the time outside of the regular inmates were Lawyer Jennings, Superintendent Hanscomb of the Boston Pinkerton agency, City Marshal Hilliard, Capt. Desmond, State Detective Seaver, Sergt. Edson and Officer Quigley. Charles H. Bryant the mason, was called in, and every fire place was opened and examined. Nothing could be found of the axe, and noting looked as though it had been disturbed. The wood in the cellar was turned over, and every inch of the building was sounded in the endeavor to find some recent hiding place, but once more the police were baffled and the conclusion was arrived at that the weapon had been conveyed from the premises.

City Missionary Buck in an interview expressed himself as a firm believer in Lizzie Borden's innocence. He said: "Aside from her christian character, her actions at the time of the murder count with me as indicating ignorance of the crime. I called on her in less than one hour after the discovery of her father's body. I asked her if there was anyone she suspected, and she replied in tears that she did not know of a person in the world who could have a motive for murdering her father. She highly endorsed the character of the Swede farm hand in Mr. Borden's employ, and said he was above suspicion.A guilty person takes every opportunity to throw suspicion on the innocent. Lizzie Borden did not do that."

As the case is involved at present it looks as if much would depend upon medical testimony. Dr. Dolan is taking care of that end of the case and will have the best experts obtainable to assist. In company with Assistant Marshal Fleet, Drs. Dolan and Leary visited the receiving vault Sunday and made a further examination of the bodies, taking measurements of the wounds and notes of other matters which will be of use when testimony is needed in these directions.

Late Sunday night it was learned that something of a sensational character is likely to occur. Just exactly what it will be could not be ascertained. It is believed that Medical Examiner Dolan will spring a surprise. He has been working harder than any man interested in the case, and he has had the least to say. It is believed that he will introduce some very important evidence at the inquest. It is probable that he will have the bloody clothes worn by the murdered people, which are buried in the yard of the Borden house, in the rear of the barn, dug up and produced in court. These clothes were buried at the request of Mr. Morse, who still remains at the house.

Dr. Bowen, the family physician of the Borden family, is likely to be a prominent witness before the inquest hearing. It is supposed that he knows considerably more about the status of the relations of the Borden family, in a professional way, than he has told, and that he may be brought out at the hearing. It is understood that he does not think Lizzie Borden is guilty of the crime, and that she is not insane or has ever showed any signs of insanity. Dr. Bowen was closeted with Mayor Coughlin in Marshal Hillard's private office for over an hour last evening, but what the interview was all about could not be learned. It was thought that an effort was made to glean from him something further about the social relations of the members of the Borden family.

This morning Dr. Dolan heard from the package in which were sent the viscera to Dr. Wood, the Boston chemist. Dr. Wood is not in Europe, as had been stated, but was in Boston and has received the package, the examination of which will be begun today. Dr. Dolan was interviewed relative to the spots of blood and the weapon which it is said had been discovered. He declined to state what kind of a weapon it was; neither did he care to affirm or deny a statement attributed to one of the officers in the case that hairs were found on it. From another source it is learned that the weapon in question is an axe.

AN IMPORTANT POINT.

The visit to the cemetery Sunday was an important one. The axe was taken along with Dr. Dolan and Assistant Marshal Fleet and was fitted into the wounds, with what conclusions cannot be stated at once. The blow which was delivered over the temple of both victims was with a dull edge, and it was impossible to tell whether the axe would fit the wound or not, so shattered was the bone. The cut which extended down the front of Mr. Borden's nose was in a soft part of the face, so that the entire edge of the weapon cut into the flesh. It was an easy matter to measure that, and it was found that while the exact length of the gash did not correspond with the width of the axe blade, yet it could readily have been made by such a weapon. None of the cuts on Mrs. Borden was so clean as that on the face of her husband. In every instance the axe had brought up against the skull, and it was not imbedded the entire width.

At the house this morning, the condition of things had not materially changed. It appears that no orders had been issued to prevent anybody from entering or leaving the house. Several friends of the young ladies called and were received, and about 8 o'clock Inspector Hanscom entered. Later he was joined by Lawyer Jennings, and the pair remained in the house for several hours.

The story of Mrs. Chace about a man being seen sitting on the fence at the time of the tragedy has been thoroughly sifted by Detectives Seaver and McHenry. The man who was engaged taking the pears at the time was named Patrick McGowan, a mason's helper employed by John Crowe.He stood on a pile of lumber, and at the time there were two other men employed in the yard cutting wood and drilling a stone. Both these men are confident that no person left the yard by that exit.

SAW A MAN AT MIDNIGHT.

The residence of Dr. Chagnon on Third street is situated close to the Borden property, both being divided by a fence about seven feet high. Mrs. Chagnon and her daughter, Martha, say that Wednesday night about 12 o'clock they distinctly saw a man jump over the fence into the Borden yard, and subsequently they heard a slight noise in the barn. The women were much frightened and told the story to the doctor on the morning of the day when the murder took place. Owing to the darkness of the street, they could not see the man plainly enough to give any description of his appearance.

NOTES OF THE AFFAIR.

Seven out of the nine stories that were reported to the police have been investigated, and every one found to be a myth.

Dr. Bowen said this noon that the Bordens were suffering from nervous prostration. Lizzie is somewhat the worse, as it was not until after returning from the funeral Saturday that she knew of the suspicion that was cast on her.

The statement of Mr. Morse that he had not been in the horse business since his return from the west was proven today by a visit to Westport by Officer Medley.

The Mrs. Borden who threw her three children into the cistern of the house south of Mr. Borden's residence is in no way related to any of the deceased. Thus no claim of insanity can be drawn from that quarter.

Marshal Hilliard ordered William Niles to be present at the house at 2:30 p. m. to dig up the clothes which were ordered to be buried behind the barn.

MINISTER JUBB

Appeals to the People to Refrain from Causeless Innuendos.

Mr. and Mrs. Borden were members of the Central Congregational church. Lizzie has been a teacher in the mission school connected with the parish, and has always been very active in the young people's societies and the work of the church. Sunday the central church worshippers met with the First Church congregation in the stone church on Main street. All of the pews were filled, many being in their seats some half hour before the service began. It was supposed that the Rev. W. Walker Jubb, who occupied the pulpit, would make some allusion to the awful experiences through which one family in his charge had been compelled to pass during the week, and the supposition was correct.

Mr. Jubb read for the morning lesson a portion of Matthew, containing the significant words which imply that what is concealed shall be revealed. In his prayer, Mr. Jubb evoked the divine blessing on the community, rendering thanks for the blessings bestowed on many, and, pausing, referred to the murder of two innocent persons. He prayed fervently that right might prevail, and that in good time the terrible mystery might be cleared away; that the people of the city might do everything in their power to assist the authorities, and asked for divine guidance for the police, that they might prosecute unflinchingly and unceasingly the search for the murderer. Mr. Jubb prayed that their hands might be strengthened, that their movements might be characterized by discretion, and that wisdom and great power of discernment might be given to them in their work. "And while we hope," he continued, "for the triumph of justice, let our acts be tempered with mercy. Help us to refrain from giving voice to those insinuations and innuendoes which we have no right to utter. Save us from blasting a life, innocent and blameless; keep us from taking the sweetness from a future by our ill-advised words, and let us be charitable as we remember the poor, grief-stricken family and minister unto them."

The clergyman asked that those who were writing of the crime might be careful of the reputations of the living, which could so easily be undermined.

For his text Mr. Jubb took the first chapter of ecclesiastes, ninth verse: "The thing that hath been is that which shall be; and that which is done is that which shall be done; and there is no new thing under the sun." The speaker considered the monotonies of life, and expatiated on the causes of indifference in persons who would be nothing if not geniuses, drawing lessons from successes in humble sphere. At the end of the sermon Mr. Jubb stepped to the side of the pulpit and said slowly and impressively: "I cannot close my sermon this morning without speaking of the horrible crime that has startled our beloved city this week, ruthlessly taking from our church household two respected and esteemed members. I cannot close without referring to my pain and surprise at the atrocity of the outrage. A more brutal, cunning, daring and fiendish murder I never heard of in all my life. What must have been the person who could have been guilty of such a revolting crime? One to commit such a murder must have been without heart, without soul, a fiend incarnate, the very vilest of degraded and depraved humanity, or he must have been a maniac. The circumstances, execution and all the surroundings cover it with mystery profound. Explanations and evidence as to both perpetrator and motive are shrouded in a mystery that is almost inexplicable. That such a crime could have been committed during the busy hours of the day, right in the heart of a populous city, is passing comprehension. As we ponder, we exclaim in our perplexity, Why was the deed done? What could have induced anybody to engage in such a butchery? Where is the motive? When men resort to crime it is for plunder, for gain, from enmity, in sudden anger or for revenge Strangely, nothing of this nature enters into this case, and again I ask—what was the motive? I believe, and am only voicing your feelings fully when I say that I hope the criminal will be speedily brought to justice. This city cannot afford to have in its midst such an inhuman brute as the murderer of Andrew J. Borden and his wife. Why, a man who could conceive and execute such a murder as that would not hesitate to burn the city.

"I trust that the police may do their duty and lose no opportunity which might lead to the capture of the criminal. I would impress upon them that they should not say too much and thus unconsciously assist in defeating the ends of justice. I also trust that the press (and I say this because I recognize its influence and power), I trust that it will use discretion in disseminating its theories and conclusions, and that pens may be guided by consideration and charity. I would wish the papers to remember that by casting a groundless or undeserved insinuation they may blacken and blast a life forever, like a tree smitten by a bolt of lightning; a life which has always commanded respect, whose acts and motives have always been pure and holy. Let us ourselves curb our tongues and preserve a blameless life from undeserved suspicions. I think I have a right to ask for the prayers of this church and of my own congregation. The murdered husband and wife were members of this church, and a daughter now stands in the same relation to each one of you, as you, as church members, do to each other. God help and comfort her. Poor, stricken girls, may they both be comforted, and may they both realize how fully God is their refuge."

DEAD BEFORE THE BUTCHERY.

A New Bedford Man's Theory of the Small Flow of Blood.

Josiah A. Hunt, keeper of the house of correction, who has had an extensive experience as an officer of the law in this city, in speaking of the tragedy advanced a theory which has thus far escaped the notice of the police, or, if it has not, they are putting the public on the wrong scent.

Said Mr. Hunt: "It is my opinion that both Mr. Borden and his wife were dead before the murderers struck a blow, probably poisoned by the use of prussic acid, which would cause instant death. The use of a hatchet was simply to mislead those finding the bodies. I believe this to be the real state of the case, for if they had been alive when the first blow was struck, the action of the heart would have been sufficient to have caused the blood to spatter more freely than is shown from the accounts furnished by the papers. There was altogether too much of a butchery for so little spattering of blood.

The Fall River Herald

THE New Bedford Journal accuses the HERALD of being discourteous in intimating that the alleged communication from the spirit world about the Borden murders was a concoction. It certainly had every appearance of being a fake, but as our contemporary declares that the letter was obtained from the alleged recipient, the HERALD will apologize. We feel certain that the Journal editor discredited the statement, although giving it publicity. The author is probably a victim of mild insanity.

The Fall River Herald

NO CLEARER!

The Solution of the Borden Mystery Still Delayed.

POLICE WORKING ON CLUES AND THEORIES

That Might Lead to the Perpetration of the Crime.

BODIES OF THE VICTIMS CONVEYED TO OAK GROVE CEMETERY.

Mr. Borden's Closeness in Handling His Money.

All day Thursday the people who have been interested in working up the Borden murder case were busily concerned in establishing theories to explain the circumstances, and then quickly abandoning those theories for some other that looked attractive at first sight. All this meant that nothing definite had been found, and only circumstantial evidence was at hand.

Upon this a host of theories have been builded. The poison feature spoken of in Friday's HERALD is being made prominent, but unless the authorities have kept to themselves important facts which the other workers on the case have not discovered, there is little satisfaction to be gained from what is known.

THE CROWD FOLLOWS MORSE.

Interest still holds at fever heat and wil not be satisfied until the impenetrable mystery which surrounds the case is pierced. Hundreds of people throng the street in front of the house and eye anybody who enters the premises with eagerness. An example of the popular curiosity was furnished about 8 o'clock Friday night. At that time Mr. Morse and the servant came out of the house and turned down Second street. Somebody in the crowd knew him and the word was passed along: "There's Morse." At once the crowd took it up and started down the street after the couple. People on Main street saw the commotion and rushed into Second street to see what was the matter. When Mr. Morse dropped a letter in the box fully 1000 people were standing around the postoffice corridors and crowding up the steps to see him do it. This shows the state of the popular mind wrought up to the intensest interest in the case.

THE POISON THEORY.

Facts may develop that will show the importance of the poison episode, but as yet the facts are meager. It appears that Lizzie Borden was ill with the rest of the family, and Dr. Bowen was called to attend them. Lizzie had told a friend the day before the murder that she was afraid somebody had tampered with the milk which had been left at the house. She seemed very much disturbed about it and remarked: "I am afraid that father has an enemy." Little was thought of the matter then, but in the light of subsequent developments this may prove to be important.

Relative to the poisoning Dr. Bowen said: "On Wednesday morning last, about 9 o'clock, Mrs. Borden came across the shed, and, entering our house, commenced conversation with my wife. She said: 'I am afraid my husband and I were poisoned last night. We ate supper as usual, and had nothing out of the ordinary on the table. About 9 o'clock we were both taken sick with terrible fits of vomiting and pains in the stomach. We finally got easier and so did not send for the doctor in the night. I thought, however, I would come over and see him this morning.' Therewith she came into my presence, and I asked her in a general way her symptoms. I could not gather from her statements any particular opinion as to the cause of the illness, but at this time in the year such troubles are not infrequent, a condition due to many causes.

"A little later in the forenoon I went over to see Mr. Borden. I found him reclining on the sofa in the sitting-room. I asked him how he was, and if he thought anything had poisoned him. He laughed and said he guessed there was not very much the matter with him. We sat talking some little time and then I went out. That was the last time I talked with him.

"That is the whole basis for the talk of poison," continued Dr. Bowen, "and, personally, I do not take any stock in the theory. That is, I see nothing, thus far, sufficiently strong to indicate it. It is a very serious matter to make reflections and insinuations against a woman of unstained character as some of the papers are doing in their reports of this case, as they relate to Lizzie Borden," continued the doctor. I have known her for many years, and have seen her several times since the tragedy. I believe her absolutely innocent of even a guilty knowledge of the crime. I will not say there may not have been occasional family differences between Mr. Borden and the girls. That is a matter I was in a position to know little about, but so far as I ever observed the inter-family relations were cordial.

SHE SAW A MAN.

Mrs. Chace, who lives over the store of Vernon Wade's grocery, the second house south of the scene of the tragedy, says that about 11 o'clock she was on the roof of a building east of her house hanging clothes. While there she could overlook Mr. Borden's yard. At the time a man was sitting on the fence filling his pockets with pears. He appeared to be a medium sized man, but as he was in a crouched position it was impossible for her to tell his height accurately. On looking up he noticed her watching him, and immediately jumped the fence and passed through the east end of Dr. Kelly's property to Third street.

A STARTLING THEORY

Gained some believers Friday night who put more faith in the poisoning story than the evidence seems to warrant. Was it not possible that the victims had been rendered unconscious by poison before the butchery began? The attitude in which Mr. Borden was found may have given support to this theory, but it is not so easy to explain why Mrs. Borden was found stretched at length on the floor where she had been stricken down by the murderous blow. Had she felt the effects of the poison slowly creeping over her, as it could be supposed that her husband did, was it not probable that she would have sought a resting place?

The trouble with the idea is that Mr. Borden was seen on the street half an hour before the news of his death was flashed over the country. During that half hour, it is known that he walked from his block on Main street to his home on Second street, exchanged his street coat for a house coat and sat down to read a paper. If he took poison after his trip down town it must have been prussic acid, for nothing else would have produced death so quickly. Professionals contended that there was nothing to indicate a dose of poison heavy enough to cause death or drowsiness. Poisons do not compose people to sleep, as a rule, and if morphine had been administered there would have been traces of it in the physical appearance of the man and woman.

CLOSE IN MONEY MATTERS.

Hiram Harrington, 40 Fourth street, is married to Laurana, Mr. Borden's only sister. A reporter who interviewed him gathered the following story: "My wife, being an only sister, was very fond of Mr. Borden and always subservient to his will, and by her intimacy with his affairs I have become acquainted with a good deal of the family history during years past. Mr. Borden was an exceedingly hard man concerning money matters, determined and stubborn, and when once he got an idea nothing could change him. He was too hard for me

"When his father died some years ago he offered my wife the old homestead on Ferry street for a certain sum of money. My wife preferred to take the money, and after the agreements were all signed, to show how close he was, he wanted my wife to pay an additional $3 for water tax upon the homestead."

"What do you think was the motive for the crime?" asked the reporter.

"Money, unquestionably money," replied Mr. Harrington. "If Mr. Borden died, he would have left something over $500,000, and all I will say is that, in my opinion, that furnishes the only motive, and a sufficient one, for the double murder. I have heard so much now that I would not be surprised at the arrest any time of the person to whom in my opinion suspicion strongly points, although right down in my heart I could not say I believed the party guilty.

"Last evening I had a long interview with Lizzie Borden, who has refused to see anyone else. I questioned her very carefully as to her story of the crime. She was very composed, showed no signs of any emotion or were there any traces of grief upon her countenance. That did not surprise me, as she is not naturally emotional. I asked her what she knew of her father's death, and, after telling of the unimportant events of the early morning, she said her father came home about 10:30. She was in the kitchen at the time, she said, but went into the sitting room when her father arrived. She was very solicitous concerning him, and assisted him to remove his coat and put on his dressing-gown; asked concernedly how he fell, as he had been weak from a cholera morbus attack the day before. She told me she helped him to get a comfortable reclining position on the lounge, and asked him if he did not wish the blinds closed to keep out the sun, so he could have a nice nap. She pressed him to allow her to place an afghan over him, but he said he did not need it. Then she asked him tenderly several times if he was perfectly comfortable, if there was anything she could do for him, and upon receiving assurance to the negative she withdrew. All these things showed a solicitude and a thoughtfulness that I never had heard was a part of her nature or custom before. She described these little acts of courtesy minutely.

"I then questioned her very carefully as to the time she left the house, and she told me positively that it was about 10:45. She said she saw her father on the lounge as she passed out. On leaving the house she says she went directly to the barn to obtain some lead. She informed me that it was her intention to go to Marion on a vacation, and she wanted the lead in the barn loft to make some sinkers. She was a very enthusiastic angler. I went over the ground several times, and she repeated the same story. She told me it was hard to place the exact time she was in the barn, as she was cutting the lead into sizable sinkers, but thought she was absent some 20 minutes. Then she thought again, and said it might have been 30 minutes. Then she entered the house and went to the sitting room, as she says she was anxious concerning her father's health. 'I discovered him dead,' she said, 'and cried for Bridget, who was upstairs in her room.'

"'Did you go and look for your stepmother?'" I asked. 'Who found her?' But she did not reply. I pressed her for some idea of the motive and the author of the act, and, after she had thought a moment, she said, calmly: 'A year ago last spring our house was broken into while father and mother were at Swansey, and a large amount of money stolen, together with diamonds. You never heard of it because father did not want it mentioned, so as to give the detectives a chance to recover the property. That may have some connection with the murder. Then I have seen strange men around the house. A few months ago I was coming through the back yard, and, as I approached the side door, I saw a man there examining the door and premises. I did not mention it to anyone. The other day I saw the same man hanging about the house, evidently watching us. I became frightened and told my parents about it. I also wrote to my sister at Fairhaven about it.' Miss Borden then gave it as her opinion that the strange man had a direct connection with the murder, but she could not see why the house was not robbed, and did not know of anyone who would desire revenge upon her father."

Mr. Harrington was asked if he knew whether or not there were dissensions in the Borden family. "Yes, there were, although it has been always kept very quiet. For nearly ten years there have been constant disputes between the daughters and their father and stepmother. Mr. Borden gave her some bank stock and the girls thought they ought to be treated as evenly as the mother. I guess Mr. Borden did try to do it, for he deeded to the daughters, Emma L. and Lizzie A., the homestead on Ferry street, an estate of 120 rods of land with a house and barn, all valued at $3000. This was in 1887.

"The trouble about money matters did not diminish, nor the acerbity of the family ruptures lessen, and Mr. Borden gave each girl ten shares in the Crystal Spring Bleachery company, which he paid $100 a share for. They sold them soon after for less than $40 per share. He also gave them some bank stock at various times, allowing them, of course, the entire income from them. In addition to this he gave them a weekly stipend, amounting to $200 a year.

"In spite of all this the dispute about their not being allowed enough went on with equal bitterness. Lizzie did most of the demonstrative contention, as Emma is very quiet and unassuming, and would feel very deeply any disparaging or angry word from her father. Lizzie, on the contrary, was haughty and domineering with the stubborn will of her father and bound to contest for her rights. There were many animated interviews between father and daughter on this point. Lizzie is of a repellant disposition, and after an unsuccessful passage with her father would become sulky and refuse to speak to him for days at a time. She moved in the best society in Fall River, was a member of the Congregational church, and is a brilliant conversationalist. She thought she ought to entertain as others did, and felt that with her father's wealth she was expected to hold her end up with others of her set. Her father's constant refusal to allow her to entertain lavishly angered her. I have heard many bitter things she has said of her father, and know she was deeply resentful of her father's maintained stand in this matter.

"This house on Ferry street was an old one, and was in constant need of repairs. There were two tenants paying $16.50 and $14 a month, but with taxes and repairs there was very little income from the property. It was a great deal of trouble for the girls to keep the house in repair, and a month or two ago they got disgusted and deeded the house back to their father."

AN INTERESTING LEGAL PHASE

of the case is involved in the question: Who was killed first? There is a diversity of opinion in this phase of the case, and there is little to show which side has taken the correct stand. The police at present are working on the theory that Mrs. Borden was killed first, and with that involved the only motive which can now be assigned for the crime—that of gain.

Quite a tidy sum, about $100,000, is the issue in the case. The amount on the basis that Mr. Borden was worth in the vicinity of $200,000 represents the one-third of an estate termed the widows' dower. If the wife was killed first this would not be taken into consideration, but if the murderer struck down the old gentleman in the beginning, the one-third share goes to the heirs of Mrs. Borden, even if she was a widow but five seconds. Under the latter case, the Misses Borden, who are not the heirs of Mrs. Borden, will be entitled, in the division of the property, to only two-thirds of the estate, and the $100,000 or so will go to the nearest kin of Mrs. Borden. If, however, it is decided the other way, that the wife died first, the entire estate will be distributed between the two daughters.

It may, however, be less difficult to prove that there was an hour or so between the time of the murder of Mrs. Borden and that of her husband. Her movements are not accounted for after 9 o'clock in the morning, at which time she went upstairs to arrange the apartment in which Mr. Morse slept the night before. How much time was required in this work cannot be estimated. It certainly was completed when the murder was committed, whether 15 minutes, an hour, or two hours after she went upstairs.

A TELL TALE HAIR.

The story started from a "high police official" as usual that a hatchet had been found Friday in the cellar of the house that had been recently scoured. It was a lather's hatchet with a claw hammer end. Every trace of blood had been removed, but a tell tale hair clung to one of the claws. It was a hair from Mrs. Borden's head, although the horrible butchery had bidden the place where it had been removed from the head.

The Police authorities still maintain that the deadly weapon has not been discovered, and they persist in the belief that it was a long handled axe, although it may have been a hatchet. Search high and low has been made for it. The cellar has been scoured, the yarn has been hunted through, search parties have turned the interior of the barn upside down, but have found nothing.

John V. Morse has been interested in the search. He wanted to hire somebody to bury the bloody clothes. Towards the close of the afternoon Morse grew irritable, and had quite an altercation with David P. Keefe, who hired a man to bury the blood-stained clothes and pieces of the skull for him. Keefe charged $5 for the work, and Morse pronounced it robbery. Keefe said he wouldn't do the job for $100, though under some circumstances he allowed that he might be glad to do it for nothing. Morse finally paid $3. Later he locked the barn when a couple of Boston newspapor men were inside, and found considerable fault with the liberties people took with the premises. He was reminded that a reward of $5000 had been offered, and that everybody was intensely interested.

THE FUNERAL SERVICES

took place at 11 o'clock, and were strictly private. The bodies were laid out in the dining room, with their heads toward the east. The coffins were plain and covered with black broadcloth. A wreath of ivy lay on the casket containing the remains of Mr. Borden, while a bouquet of roses occupied a similar place on Mrs. Borden's. The services consisted of an invocation and reading of scripture by Dr. Adams of the First Congregational church, after which prayer was offered by the Rev. Mr. Buck.

Among the parties who were present and accompanied the remains to their final resting place were the following: Southard H. Miller and wife, Dr. Bowen and wife, Mrs. Adelaide Churchill, Miss Mary Ann Borden, of whose estate Mr. Borden was the guardian; Frank Miller, George Whitehead and wife, the latter being a half-sister to Mrs. Borden; Mrs. Oliver Gray and daughter, the former being the step-mother to Mrs. Borden; Mrs. J. L. Fish of Hartford, a sister of Mrs. Borden; Mrs. J. D. Burt, William Wilcox and wife, Mrs. Restcome Case, Mrs. John Durfee, Hiram Harrington, brotherinlaw of Mr. Borden.

For the family Miss Lizzie was the first to appear, and, escorted by Undertaker Winward, she took her place in the coach. No veil covered her face, and she walked with a firm and steady step to her seat in the carriage. Nothing in her manner would indicate that the finger of suspicion was pointed toward her, although it was easy to see that the burden of grief she was carrying was heavy. Emma Borden followed, her step and carriage being much weaker than her sister. The remains of Mr. Borden were then placed in the hearse by Abram G. Hart, George W. Dean, Jerome C. Borden, Richard B. Borden, James M. Osborn and Andrew Borden as pallbearers. Mrs. Borden's remains followed, with James C. Eddy, Henry S. Buffington, Frank L. Almy, J. Henry Wells, Simeon B. Chace, and John H. Boone as bearers. Dr. Adams and the Rev. Mr. Buck followed, accompanied by Mr. Morse. On their appearance the latter was the target of all eyes. He appeared to realize the fact, but held his head high and walked firmly to his seat in the carriage. The funeral cortege then proceeded to the Oak Grove cemetery;

LIZZIE ANDREW BORDEN

when there the final interment took place. The services were read by Dr. Adams, after which benediction was offered by the Rev. Mr. Buck. A return to the house was then made, and the victims of the most puzzling tragedy in the history of this country were left to rest beneath the clay.

HAVE SEEN NO PAPERS.

The house has been carefully guarded and orders were issued to admit nobody who had no business there. A relative, who came from Fairhaven, could not get into the house. Officer Hyde, who has stood guard over the side door, was the Cerebus who drove away inquisitive reporters. It appears that no newspapers have been received inside the house since the murder, and that up to the time of the funeral neither of the sisters suspected the cruel suspicions which the police had formed. The Misses Borden were beginning to feel the strain terribly. Besides the kind friends who have sacrificed their own comfort to relieve the stricken daughters, they have seen nobody to talk to since the murder. The newspaper stories have been kept from Lizzie, but will be broken to her after the funeral, either by friends or officers of the law. Up to the present, Marshal Hilliard has respected the feelings of the daughters, knowing that he would be able to find either of them when he wanted to interview her.

As soon as the funeral cortege passed out of sight of the house, Marshal Hilliard, Assistant Marshal Fleet and Detective Seaver entered by the side door and proceeded to examine all the inmates who had not gone to the grave. They were closeted with them for a long time.

TO DISCOVER A MOTIVE.

An effort is being made to discover a motive in the family relations of the Bordens. Their friends admit that things were not as pleasant as they might have been in the house. Mrs. Borden was not the mother of the girls and the father was not over liberal with them. Some stories that have been written concerning these relations, however, are regarded as the grossest exaggeration. If all that has been written should prove on further investigation to be true, a person will fail to find in the family relations anything so strained as to encourage the perpetration of one of the most startling crimes in the history of the country.

It is difficult to follow the conclusions of the police without agreeing that the work was that of a maniac. Such cruelty can hardly be conceived to have been planned and carried out by a sane person, but appears rather to be the wonderful cunning of a deranged mind. A leading physician said at noon that he was fully convinced that the act was not done by a man, as all authorities agreed in saying that hacking is almost a positive sign of the deed of a woman who is unconscious of what she is doing.

The New York Herald

MRS. BORDEN WAS DEAD A FULL HOUR BEFORE HER HUSBAND CAME.

Developments at Fall River Show That Mr. Borden Returned Home To Be Murdered Long After His Wife Had Been Killed.

TOOK GREAT RISKS AFTER THE FIRST CRIME.

The Murderer Must Have Remained in the House Waiting for His Second Victim and in Constant Danger of Discovery.

DETECTIVE HANSCOM'S INFLUENCE.

He Has Been Employed by the Borden Family, and Is Believed to Have Caused the Police to Change Some of Their Plans.

SEARCHING FOR TRACES OF POISON.

[BY TELEGRAPH TO THE HERALD.]

FALL RIVER, Mass., August 7, 1892.—Policemen, owl-like and solemn, made a cordon all day around the queer old house where on Thursday a harmless old man and his wife were so cruelly butchered.

All day other policemen, equally owl-like and equally silent, careered over the town on a kind of hopeless hunting.

All day the mysterious chief of the owl-like police and the more mysterious country detective went hither and thither in strange fashion.

Yet at the end of their day of inscrutable labors they knew apparently no more about the murder of A. J. Borden and his wife than they knew at the beginning, and no more than the crowds that gaped all day over the palings about the grewsome house. Still there were actual developments enough and indications enough to induce action in a police force not divided against itself and not ruled by twenty heads instead of one.

For one thing there was news from Boston about the chemical analyses that are being made there. Medical Examiner Dolan, who holds a position like to that of a coroner in New York, received this news and except to the police refused to tell exactly what it was. The medical examiner is a firm and a shrewd and clear headed man, and nothing was to be gained from him, but it was repeatedly asserted during the day from a source that led back to the police that poison had been discovered in the contents of the stomachs sent to Boston for analysis.

NOT SETTLED BY HILLARD'S DENIALS.

Now, this is one of the reports that cannot be authentically fathered and, of course, Chief of Police Hillard denies it. He denies everything, but for all that it seems to rest on good authority. Just as soon as the medical examiner got the word, whatever it was, he went quickly, with an assistant, to the cemetery, where the bodies are still in the receiving vault, and removed organs which are supposed to be wanted for further tests. It is quite certain that this would not have been thought necessary if no discoveries had been made in the stomach analyses. Yet the police made no move, notwithstanding that the contingency that a discovery of poison has been supposed to have but one meaning, and it is very well known who attempted to buy poison only the day before the murder.

There is something strange about this. It is notorious now that yesterday the police had made all their arrangements for the first arrest in the case. It was distinctly understood that after the family had returned from the funeral, a member of it who has been under suspicion since Thursday night should be taken into custody. For some reason this plan was abandoned. Yesterday morning there appeared on the scene Emory D. Hanscom, of Boston, assistant manager of Pinkertons' New England agency, and a very able detective. But Mr. Hanscom was not employed by the authorities, nor for the purpose of tracing the wonderfully clever assassin who produced this puzzling mystery. He was and is employed by the family to look after its interests.

HANSCOM'S PROTECTING INFLUENCE.

What a family so situated may want of a private detective I cannot imagine, but there is a story that he exerted his influence to prevent their arrest, and that was the reason the police changed their plan.

Mr. Hanscom's time is chiefly spent about the Mellen house in affable conversation with the newspaper men in whose affections he has made great progress, but if anybody asks him what he is doing here he says he has come to fish, and if asked what he thinks of the case he says he has scarcely heard of it; only he thinks it would be a shame to arrest any person without evidence enough to convict. That, by the way, exactly coincides with the present opinion of the tall and stately Chief Hillard, when he is asked why he does not make a move in the case, when the suspicion seems to be so obvious and the suspected persons are having a fine opportunity for communication, if not for escape.

Nevertheless the weird story is working itself clear, without the aid of the police, of the vast mass of inventions and lies that formerly clogged it. There was, for example, a fine circumstantial story let loose in the morning papers about the "unknown man," famous in New York police reports. This mysterious being called last Monday at Mr. Borden's house, leaving a companion in a buggy outside. Just before the time of the murder, that is about half-past ten Thursday morning, he called again and was afterward seen climbing over the fence at the rear of the house, being easily distinguishable by a pair of baseball shoes and his odd patterned trousers. Even the name of the witness, a respectable woman who lives opposite the Bordens, was given to bolster up this interesting narrative. Then the story led to a neighboring village and a band of gypsy horse dealers, and then the strange man disappears.

SOME YARNS DISPROVED.

Patient inquiry disposes of this yarn. There was no such caller at Mr. Borden's and the witness summoned to say there was utterly denied that she said anything of the kind. Then there was also an interesting anecdote to the effect that when the Bordens' servant girl heard of the murder she said, "It was the Portugee," but it appears that the servant girl said nothing of the kind, and there is no "Portugee" known in this part of the world available for the character of the murderer.

Stories of quarrels with various persons, of unknown enemies and secret plots have readily been destroyed by application to Mr. Borden's acquaintances. Mr. Borden did not quarrel and it is inconceivable that he had any secret enemies. It might be interesting to know the source of all these imaginings which cloud more or less a clear view of what facts have been settled.

The case no doubt is pretty dark, and yet I think the most puzzling thing about it is to go to the house and examine the premises and then tell how the murders could have been committed by an assassin who was able to make his escape from such a place. The old fashioned frame house of the Bordens stands in the middle of a block on a street that is half a residence and half a business street, and in the midst of almost the busiest part of Fall River. The front wall is only sixteen feet from the sidewalk, where at all hours of the day people are passing, for the street is a main thoroughfare. The next house on the north is only twenty feet away.

The next house on the south is twenty-four feet away. Both have many windows opening upon the Borden house.

IN PLAIN VIEW ALL AROUND.

There is a small yard at the rear, surrounded by a high unbroken board fence guarded by barbed wire. On all sides are the yards of neighbors and houses. A small barn stands at one side of the Borden yard. It is not used now except for a storehouse. The house is very old. On the north side there is an entrance going into the kitchen and the sitting room, and a flight of stairs leading to the second story. The only other entrance is the front door opening from the street. These are dry details, but they are necessary to understand this remarkable story.

Mr. Borden owned a great deal of real estate, was president of a savings bank and had other interests, and Thursday morning, as usual, went about town looking after his affairs. All that is positively known about his taking off is quickly told. He started for home about half-past ten. About a quarter-past eleven o'clock his servant girl ran over to Dr. Bowen, who lives just across the narrow street, and told him that her master had been murdered. Dr. Bowen, going with the girl, found Mr. Borden lying dead on the lounge in the sitting room, his head mangled in the manner before described. A few minutes afterward the body of the wife was discovered in a room up stairs, the second one from the street on the south of the house.

There were two persons in or about the house at the time of the murder. These were Lizzie Borden, the second daughter, and the servant girl, named Sullivan. Of course their stories of what they observed should be of the greatest importance.

LIZZIE BORDEN'S STORY.

Sifted of some gratutious additions what Lizzie Borden told the police was when her father came home he lay down in the sitting room and read his paper. The servant girl was up stairs. She herself went out to the barn to get some lead sinkers to use on a fishing trip she was going to take. She was gone about twenty minutes, and when she came back found her father butchered. She called to the servant girl, who brought Dr. Bowen. She heard nothing and saw nothing of the murderer. The servant girl says she was at work cleaning windows in the front room up stairs and she heard nothing until Miss Lizzie called her.

But there are ascertained facts with which Miss Lizzie's story does not fit. Supposing the murderer to have been somebody who entered the house and then escaped from it after his bloody deed, how did he get away? Not out of the front door, certainly, for then he would have been seen by somebody in the passing throngs. The only other exit was the back door. But that is directly opposite a window in the adjoining house, and at that window sat during all this time Mrs. Buffen, the lady of the house, and she says nobody went in or out of the door until the servant ran out on her way to Dr. Bowen's.

But supposing the murderer to have got into the back yard unobserved by Mrs. Buffen, he must then climb the high board fence and get over the barbed wire without being seen. And when he had done that he would be in the yard of a neighbor, from which the only way out was past the neighbor's house and windows and very front door upon a street almost as much travelled as the one in front.

The fence is covered with dust and shows no signs that anybody has climbed it; the barbed wire has not been disturbed nor torn anybody's clothing. Nobody was seen in Mr. Borden's nor any of the yards.

These considerations are entirely aside from the fact that there was no apparent motive for the murder, Mr. Borden not being robbed, and nothing in the house being disturbed. There is still more to this. Neither the servant girl nor the people in the adjacent houses heard an outcry nor a sound of a struggle. Yet Mr. Borden was in fair health and Mrs. Borden was a robust, powerful woman. Therefore it is argued that either they must have been under the influence of drugs or their assailant was a person of whom they had no fear.

MRS. BORDEN KILLED FIRST.

More remarkable than this even, the results of to-day's investigation satisfied Medical Examiner Dolan that Mrs. Borden was killed at least an hour before her husband. This appears from the statement of Dr. Bowen, that when he arrived Mr. Borden's body was warm and the blood was flowing, but Mrs. Borden's body was cold and stiff. During the hour that elapsed where was the murderer? He must have been concealed somewhere about the house. But it would have been impossible for an outsider to know when Mr. Borden would come home. The murderer must, therefore, have stayed upon the very scene of his first crime, not knowing what moment it might be discovered and he with it, though immediately after his second murder he disappeared so amazingly that no one can guess how he went.

The first question Dr. Bowen asked of Lizzie when he reached Mr. Borden's side was, "Where is your mother?"

"She's gone out," said Lizzie. "She went out two hours ago to see a sick friend who wrote a note asking her to go and see her."

A few minutes afterward Mrs. Borden's body was found up stairs. No trace of any such note has been discovered anywhere about the house, and although every man, woman and child in Fall River has heard about it nobody has come forward to acknowledge the writing of it. When Lizzie found that her father had been murdered she called for the servant girl, not for her mother. The note would account for this strange omission if the note or any trace of it could be found.

MRS. BORDEN'S WOUNDS.

The wounds on Mrs. Borden's head offer a wide field for theorizing. First she was struck a straight blow in front of her forehead, delivered either when she was standing or when she reclined upon her back. This was with the edge of the hatchet. The other blows were along the side of the head, and dealt with the back of the hatchet. The body lay face downward on the floor six feet from the bed. Yet the servant girl at work on the same floor did not hear it fall. How did it get into that position? That is one of the puzzles for which nobody has suggested an adequate solution.

The hemorrhage was very small from both bodies. This was what started and gave color to the idea that Mr. and Mrs. Borden had been poisoned before they were butchered. Then it was discovered that the day of the murder a woman, said to be Miss Lizzie Borden, had tried to obtain prussic acid at a neighboring drug store. To-day I learned from a very fair sort of witness that on Wednesday almost the whole family became suddenly sick and that Mrs. Borden said she thought it was something in the food. This witness is John V. Morse, the brother of Mr. Borden's first wife and an inmate of the house, who has not gone entirely free from suspicion notwithstanding it appears he was not in the neighborhood at the time of the murder. I saw Mr. Morse at the Borden house this morning. He is a commonplace looking man, about forty years old, tall, lank, with a ragged beard and shallow, gray eyes.

WHAT MR. MORSE SAYS.

He has not been willing to say much for publication heretofore, but to-day he consented to tell the HERALD his full story. He said:—

"I returned to Fall River from New Bedford on Wednesday afternoon; and after a drive to Swansea and back came to Mr. Borden's house and stayed that night. The next morning I had breakfast about seven o'clock and at a quarter to nine I left. Mrs. Borden was up stairs. I hadn't seen her since eight o'clock. Mr. Borden left me at the door, asking me to come home to dinner. I went to the Post Office and several other places about town and finally to Daniel Emery's, at No. 4 Weybosett street. I stayed there until between quarter after and half-past eleven, when I started for home by street car. It was twenty minutes to twelve when I got home and heard of the murders. The house was full of policemen and people. That is all I know about it."

"Mr. Morse," I said, "it has been asserted that when Lizzie Borden was away the week before the murder she went to New Bedford to see you."

"That is not true," said Morse vehemently. "She did not see me. I didn't get any letters from her, either, though I heard she was at Marion."

Mr. Morse admitted that there had been ill feeling between Mrs. Borden and her step-daughters, but he would not discuss that matter further. Lizzie, he said, was a peculiar girl, often given to fits of sullenness. His statement about his whereabouts during the morning of the murder has been fully corroborated, and persons who were on the street car with him when he went home testified to that fact. Perhaps it was only Mr. Morse's furtive and unhappy manner when he talks that directed any suspicion toward him.

OPEN WAR ON MRS. BORDEN.

The Borden household must have been a rather grim sort of a place. Mr. Borden himself, though perfectly respectable and upright, was not particularly cheerful, and between his wife and her stepdaughters there was open war. The elder daughter, Emma, is described as of a mild and gentle disposition, but there was little mildness about Lizzie, seven years her junior.

Mr. Borden was worth half a million dollars, and, though penurious as a rule was inclined to be generous to his household, but Lizzie resented his liberality toward the stepmother. Her own mother died in giving birth to her and she has been odd all her life. She grew up to be much of a recluse. She is far from homely, though not particularly handsome, but she never had a lover, she has avoided the company of young men and has never gone into society. She has her defenders, who say she has an amiable disposition. The allegations to the contrary may be mere ill natured gossip.

One thing is certain. She has wonderful self-possession. When with Dr. Bowen she stood by her father's body, when her mother was discovered murdered, at the time of the funeral, and on all other occasions since this story began she has manifested, they say, almost unshaken calmness. She is a masculine looking woman, with a strong, resolute, unsympathetic face. She is robustly built, thirty-three years old and of average height. Her voice has a peculiar guttural harshness. Her hair is brown and long, her eyes brown and steady. Her self-possession is expressed in her looks. I do not think she is afraid of many things. She must know that she is under constant police espionage and suspicion, but there is nothing in her appearance to show that she is concerned about it. She declined to-day to make any statement about her case.

ALDERMEN AGAINST MAYOR.

The Mayor of Fall River is the real head of the police force, though at present his direction of it is hampered by the opposition of a majority of the Board of Aldermen, who will not confirm his appointments nor assist in his plans. The present Mayor is Dr. Coughlin. He has taken as active an interest in the Borden case as any detective here, and has formed his theory of the mystery, which is not different from that held by some others. Mayor Coughlin said to-night that the inquest would probably begin on Tuesday, when he thought Professor Woods, of Harvard, who is making the analysis of the stomach, would make his report.

Patrolman Hayes distinguished himself to-night by suddenly reporting that on the morning of the murder he had seen a man loitering about in front of the Borden residence. He gave a sort of half description of the man. As nobody else saw him and Hayes did not explain why he had held back his information the clew is not regarded as greatly important.

When the house was searched yesterday afternoon two hatchets and two axes were found and taken to Police Headquarters. One of the hatchets was stained and looked as if an attempt might have been made to clean it. It was turned over to a local physician that the stains might be analyzed. It was said this afternoon that experts had decided that the stains were blood.

Chief of Police Hilliard denied that there was anything in this. He said that some people thought the stains were blood and some said they were only rust, but nobody could tell until a scientific test had been made. As to the fact that no arrest had been made, Chief Hilliard said that the police were working slowly but surely, taking up one clew after another, and when they reached one that seemed to be upheld with testimony enough to convict they would make an arrest. He predicted that would be within two or three days.

EXCITED BY AN OLD WOMAN'S DEATH.

Excitement in police circles ran high this evening when it was reported that an unknown woman had been found murdered in a lonely spot in South Somerset, near William's Pond. Investigation showed that Mary Gifford, aged seventy years, was dead and had been found lying in some bushes near a stone wall, her position indicating that she had fallen naturally from weakness. There were two bottles found near her, both of which smelled strongly of liquor. Medical Examiner Dolan was in doubt as to whether or not the woman had been treated violently before death, and he proposes to hold an autopsy to-morrow or next day. Mrs. Gifford was well known in police circles as "Portsmouth Mary," and a dissolute character.

At a late hour it is reported that the suspicions of blood spots on the hatchet in possession of the police are well founded and that there is every reason to believe that members of the family are directly accountable for the death of the two victims.

The Fall River Herald

A GREAT deal of nonsense has been printed about the Borden murder mystery, but hardly anything equals the foolish statements that the muddle between the mayor and the combination over the police appointments has interfered with the investigation. No basis has been afforded for the report. The police are obeying orders from the marshal, and every member of the department who has been assigned a task has discharged it faithfully. There is no shirking, nobody is grumbling. If dissatisfaction was apparent to correspondents, is it not extraordinary that nobody else has perceived it?

CONSULT EDITOR HARRIS.

Marshal Hilliard should consult Editor Harris of the Newport Observer and ask his advice as to the best course to pursue in fixing the responsibility for the Borden murder. The editor is too modest, too anxious to avoid notoriety, to come to this city and prove that he is entitled to the reward of $5000. We do not wish it to be understood that the money would not be gratefully received and suitably acknowledged.

After reading the Monday morning accounts of no change in the situation our editorial brother seized his pencil and dashed off an observation which began with "the Fall River police are making a dreadfully bungling mess of the Borden murder affair." This was a catch line, but the reader who followed the article to the end found no ground for the indictment, which closed with likening our faithful police "to a lot of country bumpkins." The qualitative, "country," was superfluous, but the Observer's observer did not bother over such a triviality.

Why has Brother Harris suppressed his theory? Is he waiting to be asked to vouchsafe the information? People who are so prone to criticise ought to be ever ready to point out mistakes. The HERALD's columns are open to him for the presentation of his ideas, and we are sure that the marshal would welcome views that would tend to illumine the darkness in which the police are now working.

Rev. WILLIAM WALKER JUBB
Pastor of the Central Congregational Church 1891 - 1896

Rev. EDWIN AUGUSTUS BUCK
Fall River City Missionary 1867 - 1903

The New York Herald

BORDEN MYSTERY MAY SOON BE SOLVED.

Fall River Police and Prosecuting Officials Consider the Evidence Collected and Discuss the Advisability of Arresting the Suspected Persons.

DOLAN'S SIGNIFICANT EXHIBITS.

He Brings to the Conference an Axe and Dress Which May Play an Important Part in Discovering the Murderer.

ACTIVITY OF THE POLICE.

Again Is the House Where the Crime Was Committed Searched—The Family Still Under Surveillance.

[BY TELEGRAPH TO THE HERALD.]

FALL RIVER, Mass., August 8, 1892.—For a long time this afternoon and this evening the Borden horror hung upon the verge of a climax as startling as the crime itself. In a private room at police headquarters, District Attorney Knowlton and Chief Hilliard conferred from five o'clock in the afternoon until late at night, and the subject of their conference was whether there is evidence enough to warrant the arrest of three persons well known in Fall River on the charge of murder. They had before them all the facts which the police have been able to collect and Detectives Seaver and Rhodes, who have done some of the collecting.

Chief Hilliard further exhibited some articles of testimony which throw a new light on the work of the police. The conference had not been going on long when a patrolman came in with one of the registers in which druggists are required to enter all sales of dangerous drugs. He took this book directly into the room where Knowlton and Hilliard were at work. What it showed nobody knows but the police and the District Attorney, but ever since the murder there has been talk of some such book said to contain a record of the purchase of poison by a member of the Borden household.

SENSATIONS IN PLENTY.

There was rather a sensational beginning in view of Chief Hilliard's repeated declaration that he was all in the dark for clews or testimony. In a few minutes there were more surprising developments. Medical Examiner Dolan came to the back door of the headquarters and carried under his arm a box in which were a hatchet and a dress. It was not intended that any one should know either of Dr. Dolan's coming or what he brought with him, but two or three reporters happened to be at the rear entrance to headquarters when he drove up and the lap robe which covered the box fell to the ground as he was lifting the box from his carriage. The dress

JOHN V. MORSE.

and the hatchet were plainly seen. There was something else in the box which I could not make out. Dr. Dolan whisked into the conference room as rapidly as possible. It has been strenuously asserted for the last two days that the police have in their possession a dress found in the Borden house on which was a drop of blood. The police have as strenuously denied it. It has also been asserted that the stained axe or hatchet found in the Borden house, as described in yesterday's HERALD, had been discovered to be stained with blood. The police have vigorously denied this also.

Why these things should be brought to the conference if they had none of the significance that had been given to them one man can guess at as well as another. Just what happened at the conference of course the District Attorney and the Chief of Police would not make public. All the subordinates about headquarters knew perfectly well that the general subject discussed was the arrests I have mentioned, and they did not hesitate to say so. It is an easy surmise that Chief Hilliard detailed to the District Attorney how he had worked out every theory that had been suggested and how they all had failed. No doubt he explained all about the man on the fence and the man with the baseball shoes and the rest of the myths that have collected about the story.

NO NEED FOR HASTE.

But, according to a report that came out at nine o'clock, the District Attorney thought that there was no necessity of proceeding hastily in the case, and soon afterward Detective Seaver gave it out authoritatively that there would be no arrests to-night. Then Mr. Knowlton and Chief Hilliard went away. Mr. Knowlton intimated that the conference would be resumed to-morrow. Although, under the law, he is really charged with the early steps for the prosecution of criminals, this is his first appearance on this scene. He has been down at Marion summering.

The Borden household is under close surveillance. They are at liberty to leave the house if they choose, but wherever they go a policeman follows them, and if they attempt to leave town his orders are to take them into custody.

Very little has been said of Bridget Sullivan, the servant girl of the Bordens, and yet it is possible if she were closely examined she might be able to tell something of value. On Saturday night this girl left the house and stayed away until Monday morning at the home of a friend of hers, a woman named Harrington. The police let her go without opposition. No doubt the girl is honest. Nevertheless, it is obvious that under some circumstances a person in her position might, if she pleased, take with her any article the discovery of which about the house would be disagreeable.

A despatch from Hartford, Conn., reports one George B. Fish as directly charging Lizzie Borden and Morse with a knowledge of the murder. This Fish married the sister of the murdered Mrs. Borden. He is not on good terms with the family and as it is impossible that he should know anything about it his talk is not given any weight here.

The inquest will be held to-morrow morning in Judge Blaisdell's court.

POLICE WAKING UP.

The police spent the day in an activity that partly atoned for their extraordinary tardiness in the beginning of the case. In the morning they went up and researched the Borden house. There is something very odd about these house searching tactics. It was not until hours after the murder that there was any searching at all. Then one room in the house was not entered because its inmate earnestly requested that it should not be disturbed, and it does not appear that the rest of the building was thoroughly examined.

When the police finally got time to examine the whole house it was Saturday afternoon, two days after the murder, and there is no telling what might have happened in the meantime. Even then they must have forgotten something, for today they went over the ground again. Perhaps it was the chimneys. They spent most of their time at the house looking up the chimneys. I do not think they discovered anything. Four days after the murder there would probably not be much left for them to discover.

In other directions they had better success. They have been steadily narrowing down the various hypotheses that have been suggested to account for this extraordinary mystery, and to-day they disposed of almost the last—except one. It must be admitted that Chief Hilliard's idea was not a bad one. He says that he took up every theory or incident that was reported and impartially sifted it to the bottom. In this way he satisfied himself to-day that a great many things were not true, even if he hit upon nothing momentous that was true. As I told in the HERALD to-day, the great puzzle, on the theory that the murder was committed by somebody outside of the family, is to tell how the assassin got into the house and got out of it unobserved. The only incident that has offered as a possible explanation of this inscrutable problem is a statement of a boy that on Thursday morning, the morning of the murder, he saw a man on the fence at the rear of the Borden house. Great stress has been laid on this as showing how the murderer got away.

But the man whom the boy saw was found to day and turned out to be a harmless mason. There are pear trees in the Borden back yard and the pears are about ripe. The mason was at work in the yard immediately behind the Bordens' and he climbed up the fence to get a pear. The boy identified the mason and the mason acknowledged his share in the performance, and thus disposed of another promising clew.

But at the same time he added another to the many reasons which make it seem inexplicable how the murderer, supposing him to be an outsider, made his escape. This mason was at work directly in the rear of the Borden house, yet he saw no one scale the Borden fence, although it was only a few feet away. Three sides of the house are thus found to have been practically under guard. At the north Mrs. Buffinton sat at her open window, twenty feet from the only rear exit from the Borden house; the mason at work directly back of the yard. On the south Mrs. Chace, the next neighbor but one, was out upon her kitchen extension, which commanded the Borden yard. The only chance that is left, therefore, is that the murderer escaped from the front door and got away unnoticed by the people in the street. Mrs. Bowen, wife of the family doctor, sat at her front window all the time and she saw nobody come in or go out. Neither did any of the other neighbors, though when Sarah came out to get Dr. Bowen a few minutes later they all saw her and wondered what was the matter.

THE CELLAR DOOR WAS BARRED.

To combat the obvious improbability that anybody could come out of the side door directly in front of Mrs. Buffinton, not twenty feet away, and still be unobserved, Detective Hanscom suggested to-day the cellar door theory. In the back of the house there is an old passageway leading into the basement, and it was Mr. Hanscom's theory that after the murderer had finished his work he got into the cellar and thence out of this exit. He would then be in the back yard, and Mr. Hanscom seemed to think that if he was a person of marvelous stealth and unaccountable luck he might be able to get out of the yard and over the fence and the barbed wire. The great trouble about this theory is that the basement entrance has been closed up for years, and the only way the murderer could have got out of it was to hammer down the door.

REAR OF BORDEN HOUSE, SHOWING THE BARN.

There was also some story about two men who had quarrelled with Mr. Borden a few days before the murder about some wages they said were due them. These two men were hunted up today and proved to be inoffensive fellows whose difference with the murdered man had been of a very mild type. There was further a story about a quarrel over a horse trade and it was proved that there was nothing in it. With these and the theories disproved yesterday the last suggestion of an outside perpetrator disappeared, unless, indeed, the murderer was some strange kind of a maniac, superhumanly cunning and incredibly stealthy, who killed for no purpose and then stole away before men's very eyes.

SEEKING A MOTIVE.

What motive could any one have to murder the poor old man and his wife, what motive could even a member of the family have? and here all the theorists come to the ground together. It is admitted that so far as known not a soul outside the family had any grudge to sate or end to gain by these murders. The only advantage that Mr. Borden's death would bring about to anybody in the family would be through distribution of the estate.

Mr. Borden had made no will. There is some slight reason to think that he may have intended to make a will very soon, for he had taken some steps toward an inventory of his estate, but this is too intangible to indicate anything. In this connection it has been pointed out that if Mrs. Borden died first, even by a moment, her relatives would have no share in the estate and the two daughters would inherit it all, but if Mr. Borden died first then his wife's relatives would inherit her widow's third. It is certain now that Mrs. Borden died first. However, there is no plausible explanation of a motive suggested by this fact, and turn the case whichever way you will the murder looks like nothing but an outburst of cunning and ferocious insanity.

HANSCOM BARRED OUT.

The Bordens are a hot blooded race. To be "as fiery as a Borden" is an old byword in Fall River, where the family is large and has many branches. But it never has been suspected that anything like a homicidal tendency ran in the blood. Detective Hanscom, whom I have mentioned as suggesting an impossible theory, is the person whom the Borden girls have employed to look after their interests. He used to be an inspector of Boston police and is no doubt as shrewd as he is suave, but somehow the police of Fall River have taken no fancy to him. He has not worked with them in any way, in fact he has not worked at all except to visit the house every day, and they do not believe that his efforts will tend to further theirs. An order was issued yesterday that the guards about the house should carefully exclude all callers except certain specified friends of the family. This did not bar out Hanscom by name, but it did in effect, and that is what the police were after.

The Fall River Herald

INQUEST BEGUN.

Judge Blaisdell Listens to the Evidence

GATHERED BY THE POLICE IN THE BORDEN CASE.

Midnight Conference With the District Attorney.

ALD. BEATTIE STATES HIS VIEWS ON THE AFFAIR.

Lizzie Borden Taken to the Central Police Station.

The central police station was the center of all interest in the Borden case Monday afternoon and night. Rumors of arrests were thick in the air, and there was a hustling and bustling that indicated that something was going to be done. Officers hurried to and fro with an anxious look on their faces. Everybody was on the qui vive, and it was expected that a sensation might occur at any moment, but the moments dragged along into hours and nothing happened. There was the stage and the stage setting with all of the supporting company, but none of the principal characters arrived on the stage.

It was known that City Marshal Hilliard and his allies had reached the point where they needed legal advice and that the marshal had sent for Hosea M. Knowlton, the district attorney. Shortly after 5 o'clock the district attorney came. He held a brief consultation with the marshal, a long talk with Medical Examiner Dolan, and again it looked as if a move was about to be made.

Timothy Sullivan, a conductor for the Globe Street Railway Co., who saw Mr. Borden on the morning of the murder and could fix the time accurately, appeared at the station house; so did Officer Harrington with a book on his arm. It closely resembled the book which druggists use for keeping a record of prescriptions and the names of persons purchasing drugs. Excitement bubbled up and boiled over. Then it died down a little. District Attorney Knowlton went out to the Mellen house to supper. At 8 o'clock Marshal Hilliard and State Officer Seaver left the central station and walked to the hotel. They met the medical examiner, and with the district attorney reviewed the case from beginning to end.

Medical Examiner Dolan went to the Borden house in the afternoon and had the clothing worn by the victims of the murder dug up and spread on the grass for examination. There were certain parts that he wanted for further investigation, and he carried them away with him and had the remnants buried behind the barn.

Mr. Morse walked down town in the afternoon and paused on his way to and from the postoffice to converse with friends whom he met. Nobody interfered with him, but Officer Devine never lost sight of him for an instant. There was nothing going on about the Borden premises to attract attention except the squad of policemen who are still kept on guard about the place.

POLICE REPORTS SUBMITTED.

If it was quiet on Second street, there was plenty doing at the central station to keep the men interested in the case wide awake. Orders had been issued by Marshal Hilliard that every officer who had had any clue to work out should make a minute report of the same and submit it in writing for further examination by the head of the department and to be laid before the district attorney. After all the special work had been written up, the marshal had a stack of papers a yard high. These he thrust into a big box and waited. He was listening to hear a call from District Attorney Knowlton, whom he had been awaiting all afternoon.

About 5:30 o'clock the marshal's private wire set the telephone bell ringing, and a voice announced that the district attorney was at the Mellen house and ready to begin business. Tucking the big box under his arm, Marshal Hilliard started out of the office with Detective Seaver close to his heels. They walked rapidly up to the hotel and met the district attorney in parlor B, on the second floor.

Here that precious casket, which contained the written results of four days' work by the Fall River police department in their hunt for the key to the most intricate riddle of crime that has ever been perpetrated in this state, was laid open before the district attorney. The most important papers were selected from the bundle, and the three men discussed the case in an informal way. An hour was finally set at 10 o'clock to meet in the same place to review the entire situation in a systematic way and to determine

HOW TO PROCEED.

At that hour the men got together again, Mayor Coughlin and Medical Examiner Dolan being with them. All hands took off their coats and settled to the task in hand without any preliminary delay. The marshal began at the beginning and continued to the end.

THERE WAS A STUMBLING BLOCK

which puzzled the district attorney and his assistants. On the day of the murder Miss Lizzie had explained that she went to the loft of the barn for the lead, and an officer who was examining the premises also went to the loft. It was covered with dust and there were no tracks to prove that any person had been there for weeks. He took particular notice of the fact, and reported back that he had walked about on the dust-covered floor on purpose to discover whether or not his own feet left any tracks. He said that they did and thought it singular that anybody could have visited the floor a short time before him and make no impression on the dust. The lower floor of the stable told no such tale, as it was evident that it had been used more frequently and the dust had not accumulated there. The conclusion reached was that in the excitement incident to the awful discovery, Miss Borden had forgotten just where she went for the lead. When she found her father lying on the lounge, she ran to the stairs and ascended three or four steps to call Maggie. Maggie is the name by which Bridget Sullivan was called by members of the family. She did not call for her stepmother, because, as she stated afterward, she did not think she was in.

THE MISSING LETTER.

Then came the history of the mysterious letter. Miss Lizzie had said that on the morning of the tragedy her stepmother received a letter asking her to visit a sick friend.She knew that at about 9 o'clock the stepmother went up stairs to put shams on the pillows, and she did not see her again. It was that letter that led her to believe that her stepmother had gone out. Here was stumbling block number two. The officers had searched all over the house for that letter, the marshal said, but had failed to find any trace of it. Miss Lizzie had feared that it had been burned in the kitchen stove.

The marshal, medical examiner and the mayor carefully rehearsed, step by step, the summoning of Dr. Bowen, who was not at home when the murder was committed, and his ghastly discovery on the second floor. No theory other than that Mrs. Borden was murdered first was entertained, and Mayor Coughlin was positive that the murderer had closed the door after the deed had been accomplished. Lizzie Borden's demeanor during the many interviews which the police have had with her was described at length, and the story of John W. Morse's whereabouts was retold.

As the night wore on it began to grow very certain that nothing would be done. There was no excuse for doing it at that hour. The persons to whom the only suspicions of any account were pointed were already under arrest for all intents and purposes. If there had been no reason why they should have been arrested in the day time it was certain that no new discoveries had been made that would compel the police to act before daylight came around again, and the wiser nighthawks on the lookout for news flew home to bed.

When the marshal and others left the district attorney they went to the central station. On their return they had another bundle of papers, said to have been warrants, but on that point nobody was positive, as the authorities refused to state what their errand had been. Each of the men referred enquirers to Mr. Knowlton, who said that he was not ready to make any statement at that time. At 1 o'clock the marshal and the mayor were in the central station discussing the situation. It was evident that no arrests were to be made after all.

It was reported that everything was ready to make an arrest. The warrants had been written out in all the details, and all that was wanting were the final signatures to make them valid. This statement has been positively denied and the nearest anybody came to being put into jail was that a couple of blank forms were enclosed in Marshal Hilliard's bundle just to be there if they were needed.

PUBLIC OPINION.

It is certain that public opinion is wavering in the conclusion it so firmly hugged to itself since Thursday night, and when a man is asked today for a theory, he is ready to admit that he has none. The friends of Lizzie Borden rallied so promptly to her support, and so general has been the testimony to her womanly characteristics that people who were led to conclude from printed statements of her coldness and lack of emotion, a nature quite devoid of feeling which could have slaughtered right and left without a fluttering of conscience, have had their theories severely shaken.

It is understood that members of the other Borden families distantly related to that of Andrew J. Borden have prepared themselves for united action in whatever direction may seem necessary. Nothing of the nature of a compact has been made, but the matter has been talked over from a family standpoint, and its wealthy members have volunteered to do what they believe to be necessary in the interests of justice. Detective Hanscom's services were secured at their suggestion, and while his work is independent of the local police it is directed to the same end—to discover the missing murderer.

So general became the popular demand for an arrest and so unanimously did public sentiment point to one person as the perpetrator of the double murder that the family became alarmed and lost no time in exerting itself to such measures as would secure at least a stay in the proceedings until there was no reasonable doubt as to the guilt of the person suspected. It was for this purpose that Lawyer Jennings has been so active in the case, and with what success is clearly evident to everybody.

MR. MORSE TALKS.

About 5 o'clock Mr. Morse came down to a drug store to make a purchase, greeted the mayor and said: "Miss Lizzie Borden is much better today than she has been, and, under the circumstances, is as well as could be expected. We are all hopeful that the murderer will be discovered, and are anxious to assist in the work. All of us at the house are at a disadvantage, however, as we cannot offer any knowledge to guide the detectives or even surmise.

"I see that there has been some insinuating aspersions on the family for employing Mr. Hanscom, and insincere motives are ascribed to us. As to that no one in the town is more deeply concerned in the case than the daughters, and they offered the $5000 reward in the hope it might be productive of results. With only the desire to apprehend the murderer governing their actions, by advice of counsel, the daughters took a proper and consistent course in employing a competent detective to prosecute the investigation. We determined to employ the best talent and were advised to engage the Pinkertons, a most reputable firm, and they are at work to apprehend the murderer and for no other purpose."

IN THE COURT ROOM.

Immediately on the adjournment of the district court this morning the judge retired to his office on Bedford street, only to return in a few minutes to the court building. Previous to this District Attorney Knowlton, Medical Examiner Dolan and Detective Seaver had arrived and were in earnest consultation with the city marshal. Officers started from the station in all directions, and it was soon apparent that something of importance was about to take place. The members of the party who had been in consultation in the marshal's office proceeded upstairs and the first legal proceedings in the case commenced. Miss White, the stenographer, took notes for Mr. Knowlton. Nobody outside of the officials was allowed in the room, and it was impossible to obtain any information as to what took place.

Bridget Sullivan, the domestic, was the first to arrive at the station. She was escorted from the house by Officer Doherty. Miss Sullivan was dressed in black, and her countenance indicated that she thoroughly realizes the position in which she is placed. If an honest appearing face was to acquit a person of a crime Miss Sullivan has that face.

From the time Miss Sullivan went up stairs, 9:45 o'clock, until 11:20 nothing indicated that an inquest was being held. An officer was placed at the head of the stairs and no one was allowed to approach within hearing distance of the room. At the time mentioned Judge Blaisdell came from the court and hurried toward his law office. A HERALD reporter started in pursuit and met his honor as he was returning from the office. In answer to a question as to whether an inquest or examination was going on he replied that he could answer that it was the former. On again being asked as to whether the warrants would be issued for the arrest of any of the suspected parties at the close of the inquest he refused to be quoted, stating that as soon as the matter was over he would be only too glad to converse.

At 12:15 a recess was taken until 2 o'clock, the witness being placed in charge of Matron Russell. District Attorney Knowlton would not say a word.

SHERIFF KIRBY OF WESTPORT

was interviewed Monday in regard to the investigations being made in his town, with a view of connecting some well-known shady characters of the place with the crime. He said: "I know that the officers have been working here, but, so far as I know, have not been made any progress towards a solution of the mystery. They first started to follow up Lincoln and Cooper, the two western dealers who are here at present, but they soon gave up that scent. I can say this much, that not the slighest suspicion attaches to any member of the Borden family so far as any dealings in Westport may be concerned." Throughout New Bedford there is a strong feeling that either the guilty party or parties or someone with a guilty knowledge are located in this section, and increased efforts will be made in this direction.

PROCEEDING CAUTIOUSLY.

A remark that is going the rounds is that if the parties at present suspected were poor people they would have been locked up long before now. This the police deny in the strongest language. As soon as a piece of evidence that is strong enough to warrant the arrest of any person is found, that party, no matter who it may be, will be placed under arrest. Marshal Hilliard has been sifting the evidence in a cool and careful manner, examinnig every possible theory and clue that would lead to a solution of the mystery. In the work he has acted impartially, and from the first determined to show partiality to none.

LIZZIE TAKEN TO THE STATION.

At 1:45 o'clock Marshal Hilliard and Officer Harrington left the central station in one of Stone's hacks. The uniform of the marshal as he drove up Second street attracted the attention of pedestrians, and in less time than it takes to write fully 500 people had assembled on the opposite side of the street facing the Borden mansion. Mrs. George Brigham left the house and was seen to enter Dr. Bowen's office. The supposition immediately became general that Lizzie, whom the officers wished to convey as a witness in the inquest, had broken down under the strain. Such was not the case, however, as when she came to take her place in the carriage her step was light and, other than a care-worn expression, nothing indicated the terrible mental strain that she was undergoing.

In the past few days Lizzie has terribly aged. The full round cheeks that friends of her former days remember have entirely disappeared, although the bright eyes and haughty expression are still retained. There was not a falter in the step as she came down the stairs, and from her every movement the woman would be the last person to suspect of the crime. In fact, her step was such as would indicate that she was going to a picnic instead of attending an inquest.

BRIDGET SULLIVAN

All along the road crowds of people had gathered, and when the hack turned back toward the station there was a mad rush for the alley. The four passengers alighted from the hack and passed into the station, going at once to the court room above.

After they had passed up the stairs, Officer Barker took his place on the landing and forbade anybody passing the staircase beyond the clerk's office. In the court room were Judge Blaisdell, Marshal Hilliard, Dr. Dolan, Detective Seaver and the district attorney. Andrew Jennings went into the marshal's office, but was not present at the inquest. Miss Borden was questioned closely as to her doings and those of the rest of the family. At the time of going to press the examination was still progressing.

NOTES.

Detective Richards of Newport was in town today, but said it was on other business than the Borden affair. In speaking of the tragedy he said it was very mysterious, but he thought it would not be long before the officers here had sifted the matter.

Photographer Walsh took an inside view of the cell room this morning.

In speaking of the handling of the case

District Attorney Knowlton stated that it more than pleases him. As everyone under suspicion was under close police surveillance, it was better to examine everything before precipitating matters.

WE'VE GOT IT.

Ald. Beattie Gives His Views on the Murder Mystery.

"I understand," said a reporter to Ald. John Beattie, "that you have a theory regarding this mystery which gives some promise of its solution."

He was at the police headquarters today, the apparent object being to impress upon the powers that be that his theory—it is his only—might have been very useful to the police at an earlier stage of the game.

"Well," he said, as he answered somewhat shyly to the line thrown out, "my theory—and it is mine alone—is one formed from the circumstances of the case. The brain which devised this crime was cunning enough to devise beforehand the means to escape detection. Supposing it was a woman, she was cunning enough to wear a loose wrapper which would have covered her clothes and gloves which would have protected her hands from the stains of blood. If so, there was time to burn both wrapper and gloves in the hot ironing fire which is known to have been burning in the kitchen on the day of the tragedy. The ashes would have shown whether or not such material was consumed in the kitchen stove.

"Again, it is hard to believe that the murderer, if there was one, escaped by the side door. He might have gone out the cellar door, as a matter of fact, and escaped by scaling the fence in the rear of the yard. On the day they buried the blood-stained clothes, I noticed that they were about to bury a piece of the skull which had been cut away from the head of one of the victims by the axe of the murderer. I told Officer Chace to preserve it. He wrapped it up in a piece of paper and is carrying it around with him. The appearance of that portion of its surface which was cleanly cut by the axe might give some clue as to the exact nature of the weapon in regard to the smoothness of its blade or the cleanness of the blade.

"The police sealed up nothing on the day of the murder. Had they sealed up the cellar door, placed two officers in the house with instructions to examine everything and note what went on there, told the inmates to keep quiet and allowed absolutely no one to enter the house for the time being, some definite action might have been taken before this—an arrest made possibly."

MYSTERIOUS ROBBERY

And Its Relation to the Killing of the Bordens.

Much has been heard about a mysterious robbery which took place at the Borden house about a year ago. Detectives were put on the search, but they could never find any trace of the missing articles. This case is recalled at present as indicating that somebody had before visited the house very mysteriously, perpetrated a crime and departed.

The robbery was done June 24 of last year. How the entrance was effected is not known. The only article in the house that was disturbed was a small desk belonging to Andrew J. Borden. This was rummaged through and through. A lady's gold watch with a chain and locket, a bunch of horse car tickets and a small sum of money were stolen.

Mr. Borden was in Swansey at the time, but when he learned about the break he hastened to inform the local police. Capt. Desmond, then inspector of the department, was detailed to look after the stolen articles. He made a long search, but could find no trace of the missing valuables.

STATE OFFICER GEORGE SEAVER

CITY MARSHAL RUFUS HILLIARD

The New York Herald

GATHERING EVIDENCE OF THE BORDEN MURDER.

Lizzie Borden and Bridget Sullivan Examined by the Officers of the Law Behind Locked Doors.

AUTHORITIES WORK IN SILENCE.

They Refuse to Make Public Any of the Evidence Which They Have Secured up to This Time.

NO ARRESTS HAVE AS YET BEEN MADE.

The Whole Trend of the Developments Thus Far, However, Points to the Accuracy of the Police Solution of the Mystery.

[BY TELEGRAPH TO THE HERALD.]

FALL RIVER, Mass., August 9, 1892.—Certainly on the face of things, the devolpments in the mystery of the Borden butchery trend steadily in one direction. It may be utterly wrong; the person around whom the lines of evidence gathered by the police seem to be closing may be perfectly innocent; there may still be some strange, horrible, unsuspected secret behind this story. If that is so, then the person so clearly indicated by the efforts and clearly evident theory of the police, is the victim of a combination of circumstances and misdirected zeal far stranger than the murder itself.

All the developments of the day seemed to bring out more clearly the solution which the local authorities have formed of the case and upon which they were ready last night to submit to the test of an arrest. They showed plainly, moreover, the possession of facts not hitherto known, and some investigations of great importance.

The tendency of all these and of one or two unexpected happenings was all in the same direction—a direction indicated in these despatches several days ago.

Instead of an inquest into the murders, the authorities began this morning a sort of secret judicial inquiry, permitted under the laws of Massachusetts. This was conducted by the District Attorney in the court room over the police headquarters.

GRIM AND SELF-COMPOSED.

To this place Miss Lizzie Borden, daughter of the murdered man, was brought and closely examined during four hours In any view of the case it must have been a very trying and painful ordeal. Yet it was noted that this extraordinary woman was grim and self-composed when she came to the place of trial, and no less grim and self-composed when she went away.

What she testified to is an official secret, but the guards were not withdrawn from the Borden house when she had done.

Bridget Sullivan, the servant girl, was also a witness at the inquiry, and there are stories of an admission in her testimony confirmatory of the theory of the police. There are, too, new discoveries that contradict any other hypothesis.

Besides the District Attorney, who is a clear headed and shrewd New England lawyer, there were present at the inquiry Chief Hilliard, who I think ceased some time ago to entertain much doubt about the murderer; Dr. Dolan, the medical examiner; Judge Blaisdell, the criminal magistrate of this court, and the stenographer.

Everybody else was strictly excluded, and guards were placed at the doors and on the stairs to see that the exclusion was enforced. Later in the day the importance of the proceedings was increased by the coming of Dr. Wood, the State chemist, who is making the analysis of the intestines sent to him last week, and has examined certain blood stains bearing on the case, and in the afternoon Attorney General Pillsbury came from Boston to consult with the District Attorney.

Woonsocket Call

It has been suggested that Lizzie Borden may be insane. That would be the natural explanation of her deed if she be shown to have been guilty of the atrocious crime charged upon her, but there are some people who think it would not be a bad idea to institute inquiry into the sanity of the Fall River police.

The action of Judge Blaisdell of Fall River in presiding over the preliminary trial of Lizzie Borden, and also over the inquest on bodies of her murdered parents, may be technically legal, but it is highly unsatisfactory to the general public, and does not savor of that rigid impartiality that should govern all judicial proceedings. We may be doing the Fall River authorities great injustice, and if we are, none will regret it more than we will, but it certainly seems as though they were anxious to obtain all the notoriety possible out of this unfortunate affair.

Providence Journal

We are thus reduced to the conclusion that the murderer was impelled simply by a kind of homicidal mania, as "Jack, the ripper," and other mysterious criminals have been impelled. In that case, while the mind of the community would be relieved in so far as the removal of existing suspicions is concerned, it would at the same time be thrown into a greater state of excitement than ever with the possibility before it of similar scenes of horror. A person who, not belonging to the family, can get free access to a house in a populous neighborhood in broad daylight, can avoid being seen by any member of the household and can commit two atrocious crimes at an interval of at least an hour and escape undetected and unsuspected is about the most dangerous being to have at large that can easily be imagined.

The Fall River Herald

STILL UNSETTLED!

Police No Nearer a Solution of the Mystery.

A SOMERSET MAN'S AXE SUBJECTED TO SCRUTINY.

A Painter's Suspicion Led to a Useless Journey.

MISS SULLIVAN UNDERGOING A SEARCHING EXAMINATION.

The Attorney General Invited to a Conference About the Case.

The judicial inquiry, examination, inquest or whatever it was, held before Judge Blaisdell in the district court room Tuesday, gave the first day of rest the inspectors who have been working up the details of the Borden murder mystery have known since Thursday. Popular interest centered in the systematic inquiry that was to be made, and it was believed that unless something new and convincing was drawn from the story of Bridget Sullivan, who was to talk in a place free from the awful spectre of the lifeless, mangled corpses of those who had been her benefactors, the inquest would amount to little indeed. It was not expected to gather much that was new from Lizzie Borden. If she had nothing to conceal, she is a woman of keen enough perceptions to have seen the importance of telling everything to the police that would be of assistance to them. In the numerous conversations they have had with her, opportunity was given to hear her whole story under different surroundings, and it was not likely that anything new would be gathered when she was confronted by Judge Blaisdell and the imposing presence of District Attorney Knowlton. If the woman had anything to conceal, the chances for getting it out of her by a judicial examination were not good. If she has been able to withstand the terrific nervous strain of the past five days and disclose nothing, the public is bound to choose one of two conclusions: either she has nothing to tell, or will not tell it for many a long day after popular interest in the case has died a wasting death.

Attention has been called to certain inconsistencies in her stories to the officials at different times, but they cannot be called significant. Feminine delicacy would prevent her from discussing the details of her visit to the barn before so fine looking a young man as Officer Harrington, who was the first to talk to her after the murder was discovered. As to the hunt for lead, the officials have probably found out whether such a thing was kept in the barn, and if it had already been cut for sinkers. The second inconsistency is said to be the length of time Lizzie Borden was outside the house. Anybody who goes out without marking the time particularly knows how difficult it is to estimate exactly how long one has been away. The third discrepancy in stories is that told by Eli Bence, the druggist, who is certain that Miss Borden called at his store for prussic acid, and that told by the young woman, who is as certain that she did not ask for the poison or visit the store. This is the most important of the three, as there can be no error of judgment or anything else in it. The return of the chemist may throw some light upon the case from which it may be possible to infer whether or not the visit was made.

THE INQUEST.

Bridget Sullivan's Examination Lasted Until 5 O'clock Tuesday.

People who watched Bridget Sullivan go through the street to the police station to be examined sincerely pitied her. The woman seemed to be dazed and unconscious of the curiosity she was exciting along the street. She was not invited to take a companion with her to be a friendly support in the strange surroundings, and she was obliged to walk to the station. People wondered why the girl was not entitled to the same consideration that was shown Miss Borden, who was as carefully guarded from the eyes of the curious as a closed carriage could do it.

Miss Sullivan was kept on the stand from 10 o'clock until 5 o'clock in the afternoon. She was in deep distress and, if she had not already cried her eyes out, would probably have been very much agitated. On the contrary, while tremulous in voice, and now and then crying a little, she was calm enough to receive the interrogatories without exhibiting much emotion and answered them comprehensively. The first question put to her was in regard to her whereabouts all through the morning of Thursday up to the time of the murder. She answered that she had been doing her regular work in the kitchen on the first floor. She had washed the breakfast dishes. She saw Miss Lizzie pass through the kitchen after breakfast time and the young lady might have passed through again.

At 5 o'clock Miss Sullivan left the police station in company with Officer Doherty and passed down Court square. She was dressed in a green gown with hat to match, and appeared to be nervous and excited. Nobody knew her, however, and she attracted no attention whatever. She went to the Borden house for a bundle and, still accompanied by Officer Doherty, walked to 95 Division street, where her cousin, Patrick Harrington, lives, and where she passed the night. She was allowed to go on her own recognizance and seemed to be much relieved to get away from the Borden house. The government impressed her with the necessity of saying nothing about the proceedings at the inquest, and she was warned not to talk with anybody regarding her testimony.

Bridget Sullivan is one of 14 children. She came to this country six years ago. For three years she worked for a number of families in this city and the police say that she bears an excellent reputation. For the last three years she has lived with the

AS MR. BORDEN'S BODY WAS FOUND

Borden family and for some time past has been threatening to return to Ireland. She says that Mrs. Borden was a very kind mistress and that she was much attached to her. Mrs. Borden used to talk to her about going home to Ireland, and used to tell her that she would be lonely without her. Accordingly, the young woman says that she did not have the heart to leave, but she never expected to be in an awful predicament like this. She had been terrified ever since the tragedy, she said.

It was whispered in police circles during the evening that there was something very significant in the fact that the only government witness, with the exception of Lizzie Borden, and a person on whom the prosecution must rely to explain certain occurrences before and after the tragedy, was allowed to go on her own recognizances, and at 6 o'clock the bearing of the officials who have worked up the case indicated that they were in possession of information which they considered as very valuable and which they had hitherto been unable to secure.

ATTORNEY GENERAL PILLSBURY.

The presence of Attorney General Pillsbury, who came to town at 2:30 o'clock Tuesday at the request of Mr. Knowlton, evidently to advise with the latter as to certain details of the case, indicated that the government was by no means dead sure of its ground and did not care to proceed with arrests until every contingency was examined. The two eminent legal lights conferred at the Mellen house, during which time a recess was had in the inquest.

The attorney general left the city at 3:40 and the inquest was resumed. Mr. Pillsbury was a trifle sarcastic. He said, just before he left, that he did not think the case was so mysterious as had been reported, and joked with the press representatives concerning their clues. He was informed that the murder was mysterious enough to baffle the police, and that five days had elapsed and there had been no arrest. Somebody took the pains to further inform him that the evidence was entirely circumstantial. "You newspaper men know, or ought to know," said Mr. Pillsbury, "that you may not be in a position to pronounce on the case. There may be some things that you have not heard of and which may have an important bearing." The reply was to the effect that the head men who had been working on the murder had allowed at noon that they had no other evidence and that they ought to be pretty good authority. "Police officers do not always tell all they know," was the parting shot of the attorney general.

THE EXPERT CHEMIST.

Another visitor to the city who commanded the attention of the interviewers was Prof. Wood, the expert chemist of Boston, who decided it to be worth his while to come down and look over the ground in person. He was closeted with Dr. Dolan for awhile. The bits of clothing and other souvenirs taken from the pile buried behind the Borden barn were turned over to him for further examination. Just what he did here is not known.

"Have you examined any axe, professor?" was asked.

Prof. Wood hesitated a moment and said: "I have seen an axe."

"Will you make an examination down here?" was the next question.

"I do not expect to," was the reply. "I could not very well bring down my laboratory."

About 7 o'clock all the prominent officials in the case disappeared to get a little rest. District Attorney Knowlton went to the Mellen house, and Mr. Seaver went down to dine with Marshal Hilliard at his home on Durfee street. It had been given out early in the afternoon that no arrests were probable at once on the evidence now at hand, and there was little of interest around police headquarters up to midnight.

A FRUITLESS RIDE.

Police Call at a House in South Somerset for Evidence.

About 6 o'clock Tuesday afternoon there was unusual commotion around the station. Officer Harrington drove up in a carryall, and Officer Medley and Peleg

AS MRS. BORDEN'S BODY WAS FOUND

Brightman got in. They drove down North Main street and disappeared in the direction of the bridge.

Mr. Brightman is a painter in the employ of George E. Hoar & Son. Last Friday he was sent to set glass in the windows of a cottage on the Brayton farm at the point. One of the windows furnishes light for a bedroom, but opens into a porch and not into the daylight direct. On one side of this is a shelf, and on the shelf Mr. Brightman found a strange package. It was rolled in cloth, and the handle of an axe could be seen from the end of the bundle. Brightman unrolled the cloth, and there he found a gory axe dyed in real blood carefully concealed in its folds. When he came home he told his employers about the ghastly find, and they tried to persuade him to tell the police about it. He was very reluctant to do so, not desiring to be drawn into the case as a witness; but Tuesday he went to the marshal and made a clean breast of the whole thing.

It was to find that hatchet that Officers Harrington and Medley drove Mr. Brightman across the river. They turned through the road leading to Brayton's point, opened a gate, crossed to a pair of bars, through another gate, over a sand hill, around a frog pond, up to another gate. That brought them to a little cottage where Joseph Silvia lived. Joseph was at home, and his wife and sister were there too. There were several bright-eyed youngsters playing around the house. Sure enough there was the axe, and there was the bloody cloth. The axe had a short handle and a big head, and the cloth had buttons on it. The axe had been wiped and the cloth was hung upon a nail That did not deceive the officers, and they called for the wondering Joseph.

"Whose blood—no, whose axe is that?" asked the tall man.

"Alas, it is my own," replied Joseph, with eyes cast down.

"Whose tennis suit is that hung upon the nail?" continued the inquisitor.

But Joseph's black-eyed wife plucked her husband's coat from behind and looked abashed. The man hesitated, and the short officer whispered something to the tall officer.

"I beg your pardon, madam, if they're yours; I didn't notice the buttons," quickly the tall man explained. "But there are bloodstains there, if I mistake not. Whence came they?"

Then the wife rushed to her husband's rescue: "You see, we wanted a chicken for dinner last Thursday, and Joseph keeps them to put the chicken in to keep the blood off the feathers when he chops the head off. It's a first rate idea, and he can kill two at a time, you see, if he puts one through here and the other through here," and the careful housewife explained the practical use to which an old garment could be put after it had passed the stage of ordinary usefulness.

"Oh, yes," said the officers, as they filed in ones out of the house. Then they drove back home through the seven gates, and over the hill past the frog pond.

KEEPING HER PROMISE.

Miss Sullivan Refuses to Say a Word About the Murder.

The fact that Bridget Sullivan, the domestic, had left the Borden mansion and taken refuge with her cousin on Division street led most people to believe that her further presence in connection with the case was not needed. This is not so, for though her testimony yesterday did not throw any new light on the matter, yet she is under police surveillance at her present abode. She is faithfully keeping the promise made to Attorney General Pillsbury not to speak about the case, and would not converse about anything in connection with the matter.

Shortly after Miss Sullivan arrived in this city she secured a situation as cook at Milton Reed's residence, and the reporter made a call on that gentleman. In answer to a question as to how his health was he stated that it was much improved. He returned last night from a sojourn at Saratoga. "You would be surprised," he said, "at the interest that is taken in the Borden case outside the city. It is the principal topic of conversation wherever I have been, and from the subtlety of its perpetration it is not to be wondered at. While I am not conversant with all the facts connected with the murder, still I cannot believe that Lizzie is guilty of the crime. I have known the young lady for some years, but I never gave her credit for the determination that would be necessary to accomplish the murder of her father and mother. The deed is one of the most atrocious that has ever been committed to my knowledge, and to have participated in it Miss Borden must have been a regular Lady Macbeth, which I do not think she is." He stated that the reported interviews held with Ald. Beattie, David Keefe and other celebrities in the case which appeared in the out of town papers highly amused him.

MISS BORDEN AT THE STATION.

Shortly before 10 o'clock this morning Marshal Hilliard appeared with a closed carriage in front of the Borden residence to convey Lizzie to the central station for a continuance of the inquest. She came out af the nouse with the same cool expression as before, though this morning her personal condition was much improved. Her eyes were much brighter, as though she had enjoyed a good night's repose, while all her actions indicated a person who had been relieved from a terrible load. She was dressed in a navy blue suit, with a hat of blue lace, with a blue feather and white trimmings. When she arrived at the station Miss Borden was taken to the matron's room, where she was detained until the district court was over.

The inquest was commenced at 10:15, and the parties present were the same as yesterday. At 11:15 Miss Borden emerged from the court room and entered the matron's apartment, where her friend, Mrs. Brigham, had been awaiting her. After the door was closed Miss Borden sank on the cot there in a very exhausted condition, and in a few minutes was in a light slumber, Mrs. Brigham fanning her all the time. In the meantime the marshal had made another trip to the house and returned with Mr. Morse. He was subjected to an examination until 12:30, when all parties went to dinner, Miss Borden, Mrs. Brigham and Mr. Morse being taken to the Second street house under the escort of the marshal.

The inquest which was adjourned at noon was resumed at 2:20 o'clock. Emma Borden and Dr. Bowen were called and were driAen to the station together in a carriage with Marshal Hilliard. The same secrecy was maintained, and the officer remained still on guard at the head of the stairway. The Rev. John Brown wanted to get in at the morning hearing, not knowing that it was secret, but the sentinel at the head of the stairs stopped him.

District Attorney Knowlton was seen previous to the opening of the afternoon session and said he could not answer the question as to whether the evidence was of a nature that would warrant the arrest of any of the parties suspected. He also refused to answer whether the evidence as heard from Bridget Sullivan was of such a nature as would cast suspicion on any person. All he would say was that as Mr. Jennings had made a visit to Boston today the news gatherer might obtain a few lines there. A visit to the lawyer's office disclosed the fact that Mr. Jennings was in Boston at an auditor's hearing and not in connection with the Borden case.

MR. BORDEN'S ESTATE.

A story was printed in the New York papers today which attributed to a business associate of Andrew J. Borden the statement that not only had Mr. Borden begun to take an inventory of his property for the sake of preparing a will, but he had even gone farther and made known certain provisions. Among his property were a small block of Union national bank stock and a larger one of the B. M. C. Durfee Safe Deposit and Trust company. This was to go to Mrs.Borden's heirs, it was claimed, in the proportion of ten shares to the wife and one to the daughters. The "business associate" is quoted further as saying that this proportion was to be followed with the rest of the estate. The story is not given much credit by other business associates of Mr. Borden, who say that it was not the man's custom to discuss his private personal affairs with anybody. They think it extremely doubtful that Andrew Borden told anybody about his will even if it was true that he was engaged in preparing one.

ANOTHER SEARCH.

Another search was made of the house this noon. The officers were assisted by a carpenter. A panel in the room where Mrs. Borden was killed which was spattered with blood was cut out and taken to the station. A quantity of lead such as is used in water spouts, besides a number of papers, was also carried away. No new clue was found. It is probably the intention to discover if the blood on the panel is the same as that reported on the hatchet said to be possession of the police.

The New York Herald

Fall River's police and detectives may have committed the Borden murder and then tried to shield themselves by throwing the blame on the mourners. This theory is quite as good as any which the police and detectives have outlined.

The New York Press

It is no wonder that the people of Fall River are dazed by such a tragedy, and that, in their eagerness to detect and punish the guilty, they have perhaps been led to do injustice to the innocent. The case is one for careful and cautious but thorough and fearless scrutiny. Every person supposed to be capable in any way of throwing light upon the horrid affair or whose actions in any way require explanation should be summoned before the coroner and required to submit to a searching examination. A refusal to testify would amount to an admission of guilty knowledge. The state of Massachusetts cannot afford to allow such a foul crime to go unavenged if human agency can bring the guilty to justice.

VIEW OF THE VICINITY OF THE MURDERS I-Borden house. II-Borden barn. III-The well. IV-Fence. V-Side entrance. VI-Churchill residence. VII-Dr. Bowen's house. VIII-Dr. Chagnon's house. IX-Kelley house. X-Yard from which officers watched Borden house. XI-Kelley's barn. XII-Pear orchard.

The New York Times

THE BORDEN MURDER MYSTERY

THE INQUEST ADJOURNED-NO CLUES TO THE MURDERERS

FALL RIVER, Mass., Aug 10 - To-night it cannot be said that the police have any substantial clue to the murderers of Mr. and Mrs. Andrew J. Borden. Theories are plentiful, but reliable evidence is wanting. At 5 o'clock this afternoon State Detective Seaver handed the following bulletin to the reporters:

"The inquest was continued at 10 o'clock to-day. The witnesses examined were Miss Lizzie Borden, John V. Morse, Emma L. Borden, Dr. S. W. Bowen, Adelaide B. Churchill and Hiram C. Harrington. Adjourned until 10 a.m. Thursday; nothing developed for publication."

This was all that was given out after examinations lasting more than four and a half hours. The principal witness was Lizzie Borden. The change in Miss Borden's appearance after her examination was the chief topic of conversation in the police station to-night. Whatever the police may think of the strength of their clues, it is certain that the opinions of Miss Borden's many friends are entirely in favor of her innocence. This feeling is gaining more adherents every hour. Dr. Bowen told a straightforward story, covering the time since he was called to the Borden house a few days before the murder. He incidentally gave some evidence which startled the authorities.

The nature of this will not be given for publication, but it was learned that to-morrow an examination of the dead bodies will be made at Oak Grove Cemetery. Hiram Harrington could give little testimony regarding the circumstances surrounding the murders, as he said that he was not in the vicinity when they occurred. Taken all together, in connection with an authoritative statement volunteered to-night, the police have presented very insufficient and meagre evidence against any member of the family.

Prof. Wood, the analyst, appeared at the station early to-day in companmy with Medical Examiner Dolan. Shortly after the inquest was resumed the two men were admitted and were behind closed doors twenty minutes. When they reappeared they were followed by a couple of policemen carrying a trunk containing bloody clothing and other evidences of the crime.

Prof. Wood took the 11:03 train for Boston and the steamer trunk was checked for the same place.

A carpenter was at work in the Borden house this afternoon. Shortly before 2 o'clock Marshal Hilliard, Detective Seaver and Officer Harrington arrived at the police station carrying three boxes. Two were wrapped up and one was open. The open one contained sheet lead and was taken from the barn where Miss Lizzie Borden said she had gone to look for lead for sinkers.

The inquest was resumed at 2:30 o'clock.

The Fall River Herald

NO ARREST YET.

Marshal Hilliard Makes a General Statement

OF THE WORK OF THE POLICE DEPARTMENT.

No Nearer a Solution Than a Week Ago.

DR. HANDY'S SUSPICIOUS CHARACTER IDENTIFIED.

The Inquest Deals with the Poison Theory.

There was nothing for searchers after information concerning the Borden tragedy to do Wednesday but to await developments. No new clues were advanced as far as could be learned, and the officers who had been detailed to look up the special features of the case were busy helping along the inquest by summoning witnesses and doing similar duty.

The coming and going of important witnesses in the case served to keep alive the interest, and whenever the grating of carriage wheels was heard in the roadway there was a rush into the alley to see who had arrived. Every effort was made to get at some idea of what was being said in the inquest, and to learn whether any new disclosures had been made. There are a hundred details about which the public is not clear, and a course of argument has to jump the breaks in the chain of circumstantial evidence.

The officers and the witnesses were the only persons who could talk on these matters. Atty. Knowlton represented the former. He talked on paper, and what he said on his bulletins bore the merit of conciseness if it did not tend to clear certain difficulties in the popular mind. As to the witnesses, it had been impressed upon their minds evidently with an indelible impression that they were not to talk about the inquest, and every one of them followed instructions carefully.

A VALUABLE WITNESS.

Bridget Sullivan proved herself a most valuable witness, and it is no wonder that she is carefully guarded at the house of her cousin on Division street. It will be remembered that the story told all along has sent her to the third floor of the house to wash windows and that nobody has been able to ascertain when she ascended the stairs. She told the district attorney that she did not go to the third story to wash windows at all. Mr. Morse and Mr. Borden both left the house when Mrs. Borden was alive. One went down town on business, and one went to Weybosset street to call on friends. At 9:30 Bridget Sullivan, acting under Lizzie Borden's orders, went outside to wash windows. There were 11 windows, and she did not get through until 10:30. While she was on the north side of the house she commanded a view of one door, and while she was on the south side, she was close to another door. Nobody entered or left the house while she was washing these windows.

Just as she had completed her work, she saw Mr. Borden coming across the street and she hurried across the lower floor to let him in. The government has fixed the time at which he entered. The servant then attended to one or two other matters in the kitchen and went upstairs. As she passed through the sitting room she saw Mr. Borden on the lounge, and Lizzie was ironing, according to her testimony. Bridget Sullivan went to the third story where her room was situated to lie down a few moments, as her back ached. The next that she knew Lizzie called her and she went down to gaze on the awful scene which had startled the young woman who had summoned her. John Morse was not in the house.

Medical Examiner Dolan has testified that Mrs. Borden was slaughtered some time before Mr. Borden came in. She might have been dead half or three-quarters of an hour. Accordingly, the man who was concealed in the house came in before 9:30, when the servant started to clean the windows on the outside. He did not leave before 10:30, and he could not leave the side door for some minutes after that, as Miss Sullivan did not go up stairs to her room until after 10:30. In other words the servant was practically on guard for an hour, and the man who did the deed must have killed Mr. and Mrs. Borden after he returned from town, or he must have concealed himself in the house at an early hour and waited.

This latter theory gains the most supporters on the ground that it would have been almost a physical impossibility to have done both deeds in the time allotted and escape without such great haste as would have attracted the attention of the neighbors; or if no escape was planned, to so effectually conceal the bloody weapon that a thorough ransacking of the house has failed to reveal it.

POINTS NOT REVEALED.

Of the above-named witnesses Lizzie Borden could make plain several points on which the public has never been fully informed. Perhaps she could account for the time after her mother disappeared at 9 o'clock, and how she herself was occupied until she entered the barn. A friend of hers, Mrs. Charles J. Holmes, has said that she was ironing. It was Thursday, and the ironing is usually over before that day, unless there has been rain and the clothes could not be dried. If she was uncommonly busy, on account of her contemplated visit to Marion, it is in order to explain why the servant did not assist her instead of going into the third story to wash windows. This Miss Sullivan does by saying that Lizzie always ironed her handkerchiefs.

Mrs. Churchill could relate her experience with Miss Borden a few moments after the murder was discovered. She could describe her appearance and bearing, explain how she bore the second shock which came to her after her mother's tragic death was announced, and, perhaps, tell how she had carried herself since the tragedy, and what she had to say in relation to it.

Thomas Walker, 11 Division street, went to the station to say that the statement published concerning trouble with the Whiteheads was not true. He had with him a note from Mrs. Whitehead which said: "I emphatically deny that I said I was afraid of Mr. Walker."

Another woman dropped into the case Wednesday afternoon, but she did not stay long. A lad who drives for Wilkinson, ice cream man, said he saw a woman come out of the Borden yard about 10:30 o'clock Thursday. Officers Harrington and Doherty went to work to find this woman, and they succeeded in discovering that Ellen Eagan was passing that way Thursday morning when she was seized with a sudden illness. She went into the first yard she came to, but it was Dr. Kelly's yard, which is next to the Borden house, and the boy was mistaken.

Perley S. Cooper, the horse dealer about whom an elegantly written story was published Saturday, came from Westport today to explain that he was in New Bedford last Thursday and could give evidence satisfactory to the marshal that he was not the man sought. Kerouack could not be found to identify him as the man who climbed the fence last Thursday, but that did not matter, because Kerouack has already stated that the street was crowded with people when he saw the man, and that it was after the news of the murder had been spread.

Dr. Frank W. Draper, the noted medical examiner of Suffolk county who gave expert evidence in the Almy murder case, was in this city yesterday afternoon. His visit was kept secret, but it is known that he was called on by a number of officials interested in the case.

The inquest was continued at the central station all the morning. The same precautions to ensure safety from intrusion were maintained, and as the witnesses were instructed to say nothing about the proceedings it was impossible to learn anything definite. Among the witnesses examined were Officer Allen, Charles Sawyer, Mrs. Perry Gifford and Mrs. Whitehead, a sister of the murdered woman. At 12:20 the inquest adjourned until 2 o'clock.

The inquest was resumed at 2 o'clock and Charles Sawyer was placed upon the stand. The other witnesses summoned for the afternoon hearing were Eli Bence, Fred Hart and Frank Kilroy. The first two are clerks for D. R. Smith, druggist. It is evident from this that the prussic acid episode will be thoroughly sifted and that the authorities have enough confidence in it to give it prominence at the hearing.

It is reported that a further examination of the remains are to be made this afternoon. Policemen have been on guard at the tomb to prevent the bodies from molestation.

Evidence of unpleasant relationship between members of the Borden family continue to be given out, together with stories of Lizzie Borden's womanly attributes. Mrs. Gray, stepmother of Mrs. Borden says that Mrs. Borden was never treated as she should have been in the house. Kindly feelings were almost unknown.

The Falll River tragedy is compared to some of Gaboriau's novels. It will have to be allowed, however, that Vidocq is left out of this tragedy in real life.—Boston Herald.

Medical Examiner Dolan visited the vault again this forenoon and remained there about two hours.

The reason why the board of aldermen gave the city marshal permission to engage more constables was because District Attorney Knowlton sent a letter to Mayor Coughlin, stating that he desired a large number of men at his disposal, and suggested that it would be a good idea to have extra men to look after the welfare of the city.

A MYSTERY EXPLAINED.

"Mike, the Soldier," the Man Seen by Dr. Handy.

The labors of Detective McHenry and Officer Medley yesterday were confined to ascertaining the foundation for the latest theory advanced in connection with the case. Dr. Handy asserted that while driving by the Borden house at about 10:30 on the day of the murder, he noticed a man walking slowly by the house. In his profession the doctor meets and passes many people, but he says his attention was never attracted to a person on the street before as it was to this man. So much was he impressed with the man's appearance that he turned about in his carriage to obtain a second look at him. He described him as being a man about five feet four inches in height, of medium weight and wearing a dark mustache. His face, the physician says, was deathly white, and he presented the appearance of being extremely agitated. He was about 24 years of age, and was unquestionably excited over something. This description tallied almost exactly with that given by Officer Hyde of a man whom he said he saw in the vicinity of Second street Thursday morning. From the first the police authorities took no stock in the suggestions that this man was in any way connected with the murder, for the reason that, after an occurrence of this nature, there invariably appear descriptions of suspicious-looking individuals whom the discoverers feel confident are in some way connected with the affair.

The chase was not a difficult one, and the individual was located promptly by the officers. He was Michael Graham, better known as "Mike, the soldier," a weaver employed in Border City mill No. 2, and for some days previous to last Thursday he had been drinking freely. The officers learned that Graham was in the vicinity of the Borden house just before 10 o'clock on the morning of the murder and that his physical condition, as a result of his excesses, was such as to render his countenance almost ghastly in its color. He reached the mill where he is employed shortly after 10 o'clock and his condition was at once apparent, and the men in charge there declined to allow him to go to work. The officers found the saloons in which Graham spent Wednesday night and learned there that he drank immoderately, and was feeling badly as a result. The description of Graham corresponded in every particular with that given by Officer Hyde, who furnished more details as to the clothing of the man than could be advanced by Dr. Handy. His trousers were of a peculiar texture and hue, and were rendered extremely noticeable on this account. This in itself was believed to be sufficient identification, but in all other particulars there was an unmistaken similarity, and the authorities arrived at once at the conclusion that the man was identical with the person described by Dr. Handy and the police officer. The explosion of this theory afforded much satisfaction to the authorities.

AN OFFICAL STATEMENT

of the Work of the Police Given to Reporters by the Marshal.

Marshal Hilliard received a representative of each of the local papers today and made the first extended statement that he has made for publication since the case opened. He said that it has been reported and the impression was quite general that all the work of the police was confined to the Borden house. This was by no mean true. Clues, however remote, had been followed out to the end. It did not matter where they led, officers were dispatched at once to fathom them. The marshal will spare no expense to trace the murderer, and his untiring efforts night and day are proof that he will spare no pains.

He declared emphatically that the stories of the disclosures of the inquest were "faked" by the writers. All of them were natural conclusions from evidence already laid before the public, and were merely a review of the same. Whatever new points had been brought out by the inquiry thus far had been carefully guarded and had not been gained by the newspapers.

As to the statements that the police inquiry centered solely in the Borden house, the marshal stated that whatever was being done there had been done at the direction of the medical examiner or the district attorney. Since last Saturday but one question had been asked of the Borden family by the police, except at the inquest, and that related to business relations Mr. Borden was said to have had with a certain individual. The family did not know that he had had any dealings with such a man.

TWO COUSINS TALK.

They Believe in the Innocence of Lizzie and Morse.

PROVIDENCE, Aug. 11.—Two cousins of the murdered Andrew J. Borden and his wife, living in Warren, were seen and talked at some length about the murder. They were Henrietta and Eliza Morse,and are cousins of John V. Morse.

Henrietta Morse took the initiatory in the conversation, and was loud in her denunciations of the manner in which the character of John V. Morse and Lizzie Borden had been handled. She was positive that neither had any hand in the horrible deed, and was equally positive that, when the guilty party, or parties, were discovered, it would be found that they were outside the family.

As regards the conduct of Lizzie Borden since the murder, she stated that Lizzie had always been a peculiar woman, and said that her entire life had been characterized by the calm and cool demeanor which is considered evidence of guilt by the police. She stated that she had known the family almost as well as her own, and that to her knowledge there had not been anything wrong or any trouble with any member of the household. John V. Morse and Andrew J. Borden were always on the best of terms, and, as far as she knew, nothing had ever occurred to disturb the serenity of the relationship.

Eliza Morse, a sister of Miss Henrietta, stated that she had been to Fall River on Monday afternoon, and saw Morse and talked with him. She said that he seemed worried and extremely anxious about the turn the affair had taken, but when asked as to her opinion as to his guilt or innocence, she boldly asserted her belief in his thorough innocence. Both women seemed very much angered by the suspicions cast upon their relatives, and each expressed the desire that the guilty party be brought to justice soon.

BENNY BUFFINGTON

Talks Interestingly of the Mystery and Gives a Theory.

Benjamin Buffington was one of the first persons at the Borden house last Thursday, made an examination of the premises, talked with Bridget Sullivan and Lizzie Borden and made inquiries in the houses surrounding the Borden residence concerning what their inmates had seen or heard. Mr. Buffington said Wednesday: "I made my examination of the place of the crime about 1 o'clock last Thursday; I came away with a theory of the cause of it. The theory I am not going to state, but I will say that this is a crime unlike any other crime. The motive was not robbery, revenge or spite. It was the removal of somebody out of the way. I did not get into the house or think it was necessary. I went into the barn, looked about the fences and went

THE DRESS-GOODS SALE AT SARGENT'S WHERE LIZZIE PLANNED TO SHOP

Monday	Monday	Monday
THE FRANK	E. SARGENT	COMPANY.
GREAT	EST OFFERIN	G YET.
Special Sale M	onday. All on On	e Long Counter.

over into the yard surrounding the house. There is nobody who could have told from the condition of the barn that anybody had or had not been in there. There wasn't enough dust on the floor for anybody's footsteps to have left marks in it, so whether Lizzie Borden went in there or not can't be said for certain. The ground on both sides of the fences showed no signs of any person having jumped the fence, although a person might have jumped the highest fence, even with a cleaver concealed about him, without much trouble. According to what one of the oldest doctors tells me, Mrs. Borden must have been killed about 9:30 o'clock. The weapon it was done with must have been thin edged, something like a cleaver. If it had been an axe or hatchet, the thickness of the blade just above would have caused wounds that opened wider and blood would have been spattered. Mr. Borden's death I place at between five minutes of 11 and five minutes past. Bridget Sullivan told me that she heard the clock strike 11 just before Miss Lizzie called her down stairs. Now you have heard people talk about the inactivity of the police. Let me tell you that the police can't go ahead when they haven't evidence to convict.

"I had a case of murder up between here and Boston, when I was state officer. A companion of the man I suspected told me all about it under a promise that I would not use it unless I got other testimony. As hard as I tried I could not get other evidence to convict, and I had to give it up. I had promised and only got my information by the promise, and I never broke my word. I couldn't ask the companion to turn state's evidence. The man who committed the crime is now in jail. We pushed him hard enough on other cases to shut him up.

"In this Borden case they may have been running up against an equally great difficulty in getting evidence. It is hard to break some people down. What can the police do when they cannot get evidence? They can't do anything in this case until they get somebody to give a fairly plain clue; but I believe this case is coming to light just as sure as fate. It will come inside of 24 hours. There is somebody who can tell you what actually transpired in that house, whether it was a man's or a woman's hand which killed Mr. and Mrs. Borden, whether the weapon is in the house now or has been taken away, and whether the person that did it had on gloves and apron and then burned them up." Mr. Buffington would not say any more at this time, but said that in the future, if an arrest was made, he would be ready to give his theory and a sketch of the family.

Did he Have a Presentiment.

Did Andrew J. Borden, after living almost to the period allotted to man, have a presentiment that he would suddenly be taken ill or meet death? The remark he made to his daughter Emma just before she left home to go to Fairhaven indicates that he had something on his mind, for he was never known to make a statement before like it.

Notwithstanding the numerous times they have been away from home, he said: "Emma, if I should want you immediately while you are away, where shall I find you?" His inquiry had a pronounced effect on his daughter, and she inquired why he asked the question. He remarked: "Nothing in particular, only I feel that I would like to know in case anything should happen." Emma gave him the required information, and he apparently felt much better because of it. This is a peculiar fact in view of the terrible tragedy.

Detective Hanscom Still Active.

Though Detective Hanscom has received but little newspaper attention during the past few days, that active individual is very much in the case, and from his position views with apparent equanimity the efforts of the officers and the government. Mr. Hanscom declines to be interviewed regarding his work here, and as far as can be observed limits his consultations to numerous visits to Andrew J. Jennings, the legal adviser of the Borden family, and apparently there is some curiosity at police headquarters as to the exact nature of the labors which are being performed by Mr. Hanscom, the general presumption being, of course, that he is here for the personal protection of Lizzie Borden.

Mr. Hanscom says he has no new theory to advance in the case, nothing in fact beyond what he has already said. He says the ferreting out of the mystery is in very capable hands, and that the police, under Marshal Hilliard, are doing good work. Mr. Hanscom smiles when he says this, for he knows that the local police authorities do not like his presence here in the employ of the Borden family, and have expressed themselves in very strong terms regarding the doubts which the Pinkerton man has cast upon a portion of their accumulated wisdom.

He did speak a few sentences yesterday when asked if there was any truth in the story advanced by one of the government officers to the effect that Detective Hanscom had two asssistants here whose sole duty it was to shadow Officer Seaver and Marshal Hilliard and ascertain the clues upon which they were working, and Mr. Hanscomb's reply to this was that there were some stories the absurdity of which showed that they required no answer. He said that he was in Fall River not to ascertain what other people were doing, but to attend to his own affairs.

The Policeman's Lot.

The policemen who are doing sentinel and spy duty around the Borden home are a very patient set, but it is clear that they long for the time when they can get back to patrol duty. It is not that they have much to do; the yard is not large enough to permit of much exercise, and there is too much of a sameness about the place.

"Many curious people pass here?" repeated an officer in reply to a reporter's query. "I should say that they did. You'd be surprised to see the number in an hour. I don't think I exaggerate when I say that fully 3000 strangers, persons who came here out of curiosity, passed here today. They go up one side of the street as far as Spring street and come down on the other. A good many come in carriages and wagons, and the way they stare is a caution. One man in particular attracted my attention. He was well dressed, and I'll bet he spent all of four hours in this vicinity. I don't know what his business was, but he talked with everybody who would speak about the tragedy. It may seem strange that we are on duty here, but I really belive that if we weren't here everything would be ripped to pieces by persons who wanted something to show as having been owned by Mr. Borden."

The New York Times

MISS BORDEN ARRESTED

CHARGED WITH MURDERING HER FATHER AND HIS WIFE.

SHE APPEARED CALM WHEN THE WARRANT WAS READ TO HER—ANOTHER AUTOPSY UPON THE BODIES OF MR. AND MRS. BORDEN—WHAT WAS DONE AT THE INQUEST.

FALL RIVER, Mass., Aug. 11.-Lizzie Borden is under arrest charged with murdering her father and step-mother last Thursday morning at their home on Second Street.

She was brought into the Second District Court room about 3 o'clock this afternoon, presumably to give further evidence at the inquest. Miss Borden was accompanied by her sister and Mrs. Brigham. As was the case yesterday, all the proceedings were carried on behind locked doors.

When Miss Lizzie returned from the third inquiry she was a physical and mental wreck and was conducted to the matron's room. The inquest was adjourned about 4 o'clock.

District Attorney Knowlton and other officials went to the Marshal's private office, where they remained closeted for two hours.

Shortly after 6 o'clock City Marshal Hilliard and District Attorney Knowlton drove to the home of Andrew Jennings, who had been the family's attorney for some years. They returned at about 7 o'clock, and went into the matron's room, where Lizzie was lying on the sofa.

The reading of the warrant was waived. The lady took the announcement of her arrest with surprising calmness. Two women who were with her were much more visibly affected.

The excitement on the street was very great when the news of the arrest became known, although some hours previous it was generally understood that Miss Borden was soon to be made a prisoner.

Miss Borden was searched by Mrs. Russell shortly after she was formally placed in custody.

Marshal Hilliard said to-day, in answer to questions as to whether or not the police had given up all hopes of locating a murderer outside of the Borden family, that three clues were already being run down and none of them would in any way implicate a member of the household. He said he had not been stinted in money nor men by the City Government because of political complications.

It has been proved that the milk drank by the Borden family was not poisoned when it was taken from the Borden farm and brought to the city. Members of the family in charge of the farm drank it, and they were affected in no noticeable way.

THE FALL RIVER COURTHOUSE

A PROPHETIC MUSICALE?

(From the Fall River Globe August 8, 1892)

Band Concert Tonight.

The following is the program of the concert to be given by Jones' band on the north park this evening:

1. March, "Ta-Ra-Ra-Boom-De-a," J. H. Taylor
3. Overture, "La Ruch D'Or." Bresprant
3. Waltzes, "Sounds from Erin," C. W. Bennett
4. Skirt dance, J. O. Casey
5. Potpourri, "O Fair Dove, O Fond Dove," E. Beyer
6. Polka, "Hit or Miss," Linter

The New York Herald

LIZZIE BORDEN UNDER ARREST.

Fall River Police Take Her in Custody, Charged with the Murder of Her Father and Stepmother.

UTTER COLLAPSE OF THE PRISONER.

When the Warrant Was Shown Her the Accused Woman Lost Her Nerve and Was Taken to the Matron's Room Instead of a Cell.

REFUSED TO MAKE EXPLANATIONS.

Confronted by Witnesses Who Told Damaging Stories About Her She Declined to Say Anything Further—To Be Taken Into Court To-Day.

[BY TELEGRAPH TO THE HERALD.]

FALL RIVER, Mass., August 11, 1892.—Lizzie A. Borden, the younger daughter of Andrew J. Borden, was arrested at ten minutes past seven o'clock to-night charged with the murder and inhuman butchery of her father and mother.

This long expected and much predicted climax in the strange Borden mystery occurred in the courtroom over the central police station, where all the afternoon the inquiry into the murder had gone on with Lizzie Borden as the leading witness.

The wonderful courage and self-possession that have sustained this extraordinary woman abandoned her in her chief hour of need. Very likely she had not been without some expectation that possibly such a fate was in store for her, yet at the reading of the warrant she fell into a fit of abject and pitiable terror. A fit of violent trembling seized her, and so complete was the collapse of her physical system, weakened, no doubt, by the prolonged and terrible strain, that instead of the cell that had been prepared for her the matron's room in the central station was made her prison.

She is there now under close guard and lock and key. Ten minutes after the poor trembling, half fainting creature had been almost carried into these quarters she could hear the newsboys in the streets crying the news of her arrest, and the solution of the mystery and the clattering feet of the people who thronged to the station house with the hope of catching a glimpse of her.

THE NEXT STEP.

The next step in the procedure will be to bring her before the committing magistrate, who, in this case, is Judge Blaisdell. Under the Massachusetts law, either side has in such cases opportunity to move for a continuance of the hearing to any date within two weeks. In this case the State will undoubtedly ask for such a continuance, which will be granted, and in the meantime Lizzie Borden will be a close prisoner in the matron's room, if her condition demands it.

The arrest had been expected all day. Lizzie Borden and her sister were brought down to the inquest again to continue their testimony. Instead of arrest what was wanted of her just then was to give her a last chance to explain some of the circumstances that look so black against her and the discrepancies in her statement.

She found there Bridget Sullivan, Eli Bence, the clerk from Smith's drug store, from whom she tried to buy poison; another drug clerk, Frank Kilroy by name, and Medical Student Fred Hart.

SHE SAID NOTHING.

Lizzie did not say anything, and still paid no heed to what was going on about her. Emma Borden looked into her sister's face, and the tears began to run down her face, but she did not say anything. Mr. Jennings addressed a few words of hope and comfort to his unfortunate client and bade her goodby. Emma Borden went with her. She did not kiss her sister or even bid her goodby, but went crying down stairs and through the police guard room filled with curious people.

I don't think she saw any of them, hard as they stared at her. Then, still accompanied by Mr. Jennings and Mrs. Brigham, she went home, where she is now save one the only inmate of the household who was there eight days ago.

During the afternoon by the Chief's orders one of the matrons had fitted up one of the cells down stairs for Lizzie's reception, but as the Chief stood and looked at her, after the serving of the warrant, he concluded that a cell was no place for a human being so crushed and broken. He gave orders instead that she should occupy the matron's sleeping room, a large, well furnished apartment on the second floor.

Matron Russell had been summoned as soon as the arrest was made. She now led Lizzie into the room which is to be her prison quarters.

Up to this time the girl had not said a word nor indicated in any way a consciousness of her position. She arose and, the matron taking her arm, they walked away together. She was taken ill and the matron placed her upon a couch.

After a time she recovered some of that impenetrable bearing she had shown, though she was far from the Lizzie Borden of old. She would not converse much with the good hearted matron and soon went to bed.

PRELIMINARY EXAMINATION.

To-morrow she is to be arraigned before Judge Blaisdell for examination to determine whether there is evidence enough to have her committed to the Grand Jury.

The law in this State allows a wide latitude for preliminary examinations. The State is probably not well prepared to go ahead. Mr. Borden's safe has not been opened yet. No doubt there is other evidence the authorities will want to develop. District Attorney Knowlton will probably ask for a continuance for ten days or two weeks, which will be granted, and the prisoner will be remanded without bail.

If, when examination takes place, Judge Blaisdell does not think there is enough evidence against her to warrant the Grand Jury's investigation, he will discharge her. In that case she will have no ground for action against Hillyard nor anybody else. If the action of the Grand Jury is invoked she may be indicted in September and come to trial during the winter.

Her counsel, Mr. Jennings, refuses to give any opinion about the turn the case has taken, nor will he offer any reply to the charges against his client.

PARTICULAR TWO

THE INQUEST TESTIMONY

LIZZIE BORDEN'S INQUEST TESTIMONY

Q. (Mr. Knowlton) Give me your full name.
A. Lizzie Andrew Borden.
Q. Is it Lizzie or Elizabeth?
A. Lizzie.
Q. You were so christened?
A. I was so christened.
Q. What is your age, please?
A. Thirty-two.
Q. Your mother is not living?
A. No sir.
Q. When did she die?
A. She died when I was two-and-a-half years old.
Q. You do not remember her then?
A. No sir.
Q. What was your father's age?
A. He was 70 next month.
Q. What was his whole name?
A. Andrew Jackson Borden.
Q. And your stepmother, what is her whole name?
A. Abby Durfee Borden.
Q. How long had your father been married to your stepmother?
A. I think about 27 years.
Q. How much of that time have they lived in that house on Second Street?
A. I think, I am not sure, but I think about 20 years last May.
Q. Always occupied the whole house?
A. Yes sir.
Q. Somebody told me it was once fitted up for two tenements.
A. When we bought it it was for two tenements and the man we bought it off of stayed there a few months until he finished his own house. After he finished his own house and moved into it, there was no one else moved in. We always had the whole.
Q. Have you any idea how much your father was worth?
A. No sir.
Q. Have you ever heard him say?
A. No sir.
Q. Have you ever formed any opinion?
A. No sir.
Q. Do you know something about his real estate?
A. About what?
Q. His real estate.
A. I know what real estate he owned; part of it. I don't know whether or not I know it all or not.
Q. Tell me what you know of.
A. He owns two farms in Swansea, the place on Second Street and the A.J. Borden

Building and corner and the land on South Main Street where McMannus is and then a short time ago, he bought some real estate up further south that formerly, he said, belonged to a Mr. Birch.

Q. Did you ever deed him any property?
A. He gave us, some years ago, Grandfather Borden's house on Ferry Street and he bought that back from us some weeks ago. I don't know just how many.
Q. As near as you can recall.
A. Well, I should say in June, but I am not sure.
Q. What do you mean by 'bought it back'?
A. He bought it of us and gave us the money for it.
Q. How much was it?
A. How much money? He gave us $5,000 for it.
Q. Did you pay him anything when you took a deed from him?
A. Pay him anything? No sir.
Q. How long ago was it you took a deed from him?
A. When he gave it to us?
Q. Yes.
A. I can't tell you. I should think five years.
Q. Did you have any other business transactions with him besides that?
A. No sir.
Q. In real estate?
A. No sir.
Q. Or in personal property?
A. No sir.
Q. Never?
A. Never.
Q. No transfer of property one way or another?
A. No sir.
Q. At no time?
A. No sir.
Q. And I understand he paid you the cash for this property?
A. Yes sir.
Q. You and Emma equally?
A. Yes sir.
Q. How many children has your father?
A. Only two.
Q. Only you two?
A. Yes sir.
Q. Any others ever?
A. One that died.
Q. Did you know of your father making a will?
A. No sir, except I heard somebody say once that there was one several years ago. That is all I ever heard.
Q. Who did you hear say so?
A. I think it was Mr. Morse.
Q. What Morse?

A. Uncle John V. Morse.
Q. How long ago?
A. How long ago I heard him say it? I have not any idea.
Q. What did he say about it?
A. Nothing except just that.
Q. What?
A. That Mr. Borden had a will.
Q. Did you ask your father?
A. I did not.
Q. Did he ever mention the subject of a will to you?
A. He did not.
Q. He never told you that he had made a will or had not?
A. No sir.
Q. Did he have a marriage settlement with your stepmother that you know of?
A. I never knew of any.
Q. Had you heard anything of his proposing to make a will?
A. No sir.
Q. Do you know of anybody that your father was on bad terms with?
A. There was a man that came there that he had trouble with. I don't know who the man was.
Q. When?
A. I cannot locate the time exactly. It was within two weeks. That is, I don't know the date or day of the month.
Q. Tell all you saw and heard.
A. I did not see anything. I heard the bell ring and father went to the door and let him in. I did not hear anything for some time except just the voices. Then I heard the man say, "I would like to have that place; I would like to have that store." Father said, "I am not willing to let your business go in there." And the man said, "I thought with your reputation for liking money, you would let your store for anything." Father said, "You are mistaken." Then they talked a while and then their voices were louder and I heard father order him out and went to the front door with him.
Q. What did he say?
A. He said he had stayed long enough and he would thank him to go.
Q. Did he say anything about coming again?
A. No sir.
Q. Did your father say anything about coming again, or did he?
A. No sir.
Q. Have you any idea who that was?
A. No sir. I think it was a man from out of town because he said he was going home to see his partner.
Q. Have you had any efforts made to find him?
A. We have had a detective; that is all I know.
Q. You have not found him?
A. Not that I know of.
Q. You can't give us any other idea about it?

A. Nothing but what I have told you.
Q. Beside that, do you know of anybody that your father had bad feelings toward or who had bad feelings toward your father?
A. I know of one man who has not been friendly with him. They have not been friendly for years.
Q. Who?
A. Mr. Hiram C. Harrington.
Q. What relation is he to him?
A. He is my father's brother-in-law.
Q. Your mother's brother?
A. My father's only sister married Mr. Harrington.
Q. Anybody else that was on bad terms with your father or that your father was on bad terms with?
A. Not that I know of.
Q. You have no reason to suppose that the man you spoke of a week or two ago had ever seen your father before or has since?
A. No sir.
Q. Do you know of anybody that was on bad terms with your stepmother?
A. No sir.
Q. Or that your stepmother was on bad terms with?
A. No sir.
Q. Had your stepmother any property?
A. I don't know. Only that she had half the house that belonged to her father.
Q. Where was that?
A. On Fourth Street.
Q. Who lives in it?
A. Her half-sister.
Q. Any other property besides that that you know of?
A. I don't know.
Q. Did you ever know of any?
A. No sir.
Q. Did you understand that she was worth anything more than that?
A. I never knew.
Q. Did you ever have any trouble with your stepmother?
A. No sir.
Q. Have you within six months had any words with her?
A. No sir.
Q. Within a year?
A. No sir.
Q. Within two years?
A. I think not.
Q. When last that you know of?
A. About five years ago.
Q. What about?
A. Her stepsister, half-sister.
Q. What name?

A. Her name now is Mrs. George W. Whitehead.
Q. Nothing more than hard words?
A. No sir. They were not hard words. It was simply a difference of opinion.
Q. You have been on pleasant terms with your stepmother since then?
A. Yes sir.
Q. Cordial?
A. It depends upon one's idea of cordiality perhaps.
Q. According to your idea of cordiality?
A. We were friendly; very friendly.
Q. Cordial, according to your idea of cordiality?
A. Quite so.
Q. What do you mean by "quite so?"
A. Quite cordial. I do not mean the dearest of friends in the world, but very kindly feelings and pleasant. I do not know how to answer you any better than that.
Q. You did not regard her as your mother?
A. Not exactly, no; although she came there when I was very young.
Q. Were your relations toward her that of daughter and mother?
A. In some ways it was and in some it was not.
Q. In what ways was it?
A. I decline to answer.
Q. Why?
A. Because I don't know how to answer it.
Q. In what ways was it not?
A. I did not call her mother.
Q. What name did she go by?
A. Mrs. Borden.
Q. When did you begin to call her Mrs. Borden?
A. I should think five or six years ago.
Q. Before that time you had called her mother?
A. Yes sir.
Q. What led to the change?
A. The affair with her step-sister.
Q. So that the affair was serious enough to have you change from calling her mother, do you mean?
A. I did not choose to call her mother.
Q. Have you ever called her mother since?
A. Yes, occasionally.
Q. To her face, I mean?
A. Yes.
Q. Often?
A. No sir.
Q. Seldom?
A. Seldom.
Q. Your usual address was Mrs. Borden?
A. Yes sir.
Q. Did your sister Emma call her mother?

A. She always called her Abby from the time she came into the family.
Q. Is your sister Emma older than you?
A. Yes sir.
Q. What is her age?
A. She is 10 years older than I am. She was somewhere about 14 when she came there.
Q. What was your stepmother's age?
A. I don't know. I asked her sister Saturday and she said 64. I told them 67. I did not know. I told as nearly as I knew. I did not know there was so much difference between her and my father.
Q. Why did you leave off calling her mother?
A. Because I wanted to.
Q. Is that all the reason you have to give me?
A. I have not any other answer.
Q. Can't you give me any better reason than that?
A. I have not any reason to give except that I did not want to.
Q. In what respects were the relations between you and her that of mother and daughter, besides not calling her mother?
A. I don't know that any of the relations were changed. I had never been to her as a mother in many things. I always went to my sister because she was older and had the care of me after my mother died.
Q. In what respects were the relations between you and her that of mother and daughter?
A. That is the same question you asked before. I can't answer you any better now than I did before.
Q. You did not say before you could not answer, but that you declined to answer.
A. I decline to answer because I do not know what to say.
Q. That is the only reason?
A. Yes sir.
Q. You called your father, father?
A. Always.
Q. Were your father and mother happily united?
A. Why, I don't know but that they were.
Q. Why do you hesitate?
A. Because I don't know but that they were and I am telling the truth as nearly as I know it.
Q. Do you mean me to understand that they were happy entirely or not?
A. So far as I know they were.
Q. Why did you hesitate then?
A. Because I did not know how to answer you any better than what came into my mind. I was trying to think if I was telling it as I should, that's all.
Q. Do you have any difficulty in telling it as you should; any difficulty in answering my questions?
A. Some of your questions I have difficulty answering because I don't know just how you mean them.
Q. Did you ever know of any difficulty between her and your father?

A. No sir.
Q. Did he seem to be affectionate?
A. I think so.
Q. As man and woman who are married ought to be?
A. So far as I have ever had any chance of judging.
Q. They were?
A. Yes.
Q. What dress did you wear the day they were killed?
A. I had on a navy blue, sort of a Bengaline silk skirt with a navy blue blouse. In the afternoon, they thought I had better change it. I put on a pink wrapper.
Q. Did you change your clothing before the afternoon?
A. No sir.
Q. You dressed in the morning as you have described and kept that clothing on until afternoon?
A. Yes sir.
Q. When did Morse come there first? I don't mean this visit. I mean as a visitor, John V. Morse?
A. Do you mean this day that he came and stayed all night?
Q. No. Was this visit the first to your house?
A. He has been in the east a year or more.
Q. Since he has been in the east, has he been in the habit of coming to your house?
A. Yes; came in any time he wanted to.
Q. Before that, had be been at your house---before he came east?
A. Yes, he has been here, if you remember the winter that the river was frozen over and they went across, he was here that winter, some 14 years ago, was it not?
Q. I am not answering questions but asking them.
A. I don't remember the date. He was here that winter.
Q. Has he been here since?
A. He has been here once since. I don't know whether he has or not since.
Q. How many times this last year has he been at your house?
A. None at all to speak of. Nothing more than a night or two at a time.
Q. How often did he come to spend a night or two?
A. Really, I don't know. I am away so much myself.
Q. Your last answer is that you don't know how much he had been here because you had been away yourself so much?
A. Yes.
Q. That is true the last year or since he has been east?
A. I have not been away the last year so much but other times I have been away when he has been here.
Q. Do I understand you to say that his last visit before this one was 14 years ago?
A. No. He has been here once between the two.
Q. How long did he stay then?
A. I don't know.
Q. How long ago was that?
A. I don't know.
Q. Give me your best remembrance.

A. Five or six years; perhaps six.
Q. How long has he been east this time?
A. I think over a year. I'm not sure.
Q. During the last year, how much of the time has he been at your house?
A. Very little that I know of.
Q. Your answer to that question before was, "I don't know because I have been away so much myself."
A. I did not mean I had been away very much myself in the last year.
Q. How much have you been away the last year?
A. I have been away a great deal in the daytime; occasionally at night.
Q. Where in the daytime? Any particular place?
A. No. Around town.
Q. When you go off nights, where?
A. Never, unless I have been off on a visit.
Q. When was the last time when you have been away for more than a night or two before this affair?
A. I don't think I have been away to stay more than a night or two since I came from abroad, except about three or four weeks ago I was in New Bedford for three or four days.
Q. Where at New Bedford?
A. At 20 Madison Street.
Q. How long ago were you abroad?
A. I was abroad in 1890.
Q. When did he come to the house the last time before your father and mother were killed?
A. He stayed there all night Wednesday night.
Q. My question is when he came there.
A. I don't know. I was not home when he came. I was out.
Q. When did you first see him there?
A. I did not see him at all.
Q. How did you know he was there?
A. I heard his voice.
Q. You did not see him Wednesday evening?
A. I did not. I was out Wednesday evening.
Q. You did not see him Thursday morning?
A. I did not. He was out when I came downstairs.
Q. When was the first time you saw him?
A. Thursday noon.
Q. You had never seen him before that?
A. No sir.
Q. Where were you Wednesday evening?
A. I spent the evening with Miss Russell.
Q. As near as you can remember, when did you return?
A. About nine o'clock at night.
Q. The family had then retired?
A. I don't know whether they had or not. I went right to my room. I don't

remember.

Q. You did not look to see?

A. No sir.

Q. Which door did you come in at?

A. The front door.

Q. Did you lock it?

A. Yes sir.

Q. For the night?

A. Yes sir.

Q. And went right upstairs to your room?

A. Yes sir.

Q. When was it that you heard the voice of Mr. Morse?

A. I heard him down there about supper time---. No, it was earlier than that. I heard him down there somewhere about three o'clock, I think. I was in my room Wednesday, not feeling well, all day.

Q. Did you eat supper at home Wednesday night?

A. I was at home. I did not eat any supper because I did not feel able to eat supper. I had been sick.

Q. You did not come down to supper?

A. No sir.

Q. Did you hear him eating supper?

A. No sir. I did not know whether he was there or not.

Q. You heard him in the afternoon?

A. Yes sir.

Q. Did you hear him go away?

A. I did not.

Q. You did not go down to see him?

A. No sir.

Q. Was you in bed?

A. No sir, I was on the lounge.

Q. Why did you not go down?

A. I did not care to go down and I was not feeling well and kept to my room all day.

Q. You felt better in the evening?

A. Not very much better. I thought I would go out and see if the air would make me feel any better.

Q. When you came back at nine o'clock, you did not look in to see if the family were up?

A. No sir.

Q. Why not?

A. I very rarely do when I come in.

Q. You go right to your room?

A. Yes sir.

Q. Did you have a night key?

A. Yes sir.

Q. How did you know it was right to lock the front door?

A. That was always my business.

Q. How many locks did you fasten?
A. The spring locks itself and there is a key to turn and you manipulate the bolt.
Q. You manipulated all those?
A. I used them all.
Q. Then you went to bed?
A. Yes, directly.
Q. When you got up the next morning, did you see Mr. Morse?
A. I did not.
Q. Had the family breakfasted when you came down?
A. Yes sir.
Q. What time did you come downstairs?
A. As near as I can remember, it was a few minutes before nine.
Q. Who did you find downstairs when you came down?
A. Maggie and Mrs. Borden.
Q. Did you inquire for Mr. Morse?
A. No sir.
Q. Did you suppose he had gone?
A. I did not know whether he had or not. He was not there.
Q. Your father was there?
A. Yes sir.
Q. Then you found him?
A. Yes sir.
Q. Did you speak either to your father or Mrs. Borden?
A. I spoke to them all.
Q. About Mr. Morse?
A. I did not mention him.
Q. Did not inquire anything about him?
A. No sir.
Q. How long before that time had he been at the house?
A. I don't know.
Q. As near as you can tell.
A. I don't know. He was there in June some time. I don't know whether he was there after that or not.
Q. Why did you not go to Marion with the party that went?
A. Because they went sooner than I could and I was going Monday.
Q. Why did they go sooner than you could? What was there to keep you?
A. I had taken the secretaryship and treasurer of our C.E. Society, had the charge, and the roll call was the first Sunday in August and I felt I must be there and attend to that part of the business.
Q. Where was your sister Emma that day?
A. What day?
Q. The day your father and Mrs. Borden were killed.
A. She had been in Fairhaven.
Q. Had you written to her?
A. Yes sir.
Q. When was the last time you wrote to her?

A. Thursday morning; and my father mailed the letter for me.
Q. Did she get it at Fairhaven?
A. No sir, it was sent back. She did not get it at Fairhaven for we telegraphed for her and she got home here Thursday afternoon and the letter was sent back to this post office.
Q. How long had she been in Fairhaven?
A. Just two weeks to the day.
Q. You did not visit in Fairhaven?
A. No sir.
Q. Had there been anybody else around the house that week, or premises?
A. No one that I know of except the man that called to see him on this business about the store.
Q. Was that that week?
A. Yes sir.
Q. I misunderstand you probably. I thought you said a week or two before.
A. No, I said that week. There was a man came the week before and gave up some keys and I took them.
Q. Do you remember of anybody else being then around the premises that week?
A. Nobody that I know of or saw.
Q. Nobody at work there?
A. No sir.
Q. Nobody doing any chores there?
A. No sir, not that I know of.
Q. Nobody had access to the house so far as you know during that time?
A. No sir.
Q. I ask you once more how it happened that, knowing Mr. Morse was at your house you did not step in and greet him before you retired.
A. I have no reason except that I was not feeling well Wednesday and so did not come down.
Q. No, you were down when you came in from out.
A. Do you mean Wednesdsay night?
Q. Yes.
A. Because I hardly ever do go in. I generally went right up to my room and I did that night.
Q. Could you then get to your room from the back hall?
A. No sir.
Q. From the back stairs?
A. No sir.
Q. Why not? What would hinder?
A. Father's bedroom door was kept locked and his door into my room was locked and hooked, too, I think and I had no keys.
Q. That was the custom of the establishment?
A. It had always been so.
Q. It was so Wednesday and so Thursday?
A. It was so Wednesday but Thursday they broke the door open.
Q. That was after the crowd came. Before the crowd came?

A. It was so.
Q. There was no access, except one had a key, and one would have to have two keys?
A. They would have to have two keys if they went up the back way to get into my room. If they were in my room, they would have to have a key to get into his room and another key to get into the back stairs.
Q. Where did Mr. Morse sleep?
A. In the next room, over the parlor in front of the stairs.
Q. Right up the stairs where your room was?
A. Yes sir.
Q. How far from your room?
A. A door opened into it.
Q. The two rooms connected directly?
A. By one door, that is all.
Q. Not through the hall?
A. No sir.
Q. Was the door locked?
A. It has been locked and bolted and a large writing desk in my room kept up against it.
Q. Then it was not a practical opening?
A. No sir.
Q. How otherwise do you get from your room to the other room?
A. I have to go into the front hall.
Q. How far apart are the two doors?
A. Very near. I don't think more than so far. (Indicating)
Q. Was it your habit when you were in your room to keep your door shut?
A. Yes sir.
Q. That time---that Wednesday afternoon?
A. My door was open part of the time and part of the time I tried to get a nap and their voices annoyed me and I closed it. I kept it open in summer, more or less, and closed in winter.
Q. Then, unless for some special reason, you kept your door open in the summer?
A. Yes sir, if it was a warm day. If it was a cool day, I should have closed it.
Q. Where was your father when you came down Thursday morning?
A. Sitting in the sitting room in his large chair, reading the Providence Journal.
Q. Where was your mother? Do you prefer me to call her Mrs. Borden?
A. I had as soon you call her mother. She was in the dining room with a feather duster dusting.
Q. When she dusted, did she wear something over her head?
A. Sometimes when she swept, but not when dusting.
Q. Where was Maggie?
A. Just came in the back door with the long pole, brush and put the brush on the handle. and getting her pail of water. She was going to wash the windows around the house. She said Mrs. Borden wanted her to.
Q. Did you get your breakfast that morning?
A. I did not eat any breakfast. I did not feel as though I wanted any.
Q. Did you get any breakfast that morning?

A. I don't know whether I ate half a banana. I don't think I did.
Q. You drank no tea or coffee that morning?
A. No sir.
Q. And ate no cookies?
A. I don't know whether I did or not. We had some molasses cookies. I don't know whether I ate any that morning or not.
Q. Were the breakfast things put away when you got down?
A. Everything except the coffee pot. I'm not sure whether that was on the stove or not.
Q. You said nothing about Mr. Morse to your father or mother?
A. No sir.
Q. What was the next thing that happened after you got down?
A. Maggie went out of doors to wash the windows and father came out into the kitchen and said he did not know whether he would go down to the post office or not. And then I sprinkled some handkerchiefs to iron.
Q. Tell us again what time you came downstairs.
A. It was a little before nine, I should say. About quarter. I don't know sure.
Q. Did your father go down town?
A. He went down later.
Q. What time did he start away?
A. I don't know.
Q. What were you doing when he started away?
A. I was in the dining room, I think. Yes, I had just commenced, I think, to iron.

Q. It may seem a foolish question. How much of an ironing did you have?
A. I only had about eight or ten of my best handkerchiefs.
Q. Did you let your father out?
A. No sir, he went out himself.
Q. Did you fasten the door after him?
A. No sir.
Q. Did Maggie?
A. I don't know. When she went upstairs, she always locked the door. She had charge of the back door.
Q. Did she go out after a brush before your father went away?
A. I think so.
Q. Did you say anything to Maggie?
A. I did not.
Q. Did you say anything about washing the windows?
A. No sir.
Q. Did you speak to her?
A. I think I told her I did not want any breakfast.
Q. You do not remember of talking about washing the windows?
A. I don't remember whether I did or not. I don't remember it. Yes, I remember. Yes, I asked her to shut the parlor blinds when she got through because the sun was so hot.
Q. About what time do you think your father went downtown?

A. I don't know. It must have been about nine o'clock. I don't know what time it was.
Q. You think at that time you had begun to iron your handkerchiefs?
A. Yes sir.
Q. How long a job was that?
A. I did not finish them. My flats were not hot enough.
Q. How long a job would it have been if the flats had been right?
A. If they had been hot, not more than 20 minutes, perhaps.
Q. How long did you work on the job?
A. I don't know, sir.
Q. How long was your father gone?
A. I don't know that.
Q. Where were you when he returned?
A. I was down in the kitchen.
Q. What doing?
A. Reading an old magazine that had been left in the cupboard, an old Harper's magazine.
Q. Had you got through ironing?
A. No sir.
Q. Had you stopped ironing?
A. Stopped for the flats.
Q. Were you waiting for them to be hot?
A. Yes sir.
Q. Was there a fire in the stove?
A. Yes sir.
Q. When your father went away, you were ironing then?
A. I had not commenced, but I was getting the little ironing board and the flannel.
Q. Are you sure you were in the kitchen when your father returned?
A. I am not sure whether I was there or in the dining room.
Q. Did you go back to your room before your father returned?
A. I think I did carry up some clean clothes.
Q. Did you stay there?
A. No sir.
Q. Did you spend any time up the front stairs before your father returned?
A. No sir.
Q. Or after he returned?
A. No sir. I did stay in my room long enough when I went up to sew a little piece of tape on a garment.
Q. Was that the time when your father came home?
A. He came home after I came downstairs.
Q. You were not upstairs when he came home?
A. I was not upstairs when he came home, no sir.
Q. What was Maggie doing when your father came home?
A. I don't know whether she was there or whether she had gone upstairs. I can't remember.
Q. Who let your father in?

A. I think he came to the front door and rang the bell and I think Maggie let him in and he said he had forgotten his key. So I think she must have been downstairs.
Q. His key would have done him no good if the locks were left as you left them?
A. But they were always unbolted in the morning.
Q. Who unbolted them that morning?
A. I don't think they had been unbolted. Maggie can tell you.
Q. If he had not forgotten his key, it would have been no good.
A. No, he had his key and could not get in. I understood Maggie to say he said he had forgotten his key.
Q. You did not hear him say anything about it?
A. I heard his voice, but I don't know what he said.
Q. I understood you to say he said he had forgotten his key.
A. No, it was Maggie said he said he had forgotten his key.
Q. Where was Maggie when the bell rang?
A. I don't know, sir.
Q. Where were you when the bell rang?
A. I think in my room upstairs.
Q. Then you were upstairs when your father came home?
A. I don't know sure, but I think so.
Q. What were you doing?
A. As I say, I took up these clean clothes and stopped and basted a little piece of tape on a garment.
Q. Did you come down before your father was let in?
A. I was on the stairs coming down when she let him in.
Q. Then you were upstairs when your father came to the house on his return?
A. I think I was.
Q. How long had you been there?
A. I had only been upstairs long enough to take the clothes up and baste the little loop on the sleeve. I don't think I had been up there over five minutes.
Q. Was Maggie still engaged in washing windows when your father got back?
A. I don't know.
Q. You remember, Miss Borden, I will call to your attention to it so as to see if I have any misunderstanding, not for the purpose of confusing you, you remember that you told me several times that you were downstairs and not upstairs when your father came home? You have forgotten, perhaps?
A. I don't know what I have said. I have answered so many questions and I am so confused I don't know one thing from another. I am telling you just as nearly as I know how.
Q. Calling your attention to what you said about that a few minutes ago, and now again to the circumstances, you have said you were upstairs when the bell rang and were on the stairs when Maggie let your father in, which now is your recollection of the true statement of the matter? That you were downstairs when the bell rang and your father came?
A. I think I was downstairs in the kitchen.
Q. And then you were not upstairs?
A. I think I was not because I went up almost immediately, as soon as I went down,

and then came down again and stayed down.

Q. What had you in your mind when you said you were on the stairs as Maggie let your father in?

A. The other day somebody came there and she let them in and I was on the stairs. I don't know whether the morning before or when it was.

Q. You understood I was asking you exactly and explicitly about this fatal day?

A. Yes sir.

Q. I now call your attention to the fact that you had specifically told me you had gone upstairs and had been there about five minutes when the bell rang and were on your way down and were on the stairs when Maggie let your father in that day.

A. Yes, I said that. And then I said I did not know whether I was on the stairs or in the kitchen.

Q. Now how will you have it?

A. I think, as nearly as I know, I think I was in the kitchen.

Q. How long was your father gone?

A. I don't know, sir. Not very long.

Q. An hour?

A. I should not think so.

Q. Will you give me the best story you can, so far as your recollection serves you, of your time while he was gone?

A. I sprinkled my handkerchiefs and got my ironing board and took them in the dining room. I took the ironing board in the dining room and left the handkerchiefs in the kitchen on the table and whether I ate any cookies or not, I don't remember. Then I sat down looking at the magazine, waiting for the flats to heat. Then I went in the sitting room and got the Providence Journal and took that into the kitchen. I don't recollect of doing anything else.

Q. Which did you read first, the Journal or the magazine?

A. The magazine.

Q. You told me you were reading the magazine when your father came back.

A. I said in the kitchen, yes.

Q. Was that so?

A. Yes, I took the Journal out to read and had not read it. I had it near me.

Q. You said a minute or two ago you read the magazine a while and then went and got the Journal and took it out to read.

A. I did, but I did not read it. I tried my flats then.

Q. And went back to reading the magazine?

A. I took the magazine up again, yes.

Q. When did you last see your mother?

A. I did not see her after when I went down in the morning and she was dusting the dining room.

Q. Where did you or she go then?

A. I don't know where she went. I know where I was.

Q. Did you or she leave the dining room first?

A. I think I did. I left her in the dining room.

Q. You never saw her or heard her afterwards?

A. No sir.

Q. Did she say anything about making the bed?
A. She said she had been up and made the bed up fresh and had dusted the room and left it all in order. She was going to put some fresh pillow slips on the small pillows at the foot of the bed and was going to close the room because she was going to have company Monday and she wanted everything in order.
Q. How long would it take to put on the pillow slips?
A. About two minutes.
Q. How long to do the rest of the things?
A. She had done that when I came down.
Q. All that was left was what?
A. To put on the pillow slips.
Q. Can you give me any suggestion as to what occupied her when she was up there, when she was struck dead?
A. I don't know of anything except she had some cotton cloth pillow cases up there and she said she was going to commence to work on them. That is all I know. And the sewing machine was up there.
Q. Whereabouts was the sewing machine?
A. In the corner between the north and west side.
Q. Did you hear the sewing machine going?
A. I did not.
Q. Did you see anything to indicate that the sewing machine had been used that morning?
A. I had not. I did not go in there until after everybody had been in there and the room had been overhauled.
Q. If she had remained downstairs, you would undoubtedly seen her?
A. If she had remained downstairs, I should have. If she had remained in her room, I should not have.
Q. Where was that?
A. Over the kitchen.
Q. To get to that room she would have to go through the kitchen?
A. To get up the back stairs.
Q. That is the way she was in the habit of going?
A. Yes sir, because the other doors were locked.
Q. If she had remained downstairs or had gone to her own room, you undoubtedly would have seen her?
A. I should have seen her if she had stayed downstairs. If she had gone to her room, I would not have seen her.
Q. She was found a little after 11 in the spare room. If she had gone to her own room, she must have gone through the kitchen and up the back stairs and subsequently have gone down and gone back again?
A. Yes sir.
Q. Have you any reason to suppose you would not have seen her if she had spent any portion of the time in her room or downstairs?
A. There is no reason why I should not have seen her if she had been down there, except when I first came downstairs, for two or three minutes, I went down cellar to the water closet.

Q. After that, you were where you practically commanded the view of the first story the rest of the time?
A. I think so.
Q. When you went upstairs for a short time, as you say you did, you then went in sight of the sewing machine?
A. No, I did not see the sewing machine because she had shut that room up.
Q. What do you mean?
A. I mean the door was closed. She said she wanted it kept closed to keep the dust and everything out.
Q. Was it a room with a window?
A. It has three windows.
Q. A large room?
A. The size of the parlor; a pretty fair-sized room.
Q. It is the guest room?
A. Yes, the spare room.
Q. Where the sewing machine was was the guest room?
A. Yes sir.
Q. I ask again, perhaps you have answered all you care to, what explanation can you give, can you suggest, as to what she was doing from the time she said she had got the work all done in the spare room, until 11 o'clock?
A. I suppose she went up and made her own bed.
Q. That would be in the back part?
A. Yes sir.
Q. She would have to go by you twice to do that?
A. Unless she went when I was in my room that few minutes.
Q. That would not be time enough for her to go and make her own bed and come back again.
A. Sometimes she stayed up longer and sometimes shorter. I don't know.
Q. Otherwise than that, she would have to go in your sight?
A. I should have to have seen her once. I don't know that I need to have seen her more than once.
Q. You did not see her at all?
A. No sir, not after the dining room.
Q. What explanation can you suggest as to the whereabouts of your mother from the time you saw her in the dining room and she said her work in the spare room was all done, until 11 o'clock?
A. I don't know. I think she went back into the spare room and whether she came back again or not, I don't know. That has always been a mystery.
Q. Can you think of anything she could be doing in the spare room?
A. Yes sir. I know what she used to do sometimes. She kept her best cape she wore on the street in there and she used occasionally to go up there to get it and to take it into her room. She kept a great deal in the guest room drawers. She used to go up there and get things and put things. She used those drawers for her own use.
Q. That connects her with her own room again, to reach which she had to go downstairs and come up again.

A. Yes.

Q. Assuming that she did not go into her own room, I understand you to say she could not have gone to her own room without your seeing her.

A. She could while I was down cellar.

Q. You went down immediately you came down, within a few minutes, and you did not see her when you came back.

A. No sir.

Q. After the time she must have remained in the guest chamber?

A. I don't know.

Q. So far as you can judge?

A. So far as I can judge she might have been out of the house or in the house.

Q. Had you any knowledge of her going out of the house?

A. No sir.

Q. Had you any knowledge of her going out of the house?

A. She told me she had had a note. Somebody was sick and she said, "I am going to get the dinner on the way" and asked me what I wanted for dinner.

Q. Did you tell her?

A. Yes, I told her I did not want anything.

Q. Then why did you not suppose she had gone?

A. I supposed she had gone.

Q. Did you hear her come back?

A. I did not hear her go or come back, but I supposed she went.

Q. When you found your father dead, you supposed your mother had gone?

A. I did not know. I said to the people who came in, "I don't know whether Mrs. Borden is out or in. I wish you would see if she is in her room".

Q. You supposed she was out at the time?

A. I understood so. I did not suppose anything about it.

Q. Did she tell you where she was going?

A. No sir.

Q. Did she tell you who the note was from?

A. No sir.

Q. Did you ever see the note?

A. No sir.

Q. Do you know where it is now?

A. No sir.

Q. She said she was going out that morning?

A. Yes sir.

(END OF QUESTIONING. THE HEARING CONTINUED ON AUGUST 10)

Q. I shall have to ask you once more about that morning. Do you know what the family ate for breakfast?

A. No sir.

Q. Had the breakfast all been cleared away when you got down?

A. Yes sir.

Q. I want you to tell me just where you found the people when you got down that

you did find there.
A. I found Mrs. Borden in the dining room. I found my father in the sitting room.
Q. And Maggie?
A. Maggie was coming in the back door with her pail and brush.
Q. Tell me what talk you had with your mother at that time.
A. She asked me how I felt. I said that I felt better than I did Tuesday, but I did not want any breakfast. She asked me what I wanted for dinner. I told her nothing. She said she was going out and would get the dinner. That is the last I saw her, or said anything to her.
Q. Where did you go then?
A. Into the kitchen.
Q. Where then?
A. Down cellar.
Q. Gone perhaps five minutes?
A. Perhaps. Not more than that. Possibly a little bit more.
Q. When you came back, did you see your mother?
A. I did not. I supposed she had gone out.
Q. She did not tell you where she was going?
A. No sir.
Q. When you came back, was your father there?
A. Yes sir.
Q. What was he doing?
A. Reading the paper.
Q. Did you eat any breakfast?
A. No sir. I don't remember whether I ate a molasses cookie or not. I did not eat any regularly prepared breakfast.
Q. Was it usual for your mother to go out?
A. Yes sir, she went out every morning nearly and did the marketing.
Q. Was it usual for her to be gone away from dinner?
A. Yes sir, sometimes. Not very often.
Q. How often, say?
A. Oh, I should not think more than---. Well, I don't know, more than once in three months, perhaps.
Q. Now I call your attention to the fact that twice yesterday you told me, with some explicitness, that when your father came in, you were just coming downstairs.
A. No, I did not. I beg your pardon.
Q. That you were on the stairs at the time your father was let in, you said with some explicitiness. Do you now say you did not say so?
A. I said I thought first I was on the stairs; then I remembered I was in the kitchen when he came in.
Q. First you thought you were in the kitchen; afterwards, you remembered you were on the stairs?
A. As I said, I thought I was on the stairs. Then I said I knew I was in the kitchen. I still say that now. I was in the kitchen.
Q. Did you go into the front part of the house after your father came in?
A. After he came in from down street, I was in the sitting room with him.

Q. Did you go into the front hall afterwards?
A. No sir.
Q. At no time?
A. No sir.
Q. Excepting the two or three minutes you were down cellar, were you away from the house until your father came in?
A. No sir.
Q. You were always in the kitchen or dining room, excepting when you went upstairs?
A. I went upstairs before he went out.
Q. You mean you went up there to sew a button on?
A. I basted a piece of tape on.
Q. Do you remember you did not say that yesterday?
A. I don't think you asked me. I told you yesterday I went upstairs directly after I came up from down cellar, with the clean clothes.
Q. You now say after your father went out, you did not go upstairs at all?
A. No sir, I did not.
Q. When Maggie came in there washing the windows, you did not appear from the front part of the house?
A. No sir.
Q. When your father was let in, you did not appear from upstairs?
A. No sir, I was in the kitchen.
Q. That is so?
A. Yes sir, to the best of my knowledge.
Q. After your father went out, you remained there, either in the kitchen or dining room all the time?
A. I went into the sitting room long enough to direct some paper wrappers.
Q. One of the three rooms?
A. Yes sir.
Q. So it would have been extremely difficult for anybody to have gone through the kitchen and dining room and front hall without your seeing them?
A. They could have gone from the kitchen into the sitting room while I was in the dining room, if there was anybody to go.
Q. Then into the front hall?
A. Yes sir.
Q. You were in the dining room ironing?
A. Yes sir, part of the time.
Q. You were in all the three rooms?
A. Yes sir.
Q. A large portion of that time the girl was out of doors?
A. I don't know where she was. I did not see her. I supposed she was out of doors, as she had the pail and brush.
Q. You knew she was washing windows?
A. She told me she was going to. I did not see her do it.
Q. For a large portion of the time, you did not see the girl?
A. No sir.
Q. So far as you know, you were alone in the lower part of the house a large portion

of the time after your father went away and before he came back?

A. My father did not go away, I think, until somewhere about 10, as near as I can remember. He was with me downstairs.

Q. A large portion of the time after your father went away and before he came back, so far as you know, you were alone in the house?

A. Maggie had come in and gone upstairs.

Q. After he went out and before he came back, a large portion of the time after your father went out and before he came back, so far as you know, you were the only person in the house?

A. So far as I know, I was.

Q. And during that time, so far as you know, the front door was locked?

A. So far as I know.

Q. And never was unlocked at all?

A. I don't think it was.

Q. Even after your father came home, it was locked up again?

A. I don't know whether she locked it up again after that or not.

Q. It locks itself?

A. The spring lock opens.

Q. It fastens it so it cannot be opened from the outside?

A. Sometimes you can press it open.

Q. Have you any reason to suppose the spring lock was left so it could be pressed open from the outside?

A. I have no reason to suppose so.

Q. Nothing about the lock was changed before the public came?

A. Nothing that I know of.

Q. What were you doing in the kitchen when your father came home?

A. I think I was eating a pear when he came in.

Q. What had you been doing before that?

A. Been reading a magazine.

Q. Were you making preparations to iron again?

A. I had sprinkled my clothes and was waiting for the flat. I sprinkled the clothes before he went out.

Q. Had you built up the fire again?

A. I put in a stick of wood. There was a few sparks. I put in a stick of wood to try to heat the flat.

Q. You had then started the fire?

A. Yes sir.

Q. The fire was burning when he came in?

A. No sir, but it was smoldering and smoking as though it would come up.

Q. Did it come up after he came in?

A. No sir.

Q. Did you do any more ironing?

A. I did not. I went in with him and did not finish.

Q. You did not iron any more after your father came in?

A. No sir.

Q. Was the ironing board put away?

A. No sir, it was on the dining room table.
Q. When was it put away?
A. I don't know. Somebody put it away after the affair happened.
Q. You did not put it away?
A. No sir.
Q. Was it on the dining room table when you found your father killed?
A. I suppose so.
Q. You had not put it away then?
A. I had not touched it.
Q. How soon after your father came in before Maggie went upstairs?
A. I don't know. I did not see her.
Q. Did you see her after your father came in?
A. Not after she let him in.
Q. How long was your father in the house before you found him killed?
A. I don't know exactly because I went out to the barn. I don't know what time he came home. I don't think he had been home more than 15 or 20 minutes. I am not sure.
Q. When you went out to the barn, where did you leave your father?
A. He had laid down on the living room lounge, taken off his shoes and put on his slippers and taken off his coat and put on the reefer. I asked him if he wanted the window left that way.
Q. Where did you leave him?
A. On the sofa.
Q. Was he asleep?
A. No sir.
Q. Was he reading?
A. No sir.
Q. What was the last thing you said to him?
A. I asked him if he wanted the window left that way. Then I went into the kitchen and from there to the barn.
Q. Whereabouts in the barn did you go?
A. Upstairs.
Q. To the second story of the barn?
A. Yes sir.
Q. How long did you remain there?
A. I don't know. Fifteen or 20 minutes.
Q. What doing?
A. Trying to find lead for a sinker.
Q. What made you think there would be lead for a sinker up there?
A. Because there was some there.
Q. Was there not some by the door?
A. Some pieces of lead by the open door, but there was a box full of old things upstairs.
Q. Did you bring any sinker back from the barn?
A. Nothing but a piece of a chip I picked up on the floor.
Q. Where was that box you say was upstairs, containing lead?

A. There was a kind of a work bench.
Q. Is it there now?
A. I don't know sir.
Q. How long since you have seen it there?
A. I have not been out there since that day.
Q. Had you been in the barn before?
A. That day? No sir.
Q. How long since you had been in the barn before?
A. I don't think I had been into it, I don't know as I had, in three months.
Q. When you went out, did you unfasten the screen door?
A. I unhooked it to get out.
Q. It was hooked until you went out?
A. Yes sir.
Q. It had been left hooked by Bridget, if she was the last one in?
A. I suppose so. I don't know.
Q. Do you know when she did get through washing the outside?
A. I don't know.
Q. Did you know she washed the windows inside?
A. I don't know.
Q. Did you see her washing the windows inside?
A. I don't know.
Q. You don't know whether she washed the dining room window and sitting room windows inside?
A. I did not see her.
Q. If she did, would you not have seen her?
A. I don't know. She might be in one room and I in another.
Q. Do you think she might have gone to work and washed all the windows in the dining room and you not know it?
A. I don't know, I am sure, whether I should or not. I might have seen her and not know it.
Q. Miss Borden, I am trying in good faith to get all the doings that morning, of yourself and Miss Sullivan and I have not succeeded in doing it. Do you desire to give me any information or not?
A. I don't know it! I don't know what your name is!
Q. It is certain beyond reasonable doubt she was engaged in washing the windows in the dining room or sitting room when your father came home. Do you mean to say you know nothing of either of those operations?
A. I knew she washed the windows outside; that is, she told me so. She did not wash the windows in the kitchen because I was in the kitchen most of the time.
Q. The dining room and sitting room, I said.
A. I don't know.
Q. It is reasonably certain she washed the windows in the dining room and sitting room inside while your father was out and was engaged in that operation when your father came home. Do you mean to say you know nothing of it?
A. I don't know whether she washed the windows in the sitting room and dining room or not.

Q. Can you give me any information how it happened at that particular time you should go into the chamber of the barn to find a sinker to go to Marion with to fish the next Monday?
A. I was going to finish my ironing. My flats were not hot. I said to myself, "I will go and try and find that sinker. Perhaps by the time I get back, the flats will be hot". That is the only reason.
Q. How long had you been reading an old magazine before you went to the barn at all?
A. Perhaps half an hour.
Q. Had you got a fish line?
A. Not here. We had some at the farm.
Q. Had you got a fish hook?
A. No sir.
Q. Had you got any apparatus for fishing at all?
A. Yes, over there.
Q. Had you any sinkers over there?
A. I think there were some. It is so long since I have been there, I think there were some.
Q. You had no reason to suppose you were lacking sinkers?
A. I don't think there were any on my lines.
Q. Where were your lines?
A. My fish lines were at the farm here.
Q. What made you think there were no sinkers at the farm on your lines?
A. Because some time ago when I was there, I had none.
Q. How long since you used the fish lines?
A. Five years, perhaps.
Q. You left them at the farm then?
A. Yes sir.
Q. And you have not seen them since?
A. Yes sir.
Q. It occured to you after your father came in it would be a good time to go to the barn after sinkers and you had no reason to suppose there was not abundance of sinkers at the farm and abundance of lines?
A. The last time I was there, there were some lines.
Q. Did you not say before you presumed there were sinkers at the farm?
A. I don't think I said so.
Q. You did say so exactly. Do you now say you presume there were not sinkers at the farm?
A. I don't think there were any fishing lines suitable to use at the farm. I don't think there were any sinkers on any line that had been mine.
Q. Do you remember telling me you presumed there were lines and sinkers and hooks at the farm?
A. I said there were lines, I thought, and perhaps hooks. I did not say I thought there were sinkers on my lines. There was another box of lines over there beside mine.
Q. You thought there were not sinkers?
A. Not on my lines.

Q. Not sinkers at the farm?
A. I don't think there were any sinkers at the farm. I don't know whether there were or not.
Q. Did you then think there were no sinkers at the farm?
A. I thought there were no sinkers anywhere or I should not have been trying to find some.
Q. You thought there were no sinkers at the farm to be had?
A. I thought there were no sinkers at the farm to be had.
Q. That is the reason you went into the second story of the barn to look for a sinker?
A. Yes sir.
Q. What made you think you would find sinkers there?
A. I heard father say, and I knew there was lead there.
Q. What made you think you would find sinkers there?
A. I went to see because there was lead there.
Q. You thought there might be lead there made into sinkers?
A. I thought there might be lead with a hole in it.
Q. Did you examine the lead that was downstairs near the door?
A. No sir.
Q. Why not?
A. I don't know.
Q. You went straight to the upper story of the barn?
A. No, I went under the pear tree and got some pears first.
Q. Then went to the second story of the barn to look for sinkers for lines you had at the farm, as you supposed, as you had seen them there five years before that time?
A. I went up to get some sinkers if I could find them. I did not intend to go to the farm for lines. I was going to buy some lines here.
Q. You then had no intention of using your lines at Marion?
A. I could not get them.
Q. You had no intention of using your own line and hooks at the farm?
A. No sir.
Q. What was the use of telling me a while ago you had no sinkers on your line at the farm?
A. I thought I made you understand that those lines at the farm were no good to use.
Q. Did you not mean for me to understand one of the reasons you were searching for sinkers was that the lines you had at the farm, as you remembered then, had no sinkers on them?
A. I said the lines at the farm had no sinkers.
Q. I did not ask you what you said. Did you not mean for me to understand that?
A. I meant for you to understand I wanted the sinkers and was going to have new lines.
Q. You had not then bought your lines?
A. No sir, I was going out Thursday noon.
Q. You had not bought any apparatus for fishing?
A. No hooks.
Q. Had bought nothing connected with your fishing trip?
A. No sir.

Q. Was going to go fishing the next Monday, were you?
A. I don't know that we should go fishing Monday.
Q. Going to the place to go fishing Monday?
A. Yes sir.
Q. This was Thursday and you had no idea of using any fishing apparatus before the next Monday?
A. No sir.
Q. You had no fishing apparatus you were proposing to use the next Monday until then?
A. No sir, not until I bought it.
Q. You had not bought anything?
A. No sir.
Q. Had you started to buy anything?
A. No sir.
Q. The first thing in preparation for your fishing trip the next Monday was to go to the loft of that barn to find some old sinkers to put on some hooks and lines that you had not then bought?
A. I thought if I found no sinkers, I would have to buy the sinkers when I bought the lines.
Q. You thought you would be saving something by hunting in the loft of the barn before you went to see whether you should need them or not?
A. I thought I would find out whether there were any sinkers before I bought the lines and if there was, I should not have to buy any sinkers. If there were some, I should only have to buy the lines and the hooks.
Q. You began the collection of your fishing apparatus by searching for the sinkers in the barn?
A. Yes sir.
Q. You were searching in a box of old stuff in the loft of the barn?
A. Yes sir, upstairs.
Q. That you had never looked at before?
A. I had seen them.
Q. Never examined them before?
A. No sir.
Q. All the reason you supposed there was sinkers there was your father had told you there was lead in the barn?
A. Yes, lead. And one day I wanted some old nails. He said there was some in the barn.
Q. All the reason that gave you to think there was sinkers was your father said there was old lead in the barn?
A. Yes sir.
Q. Did he mention the place in the barn?
A. I think he said upstairs. I'm not sure.
Q. Where did you look upstairs?
A. On that work-bench like.
Q. In anything?
A. Yes. In a box---sort of a box. And then some things lying right on the side that

was not in the box.
Q. How large a box was it?
A. I could not tell you. It was probably covered up---with lumber, I think.
Q. Give me the best idea of the size of the box you can.
A. Well, I should say I don't know. I have not any idea.
Q. Give me the best idea you have.
A. I have given you the best idea I have.
Q. What is the best idea you have?
A. About that large. (Measuring with her hands)
Q. That long?
A. Yes.
Q. How wide?
A. I don't know.
Q. Give me the best idea you have.
A. Perhaps about as wide as it was long.
Q. How high?
A. It was not very high.
Q. About how high?
A. (Witness measures with her hands).
Q. About twice the length of your forefinger?
A. I should think so. Not quite.
Q. What was in the box?
A. Nails and some old locks and I don't know but there was a doorknob.
Q. Anything else?
A. I don't remember anything else.
Q. Any lead?
A. Yes, some pieces of tea-lead like.
Q. Foil. What we call tinfoil; the same you use on tea chests?
A. I don't remember seeing any tinfoil; not as thin as that.
Q. Tea chest lead?
A. No sir.
Q. What did you see in shape of lead?
A. Flat pieces of lead a little bigger than that. Some of them were doubled together.
Q. How many?
A. I could not tell you.
Q. Where else did you look beside in the box?
A. I did not look anywhere for lead except on the work bench.
Q. How full was the box?
A. It was not nearly as full as it could have been.
Q. You looked on the bench. Beside that, where else?
A. Nowhere except on the bench.
Q. Did you look for anything else beside lead?
A. No sir.
Q. When you got through looking for lead, did you come down?
A. No sir. I went to the west window over the hay, to the west window, and the curtain was slanted a little. I pulled it down.

Q. What else?
A. Nothing.
Q. That is all you did?
A. Yes sir.
Q. That is the second story of the barn.
A. Yes sir.
Q. Was the window open?
A. I think not.
Q. Hot?
A. Very hot.
Q. How long do you think you were up there?
A. Not more than 15 or 20 minutes, I should not think.
Q. Should you think what you have told me would occupy four minutes?
A. Yes, because I ate some pears up there.
Q. Do you think all you have told me would take you four minutes?
A. I ate some pears up there.
Q. I asked you to tell me all you did.
A. I told you all I did.
Q. Do you mean to say you stopped your work and then, additional to that, sat still and ate some pears?
A. While I was looking out of the window, yes sir.
Q. Will you tell me all you did in the second story of the barn?
A. I think I told you all I did that I can remember.
Q. Is there anything else?
A. I told you that I took some pears up from the ground when I went up. I stopped under the pear tree and took some pears up when I went up.
Q. Have you now told me everything you did up in the second story of the barn?
A. Yes sir.
Q. I now call your attention and ask you to say whether all you have told me---. I don't suppose you stayed there any longer than was necessary?
A. No sir, because it was close.
Q. Can you give me any explanation why all you have told me would occupy more than three minutes?
A. Yes. It would take me more than three minutes.
Q. To look in that box that you have described the size of on the bench and put down the curtain and then get out as soon as you conveniently could; would you say you were occupied in that business 20 minutes?
A. I think so because I did not look at the box when I first went up.
Q. What did you do?
A. I ate my pears.
Q. Stood there eating the pears, doing nothing?
A. I was looking out of the window.
Q. Stood there looking out of the window, eating the pears?
A. I should think so.
Q. How many did you eat?
A. Three, I think.

Q. You were feeling better than you did in the morning?
A. Better than I did the night before.
Q. You were feeling better than you were in the morning?
A. I felt better in the morning than I did the night before.
Q. That is not what I asked you. You were then, when you were in that hay loft, looking out the window and eating three pears, feeling better, were you not, than you were in the morning when you could not eat any breakfast?
A. I never eat any breakfast.
Q. You did not answer my question and you will, if I have to put it all day. Were you then when you were eating those three pears in that hot loft, looking out that closed window, feeling better than you were in the morning when you ate no breakfast?
A. I was feeling well enough to eat the pears.
Q. Were you feeling better than you were in the morning?
A. I don't think I felt very sick in the morning, only---. Yes, I don't know but I did feel better. As I say, I don't know whether I ate any breakfast or not or whether I ate a cookie.
Q. Were you then feeling better than you did in the morning?
A. I don't know how to answer you because I told you I felt better in the morning anyway.
Q. Do you understand my question? My question is whether, when you were in the loft of that barn, you were feeling better than you were in the morning when you got up?
A. No, I felt about the same.
Q. Were you feeling better than you were when you told your mother you did not care for any dinner?
A. No sir, I felt about the same.
Q. Well enough to eat pears, but not well enough to eat anything for dinner?
A. She asked me if I wanted any meat.
Q. I ask you why you should select that place, which was the only place which would put you out of sight of the house, to eat those three pears in?
A. I cannot tell you any reason.
Q. You observe that fact, do you not? You have put yourself in the only place perhaps, where it would be impossible for you to see a person going into the house?
A. Yes sir, I should have seen them from the front window.
Q. From anywhere in the yard?
A. No sir, not unless from the end of the barn.
Q. Ordinarily in the yard you could see them and in the kitchen where you had been, you could have seen them?
A. I don't think I understand.
Q. When you were in the kitchen, you could see persons who came in at the back door?
A. Yes sir.
Q. When you were in the yard, unless you went around the corner of the house, you could see them come in at the back door?

A. No sir, not unless I was at the corner of the barn. The minute I turned, I could not.
Q. What was there?
A. A little jog, like. The walk turns.
Q. I ask you again to explain to me why you took those pears from the pear tree?
A. I did not take them from the pear tree.
Q. From the ground, wherever you took them from. I thank you for correcting me. Going into the barn, going upstairs into the hottest place in the barn, inthe rear of the barn, the hottest place, and there standing and eating those pears that morning?
A. I beg your pardon. I was not in the rear of the barn. I was in the other end of the barn that faced the street.
Q. Where you could see anyone coming into the house?
A. Yes sir.
Q. Did you not tell me you could not?
A, Before I went into the barn---at the jog on the outside.
Q. You now say when you were eating the pears, you could see the back door?
A. Yes sir.
Q. So nobody could come in at that time without your seeing them?
A. I don't see how they could.
Q. After you got done eating your pears, you began your search?
A. Yes sir.
Q. Then you did not see into the house?
A. No sir, because the bench is at the other end.
Q. Now, I have asked you over and over again, and will continue the inquiry, whether anything you did at the bench would occupy more than three minutes?
A. Yes, I think it would because I pulled over quite a lot of boards in looking.
Q. To get at the box?
A. Yes sir.
Q. Taking all that, what is the amount of time you think you occupied in looking for that piece of lead which you did not find?
A. Well, I should think perhaps I was 10 minutes.
Q. Looking over those old things?
A. Yes sir, on the bench.
Q. Now can you explain why you were 10 minutes doing it?
A. No, only that I can't do anything in a minute.
Q. When you came down from the barn, what did you do then?
A. Came into the kitchen.
Q. What did you do then?
A. I went into the dining room and laid down my hat.
Q. What did you do then?
A. Opened the sitting room door and went into the sitting room; or pushed it open. It was not latched.
Q. What did you do then?
A. I found my father and rushed to the foot of the stairs.
Q. What were you going into the sitting room for?

A. To go upstairs.
Q. What for?
A. To sit down.
Q. What had become of the ironing?
A. The fire had gone out.
Q. I thought you went out because the fire was not hot enough to heat the flats.
A. I thought it would burn, but the fire had not caught from the few sparks.
Q. So you gave up the ironing and was going upstairs?
A. Yes sir, I thought I would wait till Maggie got dinner and heat the flats again.
Q. When you saw your father, where was he?
A. On the sofa.
Q. What was his position?
A. Lying down.
Q Describe anything else you noticed at that time.
A. I did not notice anything else, I was so frightened and horrified. I ran to the foot of the stairs and called Maggie.
Q. Did you notice that he had been cut?
A. Yes, that is what made me afraid.
Q. Did you notice that he was dead?
A. I did not know whether he was or not.
Q. Did you make any search for your mother?
A. No sir.
Q. Why not?
A. I thought she was out of the house. I thought she had gone out. I called Maggie to go to Dr. Bowen's. When they came in, I said, "I don't know where Mrs. Borden is." I thought she had gone out.
Q. Did you tell Maggie you thought your mother had come in?
A. No sir.
Q. That you thought you heard her come in?
A. No sir.
Q. Did you say to anybody that you thought she was killed upstairs?
A. No sir.
Q. To anybody?
A. No sir.
Q. You made no effort to find your mother at all?
A. No sir.
Q. Who did you send Maggie for?
A. Dr. Bowen. She came back and said Dr. Bowen was not there.
Q. What did you tell Maggie?
A. I told her he was hurt.
Q. When you first told her?
A. I says, "Go for Dr. Bowen as soon as you can. I think father is hurt."
Q. Did you then know that he was dead?
A. No sir.
Q. You saw him?
A. Yes sir.

Q. You went into the room?
A. No sir.
Q. Looked in at the door?
A. I opened the door and rushed back.
Q. Saw his face?
A. No, I did not see his face because he was all covered with blood.
Q. You saw where the face was bleeding?
A. Yes sir.
Q. Did you see the blood on the floor?
A. No sir.
Q. You saw his face covered with blood?
A. Yes sir.
Q. Did you see his eye-ball hanging out?
A. No sir.
Q. See the gashes where his face was laid open?
A. No sir.
Q. Nothing of that kind?
A. No sir. **(WITNESS COVERS HER FACE WITH HER HAND FOR A MINUTE OR TWO, THEN EXAMINATION IS RESUMED.)**
Q. Do you know of any employment that would occupy your mother for the two hours between nine and 11 in the front room?
A. Not unless she was sewing.
Q. If she had been sewing you would have heard the machine.
A. She did not always use the machine.
Q. Did you see or were there found anything to indicate that she was sewing up there?
A. I don't know. She had given me a few weeks before some pillow cases to make.
Q. My question is not that. Did you see, or were there found, anything to indicate that she had done any sewing in that room that morning?
A. I don't know. I was not allowed in that room. I did not see it.
Q. Was that the room where she usually sewed?
A. No sir.
Q. Did you ever know of her using that room for sewing?
A. Yes sir.
Q. When?
A. Whenever she wanted to use the machine.
Q. When she did not want to use the machine, did you know she used that room for sewing?
A. Not unless she went up to sew a button on, or something.
Q. She did not use it as a sitting room?
A. No sir.
Q. Leaving out the sewing, do you know of anything else that would occupy her for two hours in that room?
A. No, not if she had made the bed up and she said she had when I went down.
Q. Assuming the bed was made?
A. I don't know anything.
Q. Did she say she had done the work?

A. She said she had made the bed and was going to put on the pillow cases, about 9 o'clock.
Q. I ask you now again, remembering that---.
A. I told you that yesterday.
Q. Never mind about yesterday. Tell me all the talk you had with your mother when she came down in the morning.
A. She asked me how I felt. I said I felt better but did not want any breakfast. She said what kind of meat did I want for dinner. I said I did not want any. She said she was going out; somebody was sick, and she would get the dinner, get the meat, order the meat. And I think she said something about the weather being hotter, or something; and I don't remember that she said anything else. I said to her, "Won't you change your dress before you go out?" She had on an old one. She said, "No, this is good enough." That is all I can remember.
Q. In this narrative you have not again said anything about her having said that she had made the bed.
A. I told you that she said she made the bed.
Q. In this time saying, you did not put that in. I want that conversation that you had with her that morning. I beg your pardon again. In this time of telling me, you did not say anything about her having received a note.
A. I told you that before.
Q. Miss Borden, I want you now to tell me all the talk you had with your mother when she came down, and all the talk she had with you. Please begin again.
A. She asked me how I felt. I told her. She asked me what I wanted for dinner. I told her not anything. What kind of meat I wanted for dinner. I told her not any. She said she had been up and made the spare bed and was going to take up some linen pillow cases for the small pillows at the foot and then the room was done. She says, "I have had a note from somebody that is sick and I am going out and I will get the dinner at the same time." I think she said something about the weather, I don't know. She also asked me if I would direct some paper wrappers for her, which I did.
Q. She said she had had a note?
A. Yes sir.
Q. You told me yesterday you never saw the note.
A. No sir, I never did.
Q. You looked for it?
A. No sir, but the rest have.
Q. She did not say where she was going?
A. No sir.
Q. Does she usually tell you where she is going?
A. She does not generally tell me.
Q. Did she say when she was coming back?
A. No sir.
Q. Did you know that Mr. Morse was coming to dinner?
A. No sir, I knew nothing about him.
Q. Was he at dinner the day before?
A. Wednesday noon? I don't know. I didn't see him. I don't think he was.

Q. Were you at dinner?
A. I was in the house. I don't know whether I went down to dinner or not. I was not feeling well.
Q. Whether you ate dinner or not?
A. I don't remember.
Q. Do you remember who was at dinner the day before?
A. No sir, I don't remember because I don't know whether I was down myself or not.
Q. Were you at tea Wednesday night?
A. I went down, but I think---I don't know---whether I had any tea or not.
Q. Did you sit down with the family?
A. I think I did, but I'm not sure.
Q. Was Mr. Morse there?
A. No sir, I did not see him.
Q. Who were there to tea?
A. Nobody.
Q. The family were there, I suppose.
A. Yes sir. I mean nobody but the family.
Q. Did you have an apron on Thursday?
A. Did I what?
Q. Have an apron on Thursday.
A. No sir, I don't think I did.
Q. Do you remember whether you did or not?
A. I don't remember for sure, but I don't think I did.
Q. You had aprons, of course?
A. I had aprons, yes sir.
Q. Will you try and think whether you did or not?
A. I don't think I did.
Q. Will you try and remember?
A. I had no occasion for an apron on that morning.
Q. If you can remember, I wish you would.
A. I don't remember.
Q. That is all the answer you can give me about that?
A. Yes sir.
Q. Did you have any occasion to use the axe or hatchet?
A. No sir.
Q. Did you know where they were?
A. I knew there was an old axe down cellar. That is all I knew.
Q. Did you know anything about a hatchet down cellar?
A. No sir.
Q. Where was the old axe down cellar?
A. The last time I saw it, it was stuck in the old chopping block.
Q. Was that the only axe or hatchet down cellar?
A. It was all I knew about.
Q. When was the last time you knew of it?
A. When our farmer came to chop wood.
Q. When was that?

A. I think a year ago last winter. I think there was so much wood on hand, he did not come last winter.
Q. Do you know of anything that would occasion the use of an axe or hatchet?
A. No sir.
Q. Do you know of anything that would occasion the getting of blood on an axe or hatchet down cellar?
A. No sir.
Q. I do not say there was, but assuming an axe or hatchet was found down cellar with blood on it?
A. No sir.
Q. Do you know whether there was a hatchet down there before this murder?
A. I don't know.
Q. You are not able to say your father did not own a hatchet?
A. I don't know whether he did or not.
Q. Did you know that there was found at the foot of the stairs a hatchet and axe?
A. No sir, I did not.
Q. Assume that is so, can you give me any explanation of how they came there?
A. No sir.
Q. Assume they had blood on them, can you give any occasion for there being blood on them?
A. No sir.
Q. Can you tell of the killing of any animal? Or any other operation that would lead to their being cast there, with blood on them?
A. No sir. He killed some pigeons in the barn last May or June.
Q. What with?
A. I don't know, but I thought he wrung their necks.
Q. What made you think so?
A. I think he said so.
Q. Did anything else make you think so?
A. All but three or four had their heads on. That is what made me think so.
Q. Did all of them come into the house?
A. I think so.
Q. Those that came into the house were all headless?
A. Two or three had them on.
Q. Were any with their heads off?
A. Yes sir.
Q. Cut off or twisted off?
A. I don't know which.
Q. How did they look?
A. I don't know, their heads were gone, that is all.
Q. Did you tell anybody they looked as though they were twisted off?
A. I don't remember whether I did or not. The skin, I think, was very tender. I said, "Why are these heads off?" I think I remember of telling somebody that he said they twisted off.
Q. Did they look as if they were cut off?
A. I don't know. I did not look at that particularly.

Q. Is there anything else besides that that would lead, in your opinion so far as you can remember, to the finding of instruments in the cellar with blood on them?
A. I know of nothing else that was done.
Q. **(By Judge Blaisdell)** Was there any effort made by the witness to notify Mrs. Borden of the fact that Mr. Borden was found?
Q. **(By Knowlton)** Did you make any effort to notify Mrs. Borden of your father being killed?
A. No sir. When I found him, I rushed right to the foot of the stairs for Maggie. I supposed Mrs. Borden was out. I did not think anything about her at the time, I was so---.
Q. At any time, did you say anything about her to anybody?
A. No sir.
Q. To the effect that she was out?
A. I told father when he came in.
Q. After your father was killed?
A. No sir.
Q. Did you say you thought she was upstairs?
A. No sir.
Q. Did you ask them to look upstasirs?
A. No sir.
Q. Did you suggest to anybody to search upstairs?
A. I said, "I don't know where Mrs. Borden is." That is all I said.
Q. You did not suggest that any search be made for her?
Q. No sir.
Q. You did not make any yourself?
A. No sir.
Q. I want you to give me all that you did, by way of word or deed, to see whether your mother was dead or not, when you found your father was dead.
A. I did not do anything except what I said to Mrs. Churchill. I said to her, "I don't know where Mrs. Borden is. I think she is out, but I wish you would look."
Q. You did ask her to look?
A. I said that to Mrs. Churchill.
Q. Where did you intend for her to look?
A. In Mrs. Borden's room.
Q. When you went out to the barn, did you leave the door shut, the screen door?
A. I left it shut.
Q. When you came back did you find it shut or open?
A. No sir, I found it open.
Q. Can you tell me anything else that you did that you have not told me, during your absence from the house?
A. No sir.
Q. Can you tell me when it was that you came back from the barn, what time it was?
A. I am not sure, but I think it must have been after 10, because I think he told me he did not think he should go out until 10. When he went out, I did not look at the clock to see what time it was. I think he did not go out until 10, or a little after. He was not gone so very long.

Q. Will you give me the best judgment you can as to the time your father got back? If you have not any, it is sufficient to say so.
A. No sir, I have not any.
Q. Can you give me any judgment as to the length of time that elapsed after he came back and before you went to the barn?
A. I went right out to the barn.
Q. How soon after he came back?
A. I should think not less than five minutes. I saw him taking off his shoes and lying down. It only took him two or three minutes to do it. I went right out.
Q. When he came into the house, did he not go into the dining room first?
A. I don't know.
Q. And there sit down?
A. I don't know.
Q. Why don't you know?
A. Because I was in the kitchen.
Q. It might have happened and you not have known it?
A. Yes sir.
Q. You heard the bell ring?
A. Yes sir.
Q. And you knew when he came in?
A. Yes sir.
Q. You did not see him?
A. No sir.
Q. When did you first see him?
A. I went into the sitting room and he was there. I don't know whether he had been in the dining room before or not.
Q. What made you go into the sitting room?
A. Because I wanted to ask him a question.
Q. What question?
A. Whether there was any mail for me.
Q. Did you not ask him that question in the dining room?
A. No sir, I think not,
Q. Was he not in the dining room sitting down?
A. I don't remember his being in the dining room sitting down.
Q. At that time, was not Maggie washing the windows in the sitting room?
A. I thought I asked him for the mail in the sitting room. I am not sure.
Q. Was not the reason he went into the dining room because she was in the sitting room washing windows?
A. I don't know.
Q. Did he not go upstairs to his room before he sat down in the sitting room?
A. I did not see him go.
Q. He had the key to his room down there?
A. I don't know whether he had it. It was kept on the shelf.
Q. Don't you remember he took the key and went into his own room and then came back?
A. No sir.

Q. You don't remember anything of that kind?
A. No sir. I do not think he did go upstairs either.
Q. You will swear he did not?
A. I did not see him.
Q. You swear you did not see him?
A. Yes sir.
Q. You were either in the kitchen or sitting room all the time?
A. Yes sir.
Q. He could not have gone up without he had gone through the kitchen?
A. No sir.
Q. When you did go into the sitting room to ask him a question, if it was the sitting room, what took place then?
A. I asked him if he had any mail. He said, "None for you." He had a letter in his hand. I supposed it was for himself. I asked him how he felt. He said, "About the same." He said he should lie down. I asked him if he thought he should have a nap. He said he should try to. I asked him if he wanted the window left the way it was or if he felt a draught. He said, "No." That is all.
Q. Did you help him about lying down?
A. No sir.
Q. Fix his pillows or head?
A. No sir. I did not touch the sofa.
Q. Did he lie down before you left the room?
A. Yes sir.
Q. Did anything else take place?
A. Not that I remember of.
Q. Was he then under medical treatment?
A. No sir.
Q. The doctor had not given him any medicine that you know of?
A. No sir. He took some medicine; it was not doctor's medicine. It was what we gave him.
Q. What was it?
A. We gave him castor oil first and then Garfield tea.
Q. When was that?
A. He took the castor oil some time Wednesday. I think some time Wednesday noon and I think the tea Wednesday night. Mrs. Borden gave it to him. She went over to see the doctor.
Q. When did you first consult Mr. Jennings?
A. I can't tell you that. I think my sister sent for him. I don't know.
Q. Was it you or your sister?
A. My sister.
Q. You did not send for him?
A. I did not send for him. She said did we think we should have him. I said do as she thought best. I don't know when he came first.
Q. Now, tell me once more, if you please, the particulars of that trouble that you had with your mother four or five years ago.
A. Her father's house on Ferry Street was for sale---.

Q. Whose father's house?

A. Mrs. Borden's father's house. She had a stepmother and a half-sister, Mrs. Borden did, and this house was left to the stepmother and a half-sister, if I understand it right, and the house was for sale. The stepmother, Mrs. Oliver Gray, wanted to sell it and my father bought out the Widow Gray's share. She did not tell me and he did not tell me, but some outsiders said he gave it to her; put it in her name. I said if he gave that to her, he ought to give us something. Told Mrs. Borden so. She did not care anything about the house herself. She wanted it so this half-sister could have a home because she had married a man that was not doing the best he could and she thought her sister was having as very hard time and wanted her to have a home. And we always thought she persuaded father to buy it. At any rate, he did buy it and I am quite sure she did persuade him. I said what he did for her, he ought to do for his own children. So, he gave us grandfather's house. That was all the trouble we ever had.

Q. You have not stated any trouble yet between you and her.

A. I said there was feeling four or five years ago when I stopped calling her mother. I told you that yesterday.

Q. That is all there is to it then?

A. Yes sir.

Q. You had no words with your stepmother then?

A. I talked with her about it and said what he did for her, he ought to do for us. That is all the words we had.

Q. That is the occasion of his giving you the house that you sold back to him?

A. Yes sir.

Q. Did your mother leave any property?

A. I don't know.

Q. Your own mother?

A. No sir, not that I know of.

Q. Did you ever see that thing? **(Pointing to a wooden club)**

A. Yes, I think I have.

Q. What is it?

A. My father used to keep something similar to this, that looked very much like it, under his bed. He whittled it out himself at the farm one time.

Q. How long since you have seen it?

A. I have not seen it in years.

Q. How many years?

A. I could not tell you. I should think 10 or 15 years. Not since I was quite a little girl, if that is the one. I can't swear that it is the one. It was about that size.

Q. **(Marks it with a cross)** How many years, 10 or 15?

A. I was a litle girl. It must have been as much as that.

Q. When was the last time the windows were washed before that day?

A. I don't know.

Q. Why don't you know?

A. Because I had nothing to do with the work downstairs.

Q. When was the last time that you ate with the family that you can swear to before your mother was killed?

A. Well, I ate with them all day Tuesday. That is, what little we ate. We sat down at the table and I think I sat down to the table with them Wednesday night, but I am not sure.
Q. All day Tuesday?
A. I was down at the table.
Q. I understand you to say you did not come down to breakfast.
A. That was Wednesday morning.
Q. I understood you to say that you did not come down to breakfast.
A. I came down but I did not eat breakfast with them. I did not eat any breakfast. Frequently, I would go into the dining room and sit down to the table with them and not eat any breakfast.
Q. Did you give to the officer the same skirt you had on the day of the tragedy?
A. Yes sir.
Q. Do you know whether there was any blood on the skirt?
A. No sir.
Q. Assume that there was, do you know how it came there?
A. No sir.
Q. Have you any explanation of how it might come there?
A. No sir.
Q. Did you know there was any blood on the skirt you gave them?
A. No sir.
Q. Assume that there was. Can you give any explanation of how it came there on the dress skirt?
A. No sir.
Q. Have you offered any?
A. No sir.
Q Have you ever offered any?
A. No sir.
Q. Have you said it came from flea bites?
A. On the petticoats, I said there was a flea bite. I said it might have been. You said you meant the dress skirt.
Q. I did. Have you offered any explanation how that came there?
A. I told those men that were at the house that I had had fleas. That is all.
Q. Did you offer that as an explanation?
A. I said that was the only explanation that I knew of.
Q. Assuming that the blood came from the outside, can you give any explanation of how it came there?
A. No sir.
Q. You cannot now?
A. No sir.
Q. What shoes did you have on that day?
A. A pair of ties.
Q. What color?
A. Black.
Q. Will you give them to the officer?
A. Yes.

Q. Where are they?
A. At home.
Q. What stockings did you have on that day?
A. Black.
Q. Where are they?
A. At home.
Q. Have they been washed?
A. I don't know.
Q. Will you give them to the officer?
A. Yes sir.
Q. The window you was at is the window that is nearest the street in the barn?
A. Yes sir, the west window.
Q. The pears you ate you got from under the tree in the yard?
A. Yes sir.
Q. How long were you under the pear tree?
A. I think I was under there very nearly four or fiveminutes. I stood looking around. I looked up at the pigeon house that they have closed up. It was no more than five minutes, perhaps not as long. I can't say sure.
Q. **(By Judge Blaisdell)** Was this witness on Thursday morning in the front hall of front stairs or front chamber, any part of the house at all?
Q. What do you say to that?
A. I had to come down the front stairs to get into the kitchen.
Q. When you came down first?
A. Yes sir.
Q. Were you afterwards?
A. No sir.
Q. Not at all?
A. Except the few minutes I went up with the clean clothes and I had to come back again.
Q. That you now say was before Mr. Borden went away?
A. Yes sir.

(HEARING ADJOURNED. LIZZIE BORDEN RECALLED AUGUST 11th)

Q. Is there anything you would like to correct in your previous testimony?
A. No sir.
Q. Did you buy a dress pattern in New Bedford?
A. A dress pattern?
Q. Yes.
A. I think I did.
Q. Where is it?
A. It is at home.
Q. Where?
A. Where at home?
Q. Please.
A. It is in a trunk.

Q. In your room?
A. No sir, in the attic.
Q. Not made up?
A. Oh, no sir.
Q. Where did you buy it?
A. I don't know the name of the store.
Q. On the principal street there?
A. I think it was on the street that Hutchinson's book store is on. I am not positive.
Q. What kind of a one was it, please?
A. It was a pink stripe and a white stripe and a blue stripe corded gingham.
Q. Your attention has already been called to the circumstances of going into the drug store of Smith's on the corner of Columbia and Main Streets, by some officer, has it not, on the day before the tragedy?
A. I don't know whether some officer has asked me. Somebody has spoken of it to me. I don't know who it was.
Q. Did that take place?
A. It did not.
Q. Do you know where the drugstore is?
A. I don't.
Q. Did you go into any drugstore and inquire for prussic acid?
A. I did not.
Q. Where were you on Wednesday morning that you remember?
A. At home.
Q. All the time?
A. All day, until Wednesday night.
Q. Nobody there but your parents and yourself and the servant?
A. Why, Mr. Morse came sometime in the afternoon, or at noon time, I suppose. I did not see him.
Q. He did not come to see you?
A. No sir. I did not see him.
Q. He did not come until afternoon anyway, did he?
A. I don't think he did. I'm not sure.
Q. Did you dine with the family that day?
A. I was downstairs, yes sir. I did not eat any breakfast with them.
Q. Did you go into the drugstore for any purpose whatever?
A. I did not.
Q. I think you said yesterday that you did not go into the room where your father lay, after he was killed, on the sofa, but only looked in at the door.
A. I looked in. I did not go in.
Q. You did not step into the room at all?
A. I did not.
Q. Did you ever, after your mother was found killed, any more than go through it to go upstairs?
A. When they took me upstairs, they took me through that room.
Q. Otherwise than that, did you go into it?
A. No sir.

Q. Let me refresh your memory. You came down in the night to get some water with Miss Russell, along towards night, or in the evening, to get some water with Miss Russell?
A. Thursday night? I don't remember it.
Q. Don't you remember coming down some time to get some toilet water?
A. No sir. There was no toilet water downstairs.
Q. Or to empty the slops?
A. I don't know whether I did Thursday evening or not. I am not sure.
Q. You think it may have been some other evening?
A. I don't remember coming down with her to do such a thing. I may have. I can't tell whether it was Thursday evening or any other evening.
Q. Other than that, if it did take place, you don't recollect going into that room for any purpose at any time?
A. No sir.
Q. Was the dress that was given the officers the same dress that you wore that morning?
A. Yes sir.
Q. The India silk?
A. No sir. It is not an India silk. It is silk and linen. Some call it Bengaline silk.
Q. Something like that dress there? **(Pongee)**
A. No, it was not like that.
Q. Did you give to the officer the same shoes and stockings that you wore?
A. I did, sir.
Q. Do you remember where you took them off?
A. I wore the shoes ever after that, all around the house Friday and all day Thursday and all day Friday and Saturday until I put on my shoes for the street.
Q. That is to say you wore them all that day, Thursday, until you took them off for the night?
A. Yes sir.
Q. Did you tell us yesterday all the errand that you had at the barn?
A. Yes sir.
Q. You have nothing to add to what you said?
A. No sir.
Q. Miss Borden, of course you appreciate the anxiety that everybody has to find the author of this tragedy, and the questions that I put to you have been in that direction. I now ask you if you can furnish any other fact, or give any other, even suspicion, that will assist the officers in any way in this matter.
A. About two weeks ago---.
Q. Was you going to tell the occurence about the man that called at the house?
A. No sir. It was after my sister went away. I came home from Miss Russell's one night and as I came up, I always glanced towards the side door. As I came along by the carriage-way, I saw a shadow on the side steps. I did not stop walking, but I walked slower. Somebody ran down the steps, around the east end of the house. I thought it was a man because I saw no skirts and I was frightened, and, of course, I did not go around to see. I hurried in the front door as fast as I could and locked it.

Q. What time of the night was that?
A. I think about a quarter of 9. It was not after 9 o'clock, anyway.
Q. Do you remember what night that was?
A. No sir, I don't. I saw somebody run around the house once before last winter.
Q. One thing at a time. Do you recollect about how long that occurence was?
A. It was after my sister went away. She has been away two weeks today, so it must have been within two weeks.
Q. Two weeks today? Or two weeks at the time of the murder?
A. Is not today Thursday?
A. Yes, but that would be three weeks. I thought you said the day your father was murdered, she had been away just two weeks.
A. Yes, she had.
Q. Then, it would be three weeks today your sister went away. A week has elapsed.
A. Yes, it would be three weeks.
Q. You mean it was some time within the two weeks that your sister was away?
A. Yes. I had forgotten that a whole week had passed since the affair.
Q. Different from that, you cannot state?
A. No sir. I don't know what the date was.
Q. This form, when you first saw it, was on the steps of the backdoor?
A. Yes sir.
Q. Went down the rear steps?
A. Went down toward the barn.
Q. Around the back side of the house?
A. Disappeared in the dark. I don't know where they went.
Q. Have you ever mentioned that before?
A. Yes sir, I told Mr. Jennings.
Q. To any officer?
A. I don't think I have, unless I told Mr. Hanscomb.
Q. What was you going to say about last winter?
A. Last winter when I was coming home from church one Thursday evening, I saw somebody run around the house again. I told my father of that.
Q. Did you tell your father of this last one?
A. No sir.
Q. Of course you could not identify who it was either time?
A. No, I could not identify who it was, but it was not a very tall person.
Q. Have you sealskin sacks?
A. Yes sir.
Q. Where are they?
A. Hanging in a large white bag in the attic, each one separate.
Q. Put away for the summer?
A. Yes sir.
Q. Do you ever use prussic acid on your sacks?
A. Acid? No sir, I don't use anything on them.
Q. Is there anything else you can suggest that even amounts to anything whatever?
A. I know of nothing else, except the man who came and father ordered him out. That is all I know.

Q. That you told about the other day?
A. I think I did, yes sir.
Q. You have not been able to find that man?
A. I have not. I don't know whether anybody else has or not.
Q. Have you caused search to be made for him?
A. Yes sir.
Q. When was the offer of reward made for the detection of the criminals?
A. I think it was made Friday.
Q. Who suggested that?
A. We suggested it ourselves and asked Mr. Buck if he did not think it was a good plan.
Q. Whose suggestion was it, yours or Emma's?
A. I don't remember. I think it was mine.

(THE EXAMINATION ENDED)

PARTICULAR THREE

THE PRELIMINARY HEARING

The Fall River Herald

NOTHING NEW

Disclosed About the Murder of the Bordens.

THE POLICE CONTINUE THE SEARCH FOR CLUES

But Find Great Difficulty in Getting Them.

PARSON JUBB'S DENUNCIATION OF THE AUTHORITIES

For the Examination of the Suspect at the Inquest.

Another day has passed and nothing of a startling or important nature has been discovered by the police that will throw any new light on the Borden tragedy. Clue after clue and possibility after possibility have been thoroughly considered, only to leave the conditions in the same relative position. In this state they will remain, in all probability, until after the examination, and even then enough evidence may not be introduced to convince the most skeptical mind of Lizzie Borden's innocence or guilt.

Even should the prisoner be adjudged probably guilty and held for the grand jury, it is stated by her most enthusiastic supporters that it will not change their minds as to her innocence. They contend that the examination, while not a farce, will not contain the principles of justice that a suspected person should expect. With the facts of the case already placed before the magistrate who will preside, and while they claim his mind will not be prejudiced by them, it is hard for these supporters to see how whatever evidence may be presented will not have more than ordinary weight.

The leaders against the star chamber inquest which are appearing throughout the country are not directed principally against the city marshal. According to the statutes, the judge of the district court is the party who shall preside at an examination of that kind, and it is he alone who shall decide whether the general public shall be admitted or not. Whether it was his wish that the witnesses should be examined in private, or he was influenced in the matter by an official or officials connected with the case, cannot be learned. There can be no question that the publicity that has been given to this so-called inquest has done more toward moulding public opinion in favor of Miss Borden than even her wonderful self-possession and claim of innocence. The constitution of the United States provides for a fair and impartial hearing for all parties suspected of a crime, and the force of the saying that they shall be considered innocent until proven guilty is recognized by all. If this case went to the grand jury without a thorough examination in the lower court, the party would appear before the jury a convicted criminal and, instead of being proven guilty, would have to prove innocence. This is more apparent when it is admitted by the government officials that the evidence in their hands so far is purely circumstantial, and if given out at the present time the defence would have an opportunity to disprove it.

That the police were strong believers in Miss Borden's innocence at the outset no one who has followed the case can doubt. It was only when the evidence, as they found it, pointed so strongly to the accused that they believed in her guilt. Every clue was worked by the officers in the endeavor to dispel this feeling, but as they all were myths they had to be abandoned. While the city marshal swore out the warrant, there can be no doubt that it was on the instructions of the district attorney, and the latter's professional reputation will have to stand the brunt.

NO DISCRIMINATION.

Miss Sullivan Preferred to Walk to and from the Station.

"Yes, I know that a great deal of adverse criticism has been indulged in at the seeming discrimination between Miss Borden and Miss Sullivan by the police," said an official who is authorized to speak definitely, "in the matter of riding to and from the central station. Now what does a half a dollar or a dollar for hack hire amount to? The trouble is that you reporters get only the surface facts, and public opinion is influenced thereby. I know what I say when I tell you that there was no favoritism shown Miss Borden. When Officer Doherty went for Bridget Sullivan he gave her the choice of walking or riding, and she preferred to walk. She had done nothing for which she should desire to shun the public gaze, and she knew that she would excite less notice by going afoot than if she went in a hack. As it was, very few persons were aware of the fact that the servant was at the police station. How differently it was with Lizzie Borden I needn't say."

"Why is an officer kept at her stopping place?" asked the reporter.

"Not because we fear that she will decamp, or that she is under suspicion, I can assure you truthfully. It is to protect her from annoyance and to guard the interests of the commonwealth in the case; in what way I am not at liberty to declare. Reporters can make themselves very obnoxious at times."

DR. HANDY'S MAN.

The Mysterious Individual Who Attracted his Attention on Second Street.

As far as is known the man seen by Dr. Handy has never yet been located, although several men have been brought forward as the mysterious stranger, but none of them has yet been identified by the doctor. Dr. Handy is very positive concerning his man. Said he: "I saw this man as near as I can recollect on the day of the murder about 10:30 a. m. I was driving down Second street in my carriage, when my attention was called to this man's movements. Now, I see a thousand people on the street every day whom I never notice or give a thought to, but this man was most extraordinary, and had a face that is imprinted upon my memory now as plainly as when I saw him.

"Now I know Lizzie Borden well, and I do not even think she did or could commit such a murder. In the first place she did not know how to use an axe with any skill, and you won't find one woman in 500 who could strike 26 blows at an object as small as a human head and make but one mistake, especially under such circumstances as these were made. Lizzie could have no motive, as those stories of dissensions in the family have been greatly exaggerated. We were very near friends of theirs, and we never heard anything about it; everything in the girl's life is in direct refutation of the charge. Again, her story was so plausible to us who know it. Lizzie was a great fisherman, and when my daughter went to Marion she and all the girls were going to have fishlines. Lizzie was going down to my cottage on Thursday, and what was more natural than for her to think of the sinker she would require there and go into the barn in search of one? Lizzie has told a straight story, and her statements have all been given a wrong meaning.

"A good many people question the right to bring her down to the inquest, when she was a suspect and virtually a defendant, to give testimony that may be used against her. I think she should at least have been allowed counsel, considering the position she was placed in. I don't see what evidence they have against her that would warrant an arrest anyway. I often wonder why Bridget Sullivan was not also arrested as well as Lizzie. There was as much ground for the arrest of one as another. Bridget Sullivan may know something about this murder, and she may also be telling things to save herself.

"You can depend upon it, if the man I saw is an accomplice, he was not one with Lizzie Borden. I do not see how they can reasonably contend that Lizzie had time to burn any bloody clothing after the murder was committed, and none was found about the house.

"I regard the story of the officer who saw no footprints on the barnloft floor and concluded Lizzie had not been there as absurd. I do not think the axe with its two spots of alleged blood upon it amounts to much. Lizzie Borden will be proven innocent."

The police claimed one Michael Graham was the man Dr. Handy saw, but although he has not seen Graham he has been furnished with a description of him, and he says he bears no resemblance to the weird stranger Dr. Handy saw near the Borden house.

POLICE CRITICS.

Editorial Fault-Finding that is Based on a Misconception.

Monday City Marshal Hilliard had something to say about the criticism which certain newspapers were making. He said that those newspapers had not printed the information which was in the possession of the government for the very good reason that they didn't have it to print. They were basing their editorial comments on such opinions as they were able to form from their news columns, and were thus attempting to influence public sentiment and prove that the police had blundered. The government, if it had the welfare of the community at heart, could not consistently give away its case, and nothing but the peculiar circumstances which surrounded this murder and distinguished it from any other murder prompted people to demand that a full expose should be made on the spot. It was manifestly unfair, he continued, to assume that because everything had not been revealed there was nothing to reveal. The police had all along been influenced in Lizzie Borden's favor. It was natural to be so influenced, and every theory that could be advanced to divert suspicion from her had been followed to a legitimate conclusion; but before the inquest had been concluded and before a preliminary hearing had been held, some of the papers were claiming that a foul injustice had been done. When all the facts were fully known, it would be in order to bring in a verdict and condemn or exonerate the government, but until the facts were known it was both idle and wrong to pronounce on the case.

"I started," he said, "on an outside clue within half an hour of the discovery of the tragedy on information furnished by members of the family. I have chased down more than 100 outside clues within 10 days. My officers were as sceptical as I was about who committed these crimes, and it was not until all the evidence was in that action was taken. You and every other citizen must remember that the newspapers have not given anything near the facts disclosed at the inquest. This case will depend on circumstantial evidence wholly, and the people's interests cannot be subserved by throwing the evidence into the hands of the defence until a hearing or trial takes place. You and the public may rest assured of this fact: The district attorney and myself are satisfied that the public authorities have ample causes for holding this girl, and she has not been imprisoned in haste nor without a full understanding of what her arrest means.

"A great deal of nonsense is being published in connection with the case about the Borden family honor. On this point the most important member of the Borden family said for publication this morning: The honor of the Bordens, whose names are so closely allied with the prosperity of the town, is not to be affected by a police suspicion perhaps resting justly on Lizzie Borden. No true Borden has ever placed a stumbling block in the way of the law, and no member of my family will in any way hamper the police in their investigation. The statement that fifteen millions of Borden money will be used in balking the authorities is untrue and ill advised."

THE FAMILY MINISTER TALKS.

He Scores the Police and Tells of Lizzie's Home Life.

A staff correspondent of the Boston Post, writing from Taunton, says: Emma Borden arrived this morning by the 8 o'clock train and remained through the day until the 3:30 train with her sister Lizzie at the jail.

The Rev. W. Walker Jubb of the Central church of Fall River, who preached yesterday in New Bedford, came over at 9 o'clock and went at once to the jail, where he was admitted, and remained an hour with the sisters, returning to Fall River on the noon train.

"Believe in Lizzie's innocence? Indeed I do, absolutely, and I think her incarceration at the hands of the trial justice a travesty on justice," said the minister. "I would think that common decency would have caused Judge Blaisdell to step aside, after having once given judgment so far as to order the issuing of a warrant.

"The star chamber proceeding by which they secured this evidence which they claim to have is a relic of barbarism.

The thing cannot be put too strongly in condemnation. They say it was merely to secure her statement uninfluenced by a lawyer's checks and restraints.

"Are we to understand that this girl was four hours making her statement? She was four hours on the stand at one time during this star chamber sitting and that was not enough. She was called repeatedly afterwards. How many questions do you suppose were asked her in that time which should not have been asked her at all under the law—questions improper in kind and form? And every word was taken down, of course, and twisted no doubt to be used against her in the trial for her life. I tell you it is an outrage. They have not enough evidence in to hold anyone for 24 hours, but because they can find no other explanation of the murder they suspect her and say so, and then bend their energies to substantiate the statements.

"Think of the manner in which they got that drug clerk to positively identify Lizzie as the woman who bought prussic acid. Instead of bringing the two together where there were other women and asking him to point her out, they take him into her presence and ask him is this the woman. Now it turns out that several women were being employed at that time to buy poison for the purpose of testing the druggists as to whether they were fulfilling the provisions of the law in selling it. That explanation will no doubt kill off the one most suspicious circumstance weighing against Lizzie.

"It is argued that the relations between Mrs. Borden and Lizzie were such that the former would not have told her the contents of the letter in any event. Now that is all nonsense. I had a long talk with Lizzie this morning. She told me that they were all on better terms during the past two years than they had ever been. She did not try to represent that there was any demonstration of affection between them, but she said they were by no means unfriendly. The girls had always been independent, going and coming without asking anyone. Very often, however, and more especially of late, Mrs. Borden would say, as she saw the girls dressing to go out: "Well, where are you off to now, Lizzie?" or some such remark. "To use Lizzie's own words," continued Mr. Jubb, "she said, 'In all our lives there never has been a harsh word passed between Mrs. Borden and myself. There has simply been the consciousness that she was not my mother. I can freely say that she has been as good a stepmother to me as many stepmothers are. Only a few days ago at dinner she said to me: "Lizzie, I wish you would help me to fit a dress after dinner, will you?" and of course I did so, helping her to drape the dress to the best of my ability. That does not look as though we were very bitter toward each other, does it?"

"To my mind," said Mr. Jubb, resuming his own thread of the talk, "it is an impossibility for this girl to have committed that deed. From the moral side of it we must first believe her insane to be capable of it without a greater motive than has been made apparent. There are no other evidences of insanity in her whole life before or since the murder, nor any in her family so far as I can learn.

"Now, as to the evidence not touching on the marvellous cunning and nerve which she must have exercised, and which has been discussed in the papers, I would like to call your attention to the entire absence of any sign about her of the deed. It has not been attempted to show that she changed her dress after either or both the murders. It has been shown that blood splashed from both the victims in all directions, and for some distance. How could it be possible that not a drop fell upon her dress? It would be very singular if she could commit one such murder and escape in that manner, but to do two, it is beyond reason.

"And does Lizzie say nothing concerning the injustice of the charge?" was asked.

"No, or very little. She is willing to wait and be cleared by an investigation. Emma said to me this morning: 'Mr. Jubb, Lizzie is as innocent of this crime as I am, who was not there. I cannot see the slightest motive she might have, either in the way of money or revenge, for of the first she had all she needed, and of the latter there was no reason.'

"Lizzie was very fond of her father. She asks why don't they go to the bank and find out just how much ready cash she has to her credit? That would dispose of the question of money. They said that her father would not give her what money she wanted to take a vacation. What folly! She wanted to go to Marion for a few days. How much do you suppose she would need for that, and is it reasonable that with the pleasures of a holiday in her thoughts she would turn to thinking of murder?

SHERIFF WRIGHT - IN CHARGE OF THE BRISTOL COUNTY JAIL

"I was talking to Mrs. Holmes about this question of the feeling between father and daughter the other day," the minister went on, "and she corroborates the statements of the girls. She was very intimate with them, as everybody knows, and she says they were on excellent terms. Mr. Holmes, by the way, is the leading deacon in my church, of which Mr. Borden was also a member. He never attended, however, out of pique toward Mr. Holmes. Mr. Borden had a piece of property that the corporation desired to buy, but would not accede to Mr. Borden's price. Mr. Holmes voted against paying the price, as he thought it too high, and as a result Mr. Borden never attended the church afterwards."

Mr. Jubb says that Lizzie is looking well and bearing up in a manner that surprises him. She does not read the papers and knows only what these friends see fit to tell her. Emma took a copy of the Metropolitan, a paper which she thought gave a very fair statement of the case, but Mr. Jubb advised her against reading it, and she followed the advice.

Profound Sympathy Offered.

The Woman's Christian Temperance union and the Young Women's union held a special meeting Monday night and passed the following resolution:

"We offer our profound sympathy to Miss Lizzie A. Borden in the sad and painful bereavement which has befallen her by the recent tragic death of her parents. We would also declare our unshaken faith in her as a fellow worker and sister tenderly beloved, and would assure her of our constant earnest prayers that she may be supported under the unprecedented trials and sorrows now resting upon her."

Miss Borden is treasurer of the Young Women's union and has been prominent in union work.

VARIOUS PRESS OPINIONS

New Bedford Journal

The spirit message from Andrew J. Borden is the talk of the town and it made a big sensation in Fall River and other cities where interest in the Borden tragedy is felt. The gentleman who got it didn't carry out his intention to go to Fall River yesterday. The reason was, he says, that he received another message which commanded him not to go yet; instead he went to Onset, and here he received strange confirmations from a clairvoyant (the New Bedford woman was a trance medium) of the Borden message.

"You have had a message from Andrew J. Borden?" said the clairvoyant.

"Yes."

"It tells you where the hatchet with which he was murdered can be found."

"Yes."

"But it doesn't say anything about trees, does it?"

"No."

The clairvoyant then went on to describe the location of certain trees which are near the place where the hatchet is to be found. The New Bedford man says that the Onset clairvoyant and the local medium are quite ignorant of each other's existence. He has also been advised that further advices from Andrew J. Borden are coming to him from the New Bedford medium, and he proposes to wait until later in the week before he goes over to Fall River.

The Boston Record

We have not space to print the letters which come to us, commending the stand we have taken in favor of not convicting Lizzie Borden, without at least some evidence to prove it. She may be guilty, but no right minded person can believe it except it is absolutely proven, for, if so, all the belief in surroundings, appearances and indications will be shattered in an instant. It is human nature that is as much on trial as Lizzie Borden.

The Lowell Times

The statistics of crime show that poison is the usual weapon of the murderess. Occasionally frenzied women use revolvers; but an edged tool is scarcely ever used by that sex. Did Miss Borden deliberately choose the coarsest device in her reach? Is she a feminine Jesse Pomeroy? If so, is it not unaccountable that her first exhibition of this proclivity should have occurred at this age and in this way? We are not attempting to forestall the action of a jury, but many of the papers are doing so by daily condemning Miss Borden.

The Concord Patriot

The arrest of Lizzie Borden, charged with the murder of her father and stepmother at Fall River, has finally been made, but does not seem to us to be justified by any evidence that has yet been made public. We cannot recall a more brutal crime or one that gave evidence of more devlish malignity or greater depravity. It not only required a fiend's heart, but a giant's strength, and to believe that it could have been committed by a physically weak woman, whose entire life has been one of refined influences, of christian profession and work of filial devotion, of modesty and self-abnegation, is to set aside as of no value all that experience and observation have taught us. The officials are evidently striking out wildly, and, we think, more in deference to a public clamor that something shall be done than from any grounds of suspicion have they made the arrest.

A CONTEMPORARY ADVERTISEMENT

CASES OF INSANITY

From the Effects of

"LA GRIPPE"

Are Alarmingly Prevalent.

SUICIDES

From the

SAME CAUSE

Are Announced in Every Paper.

Would You be Rid of the Awful Effects of La Grippe?

There is BUT ONE SURE REMEDY that NEVER FAILS, viz:

DANA'S

SARSAPARILLA.

We Guarantee to CURE you or REFUND your money.

COULD WE DO MORE?

ISN'T IT WORTH A TRIAL?

The Fall River Herald

THE POLICE MOVE.

Lizzie Borden Arrested for Killing Her Father.

THE WARRANT SERVED AT THE CENTRAL STATION

In Presence of Her Sister and Mr. Jennings.

A PLEA OF NOT GUILTY ON ARRAIGNMENT.

A Suspicion That Others Were Concerned in the Tragedy.

After a judicial examination of the evidence gathered by the police, it was decided at 7 o'clock Thursday night to formally charge Lizzie A. Borden with the killing of Andrew J. Borden, her father, and Abbie D. Borden, her stepmother, on the morning of Thursday, Aug. 4.

This enquiry lasted three days and was minute and exhaustive. Judge Blaisdell heard the evidence and so did District Attorney Knowlton, two keen legal minds, and when they had looked into the case they said that the theory already adopted by the police was so apparently correct that they were justified in holding the person whom they suspected to be guilty of the atrocious crime.

Quickly was the decision reached, and no time was lost in carrying out the determination. Everything had been so arranged by Marshal Hilliard that when the time arrived to act the person who was wanted was right at hand within the precincts of the law, whither she had been summoned early in the afternoon to give testimony at the inquest. The serving of the warrant was done quietly by Marshal Hilliard in the presence of Detective George Seaver, Andrew J. Jennings, Esq., and Matron Russell. The accused was lying on the lounge and did not rise. The lawyer waived the reading of the warrant, and the prisoner was turned over to the care of the matron.

At 7:10 o'clock the news reached the public ear. Knots of people gathered on the street corners and in doorways to discuss the case quietly among themselves. Each had an idea concerning the guilt of the prisoner and the arrest served to vindicate those who had held from the first that Lizzie Borden was guilty. People who had hitherto believed her falsely accused on the evidence they had heard shrugged their shoulders and reluctantly admitted that something important was known to the police that had not been made public. The family friends and intimates stood loyally out for the innocence of the girl. They could not and would not believe her guilty of the fiendish crime of which she had been charged. After the first excitement of the news was over, people went home and the streets at 11 o'clock exhibited their usual quiet.

At the police station there was a manifest feeling of relief. The intense activity characteristic of the place during the past seven days was relaxed, and the officers felt that they had earned a rest.

At midnight the town was quiet. There were, however, tearful eyes that never closed throughout the weary hours of darkness; a sister overwhelmed with grief, stricken down with the burden of a day of unutterable woe; friends who tossed on feverish pillows to whom soothing sleep was stranger; yet for all that, there was a feeling in the popular mind that a weight of uncertainty and doubt, intensely wearing, had been removed.

THE INQUEST,

which began Tuesday morning at 10 o'clock, was completed shortly after 5 o'clock Thursday afternoon. The last witnesses were Eli Bence and Fred Hart, clerks in D. R. Smith's drug-store, who testified concerning the purchase of poison. Frank Kilroy was called to tell about seeing Mr. Borden on the street.

It was considered significant, however, when a carriage was seen to roll up Court square and stop at the side entrance to the central station about 3:20 o'clock. A crowd of curious watchers hovered around and saw three ladies and Marshal Hilliard alight. They were Emma Borden, Lizzie Borden and Mrs. George Brigham. The crowd rushed forward to get a better view, but the arrivals had disappeared into the station house and were conducted to the room of the police matrons, ostensibly to wait until they were called to testify again in the inquest. People who saw Lizzie Borden enter the building felt certain that she would come out of it free forever, or that she would spend the night there and many a long hour afterwards in some other place of confinement.

COURT SQUARE WAS POPULATED

even more closely than at any previous time since the murder. People seemed to be satisfied that something was to be done, and they determined to be on the ground early, prepared to stay till all was over. At 3:20 the closed carriage, which is becoming almost as familiar a sight as the patrol wagon, rattled over the rough driveway in the alley. Half a dozen men were standing near the station. In three seconds 200 men, women and children swarmed around the coach.

The warrant reads "that Lizzie A. Borden of Fall River in the county of Bristol, at Fall River, on the fourth day of August, 1892, in and upon one Andrew J. Borden, feloniously, wilfully and of malice aforethought, did make an assault, and that said Lizzie A. Borden then and there, with a certain weapon, to wit, a hatchet, the said Andrew J. Borden, in and upon the head of the said Andrew J. Borden, then and there feloniously, wilfully and of malice aforethought, did strike, giving unto the said Andrew J. Borden, then and there with the hatchet aforesaid, by the stroke aforesaid in manner aforesaid, in and upon the head of the said Andrew J. Borden, one mortal wound, of which said mortal wound said Andrew J. Borden did die."

BEFORE THE POLICE STATION AFTER THE ARREST OF MISS BORDEN.

PREPARED THE WARRANT.

After the inquest was closed, District Attorney Knowlton disappeared with Marshal Hilliard and visited the Second street house. Judge Blaisdell retired to his office and Detective Seaver went out into the guard room to smoke a cigar. Miss White, the stenographer, was dismissed for the night. About 6 o'clock, Judge Blaisdell returned to the station, Mr. Knowlton arrived in Dr. Dolan's carriage, and Clerk Leonard put in an appearance. All these signs were noted by the crowd of newspaper men, and they felt that the affair was about to culminate in an arrest. The officials met in the clerk's room, where a warrant was drawn up in due form charging Lizzie A. Borden with committing the crime of homicide. This was signed in due form and all that remained to be done was to make service on the young woman.

Soon Marshal Hilliard came out accompanied by Mr. Knowlton, and as they entered a carriage a telephone message informed Andrew J. Jennings that the two men were about to pay him a visit at his residence. This information obtained but little publicity, and not a few in the assembled crowds believed that Mr. Knowlton was being driven to the Boston train. The marshal and the district attorney proceeded to Mr. Jennings' residence and informed that gentleman that the government had decided upon the

ARREST OF LIZZIE BORDEN,

and, recognizing that his presence at the station would be desirable, had deemed it wise to notify him of the decision arrived at and the contemplated action. Mr. Jennings was not apparently greatly surprised, and at once made preparations to visit his client. The officials returned to the court room and were followed in a few moments by the attorney.

At the suggestion of the officers Mr. Jennings was entrusted with the duty of breaking the news to his client. He found her reclining upon a lounge in the matron's room, and Emma and Mrs. Brigham seated near her. As delicately as he could do so, Mr. Jennings informed the ladies of the decision of the court. The appalling news fell upon the accused with crushing weight. She seemed dazed and unable to thoroughly comprehend the situation. Emma bore the ordeal well and rushed to her sister's side to comfort her. Very soon the marshal and Officer Seaver appeared. Lizzie Borden tried to rise, but failed. The marshal was evidently affected by the scene, as was the detective who was to witness the service.

"We have a warrant for your arrest," said Marshal Hilliard, looking towards the accused. She raised her head for a moment and then dropped back.

"My client will waive the reading of it," said Mr. Jennings.

The marshal then assured Mr. Jennings that he was at liberty to see the prisoner whenever he chose, and that directions would be given for her comfort during the night. There was nothing more for the marshal to do and he retired. Mr. Jennings left very soon and went to the Borden house.

Emma and Mrs. Brigham took a tearful leave of the accused and were driven rapidly up Second street. Soon afterwards, Mr. Jennings returned with Dr. Bowen, bearing articles of clothing and necessities for the comfort of the prisoner. She was left in care of Matrons Reagan and Russell, both of whom were upon duty at the time of the arrest. Later in night Dr. Bowen again called, and it was reported that the prisoner was quite ill. The doctor remained with her a short time only, and at 9 o'clock the matron's room was closed for the night.

THE ARRAIGNMENT.

A Plea of Not Guilty Entered and Ready for Trial Announced.

As early as 8 o'clock a crowd commenced to assemble about the station door eager to obtain entrance in the court room to witness the arraignment of Miss Borden. When the doors were opened only enough to fill the seating capacity of the room was allowed to enter, and officers were placed at both entrances to keep all others out.

About five minutes past 9 o'clock Miss Borden came from the matron's room, leaning on the arm of the Rev. E. A. Buck. She appeared cool and calm, while her face bore a stoical expression. She first sat in the dock, but Marshal Hilliard took her to a seat beside her counsel, Andrew J. Jennings. She did not turn her head to gaze at anyone, but seemed to make the corner of the clerk's desk the object of her attention. When she arose to sign a legal document that her counsel was preparing, there was not a tremor on her face, or a shake of her hand as she took the pen.

"What is your plea, Lizzie A. Borden?" asked Clerk Leonard.

"Not guilty," was the response in a clear and precise tone that could be heard all over the court room.

POLICE SATISFIED

Of Their Ability to Sustain the Charge Against the Prisoner.

A load of anxiety was lifted from the minds of the police officials when the thing was over. Night and day have they worked on the case, and wherever a clue pointed they were obliged to follow. City Marshal Hilliard and Detective George Seaver of Taunton have worked together, and Assistant Marshal Fleet has taken care that orders issued were obeyed. The routine duty of the marshal's office has fallen to his lot as well as special duty in connection with this case.

A HERALD reporter who called upon Marshal Hilliard, Detective Seaver and Assistant Marshal Fleet was met with a courteous refusal to talk about the case. "We are too tired tonight to talk, and we shall proceed to get home and to bed just as soon as we can." A talk with officials of the case may be summed up as follows:

"We are quite satisfied that when this case comes to a trial we shall be able to establish the theory we adopted at the start. Why, the papers talk about not having searched the house until several days after the murder. In fact, that house was as thoroughly gone through from cellar to garret within an hour after the last crime as would reveal any evidence that could have been discovered without a minute search of all the rooms such as has followed. Lizzie Borden's room was examined before she knew anything about it. A theory was formed on the spot, and that theory has been maintained ever since. As to the evidence in the hands of the police, it is safe to say that the public have not realized how strong it was. We did not propose to show our hand and let anybody see what we were going to do, so that they might stop us. When the case is publicly heard people will be satisfied with the evidence we shall offer, and so will the jury."

The special working of clues devolved upon Detectives Seaver, McHenry of Providence, Officers Medley, Harrington and Doherty, and those officers were directed to sleep as long as they wanted to this morning. At the Borden house Officer Chace stood guard at the front door by day and Officers McCarty and Reagan, second, at night. Officer Hyde looked out for the rear in the daytime and Officers Dyson, Minnehan and Ferguson assisted after dark. Officer Devine shadowed Mr. Morse and Officer Linnehan helped at night. All the other men on the force have been called to take a turn at the extra duty. Officer Feeney has hunted down some good clues.

POLICE SUSPICIONS.

The police guard is still maintained at the house. The city marshal was asked if the guards at the Borden house and of Bridget Sullivan would be removed. "No, sir," he replied, "and they "won't be for some time yet." The condition of the case at this stage is therefore as follows: The police believe that Lizzie Borden was not alone in the commission of the two crimes of last Thursday, and they have evidence in their possession which makes them consider it necessary to go further in the direction of the people interested in affairs at the Borden house than they have hitherto been expected to go. They suspect that Lizzie had a confederate or assistants.

MYSTERIOUS STRANGER

Conveyed to Newport Last Week by Gideon Manchester.

The clue given by Dr. Handy is one that should be followed up, and most certainly will be. It is not only important that the mysterious stranger should be located, but absolutely necessary. If the man is found and is able to prove that he is in no way connected with the murder, the government's case would be considerably straightened. If he was a paid confederate, it is likely that he would not be able to bear up against a rigid cross-examination. The strange actions of the man when seen by Dr. Handy, his nervous appearance, conclusively prove that he was in some way connected with the crime. If he was not, his disappearance should be accounted for.

A Lawyer's View.

It is evident that the prosecution was surprised because Lawyer Jennings did not waive examination. Though Judge Blaisdell advised that step, Mr. Jennings declined. A prominent criminal attorney said this morning that Mr. Jennings made a mistake in objectigg to Judge Blaisdell conducting the examination. If he allowed him to do so, he thought that Mr. Jennings would have no difficulty in getting his client released on a writ of habeas corpus till indicted by the grand jury. As Lizzie Borden was really charged by the people and the police with the crime since the first day," continued the lawyer, "they had no right to summon her to testify against herself. This is a right guaranteed by the constitution."

The New York Times

LIZZIE BORDEN IN JAIL

SHE PLEADED NOT GUILTY OF MURDER WHEN ARRAIGNED IN COURT

FALL RIVER, Mass., Aug 12-Lizzie A. Borden who is charged with killing her father and stepmother, is in the Bristol County Jail at Taunton to-night, where she was taken this afternoon by City Marshal Hilliard. She is being cared for by Sheriff Andrew R. Wright and wife, who formerly lived here and were fast friends of the Bordens. Mrs. Wright showed much feeling when Miss Borden entered the jail in custody of Marshal Hilliard and Detective Seaver and accompanied by the Rev. E. A. Buck, the city missionary.

There was a great crowd in Taunton when the train arrived on which the prisoner was taken from this city. Miss Borden was taken from the Central Police Station about 3 o'clock and when she reached the railroad station the services of a large force of policemen were required to keep back the great crowd of curiously disposed persons who pressed about her. The prisoner was arraigned in the Second District Court, before Judge J. C. Blaisdell, this morning. The room was crowded to suffocation. Mr. Morse, Bridget Sullivan, Emma Borden and City Missionary Buck were present. Miss Borden was represented by Andrew J. Jennings.

The trial was begun by the entering of a plea signed and sworn to by the prisoner. It recited that the prisoner objected to the opening of a trial before a Justice who was already sitting at an inquest held to determine who committed the crime charged against her. This plea was overruled for the time being, and the Judge asked for the reading of the complaint. The reading was waived and Mr. Jennings said he would enter a plea of not guilty. District Attorney Knowlton, who was conducting the State's case, insisted that Miss Borden plead herself.

Augustus B. Leonard, Clerk of the Court, asked her to stand up, which she did firmly and without assistance. She was then asked to plead to the charges of homicide, and did so in a very weak voice at first, saying, "Not guilty."

The Clerk did not hear her, and she raised her voice and said in quite a loud tone, "Not guilty!" putting strong emphasis on the first word.

Mr. Jennings then began to argue for the acceptance of his plea' that his client should not be examined before the court where she had already been examined at an inquest.

District Attorney Knowlton entered a demurrer against the plea and the demurrer was sustained. Mr. Jennings filed an exception. He moved for a trial at once. District Attorney Knowlton objected on the ground that an inquest was still going on. He asked for a continuance until Monday, August 22, and it was granted.

Miss Borden was asked to stand up and was committed without bail. She left the courtroom leaning on Rev. Buck's arm and was closely followed by City Marshal Hilliard, who again placed her for the time in charge of Matron Russell.

It is said to-night that the police have in their possession the hatchet which it is supposed was used in killing the Bordens. It is described as what is known among farmers as the thrash-wood hatchet, save for a claw on the side of the head nearest the handle. It was found, reports say, in the cellar of the Borden house, and spots of blood were upon the blade and handle. Marshal Hilliard said there was a great deal yet to be proved before the crime could be fastened upon Miss Borden. Much had been learned, but for all that he could see the trial would be long and tedious.

There is a report of an unsuccessful search made in the Chace mill woods ponds, which, according to the statement of a man named Ward, contained evidences of the crime. Officers Doherty and Harrington found nothing suspicious there.

The Fall River Herald

GIVEN a pencil, a ream of paper, and an easy conscience, and some newspaper men can tell the most plausible tales about the Borden mystery.

The Boston Advertiser

BEHIND THE BARS.

MISS LIZZIE BORDEN IN TAUNTON JAIL.

THE CURTAIN FALLS ON THE FIRST ACT OF THE FALL RIVER TRAGEDY.

A Crowd Follows the Carriage Containing the Prisoner, and Police Force Is Necessary to Restrain Them—Strong Rumors that the Weapon Used in the Murder Has Been Discovered—A Great Deal Yet to be Proven.

TAUNTON, Aug. 12.—Miss Lizzie Borden entered a cell at Taunton jail, at 4:25 this afternoon. Her entry into the city took the form of a public ceremonial. The excitement was high. Arriving at the central passenger station, Miss Borden was conducted to a curtained hack by Minister Buck and City Marshal Hilliard, Detective Seaver acting as guard and clearing the way. The only sign of interest she manifested was when Taunton was reached, when she aroused from her lethargy for a second, then dropped her head on her hand and closed her eyes. Arriving at the jail she was at once placed in a cell, the minister conducted her to the door and Marshal Hilliard seeing that the door was properly secured. Mrs. Wright, wife of Sheriff Wright, an old friend of the Borden family, hurried to the cell with a glass of water, which the prisoner eargerly drank. When Miss Borden entered the jail office, her face was composed and there was no sign of consciousness given as she passed towards the corridor, apparently seeing nothing and noticing nothing. The sheriff stood by the inner door, and he was affected almost to tears, as he saw the daughter of his old friend passing to apartments usually occupied by the most degraded females. Minister Buck emerged from the cell room white and agitated, and not disposed to talk. After the marshal had made his returns he and Mr. Buck left the jail, and the sheriff was left with his new charge.

THE DEPARTURE.

A Crowd Surges About the Carriage Containing the Prisoner—Rumors That the Murderous Weapon Has Been Found.

FALL RIVER, Aug. 12.—Miss Borden was taken from the central police station about 3:19 P.M. today, and was conveyed to the railroad station, where she was put aboard the train leaving for Boston at 3:39. Court sq. was crowded with people, requiring the services of a large force of police to keep them back. Immediately after the hack started towards the depot, two hacks containing eight reporters hurried after it. The carriages were driven very rapidly by a circuitous route and attracted much attention. Many persons in the crowd followed the carriages, and when they arrived at the depot, they found a great gathering of people. Marshal Hilliard stepped from the carriage, but the others remained inside until the arrival of the train. When the tickst master called out the arrival of the train, the crowd surged toward the carriages and the services o several policemen were necessary to keep the curious people from crowding in on the hackman who stood at the door of the vehicle.

Detective Seaver came from the carriage first, closely followed by Mr. Buck and Miss Borden. The latter was neatly attired in a blue dress and a black velvet bonnet, the latter partially covered by a blue veil. As she passed from the depot to the train, she weakened perceptibly and leaned heavily on the arms of Mr. Buck and Marshal Hilliard. She sat in the seat with Mr. Buck during the trip to Taunton, and the detective and Marshal Hilliard sat directly behind her. She did not open her lips from the time the train left Fall River until it stopped at Taunton station, and she took little or no notice of passing stations or scenes inside the car. She did not look up once from the moment she left Fall River until she reached North Dighton.

This afternoon and evening there were the strongest rumors that the police have procured the hatchet with which the crime was committed. The police are in possession of a peculiar hatchet, and the rumor that this particular hatchet was used, is greatly strengthened by the strong wording of City Marshal Hilliard's complaint, published today. No hatchet like the one in custody can be found in the local hardware stores. Its greatest peculiarity is a claw on the side of the head nearest the handle. The handle is about 2½ feet long and the top of the head is about 1½x4in. It is said that the head of the hatchet fits into the murderous wounds in Mrs. Borden's head. The blade of the implement is represented as being very thin and very sharp, measuring about 5½ inches in the widest part. It is what is known among farmers as an old fashioned thrash wood hatchet, except for the strange claw. A hardware man says that such hatchets are probably used in laying heavy planking where spikes are driven, the claw being used in pulling out spikes.

When the police authorities were asked if such a hatchet was in their custody they would neither admit nor deny it. The matter, with all other evidence, is now in control of District Attorney Knowlton. The connection of the hatchet with a bloody deed of some kind is almost beyond doubt as spots of blood have been found on the blade and handle. Certain clothes covered with blood, found in the cellar where the hatchet was found, are said to have an important bearing on this part of the case.

Tonight Marshal Hilliard said there was a great deal yet to be proven before the crime could be finally fastened upon Miss Borden. Much had been learned, but for all that he could see, the trial would be

LIZZIE LEAVES FOR PRISON ESCORTED BY REV. BUCK AND MARSHAL HILLIARD

long and tedious. Medical Examiner Dolan says that a great deal will depend on the accuracy of the medical examination of the body and the analysis of the parts sent to Boston. Tonight affairs are more quiet in police circles than for many hours. There is the report of an unsuccessful search made in the Chace Mill wood's ponds, which, according to the statement of a man named Ward, contained evidence of the crime. Officers Doherty and Harrington found nothing suspicious there.

The strongest evidence against Miss Lizzie Borden she is understood to have introduced herself. One of the officials who was present stated last night that as she proceeded with her story the case against her grew blacker and blacker. The most important parts of her testimony were tested. On the point of the time that she remained in the loft great stress was brought to bear.

It was held that the loft on a hot day was like an oven, and it was considered improbable, to say the least, that a refined and cultured lady, unaccustomed to hardship, would remain in such a place for 20 minutes unless something imperative demanded it, when she could have remained quietly in a cool room within doors and waited until a cooler part of the day before making her search for the lead or whatever else she was after. She was forced to repeat her story time after time. Inconsistencies did not necessarily have great weight, but parts of her story were regarded as improbable.

Medical Examiner Dolan refused to divulge any of the secrets of the inquest when approached, but willingly submitted to an interview. He stated that the arrest did not result from the investigation into the medical and surgical side of the case. His part of the investigation remained just where it was on the day after the murders, with the exception that an autopsy had been held and the new cut found on Mrs. Borden's body. The medical examiner wanted it understood that no autopsy occurred before yesterday. On the day of the murder there was no examination of the bodies away from the heads. He had removed the stomachs against almost the unanimous opposition of all the others engaged upon the case. They had insisted that the cause of death in each case was too evident to require any further investigation. When Attorney General Pillsbury was called into the case he thoroughly approved of the course pursued by the medical examiner, and insisted that everything that might in any possible way throw light upon the case should be torn up or cut up, whichever was required.

Dr. Dolan has little faith in the poison theory, and has had little since early in the investigation. The only evidence that he expects from the return of the analysis of the stomachs and their contents, is as to the time of the murders. The extent of digestion will determine positively which was killed first and how long a time elapsed between the killing of the first and the killing of the second. The arrest yesterday was not the result of any return from Prof. Wood, as he has made none. No word is expected from him concerning the analysis for a week and possibly nothing will be heard for two weeks.

Now that action has been taken by the police Medical Examiner Dolan will not object to being named as the author of the hypothetical poisoning case given in Wednesday's second edition of the News. This case was widely circulated and very generally accepted as strong proof that Lizzie Borden did not use prussic acid. No one doubted that she would have committed suicide, had she been in possession of such a poison, as soon as she learned that she was suspected.

This morning Marshal Hilliard was asked directly if he would state whether an important discovery made yesterday after 12 o'clock led to the arrest, or whether the arrest resulted from the gradual accumulation of evidence under the direction of the district attorney.

The marshal referred the questioner to District Attorney Knowlton, who was in the office. The district attorney gave what he seemed to consider a satisfactory answer. "A letter had been received from a clairvoyant in Newport, who had predicted the weapon was a long-handled carving knife which would be found concealed in the chicken coop located west of the house. That would bring the coop into the street. The officers found the coop, searched it, found the knife and the arrest followed as a natural consequence." The official seemed much surprised that no thanks were returned for this answer.

Editor Milne renews strongly tonight in the News his plea for suspension of judgment, saying: "The crime with which Miss Borden is charged is so utterly unnatural and motiveless, and is in such violent contrast with her character as hitherto established in this community, the consequent presumption against her guilt is so strong that she is entitled to the consideration which we ask.

"The act, which is unspeakably atrocious in any event, is so much more awful on the theory that she is the guilty party, that every sensitive heart ought to long for her exoneration from the crushing charge which now stands against her. Of course the foremost desire of all right-thinking people will be that the truth may come to light, whatever it reveals; but at the same time the hope ought to be fervently cherished that the disclosure of the truth may set free from suspicion the young woman whose charitable and Christian life has never before been called in question. The real interest of the public lies along that line."

The New York Recorder

Mr. Rufus H. Hilliard's complaint is assuredly a most astounding document. City Marshal Hilliard, on oath, complains that Miss Borden did assault and kill her father, Andrew J. Borden, with a hatchet, and "willfully and of her malice aforethought did kill and murder." Now, this may be in due form of law, but is it fair? Is it warranted by any facts which the police have so far shown themselves able to prove? We do not believe that any fair-minded person who has followed the daily developments in this remarkable case will say "yes" to either question.

Is it not the usual and much more decent procedure, in cases where positive proofs are absent or as yet undisclosed, for a complaining officer to make oath and say that he believes that the accused person did the deed of which he or she is suspected? We have certainly so understood the theory and practice of American criminal law. Since when did the maxim that "the citizen must be presumed to be innocent till he is proven to be guilty cease to be a fundamental one in every American court?

Yet Marshal Hilliard brushes this maxim entirely aside and swears positively, without qualification of any sort, that Miss Borden has committed murder. This goes too far, much too far. It savors of an overzealous attempt to set up a police theory, take everything for granted and proceed to arbitrarily fit the facts to the theory. This is not American justice on fair-play lines. And it will not go down in this country.

Miss Borden may be guilty as charged, but she is entitled to be decently, calmly and deliberately tried before she is branded as a murderess. We do not hesitate to say that City Marshal Hilliard's complaint, and the proceedings taken thereon, were in outrageous defiance of the American doctrine that every person must be assumed to be innocent of crime until he or she is shown to be guilty.

The New York Herald

HER FATHER'S MURDER CHARGED AGAINST HER.

Lizzie Borden, Brought Before Judge Blaisdell, Pleads Not Guilty and the Examination Is Postponed.

OBJECTIONS TO THE JUSTICE.

The Accused Woman's Counsel Enters a Formal Protest Against His Hearing the Case, Which Is Promptly Overruled.

TAKEN TO THE TAUNTON JAIL.

For Ten Days the Prisoner Must Wait in a Cell Before the Hearing—Outline of the Evidence—Great Family Influence.

[BY TELEGRAPH TO THE HERALD.]

FALL RIVER, Mass., August 12, 1892.—Lizzie A. Borden, accused of the murder of her father and stepmother, is now a prisoner in the County Jail at Taunton, held without bail for the continuance of her examination. She was publicly arraigned before Judge Blaisdell this morning and charged with the crime. It was at the request of the prosecution that further consideration of the case was postponed ten days without bringing forth any of the evidence laid against her.

The trying ordeal of the public arraignment in a court room, crowded with curiously staring and unsympathetic people, she bore without much concern, but more like one who did not fully understand her position than with the composure of courage.

The inquest is not yet concluded. It will be resumed on Monday. Except for that there will be nothing developed in the Borden case until August 22, when Lizzie will again face her accusers and much of the testimony of the prosecution will have to be disclosed at the continuance of the preliminary examination.

Lizzie passed the night on the couch in the matron's room, and after twelve o'clock slept well. Before that she had been nervous and restless, but all Matron Russell's efforts to cheer or relieve her were steadily repulsed. She awoke this morning very much like the Lizzie Borden of old.

SHE WOULD NOT TALK.

The matron told her she could have anything she wanted to eat, but she had little appetite. She would not talk except when absolutely necessary, and then in monosyllables. As far as she could

TOMB IN WHICH THE BORDEN BODIES REST.

she ignored the matron's presence and stared straight ahead of her. Early in the morning the Rev. E. A. Buck, pastor of the First Congregational Church, which Lizzie attended, called upon her and talked to her. Mr. Jennings, her counsel, came just before nine and told her a few things about what she might expect.

The clerk motioned to Lizzie Borden, and she stood up and faced him. "This is a complaint," he said, in the true court sing song, "charging you with homicide. What say you? Are you guilty or not guilty?"

"Not guilty," said Lizzie in a very low voice. The clerk did not hear her well. "What?" he demanded.

"Not guilty," she said again in a loud and clear voice, audible all over the court room, and with an emphatic accent on "not."

The plea was entered and Mr. Jennings went on to protest once more against the present proceedings. "Although it has been common report," he said, "and admitted by the authorities that Miss Borden was under suspicion in this case, she was not allowed to be represented by counsel at the inquest. I spoke to both of you gentlemen about permitting me to be present when such grave interests of my client were at stake and you refused. All the evidence against her has been concealed from her and she has been subjected to a severe examination without the benefit of counsel.

"The inquest is still open. You, hearing this case as Judge, are also hearing evidence against her in another court to which she is not admitted. You are a prejudiced magistrate.

SAYS THE JUDGE IS PARTIAL.

"It is beyond human nature," said Mr. Jennings, "to suppose that Your Honor could have heard all the evidence at the inquest and not be prejudiced against this woman. I submit that Your Honor is acting in a double capacity, and therefore you cannot be unbiassed. This takes from my client her constitutional right to be heard before a court of unprejudiced opinion.

"Besides, the evidence that you have heard may have been, for all we know, incompetent or inadmissible. I submit that these proceedings are not before an impartial magistrate."

"The Commonwealth demurs to the plea," said Mr. Knowlton in his cool, metallic voice, "and asks that it be overruled. There is nothing extraordinary in these proceedings. They are exactly in line with the provisions of the statutes and with precedent. More than twenty times within my memory has this proceeding had an exact parallel. It has not before attracted such widespread attention, because the instances were not preceded by such an unusual case as this. The inquest has nothing whatever to do with the arraignment of this defendant, neither has it to do with this complaint. They are separate and distinct."

A GLARING DIFFERENCE.

Mr. Jennings is a small man but a hard fighter.

He jumped to his feet and said:—"The difference between this proceeding and the inquest is apparent and glaring." The police, after determining in their own minds who was the guilty party, have ordered an inquest, which is still on, and in place of arresting the suspect at the time they seek to try her in secret without the protection of her counsel. They did not arrest her and try her in open court, where she would have a chance to be defended in the regular way."

"I don't think the police and the officers of the inquest should be arraigned at this stage of the proceedings," said Mr. Knowlton.

The Court interposed. "The counsel for the defendant mistakes the statutes," he said. "They provide for an inquest. If the evidence at the inquest points to it the Judge's duty is to issue a warrant. Isn't that my province and duty?"

"I don't question your power to do it," Mr. Jennings snapped.

"Plea overruled and demurrer sustained," said the Court.

"Except!" said Mr. Jennings, sharply. "Now we are ready for trial."

But the Commonwealth was not ready if Mr. Jennings was. He said that the completion of the inquest would take some time and he would not be ready to proceed for a week or ten days. He moved a continuance until Monday, August 22. "My client," said Mr. Jennings, "is ready and anxious to proceed to the trial at the earliest possible moment."

However, Mr. Knowlton's suggestion prevailed. Then he said that he had two important witnesses, John V. Morse and Bridget Sullivan, and he asked that they be put under bonds for their appearance at the trial. The Court fixed their bonds at $500 each. They were brought across the court room and took seats on the prisoners' bench by the side of Pastor Buck, who had insisted upon remaining there until Lizzie's case was concluded.

COMMITTED WITHOUT BAIL.

"Lizzie Borden, stand up," said the clerk. Lizzie rose to her feet. "By the order of this Court this case is continued until August 22 and you are ordered to stand committed without bail."

District Attorney Knowlton has steadily refused to make any statements about the case while it was under investigation, but to-day he was willing to defend himself from the charge of injustice in excluding Lizzie's counsel from the inquest.

PERFECTLY REGULAR.

"It was perfectly regular and in accordance with precedents," he said. "The witnesses summoned were obliged to choose between one of the three things—tell all they knew bearing on the subject in which they were supposed to be informed, go to jail for contempt if they didn't, or set up the plea of exemption on the ground that their testimony would criminate themselves. Any evidence given by a witness at the inquest could be used against him at a trial in the courts. This may seem hard, but the law allows it and the Court awards it."

Mr. Knowlton did not think there would be a session of the Grand Jury before the regular term of the Superior Court in November, so that if Lizzie is held on the preliminary examination, a week from Monday, she will have to stay in jail three months.

Bail for Bridget Sullivan and John V. Morse was offered as soon as Court adjourned by John C. Milne and Frank Almy, proprietors of a Fall River newspaper which has been interested in Lizzie Borden's behalf.

The two witnesses were released and went home. The police espionage under which they have been so long ceased, but both refused to make any statements about their testimony.

LACKS AN IMPORTANT LINK.

This is briefly the outline of the case against Lizzie Borden. It will appear at once that it is not a very strong chain and lacks the most important link of all—the motive. True, the discovery of a will may indicate something of that kind, or it may be argued that the bitter feud at home furnished the motive; but neither of these will seem a sufficient reason for such a butchery in a rational being.

But perhaps she is not a rational being. In Fall River the opinion of nine in every ten persons is, that whether guilty or not, if she keeps still she will never be convicted. It is hard to convict a woman on circumstantial evidence, and the prosecution has nothing else.

As to the defence, nobody who knows will say what that will be. Mr. Jennings, Lizzie's counsel, absolutely declines to say a word in her behalf, to explain any of the circumstances that look so black against her, or to try to justify any of her statements to the known facts. His one answer to every question put to him on these points or as to what would be done to protect Lizzie's interests was "I have nothing to say."

WOULD EXPRESS NO OPINION.

He would not even express an opinion about the proceedings taken against her further than he expressed this morning in court. Emma Borden has shut herself up in the house and declines to answer any questions. Of the other persons who might in the ordinary meaning of the word be called the prisoner's personal friends, there are so few that it is a hopeless task to try to get any authoritative utterances in her defence.

Still, it must not be supposed that Lizzie Borden is hopeless and friendless. She has back of her a great fortune that may be spent for relief, and perhaps the most powerful family interest to be found in New England. The Bordens are a very old and very large family. They have been in Fall River ever since it was founded, in 1820, and they have multiplied and branched out until there are more Bordens in Fall River many times over than people of any other name.

The safe in Mr. Borden's house, which made so much trouble yesterday, was opened this morning after a prodigious effort. The expert from Boston worked all yesterday afternoon on the simple old fashioned lock and couldn't stir it. This morning he resumed the job and just as he concluded that he would never get at it without dynamite the door swung open.

The reward for all this effort was not great, not so far as a hasty examination could show. There were some money and a pile of papers, but no trace of a will and nothing else that bore on the case. District Attorney Knowlton took charge of the papers.

Miss Lizzie Borden Safe in a Cell in Taunton Jail.

[BY TELEGRAPH TO THE HERALD.]

TAUNTON, Mass., August 12, 1892.—The train which brought Lizzie Borden to the County Jail reached here at twenty minutes past four. Almost the whole town had assembled to meet it. The policemen hurried Lizzie into a coach and drove rapidly to the jail, followed by a great crowd. Sheriff Wright, who had charge of the jail, used to live in Fall River and his family was very intimate with the Bordens.

Isabella Wright, the Sheriff's daughter, was a schoolmate of Lizzie. There was an affecting scene when they received their prisoner. Mrs. Wright broke down and cried. The family treated Lizzie with the greatest kindness, and she will not lack for every possible comfort at their hands. She went through the meeting with her former friends and the ordeal of giving her pedigree without emotion. None are allowed to see her cell. Lizzie's pastor, the Rev. Mr. Buck, accompanied her to Taunton and did not leave her until she was taken away to be locked up.

Boston Record

If Miss Lizzie Borden of Fall River is half as plucky and determined as she is given credit for, she will, on the theory that she is innocent of the murder of her father and mother, as every one must believe until there is strong evidence to the contrary, along about Oct. 1 bring some libel suits that will net her a handsome return finencially and also set her right in other ways before the community.

Woonsocket Call

The Borden case at Fall River is apparently as much a mystery as ever, and apparently because the police are either incompetent or wilfully stubborn. Nearly a week has passed since the murder was committed, and although the entire police department has been at work on the case, so far as the public is informed they are no nearer a solution than when they started. In the first place they made a grave mistake in not doing what every intelligent official should know enough to do at the start and that is, make a thorough examination of the premises.

The New York Herald

CHAIN OF EVIDENCE AGAINST LIZZIE BORDEN.

The Blood Stained Hatchet with Which the Double Murder Was Probably Committed Belonged in the House.

LOOKING FOR A MOTIVE.

Andrew J. Borden Was About to Make a Will, the Authorities Say, and They Depend on This As Furnishing the Missing Link.

BOTH SIDES ARE RETICENT.

The State Will Endeavor to Hold Back Its Evidence at the Preliminary Hearing, and Lawyer Jennings Orders His Client to Keep Silent.

[BY TELEGRAPH TO THE HERALD.]

FALL RIVER, Mass., August 13, 1892.—It seems that the hatchet believed by the police to have been used in the murder of the Bordens was not an old fashioned one, as has been described, but one of recent manufacture. It was purchased by Mr. Borden about a year ago—probably last fall—and had been used very little by any members of the family. It was kept on a shelf in the cellar. When, however, the cellar was searched on the day of the tragedy it was not discovered in its regular place. It lay on the floor near one of the axes used to split wood, a most unusual place for it.

The hairs were easily detected on it, but the stains which looked like blood had first to be subjected to a microscopic test before their nature was established for a certainty. It was thought that they might possibly have been caused by rust. When the physicians held the glass over the spots they found there was no iron rust about them—that they were probably human blood. There was another weapon found by the police in their search of the house. It was a peculiar looking club, and bore marks of having been stained by blood. It was not "turned up" until the very careful search, which was made the day of the funeral—last Saturday—and the following Monday the police denied all knowledge of it.

A MYSTERIOUS CLUB.

The doctors have failed to find any wounds that were in any probability caused by such a weapon of wood, but there is no question that one was found. Chief Hilliard stated this morning that the hatchet was the only iron weapon which he thought had any connection with the tragedy, laying particular stress on the word iron. The club was found in the room where Mrs. Borden lay dead, the apartment in which John V. Morse slept the night before the murder. That it was well hidden is shown by the fact that it was not found until a most thorough and exacting search was made.

Deputy Sheriff Graham said this morning that with the axe hatchet or hatchet axe and its handle of two feet long it would have been utterly impossible for Lizzie Borden to come up behind Mrs. Borden and strike her so as to bury the blade through her dress under the shoulder, for the reason that when she aimed and struck a blow the very weight of the blade would cause the hatchet to glance, and it would swing off sideways in the nature of things. How a woman holds a hatchet and delivers a blow with it, and how this hatchet must have been held, is a most interesting feature in this case.

The point raised as to the right of Judge Blaisdell to preside will be carried up to the Supreme Court.

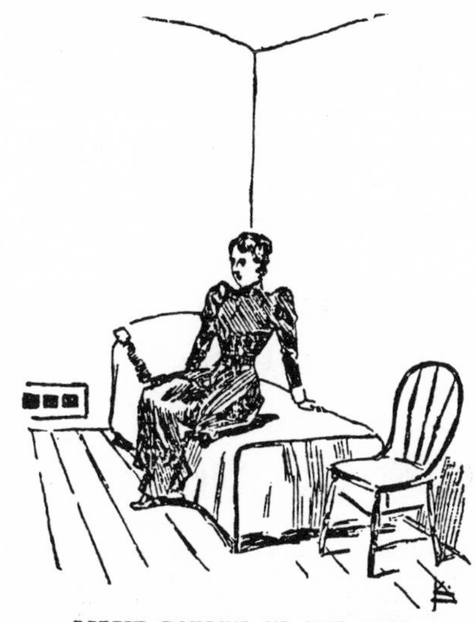

LIZZIE BORDEN IN HER CELL.

INTEREST SUBSIDING.

With the removal of Lizzie A. Borden from this city to the County Jail at Taurton, where she will remain until the preliminary hearing to be held here on Monday, August 22, interest in the dual murder case has seemingly begun to droop. The guards have been removed from around the house and now only one patrolman, on whose beat the brown mansion stands, passes by it once every half hour.

Chief Hilliard said to me to-day that Mr. Borden was about to make a will. This statement was made to the Chief by a man whose name he declines to mention. He avers, however, that the old gentleman had been at work making an inventory of his property during the ten days preceding his murder. Mr. Borden had even departed from his usual retieence about his own private affairs and had told Chief Hilliard's informant that he intended to devise his property "according to his own ideas."

Mrs. Borden was placed in the position that nine out of ten stepmothers are. She was heartily disliked by her stepchildren, Emma and Lizzie. Mr. Borden, on the contrary, had a great affection for his second wife and was greatly influenced by her.

John V. Morse knew of the fact that Mr. Borden was about to draw up the instrument, so did Lizzie and Emma. All three had the same dislike for Mrs. Borden, whose hand had been plainly seen in some of the murdered man's charities. Mr. Borden, resented on all possible occasions the attitude of his daughters toward his wife, and his object in making a will could be for naught else than to leave Mrs. Borden in better financial condition than she would be if he died intestate. Her share of the real estate, if he died without a will, amounting to about $60,000, she would not own, but hold in trust for her daughters, drawing only the interest upon it. At four per cent this real estate would yield her only about $2,400 per year. This would be enough to live on, but could never make her wealthy. Now, it is known that Mrs. Borden, who could not be called a designing woman, did nevertheless tell some of her intimate friends that if Mr. Borden died first she was to be well taken care of.

A visit to the Second street house was made to-night, but Morse and Miss Emma decline to talk. They did state, however, that Lizzie was kindly treated in the Taunton jail, and she was in good health and spirits. They were certain, they said, to prove her innocence.

An unnatural feature of this case is the fact that Emma and Lizzie occupied the room in which their stepmother was murdered the next night after the body was found. Emma still continues to sleep there.

Emma Borden Visits Her Sister In the Lynn Jail.

TAUNTON, Mass., August 13, 1892.—Miss Borden passed a comfortable night and this morning was cheerful to an unusual degree, brought about perhaps by the prospect of a visit from her sister. Mr. Jennings and Miss Emma Borden came up this morning, and the former after a brief conversation went away, leaving Emma in the cell with her sister.

The two conversed in low tones for some time, but there were no tears, no complainings, and the whole affair had the appearance of a simple, ordinary, every day visit between friends. During part of the time Lizzie was occupied with some sewing which she had brought with her. It is understood that under no circumstances will she open her mouth, and Mr. Jennings, her counsel, will do all the talking necessary.

OPINIONS FROM OTHER NEWSPAPERS

New Bedford Mercury

A Fall River friend of the Bordens said to a Mercury reporter: "Two years ago Lizzie went to Europe. Since that time she has yearned to travel. She said that there was something outside of the little circle in which she lived, and she has continually fretted at her restraint. One of the young ladies who is now at Marion was accustomed to urge her to make her father more liberal, telling her that he could very well afford to let her do as the other girls were doing.

"Every one knew that there was ill feeling in the home. Mr. Borden give his wife stocks to the value of $5000 and when the daughters learned of it they were very angry, feeling that she was making an attempt to get Mr. Borden to make his property over to her. To conciliate them, Mr. Borden gave them stocks of an equal face value, but they turned out to be worth very little and the daughters were more annoyed than before. Lizzie Borden is an intensely determined girl. You cannot talk with her five minutes without seeing that." A New Bedford physician is quite sure that the analysis will show that the Bordens died of poisoning and were hacked afterward to divert suspicion from the household. In no other way can the lack of blood about the rooms where the murders were committed be explained.

The Fall River Herald

What Fall River Folks Say.

"It is too bad, too bad," said City Missionary Buck. "And yet I am not so much surprised, as I have felt all along since the inquest began that it would come to this. I know Lizzie Borden too well to believe for a moment in her guilt. Why do I think her innocent? Because I know her so intimately as to think and believe the best always of her. I have seen her every day since the murder, and a nobler and more innocent appearing woman I never saw.

"She was calm and talked about the crime much more composedly than she could have if she were guilty. I know her mind was not troubled by any knowledge of guilt, and her appearance to me since the murder is enough to assure her innocence."

Said Alderman Beattie: "I am sorry that it was found necessary to arrest Lizzie Borden, but I am anxious to see justice prevail. We hate to believe, we find it hard to think, that a girl brought up as well and with the intellectual associations she has had would commit such a crime as this. Lizzie Borden has lots of friends who believe in her innocence, and who will work hard to establish it. I have always wondered why the servant girl was not arrested at first, as she was the only person in the house at the time of the murder."

C. S. Sawyer believes thoroughly in Lizzie's innocence.

Said he: "When I was on guard outside, on the day of the murder, Bridget told of a Portuguese employee of Mr. Borden, and suggested that he might have committed the crime. Lizzie was completely prostrated by the shock she had received, but as soon as she heard of Bridget's story she sent Miss Russell out to me to deny the possibility of the story.

"Miss Russell said Lizzie was worried lest the Portuguese employee, who, she said, was a worthy man, should hear that he was suspected, for she feared, owing to his sensitive nature, it might kill him."

"I am sorry," said Hiram Farrington. "I wish it could not have happened," and he turned sadly into his doorway, fearful that the news would be read in his face by his in alid wife.

New Bedford Excited.

NEW BEDFORD, Aug. 12.—Quite a lot of excitement was caused about the city, this afternoon, over the report that a Frenchman had been arrested on suspicion that he was the man talked about in connection with the Borden murder case. The report spread with surprising rapidity, and the whole city was agog with the news that the murderer of the Borden's had been captured here. The report proved to be groundless.

THE CHARGE AND PLEA.

Full Text of the Complaint Against Miss Lizzie Borden and Her Answer.

FALL RIVER, Aug. 12.—The following is the complaint to which Miss Lizzie Borden pleaded in court today:—

To Augustus B. Leonard, clerk of the second district court:—

Rufus B. Hilliard, city marshal of Fall River, in behalf of said Commonwealth, on oath, complains that Lizzie A. Borden of Fall River, on the fourth day of August, in the year of our Lord 1892, in and upon one Andrew J. Borden, feloniously, wilfully and of her malice aforethought, did make an assault; and that the said Lizzie A. Borden then and there with a certain weapon, to wit, a hatchet, in and upon the head of said Andrew J. Borden feloniously, wilfully and of her malice aforethought did strike, giving unto the said Andrew J. Borden then and there, with the hatchet aforesaid, by the stroke aforesaid, in manner aforesaid, in and upon the head of the aforesaid Andrew J. Borden, one mortal wound; the said Andrew J. Borden then and there instantly died. And so the complainant aforesaid, upon his oath aforesaid, further complains and says that the said Lizzie A. Borden the said Andrew J. Borden, in manner and form aforesaid, then and there feloniously and wilfully and of her malice aforethought did kill and murder.

R. B. HILLIARD.

Aug. 11, 1892.

The defence submitted the following answer:—

COMMONWEALTH VS. LIZZIE A. BORDEN.
COMPLAINT FOR HOMICIDE.
Defendant's Plea.

And now comes the defendant in the above-entitled complaint, and before pleading thereto says that Hon. Josiah C. Blaisdell, the presiding justice of the second court of Bristol, before which said complaint is returnable, has been and, as the defendant is informed and believes, still is engaged as the presiding magistrate at an inquest upon the death of the said Andrew J. Borden, the person whom it is alleged in said complaint the defendant killed; and has received and heard, and is still engaged in receiving and hearing, evidence in relation to said killing and to said defendant's connection therewith, which she is not and has not been allowed to hear or know the purport of.

Wherefore, she says that the said Hon. Josiah C. Blaisdell is disqualified to hear this complaint, and she objects to his so doing, and all this she is ready to verify.

LIZZIE A. BORDEN.

Sworn to before A. J. Jennings, justice of the peace.

THE ARRAIGNMENT.

Miss Lizzie Borden Pleads Not Guilty and Will Have a Hearing Aug. 22.

FALL RIVER, Aug. 12.—Lizzie A. Borden was arraigned in the second district court before Judge J. C. Blaisdell this morning on charges of homicide arising from the killing of her father and stepmother. The court room was crowded to suffocation by a motley crowd of curious people in no way directly interested and Miss Borden's friends at court were very few in number. Mr. Morse, Bridget Sullivan, Miss Emma Borden and City Missionary Buck were present.

Miss Borden, the prisoner, was represented by A. J. Jennings. She was dressed in a dark blue tailor-made gown, and wore a black lace hat, adorned with a few red berries. She looked better than she did last night just before her arrest.

She entered the court room leaning on Missionary Buck's arm. She was somewhat nervous, but did not show feeling by either tears or trembling. She was given a seat beside her counsel and her sister Emma, and Rev. E. A. Buck occupied a seat in front of the prisoner's dock. The trial was commenced by the entering of a plea signed and sworn to by the prisoner.

It recited that the prisoner objected to the opening of a trial before a justice who was already sitting at an inquest held to determine who committed the crime charged against her. This plea was overruled for the time being and the judge asked for the reading of the complaint. The reading was waived, and Mr. Jennings said he would enter a plea of not guilty. District Attorney Knowlton, who was conducting the government's case, insisted that Miss Borden plead herself.

"The inquest was not held until after long a delay," said Mr. Jennings: "until it was common report that the police had openly admitted that they suspected Miss Lizzie Borden as the murderess. She was not represented by counsel at this inquest; neither did she have an opportunity of hearing what was testified to by the other witnesses.

"The same judge who sat on the inquest, which is now going on, is the one before which this case comes up for trial, and I submit that it is beyond the bounds of human nature to suppose that your honor can fail to be prejudiced.

"She was probably subjected to a severe examination at that inquest, but I do not know how many questions she may have been asked. Neither do I know what questions may have been put by the district attorney to which exceptions might have been raised, and it seems to me it would not be right to try this case, after listening to perhaps incompetent and inadmissible evidence.

"I submit that it is not allowing the case to be tried before an impartial magistrate, a privilege which the law gives every man. I submit that the plea should be sustained.

"Let me illustrate. Supposing a complaint should be made to your honor in relation to an offence, and the witnesses for the prosecution were called into your private office. After you had heard their stories, suppose that you had brought the case into open court and then proceeded with the evidence. That is about the the in which this matter appears to me."

The district attorney was quickly on his feet.

"My brother is in error," he began, "in assuming that there was any unreasonable delay. The authorities cannot take action until the medical examiner has made a report to them, and within 24 hours after this report had been received this inquest was started.

"The method of procedure is strictly proper and in accordance with the law and with custom."

Judge Blaisdell then rendered his decision, in the course of which he reviewed the case at length; said it was the duty of the magistrate to hear the inquest and cause the warrant, not on the previous assumption that the defendant was guilty, but because of the evidence presented to him at the official hearing.

"The pleading must, therefore, be overruled and the demurrer sustained," he concluded.

"I wish to take exception to your honor's ruling," said Mr. Jennings, and the exception was noted.

Mr. Jennings said his client was ready to go on with the trial.

The Fall River Herald

TAKEN TO TAUNTON.

Lizzie Borden Placed in the Sheriff's Care

UNTIL THE DAY SET FOR HER EXAMINATION.

Exhibits No Emotion During Her Transfer.

The Best of Criminal Lawyers to Be Engaged.

The Police Continue the Search for Evidence.

Already it is possible to notice the feeling of relief which has come upon the city after the severe trial of the week. The thought that an assassin could steal into a house in broad daylight and for a pastime hack to pieces two unsuspecting people, escaping again undetected and leaving behind him as the only souvenir of his visit the reeking corpses of his victims was a horrible one, and led to speculating whether there were not dangers in the gathering together of human beings into society that were commensurate with the advantages.

A person cannot always be on the watch to the right and to the left, before and behind, ever on the alert to ward off the blow aimed at his life. There must be times of relaxation, and unless society can guarantee a large measure of safety in such hours, society is a failure. In such circumstances as surrounded the Borden killing, unless the perpetrator of the deed can be detected, anarchy finds a strong argument. People probably did not think this thought out in detail when the news of an arrest was given out, but it was the underlying principle of the general relief that accompanied the announcement. An arrest of any person whatsoever was certain to generate this feeling, for it was an earnest that the authorities to whom the people look for protection had been on the alert and had worked over the combination of circumstances with a reasonable prospect of success. If they had succeeded in detecting the murderer in the face of thé gigantic difficulties which surrounded them in the Borden case—circumstances the like of which have rarely been combined in any criminal case on record—it is a warning to the evil-disposed and a protection to the people.

As to the arrest of Lizzie Borden herself, hardly a person in the city does not pity her. There is a genuine sorrow that the deductions of the police have led them to take the step they have found necessary. It must be borne in mind, too, that she is not a murderer until the crime has been proved. Conclusions built on overwhelming evidence of circumstances are sometimes in error. The police may have made a mistake, and thousands of people sincerely hope that they have for the girl's sake. This feeling, however, does not interfere with the satisfaction that the work of the authorities has been earnest and has led to a definite conclusion.

AFTER THE ARRAIGNMENT in the district court Friday morning, Lizzie Borden was transferred to the matron's room in the central station. There she was received by her sister and Mr. Morse. The relatives were left together for some little time while the proceedings were being completed inside the court room. They remained together until Mr. Morse and Bridget Sullivan were called before the court and bound over in $500 each to appear at the hearing Aug. 22. Lizzie Borden spent the day comfortably in the matron's room when she was alone, reading from a book. Friends had sent in flowers, and the Rev. E. A. Buck dropped in to offer spiritual comfort. Matron Reagan, who had relieved Matron Russell, was with her until train time.

The preparations for the journey to Taunton were simple. At 3:20 Court square was choked with sightseers; it will probably not be so choked again until a week from next Monday, when the prisoner will be brought back for the hearing. One carriage drew up at the main entrance and Miss Emma Borden and Andrew J. Jennings, Esq., entered it and were driven to the depot. Lizzie Borden, the prisoner, stepped into a carriage which was in waiting at the side entrance and was also driven off. To all outward appearances, she was as calm as though she had been going for a visit to relatives. The Rev. E. A. Buck, City Marshal Hilliard and State Officer Seaver accompanied her. A small valise containing the prisoner's clothing was placed on the box, and the curtain descended on the first act. The representatives of the press followed the carriage containing the prisoner in cabs, and at 3:30 Court square was quiet.

TAUNTON WAS REACHED AT 4:20 O'CLOCK.

Awaiting her arrival was a gathering of hundreds, and they crowded about every car. Officer Seaver, in order to attract their attention, hurried to the north end of the station, and the throng hurried in that direction. At this time Mr. Hillsrd and Mr. Buck escorted the prisoner from the south end of the station and into a carriage. Mr. Seaver joined them, and the crowd found itself disappointed. After the vehicle rolled the cabs of the newspaper men.

Taunton jail is not far removed from the center of the city and is a picturesque looking stone structure. On the outside of the structure ivy grows in profusion, and the building does not resemble, except in the material of its construction, the generally accepted appearance of a place of confinement. It has accommodations for 65 prisoners, and the women's department is on the southeast side. In this portion of the building there are but nine cells, and before the arrival of Lizzie Borden but five of these were occupied. The prisoners were confined for offences of a minor nature, as it is not customary for the officials of Bristol county to send many women to Taunton, the majority being committed to the jail at New Bedford, where there is employment for them. The matron is Mrs. Wright, wife of Sheriff Andrew J. Wright, keeper of the jail, and her personal attention is given to the female prisoners.

The officers had been notified of the coming of Miss Borden, and her arrival was unattended by any unusual ceremony inside the jail. Her step was firmer than ever as, unassisted, she walked up the three steps and into the office of the keeper. From there she was directed to the corridor which runs along the cells of the women's department, and here Mr. Hilliard left her. Returning to the office he handed the committing mittimus to Sheriff Wright, who examined and found it correct.

In the meanwhile Lizzie Borden was alone with the clergyman. He spoke words of cheer to her and left her in the care of the matron. Mr. Buck said she was not shocked at the sight of the cells, and, knowing that she was innocent, accepted the situation with a calm resignation. He said her friends would call upon her from time to time, this being allowed by the institution.

The cell in which Lizzie Borden is confined is nine and one-half feet high and seven and one-half feet wide. Across the corridor, looking through the iron bars, her gaze will rest upon whitewashed walls. The furniture of the cell consists of a bedstead, chair and washbowl, and she will spend her time in reading. All the papers regularly subscribed for by her father will be forwarded to her, but they do not include the daily newspapers. At her personal request she has seen none of these and will not do so. Consequently she is not familiar with the comments of the papers regarding the case. Taken in charge by the matron, Lizzie Borden was escorted to the cell, and the iron doors clanged behind her.

WONDERFUL FORTITUDE.

Lizzie A. Borden now occupies a small cell in the women's department of the Bristol county jail. Of all the trying scenes through which the young woman has passed, this parting from her relatives and departure from the city of her home under the charge of police officers, to mix with low criminals of both sexes, might well be supposed to be the most severe; but beyond an evident loss of strength as she entered the train at Fall River there was no evidence of anything approaching physical prostration, and her step as she alighted from the carriage at the entrance to the Taunton jail was firmer than at any time during the journey.

"She is a remarkable woman," said Marshal Hilliard, "and is possessed of wonderful power of fortitude."

"She still retains the same christian spirit of resignation as at the outset," remarked Rev. E. A. Buck, her pastor, "and her calmness is the calmness of innocence."

Whichever view may be correct, this prisoner is certainly a remarkable woman. Her demeanor is going far to cause a retention of the interest in this case, which the people do not appear at all inclined to drop, even though the government authorities express themselves satisfied that the murderer of Mr. and Mrs. Borden is now in custody. Viewed by hundreds of people in Fall River and Taunton (the crowd awaiting her arrival in the latter city being enormous), the only evidence of agitation upon her countenance was a slight flush, and even the loud remarks of the girls as they pointed her out to each other apparently failed to disturb her equanimity. Certainly in Lizzie Borden some of the weaknesses of her sex are conspicuously absent.

MRS. WRIGHT PAINED.

Perhaps no person in Taunton experienced a greater surprise and shock at the arrival of the accused than Mrs. Wright, the matron, in whose care the prisoner is. Sheriff Wright was for several years a resident of Fall River, and at one time held the position of marshal. Mr. and Mrs Wright were well acquainted with the Borden family, but the first names of their acquaintances had slipped from their memory, and the sheriff and his wife did not connect the Borden they formerly knew with the prominent actors in this tragedy.

When Lizzie entered the presence of the matron, the latter noticed something familiar in the countenance of the young woman, and after the retirement of Rev. E. A. Buck commenced to question her. Finally, after a number of questions, Mrs. Wright asked, "Are you not the Lizzie Borden who used as a child to play with my daughter Isabel?" The answer was an affirmative one, and the information touched Mrs. Wright to the quick. When she appeared in the keeper's office a few moments later her eyes were moist with tears.

MR. BORDEN'S SAFE.

An Expectation Not Realized—The Contents Gives No Clue.

It was rumored about the city Friday afternoon that a will had been found among the private papers which the opening of Andrew J. Borden's safe had revealed. This was afterwards denied by the authorities, who gave out the information that the papers consisted of deeds, insurance policies and similar documents, together with a large amount of cash. The papers were tied in a bundle and deposited in the vaults of the B. M. C. Durfee bank and will be turned over to the administrator of the estate whenever he is appointed.

It was expected that the little safe might reveal a secret or two that would shed light upon the motive which led to the crime, some memorandum or other that signified the intentions of the man in the final disposition of his property. All along in the investigation an attempt has been made to discover a reason for the crime. Every avenue of information has been travelled to the end to learn whether Mr. Borden ever had had difficulties of a social or business nature that would have incurred anybody's hatred to so malignant a degree as to lay him liable to the cowardly attack that ended his life. Nobody could be found who was likely to cherish such a feeling. Robbery was not the motive because nothing was stolen, so far as has been learned, and certainly no looting of the house was planned unless the murderer was frightened away after he had thought he had cleared the course of all the obstacles to a complete clearing out of the valuables in the house. This is by no means probable.

The only conclusion left, in the search for a motive, was the desire to gain possession of property, or the fear that it was about to slip into other hands than those by whose self-denial the building up of a fortune has been made possible. The police worked up the case with an eye fixed upon that possibility, and they have not yet abandoned it. A. J. Borden possessed real estate valued at $173,000, according to the tax assessors of Fall River; personal property worth at a moderate appraisal, $30,000 more. His wife had about $5000 in her own name. The two girls owned personally property, principally mill stocks, valued at about $10,000 each. The family was better off than several families of the Fall River Bordens who live in grand style. Mr. Borden, it is said, early set his heart on accumulating wealth for its own sake, so

THE BRISTOL COUNTY JAIL AT TAUNTON

he never spent it freely. It is alleged now that Mrs. Borden, who was a second wife, on more than one occasion spoke of having a large part of the property when her husband died. She may have meant that her husband was going to leave her property in his will, or she expected to have large property from her dower rights in case her husband died intestate. About the first suggestion one can say nothing definite. A. J. Jennings is perhaps the only man who can state whether Mr. Borden was making an inventory of his property, preliminary to writing his will, and whether Mr. Borden intended to divide his estate unequally between his wife and his daughters. If Mrs. Borden anticipated having a large estate in fee left her by the death of her husband, she was mistaken. The law in the case is confusing, but a statement of its application to the Borden case is easily made. Had Mr. Borden alone died and died intestate, Mrs. Borden would have received in the discretion of the court of probate not exceeding $5000 in real estate in fee, one half of all the real estate for use during her lifetime, with reference back to the children at her death, and such a fraction of the personal estate as the court of probate in its discretion allowed, this also for use during lifetime only. In a word, Mrs. Borden could have hoped to secure only rights to property which would depart from her control at the end of her life. In case Mr. Borden wished he could have entirely disinherited his children.

FOOTPRINTS IN THE BARN.

Why Did Not Officer Medley See John Donnelly's Tracks?

"Before saying anthing about what I saw in the Borden house, I wish to call attention to a point that seems not to have reached the inquest," said Charles H. Bryant. "John Donnelly, the hackman, was among the first to enter the barn, and walked all over the loft. Then up goes Officer Medley and takes a walk around and goes before the coroner with the highly important information that he examined the dust covered floor of the barn very carefully and could find no tracks, although he said he could easily distinguish his own. Now if he could distinguish his own so easily, why didn't he find John Donnelly's, and if he couldn't find John Donnelly's heavy prints, how could he expect to find Lizzie Borden's? The air is full of theories. I'd like to hear a few people explain that.

"I was engaged as an expert," said Bryant, "and carried out the instructions of the authorities. I do not know Lizzie nor Emma Borden, one from the other, but both were in the house and gave me every assistance. Indeed, if anything, I thought they were over anxious that I should make a complete examination.

"So far as the chimneys were concerned I saw at a glance that it was useless to tear them open, for I could see through every flue in the house, and I told them so, but still the district attorney told me to go ahead, and I dug into them. That finished, I asked Miss Borden if there were any flues in the garret, such as might have been put in for a stove at some time, and she said she did not know, but I had better look. I made a careful examination, but found nothing. Then we made inquiries about an alleged cistern said to be in the cellar, and the girls said there had been at some time, but it was an old wooden affair, which had doubtless been filled up; at any rate she had not seen it for a long time. They told us what part of the cellar it had been in, and we pried round there for some time with a crowbar and found nothing.

"During the whole time the girls, as I say, were at our service and expressed every willingness to show us through the house, giving us the keys to all the rooms. I was in every room in the house except the front entry and observed things closely all the while. I may say that the house is furnished very plainly—notably so. The ordinary American mechanic with an ordinary salary has his house furnished as well. There was nothing in the house to indicate the wealth of the people who lived there."

"Did you know Andrew J. Borden?"

"Not intimately, but I know he was a close-fisted business man. Here's an incident: As one of a committee of the Knights of Pythias I called upon him to see about leasing his lot on Main and Anawan streets where his big block now stands. He said he could call at the lodge rooms the next night and did so, and without any ado went straight to the business. He said he would lease the lot for a term of twenty or fifty years on a sliding scale of its assessed valuation, asking nothing but six percent. on that amount. That struck us as very favorable; then he added as the condition that we build a structure costing not less than $65,000. That was all right. Then he added that at the end of the lease the building should belong to the estate.That knocked the whole thing. But you see how careful he was on behalf of his heirs, for he must have been dead at the expiration of the lease by 30 years at least,living his allotted time. We wanted him to provide for the sale to the estate at a figure to be fixed by judges, but he had said his say and would hear to nothing else. That is an incident fairly illustrative of Andrew J. Borden's character. He is well known to have been a hard business man, but I do not know that his treatment of his daughters was such as to furnish a possible motive for such a deed as this."

"I was passing the house on the day of the murder soon after the police arrived on the scene," said John Donnelly, "and an officer asked me to come and look around. You know it was the day of the policemen's picnic and the force was short. I told him it was none of my business,but he said it was the business of every citizen. So I called Charley Cook and we two examined the grounds, the fences and windows, and found nothing of a suspicious nature. Then we went into the barn and climbed into the loft. We were among the first, if not the first, persons to go into the loft after the murder. I noticed the little pile of hay—hay that had been cut from the Borden yard—and remarked that it looked as though some one had been sleeping or lying upon it, but I saw nothing there of a more suspicious nature than that."

To Continue the Investigation.

"Shall you rest your investigations in the case with the arrest of Lizzie Borden?" asked a HERALD reporter of Marshal Hilliard today.

"By no means," was the reply. "Every reasonable clue that is offered will be investigated. We have three men at work on out of town clues today, and we hold two officers for special duty in the city. The guard we have left at the house consists of but one officer in citizen's dress, at the request of the family, to drive away curiosity seekers who might annoy the family."

The latest clue (and this incident illustrates the willingness of the police to still follow clues) was run to earth yesterday afternoon. For some time past a man has haunted the central station with a story about another man. The other man had been seen diving in and out of the swamp land near the Chace mill. Smoke was seen rising from this same swamp land, and the conclusion arrived at was that the man should be captured and the fire which made the smoke stamped out. Accordingly,Officers Harrington and Doherty went over the Chace mill district yesterday and came back as wise as they went. The report that came from Stone Bridge of a man who was driven to Newport Thursday by Gideon Manchester and who was unusually nervous and talked about the murder all the way is being investigated. This man is said to correspond to Dr. Handy's man.

NEWSPAPER MEN GO HOME.

The Borden case will be kept constantly before the public by the report of proceedings from time to time as they occur, but the murder and the accompanying incidents will gradually lose their prominence in the newspapers after this week. Friday night the representatives of the New York papers, of which the Sun, World, Herald and Recorder had special men in the city during the week, returned home, and the Boston men who represented the Herald, Globe, Post and Journal will leave today or Monday.

Immense amount of matter has been handled at the telegraph offices. Manager Coffin of the Western Union and Manager Reagan of the Postal Telegraph offices in this city have worked night and day to accommodate the newspapers. Operators have been secured from every place where a man could be spared. For all that the resources of the offices were taxed to the utmost, and it is estimated that 100,000 words a night were the average for the two offices in the first days succeeding the tragedy.

Quiet at the Station.

A visitor to the central station today would never imagine from the quietness that prevails that it had been the scene of more than feverish excitement for the past nine days. Everything is proceeding as though a person accused of one of the most horrible crimes perpetrated in the christian era had never been lodged within its walls,and that person an individual who had beed reared in this city and been prominent in church missions and charities. A smile of contentment is noticeable on the officials' faces now that Miss Borden is not in their custody, although a feeling of sorrow is expressed at the young woman's connection with the unfortunate affair.

Every member of the force has worked with energy in the matter, and even if they do not prove their case it will be impossible to ascribe it to any blunder on their part. The officials have been more than ready to listen to clues and to theories on the question, and no matter from where they eminated all have been thoroughly examined. It is freely said that if Mr. Jennings persists in having an examination a week from Monday the evidence presented by the government will bê of such a nature as to leave no doubt in the public's mind as to the perpetrator of the crime.

Strong Legal Talent.

Lawyer Jennings, Minister Buck and Emma Borden paid a flying visit to Taunton this morning, remaining at the jail but a short time. It was said that Lizzie was bearing up under her heavy burden with more than christian fortitude, and that the rest in her new quarters, if rest it could be called, was taken with a determination to retain the little strength and self-possession she is now mistress of for the severe and rigid torture of a public examination.

Mr. Buck was asked about the employment of extra legal talent and stated that the best obtainable would be secured for the defendant. He would not answer the question as to whether Burke Cockran or Gen. Butler had been retained.

That Manchester Story.

The clue given in Friday's HERALD, telling of the supposed whereabouts of the mysterious man seen by Dr. Handy, was followed up by a HERALD reporter Friday night. Gideon Manchester, by whom the story was told, was interviewed at his post, the Stone Bridge draw. Manchester's home is just across on the Portsmouth side. In response to inquiries the draw tender said that as he got the story the man answered in every way the description given by Dr. Handy. The man who drove him to Newport was Oscar Manchester, postmaster of the Newton office. Gideon said he was not certain that he was the one, but acting on the information the scribe drove to Newton.

Oscar Manchester was in bed, but was quickly routed out. He emphatically denied that he had driven a stranger to Newport; he appeared somewhat staggered when the the question direct was put to him. He was pretty sure, however, that John Manchester, living at Bristol Ferry, was the one who conveyed the stranger.

John Manchester of Bristol Ferry goes to Newport every day, and he is probably the man who carried the mysteriouse fellow.

NOTES.

Detective Hanscom was in the city last night. He had a conference with Andrew Jennings and left for Boston on the 9:40 train. The purpose of his visit could not be learned. It was concluded that he is at work on clues out of town and has by no means been dismissed from the case. Hanscom bears the reputation of being one of the shrewdest men in the Pinkerton service, and it will be interesting to know the direction of his work and his theory on the case. What he is doing apparently with the greatest success is keeping still. He may be heard from later on and before the hearing Aug. 22.

The inquest, Judge Blaisdell decided last night, would not be reopened before Monday. The delay is to give the police time to work out some points they are in possession of, because all the authorities are tired out.

Medical Examiner Dolan has not yet heard from the chemical analyses. He says that the stories which came from Boston last night describing the axe were "faked."

It is the opinion of most of the lawyers of this city that Judge Blaisdell was the only person who had a right to preside at the inquest. It was not right to assume that his mind would be prejudiced by the testimony he had heard. Miss Borden had entered the room and had given all the information she knew of the matter. She did not go as a criminal, but as a witness, and if her own testimony or that of others pointed toward her the judge was in duty bound to issue a warrant for her arrest. It would not be right to place a special justice on the bench at the preliminary examination, as it would seem as though he tried to throw the responsibility off his shoulders. By Mr. Jennings forcing an examination, he will compel the government to show its hand somewhat, and thus when the case goes to the supreme court the attorney for the defence will not be as much in the dark as at present.

The bodies of Mr. and Mrs. Borden in the vault at the Oak Grove cemetery are still guarded day and night by the police.

A Taunton dispatch says: Miss Borden passed a comfortable night and this morning was cheerful to an unusual degree, brought about perhaps by the prospect of a visit from her sister. Mr. Jennings and Emma came up this morning, and the former after a brief conversation, went away, leaving Emma in the cell with her sister. The two conversed in low tones for some time, but there were no tears, no complainings, and the whole affair had the appearance of a simple, ordinary every-day visit between friends. During part of the time Lizzie was occupied with some sewing which she had brought with her. It is understood that the coming examination has no terrors for her, for under no circumstances will she open her mouth and Mr. Jennings will do all the talking necessary.

OPINIONS FROM OTHER NEWSPAPERS

The Providence Journal

If the Fall River police want to find the real criminal in the Borden case they had better keep a sharp eye on the newspaper correspondents who are there. A Boston contemporary publishes pictures of them, and we are free to say that we have seldom seen a more villainous looking lot. The only consoling reflection is that perhaps these alleged portraits do not do the subjects full justice.

The Newport Observer

Certainly, their star-chamber procedure is little calculated to inspire public confidence in their course in treating Miss Borden as an accused and at the same time denying her the advice of counsel and friends, in order to scrape together enough circumstantial evidence to warrant the arrest. The interest of a community and of every member in it requires that in all judicial proceedings, especially in those of a criminal nature, there should be the fullest publicity.

The Lowell Times

In our judgment, if the Fall River authorities have erred, the error has been not in being slothful or inactive, but in sticking too closely to the first impression that a member of the household must be the guilty one. That Lizzie Borden is guilty can only be accepted after every other possibility is exploded, and even then it must rest on something much more tangible than anything now known.

The Boston Record

The case has not ceased by any means to be a mystery of the most notable order. The terrible problem is still unsolved. Hundreds of people in Fall River, including her most intimate friends and the most conservative authorities, still believe Miss Borden innocent. This appears fully in today's despatches. Until the girl's guilt shall have been proven beyond a doubt, it is no more than common charity to hold aloof and suspend judgment.

New Bedford Journal

It must be presumed that the inquest in the Borden case has brought out some important facts not yet in the possession of the public, otherwise it is hardly conceivable that the authorities could have decided to arrest Miss Borden. The arrest deepens rather than lessens the mystery. The young woman may know more about the murders than she tells, but that she should herself have struck the fatal blow seems to us impossible.

The Fall River Herald

DIVIDED OPINION

As to the Guilt of the Taunton Prisoner.

CONFIDENCE OF THE CHURCH PEOPLE IN INNOCENCE.

Clues Inquired into and Proved to be Worthless.

A NEW BEDFORD MAN'S LETTER FROM THE OTHER WORLD.

A. J. Borden Speaks to the Public Through a Medium.

Although Lizzie Borden is behind the bars at Taunton accused of the murder of her father, the public mind is beginning to waver as to the chances of conviction. Now that the excitement attending the tragedy has somewhat abated, people are calmly considering the possibilities of the trial.

Of course it is impossible to tell what evidence the government has kept back, but from what is publicly known it is not thought by the legal minds of the city that the prisoner can be convicted. The fact that the government specifically charges that the deed was perpetrated with a hatchet would indicate that the district attorney felt sure of a conviction on that line. This is more strongly indicated when it is known that to issue the warrant it would not be necessary to specify the weapon with which the deed was committed.

What facts were given at the inquest is unknown to the general public, although statements have been made about discrepancies. As to the length of time she spent in the barn it is possible that the young woman may be wrong, but that is not considered of much moment when it is remembered that but few people can accurately account for their every movement during the day. People are also wondering why this hatchet with its speck of blood or rust was allowed to remain in the station house for two days before it was subjected to a powerful glass. Even if it was done in that time the police are very reticent, and it is impossible to learn what the substance was that marked the hatchet.

No matter where a person goes—in the city, in the country, on the river or at the seashore—the murder continues to be the principal theme of conversation. People can hardly believe that a young woman, highly educated and on whom the breath of scandal had never fallen, could coolly and calmly carry out the fiendish plot, or to even have been an accessory to it. The thought that after killing her stepmother she could go about the house for an hour awaiting the arrival of her father, and, after seeing him comfortably resting on the sofa, steal up behind him and brutally hack him to pieces is something terrible to contemplate. The cool manner in which she has conducted herself since the crime has made a great many people marvel. To some it is an indication of innocence, while others say it is an indication of what the young woman could do if she had made her mind up.

The stand taken by Mr. Jennings in demanding an immediate trial had much to do in turning the tide of sympathy in favor of the accused. By doing this the course pursued at the star chamber examination will have to be exposed to a great degree, but the government will fight hard not to introduce any more evidence than is necessary to bind Miss Borden to appear before the grand jury. Whether the girl is guilty or not, fair-minded people hold that the law should be used to protect as well as punish, and the keeping back of testimony, and especially so when it is of a circumstantial nature, is held to be unjust. The government has all opportunities to form theories, and the defence is expected to answer in a moment what it will take the police three months to build up. On this point it is thought to be no more than right that all the evidence should be given to the public on Monday next.

Another question that is being talked about is the positson which Judge Blaisdell holds. There is no question but what he is right in his stand, but people interested in the case ask if he considered that there was enough evidence at the time of the inquest to cause an arrest, how it will be possible when the matter comes before his attention again for the prisoner to be released? There can be no question as to how Lawyer Jennings will fight. He will endeavor to have the prisoner discharged at the hearing, and as a result the government will have to show considerable more evidence than has been given out to satisfy the public mind that Miss Borden should be retained in custody.

PINKERTON'S VIEW.

He Seems to Think the Crime Committed by an Insane Person.

Robert Pinkerton gave his views on the Borden murders to a New York reporter Saturday. He said he had not studied the case from a detective's standpoint, but only through the newspapers.

When asked if he thought the murderer an insane person, he said: "Judging from what I have read about the case, it seems to me that the person who killed Mr. and Mrs. Borden must have been insane, but I would not care to be quoted as advancing an insanity theory."

Continuing he said: "It seems strange that there are no more conclusive clues to be followed if the reports of bloodstained walls and ceiling are true. If they are in such a condition the murderer must have gone away with blood stains on his clothing. Now where are these bloody clothes? The mere fact that Miss Borden has told conflicting stories is more in her favor than if she had unhesitatingly stuck to the same tale, as an innocent person is more likely to make conflicting statements than is a guilty one."

Concerning the Pinkerton detective who was placed on the case and who was severely criticised by the Fall River authorities, he said: "The authorities seem to have thought that our detective was brought into the case for the purpose of protecting Lizzie Borden from them. Such was not the case. He was hired by the family to follow any clues that might lead to the detection of the criminal. He has been removed at my suggestion, as I thought it unwise to have a private on the case until the authorities had reached some decision." The lawyer who has charge of Miss Borden's interests Mr. Pinkerton considers a very clever man, and thinks her interests will not suffer while under his care.

A Talk with Matron Wright.

"Miss Borden," said Matron Wright of the Taunton jail, "is remarkably calm and self-contained, even cheerful; today I allowed her to walk in the corridor after her sister came. They walked up and down for some time, talking, even conversing with one of the prisoners, who told her story, and for whom they expressed their sympathy. Miss Borden, despite her calm, did not sleep at all Friday night, nor eat anything from the time she entered until noon Saturday; then she and her sister dined together, a nice dinner being sent over from the hotel, where we ordered it at their request.

"Believe her guilty?

"No, I can't. I said so to her when she first came, and the only emotion she has shown came then. She looked up at me quickly, and said in a surprised way: "'Oh! you don't? Oh, Mrs. Wright!' and she threw her arms about me, as if it was more than she could stand of relief to find any one who had not turned against her outside of her own sister and most intimate friends.

"It is my duty to look over whatever a woman committed here brings with her. Miss Borden had beside her clothes, a folding bag filled with books."

"What were they?"

"Her bible, her testament, and so on, every one of them a religious work of some description. She has not felt like reading any yet, but it will help to make the time less long for her."

Sympathy in Taunton.

There is a strong feeling of sympathy expressed here for Lizzie Borden, says a Taunton correspondent, strong because the family had many friends here and the general character of Lizzie as understood by those friends pecluded any possibility of their believing at this stage in anything but her entire innocence.

The prison physician remarked as she passed from view: "That woman is a study, a wonder." Mrs. Wright, her motherly instincts alert, went to the cell in which Miss Borden had been placed with a refreshing glass of water and the young lady then showed the first signs of interest in her surroundings and her thanks for the boon came straight from the heart.

Taunton jail has had the honor of sheltering many of Fall River's distinguished citizens, but the latest accession in this line is the strangest and most distinguished of all. And she is one of the now celebrated Central church flock, too, from whose portals there appears to have come so many erring ones, as those who will recollect the Hathaway-Chace-Stickney muddle may call to mind.

IN THE JAIL.

The Rules Not Relaxed for Sunday Observance by the Sheriff.

As became the Sabbath, absolute quiet, so for as might be, prevailed in and about the present abiding place of Lizzie Borden. Here, to be sure, the Sunday pedestrian, with his wife and children, sweetheart or friend, went out of his way to pass down Hodges avenue and stop before the Bristol county jail—with which most of them were quite familiar—and look up at its barred windows. They wondered just where her cell was, and discussed the awful deed with which she is charged. People who were taking their Sunday outing behind horses drove around that way, and the conversation, if it had not been dwelling upon it before, then took the turn of wondering if she could possibly have done it.

A few people—they were women all—came to the town from distances as far as Boston, in the hope of being permitted to attend the Sunday services in the jail, and thus perhaps get a glimpse of the woman about whom all New England is talking; but for the reason that there are no Sunday services during August they were not permitted beyond the office, where Sheriff Wright remains on guard.

The rules of the prison say that no visitors shall be admitted on Sunday. So far as Lizzie Borden is concerned, these rules, says the sheriff, shall be adhered to on all other days, save with regard to her sister, her lawyer, her pastor and, if need be, her doctor. "I do not believe that the public has a right to know anything of this girl's life within these walls; when she gets up and when she lies down, and what she eats and drinks, and when she does either," says the sheriff. "She herself wishes not to be disturbed, and I am not going to allow her to be disturbed. Nor shall I relate these petty incidents of her life here."

That the public, the right-thinking public, will commend the sheriff's stand in this regard there can be no question. Miss Borden has been made as comfortable in her quarters as is possible under the regulations. Mrs. Wright's sympathetic hand has changed the prison pillow and placed in its stead a soft one from her own bed, also a rocking chair and stool. Some bright bits of color and other things calculated to soften the abrupt contrast with the unhappy girl's own room in the desolated home at Fall River have found their way into the prison cell. Her friends may be reassured in the thought of this kindly woman's constant presence with her in the prison.

"Does not the fact that this prisoner has not been convicted of any crime as yet exempt her from the regulations that apply to others?" was asked by the sheriff.

"She can buy what she wishes to eat and it will be brought to her, and have other little comforts that may be supplied to her; otherwise, there is no difference," he replied.

The prisoners in the Taunton jail are required to rise at 6 o'clock. Their breakfast of fish hash, bread and coffee is served at 7. On Sunday a dinner of meat, a few vegetables and water is served after 1 o'clock. Lizzie arose with the others at 6 o'clock and made her own bed. She had slept brokenly, but was still refreshed. She drank a cup of coffee and a mere bite of bread, but wanted nothing more until noon. A little after that hour an expressman brought a dinner from the bill of fare of the City hotel, some blocks away, made up of tempting dishes. Of this she partook quite heartily. She is reported not to have suffered a return of the nausea, which overtook her on the day of her arrest, and of which she stands in dread. She maintains that poise which has been the wonder of all since this tragedy and its mystery has turned so many eyes upon her.

LOTS OF ADVICE

Tendered the Marshal by Persons with Fancies of Different Kinds.

"There is no end to the letters of advice and counsel," said Mr. Hilliard Sunday, "and the theories I am receiving on this case. Persons write telling me to do this and that. I have a host of offers from clairvoyants, who offer, for so much money, to put me in the way of getting the murderer. Now, while I won't say that there is nothing in spiritualism, still they would have to convince me pretty positively that it was really a communication from any deceased friend of mine before I would give it much thought. If any man sends in a clue or statement of any suspicious man seen, even if it looks like a fake, I will send an officer who will not stop until he has run it down, but this correspondence is from cranks or people endeavoring to get some money by working on the case.

"Here is a good specimen of many of them, a letter from a woman, and reads: 'Your honor, I am a person born with the qualifications of a detective, and if you would like to try my skill in that direction I will officiate by asking suspected persons questions, thereby causing them to confess the deed if they be guilty. I should require you to send me $8 by post-office order to pay expenses for myself and husband there and back. How much would I get if I was the cause of the guilty parties confessing the truth?'

"It is needless to say that I hardly felt as though the lady's services were required. There are a number of others like this from women who rate their ability to obtain confessions very highly. Here is a clairvoyart, one from Rochester, N. Y. The writer, in putting forth her abilities, is also candid enough to admit she will also be making a good thing out of the transaction. She writes:

'Dear sir—I am a great clairvoyant and I have the charm in this world that I could make the parties give out who murdered them. If you want to buy this charm you can have it. I am poor and if I can make a couple of thousand dollars it would be good for me and that would save you a great deal of trouble.'

"A charm is a good thing, but really I don't thing the one she wants $2000 for would be of enough use to warrant our purpose. I received a great many from clairvoyants, but they are all in the same general tenor of this one. They hope that I will think enough of their abilities to engage them to transmit the name of the murderer from the murdered people to me. I have found some queer people in the world since I have been at work upon this murder. Here is a man whose father was mysteriously killed, and he evidently thinks some gang like the mafia had a hand in this double murder. This man writes from Boston, and so as to be sure I had opportunities of using his idea in this case, he sent this letter written two days after the murder. This is his letter:

"'Dear sir:—Why not clear up this mystery by an examination of the retina of the eye of one or both of the murdered parties? If either were conscious at the time of the murder, the last object seen by them will be found impressed thereon. In the case of Mrs. Borden it would be a sure test, I would think, if she turned, as is supposed, and faced the assassin. Dark mysteries have been brought to light in this manner by the means of photography. Do not care to be known at present.' He signed it 'Detective,' and writes a bold hand, like a person of some education. This is the most unique of the many theories that I have received. 'Pro Bono Publico' the day after the murder sent an idea founded probably on his knowledge that there are mills here. He thinks I ought to work upon the anarchist theory. This is how he puts it:

"'Dear sir—I would suggest that you make inquiries as to whether Mr. Borden said or wrote anything to excite the hatred, malice and murderous vengeance of the anarchists during the recent Homestead troubles, and did he have any money dealing with persons who may be supposed to have sympathies with anarchists? Was the person who in angry talk threatened Mr. B. with getting even with him an anarchist? Finally, if this heinous crime cannot be traced to the door of some one in the house, a member of the family, then why not suspect the anarchists of it on general principles?'

"A number of letters are evidently written in good faith and with an honest endeavor to be of some assistance, but most of them are like those I have read. It shows how extensive the knowledge of this case has been and also the interest taken in its solution. In this murder, as in all of my cases, I do not want any innocent person convicted. I would rather any time see 20 guilty men go than one innocent be convicted. I am bound to work everything in the nature of clues or information given me."

ECCENTRIC, BUT HONEST.

John V. Morse as Known by His Far-Western Neighbors.

A Hastings, Ia., dispatch says: This place was for about 25 years, and in a sense is yet, the home of John V. Morse, upon whom some suspicion of complicity in the mysterious murder of the Bordens at Fall River, Mass., for a time rested. Miss Lizzie Borden has sent Detective Hanscom out here to investigate relative to Morse's past life.

The people of Hastings, and particularly John Davidson, Morse's brotherinlaw, are awaiting the arrival of the Pinkerton expert with much interest. Morse came here in 1869 from Illinois, where he had been a farmer with the exception of two or three years, during which, while a young man, he learned the butcher's trade. Morse has been a farmer ever since.

In Illinois he was a renter. During this period he saved up something less than $1000, and then came here and bought land; he now owns two farms, 220 acres in all, of the finest land in Miles county. Both of these farms lie directly south of Hastings, only a mile and a half from the town. One of them has a very fine, large house on it, a large barn and is otherwise as well improved as any farm in the county.

Morse has never married, but it is the theory of those who know him best that he at one time contemplated marriage and that he improved his farm with a view to marrying some day and making this place his home. He was always regarded by his neighbors as a very eccentric and peculiar man. He never, apparently, formed any close friendships, always maintaining a close reserve that checked the slightest approach to intimacy, and in all his dealings was close almost to the point of penuriousness. But he was always strictly honest. The years he spent here were years of the strictest frugality, of self-denial that amounted almost to miseriiness. Even after he became comparatively well off there was no relaxation in his frugal habits. He would drive to town in an old rattle-trap lumber wagon using a pine board for a seat when he could just as well have afforded a buggy. He would wear the same suit of clothes everywhere and on all occasions, and one suit usually lasted him two or three years. Indeed, it is pretty certain that the suit he is now wearing at Fall River is the same he wore when he left here two years ago.

WHERE BRIDGET SULLIVAN STAYED DURING THE INQUEST

WORDS FROM THE PULPIT.

The Rev. Dr. Mason's Words of Sympathy for the Stricken Miss Borden.

The Rev. Dr. Mason of the Bowdoin college church, Brunswick, Me., supplied the pulpit at the Central Congregational church Sunday morning, where union services were held. In opening the services Mr. Mason prayed tenderly and sympathetically that the Lord would be with the stricken Miss Borden in her present misery; that he would give her strength to bear up under the terrible load that is oppressing her. Dr. Mason took the simple and appropriate words "Our Father" for the text of his sermon, and during his discourse made the following reference to the Borden murder: "A great, dark cloud has settled down upon one of our families. But God is in that cloud. He is with that poor; tried, tempest-tossed girl; he will give her strength and peace; he will make her glad. It is impossible for a wrong to be done in this world that eternity will not undo. Good is coming; good out of evil; light out of darkness. The father is over all. He will vindicate, and raise and glorify."

In many of the churches the ministers referred to the sad tragedy which has so excited our city for the past ten days. At the United Presbyterian church the Rev. W. J. Martin, who had preached a week before on the tragedy,treating the causes which generaly led to deeds of violence as either the vindictive anger or the desire of speedy gain, spoke from the words, "judge not according to the appearance, but judge righteous judgment." Mr. Martin noted that the caution had reference only to the manner in which judgment should be exercised. Humanity is called to exercise its judgment faculty, and at proper times men are to express their judgments. Mere appearance is variable and, moreover, often things are not what they seem. Righteous judgment requires a proper standard and evidence. There is needed honesty of spirit and a measure of the judicial temperament, or the decrees of the mind will not be trustworthy. But given these, the right is to be sought and, when found, commended; wrong is to be traced and when discovered is to be reprobated. Praise is to be administered to them who do good, censure to them who do wrong. Suspension of judgment is altogether proper while the processes are going on with desire to attain truth and right.

Chasing Down Clues.

The police have been engaged in chasing down clues and testing statements made in many letters sent to the marshal. It is Lizzie Borden's side of the case that is now attracting the whole attention of the police. The report that Gideon Manchester, draw tender at Stone Bridge, had seen Dr. Handy's wild eyed man being driven towards Newport by his brother has been proven to be untrue. Manchester's brother has been dead three years. Officers Harrington and Doherty have been all over Rhode Island in an unsuccessful search to determine who drove the suspect to Newport.

The story Almer Coggeshall told the police about his son having heard cries from the Borden house the morning of the murder amounts to nothing. His son was at work at Forest Hill, two miles from the scene, all day Thursday, Aug. 4.

The police have spent some time running down the statement made that suspicious characters were seen going toward New Bedford, but without success.

The Prisoner's Self Control.

On Friday afternoon before the carriages arrived at the police station Miss Borden said:

"I suppose they're going to take me to Taunton, aren't they?"

"Yes, Lizzie," the matron replied, "I hear that you are going to Taunton this afternoon."

"They seem to do as they please with me," Miss Borden continued. "They have taken me from my home in a carriage, driven me back and forth and kept me here over night. Now they are going to take me to Taunton. They're having their own way now, but later on it will be my turn." Those were about the last words the prisoner uttered before she was driven to the depot.

Resolution of Confidence.

Sunday night, at the regular weekly prayer meeting of the Y. P. S. C. E. of the Central church, of which Lizzie A. Borden is one of the most active members, the following resolution was unanimously adopted to be sent to Miss Borden, with flowers: "We, the members of the Young People's society of Christian Endeavor, desire to express to our fellow member, Miss Lizzie A. Borden, our sincere sympathy with her in her present hour of trial, and our confident belief that she will soon be restored to her former place of usefulness among us."

Why She Rested.

A Taunton Gazette reporter learned from Bridget Sullivan on Sunday that the reason she lay down on the day of the Borden murders was because she was troubled with nausea that morning and vomited several times while washing windows. Previous statements from the police have been to the effect that she lay down because she was tired with the work. It is probable that this statement was held back, if made known at the inquest, as bearing on the theory that the victims may have been dosed.

Providence Journal

If Lizzie Borden committed the crime for which she has been arraignsd—and it cannot be too often insisted, in justice to her, that the whole case, so far as it has been made public, is purely hypothetical—had she any accomplices? Was the crime the result of a deep-laid plot, and did others than herself expect to profit by it? This is an aspect of the case which is by no means clear. That the police expect something of the sort has been asserted more than once. But they have held the servant and Mr. Morse—who might have been implicated—merely as witnesses upon a nominal bond, which seems to remove all suspicion from them.

The Newport News

The case has now assumed a serious aspect for Miss Borden, and even her warmest friends have occasion to fear the result. Circumstances are certainly against her, though it is too early, especially in the absence of the testimony, to form decided opinions.

Brockton Enterprise

But upon what sufficient evidence is this crusade against Lizzie Borden being conducted? She may be the murderess, but what evidence is there of it that excuses the efforts that have been put forth to prove her guilty? If the police have had cnoclusive evidence against her, why wasn't she arrested several days ago? If they had but slender support for their theories, what good reason have they for cornering this woman, heaping up evidence of no value against her and branding her, to all intents and purposes, as the slayer of Andrew J. Borden and his wife?—

The Fall River Herald

WHAT CONSTITUTES PUBLIC OPINION?

"Public opinion," says the Attleboro Sun, "thus far does not sustain the Fall River authorities in the arrest of Miss Borden." Intelligent public opinion can neither condemn nor sustain the police, for the all sufficient reason that the few facts that have percolated through the meshes of the veil of secrecy that envelops the case afford no ground upon which to predicate judgment of the guilt or innocence of the accused young woman. Everyone has his notions, but nothing, aside from the arrest of Lizzie Borden, has transpired to make them definitive.

Until the facts are disclosed at the examination it will be foolish to attempt to guage the state of the public mind. As one swallow does not make a summer, it is the height of egotism for an editor to arrogate to himself the honor of voicing public opinion when he indites his ideas. Nobody has the right to be regarded as Sir Oracle in treating of the Borden case. Everyone has the right to freedom of thought, but he has no right to reach a conclusion or to formulate a theory based on ignorance, and to condemn all who refuse to accept it.

A CONTEMPORARY ITEM

Fall River's Giddy Girls.

A citizen of this town who keeps his eyes open was talking the other evening. "There are some young girls in this city," he said with great energy, "who are going to the devil as fast as a horse can trot. They are loafing about the streets afternoons and evenings and Sundays. They dress as flashily as they dare, they have their eyes open for everything that's going on about them, and they know as much now about the 'dark side of life' as their mothers did at twenty-five. You'll find them nights about the corridors of the business blocks, talking with oversmart youths and with men, knowing everybody and known to everybody, the police included. What kind of a future are these girls laying out for themselves? And what stories do they tell their mothers to excuse themselves for the hours they are keeping? That's the part of it that gets me." Then the citizen walked away to ruminate over the degeneracy of these times.

The New York Times

NOT IMPRISONED IN HASTE

WHAT FALL RIVER'S MARSHAL SAYS OF MISS BORDEN'S ARREST

FALL RIVER, Mass., Aug 15.-The case of Lizzie Borden, charged with the murder of her father and stepmother, assumes no new features as the time for the preliminary hearing approaches. It has been noticeable here since yesterday forenoon that intelligent persons have ceased giving positive opinions on the merits of the case. Temperate-minded people will not talk at length about facts, but will argue that no fairer trial can be secured than may be had in this city. There has never been an intense feeling here against Miss Borden, despite the weight of the charge made against her. One topic of discussion relating to the crime is the small bail furnished by the principal Government witnesses, Miss Sullivan and Mr. Morse, each being held in only $500.

City Marshal Hilliard said to-day: "This case will depend on circumstantial evidence wholly, and the people's interest cannot be subserved by throwing the evidence into the hands of the defense until a hearing of the trial takes place. The District Attorney and myself are satisfied that the public authorities have ample cause for holding Miss Borden, and she has not been imprisoned in haste nor without a full understanding of what her arrest means."

The Marshal's statement has given rise to much speculation as to the character of the evidence that the prosecution can submit at the trial. The preliminary trial is not now regarded as of special importance in fixing the responsibility for the crime, except that it gives the defense an opportunity to measure the strength of the Government's case. It is an even chance that the verdict will be "probably guilty". If the verdict should be "probably not guilty," the Government could still insist on placing the case before the Grand Jury and demand an indictment over a discharge ordered by a lower court.

A great deal is being published in connection with the case about the Borden family honor. On this point the most important member of the Borden family said for publication this morning: "The honor of the Bordens, whose names are so closely allied with the prosperity of the town, is not to be affected by a police suspicion perhaps resting justly on Miss Lizzie Borden. No true Borden has ever placed a stumbling block in the way of the law and no member of my family will in any way hamper the police in their investigation."

The Fall River Herald

ILLUSTRATED AMERICAN DRAWING - EMMA, LIZZIE AND REV. BUCK

The Boston Advertiser

MISS BORDEN'S SIDE

OF THE MURDER CASE NOW ATTRACTS ATTENTION.

POLICE BELIEVE HER INSANE IF SHE COMMITTED THE MURDERS.

No Communication from Prof. Wood Regarding the Blood Stains—Letters to the City Marshal from Cranks in All Parts of the Country—The Preliminary Hearing Aug. 22 Will Probably be of Short Duration.

FALL RIVER, Aug. 14.—It is Miss Lizzie Borden's side of the murder case that is now occupying the attention of people and police in this city. A revulsion of feeling in her favor naturally followed the arrest, and, added to this, the steady work of Attorney Jennings at the time of the arraignment has done much to change public opinion concerning the girl, more particularly that position referring to a fair trial by an impartial judge. Although Miss Borden is under arrest, charged with, perhaps, the most heinous crime committed in recent years, there is little talk about the punishment that should be meted out to her. She is finding supporters and friends in most unexpected places. Ordinarily, people would say that the punishment should be as severe as the laws would sanction, but in Miss Borden's case, almost nothing is said about the punishment of the suspected criminal. The talk is almost entirely regarding her chances of proving her innocence. This fact gives additional interest to her preliminary trial and also gives the police authorities reason to think that much strong evidence will have to be given before Attorney Jennings will consent to an order for holding his client until November.

It is an open secret in police circles that the government officers believe that Miss Borden was insane at the time of the murders, if she committed them. It is well known in this city that Judge Blaisdell and District Attorney Knowlton were prejudiced in Miss Borden's favor and they must have had the strongest possible reasons for ordering her arrest. Some evidence relating to the private life of Miss Borden now in the hands of the police, bears directly on this side of the case and strengthens the opinion of the high police authorities who have said that Miss Borden was not conscious of her deeds if she was implicated.

Neither Medical Examiner Dolan nor City Marshal Hilliard have heard anything from Prof. Wood, who is analyzing the contents of the stomachs of the victims and examining and comparing the spots of blood on the axe and carpet. The former says if there is any truth in the reports that Wood has discovered that the blood upon the axe and carpets is the same, it is very strange he has not heard it officially. The police today have been engaged in chasing down clews and testing statements made in many letters sent to the marshal.

No spiritualist nor crank theorists have visited the marshal during the day, but he shows the strangest imaginable collection of letters from all parts of the country, suggesting ways and means to locate the criminal.

It is not thought now that the preliminary hearing set down for the 22nd inst., will be of long duration. It has been the policy of District Attorney Knowlton in handling capital crimes to give as little evidence as possible until the trial takes place. Attorney Jennings, who beyond question, believes in the innocence of Miss Borden, will do everything in his power to have full examination at the earliest date.

At the Central Congregational church, of which the Borden family were members, union services were held, attended by the members of the first and central churches. The pulpit was filled by Rev. Dr. Mason, Bowdoin College, Brunswick, Me. He spoke on the words, "Our Father." In opening his sermon he spoke tenderly of the young girl of his flock who was stricken down with misery. He prayed that the Lord might grant her strength to bear up under the terrible oppression now her lot. Continuing he said: "A great dark cloud has settled upon one of the families of this congregation, but God is within the cloud. He is with that poor, tried, tempest-tossed girl. He will give her strength and peace and will make her soul glad." In closing he said: "For I am persuaded that neither length nor breath, height or depth, neither things present nor to come, nor any creature, shall be able to separate us from the love of God."

THE BORDEN GENEALOGY.

A Family of Social and Business Prominence for Nine Generations.

FALL RIVER, Aug. 14.—The high social standing of all connected with the Borden tragedy is hardly realized outside of this city. The Bordens are one of the leading families, if not indeed the leading family, in Fall River. If the statement is modified by saying that the Borden and Durfee families are the most important in Fall River the assertion will be absolutely correct.

The industries of Fall River were chiefly developed in the early years of the present century through the exertions of Richard and Jefferson Borden, Bradford and Nathan Durfee and Holder Borden. These men, associated together and as individuals, built and conducted the cotton mills, organized transportation companies, formed the first of the great joint stock companies that now carry on the manufacture of cotton in the city, and in general were the creators of the industrial and financial organizations of Fall River. Of the men named, the two most conspicuous were Richard Borden and Bradford Durfee. Jefferson Borden was a brother of Richard and Holder Borden was a distant relative.

The Borden family was founded in America in 1635 by a Richard Borden, who emigrated from Wales and settled at Portsmouth, in Rhode Island. His son Matthew, born May, 1638, is recorded in the Friends' Book of Records, as the first child born of English parents in Rhode Island. The numerous descendants of this original Richard Borden, now composing a large and influential section of Fall River's wealthy and exclusive citizens, are descendants of John, the fourth son of this original Richard.

A. J. Borden, the murdered man, is in the ninth generation from the original Richard Borden, and is the son of A. B. Borden, a full cousin of the eminent manufacturers, Richard and Jefferson Borden.

A. J. Borden was born Sept. 22, 1822. For his first wife he married Sarah A. Morse, Dec. 26, 1845, and for his second wife (the murdered woman) Abbey D. Gray, June 6, 1865. By the first marriage there were three children, Emma L., Alice E., who died in youth, and Lizzie D., now under arrest on the charge of murdering her father and step-mother.

Not Killed by Mutineers.

THOMASTON, ME., Aug. 14.—The suggestion that A. J. Borden might have been murdered by one of the mutineers of the Jefferson Borden, sent to prison largely through Mr. Borden's influence, and said to have been pardoned by the efforts of interested labor men has no foundation in truth. George Miller and William Clark, the ringleaders, were sent to the marine state prison on life sentences. They are still confined here.

The New York Times

A CRANK AT FALL RIVER.

CHARLES H. PECKHAM DECLARES HE KILLED THE BORDENS.

FALL RIVER, Massachusetts---Charles H. Peckham of Central Village, Westport, Mass., walked into the Central Police Station this morning and said to Assistasnt Marshal Fleet: "Well, Mr. Marshal, I killed Mr. and Mrs. Andrew J. Borden, and I have come from home to give myself up. I went over the back fence and through the rear door of the Borden house two weeks ago to-day, and I killed both of those people out of pure love for blood. I went out the rear door and over the back fence, and walked over the New Bedford road home. I'm the murderer, and I want to be locked up."

The Marshal took him to the cellroom and searched him. He found a pocketbook with a few receipts in it, and also unearthed some official communications from the Russian Legation in Washington.

He was asked if his clothes were spotted with blood, and he replied that there were no spatters, because the first blow caused death and stopped the heart's action. He said he struck the other blows by way of precaution. He then told the Deputy Marshal that he expected no sympathy, and wanted to be held. He had borne the knowledge of his crime as long as he was able, he said, and now wanted relief of mind.

Peckham was allowed to go into the guardroom after a short confinement in a cell, and begged several uniformed officers to hang him. Assistant Marshal Fleet told him to follow him and he would accomodate him. He was taken to the cellroom and locked up again. Alderman Beattle went into the cellroom and had a long talk with him. He told the Alderman he had had some trouble with his family.

Peckham lives two and one-half miles south of Brownell's Corner in Westport, on a farm he purchased this Spring. He was in this city last Friday, and heard a great deal about Lizzie Borden's arrest. He went home, and since then has brooded so much over the affair that he became insane. He left his house between 6 and 7 o'clock this morning, despite the protestations of his wife, and walked ten miles to the police station to give himself up. He is a war veteran, and has been subject to fits of insanity for some years. He will be cared for by his friends.

OPINIONS FROM OTHER NEWSPAPERS

The Dover Democrat

Whether guilty or not guilty, it cannot be that they mean to convict Lizzie Borden anyway and hang her for the Fall River crimes. Is it an official necessity to do it, and is a vicarious sacrifice just as good as any? If so, we predict that there will be an unprecedented thundering of public opinion against it. In the utter absence of all motive for murder as there is in this case, there must be a very different and much more damaging and conclusive evidence against this woman than has yet been made public, or nothing but her perfect vindication and freedom will satisfy justice and humanity.

New York Telegram

Miss Lizzie Borden, being now behind prison bars, may thank her stars on having found a sanctuary from the sleuth hounds of the press.

The Boston Herald

While this case is in suspense, awaiting the testing of the innocence of Miss Borden, it is useless to argue her innocence or guilt, and the spectacle presented by the citizens of Fall River, in arraying themselves on opposite sides of the question, and arguing it with all the heat and ferocity that passion can import into it, is not one that is edifying, or that commends itself to public approval. The machinery of a public trial is intended to elicit the truth, and until this machinery has failed to serve its purpose the proper thing is to suspend judgment. The organization of Fall River people into church and non-church factions is too ridiculous to be maintained.

The Fall River Herald

LEGAL ASPECT

Of the Case Against Lizzie A. Borden.

LAWYER BRAGG'S POINT ON THE ACTION OF THE JUDGE.

Remedy for Mr. Jennings if His Client is Held.

Lawyer Reed Discusses the Theory of Insanity.

What if Miss Borden Should Refuse to Testify?

The nearer the day comes for the examination of Lizzie Borden for the murder of her father, the more complicated the discussions on the case become. The horror connected with the crime has greatly abated, mostly so on account of the stand that honest editors have taken that, until proven guilty, the woman should be regarded as innocent.

That a person who has to face circumstantial evidence should be allowed to have legal advice all fair-minded people will admit, and especially so when that party is one who, from her previous connection with the world, would not have the tact or knowledge to answer questions that can be construed in a manner entirely different from her intention. What questions may have been put to Miss Borden in the so-called inquest can only be learned from the stenographer's report, but as that, undoubtedly, will be kept hidden until Monday, if it is even shown then, the public and legal fraternity can only base their theory on their previous knowledge of the district attorney's shrewdness.

When Lawyer Jennings was arguing on Friday against Judge Blaisdell sitting on the bench to hold Lizzie for the crime, he evidently overlooked a point in law that would undoubtedly give his client freedom until the grand jury met in November. Of this point he was reminded in a note from Lawyer Bragg.

The penal statutes are construed strictly in the interest of the accused, their effect being limited by the express words employed and not by extended implication. Judge Blaisdell had heard the implications connecting Miss Borden with the tragedy, and therefore cannot sit in conformity with recognized law on the case. A justice who has an interest in a corporation has no right to sit in judgment on a civil suit, and why should a man who has already passed his opinion on the matter in an inquest be called on to affirm or revoke it in public? If the finding is against the prisoner, there can be no doubt that Mr. Jennings will apply for a writ of habeas corpus from the supreme court to have the woman released until the grand jury meets in November. This was the point that Mr. Bragg intended to convey, and it was immediately acquiesced in by Mr. Jennings.

Should Miss Borden be held for the grand jury these special rules which are applicable to criminal cases will undoubtedly be used by her counsel:

"The state must prove affirmatively and beyond a reasonable doubt every material allegation in the indictment.

"The testimony must be such as to exclude every reasonable hypothesis but that of the defendant's guilt.

"The corpus delicti (body of crime) must be established other than the extra-judicial admissions of the accused.

"When a specific intent is alleged in the indictment, it must be proved as laid.

"The voluntary confession of the accused when made without fear or hope of favor is competent evidence against him.

"The accused is always presumed innocent until proven guilty, and if upon the whole evidence there is a reasonable doubt of his guilt he is entitled to an acquittal."

PSYCHOLOGICAL QUESTION.

Milton Reed, Esq., Thinks the Murderer was Insane

Milton Reed, Esq., in talking about the case, said: "This case is now becoming a psychological question," said he, "and the sooner it does the better it will be for everybody concerned. Now let us look at the matter from a common sense view—and I think if a little more common sense had been used in this case it would have been better. We who have had some experience with criminals, and some knowledge of crime, know that murderers do not stand over the victims delivering blow after blow when they know the victims are dead, or when they have good reason to believe they are. It is one stroke with knife or axe, and it is all over. The deed does not appear like that of a person who was perfectly rational. In every detail it shows the stubborn and dogged brutality of the insane. Now when you re-establish it as the work of an insane person you have gone a great way towards the solution of the case.

"Try to find out who there was who might have had a monomania so aggravated as to incite him to this deed, who the person was who might have committed the murder under this mental aberration. Question them to ascertain the character of their mania. You might find men who would be mentally sound upon a hundred questions, and, upon the one hundred and first, insane. You might find them rational on a thousand questions, and a raving lunatic on the one thousand and first.

"I don't know Lizzie Borden, but there are people who are liable to know as to whether or not she was mentally weak upon any one question such as to give credit to a probability that it might have excited her to murder. At any rate, with it established as the act of a lunatic, look for the maniac. Lizzie Borden is in a very unfortunate position. If she is innocent what more pitiable than her arrest? and if she is guilty she is even more unfortunate. It seems to me that the lunatic theory is the only reasonable and common sense one, and if properly investigated it may be shown that there was no crime at all committed, but merely the work of a morally irresponsible person. What happier solution of the mystery could there be than this? I believe it will result in this. This murder is, in my opinion, purely a psychological question."

MORE FROM THE SPIRITS.

Both Mr. and Mrs. Borden Talk—The Latter Comforts Lizzie.

Two more messages have been received from the spirit world, says a correspondent of the Boston Post. Sunday evening the spirit of Andrew J. Borden knocked again at the brain of this New Bedford medium, while Monday night from 8 o'clock till 10:30 the spirit of Mrs. Borden whispered strange words that may or may not mean much.

Monday night's message from Andrew J. Borden read as follows: "No one knows where the axe is but you. Now I want you to publish when you go to the hidden scene; start early in the morning when the air is clear. Two weeks from now you will know much more about this. We want justice done to this dear woman."

"Do you mean the medium?"

"Yes; you must see, my friend, that she is well rewarded. I know that you can find the axe. A number of persons have been there, but have found no trace. Even the man who hid it cannot locate the place now. You cannot find the axe unless the medium goes with you. They have not got this man's name I gave you; don't wait too long before you go for the man."

"Shall I write to the Pinkertons?"

"Don't write; let them come to you."

"Did the man have dark circles beneath his eyes?"

"Yes."

"Were his clothes dark blue instead of a black or dark brown?"

"I cannot tell; only they were dark. When I was struck I was in the mortal, when I saw I was in the spirit; I feel I am losing my strength; I must leave you; good night. ANDREW J. BORDEN."

Monday evening the following was received from the spirit of Mrs. Borden: "This is Mrs. Borden. I have come to thank you for what you have done for us."

"Can you give us a test?"

"Tell them to take care of my things and a copied picture. I will do as much to help them. Tell Lizzie I know the window was left open; I know the man can be found. Please write this to Emma: 'I want to know the reason you don't go to Fall River.'" The reason was given and accepted by the spirit, and the influence left, signing "Wife of A. J. Borden."

STRANGE AND UNNATURAL

A Boston Newspaper Man's View of the Great Crime.

Among all strange outbursts of murderous passion the Fall River case is the most complete, says a writer in the Boston Globe. Every element of a great sensation is present. The victims were man and wife, wealthy and respectable. The accused is a woman of refinement and their daughter. The deed was done with every circumstance of furious brutality and in the open day. Thus far to the public and the press the mystery surrounding the whole case wears an impenetrable front. A week has passed, and Miss Borden enjoys the benefit of the doubt far more generally than she did in the first flash of suspicion that affected the popular judgment. Whatever the law officers may have in store for the examination, not a syllable or scrap of evidence of a motive or a temperament to fit a crime so foul, strange and unnatural is yet before the public.

It has not appeared that she is a lunatic, or, on the other hand, that she had nursed a murderous hatred of either her father or her stepmother. Mrs. Borden was by no means the first woman to fail of a stepchild's affection, and perhaps Mr. Borden was not the man to invite the fondest filial relations. How common and familiar is this situation, and yet if Miss Borden be guilty how uncommon is the sequel!

Arranged for a murder, wantonly and unaccountably savage, no hint has yet escaped her accusers of any quality in the prisoner's disposition unusual and unbecoming in innocent and tender womanhood, while her friends, among men and women alike, are unshaken in their support. Is it possible that a woman so honest and inexperienced as these neighbors believe her to be could plot a double murder with such consummate skill, and that hands so fair and clean as hers could inflict upon the faces of her father and his wife wounds too ugly for description? Judgment may well waver and await the secret evidence of the prosecutors.

Job too Much for the Spirits.

An Onset medium assured a Boston Globe reporter that there was a great diversity of opinion in the spirit world as to the identity of the person who murdered Mr. and Mrs. Borden. "You see," she said, "spirits don't know everything, at least many spirits do not. And if they didn't happen to be looking just at the moment when the murder was committed they couldn't be expected to know about it."

"But," ventured the reporter, "couldn't Mr. and Mrs. Borden be hunted up in the spirit world and solve the mystery for us?"

"Yes, I suppose they might be found somewhere if a search were instituted for them. But even if their whereabouts were discovered it's not certain that they would know who the murderer was, for Mr. Borden was asleep and Mrs. Borden's back might have been turned."

"But it would seem," the reporter urged, "that if Mr. and Mrs. Borden could be found and induced to tell all they know about the circumstances preceding the fatal deed, some clue or some corroboration of existing suspicions might be obtained."

"Yes," the medium assented vaguely, "but the trouble is that when people go suddenly into the spirit world, as Mr. and Mrs. Borden went, they are apt to be in a dazed or half-conscious state for a long while and unable to remember anything."

The medium said that spirits often find as great difficulty as mortals in solving mysteries and she wouldn't undertake the job of trying to discover the Fall River murderer.

The Portland Express

Of course, it is possible that Lizzie Borden committed the terrible crime with which she is charged and for which she is now under arrest. It is just possible and that is all. If she had desired to do it she might, under all the circumstances, have succeeded. That is what the arrest is based on. Stupidity seems to be the only attribute that the Fall River police have yet displayed in this matter.

The Fall River Herald

A CLOSED BOOK.

Lizzie Borden's Conduct Puzzling Everybody.

WESTPORTER'S ACKNOWLEDGEMENT OF GUILT.

Wanted to be Hanged at the Central Station.

A MAN WITH A BLOODY AXE SEEN AT STEEP BROOK.

Charles C. Cook Speaks About Andrew J. Borden's Will.

A famous writer has said: "Life is our dictionary; we carry it with us constantly; we cannot shut it up; page after page appears daily before us." How true a remark and yet how false. That life is our dictionary is true in one sense. It is the dictionary of one's own mind, which no one but himself, if so inclined, can read. The outer acts in life are apparent to all, but thoughts and malign feelings are often guarded more closely than a mother looks after her first born. Lizzie Borden's previous life has been a dictionary, as far as outward appearances are concerned, that has been easy for the eye to read. Reared in luxury, she has felt her position, and, although haughty, has never been so in the extreme. While of this disposition, she has been known to do a number of charitable acts that would not be expected from such a source. These deeds now are constantly before our eyes, and we cannot close the page that describes them.

The charitable are always ready and willing to look on the bright side of a question or anything that will tend to lessen the abhorrence that a general public will have for a person under suspicion. This, probably, and the fact that the woman was not allowed counsel to protect herself have done more to cause nearly the entire press of the country to rise in indignation against the so-called inquest. While they may not believe in her innocence, the right that the weak should have support is predominant.

Looking at the matter in a different light, what would the opinion be if Miss Borden's mind could be read? Standing before us is a woman whose public acts are known, and one whom we would never credit for self-possession that she has displayed. Never, without doubt, has the christian world seen such an example in a person charged with such a horrible crime. Could but the page be turned that shows her outer life and the inner exposed, we might see imprinted in large letters on the mind a prayer to give her strength to withstand the terrible ordeal of an unjust accusation, or we might see damming evidence of her guilt trying to be covered by the ocurage and coolness of a depraved mind. Such pages in our life as we are disposed to exhibit are always open to the public examination, but how many dare expose the opposite side? It is not human, and for that reason Miss Borden's courage and self-possession should not be ascribed to the wrong motives. She may be guilty, but if proven innocent how much more remarkable will she appear for being able to stand the test. Guilt will always back itself up by craft, but an innocent person has only to depend on the page of the dictionary that cannot be read by the accusers.

LAWYER BRAGG

Argues Against Judge Blaisdell's Presence at the Hearing Monday.

TO THE EDITOR OF THE HERALD:—Sir: As I have been quoted as saying certain things in relation to the Borden murder and the parties interested therein, and as what I have said has in some instances been misconstrued, I desire to set myself right through the columns of your paper by explaining the reasons for my utterances in the matter.

I have no interest in the Borden murder case other than that of a citizen of Fall River. I do not know the defendant, and I never had seen her up to the time that I gave her my seat in the police court that she might sit beside her counsel. On that day I studied her every look and motion, and drew my conclusions therefrom; and I became so well satisfied of her innocence that even a verdict of guilty returned by a competent jury would not alter my opinion in the least. In the ten years I have been engaged in the trial of criminal cases I have seen men and women who had been accused of crime in their cells and in the courts. I have conversed with and defended the innocent and the guilty, the educated and the ignorant; I have studied the different phases of their characters to such an extent that I have seldom failed in forming a correct conclusion of the parties coming under my observation, and it is from this experience that I have drawn my conclusion in the Borden case.

The assistance which I rendered to Lawyer Jennings in the police court was nothing more than is customary among brother attorneys and should not be taken in any other light than an act of fraternal courtesy. My objections to Judge Blaisdell presiding at the hearing to be given Miss Borden are not based, as has been stated by some, upon any ill feeling existing between the judge and myself, but upon the ground of the probable holding for the grand jury of Miss Borden. If held, she should be rendered free of the suspicion that the presiding justice was in any manner prejudiced against her. Both of the above named gentlemen are my friends, and the worst wish I have for either of them is that he may be with the majority in this life and with the minority in the life to come.

Regardless of what the authorities have said I have grave doubts of their being able to produce sufficient evidence at the hearing to be given Lizzie Borden Monday to convince an unprejudiced mind of probable cause of her guilt, for if Mr. Knowlton had not been convinced of the weakness of the case against her he would not have proceeded in the matter as he did. There was no desire on Miss Borden's part to run away,and if she had had a desire of that kind she could not have gone beyond the limits of the city. Mr. Knowlton had it in his power to convene the grand jury in special session, and he would have done this if he had been sure of his case; but not being sure that the evidence would warrant the grand jury in finding a bill against Lizzie, he took several days in the attempt to get evidence against her and at the same time to prejudice the mind of the judge by it. Therefore, realizing the weakness of his evidence, he opposed Mr. Jennings' motion in objection to the judge. If Mr. Knowlton should succeed in keeping Judge Blaisdell on the bench at the hearing and through incompetent evidence taken at the inquest he should hold Miss Borden to the grand jury, then, although he had a weak case, the fact that Judge Blaisdell held her would be used to induce the grand jury to return a true bill.

A. E. BRAGG.

JENNINGS HARD AT WORK.

Looking up All Important Points for Lizzie's Defence.

Lawyer Andrew J. Jennings is a very hard man to interview. He declines absolutely to talk about the Borden case, and will not allow either Emma Borden or John Vinnicum Morse to talk about the matter, either. He said that the time for him to have his say was in court, and he did not think he should have anything to discuss until that time.

When asked about the summonses issued to Marshal Hilliard and Medical Examiner Dolan to bring to the court everything in their possession, and everything that they had taken possession of, from the stomachs of the murdered persons to the pieces of carpet on which the blood from their wounds flowed, he remarked that his reason for this would be fully shown in the examination, but until then he did not wish to discuss the matter. Neither would he tell who his witnesses for the defence are to be at the examination. It is know, however, that he has been hard at work looking up all the points in the case, and his clerk, Mr. Phillips, has spent much time examining the different witnesses who are expected to appear.

Mr. Jennings has not relied on any of the Pinkerton detectives for information of this kind, and if they are still at work he is apparently unaware of the fact. All the information he has at hand, and all that will be introduced at the hearing, has, it is said, been gathered by him and Mr. Phillips. There is likely to be some interesting complications in the case if Judge Blaisdell insists on sitting at the hearing.

Lawyer Jennings' point raised at the examination last Friday is an important one, and has never been tested. He claims that as Judge Blaisdell presided at the inquest and heard all of the evidence there introduced, he is prejudiced against Miss Borden, and is, therefore, incompetent to decide whether or not there is evidence enough to find the accused probably guilty. Mr. Jennings objected at the hearing last Friday, and on the judge over-ruling the objection the lawyer entered an appeal. If Judge Blaisdell withdraws now, however, the matter will not be pushed, and there will be, accordingly, no complications.

Letters to the Marshal.

The city marshal is in receipt of lot of correspondence concerning the crime and the manner in which to convict the criminals. The following is a sample, having been written in a cramped hand on a piece of cardboard: "City marshal—I told old Borden that I would kill him. The servant girl killed Mrs. Borden. Lizzie had nothing to do with the matter. You will not get me, as when you receive this I will be on the sea. I was in jail in Maine on old Borden's account, and I meant to get even. SEE ME NOT."

Another letter was received from a prominent church organization of New York telling the marshal to proceed with his work. The writer states that when the girl is convicted it will be time to extend mercy, and that justice should not be hampered in its work. The claim is made that the Borden millions will not be used to protect the girl if she is guilty and that religious people are anxious that the matter should be thoroughly sifted.

OFFICER SEAVER

Says That He was Misrepresented About Blood Stains.

"I examined the dress worn by Lizzie Borden on the day of the murder and went over it very carefully with a glass," says State Officer Seaver. "There were only two spots on it and they were near the pocket of the skirt. I am very certain they are not blood spots, and at the time of the examination did not for a second consider them as such. They might be grease spots or stains originating from such cause, but they had not the slightest appearance of being blood. Furthermore, you may say no evidences of blood were found on any wearing apparel in Miss Borden's possession except on the skirt. I have, moreover, at no time laid special significance upon that discovery, as its presence there is explainable by natural conditions.

"It is my purpose, as it is the intent of every official in the commonwealth, to deal fairly in words and acts with the accused; and, therefore, the public can understand how righteously indignant it makes me feel to see myself quoted in the newspapers as being certain of Lizzie's guilt, the servant girl's complicity and other such insinuations, when I have not opened my mouth or said a word to anybody regarding the matter attributed to me. In reality I have not the slightest reason to think that Bridget Sullivan was involved in the murders. On the contrary, I have reasons for believing she knew nothing about them.

"What the government may consider its strongest point against the accused I am not prepared to say. I think, however, the gravity of her position is indicated by the fact that she admits being nearest to both crimes at the time they were committed. She has sworn that between 9:30 o'clock and the time of her father's return on the fatal forenoon she was all the time indoors. She says she was in her own room nearly opposite the chamber in which her mother was killed for a portion of the hour during which it is clearly evident the deed was committed. The rest of the time she was on the floor below, but within easy hearing distance of the scene of the first tragedy. The facts as to her admissions after her father's return up to the time she is alleged to have discovered his death have been previously stated in a general way, and I have no time or inclination to dwell upon them. It is not my right or privilege to talk about the government's evidence, and from further remarks in that direction you must excuse me.

"Have I said anything about Miss Borden being insane? No, I have not," replied Mr. Seaver, "and that part of the alleged interview must be included with the other fiction attributed to me. Do I think she is insane? You can answer that question as well as I. Does the crime look the work of a woman in her sober senses or not? Until experts decide it would be useless for laymen to discuss a mental condition to diagnose which the most competent specialists in the country would be needed."

Man with a Bloody Axe.

This morning a man named Lemay, who resides a short distance north of Steep Brook, reported to the marshal that on Tuesday night he saw a man sitting on a wall with a bloody axe in his lap. When Lemay asked in French if he was tired the man immediately took his departure.

Sergeant Edson and Officers Perron, Doherty, Harrington, Devine and Chace were despatched to search the woods in that neighborhood. At the time of going to press the police were still on the hunt among the woods, and their return is eagerly awaited at the central station. This is the only new clue that has been presented in the case today, and, as usual, the marshal is devoting all his energies to sifting it to the bottom.

The Inquest is Off.

District Attorney Knowlton returned from Boston Tuesday night and went on to his home in New Bedford. Yesterday morning the Taunton Gazette called him up by telephone and put the direct question, "What is to become of this Borden murder inquest?"

In reply he said with equal directness: "That is off. It has fulfilled its mission, and a return will be made upon the evidence already in."

The Handy Specter.

A Haverhill dispatch says: A man exactly resembling Dr. Handy's white-faced, evil-looking man, who is suspected of being connected with the Borden murders, was seen at the Boston & Maine depot this morning. His clothes, which were exactly like the mysterious man's, had blood spots upon them. He left for Boston.

Notes.

The question as to whether Mr. Borden made a will or not is receiving considerable attention. The HERALD is in a position to state authoritatively that no such document is in existence. C. C. Cook, the real estate agent, states that any statement attributed to him as to how Mr. Borden intended to dispose of his property is false. He has never spoken of the matter, and what is more will not do so at the present.

The marshal, in talking about who committed the crime, stated it as his belief that "whoever did it must have been temporarily insane." The reporter turned to Medical Examiner Dolan, who was present, and asked if most murderers were not insane. "Yes," replied the doctor, "when their trials come off."

The stories given out as to what Prof. Wood will testify on Monday are merely the workings of an imaginative brain. Medical Examiner Dolan, who unquestionably would be one of the first persons to hear from the professor as to the condition of the stomachs, has not received a word of information, and denies that any of the stories in circulation come from him.

Taunton Gazette

Said a prominent Tauntonian this morning: "The manner in which the Fall River people are pursuing the officers is wrong; it is almost criminal in itself. They should not lose sight of the fact that a very grave crime has been committed and that it is the bounden duty of the government to pursue every thread of evidence to the end for further evidence and finest clues. The least bit of evidence in one direction may be of such a nature as to lead to the unravelling of another thread, and that one may be of the greatest importance. Let me give you an instance of how slight a thing may lead to big results. Some years ago a Taunton man went to the city hall for aid. He had been a soldier, he said, and when he was asked what regiment he had served in replied the f-f-f-fourth regiment. The records of the fourth were looked up and sure enough he had served his full term of enlistment and appeared to stand out as an honorable man with an excellent record in army life; but that "f-f-f" stuck in the official's crop and he was sure it meant something besides "fourth," so he looked up the record of the 58th regiment, where he knew some Taunton men had been, and then he was not surprised to find that the man had enlisted in the 58th and ran away with a big bounty. It was a trifle that discovered the guilt of the man and his unworthiness to be entitled to military aid, and it may be a trifle that will show more to this Borden case than any yet dreamed of. Therefore, I say suspend judgment and assist the police all that is possible to the end that full justice shall be done."

Pawtucket Times

It is the duty of Jennings, the counsel of Lizzie Borden, to insist upon every point which he thinks might make in her favor, and his objection to the sitting of Judge Blaisdell as the examining court to decide whether Miss Borden shall be sent before the grand jury is perfectly proper. Certain newspapers appear to have taken up the matter as though Judge Blaisdell was to sit to decide the question of the guilt or the innocence of Lizzie Borden. The law of the state of Massachusetts permits Judge Blaisdell to sit, and as a justice his decision will rest upon the evidence presented to him at the sitting. As a matter of law Judge Blaisdell is right, and as a matter of justice there is nothing to indicate that he is wrong.

Providence Journal

Some of the stuff which is now being published concerning the Borden case must be taken to indicate that certain esteemed contemporaries have got down to what must be called the emptyings. It is hard to keep public interest at the highest pitch when there is a dearth of the real material to work upon.

The Fall River Herald

A STRANGE STORY

About Domestic Relations of the Bordens

TOLD BY A FALL RIVER MAN IN NEW BEDFORD.

An Alleged Wish That the Father Should Die.

LOWELL LAWYERS TALK ABOUT JUDGE BLAISDELL'S ACTION.

The Westport Farmer Recovers His Senses in a Cell.

While the majority of people have been twisting their mind in all shapes in order to find a theory or clue for the murder of Mr. and Mrs. Borden, not a few have been asking themselves what was the reason that John V. Morse left his farm in Iowa and came east at this particular time. It was the season of the year when farming duties require the most attention, and the cause must have been very urgent to have brought him to this city.

A HERALD reporter called on a member of the Borden family and asked if she could answer the question. At first a refusal was met with, but finally the following was obtained: "The cause of Mr. Morse's visit to this city was known by few members of the family. It has never been divulged, for the reason that family pride tried to conceal it. There is always a skeleton in most houses, and the home of Mr. Borden's was no exception. By members of the family it was known that Lizzie regarded Mr. Morse with more tenderness than most nieces feel for their uncles. This Mr. Borden was aware of, and he was constantly on the alert to see that the breath of scandal did not reach his home. Why should Mr. Morse make his residence at Dartmouth while on the visit if something did not prevent him accepting the hospitality of his nieces?"

"Do you know if Lizzie ever had a young man calling at the house?" was asked.

"No, I do not think she had. She used to attend church with a near neighbor, but no suspicion of wrongdoing was ever attached to that."

"Could you state as to how Mr. Borden acted as regards allowing his daughters to keep company with young men?"

"Mr. Borden, as was known by all people acquainted with him, was a very strict and stern man. He never opposed his daughters in this matter provided the parties were respectable, and it can truthfully be said that outside of the fact stated above the Bordens never gave their father an opportunity to chide them as to the company they kept. The haughty and cold nature of Lizzie was repellant to most people, and it was seldom that she was seen on the street in male company unless attended by the friend who went to and from church with her. No, I do not know whether Mr. Morse and Lizzie were in the habit of having carriage rides, but it would not be impossible for them to do so without my knowledge. The wish I have for Lizzie is that she will clear herself of the horrible charge that is preferred against her, though at present it looks very black for her."

LOWELL LAWYERS

Interviewed as to Judge Blaisdell's Determination to Sit at the Hearing.

One of the associate judges of the police court said: "It is my experience, and it is so with other judges, that the hearing of evidence on which warrants were issued in no way prejudiced my opinion. Many times the case is forgotten by the judge when it is called for trial. In any event the hearing of evidence leads to a just decision. The judge who grants the warrant has no pride of opinion in the matter and is not committed to the complainant's side simply because he authorized the arrest or summons. I have no doubt Judge Blaisdell will be absolutely impartial in conducting the preliminary hearing if he sits in the case, although he has heard the evidence in the inquest and that presented to secure a warrant. As a matter of fact the clamor that has been raised against his sitting would tend to make him favor the prisoner, as in his anxiety to be exactly fair the impulse would naturally be to her side. The case is one of unusual importance, but the proceedings of the lower court are only of moment as they affect the liberty of the accused. The police justice simply tries the issue of probable cause. If the judge should decide there was not probable cause, it would not prevent the authorities from going to the grand jury and endeavoring to get an indictment."

Other leading members of the Lowell bar thought Judge Blaisdell should not preside at the preliminary hearing.

ADDICTED TO SPELLS.

The Westport Man Forgets That He Accused Himself of Murder.

Charles H. Peckham, the self-accused murderer of the Bordens, has been released and is at work today on his Westport farm. Mrs. Peckham called at the station Thursday night and told the marshal that her husband had such spells about once a year. He was perfectly harmless, but had caused her lots of trouble. He would remain unconscious of his surroundings for two or three days, during which time he would not sleep. When he closed his eyes in repose and awoke all that he had done during his abberation would be forgotten. The cause of these spells was attributed by Mrs. Peckham to a wound he received in the war. As he was harmless, the wife asked the marshal to be allowed to take him home, and the request was granted.

Steward Cummings was directed to bring the man from the cell room. Peckham was found sleeping soundly and had to be shaken to arouse him. When he went into the guard room he immediately demanded to know what he was arrested for.

"For the murder of the Bordens," was the reply.

"What, I commit a murder? Why I would not harm a fly. There must be some mistake."

"Well, you came in this morning, and after making a confession, said you wanted to be hanged right away. How dow do you feel about the matter now?" was asked.

"I guess I want to live a few years longer," was the response.

It will be in order for some other diseased mind to bring a hatchet into the station room covered with blood and claim that it is the weapon with which the deed was committed.

The man had simply been reading and thinking incessantly about the murder, and his mind gave way temporarily beneath the strain. Suddenly the conviction that he himself was guilty fastened itself upon him. The newspapers and his abnormal imagination supplied the necessary details. Instantly he set off for Fall River. The heat was intense, and that, with the unusual exertion of fast walking, increased his mania. Hence his hurried confession and intense desire to be hanged at once and have done with it.

"He has not been strong for years," Neighbor Reed said; "and he would not harm a mouse."

The police from the moment the man entered the station house humored him and attempted to calm his mind. Never for a moment did they regard his statements seriously. Everyone was sorry for him, though the advent of a self-accused murderer has long been regarded as probable.

SEAVER'S TALKS.

The Taunton Gazette Insists that he was Correctly Reported.

Detective Seaver is reported to have denied the truth of interviews purporting to be had with him.

Crimination and recrimination about the truth of important interviews get a little tiresome after a time. The following from the Taunton Gazette shows that a question of veracity has been raised:

"Detective Seaver is quite busy now, making energetic denials of statements attributed to him in several papers, but so far as he has developed yet, he has not been heard of directly at the Gazette office. Now it happens that there were two newspaper men interested in Mr. Seaver on the evening when he talked. One was a Boston Post man and the other a Gazette man. The Post man's interview with Mr. Seaver is thus described this morning by a disinterested but reputable listener. The Post man approached and began to argue the case, and Mr. Seaver replied at first in a non-committal sort of a way: 'Perhaps that may be so;' 'can't tell,' etc., until in some manner he became piqued at a question put, or a suggestion made, and then all the Post man had to do for about fifteen minutes was to fold his hands, open his ears, and keep his thinking and memorizing apparatus hard at work. Then he went into the Western Union and told his story.

"When the Gazette man happened along a few minutes after, Mr. Seaver was sitting in a chair outside the City hotel door. There was room for two to sit down comfortably in the Western Union office; both went there, within plain sight of the operator, who was sending the Post matter in, and there Mr. Seaver and the Gazette man sat and kept talking about the matter for half an hour."

Notes.

The squad of officers detailed yesterday to search the fields and woods north of Steep Brook for the man who was seen sitting on a stone wall Tuesday night with a bloody axe in his lap, returned about 6 o'clock, footsore and weary after a fruitless search. Every conceivable nook that would shelter a person in that neighborhood was examined but no trace of man or axe was discovered. The police say that the man sitting on the wall existed in the imagination of the informant.

Providence Journal

A Crank with Glass in His Hair.

Into the central station in this city yesterday wandered a well dressed, intelligent appearing man, who said he came from Fall River. He spok to Lieut. O'Neil, who was sitting behind the desk, and said "I've come for that $5000 reward for the capture of the murderer of Mr. and Mrs. Andrew J. Borden."

"Is that so?" said the lieutenant.

"Yes," replied the Fall River crank. "I had him caged this morning, and he made a clean breast of everything, and I can lay my hands on him at any time. Where'll I go for the reward, sir?"

Lieut. O'Neil does not throw away much time generally in listening to cranks, but this fellow did not show the slightest sign of being "off" when he entered the station and so the officer got into conversation with him.

Finally the man was sent to the city hall, where he braced up beside Chief Child and began to spin off a great tale about the murder. Officer Feeley was there, and as the crank removed his hat the light so struck upon the man's head as to make it appear as though his hair was filled with small electric lights. It wasn't though, but in it must have been a good half pint of broken glass scattered all over the scalp, making it look much the same as the spangled costume of a bare-back horse rider in a circus.

Chief Child told the fellow he had better get down to Fall River by the first train and get the money. The man muttered to himself, made a double quickstep through the corridor and was soon out of sight.

Boston Post

There is no doubt that the man who walked into the Fall River police station yesterday and asked to be hanged at once for the murder of the Bordens is of unbalanced mind. Yet why is it not even more likely that he is the criminal than that Lizzie Borden should perpetrate such a butchery? Match all the known facts, and they fit much more nicely the theory that Peckham did the deed than that it was done by the woman now locked up under the terrible charge of parricide. The police have begun already to weaken in their first confidence. They have given out, within two days, the modified theory that, while it must have been Lizzie Borden who did it, she must have been acting under an impulse of insanity. That is to say, they find it impossible, after cool consideration, to make the facts fit their first theory of a deliberate, cold-blooded butchery of parents by a daughter.

Milton News

The efforts to detect evil-doers are passing the bounds of decency and law in this great and free commonwealth. Down in Fall River there is a most aggravating case at the present time, where a young woman is being cruelly persecuted by a lot of so-called minions of the law, who are bringing every effort to prove her guilty before there is the least clue on which to make a case against her. In the eyes of the law she is innocent until a court of justice has sufficient evidence to prove her guilty, and those who are at work trying to undermine her health and mind are worse than heartless and unlawful in their designs. If there is no protection in Massachusetts against the traducing of law and order, as illustrated in this case, no one is safe.

Brockton Enterprise

Miss Borden may not be guilty, and in fact the evidence thus far presented to the public seems not inconsistent with a theory of her absolute innocence. But this woman's previous good character, while it is a strong point in her favor, is nothing that necessarily absolves her totally from even the suspicion of guilt. Defaulting bank officials are generally good till found out. Members of churches are seldom suspected of crime till the revelation is made some day with the vivid suddenness of a lightning flash.

Newport Observer

The grossly stupid conduct of the city marshal and police has been outdone by Justice Blaisdell, whose intense conceit appears to be the only explanation of his extraordinary course in presiding over an inquest and finding poor Lizzie Borden guilty and then sitting in judgment upon the case in the court above. If Miss Borden is guilty, the prosecution will never have the sympathy of the populace, for its course has been as near vicious as possible, and more in the line of persecution than calm, judicial investigation. It is hoped that full and complete justice may yet be done, but if such an end is ever attained it will more than likely result from other and wiser individuals than the Fall River police officials.

Philadelphia Record

The methods adopted by the authorities seem utterly repugnant to all generally conceived notions of the rights of individuals, and to be more in keeping with the inquisitory methods of a French procureur than with our system of criminal jurisprudence. The suspected woman was subjected to a star chamber inquiry, which was dignified by the name of an inquest; she was not allowed the assistance of a lawyer, her every movement was watched and followed, she was constantly attended by an officer, her privacy was invaded at every step, and the torture under which she labored must have been mentally as great as the physical pain of the rack or thumbscrew.

A CONTEMPORARY ADVERTISEMENT FROM THE FALL RIVER GLOBE

WONDERLAND AND PLEASANT ST. Musee and Theater.

G. F. DUNBAR.................... ....Manager.

GRAND OPENING, MONDAY NEXT, AUGUST 22.

Wonderland open 4 days each week, Monday, Tuesday, Wednesday and Thursday afternoon aud evening; Pleasant street open 2 days each week, Friday and Saturday afternoon and evening.

And here is the cream of novelty for one week only. **—5— Champion Lady Sprinters —5—** In a grand international sprinting contest

BEAUTIFUL LADIES! CHARMING LADIES

STACE SHOW—Leonard and Moran, including their new star attraction.

ADMISSION ONE DIME Doors open at 1 30 and 6:30 p. m. Three shows on Saturday evenings.

The Fall River Herald

AWAITING MONDAY.

The Hearing on the Charge of Murder.

GREAT PUBLIC INTEREST FELT IN PROCEEDINGS.

A Suggestion that the Judge Take a Vacation.

A FRIEND OF THE ACCUSED ON FAMILY RELATIONS.

The Westport Farmer in a Very Bad Way.

Monday afternoon the preliminary examination of Lizzie Borden on the charge of homicide will begin. While the finding of the second district court will have no direct bearing on the disposition of the case, the binding of the young woman over to await the action of the grand jury will have considerable to do with molding public sympathy against her. On the bench will sit a justice who has already heard the evidence. If he has already formed an opinion, it will be considerably strengthened by a recapitulation of the facts of the case. While no one doubts that Judge Blaisdell will decide on the facts placed before him, it is hard for the ordinary mind to see how he will not be influenced more or less by the knowledge he already possesses. By his decision, a person will be deprived, at least, of her liberty until November, and if it cannot be proved beyond a possible doubt that Miss Borden is guilty no order should be made for her commitment. As all persons acquainted with law know, the findings of the lower court are not binding. Any person dissatisfied with the rulings of the court can appear before the grand jury and, on the presentation of sufficient evidence, that body will cause a warrant to be issued for the arrest of the suspected party even though he had been previously discharged in the lower court.

As this is a splendid time in which to enjoy a vacation, why should his honor not cast off the mantle of justice for a while and seek the health-giving ozone of the mountains or seaside? By doing so he will not lower himself in any degree, and the public's idea of fairness will be satisfied to a great degree. It may be that the question as to who would occupy the bench in his absence may have more to do with the matter than the ordinary mortal comprehends. By the laws of the state, when the justice of a state is unable to occupy his seat he shall cause the senior special justice to be notified. In that case he would have to call on Lawyer Lovatt. While it is not right to intimate that Judge Blaisdell is not influenced by other than legal means to sit on Monday, it is well known that District Attorney Knowlton and Special Justice Lovatt are not as friendly as before the Vose trial. On that occasion the justice was a witness, and in the cross-examination by the district attorney a few sharp retorts passed between the two legal lights. Mr. Knowlton soundly berated the witness for a remark he inadvertently made.

MR. JUBB EXPLAINS

What His Criticisms of the Borden Case Really Were.

"My statement that Lizzie Borden was under examination for four hours is adversely criticised. My reply is that the newspaper reports stated that her examination had lasted for four hours the first day and that it was not completed. It is not so much a question of four or three hours—it is rather a question of whether a young lady, unaccustomed to courts of justice, and with a terrible cloud of suspicion hanging over her, should be subjected to examination and cross-examination by those in whose breasts the suspicion rested, without any legal adviser to protect her. That is what I called, and call now, star chamber proceedings.

"I did not say that 'there was not evidence enough to hold any one for 24 hours.' My statement was that, from the reports published, there was not evidence enough to so far convict any one as to give them 24 hours' imprisonment. I did not say 'blood splashed from both the victims in all directions and for some distance,' but that blood was found on the bed by the side of where Mrs. Borden's body was found, and if it splashed on the bed it is reasonable to suppose that it would have splashed upon the dress of the author of the deed, and yet no evidence has been produced to the public that blood was found on Miss Lizzie Borden's dress."

Rev. Mr. Jubb goes to Boston tomorrow, and will preach at Brookline in Dr. Reuen Thomas' pulpit.

MISS BORDEN'S FRIEND.

Mrs. George Brigham Speaks on the Family's Domestic Relations.

"I wish you would stamp as a lie the allegation that Lizzie was not happy with her father and mother—her stepmother I mean. She has told me many times that these latter years have been her happiest," said Mrs. George Brigham. "The story that she would not sit at the same table with her father is a falsehood of the blackest sort.

"It has been said that Mr. Borden was angry with and did not speak to Lizzie upon her return from Europe. That, too, is a falsehood, distorted out of facts that were as contrary to the statement as could be. On the night Lizzie arrived the family had given her up and Mr. and Mrs. Borden had gone to bed. Lizzie was very tired and only spoke a few words to Emma that night and retired. The next morning Mr. Borden found her steamer chair in the hall and bounded up stairs three at a time to see and greet her, and Lizzie told me her hand ached all day he pressed it so hard. Going down town he met a man who said to him: 'Well, I would guess that some one had come home judging from your bright face this morning.'

"Mr. Borden was, as they say, not a demonstrative man, but he loved his daughters and showed it at such times when they came back after being away. He did not like them to be away from home. I could give you very many illustrations of this, showing Lizzie's kind consideration for her father and he for her. For instance, both the girls would have much preferred to live in this part of town to where they did, and often expressed the wish of course, but said that it was better for their father, more convenient to live where they did, as it was near his business interests, and so they did not urge it. On the other hand, the father, knowing the wish, told them only a short time ago to look for a house in this neighborhood.

"Now as to Mrs. Borden. While she was a very good woman, she was not at all affectionate or calculated to draw the children to her. She was simply mild and good, and so long as things went smoothly she would have very little to say about the house. So that this should not be taken as proof of any bitterness of feeling between them, for there was none. Lizzie Borden was a kind and generous girl—very generous—who would do anything in the world for anyone she thought much of. Whenever there were subscriptions to be made up she contributed liberally, and I have seen her assume debts at the church all herself. These stories of her being skimped for money are equally false with the others. While her income was scarcely in keeping with the wealth of her father, she had more money than she needed. She had the best of clothes, her room was fitted luxuriously as a parlor and bedroom, and she bought books by the set rather than by the volume.

"Now let me tell you about the arrangement for her outing at Marion just previous to the tragedy. I was invited to be of that party, and like her I could not go with those who went first, although the fact that she couldn't has been spoken of as so singular. She couldn't go because her father and mother were going to Swansey. Her mother was depending upon a certain woman to go with her as a companion, as Mr. Borden spent so much time in town that she would not remain over there alone. They found they couldn't get the woman and so gave up the idea, and Mrs. Borden told Lizzie to go on with her plans. Previous to this, Lizzie had promised to act as substitute for the secretary of the Christian Endeavor society at its meeting on Sunday—it was an important consecration and business meeting. Had it not been for this she would have gone to Marion on Saturday, but she would not break her word. It was early in the week when her mother told her she might go on with her plans, and she determined to visit her mother's cousin, Mrs. Morse, at Warren, for a couple of days, and wrote her to that effect. She was taken violently ill on Tuesday morning, and Wednesday morning, not feeling well enough, she wrote to Mrs. Morse that she could not come.

"And as to insanity?"

"There has never been a trace of it about her. She was a girl of very even temper. She never became excited. She had ideas, spoke them quietly and clearly. She could not be insane for the instant of committing the murder, and then return to her own normal self instantly—and after each of the two murders, for I think Mrs. Borden was murdered first, as do the others.

"Her conduct since the murder has been just what anyone who knew her would expect. They speak of her dry eyes. Is it not all to awful too cry about? We might weep, as all of us have, for the death of Mr. and Mrs. Borden, but this, this is too terrible; even I cannot weep in face of it. Her pride was touched at the first sign of suspicion being directed against her, and the horror of it has kept her as she is."

"Has she expressed no idea as to how or by whom it was committed?"

"I know what she thinks, but she has, of course, been closely questioned about that at the inquest, and I would not care to say anything about it before the hearing."

"Does she suspect anyone?"

"No; I can say she suspects no one."

"Can you tell me how the murders might have been committed?"

"I do not wish to add to the many theories which have been discussed, but I know that Lizzie herself has often spoken to her mother about the arrangement of the rooms and halls of the house, and how anyone might come in and go all over the house without anyone knowing it. Members of the family have often done so and spoken of it. The house is a very solid old building and any noise or jar is not easily heard. A man could have entered by the cellar way or the side door, gone upstairs and killed Mrs. Borden and afterwards gone down and hidden in the parlor, which was rarely entered by any of the family. From there he could see anyone in the sitting room and, taking opportunity, have killed Mr. Borden and passed out either by the cellar way or (which would have been easier) turned the spring latch and walked out of the front door and down street, as would a caller at the house."

"Knowing the family and its history as you do, have you no theory as to who committed this murder?"

"No, I have not. Mr. Borden was a man who spoke his mind very freely to anyone, and if they attempted to reply he would shut his teeth and walk away. Of course he had enemies, but none that I could suspect of such a deed."

A Woman's Appeal to Women.

A New York woman, writing to the New York World, says: To my mind—and I have followed the evidence closely—nothing at all decisive has yet been proven against Lizzie Borden. To be sure there are points in her story that don't hang together. That is one of the evidences to me that she is telling the truth. Any lawyer will tell you that the most reliable witness will contradict himself sometimes. Miss Borden is a clever woman, and if she had planned the murder she would have planned a better story to match it.

People in Fall River say that the Bordens quarrelled and had misunderstandings. I fancy there is not a family in this country consisting of father, stepmother and two grown daughters of which the same could not be written down. And even this is village gossip. It seems to me that Miss Borden has been arrested on village gossip and nothing else. Think of the stigma on the life of this young, proud, intelligent woman! For it is improbable that the real murderer in so blind a case will ever be discovered; it is equally improbable that Lizzie Borden can be convicted on the testimony that is adduced. But her whole life is a ruin from this time forward. I appeal to other women to join me in a remonstrance against this outrage.

The Fall River Herald

BEFORE THE BAR!

Lizzie Borden Brought Down from the Jail

TO ANSWER TO THE CHARGE OF MURDER.

A Boston Lawyer Assisting in the Defence.

TWO OUTSIDE YARNS ABOUT THE AWFUL TRAGEDY.

Views of a Well Known Novelist on the Question of Guilt.

The day has arrived for the beginning of the examination of Lizzie Borden for one of the most heinous of crimes. While this court has not final jurisdiction in the matter, yet if it can be shown to the judge that there is a doubt as to the young woman's guilt she will be discharged.

The history of the crime from the time Miss Borden found her father lying dead on a sofa with his head hacked beyond recognition is well known from Maine to California. What happened behind the closed doors at the inquest the public is ignorant of. The revelations made there were the basis for the arrest of the daughter for the murder of her father. Today's proceedings will tend to show probably whether that arrest was made to satisfy a suspicious public, or that the ends of justice demanded it.

The question as to whether Judge Blaisdell should sit on the bench after hearing the evidence at the inquest has been thoroughly ventilated, and the general opinion has been in the negative. As he intends to preside, his rulings on questions of law will be watched with more than ordinary interest.

Since her commitment in Taunton jail very little is known of the accused. Outside of visits by her sister, her minister and counsel and one friend, Miss Borden has been virtually dead to the world. But a few weeks ago this young woman's society was courted. Heir to a large property, her position in life was envied by many. Today she is placed before the bar of justice to answer a charge for which the penalty is life imprisonment.

At two minutes of 2 o'clock a number of ladies walked into the court room and filled every seat. Mrs. Dr. Bowen was greatly distressed, and hid her head in her handkerchief to hide her emotion.

As the clock struck 2 Judge Blaisdell came from his office and took his place on the bench. A stillness that was distressing then followed until ten minutes of 3, when City Marshal Hilliard, Detective Seaver, District Attorney Knowlton and Lawyers Jennings and Adams entered the room.

A consultation was held by the lawyers, when District Attorney Knowlton arose and said:

"Some part of this case requires the examination of various things that have been found by the officers. These things are now in the possession of men who are expert examiners, and they have not yet been able to build up or make even any progress. The examination is insufficient for them to call witnesses. My learned friends, as well as myself, are anxious that this evidence should be presented at the trial. I would suggest that the trial be adjourned until next Thursday morning at 10 o'clock."

The judge was agreeable and the crowds sadly departed.

JUDGE JOSIAH BLAISDELL

A FICTIONIST FACES FACTS.

Anna Katharine Green Writes in Favor of Lizzie Borden.

As a professed writer of stories in which guilt and its detection play a prominent part, I have been asked by the New York World to state my impressions concerning the very remarkable murder which has lately taken place in Fall River, and the probable culpability of the young woman upon whom the suspicions of the police have mainly fallen.

Not till my attention was specially drawn to the matter did I peruse the columns devoted to this affair, so rarely is there any feeling save revulsion, produced in me by details of this nature. But this crime is not of the ordinary type. Indeed, it is not sufficient to class it among those of an extraordinary nature. It is unique, sole, the crime of the generation as regards mystery and the shock it gives to all natural and human probabilities. When I began to read its story I found myself startled, and before I had finished the astonishing tale I was positively aghast. The circumstances—the finding of the body of an elderly man lying slain in his own home, with no evidences of struggle or surprise visible in his countenance; a servant near, his daughter within hearing distance, yet no cry heard, no sound of a fall noticed, his watch in its place, his money intact in his pockets, thus robbing the gruesome affair at the first blush of the usual motive of theft, but supplying later certain facts which bespoke a still more subtle motive in the cupidity of the daughter anxious for the fortunes she saw slipping through her hands—all this was not new to me, all this had been gone over in my mind years and years ago with creatures of my imagination, even down to the last startling detail of the proposed will he was prevented from making by his sudden death. That there were two victims here instead of one, that the time of murder was in broad daylight when doors and windows are supposed to be open and any unusual sound in so light a structure as the frame house inhabited by the Bordens would be likely to attract attention, and that the most brutal of all weapons, the axe, had been preceded by poison, are the touches whereby reality transcends romance and human nature proved to be more vindictive in its hatred and more reckless in its methods than any writer dares to make his characters in fiction. Mr. and Mrs. Borden were not only killed, but hacked, and this not because of resistance or from a desire to escape an alarm, but in face of non-resistance and an undoubted physical powerlessness, their energies having been previously paralyzed by poison if not utterly destroyed by the first blow they received. A man will strike and strike and strike again, even after death has set in, the object of his hatred, and there must have been hatred seemingly of a deeply rooted and prolonged nature at the bottom of this crime. A woman will strike and strike and strike again, perhaps with more unreasoning and unrelenting frenzy than a man, when her victim is a rival who has aroused her jealousy, or the man who has outraged her affections or robbed her of her children.

MISS LIZZIE BORDEN

But for a girl of any education or training to bring down an axe again and again upon the unresisting form of a father, who, whatever his severity had been towards her, could have aroused in her no fury of antagonism which would not have been satisfied by his mere death, is not consonant with what we know of female nature, and makes one pause when the cry goes up too loudly against her. Cruelty and the shedding of blood for blood's sake are a man's prerogative, or if they are ever found developed in a woman the cases are so rare that we may well afford to give Lizzie Borden the benefit of the doubt. I believe her innocent. To slay an aged father—even an aged mother—from motives of anger or cupidity is possible to a woman even in this day and generation, as our papers frequently show, but to needlessly hack and hew them! What motive of rage could have been strong enough to carry Lizzie Borden through what? Revenge for moneys withheld, tastes crossed or desires unsatisfied? I cannot think so.

THE CENTRAL STATION.

Marshal Hilliard Returns to His Desk After Several Days' Absence.

Sunday was the first that the marshal has been about headquarters since Thursday. In the mean time he had been out of town in consultation with the district attorney, preparing evidence for presentation at the approaching hearing. When asked how much evidence would be offered, he said that he was not prepared to answer that question, but said that he would not be surprised if the hearing consumed four or five days. It would seem from this that the government might put in the greatest part of its case for no other purpose than to vindicate the officials in charge and satisfy the public that the facts in their possession merited the action they have taken.

Alluding to some of the criticisms which have been made by the press on an imperfect knowledge of facts, Marshal Hilliard called the reporter's attention to an editorial in a Boston paper of Saturday, in which the ground was taken that Judge Blaisdell having issued the warrant for the arrest of Lizzie Borden ought not in deference to the proprieties sit on the case. As a matter of fact he did not issue the warrant, did not know that it had been issued until after it had been decided to serve it. The warrant runs to "August B. Leonard, clerk of the second Bristol district court and justice of the peace."

One of the earlier visitors of the day at the office was George W. Hathaway, the man whom Capt. Smalley of New Bedford named as the author of the story published a few days since regarding alleged differences between Miss Lizzie Borden and her father. He was particularly anxious to disavow the statement of the New Bedford man, and have the marshal and the public understand that he was citing the case of another family. As for himself, he said, he believes Miss Lizzie Borden innocent, and was not flattered at all over the notoriety he had obtained in the past few days.

Taunton Gazette

Did the Judge Consult?

It would not be surprising to learn at some future time when the excitement over Judge Blaisdell's proposed action in the Borden matter had died away that the judge had fortified himself by obtaining from his brother justices expressions of opinion as to the proper course to pursue. Neither would it be surprising if it was shown that each and all had intimated that he was all right and should go ahead, meaning that they didn't care to have the task put upon them quite as much, perhaps, as that the sitting was the correct thing. When a presiding justice says that he will not state whether or not he had any word from Judge Blaisdell in regard to the matter it seems safe to presume that he has heard something.

Lowell Times

It is common opinion in this city that the authorities of Fall River are putting the Borden family, Bridget Sullivan and John V. Morse to infernal torture. They have a right to their liberty unmolested unless the police have evidence enough to warrant the arrest of one or all of them. In justice to these people matters ought to be brought to a focus.

The Fall River Herald

MUCH CONJECTURE

As to the Reasons for the Continuance

OF THE BORDEN HEARING UNTIL THURSDAY.

The Accused Confined at the Central Station.

A REPORT THAT THE POISON THEORY WILL COUNT

Among the Points to be Urged by the Prosecution.

There was a feeling of keen disappointment about the city Monday night when it became known that the examination of Lizzie Borden had been again deferred. People who have been unsettled in their minds as to what the verdict against the prisoner should be are anxious to have the whole evidence laid before them so that they can form an opinion for themselves. Accordingly there was more or less impatience with the prosecutors because the case did not go forward according to the announcement, but so long as the public has only such an interest in the case as concerns justice and the care for general safety, the officials on the government side did not appear to be disturbed at the complaints.

The postponement was the theme of discussion everywhere, and plenty of men assured their friends that they knew its significance. As the reasons assigned for the government's action differed quite materially from one another, they gave rise to such energetic discussion as characterized the early days of the case.

It cannot be doubted that the majority of people believe that the delay is a manifestation of weakness on the part of the prosecution. Dist. Atty. Knowlton declined to give any reason other than that which he expressed in court, and the police are silent. The HERALD man who talked with Mr. Jennings got small satisfaction.

"Did you urge a postponement of the case?" was the question asked the lawyer.

"The suggestion came from the other side. We were ready for the trial, for you must bear in mind that the duty belongs to the government to show that Lizzie Borden is guilty and not to us to prove that she is innocent. Until she has been proved guilty the presumption is that she is innocent."

MISS BORDEN'S FRIENDS got a good deal of comfort out of the latest development. They reasoned that if so much value was attributed to the evidence of medical experts, it was very clear that the important disclosures reported from time to time to have been made at the inquest were not made at all, because if all of them had been described as was reported there was certainly sufficient evidence to warrant Judge Blaisdell to commit the prisoner to appear befor the grand jury.

It was told that Bridget Sullivan had said that she had seen an axe partly hidden under the lounge before Mr. Borden came home; that blood spots had been found on Miss Borden's dress and a hundred other details that were vaguely accepted as completing a chain of evidence in which there was not a single defective link.

The Prussic Acid Theory.

From information which came to me yesterday from a source which must not be revealed, says the New Bedford Mercury's correspondent, the government's case may be stronger than has been conceived, and it is this which renders the analysis of Prof. Wood a matter of the most vital importance. It has come to my knowledge that the prussic acid feature may be the sensation of the case.

It is a fact which has never been printed that Edward E. Wright, of the Wright Drug company, New Bedford, has been summoned to Fall River, and has been in consultation with District Attorney Knowlton and Marshal Hilliard. At this hearing he posted them on toxicology, with especial reference to prussic or hydrocyanic acid, which the government will attempt to prove was purchased by Lizzie Borden a few days previous to the murder. Marshal Hilliard, on his recent visit to New Bedford, was again in consultation with Mr. Wright, and now the latter is summoned to repeat his testimony.

It has several times been suggested by physicians that there was an absence of blood spurting in the rooms where the murders were committed, such as might be expected from the nature of Mr. and Mrs. Borden's wounds. This might have been explained, physicians have said, if it was shown that the victims were dead when the blows were inflicted. My informant tells me that Prof. Wood is analyzing the stomachs no less to find which of the twain was the first to die, than to see if traces of poison, of prussic acid, can be found.

THE DEFENCE.

Some of the Things That Lizzie Borden's Counsel Will Show.

Any evidence the government may put in relative to the relations of the members of the family may be offset by the testimony of Morse, Dr. Bowen, Emma Borden, Mrs. Bowen and other members of the family and friends, while the government had Hiram Harrington, Mrs. Whitehead and several other witnesses to give light on the family relations.

The defence was anxious to know all there was in the poison story and Eli Bence, Fred Hart and Frank Kilroy were on hand to tell about it. The local specials, headed by Detective Seaver, are to be put upon the stand.

The defence is going to meet Officer Medley's statement that the floor of the barn loft was so dusty that if anybody had been up there on the day of the murder he would have discovered footprints.

He says he found none, and the prosecution will introduce this testimony in its endeavor to show that Lizzie Borden never went into the barn loft at all. John Donnelly says that he and another man went up there directly after the murder and before Officer Medley arrived. They did not notice any great amount of dust on the floor, and they wonder why the officer did not detect their footprints when he visited the place afterwards.

The presence of Abram G. Hart of the Union savings bank, Cashier John T. Burrell of the Union national bank, Cashier Everett B. Cook of the First national bank and Charles C. Cook, agent of the A. J. Borden building, made it apparent that the business relations of the murdered man are to be carefully examined. Bridget Sullivan is considered the most important witness of all, but about what she will testify that is not already known can only be conjectured.

Was Not Taken Back.

It was at Lizzie Borden's request that she was allowed to remain at the central station until Thursday. The accommodations are better and saves the publicity that would have to be undergone in travelling to and from Taunton.

She is looking much better than when committed and her appetite is also improved. Her meals are brought from the Second street residence and are eaten with an apparent relish. Last night she slept soundly and looked as bright as could be this morning. Most of her time is spent reclining on a cot. She is a constant reader, the books being of a light character. One of the matrons is in constant attendance in the room and is held responsible for her charge.

Views of an Official.

"Too much importance ought not to be attached to this postponement of the case," said an official this morning who did not want to be named. "While it was technically asked for by the government, it was really for the interest of the defence. Mr. Jennings wanted Prof. Wood to be present so that he could be cross-examined. The government was satisfied to go on without him, but was willing to give the other side every opportunity it desired to make out a strong defence. It is willing to lay its whole case before the lawyers for the defence so that when the final trial shall come they will have every means of rebutting the testimony offered."

In opposition to this view, it is claimed that the case has proceeded too far to allow the lawyers to strain at courtesies. Both Mr. Knowlton and Mr. Jennings are bound to win, and the government never loses sight of the fact that only a verdict of "probably guilty" is necessary in this court. The grand jury and superior court may have to look into the evidence in turn, and then it will be done very minutely. Until then, it is thought to be unusual if Mr. Knowlton countenances any measures which are in the direct interest of Mr. Jennings.

Notes.

Detective McHenry has been the center of much speculation since Saturday. On that day he drove up to the station house accompanied by a heavily veiled woman, whom he conducted into the office of the Marshal Hilliard. At once every was asking: "Who is the veiled lady; where does she come from and what has she to do with the case?" Nobody who knew would tell and such an air mystery surrounded the coming and going that it was evident that the women had some important evidence to give. The same secrecy is maintained today, and the officials have no answer for the query: Who is the veiled lady?

VIEWS FROM OTHER NEWSPAPERS

The New York World

The police insist that they have proofs not yet disclosed to the public. But it is the evidence that is missing which shakes the belief of the people in Lizzie Borden's guilt. Where is the blood-stained axe that beat out the lives of two persons? Where are the telltale stains on the handle and on the blade? Where are the bloody clothes which the murderess must have worn?

The Providence Journal

The author of "The Leavenworth Case" has been called upon for an expert opinion on the Borden murder, and, after pointing out the close resemblance between fiction and fact, states with some show of diffidence that Miss Borden must be innocent. Criticism of the Fall River police for not applying to such an authority in the first instance is now in order.

The Boston Post

Up to this point in the Borden case, even after the authorities had fixed upon the one whom they supposed to be the criminal, there has been too much of the policy of concealment. If the counsel for the defence has succeed in breaking down this wall of secrecy and forcing the government to bring its evidence out into the light of day, a work of considerable importance has been accomplished. The ends of justice will be served by throwing open the whole case clearly on Thursday.

The New York Press

Speculations continue as to the guilt or innocence of Miss Lizzie Borden, accused of the murder of her father and stepmother. The approaching examination before a magistrate will leave the public in a better condition to judge of the truth or falsity of the charge. It may be worth noting in this connection that the late Charles O'Connor, in the last criminal case in which he ever appeared—the defence of Frank Walworth, charged with the murder of his father, Mansfield Tracy Walworth—argued that there was no authentic instance of sane and deliberate parricide. It was a startling argument, and may or may not have had an effect upon the jury, which found the young man guilty of murder in the second degree.

The Boston Advertiser

IT WAS MISS BORDEN

WHO ASKED FOR POISON AT THE DRUG STORE.

EVIDENCE WHICH THE GOVERNMENT WILL PUT FORWARD TODAY.

Much Excitement Regarding the Opening of the Borden Murder Trial in Fall River—Were the Murders Committed by a Left-Handed Person?—A New Question—Rev. Mr. Jubb Wronged—Bridget Sullivan's Talk.

FALL RIVER, Aug. 24.—Marshal Hilliard arrived from Boston tonight, and Attorney Jennings came down on the same train. The marshal stated that the government is ready to go on with the case, but declined to say whether or not the analysis was completed. It is generally believed here that Prof. Wood will be ready to go on the witness stand and testify as to what discoveries he has made up to the present time. The defence is also ready to proceed. Mr. Adams arrived here at a late hour and was in consultation with Mr. Jennings for a long time.

Tonight the question is being very generally discussed as to whether or not the assassin was left-handed. The direction of the wounds would give good grounds for supposing such statement to be well grounded. In relation to the poison theory, it was said tonight at the police station that Miss Borden has been identified by E. E. Wright of New Bedford as a person who inquired for poison of him. The Daily News says:—

"As far as we can learn the authorities do not expect to establish that prussic acid was administered to the victims. Its action as a poison is rapid. The symptoms of the sickness complained of by the household were not the symptoms of this poison. It would not tend to lessen the flow of blood as has been urged. The theory of the government on this point has been stated previously to be that the attempted purchase of poison by Miss Lizzie would show premeditation of crime and quick means of escaping legal punishment should detection be established.

"But it is hard to reconcile this theory with that of momentary insanity and complete forgetfulness and knowledge of the actual deed, which some charitably inclined officers have advanced. The mistaken identity of the drug clerks is of easier conception."

Miss Borden is in very good spirits tonight, and looks forward eagerly to tomorrow's examination. She has perfect freedom of the matron's room, but complains a little of the noise at 1 o'clock in the morning, when the policemen are going to and returning from their beats.

One of the most prominent citizens is quoted tonight as saying that he asked Mr. Borden why he was not spending the summer at his farm in Swansea, receiving the reply: "No; I have had so much difficulty in my family I have not felt like going away." It is certain that Bridget Sullivan, the servant girl, told many of her friends of quarrelling in the Borden household, some time before the murder occurred. The name and address of friends with whom she conversed are now in the hands of the police.

Despatches sent from this city today giving an account of the visit to the central police station of Rev. Mr. Jubb, contained statements cruelly wronging that gentleman. Local papers reflected the same spirit tonight to such an extent that he looked up the Associated Press reporter and made the following statement of what transpired in Miss Lizzie Borden's room:—

Rev. Mr. Jubb said: "I went into the police station and was directed to the matron's room up stairs by a policeman. I went to the door, knocked and was admitted by Matron Reagan. I told her I was Mr. Jubb and she bade me enter. I shook hands with Miss Lizzie Borden, and was about to converse with that lady when Mrs. Reagan appeared to recall that she might have violated some police rule, and asked me to step outside for a few moments. Her manner was perfectly ladylike.

"I stepped towards her, and she asked me if I would wait until she had seen Marshal Hilliard and learn if I was a proper person to talk with the prisoner. She went downstairs and learned that the marshal was out of town, but on returning saw Assistant Marshal Fleet at the head of the stairs. He gave me permission to enter the room at any time. Mrs. Reagon was about to follow his instructions when Rev. Mr. Buck appeared. We shook hands and talked a few moments. As he had a bouquet and other things in his hand I said I would not go in with him, but would return later. I felt that one minister would be plenty at a time.

"I went to the door with Mr. Buck, told Miss Lizzie I would return in the afternoon, then went downstairs. There was no such talk at the door, nor was there any such unladylike talk as was attributed to the matron and other officials. I think Mrs. Reagan's actions were perfectly proper under the circumstances. I went to Miss Lizzie's room this afternoon and remained in conversation with her for nearly half an hour.

"The exaggerated and untrue accounts of the morning's interview are attributed to persons who are nursing strong feelings against Rev. Mr. Jubb because of statements made in public some few days ago.

Le May, the Frenchman, who reported having seen a suspicious stranger in the vicinity of Thomas Thurston's house, insists that his story is correct. Two policemen are stationed at Steep Brook tonight to watch for him. A woman, plainly dressed, with short, dark hair, called at the police station, this afternoon, in search of Marshal Hilliard. Failing to find him, she returned tonight, and was closeted with him for half an hour. She refused to give her name and also declined to register at the Wilbur House, where she is stopping.

She told the marshal that she was peculiarly gifted from infancy, and went on to say that she saw in a vision Miss Lizzie Borden murdering her mother at 10:10 o'clock Thursday, Aug. 4. Later she saw Miss Lizzie pass downstairs with a hatchet in her hand, go towards her father, putting the hatchet in a corner while she smoothed the sofa pillow for her father to rest on. Still later she saw Lizzie standing at the head of the sofa hacking mercilessly at her father's skull. Marshal Hilliard says that the woman appears to be sane.

Life-sized photographs have been taken of the skull of Mr. and Mrs. Borden showing the position of the wounds, and they will be used at the trial. One half of Mrs. Borden's skull is broken in.

Late tonight Attorneys Jennings and Adams called at the police station to make inquiries concerning the truth of Le May's stories. They took notes of the progress made by the police in searching for the Steep Brook suspect.

A CONSTANT WARFARE

Had Been Going in the House of the Borden's House, Bridget Sullivan Says.

FALL RIVER, Aug. 24.—It has come to the knowledge of the public today that Bridget Sullivan had long before the tragedy at the Borden home confided to intimate friends certain facts which leave little doubt that there had been a constant warfare going on in the Second st. house. Mrs. Borden and her stepdaughters were on anything but pleasant terms with each other, although the former tried in every way to establish pleasant relations. Lizzie showed more antipathy toward the older woman than did her sister. It is supposed that at the inquest Bridget Sullivan divulged a great deal of important information of this character and furnished the government broad grounds on which to base the theory of a motive.

Another new feature of the case is a letter which Lizzie wrote to her sister Emma the Tuesday before the murder. The first knowledge of this letter came out at Lizzie's examination at the inquest in reply to the question: "Had you ever noticed any suspicious persons about the house on the day of the tragedy?" She said she did not on that day but had on the Monday night before, and had written an account of the incident to her sister Emma.

Inquiry develops the fact that on Wednesday Emma did get a letter from Lizzie in which the latter refers to her anxiety over something which happened on Monday night. When she was returning home from a call she noticed a man in the back yard just as she opened the side gate. He disappeared about the house on discovering her. After entering the house, Lizzie wrote, she was so disturbed over what she had seen that she went to one of the windows in her room commanding the back yard and watched. She saw a man, who looked like the one she had seen already, moving about, but it was quite dark and she could not give any description of him. Emma Borden showed this letter to friends in Fairhaven with whom she was visiting when she received it, and then destroyed it, she says.

It also turns out that the letter which Lizzie Borden sent to her Marion friends, and which was received by them on the day of the murder, was also destroyed because it contained reference to something which, in the opinion of the young woman to whom it was sent, might, in the light of subsequent events, be misconstrued. Some of the speculating ones are now wondering if that something was not this story of the suspicious man whom Lizzie told her sister was about the Borden house Monday night.

The Fall River Herald

ELEMENT OF TIME

To Figure Largely in the Case Tomorrow.

MANY THINGS WERE DONE IN A FEW MINUTES.

The Government and the Prussic Acid Theory.

A NEW YORK WOMAN DESCRIBES THE HOUSE

Where the Tragedy was Committed --Supprised by the Arrangements.

Having talked over the postponement of the examination of Lizzie Borden to their heart's content, people have settled down again to await the developments of Thursday. There were no striking incidents in the case Tuesday to be related. The prisoner spent the day under supervision of Mrs. Russell and Mrs. Reagan, police matrons, and her sister and intimate friends were allowed to see her.

By piecemeal, the evidence in the hands of the government continues to leak out, some of which is authentic and a good deal more of it the conclusions jumped at from a chance word dropped now and then by officials concerned in the case. This, too, may be authentic and then again it may not be. If one tries to verify the hearsay concerning the vital points of the case, he encounters a reluctance to talk that is proof against the most persistent interviewer.

People who have been out of the city since the murder are astonished at the clean cut opinions as to the guilt or innocence of the accused which are stoutly maintained by men and women who live at a distance from the scene of the tragedy. According to the view of the case accepted by their favorite journal, these people will argue until sundown or day break, and present an array of accepted facts that is truly startling to a person who has followed the case upon the ground. While outside opinion is fairly divided upon both sides, there are very few persons who admit that they have any doubt upon one side or another, according as they have reasoned out the case beforehand.

Of the evidence which has been coming to public knowledge since the inquest, it appears that any doubt that may have existed concerning the escape of a person from the Borden house on the day of the murder by way of Dr. Chagnon's yard and Third street has been cleared up by Miss Collet, who states positively that she was in Dr. Chagnon's yard all morning until after the murder had happened and would certainly have seen everybody who passed through there. The young lady is now on a visit to friends in Canada, but will return if her testimony is needed at the trial.

AN IMPORTANT POINT.

The Question of Time an Important Consideration in the Trial.

The defence will make every effort to fix the time exactly when Mr. Borden entered the house and when the alarm was given, as it will be a matter of great importance in the case. As nearly as can be figured out, the time when Mr. Borden was not visible, alive or dead, to people outside his home is within a minute or two of 20 minutes.

Accepting the theory of the government that Lizzie Borden committed the crime, a person is forced to admit that the plot was not only carefully planned, but was attended with just such marvelous good luck as has concealed the murderer until this moment, if he escaped from the house at all. As the case goes forward, additional acts on the part of somebody are being crowded into that fatal 20 minutes, which are already full to overflowing of direful events.

The story of the 20 minutes as pieced together from the scattering evidence may be reviewed. After Andrew Borden disappeared into his house, he must have gone to the kitchen to hang up his hat. Even if nothing attracted his attention in the rooms of the house so that he paused a moment or two, or even if he handed his hat to his daughter and prepared for a rest at once, the time it took him to remove his heavy coat and put on a house coat, even if the latter usually lay on the sofa where he threw his outside coat, and to compose himself to sleep, not going to the extent of falling into a doze, can be estimated to suit any reasoner on the case. Anybody can think it over and conclude for himself whether it would have been done naturally in less that six or eight minutes. Every minute must count in so short a section of time, for there is still a great deal to be done in what moments are left. The weapon must be pulled out of its temporary hiding place; it may have been only a step away, but it certainly could not have been carelessly left where Mr. Borden or the servant was likely to find it by accident. There could have been no unnatural hurrying through the house for, unless Mr. Borden were already dead, the swift movement of a person through the room must have caused him to open his eyes. He was not deaf, nor can it be believed that he was fast asleep.

Having secured the weapon the murderer delivered 11 blows, the first with such strength as to crush the hard bone above the temple, as could have been done by a full arm swinging movement. Then ten heavy blows followed. There must be no delay, no fastening of the axe's edge in the wounds, no hesitation at the sight of such work that a quarter of an hour afterwards caused sturdy men to sicken and turn away and was not without effect upon physicians accustomed to the sight of mangled corpses. How much time was consumed by such operations can only be barely conjectured; but it must be added to the time needed to leave Mr. Borden settled for a nap on the lounge and the fatal 20 minutes reduced by just so much as one makes the total.

There is yet much to be done. If Lizzie Borden used a hatchet in this fiendish work, as the police say she did, she lost no time in concealing the weapon or covering up the traces of the crime. If the axe was hidden and has not been found, two conclusions are necessary. Either a place was prepared to receive it only a few steps away from the sitting room, or it was carried to a remote part of the house and hidden where a repeated, persistent search has failed to reveal it. How much time such an act would take cannot be reckoned, but it must still be within the limit of that dreadful 20 minutes, so much of which had already been consumed by getting Andrew Borden composed for a quiet nap and then sending him into eternal sleep.

The police hint that the weapon has been found beside a sink in the cellar, and upon it are only faint signs of blood, so faint, indeed, that a microscope has been necessary to detect their nature. Here are signs of time-consuming effort. Lizzie Borden must be conceived to have rushed to the kitchen sink, not simply washed, but scraped and scoured that hatchet reeking with her father's blood, hurried to the cellar stairs and hurled it to the place where it was found. Perhaps she did not wash the bloody axe at the kitchen sink; she may have carried it into the cellar, carefully, indeed, so that not a stain should fall upon the clean surface of the wooden stairway. Then the washing and scouring must have been done below stairs. Valuable moments were used—two rooms were crossed and a winding cellar stairway was threaded. The water was poured down the sink and care taken that no tell tale drop of it should light upon the woodwork, for there were certain to be keen eyes to examine all about, so that haste must not cause mistake.

Time is flying all the while, no second to be wasted. There must yet be left of that 20 minutes enough for other things. Lizzie Borden must hurry across the house, rushing by her father, the gaping wounds and trickling blood on whose head must not excite remorse. There is no time for remorse; the servant must be called; the neighbors must be aroused; a hasty glance must be given one's clothing and hands to see that all has been neatly done. The servant must not waste valuable seconds in yielding to feminine weakness at the sight of her butchered employer; she must be hurried across the street for Dr. Bowen, yet not too eagerly because she might recall it afterwards. Again across the sitting room, again in sight of the reproaching, bleeding wounds must the woman have passed to the side door to summon Mrs. Churchill and the neighbors. Had not everything gone well thus far, extremely well?

But as if all this were not enough to crowd into the already heavily laden 20 minutes, the rumor gains currency that the woodwork had been washed after the killing to remove spots of blood. Lizzie Borden must have done this,if she did the rest. Breathless with chopping, with running into the cellar or to the kitchen sink, fearful lest somebody should come in or the servant come down stairs, she must still have all control of her faculties, move about where her father lay dead,detect the spots of blood on the casing, bring water to wash them out, empty it afterwards and rinse the cloth which did the wiping.

These are some of the things that the prosecution will show were packed into the time that elapsed when Andrew Borden entered the house and was afterwards found dead by his neighbors. Allowing 23 minutes, 25 minutes or 30 minutes, as has been variously stated, everything was done with a success that was as if under the fostering care of a power supreme for evil. It was just such luck as might have attended a murderer who stole into that Borden house on the fatal Aug. 4 and who had stolen out again, leaving behind him two bleeding corpses as the only souvenirs of his visit.

THE BORDEN HOUSE.

Mrs. Percy, the correspondent of the New York Herald, telegraphs as follows: "I went to the Borden house today. I was unable to see any member of the family. I was allowed to examine the rooms where the two murders were committed, the parlor and dining-room adjoining on the lower floor, and the bedchambers of the two sisters above, next to which Mrs. Borden was found brutally done to death by an assassin. I was surprised to find the house extremely pretty and refined in its appointments. Easy chairs, shaded lamps, books, well-chosen bits of bric-a-brac, cushions and draperies, an open piano, a hundred comforts and pleasing trifles tastefully disposed bespoke pleasantly the character of the occupants. The "spare room" is the only unattractive apartment in the house, and that is not cheaply furnished, but in heavy gloomy style of the Brussels carpet, black walnut period long passed.

"There is a great square space where the blood-stained carpet under Mrs. Borden's crushed head has been cut away. The paper underneath shows the awful discoloration where it soaked slowly through.

"Lizzie Borden's room is as dainty and charming a place as any girl need ask for. The tiny bed had a pale blue embroidered counterpane, the work of the woman who occupied it. Many books and pictures were in the room, some of them evidently gathered in that foreign journey of which we have heard so much. One thing struck me forcibly. How could Lizzie Borden have come in the dainty place and removed the traces of such fearful work without marring all the delicate purity of everything with which she had contact? Why, the washstand even is in a recess veiled by a pale silken curtain. A soiled finger pushing it aside would leave a mark, and there is none. The stairway leading from the front hall is steep and winding at the top, and the wall at one side is covered with a pale gray cartridge paper. This way, up and down, which the assassin passed bears not a trace. Truly the Borden mystery holds its own as such."

Notes.

That the government is bound to work the poison theory for all it is work is shown by the determined effort the police are making to connect it with the case. Last week a druggist from New Bedford visited Taunton jail three times in the endeavor to identify Lizzie as the party who wanted to buy prussic acid from him. He would walk up and down the corridor a number of times on each visit, but as Miss Borden kept her back toward the cell door it was impossible for him to identify her. It seems strange that the government did not bring the two parties face to face and thus settle the matter.

It is stated on the best of authority that three days previous to the murder Lizzie wrote a letter to her sister Emma in Fairhaven, complaining about a man whom she saw lurking around the house. This letter was destroyed, but its contents was shown to a number of friends in Fairhaven, and they will, if necessary, be called on to testify.

Lowell Times

Let our contemporaries possess themselves in peace as concerns Judge Blaisdell's connection with the Borden case. Judge Blaisdell presumably knows the law, and presumably too is a fair and honest man. He would not sit upon the case to the deliberate prejudice of the prisoner's cause. Beyond Judge Blaisdell, if the prisoner be held, two juries will be given opportunity to do justice by Lizzie Borden.

New York Telegram

There had been too much in the nature of star chamber proceedings already in this case. If a heretofore irreproachable and a cultivated and tenderly bred young lady is to be any longer held under the suspicion of a crime concerning which it is conceded there is at the utmost nothing but circumstantial evidence, it is of importance to the public as well as to her, that all should have the speediest opportunity possible of deriving some estimate of the nature and value of that evidence.

San Francisco Examiner

Murders occur every day, and unless near at hand provoke little notice and no comment. It is seldom that the assassination of a private citizen leads to developments that interest the whole country. The murder of Andrew J. Borden, a capitalist of Fall River, Mass., and his wife, the suspicion that fell on Mr. Borden's daughter Lizzie, her calm demeanor under the fearful charge, her examination and formal commitment, constitute an exception to the rule. The mystery of the crime is so intense, and the efforts of the detectives to fasten it upon the imprisoned daughter so determined,that the country at large is interested in knowing whether she is really guilty; whether she is a monstrous creature fit for the gallows or asylum, or simply a wronged and tortured woman, the victim of circumstances.

Viewed from a distance it would appear that the detectives had chosen to brand Lizzie as the murderer rather from lack of evidence against any one else than by reason of evidence against her. It was, at least, her misfortune to be in the vicinity and to have nothing to corroborate her statements as to how she was employed during the few fateful moments when the aged couple were hacked to death.

JUDGE BLAISDELL
CLERK LEONARD
MARSHAL HILLIARD
DIST. ATTY. KNOWLTON
ATTORNEY ADAMS
ASST. MARSHAL FLEET
OFFICER DOHERTY

DRAWN BY A SPECIAL ARTIST FOR THE ILLUSTRATED AMERICAN MAGAZINE

The Fall River Herald

AWAITING HER FATE!

Beginning of the Examination of Lizzie Borden.

THE COURT ROOM CROWDED TO THE DOORS.

Dr. Dolan Testifies as to the Wounds

AND THE WAY IN WHICH THEY COULD BE CAUSED.

Sensational Story About an Alleged Quarrel.

The second act of the great Borden tragedy began at 10 o'clock today. Everybody is familiar with the scenes of the first act: the commotion in the usually quiet neighborhood of Second street, the discovery of the murders, the hunt for the murderer, the inquest and the arrest of the daughter of the murdered man and her committal to jail. When the curtain dropped on the last scene the spectators busied themselves in discussing the denoument of the plot. How was it all to end? Here was a young woman of unblemished reputation charged with the fearful crime of slaughtering in cold blood the man who had watched over the days of her childhood, her own father. Could it be possible that one nurtured amid refined surroundings, supplied with all the comforts of life, devoted to works that appealed to the highest sympathies of womanhood could raise a murderous arm against an unwitting victim, made defenceless by sleep? If this be so, what is left to assure one that his friend, his brother, his child, for whom love springs deep in his heart and from whom there has been daily manifestation of respect at least, may not nourish in his breast a purpose to kill? Confidence in a friend is but a mockery and mankind must ever live armed against mankind.

IN THE COURT ROOM.

Big Crowd of Men and Women Anxious to Hear the Trial.

These were some of the thoughts more deeply underlying the opinions expressed by men at the close of the first act. With the postponement of the examination last Monday, the rise of the curtain on the preliminaries of the great trial was delayed to today. As on Monday, public interest manifested itself in the efforts of the curious to get places in the court room. As early as 8 o'clock the entrance to the court were blocked by the waiting crowds. The regular attendants at the proceedings found themselves out of place in the throng of tastefully dressed women and respectable citizens of leisure who were crowding to get into the building. As on the former occasion, the women were most eager to get inside, and the gallant court officer provided for them first. There were but few men in the spectators' seats, and such as gained admittance afterwards took places next to a row of prisoners up for drunkenness and minor offences.

There was no delay in beginning proceedings. The indictment had been read at the first arraignment and the woman had pleaded not guilty to the charge. Dist. Atty. Knowlton called the witnesses one by one and each was sworn in turn before he stepped upon the witness stand.

CIVIL ENGINEER KIERAN

stated that he made the plan of the Borden house, and it was correct. He showed the different rooms and the spots where the bodies were found. It is two feet 11 inches from the bed to the bureau where Mrs. Borden lay. A dot on the plan indicated where a board was taken from the floor that had a blood spot. He also had drawn a complete plan of the barn, fence and yard. There was a blood spot on the wall paper back of the sofa; there was also a spot on the south door. From the west end of the sofa to the door the distance was eight feet two inches. There was also a spot on a picture on the south side of the room, and that distance from the sofa was five feet and four inches. It is 15 feet and four inches from the house to the fence on the north side, and 23 feet and three inches on the south side; and from the house to the nearest end of the barn it is 14½ feet.

By Mr. Jennings—The sofa was placed there by Dr. Dolan and the measurements taken then; the blood spot on the door leading to the kitchen was on the casing. The spot on the picture was shown to me by Dr. Dolan. Was shown a piece of wood which fitted the place taken from the floor by Marshal Hilliard; there were two spots close together. Imagined that blood spots came from direction of sitting room. The spot of blood was on the dining room side of the door casing; to the east of the spot was the dining room door leading to the sitting room. Did not form any theory as to how the spot could pass through the door from the inside. The spot was on the frame of the door nearest to the dining room. Did not have attention called to ceiling; there was a pile of boards near the fence east of the side. The reason I did not put it on the plan was that I did not think of it.

MEDICAL EXAMINER DOLAN.

Have been medical examiner a year last month; saw bodies of Mr. and Mrs. Borden about 15 minutes of 12 o'clock on Aug. 4; saw body of Andrew Borden first lying on a lounge on the north side of house. The head of the sofa was to the west and a small sofa cushion was there; on this his head lay. His feet were on the floor and he looked as though he had been asleep; examined wounds, not thoroughly, but later in the day removed stomach and sent it to Dr. Wood of Boston by express. I saw the body of Mrs. Borden a few minutes later upstairs; it lay face down between the dressing case and bed; she was dressed in a calico dress; there was a silk pocket handkerchief on the floor near her head; it was an old one and

I could not tell whether it was cut; but it was torn. Turning back to Mr. Borden's body, when I lifted the sheet the sight was most ghastly, the worst I had ever seen. Mr. Borden lay on the side of his face. There was one wound which extended through the nose and reached as far as the chin. Another extended from the angle of the eye almost the entire length of the face.

Mr. Jennings raised objections to Dr. Dolan's reading from the record of the autopsy made one week after the crime, and the witness spoke from memory. There was one wound one and one-half inches on the forehead on the left side. Another wound, which took a piece out of the skull, reached downward to the outer ball of the eye. Another wound extended down as far as the mouth. There were ten wounds in all, and all parallel. They ranged from one and one-half to four and one-half inches. Right above the left ear, about one inch and a half, there was another wound. It was a crushing wound which carried the skull with it into the brain and made an opening about four inches. I found no other wounds on the body. I made an examination of the vital organs one week later and found no other cause of death. I found death to have been caused by a shock from these wounds. The side of Mr. Borden's head was covered with blood. It was not clotted blood. The head lay on the arm of the sofa, and the body lay at an angle on the sofa. It was 11:45 when I was at the house. The body was not cold, the blood was oozing from the wounds in the face and head. The principal flow of blood was on the lounge. There was not a great deal of blood on the floor. I think he could not have been dead over half an hour when I entered. I found blood behind the sofa. There were in one cluster of spots, discribed in the arc of a circle, 86 spots immediately behind his head. Some of the spots were minute. They were all on the wall paper. I then found on the paper above the lounge a spot which was six feet one and three-quarters inches from the floor. In fact there were two spots, the lowest one being six feet one and one-half inches from the floor. Further along towards the east were 40 more spots, the highest 58 inches from the floor. All these spots were regularly distributed. There were also spots on the mop boards behind the lounge. On the carpet were spots of blood five feet from the head. I saw two spots on the ceiling above the head, but I don't think they were human blood. I found one spot on the door jamb of the door leading from the sitting room into the dining room. This last spot was more of a stream and measured probably two and one-half inches.

Knowlton—Did you infer that this spot or stream was of a different nature from the others?

Dolan—This spot was more a line, while the others were clustered. This spot could be made by the swinging of an instrument in the hands of a murderer.

Knowlton—What was the character of the wounds on the face?

Dolan—They were incised and made by a sharp instrument.

Knowlton—What relative degree of force is required to crush a skull in that place, assuming that the weapon used was a hatchet?

Jennings—I object to that because Dr. Dolan is not an expert and has no right to give an opinion on such matters.

Dolan—I think a person with a hatchet of four or five pounds could very easily fracture a skull.

Lawyer Adams objected to the answer and said it was not responsive to the question. The objection was overruled.

Dolan—I think a person in good health could, by using moderate force, break a skull with a four or five pound hatchet. Mr. Borden was a man about 70 years of age and in excellent physical condition. He was five feet and nine inches in height and of medium build. The body of Mrs. Borden was lying on its face. I could see only part of her face. I turned the body over and found 18 distinct wounds, all but four on the right side of the head. The wounds were all in a parellel direction Some took pieces of skull out and others went through to the brain. None of the wounds on the left side went through to the brain.

MEDICAL EXAMINER DOLAN

I saw hatchets down stairs going to the left of stairs as I went down. There were three wood axes and a claw hammer hatchet. I examined the hatchet and one of the axes. The hatchet on the blade looked as though it had been washed or scraped; it would make a wound five inches in length. Afterwards I examined it with a glass and found spots of blood and two hairs on it. Then there were spots on the other three axes, but I could not say it was blood. I took a skirt, the dress skirt and underskirt belonging to Miss Borden and sent them to Prof. Wood.

A recess was then taken until 2 o'clock.

On resuming Dr. Dolan testified: I received the shoes and stockings and also gave them to Prof. Wood; also received a piece of the jamb of the door. One of those crushing blows on the skull would cause death instantly.

Cross-examination by Mr. Adams—Do not make surgery a practice; what I have done has been as medical examiner; I have had a case of homicide before; the party was Catherine O'Connor, and the cause of the death was concussion of the brain. I received no information causing me to go the Borden house that day, but was passing in making a call; went indoors on north side of house; Bridget Sullivan and Dr. Bowen were in the house at the time and met me going in; in the sitting room in which Mr. Borden lay Officers Mullally and Doherty were present; then went upstairs; and then went into the room over the downstairs parlor; the bed in the room was an ordinary one; could not say whether there was anyone in the room at the time; Dr. Bowen told me of the party upstairs; Dr. Bowen was present with me in the room, and my impression is that Drs. Tourtellot and Hartley were also present; the first I saw of her body was when entering the room I saw her feet protruding from the bottom of the bed; the woman's head was about three or four feet from the wall; the distance from the dressing case to the bed was about the length of the clerk's desk. Mrs. Borden was about the build of District Attorney Knowlton, but somewhat larger; her head was lying a little on the left side, leaving the right side of the head clearly exposed; the position of the body had not been changed until I arrived; Dr. Bowen told me so; I did not see Dr. Bowen change her position; I put my fingers in the wounds; my hand became bloody, but am confident that none dropped; I made an examination of Mr. Borden first; my hand became bloody from examining him, but none dropped; did not make an examination of the spots on the wall then; the nature of the hair cloth covering the sofa would let the blood slide off.

THE SISTERS QUARRELLED.

A Statement That the Prisoner Indulged in an Outburst.

The day before the preliminary hearing in the famous Borden murder case was eventful. It is said that there was a scene in the matron's room between Emma Borden and Lizzie Borden yesterday afternoon which surprised the prisoner's attendant. Emma entered the apartment pleasantly as usual, and to her evident surprise was greeted by Lizzie: "You gave me away, Emma, didn't you?"

"No, Lizzie, I only told Mr. Jennings what I thought he ought to know for your defence," Emma Borden replied.

"That is false," was the rejoinder, "and I know it. But, remember, I will never give in one inch! Never!"

Emma walked slowly away, and it looked as if the sisters had parted company for good.

Ever since Lizzie has been held under arrest, Emma has been very devoted to her and has shown her all the attention which could have been expected. It is not strange, therefore, that the reception accorded her yesterday afternoon surprised and shocked Matron Reagan. She did not know what to make of it. Possibly it can be explained on the ground that Lizzie had been subjected to a very severe strain during the morning. She was visited by her counsel and he talked long and earnestly with her. Matron Reagan left the room during the interview, but when it was over it was observed that Lizzie's composure had disappeared. She seemed much more nervous and excited than usual, paced the room, rubbed her hands together and was evidently suffering mentally. Matron Reagan refused to talk today about the episode, but the reporter who is responsible for it says tha it actually occurred.

Mr. Jennings went to Boston yesterday afternoon and when he returned Mr. Adams, the associate counsel for the defence in the case, alighted from the train with him. The two lawyers talked for some time in front of the Mellen house and called at police headquarters, where they questioned the captain of the night force regarding the story of the man with the gory hatchet who has been haunting Steep Boook. It is reported that Mr. Jennings talked with Emma and that later he called on Lizzie in order to clear up certain matters on which he has not been able to secure satisfactory information.

DISTRICT ATTORNEY KNOWLTON

PASTOR JUBB

Denies a Statement to the Effect that he Was Cheeky.

The statement having been made that Pastor Jubb of the Central Congregational church had created a scene at the central station Wednesday morning because he was not admitted to see Lizzie Borden, the following is given in explanation: "I went into the police station and was directed to the matron's room upstairs by a policemen. I went to the door, knocked and was admitted by Matron Reagan. I told her I was Mr. Jubb, and she bade me enter. I shook hands with Miss Lizzie Borden, and was about to converse with her, when Mrs. Reagan appeared to recall that she might have violated some police rule, and asked me to step outside a few moments. Her manner was perfectly ladylike. I stepped toward her and she asked me if I would not wait until she asked Marshal Hilliard and learn if I was a proper person to talk to the prisoner. She learned down stairs that the marshal was out of town, but on returning saw Assistant Marshal Fleet at the head of the stairs. He gave me permission to enter the room at any time. Mrs. Reagan was about to follow his instructions, when Rev. Mr. Buck appeared. We shook hands and talked a few moments. As he had a bouquet and other things in his hands, I said I would not go in with him, but would return later. I felt that one minister would be a plenty at a time. I went to the door with Mr. Buck, told Miss Lizzie I would return in the afternoon, then went down stairs. There was no such talk at the door, nor was there any such unladylike talk as was attributed to the matron and officials. I think Mrs. Reagan's actions were perfectly proper under the circumstances. I went to Miss Lizzie's room this afternoon and remained in conversation with her for nearly half an hour."

WHERE'S ROBINSKY?

Wrote a Letter from Waltham to the Sister of the Accused.

A clue on which the counsel for the defence have been hard at work since Aug. 18 is supplied by the following letter, the writer of which they are striving to find, but as yet without success:

WALTHAM, Mass., Aug. 17, '92.

Miss Emma Borden:—Dear madam: You must excuse that I take the liberty in sending you these few lines. I ought to have written to you before this, but I was unable to do so, as I was travelling every day. My name is Samuel Robinsky, I am a Jewish peddler. When the fatal murder in Fall River occurred, I was only a few miles from Fall River that day. While sitting on the roadside towards New Bedford, I met a man who was covered with blood; he told me that he worked on a farm and that he never could get his wages, so he had a fight with the farmer. He said he run away and did not get any money after all. All he had was a five dollar bill. He bought from me four handkerchiefs, one looking-glass. one necktie, collar and shoe blacking. His boots was covered with blood and he put lots of blacking on it. I helped him to fix up again and get cleaned, but by this time I did not know anything about the murder. I felt sorry for him and thought only he gave the farmer a good licking. I advised him to travel at night, which he said he would do, as he feared arrest during the day. I gave him my lunch and he gave me a quarter and told me not to say anything that I met him. He asked me what time the train left for Boston after 8 o'clock at night, and I told him. He had also a bundle with him, which was about two feet thick or big. When I was peddling I did not read any papers only Sundays, as I am studying the English language. When I was in Boston last Sunday a friend of mine told about the Fall River murder. I told him that I was in Fall River and around the neighborhood. I told him about my stranger, and my friend said: "But why did you not report this to the police?" I told him I was afraid, as they would lock me up as witness, and another thing I did not have any license, so I was afraid. I told my friend I would write to you or Mr. Jennings about the case. I read last Sunday Boston Globe and thought that I might have seen the murder; if I should see him here in Boston, I am sure, yes, dead sure, I know him again. He is of medium height, dark brown hair, reddish whiskers or moustache, weight about 135 pounds, grey suit, brown derby hat. His shoes was what they call russian leather, no blacking, or so called summer shoes; he put my blacking on to make them look black and people could not see the blood. It was about 4 o'clock noon that day; I only heard about the murder at 6 or 7 o'clock that night. I kept quiet, as I had no license and feared to be arrested. My stranger was very much afraid, he ask me a million times if he looked all right again, and I brushed him off with my shoe brush, and told him to wait till dark.

If I come again to Fall River next week I shall call on you, if you think it is necessary, but all I can swear to is the stranger which I have seen that afternoon, this is all. But if this man was the murderer I cannot say, but I shall fund him out of 100,000. Will close now will go to Fitchburg tomorrow morning and return to Boston Saturday night. Please do not say anything to the police and would be arrested. If I had known about the murder about the time I met my stranger it would have been different as I would have followed him up, and perhaps got the reward. I thought it was a poor farm hand and took pity on him, as I know as a rule farmers seldom pay their hands during summer. Hoping that my information will be of some use to you, I remain very respectfully,

SAMUEL ROBINSKY.

P. S. Please excuse paper and mistakes, as I am a foreigner.

Mr. Jennings immediately telegraphed to Mayor Mayberry of Waltham, asking if such a man lived there, and received the following reply: "Cannot find that he lives here. Am told that a peddler of that name living in Boston sometimes comes out here."

The New York Times

LIZZIE BORDEN'S HEARING

SHE LISTENS TO THE EVIDENCE WITH STRANGE CALMNESS.

FALL RIVER, Mass., Aug. 25.—Never in the history of this section has a criminal trial attracted the interest manifested at the opening to-day of the preliminary hearing of Lizzie A. Borden, charged with the brutal murder of her father and stepmother. At the Second District Court room newspaper reporters from all parts of the country, members of the bar from this and neighboring States, professional men, and clergymen jostled one another in an eager attempt to gain admittance. None but those of influence were let in, but even these were in sufficient numbers to render the temperature almost unbearable. The prosecution was conducted by District Attorney H. M. Knowlton, and Andrew J. Jennings of Fall River and Melvin O. Adams of Boston guarded the interests of the accused woman.

The remarkable feature of the day was the great calmness exhibited by Lizzie Borden. Seated beside her sister Emma, and supported by the presence of her aged pastor, the Rev. E. A. Buck, and her intimate friends, Bank Examiner Holmes and his wife, she watched the great fight being made in her behalf with apparent unconcern. Three or four times through the weary day she found something amusing in the testimony and laughed heartily. Even at the recital of the gory details of the butchery of her parents she showed no emotion and her demeanor throughout was a marvel of calmness.

The New York Times

BRIDGET TELLS HER STORY

HER TESTIMONY IN THE TRIAL OF LIZZIE A. BORDEN.

SHE DESCRIBES THE SCENES AND INCIDENTS LEADING UP TO THE DOUBLE MURDER—THE PRISONER'S RARE NERVE—OTHER WITNESSES TELL WHAT THEY KNOW.

FALL RIVER, Mass., Aug.26.-The second day of the Borden trial developed much interesting testimony and many significant incidents. Rapid progress in the examination of witnesses was made, and late in the afternoon Bridget Sullivan, the domestic, who is generally regarded as one of the most important witnesses for the prosecution, was placed upon the stand. Her testimony was unfinished when the court adjourned. John V. Morse, uncle of the Borden girls, who was at first suspected by the police as having been concerned in the murder, related his story at great length.

Through it all Lizzie Borden retained the same calm demeanor which has characterized her throughout, and only once during the day did she betray any great interest in the proceedings.

Dr. Dolan resumed his evidence at 10 o'clock. He did not measure at any time, he said, the length of the handle of the hatchet. His opinion was that it was about 18 inches to 2 feet long from the edge of the blade. He did not at any time measure the length of the blade, and could not tell its weight. His opinion was that the blows given to Mrs. Borden were when she was lying down on the floor, the assailant standing in a stooping position over her. The doctor advanced the opinion that the person might have stood with one foot under the bureau and the other turned toward the bed. The assailant's position, he said, must have been near the window, judging from the position of the wounds.

The witness could not say whether the handle was held with two hands or with but one. It might have been held by one.

"Standing in the position you describe, wouldn't the assailant of necessity have been spattered with blood himself in delivering these blows?" was asked.

"Yes, Sir, I think he would be," replied the witness.

"And wouldn't his hands be covered with blood?"

"Yes, Sir, I think it possible they would be." was the answer.

"Possibly! Do you not admit the probability?"

"No, Sir," was Dr. Dolan's positive answer.

The witness said that he never gave permission to any member of the Borden family to wash or clean up around the house. He did not remember telling Mrs. Holmes that she might do it. If Mrs. Holmes should say so he should be inclined to dispute her understanding of what he did say. There was some cleaning done by some person, but by whom he did not know. He was not prepared to say that the members of the family willfully removed them. There were blood spots, Dr. Dolan testified, on the parlor door frame and sitting room, which were removed on the day after the killing without his knowledge. There was a spot on the window glass in the parlor chamber on the outside of the pane. It looked like blood, but afterward it was proved to be dirt. The pane was rubbed to test the spot.

There was no general handling of the axes. They were not brought upstairs to the kitchen and put on the table. "The axes," said the witness, "were lying on the earth in the cellar."

"Were they bone dry? was asked.

"No, Sir," replied the doctor. "Nothing could be bone dry in a cellar."

"Was the cellar damp?"

"No, Sir."

"Was it more or less damp?"

"I don't think that is a sensible question," said the witness.

"I beg your pardon, doctor, but you are not to criticize my questions," said this interrogator.

"But I have to answer them," said the doctor, testily, "and I want them put as they should be." There was a long discussion on the coagulation of the blood.

The doctor reiterated his statement that he believed Mrs. Borden to have been dead an hour to an hour and a half before Mr. Borden. He based this, he said, not on the temperature, but on the presence of clotted blood. There was not much of the clotted blood, though. The witness said that the carpet of the room was a Brussels, with a canvas back, which, he admitted, would keep the blood at the top of the fabric where it might have dried quickly. Dr. Dolan agreed to furnish all of Mr. Borden's personal effects in his possession.

Abram G. Hart, Treasurer of the Union Savings Bank, who talked with Mr. Borden on the fatal morning, testified that he had known Borden for years. Borden was President of the bank. The witness saw him at the bank about 9:30 o'clock the morning of the day he was found dead. Borden was there about five minutes.

"I had an idea," said the witness, "that Mr. Borden did not look well. The day before there was a quarterly meeting of the Trustees, at which, as President, he should have been present. He was not there on that day, and when I saw him he explained his absence by saying that it was because he had not felt well."

John P. Burrill, cashier of the National Union Bank, testified that Mr. Borden came into the bank at 9:45 A.M. on the day of the murder. Borden stopped at the bank only a few minutes.

Everett Cook, cashier of the First National Bank, testified that Mr. Borden left that institution at 9:55 A.M. Borden, the witness testified, had offices in the same building in which the bank was situated.

Charles O. Cook, an insurance agent, testified to his business relations with Borden. Cook said he had charge of his (Borden's) business block, at the corner of Anawan and South Main Streets. Cook usually saw Borden three or four times a week, but did not see him at all on the day of the murder. He saw him pass along the street on the day before. The witness talked with Borden on the Tuesday before the murder.

"Did he say anything about making a will?" asked the District Attorney.

"No, Sir."

"Had he ever said anything to you about his will?"

"Not about making a will," replied the witness. "He said that he hadn't one."

"Were you drawing up a will when he came?"

"I was preparing a draught for somebody else."

"Did he notice your work and say 'That is something I ought to do.'?" asked the District Attorney.

"He did not. He simply said, in noticing it, that he hadn't any will of his own."

"Do you remember Officer Medley coming to you two days after the murder?"

"Yes, Sir."

"Do you remember the officer asking you about what Mr. Borden said to you that morning?"

"He asked me a great many questions."

"Do you remember telling Mr. Medley what Mr. Borden said to you that morning?", persisted the District Attorney.

"He asked me a great many questions," again replied the witness.

"Do you remember telling Mr. Medley that Mr. Borden said to you, 'What are you doing?'?" This question was objected to by Mr. Jennings and was withdrawn.

"Do you remember telling Officer Medley that Borden said to you that what you were doing was something he hadn't done and that he ought to do?

"I never said anything of the kind," was the witness's emphatic reply. This was a sharp blow at the prosecution's theory of motive and is of great interest to the defense. Mr. Cook was told that he might leave the stand.

The defense made no cross-examination.

Mrs. Caroline Kelly, who lives next door to and south of the Borden house, was next called to the stand. She said: "I saw Mr. Borden that morning walking around in his yard toward his front door. I think he then tried and opened the door. Next I saw him walking down the street in front of the house. I think he had a small white package in his hand at the time. As near as I can fix it, it was 27 or 28 minutes of 11 o'clock. I fix the time by an appointement I had with my dentist."

LAWYER ADAMS.

Dr. Dolan was recalled by the District Attorney and Mr. Adams called for the keys of the Borden house. The Medical Examiner brought forth a satchel containing the articles taken from the Borden house. The keys were first produced. Taking them to Lizzie Borden, Attorney Adams held a consultation with her. Dr. Dolan also produced a handkerchief, a letter and some tobacoo.

"Do you understand that Mr. Borden was in the habit of using tobacco?" asked Mr. Adams.

"I don't know anything about it," was the answer.

The articles were left on the desk and District Attorney Knowlton, after examining them, said:

"The engineer gave us some distances, which he said you pointed out to him. Did you do so?"

"Yes, and he made the measurements," was the answer.

"When an artery is cut, what is the result?"

asked the District Attorney.

"It spurts," was the laconic reply.

"How many such spurts did you find around Borden's body?"

"I found one formed of many spots."

"In what direction would the blood spurt from such a cluster?"

"The direction would be up and toward the wall at an oblique angle."

"Then you think the other spots were from the weapon?"

"Yes, Sir."

"Is there any way in which you could determine which were the first blows struck?"

"I must say not."

"Was the blow which caused the spurts given in life?"

"Yes, I should say so."

"Could the crushing blows not have been given in life?"

"Yes, I should say so."

Could the crushing blows not have been given while Mrs. Borden was standing?"

"They could not."

"When did you see her first?"

At about 11:45 o'clock," replied the witness, "when I first came in."

Mr. Knowlton showed the photographs of the bodies of Mr. and Mrs. Borden to Dr. Dolan and had them identified with reference to the time when they were taken and the location of the bodies when photographed. On re-cross-examination, Mr. Adams asked if the direction of an artery spurt depended on the way it was cut. The witness replied in the affirmative.

"In your testimony," said Mr. Adams, "you said the spaces on both sides of the body were equal. Now, in the photograph of the body as it lay on the floor, is not the space between the body and the bed frame much less than the space on the other?"

"Yes," said Dr. Dolan, "it looks less. The distance seems to be only about six inches."

"Was there a yardstick found near the body of Mrs. Borden?"

"I don't remember. I don't know if one was found near the foot of the body. There was one in the room though."

Johnathon Clegg, a dealer in furnishing goods, testified that he saw Mr. Borden in his store on the morning of the murder. Borden left there exactly at 10:20 o'clock. On leaving, Borden went south.

"How did you fix the time?" asked Mr. Jennings.

"I looked at the City Hall clock. I knew he was coming, as I had partly made arrangements with him to take a store in his new block, and I was watching for him."

"How do you fix the time he came into your store?"

"I should say he was there eight or nine minutes. I judge from that as to the time he came in. I went south and to the best of my knowledge he went south also."

"Did you see anything of Mr. Borden after you left the store on your way south?"

"No; I didn't see him after he left my store."

"Was Mr. Borden ever in your store before?"

"Yes, on the Tuesday before he was killed. It was sometime before dinner; I can't tell exactly what time he was there. I had an object in looking at the clock that day, as I had to go out and get back and let my clerk go to dinner before 11:30 o'clock."

DISTRICT ATTORNEY KNOWLTON.

John Cunningham, a newsdealer, testified that he was in front of a house four doors from the Borden dwelling when he heard of the murder. He saw Mrs. Churchill cross the street; he was told that Mrs. Churchill wanted a policeman, and he telephoned to the City Marshal. It was then 10:50 o'clock.

"Did you notice the cellar door of the Borden house?" asked Mr. Jennings.

"I did, particularly. I tried it and it was locked. I remained there about ten minutes, until Officer Doherty and Mullaly came. Then I went after the boy , whose name was Pearce, and who told me that Mrs. Churchill wanted the police telephoned for. Somebody said that he was the farm hand employed by Mr. Borden. I got him and took him to an officer."

On the re-direct examination, the witness said that Mrs. Churchill came out of the house and crossed the street.

Francis H. Wixon, a Deputy Sheriff, testified that he was in the Marshal's office when he heard of the murder. It was then about 10 or 15 minutes past 11 o'clock, the witness calculated, as on his way to the office he heard the bell in the Granite Block strike ll. The witness went to the Borden house five or six minutes after the message was received, and arrived there about 11:30 o'clock. There were few people in the house. The witness saw Dr. Bowen there upon his arrival. Policeman Doherty overtook the witness on the way to the house and they went in and looked at the body of Mr. Borden. He knew nothing at that time of Mrs. Borden's murder. He had a consultation with Dr. Bowen, the result of which was that the witness removed Mr. Borden's watch. He saw nothing of Lizzie Borden after the consultation. Dr. Bowen went upstairs, and the witness and the officer followed. Dr. Dolan reached the house before the witness left.

Continuing, Mr. Wixon said: "I went out in the yard and looked south. I saw a man sawing wood, and in the same lot were two other men at work. None of them had heard of the murder until I told them of it."

"Was any search made while you were there?" asked Mr. Jennings.

"A search was suggested," said the witness, "and I think that some of the officers looked about."

"After you came out of the yard did you go into the barn?"

"No."

"Did you see anybody go in?"

"I can't say; there were too many people around there. I was in the Borden yard and in the yard south of it until after 12 o'clock."

"How did you get into the south yard?"

"I climbed upon a pile of lumber and went over the fence. All I could see of the man in the yard was the top of his head. The yard I climbed over into ran out to Third Street. I couldn't even see the other two men from the fence, but by climbing on a small barn adjoining the Borden estate I saw them in a lot south of the barn. The other man must have see any person who went over the fence, if he had been looking that way."

The engineer's plans were produced and Wixon pointed out to Mr. Jennings the positions which he and the other men occupied. The first man, he said, was down to the west of the barn in the lot, twenty-five or thirty feet from the fence. He was a Frenchman. I talked to him through an interpreter. Between 3:30 and 4 P.M. the witness went back to Kelly's yard and entered the Borden house by getting up on the pile of lumber and climbing up on the fence.

The first witness in the afternoon was Joseph Shortsleeves, a carpenter and a former employee of Borden, who testified that he saw Borden at 92 South Main Street at 10:40 o'clock the day of the murders. When he left he went toward Spring Street.

James Mather, who was with Mr. Shortsleeves at the time of Borden's visit corroborated his testimony.

Mather said that Borden remained in the store three or four minutes and then went toward Spring Street. Mr. Borden was in the store, and the witness looked at the City Hall clock and the time indicated was 10:40. The reason Mather looked at the clock was because he generally ate lunch at that time and he wanted to know the hour. When the police asked him the time the following Saturday he told them it was between 10:30 and 10:45 o'clock. This was the first time he had stated the period exactly. On his way to Spring Street the witness could not tell whether Mr. Borden stopped in any of the other stores or not.

John V. Morse was the next witness. "On the death of my sister, Mr. Borden's first wife," Morse said, "Lizzie was three years old and Emma about nine years old. I was at the Borden house on Aug. 3. I came from New Bedford on the 12:35 P.M. train. I dined there. Emma was not at home." Morse did not know whether the door between his room and Lizzie's was locked or not. Mrs. Borden went to bed first that night, he said, and Mr. Borden remained up until 10 o'clock. Morse got up at 6 o'clock the next morning. Mr. Borden came down 15 minutes later. The witness remained in the sitting room until breakfast was ready. About 7 o'clock Mr. and Mrs. Borden and the witness sat at the table. This was the first time that he saw Bridget Sullivan that morning. Nothing out of the ordinary occurred at the table.

Morse left the house about 8:45, he testified, and had not seen Lizzie up to that time. Mr. Borden went to the back door with Morse and unhooked it to let the witness out. The last words Mr. Borden spoke to him were: "John, be sure and be back to dinner." The hook on the door, Morse said, was an ordinary hasp. The breakfast did not occupy more than twenty minutes, and the rest of the time was spent in the sitting room. The witness went down to the Post Office and wrote a postal card, after which he took a car to Weybosset Street to visit Daniel Emery, where he had a nephew and niece. When Mrs. Borden left the sitting room she didn't say anything, and that was the last time she was seen alive by the witness.

"I came back to Mr. Borden's after I left my nieces on a Pleasant Street car," continued Morse. "The first I learned of the murder was when Bridget told me. Mrs. Sawyer and Dr. Bowen were in the house. After I had been back a few minutes I saw Lizzie sitting on the dining room lounge. I went upstairs and looked under the bed, and saw Mrs. Borden lying there.

"I was on corresponding terms with Mr. Borden and with Emma when I was in the West. I had a letter from Lizzie but never wrote her."

On cross-examination Morse said:"In regard to the health of the Bordens, they all appeared to be sick. Mr. Borden said the milk might have been poisoned. They were first taken sick Tuesday night. Wednesday Lizzie was up stairs ill all the morning. Mrs.

Borden said it might be baker's bread that made them sick. I had no supper at the house Wednesday night, and I don't think Lizzie was in the house. I heard some person come in the front door, but I couldn't see who it was. Lizzie's door was shut when I went up stairs. The door going from the hall was also closed. As to the door that opened from Lizzie's room into the spare room, I don't know whether it was fastened or not. A desk in Lizzie's room is placed against this door. It is about five feet high."

Morse described the spare chamber, telling when he slept in it, and said that he noticed no difference in the furniture on the day of the murder. "On the next morning," said he, "I took my breakfast with the family. Mrs. Borden told Bridget to wash the windows, but I don't think she designated any certain windows. Bridget was in the kitchen when I went away. Mrs. Borden was dusting after breakfast, and Mr. Borden was talking to me most of the time. I heard no sounds from Lizzie's room. Before I went away that morning no one went out of the front door. I went out of the side door as usual and it was also Borden's custom to use the side door. After I went out Mr. Borden hooked the door.

"When I returned, I saw nobody on the streets whom I recognized. I went into the house by the north gate, and walked to a pear tree in the back yard. I came back to the screen door, and Bridget was there. She said: 'Mr. and Mrs. Borden have both been murdered.' Inside the house I found Dr. Bowen and two or three policemen. I looked at Mr. Borden and then went upstairs. I saw Mrs. Borden lying near the bed. Somebody told me that she was in that room. I did not see Lizzie at this time. When I came down stairs Lizzie was in the dining room, sitting on the lounge. There were several ladies with her. I saw no one go into the barn.

"The cellar door, I think, was open before I first went into the house. The barn door was also open. I made no examination of the barn. There were two piles of wood in the yard, the largest being 4 1/2 feet high. I made a cursory examination of the blood spots in the room after the murder. The parlor door, as far as I know, is the only place from which blood was washed. I would guess there were forty spots of blood sprinkled all over the door. The largest spot was nearest the bottom of the door. I examined the picture and saw one blood spot on it. The paper above the sofa was covered with blood. The half circle of space indicated to me that they all came from the same direction. I formed an opinion as to how the blow was struck."

"What was that opinion?" asked Mr. Jennings.

"I object," said Mr. Knowlton. "I do not think this man can give any more information than he has."

The Judge excluded the question.

Resuming, the witness said: "I saw three or four axes taken away the day after the murder, and not on the day of the murder. One axe was such as a person uses to cut trees with, while the others were blades with handles 16 inches long. The officers placed them in a rack, and I could not tell whether there was any rust on them or not."

"Bridget Sullivan," called the District Attorney, and the interest of the crowd was at once raised to a high pitch. The girl looked pale and seem frightened as she took the stand. She was handled gently by Mr. Knowlton.

"On the morning of the murder," she said, "I was washing windows, and went into the house after a dipper, after getting through with the brush. I was then very near the end of the work. I think that the sitting-room door leading from the front hall was shut. I saw nothing of Miss Lizzie nor of Mrs. Borden as I went around the house.

"There were three windows in the parlor, two in the dining room and two in the sitting room. The sink where the dipper was procured was on the east side of the kitchen. I should think it was 10:20 o'clock whenI went into the house after the dipper to finish the windows. I washed the sitting-room side of the house first, and started to wash the parlor windows, and did not see Lizzie. I saw no one from the outside while I was washing the windows. I did not see Lizzie when I returned; went inside the house. On going inside I began washing the upper part of the inside of one of the sitting room windows. I had part of one window done when I went to the front door, as I had heard some one rattling there with a key, and, supposing it to be Mr. Borden, I went to let him in. I found that the bolt was across the door and the key turned in the lock.

"While I was trying to open the door, I heard Lizzie laughing up stairs in the front hall." The witness said she was surprised to hear Lizzie laugh, but explained that she made an exclamation which she did not want to repeat, and this, she supposed, caused Lizzie to laugh. Bridget heard Lizzie talking to her father in the sitting room five or ten minutes later, and she saw Mr. Borden sitting on a chair in the dining room, reading. He had no finished reading when Lizzie came down stairs and asked him if he had any mail for her. Bridget heard Lizzie tell her father that her mother had received a note and had gone out. Bridget was washing the sitting-room windows at that time.

Mr. Borden took his room key from the mantel and went up stairs the back way. Bridget then took the stepladder and went into the dining room. She did not see Lizzie in the room, she said, nor in the kitchen.

A few minutes later she saw Mr. Borden come back, place the key on the mantel, take a book and a chair, and sit near the window.

While the other windows were being washed Lizzie took a small ironing board and, placing it on the dining-room table, began to iron. She usually ironed her own handkerchiefs. Bridget said she did not hear Mr. Borden move while the windows in the diningroom were being washed. Lizzie came to her and asked her if she was going out. If she was, Lizzie said, she wanted Bridget to lock the back door, as she herself might go out also. Mrs. Borden, Lizzie said, had received a note about a sick friend and had gone out.

The witness asked who the sick friend was, but Lizzie did not name her. Continuing, the witness said that she did not stay up stairs more than three minutes. She heard the clock strike 11, and for about three minutes she lay on the bed. She did not remove her clothes. She had time enough to get dinner at 11:30 o'clock, but didn't look at the fire, and had not seen it since she washed the dishes. She did not put the flats on the stove, she said. The dinner was to have been soup and cold mutton, and if there had been no fire the witness would have had time to prepare it, even after she woke up.

She did not go in or out of the door, she said, after she came in from dashing water on the windows. She remained ten or fifteen minutes up stairs and came down in answwwer to a summons from Lizzie, who cried, 'Come down quick; father is dead.' She hurried down and was about to go into the sitting room when Lizzie called her back and told her to go for Dr. Bowen.

"I went for Dr. Bowen," said Bridget, "but he was not at home, and I told his wife and went back and told Lizzie, and she sent me after Mrs. Russell, who lives on Borden Street. I went and told her, and then returned ahead of her. When I got back Dr. Bowen had just stepped out of his buggy, and was in the house when I got in. Mrs. Churchill was there also. Lizzie was in the kitchen. I heard Dr. Bowen say that Mr. Borden was murdered. I said: 'I wonder where Mrs. Borden is?' and Lizzie told me to go upstairs and look for her. I refused to go, and Mrs. Churchill agreed to go with me, and we went up and saw Mrs. Borden lying on the floor.

"We came back, and Mrs. Churchill told Dr. Bowen that Mrs. Borden was upstairs, and then I was taken into the cellar by two policemen, and we found some axes in a box. I never saw them before, paid no attention to the outside cellar door, but came back and asked Lizzie where she was when the people were killed.

"She said: 'I was in the yard.' I don't remember what kind of a dress Lizzie had on that morning, neither do I remember that she wore an apron."

"Was Mrs. Borden in the habit of telling you when she left the house?" asked Mr. Knowlton.

"I object," said Mr. Adams.

"Lizzie told me all that I know about Mrs. Borden's going out," said Bridget, paying no attention to the objection. The objection was, however, sustained by the court, and the answer was ruled out.

The court then adjourned until to-morrow at 10 o'clock.

CONTEMPORARY ADVERTISEMENTS

UNION MARKET!

BEEF! BEEF!

Cheaper Than Ever.

A Good Sunday's Dinner

For 25c.

3 lb STEAK 25c.

Friday & Saturday's Bargains.

Come and See Us and You Will Go Away Happy.

14 North Main Street,

OPP. WILBUR HOUSE.

PERFUMES! PERFUMES! PERFUMES!

We opened this morning a case of new perfumes, among them being some entirely

New Odors:

EASTER LILY, very fine. LILIOPTUS, a choice perfume. JAPONITA and several others. Step in and let us perfume your handkerchief.

We are Headquarters for PERFUMERY.

J. C. BRADY, - - DRUGGIST

1 Granite Block, cor. Pocasset St.

The Fall River Herald

HEADLESS TRUNKS

Of the Victims of the Tragedy

PLACED IN THE GRAVES AT OAK GROVE.

Dr. Dolan Creates a Mild Sensation Today

BY TELLING THAT THE HEADS HAD BEEN REMOVED.

Unimportant Testimony Given by John V. Morse.

The first day's hearing in the Borden case revealed no startling developments. The value of the evidence given by Dr. Dolan was variously estimated according as one had formed an opinion on the case beforehand. Some people said that they expected little that was new to be brought out in the examination of that official since they had previously been kept pretty well informed of his movements. They knew beforehand what was likely to be the nature of his testimony, and they preferred to wait until witnesses were put upon the stand who could tell something concerning the prisoner. Bridget Sullivan is one of these, and until her testimony has been heard it is perhaps not safe to form a fixed opinion on the case. The medical examiner's prominent position did not prevent some people from considering him one of the most important witnesses to help make up the chain of circumstantial evidence, and they were talking about a weakened case on the government side when the day's doings were over.

The lawyers arrived in good season and the prisoner, accompanied by her sister, Mrs. Holmes, Mrs. Brigham, Mr. Holmes and the Rev. Mr. Buck, entered the court room five minutes before the hour set for the trial. The Borden women walked to their places unassisted. Both were dressed as they were yesterday and bore themselves without any outward sign of weakness. They smiled faintly in recognition of the salute of the lawyers, and were quickly seated.

Although the hour for opening the trial had not yet arrived by three minutes or more, Judge Blaisdell entered the court and, as all the principal parties were ready, the hearing was resumed. Dr. Dolan was again called and Lawyer Adams continued the cross-examination. The Boston lawyer is traversing the ground very minutely and seemed intent on confusing the witness. Notwithstanding questions, impertinent and exasperating, Dr. Dolan answered carefully and without confusion.

Towards the close of Thursday's hearing, Dr. Dolan was questioned concerning the autopsy and presented copies of the partial report on the same. The blows, he thought, were delivered by a person standing behind. He had washed his hands before going into the cellar and before he examined the hatchet. It was one which might have made such wounds as were found on the bodies. He testified that the hatchet was sharp though not bright. He tried the edge with his thumb. There was blood on the cutting edge and some on the side, probably seven or eight spots in all. These spots were as large as two pin-heads; the blood or whatever it was was dry.

This line of cross-examination was followed this morning. The first sensation of the case was brought out by Mr. Adams when he inquired about the autopsy at Oak Grove cemetery. Dr. Dolan stated that by order of the attorney general he had removed the heads from the bodies and that the skulls had been cleaned and were in his possession. This announcement created a mild sensation in the court. Everybody's eyes turned towards the sisters to see how they took the announcement that their father's body had been buried headless. Emma's eyes filled with tears and her head sank upon her hand. Lizzie appeared for an instant startled and quickly looked toward her sister. All the morning her eyes had ranged from the counsel to the witness. They were sharp and piercing, and the shocking announcement did not dim their brilliancy.

Resuming his testimony, Dr. Dolan presented photographs of the skulls and the interior of the rooms where the bodies were found, and these were handed about for examination.

Dr. Dolan, on resuming, said that from the positions the party who struck the blows would be spattered with blood below the waist. On an examination of the window, spots were found on the outside that looked like blood, but it would be an impossibility for it to reach there. There was a spot on the inside of the window, but it was not blood. This was upstairs where Mrs. Borden lay. No authority was given to clean the room downstairs. There were some spots removed wilfully, probably the next day, from the parlor door, but the witness could not say who did it. There were eight spots on the parlor door. As far as known no spots were removed from any other place in the sitting room.

When the Oak Grove autopsy was made the wound in Mrs. Borden was first found, and everything else was the same as at the autopsy. The bodies were buried a week after. The skulls were taken away at the time by order of the attorney general. They were cleansed. The bodies are now buried without their heads, and they are in the doctor's possession. The skulls were photographed on Monday or Tuesday of this week by James A. Walsh. There was no change in the position of the parties in the first photograph that was taken, although the bed had been thoroughly searched. Photographs were then shown of the different positions in which the bodies lay at the time of the tragedy.

About the cloth that was found in the pail in the cellar the government decided to have nothing to say, as it would bring up unpleasant recollections. The clothing that was taken up when buried again was placed in a wooden box. All that clothing is now in the marshal's office. The axes I gave to Prof. Wood on Tuesday before the Oak Grove autopsy. The axes were not used by me or any other person to fit the wounds. I formed my first opinion when Mrs. Borden died when I lifted her up on the day of the murder. When I performed the autopsy in the afternoon it was all speculation as to the time of death.

Adams—Isn't it all speculation?

Dolan—As far as temperature is concerned. I should say Mrs. Borden died one hour and a half before Mr. Borden. I judge so on the clotted condition of blood under her head.

Adams—Was the blood on the carpet coagulated because of its having dried?

Dolan—It coagulated and dried because it was exposed to the air. There must have been coagulation of the spots on the paper.

Adams—How is it that the blood on the carpet did not dry then?

Dolan—The spots on the paper were so small they dried more quickly. The condition of the pine floor without carpet would indicate that Mrs. Borden had been dead one hour and a half.

Adams—Did you then examine the wounds of Mr. Borden?

Dolan—No, sir.

Adams—Did you the second time.

Dolan—Yes, sir.

Adams—I would ask you when it was that you first formed your opinion as to the length of time Mrs. Borden had been dead?

Dolan—One hour and a half.

Adams—On the second time you saw her, how long did you think she had been dead?

Dolan—An hour or two. I should say two hours.

Adams—Might it not have been three quarters of an hour?

Dolan—It might have been.

John T. Burrell, cashier of the National Union bank, told the court that he saw Mr. Borden during the first business hour of the bank. He remained about five minutes and then went out.

Everett Cook, cashier of the First national bank, of which Mr. Borden was a trustee, said he had seen Mr. Borden at 15 minutes of 10 o'clock. He went away ten minutes later.

Charles C. Cook, insurance broker, had charge of the Borden building, corner of South Main and Anawan streets. He did not see Mr. Borden on the day of the murder; the last time he saw him was onTuesday before the murder. There was no talk about a will on that day, but he had said some three days before that he never made a will. No remark was made about making one. The witness did not remember telling Officer Medley what Mr. Borden said. He did not say to Medley that Mr. Borden made the remark that a will had not been made, but he must make one.

CATHERINE KELLY

was the next witness. She said: I live in the house next to Mr. Borden on the side furtherest from Borden street. I was at home Aug. 4, the day of the murder, and I saw Mr. Borden that morning as he was going into the house. I saw him on the steps trying to open the front door. At this time I was going out. Mr. Borden had a small package in his hand. I did not stop to speak to him. It was 27 or 28 minutes to eleven when I saw him. I fix the time in this way: I was to be at the dentist's, corner of Borden and South Main streets, at 9:30, and I looked at the clock and found it was 10:35, and I was an hour late. Cross-examination by Mr. Jennings failed to shake Miss Kelly's testimony, with the exception that she was not sure that Mr. Borden went into the house; she saw him about to go in. She was certain about the time.

Dr. Dolan was recalled and produced the keys taken from Mr. Borden's clothing. Six keys on a bunch and two separate large keys were shown. There was also a partly used package of fine cut chewing tobacco. The goods were then given in custody of the court. The photographs were also given in as evidence so as to show the position of the bodies when found. The spurt of blood on the wall indicated that it came from an oblique direction. There was no way to determine whether the first blow was fatal in either case, but the spurt of blood must have been made before the heart ceased to beat, When he first saw Mrs. Borden laying on the floor the bed was all made; at this time it was close to 12 o'clock.The pictures were then explained to the different counsel, the one showing Mrs. Borden on the floor placing her much nearer the bed than the dressing case.The witness did not know of a yardstick being found, but had seen one in the room. He called for one and it was produced. There was a camp chair in the room near Mrs. Borden's feet, and it was covered with blood. It had not been placed in the photograph and was still at the Borden house. There were also a rocking chair against the window and a work basket on another chair. There was also a sewing machine in the room.

Jonathan Clegg spoke as follows: I knew Mr. Borden. I saw him that day. I first saw him opposite my store in front of Shove & Fisher's. I had occasion to see him that morning. I called him across to my store. I had considerable talk with him. It was 29 minutes past 10 o'clock exactly when Mr. Borden left my store. He went south when he left my store.That was the last time I saw him.

JOHN CUNNINGHAM.

I am a newsdealer by profession. I was opposite Mr. Hall's store on Second street when I first heard of the murder. The first information of it I got was when I noticed four or five men standing on Second street near the Borden house. I also noticed a lady run across the street. It was Mrs. Churchill. I was standing on the sidewalk, and her actions attracted my attention. While I was standing there a boy came running up to me and said that Mrs. Churchill wanted a policeman. I stepped into a shop and telephoned to the city marshal.

Knowlton—Did you talk with the marshal?

Cunningham—I did, sir.

Knowlton—How did you know the time?

Cunningham—There was a clock in the paint shop and it was ten minutes past 11 by it.

Upon cross-examination by Mr. Jennings, Cunningham said: After I talked to the marshal I telephoned to the newspapers. I then went up into the shop on business. When I reached the street again I saw Officer Allen. Mr. Allen went directly into Mr. Borden's house, and after he came out I went into the yard. I saw a man named Charles Sawyer there. Mr. Sawyer was at the side door. There were two reporters in the yard. We made a search of the yard. I tried the cellar door and found it locked. I saw nobody go into the barn.

SHERIFF FRANCIS S. WIXON.

I am a sheriff. I was in the marshal's office when the telephone message came. I took no note of the time, but I think it was about 15 minutes after 11. Before I went into the marshal's office I remember that the city hall clock struck 11 as I was turning the corner of Bedford street and Court square. The marshal and myself were conversing for ten or 15 minutes before the telephone message came. It was about 11:30 when I left.

I went into the office of Swift & Grime first and then directly to the Borden house. I first saw Dr. Bowen, and he lifted the sheet from Mr. Borden's body for me to look. I had some conversation with Dr. Bowen, and we removed the watch from Mr. Borden's pocket. Dr. Bowen made the remark that Mrs. Borden was dead, too. I went into the yard and looked over towards Dr. Chagnon's yard. I saw one man over in that yard at the east extremity of the Borden estate. The man was sawing wood. I saw two other men further along towards Second street, working. I told them what had happened and they seemed much surprised.

Mr. Wixon was then rigorously cross-examined as to the distances of the men from the fence and the time in which he saw them, but nothing contradictory was brought out.

Lizzie Borden left the room shortly before the he hearing closed, leaning on the arm of the Rev. Mr. Buck and walking very unsteadily.

The morning session closed at 12:22.

This Afternoon's Session.

At the opening of the afternoon session the court room was again crowded, most of the sight-seers being women. The drizzling rain did not dampen their ardor in the least, and weather that would prevent them from visiting a friend was no barrier when they wished to satisfy their curiosity. The court room is now cleared after every session, and the procession of females coming from the building would remind one of a bonnet show. Much the same faces are always visible, and the determination is expressed to see the examination to an end.

The first witness called was Joseph Shortsleeves, a former employee of Mr. Borden. He is a carpenter, and saw him in the building 92 South Main street. Mr. Borden was on his way home, but dropped in to see the store the witness was repairing for Jonathan Clegg. He remained three or four minutes and headed for Spring street. It was after 10:30. A friend who was in the store looked at the city hall clock, and it indicated 10:40.

James Mather, who was with Mr. Shortsleeve at the time, said he never knew Mr. Borden until that day. Mr. Borden remained in the store three or four minutes, and then went toward Spring street. Mr. Borden was in the store and the witness looked at the city hall clock, and the time indicated was 10:40. The reason Mr. Mather looked at the clock was because he generally ate a lunch at that time, and he wanted to know the hour. When the police asked him the time the following Saturday he told them that it was between 10:30 and 10:45 o'clock. This was the first time he stated the period exactly. On his way to Spring street the witness could not tell whether Mr. Borden stopped in any ofthe other stores or not.

The New York Herald

BURIED THE BORDENS WITHOUT THEIR HEADS.

By Order of the Attorney General the Skulls Were Separated from the Bodies Before They Were Interred.

TRACING THE BLOOD STAINS.

Dr. Nolan Tells the Result of His Examination of the Spots Found on the Walls and Doors.

BRIDGET SULLIVAN ON THE STAND.

She Testifies as to What Took Place Immediately Before the Murder—Matron Reagan Denies a Story.

[BY TELEGRAPH TO THE HERALD.]

FALL RIVER, Mass., August 26, 1892.—The second day of the preliminary hearing in the trial of Lizzie A. Borden for the murder of her father has been big with interest. Bridget Sullivan has been called. "Uncle" John V. Morse has given his testimony, and a sensation was furnished during the morning session which was a horrible reminder of the Paris Morgue.

The day dawned cold and gray, with a drizzling mist, but the inclement weather made no difference to the eager crowd which packed the dingy, stuffy little court room. Ladies donned their mackintoshes and ventured forth. Many men stood up through each session. Every inch of space was occupied. The Bordens came in promptly at the hour of opening the hearing, and were placed exactly as they were yesterday, Miss Lizzie immediately behind her counsel, Messrs. Adams and Jennings, and then Emma Borden, Rev. E. A. Buck, Mrs. Holmes, Mrs Brigham and Mr. Holmes. The sisters looked tired and anxious, especially Miss Emma, when they first entered, but later seemed to become absorbed in what was going on.

Miss Lizzie took an active interest in the proceedings, frequently leaning forward to speak to her lawyers, consulting with them and several times during the cross-examination making suggestions, which were evidently adopted.

DR. DOLAN RECALLED.

The first witness was Dr. Dolan, recalled this morning to testify further about the bloody stains on the doors and walls and the dark splotches on the hatchet. The examination was conducted by Mr. Adams. When in answer to the question whether when the autopsy was held in the ladies, waiting room at Oak Grove Cemetery the witness had removed anything from the bodies of Mr. and Mrs. Borden, Dr. Dolan dropped his eyes for an instant and replied in a low voice, "I did," people felt something unusual was coming.

"What did you remove?"

"I removed the skulls."

A shudder ran through the audience. Both Borden sisters dropped their heads and covered their eyes with their hands. Mr. Adams inquired in an impressive tone:—"Do you mean to say that the bodies of Mr. and Mrs. Borden were buried without the heads?"

"I do." The sensation created by this disclosure was profound. Further testimony showed that the decapitation had been done by order of the Attorney General, and that the skulls had been cleaned and photographed and are now in the possession of the medical examiner.

GETTING AT THE EXACT TIME.

A number of witnesses were examined to show the time intervening between Mr. Borden's last appearance on the street alive and the announcement that he had been found murdered. The comparison of private timepieces with the town clock and the explanations of why various people had such an accurate record of minutes and seconds on the 4th day of August before noon were not edifying. The result of it all was that the period inquired about gradually dwindled to barely twenty minutes.

The afternoon session began at a quarter past two o'clock. Bridget Sullivan was called, but had not arrived. This rather spoiled Mr. John V. Morse's début. He was summoned in place of the absent witness, and if every one had not been devoured by curiosity to know what disclosures the celebrated Bridget had to make the tall, awkward, ill looking old man who shuffled on to the witness stand would have been an object of absorbing interest.

The witness, leaning his elbows on the rail at either side, stood with his profile to the audience and made his replies in a voice so indistinct that he had to be repeatedly admonished to speak louder. Mr. Morse's evidence was devoid of sensations. A rather disconnected story was dragged out of him covering the time from his arrival at his brother-in-law's house on Wednesday noon, the day previous to the murder, until after the tragedy. He said he did not see his niece Lizzie until the murder had been discovered. Mr. Morse was dreadfully ill at ease during District Attorney Knowlton's examination. He wrung his hands and twisted and untwisted his long, gray trousered legs in excessive nervousness. When he passed into the hands of the counsel for the defence, however, he seemed to take heart, stood straightly, spoke up and faced the people.

BRIDGET SULLIVAN'S TESTIMONY.

It was late in the dark afternoon when Bridget Sullivan was called and answered. The girl was very pale, but must have learned some lessons of repression and self-control during her residence in the Borden household, for she was as composed and quiet as the two dark, robust women sitting like statues on the bench behind the lawyers.

Bridget testified that she was called Maggie in the family of Mr. Borden where she had lived for two years. Miss Emma had been away from home about two weeks at the time of the tragedy.

She described the simple breakfast partaken of by the two old people and Mr. Morse, their guest, and told how Mrs. Borden went about the lower rooms dusting and putting all to rights after breakfast. Mr. Borden saw his guest out the side door and a little later went out himself.

She saw Mrs. Borden about nine o'clock, after her husband had gone out. Did not see him go out; was out in the back yard. Mrs. Borden told Bridget to wash the windows inside and out that morning. Miss Lizzie came down stairs before she went into the back yard, and said she would like some coffee and cookies for her breakfast. It was her first appearance.

JUST BEFORE THE MURDER.

After cleaning up the kitchen Bridget went down into the cellar for pail, brushes and stick, to use for window cleaning. Miss Lizzie was at the back door. When she returned Lizzie asked if she was going to wash windows. She washed the sitting room windows first, then the parlor outside and the dining room and came indoors to wash sitting room windows inside. Saw nothing of any of the family during this time. Mr. Borden came in while she was washing the second window. She heard him trying to open the front door and let him in. Lizzie was up stairs at the time and Bridget heard her laugh at some exclamation because the door did not open readily.

Lizzie came down five or ten minutes after to the sitting room. Mr. Borden was seated in the dining room. Lizzie asked if he had any mail and told her father that Mrs. Borden had got a note from some one. He presently took the key of his room off the shelf and went up the back stairs. When he returned he sat down in a chair in the sitting room, near a window, with a book in his hand.

THE MURDER.

She was in the habit of resting a bit before getting dinner if there was time, and she lay down on the bed and heard or saw nothing more until Miss Lizzie called. "She hollered," continued the witness, "to me to come down quick, for her father was dead. I knew something was wrong, she hollered so loud. She was leaning against the door and told me to go quick for Dr. Bowen.

"The Doctor was out, and Mrs. Bowen sent me for Mrs. Russell, who lived near. When she got back Miss Lizzie was in the kitchen and Mrs. Bowen and Mrs. Churchill were at the house. It was Miss Lizzie who proposed looking for Mrs. Borden, whom, she said, she had heard come in. Bridget said she and Mrs. Churchill went up stairs together and found the mistress dead. Dr. Bowen said she had been murdered."

Here Bridget's evidence ended for to-day, and the court adjourned at half-past five P. M.

Immediately afterward an indignation meeting of irate citizens, friends of Miss Borden, assembled around her counsel's table and proceeded to denounce the entire press because a Boston paper had published a tale to the effect that Miss Emma had confessed to Mr. Jennings her sister's guilt, had been upbraided by Lizzie for giving her away and that a quarrel had ensued between the two sisters.

The account was credited to Matron Reagan, who has Lizzie Borden in custody. Matron Reagan and the other parties involved had all promptly denied the story, but it was copied by a New York paper and revived by the local press to-night.

Rev. Dr. Buck wanted Mrs. Reagan's denial put into the form of an affidavit, but was assured that a statement over her signature would serve as well for publication. Accordingly Mr. Jennings drew up the statement and gave it to Dr. Buck. He took it to Matron Reagan, who came into the corridor outside the prisoner's door. She said she was willing to sign it, but must first ask Marshal Hilliard's permission. Dr. Buck accompanied her to the Marshal's room, on the ground floor. He read over the statement, and with clouding countenance exclaimed, "If you sign that you do it without my consent." Here he discovered my presence and gave an order to clear the room.

SECURED A DENIAL.

A crowd had assembled in the hallway. Mr. Jennings hurried past into the Marshal's room, an angry altercation followed his entrance, and in a moment he rushed out, with the matron's denial of the story in his hand. He said he wished every newspaper to publish the fact that the Marshal of Fall River refused to allow a public denial of a lying statement which was simply prejudicial to his client.

Matron Reagan said to me:—"I never told the Marshal that Lizzie Borden and her sister had a spat, and I never repeated the words which the Boston paper made Lizzie say to Emma, because there was no such conversation. There is absolutely no truth in the story. Lizzie Borden greets her sister affectionately, and when she doesn't kiss her she always shakes her hand warmly. I have never left the prisoner except with her own counsel, and I know all that she has said to everybody but Mr. Jennings while I have had her in my charge."

Mrs. Reagan further said that on Wednesday afternoon, the time when the sisters are said to have quarrelled, Mrs. Charles Holmes called on the prisoner and described an incident she had seen. A man had tried to break a hen's egg between his clasped hands. He could not do so. Lizzie said she did not believe it. On her way home from here Mrs. Holmes met Mrs. Brigham and gave her an egg to fetch to Lizzie to experiment with. When Mrs. Brigham arrived Miss Emma was there before her. And the story was told over.

Lizzie was sure she could break the egg in the manner described. She jumped up from the sofa and took it between her two hands. Emma and Mrs. Brigham and Matron Reagan stepped back so it wouldn't spatter their clothes if it did break. Lizzie worked hard and tried again and again to crush it. Finally she sat down tired, saying, "Well, to think that I who can do most anything cannot crush a frail little eggshell." Emma remained until seven o'clock and not a word about the murder was spoken. They had no disagreement.

The New York Times

LIZZIE BORDEN'S ORDEAL

END OF THE FIRST WEEK OF HER TRIAL FOR MURDER.

THE DISTRICT ATTORNEY'S EFFORTS TO ENCIRCLE HER WITH A WEB OF CIRCUMSTANTIAL EVIDENCE—LACK OF DEFINITE EVIDENCE—HER REMARKABLE COOLNESS.

FALL RIVER, Mass., Aug.27.-The first week of the Borden murder trial closed at noon to-day, and after half the Government witnesses have testified there is not the slightest change in the divided opinions of the people here as to the guilt or innocence of the young woman who is accused of having brutally murdered her father and stepmother.

The only witness of the day was the domestic, Bridget Sullivan, and she was subjected to a severe cross-examination by the attorney for the defense. She stood the ordeal well, and had evidently been carefully instructed as to the manner of answering the numerous questions directed at her in rapid succession by Attorney Adams.

The District Attorney says that he is well satisfied with the development of the web of circumstantial evidence which he is endeavoring to weave about Lizzie Borden, and the Government asserts that its belief in the guilt of the young woman has increased greatly since the testimony of Bridget Sullivan. These officers say that the story of the servant shows how manifestly impossible it was for any one to enter or leave the house while Lizzie was alone with first her mother and then her father, and they further assert in answer to the query as to why this servant did not hear the fall of Mrs. Borden's body that the noise of the water splashing against the windows effectually drowned any such sound.

On Monday the prosecution expects to put Prof. Wood of Harvard upon the stand. He has had in his possession the axes found in the Borden cellar, and upon which there appeared to be what Medical Examiner Dolan thought was blood. He has also had Lizzie Borden's skirt, containing a drop of blood, and her shoes, which were also stained by some red liquid. He has made a careful analysis of all these articles and will say when he gives his testimony whether or not the analysis shows these drops to be the blood of a human being.

The attorneys for the defense make light of this, and assert that Lizzie Borden will never be convicted on expert testimony. Attorney Adams told a TIMES representative at the conclusion of to-day's hearing that no evidence presented yet made him feel at all uneasy. He has also given it as his opinion, and he is one of the shrewdest criminal lawyers in the Bay State, that something far stronger than has yet been presented will have to be made public before the presiding Justice will be justified in holding Lizzie Borden for the Grand Jury.

Thus far the prosecution has shown no motive, and in this respect the testimony of Bridget Sullivan and John V. Morse has been disappointing to the public. They expected a recital of the family relations in the Borden house and a rehearsal of troubles between the Borden girls on one side and their father and mother on the other. But no such testimony has been advanced, and the nearest approach which the Government has made toward endeavoring to show a motive was when the District Attorney questioned Insurance Agent Cook and John V. Morse regarding conversations Mr. Borden had with them in relation to certain bequests he was said to have intended to make. But this was a failure, and a motive for the fearful murder is yet to be shown.

The District Attorney says that he does not intend to put in his full case, but will only put in sufficient evidence to warrant holding the accused for the Grand Jury. The drug clerk Eli Bence, has not yet testified, and his story is awaited eagerly. It is charged that it was from him that Lizzie endeavored to purchase hydrocyanic acid, and finally bought prussic acid. The day before the murder Mr. and Mrs. Borden complained of being sick, and suggested that the bread might have contained poison. Their stomachs have also been in the possession of Prof. Wood, and he will tell whether or not they had contained any poison for hours before the couple were hacked to death. If he proves that prussic acid entered their organs, the case will look darker for the young woman than it does at present.

John C. Milne, one of Fall River's wealthy residents, was an old friend of Andrew Borden and is a firm believer in the innocence of his daughter. He is proprietor of the Evening News, and from the outset the editorial columns of his paper have been devoted to the defense of Lizzie Borden. This is the manner in which he sums up the week's doings to-night, and it may be taken as the opinion of all the supporters of the prisoner:

"There has been, up to the present, not a single item of evidence that can have weight against the defendant, and John V. Morse and Bridget Sullivan, understood to be the Government's most important witnesses, have accounted for their movements on the days previous to the murders, on the day of the murder, and on the days following. They have also told all that they knew about the movements and conversation of the other members of the family as far as they were able, and the only thing proved is what has been admitted by Miss Lizzie's adherents from the first. She was alone at the time Mr. Borden was murdered and has no one to support her statement that she was not alone. No witness has yet been called who saw any one except the members of the family around the house, but on the other hand, the Government have failed to prove conclusively that it was impossible for anyone to gain admittance to the house unseen.

"The relations between the members of the family, it was understood, were to form a prominent part of the Government's case. First came Uncle John V. Morse, who knew the habits of the family as well, probably, as any one not living in the house. Neither in direct nor in re-direct examination was he questioned upon this point. The Government did not take up the point, and the defense, of course, could not. Then came Bridget Sullivan, the servant. If any one is in a position to know of any breach, no matter how slight, between members of a family, it is the servant. Alleged reports of proceedings at the inquest stated that Bridget had given very damaging evidence upon the hard feelings exhibited by Lizzie toward Mrs. Borden. The absence of any such testimony at the trial seems to prove that the evidence given at the inquest did not leak very much after all. The will theory has been completely spoiled. Now all inquiry into the family relations, which were not so pleasant as they are in the majority of families, has been avoided, and the Government stands absolutely without a motive."

The most remarkable feature of the trial has been the demeanor of Lizzie Borden. From start to finish she has manifested no feeling of weakness, and has listened to the recital of the most cold-blooded and shocking details of the crime with a perfectly impassive and unmoved countenance. The description of the wounds by the medical examiner, his gory tale of how the skull was forced into the brains of the aged couple a dozen times, his recital of how the skulls were sawed from the bodies under his direction and the removal of the flesh from them-all these and other similarly ghastly stories the young woman heard, and was apparently unmoved. Three or four times she enjoyed a hearty laugh: for instance, when her attorney, desirous of ascertaining the space occupied by the body of her stepmother as it lay upon the floor compared the aged lady's physical proportions to those of the solidly-built District Attorney. Those who believe her insane consider this good evidence of that fact, but there is no apparent insanity in the clear blue eyes which look up now and then with apparent interest at the half a hundred busy press correspondents. Everybody, including the police officials, say she's a remarkable woman, and after her demeanor during the long hours of the trial as it has proceeded, there is no one to dispute the statement.

Lizzie and Emma Borden, accompanied by Mr. Holmes and the Rev. Mr. Buck, came promptly into court at the time for commencing proceedings to-day. There was, of course, no change in the impassive countenance of the young woman, and nobody expected to see any. Across the room was Bridget Sullivan, with her face very white and her eyes downcast. She did not look up as the prisoner and her friends entered, and she moved slowly to the witness stand when she was summoned by the District Attorney. Bridget was a most difficult witness to the press representatives, for her replies to the interrogatories of the attorney were so low as to be inaudible at a distance of ten feet from the witness stand.

Almost unconsciously perhaps the District Attorney fell into the same soft tones in directing his queries, suggesting the idea that he was intentionally handling the witness with soft gloves in a desire not to confuse her or add to her embarrassment. There was consequently much speculation as to the manner which the attorneys for the defense would assume toward the witness in their work of cross-examination.

Mr. Knowlton called Bridget Sullivan to the stand at 10:16 o'clock. Bridget continued her testimony as follows: "Mrs. Borden came down stairs Wednesday morning saying she and Mr. Borden had been sick that night. They looked pretty sick. Lizzie said she had been sick all night, too. When I came down to start the fire I used coal and wood in the kitchen fire. Used hard wood always. Miss Lizzie had been ironing eight or nine minutes when I went upstairs. There used to be a horse kept in the barn. Since the horse was kept there I have seen Lizzie go to the barn.

Mr. Knowlton--Tell me again, now, what Lizzie had to say about the note her mother received."

Bridget Sullivan--Miss Lizzie spoke about her mother going out, and said that her mother had received a note that morning.

Mr. Knowlton--Did Lizzie say anything about hearing her mother groan?

Bridget Sullivan--She said she heard her father groan.

Mr. Knowlton--Did you at any time that day see Lizzie crying?

Bridget Sullivan--No, not in all the day.

Mr. Adams conducted the cross-examination and commenced by politely asking the witness if she would be seated. The witness declined a chair, and questions commenced rapidly.

"Have you ever told your story before?"

"No, Sir."

"Didn't you tell it at the inquest?"

"Yes, Sir; on the Tuesday after the murder in this courtroom. Dr. Dolan, Mr. Knowlton, the Marshal and some others were present."

"Who asked you the questions?"

"Mr. Knowlton."

"Was it taken down?"

"Yes, Sir."

"Has it been read to you?"

"No, Sir."

"Where were you last night after the hearing?"

"In the Marshal's office."

"Did Mr. Knowlton speak to you about your testimony?"

"Yes; he had a piece of paper."

"What was it?"

"Something printed."

"Was it something you said?"

"Yes, Sir."

"What did he say about it?"

"He read a little of it."

"When did you say this?"

"I don't know."

"Had you forgotten all about it?"

"No, Sir."

"How much did he read to you?"

"About half a dozen words."

"What were they?"

"I don't remember."

"Who was there?"

"The Marshal was about there."

"The Wednesday night before the murder you went out the back door, didn't you?"

"Yes, Sir."

"These back stairs you went up and down were the same that Mr. and Mrs. Borden went up and down, were they not?"

"Yes, Sir."

"Were these stairs carpeted?"

"Yes, Sir."

All this time Mr. Adams was directing the questions at the young woman with unprecedented rapidity. She stood the ordeal very well and her stereotyped answers were "Yes, Sir," and "No, Sir", giving possible evidence of some instruction as to the manner of her replies. Bridget Sullivan continued: "Had a key when I went out that night. Left the screen door fastened and locked the other door. Never had any man call on me at the house. Never had any man from Fall River call on me there. When some one came it wasn't from Fall River. It was two months ago. Had not been out in the yard Wednesday morning. Lizzie told me she had been sick. Don't know if Lizzie went away Saturday or Sunday before the murder. Tuesday night, when they were taken sick, we had swordfish warmed over for dinner. Had baker's bread, too. Got the bread myself. Didn't see Lizzie Wednesday after breakfast. They were all sick. Wednesday morning I went down stairs after coal and kindlings. Mrs. Borden came down stairs and told me that Mr. Morse was in the house. I asker her if he slept in the attic, and she said no, in the spare chamber. That Thursday morning Mr. Borden had brought a basket of pears from the tree. He had brought in some a day or two before. They got rotten and he had dumped them under the barn.

"The only rooms I had been in Thursday morning up to breakfast time were the kitchen and dining room. Think it was before 9 o'clock when Mrs. Borden said that morning after breakfast, 'What have you got to do to-day, Maggie'? She told me that I had better wash the windows outside and in. Lizzie took her breakfast in the kitchen. She took coffee. Lizzie was in the dining room, I think, when her mother asked me what I had to do. Lizzie said coming out into the kitchen, that she was going to have a cookie and coffee for breakfaast. She sat down by the kitchen table. There were old magazines in the closet. Had seen Lizzie sit down in the kitchen sometimes and read the old magazines. When I went out into the back yard she was eating her breakfast. First saw her coming out of the dining room door to the kitchen when I was at the sink."

Continuing, in answer to Mr. Adams's questions, the witness said: "It was about an hour after she came down that she came to the screen door. During that hour I was washing up the dishes. I was out in the yard when she was at her breakfast. I felt sick that morning when I got up. I drank some of the milk but I didn't eat any of the bread. I don't know whether they drank milk before being taken sick or not. I had eaten some mutton soup and some of my own bread before being taken sick. I had not eaten any of the pears, for I am no great lover of them. I came back in again and Lizzie had her breakfast. I went to work washing windows. I didn't know where Lizzie was then, but she wasn't in the kitchen. Mr. Morse went away while I was washing the dishes, but I don't know whether this was before or after Lizzie had had her breakfast."

"When you came back was Lizzie there?"

"I didn't see. When I went out that was the last I saw of Lizzie for some time."

"Had Mr. Borden gone out?"

"I don't know. I didn't see him go out that morning."

"What did you do after that?"

"I went to washing windows."

"Lizzie had had her breakfast, Morse had gone, you didn't know where Mr. Borden was, Mrs. Borden was in the dining room, dusting?"

"Yes, Sir."

"Then you went out and got the pail and brush?"

"Yes; but not right away."

"How long before you got the pail and brush?"

"About half an hour."

"What were you doing, then?"

"Straightening up and putting away the dishes."

"What then?"

"I went down stairs into the laundry, got a pail and brush, and then went out into the barn to get a handle for the brush. I got it in one of the stalls. As I went out I spoke to Lizzie at one of the screen doors. Lizzie asked me if I was going to wash the windows, and I said yes. She followed me into the entry."

"Where did she come from?"

"I don't know."

Bridget Sullivan continued: "When I told her she needn't fasten the screen door she didn't do it. Mr. Borden was in the habit of going out the back door, but I didn't see him. I was washing the windows. I did not see Mr. Borden go out before I washed the windows. Raised the sitting-room windows to wash them from the inside. The window nearest the hall was open when I heard Mr. Borden at the front door. Can't say if the bell rang."

Mr. Adams--How was it, was Lizzie in the dining room ironing when you came in for the dipper?"

Bridget--I can't say.

Mr. Adams--Wait, take time. Are you sure you can't remember if she was there reading or ironing?

Bridget--I don't remember seeing her there.

Mr. Adams--Didn't you say that she sometimes read there?

Bridget--Yes, but not that morning.

Mr. Adams--Now are you prepared to say that you did not see Miss Lizzie sitting there in the kitchen when you came for the dipper?

Bridget--I can't rememeber.

"Did you see a pile of handkerchiefs while she was ironing?"

"Yes, sir."

"You weren't sure whether the doorbell rang or not?"

"No, sir."

"Then you went to the door?"

"Yes, sir."

"Did every one of those locks fasten?"

"Yes, sir."

"What did you say when you were opening the door?"

There was a pause for this was the question which the witness objected to answering yesterday. "I'm waiting Miss Sullivan," said Mr. Adams.

"I said, 'Oh, pshaw' and Lizzie laughed," replied the witness.

"Well, is there anything bad in that you should object to repeating it?"

"No, Sir."

Continuing, the witness said that Miss Lizzie came through the dining room. Mr. Borden, she thought, had a parcel, and he sat down in the dining room. Lizzie told her father about the note Mrs. Borden had received, but I did not hear him give any answer, and then I washed the windows in the sitting room while Mr. Borden went up stairs.

"Hasn't this house been broken into in broad daylight?" asked Mr. Adams.

"Yes, Sir."

"Weren't a gold watch and other valuables taken?"

"Yes, Sir."

"And this was in broad daylight, while you were in the house?"

"Yes, Sir."

"What were you doing then?"

"I was at my work."

"And a man came in, stole a number of articles, and escaped without being seen?"

"Yes, Sir."

"When was that?"

"Last July, I think."

"Since that time hasn't the barn been broken into?"

"Yes, Sir."

"How long ago was this?"

"I can't tell; A few months, I think."

"Was not something taken from there?"

"Yes, Sir."

During this testimony of Bridget Sullivan, Emma Borden sat with her gloved hand shading her eyes. There was a little of the flush upon the countenance of the prisoner which those who have studied her features have learned to know as an indication of emotion, and she carefully listened to every sentence as it was presented. Bridget Sullivan continued: "Lizzie came into the dining room when her father came in. I was washing windows. Miss Lizzie then took the small ironing board and placed it on the dining-room table. She ironed some handkerchiefs. Miss Lizzie told me that her mother was going out to make a sick call. It was a few minutes of 11 when I went up stairs. Did not look at my clock, but know it was a few minutes before 11. Did not take off my clothes when I lay down. Heard the clock strike 11. When Miss Lizzie called to me that her father was dead I went down and found her standing up near the door. She didn't have her hands up to her face. She wasn't crying. She told me to go to Dr. Bowen's, and after that to go after Mrs. Russell."

Mr. Adams--Did you talk with Mrs. Churchill?

Bridget--Yes.

Mr. Adams--Did you tell her that Mrs. Borden had gone away to make a sick call without telling you where she was going?

Bridget--I cannot remember.

Mr. Adams--Are you willing to say you did not tell Mrs. Churchill anything about it?

You did talk with her, didn't you?
Bridget--Yes, Sir.
Mr. Adams--Well, did you say that Mrs. Borden had gone out to make a sick call without telling you where she was going?
Bridget--I don't remember.
"Did you go up stairs before you went for Mrs. Bowen?"
"I went up to see Mrs. Borden after I went for Mrs. Bowen."
"When did you go down cellar after the tragedy?"
"I can't tell, but it was pretty soon after. I went in all the rooms with the officers. They found some axes in a little box near the furnace. This box was near the front part of the cellar. They were in a box that we used to keep starch in."
"When you saw Miss Lizzie, when she gave the alarm, what dress had she on?"
"I don't know."
"Was it light or dark?"
"I don't know."
"Did you see any blood spots on her?"
"No, Sir."
"Did you see any blood spots anywhere except in those places that have been indicated?"
"No, Sir."
"Where was this room which was burglarized?"
"Near Mrs. Borden's room."
"At the end of the back stairs down which Lizzie Borden came?"
"Yes, Sir."
Mr. Adams--Well, this room led out of Mrs. Borden's room, but you got out the back way?
Bridget--Yes, Sir.
Bridget continued: "Did not empty any pails after the tragedy. Saw several people washing their hands after the tragedy. Think I saw Mayor Coughlin wash his hands."
Judge Blaisdsell announced at this point that the hearing was adjourned to 10 o'clock Monday morning. Bridget Sullivan's testimony is not concluded, but there will be other witnesses examined before she is called again.

The Fall River Herald

Is it curiosity or sympathy that attracts so many women to the district court room? Some women are blessed in not having any household cares to bother them.

NOTHING disclosed at the Borden trial yesterday afforded any reason for judging of the innocence or guilt of the accused. Aside from the testimony respecting the weapon, the evidence of the medical examiner was not of special importance.

Notes of the Trial.

There are 43 reporters and sketchers inside the rail at the district court representing all the leading dailies of the east. Among them are six or more ladies.

Half the night force of police are kept on duty around the station house during the trial in addition to their regular duty.

OPINIONS FROM OTHER NEWSPAPERS

The Boston Globe

Dr. Dolan told his story of the Borden tragedy in court yesterday, and told it fairly well. There was no attempt at unnecessary scientific detail, nor any effort at dramatic possibilities. The story is a ghastly one at best, and diving into details did not add to its attractiveness.

The Pawtucket Times

There is little advantage in reading the accounts, more or less true, of what is going on in relation to Lizzie Borden, and as to what she says and does, and yet until this preliminary hearing is closed the public mind will be turned to this sad affair, even unconsciously. The extreme expressions of the partisans of Miss Borden have been repressed of late, there is a more sensible atmosphere in Fall River, and aside from the inevitable cranks there seems to be a disposition to secure justice. There is one fact which is as encouraging as it is patent. The prosecuting officials and the justice concerned in this affair are men of ability, of cool common sense, of that determination which is unaffected by popular clamor. If Lizzie Borden is innocent these officials will rejoice with exceeding great joy so to find it. If she is guilty, they will prove it, if they can, to the conviction of every sound mind. That is to say, they will do their duty. The further responsibility will rest in other hands.

The Boston Herald

There is nothing about this Fall River investigation to our mind more astonishing—not to say more abnormal—than the impassive coolness of the woman who is charged with the murder. The circumstances of the case are such, under the presumption of either her guilt or her innocence, as to excite her nervous system to a state approaching frenzy; yet through it all, from the beginning to the end of the events that have followed the discovery of the crime, no one has been calmer than this person who is more nearly affected by it than any other. It would be astonishing in a man of the strongest nerve and the most unlimited control of self; in a woman not very far past the age of girlhood it is so amazing as to seem incredible were not the facts before the public eye. There is nothing that tends more to induce the belief of insanity in the case than this most extraordinary exhibition.

The Fall River Herald

IRON OR LEAD?

Why Did Lizzie Borden Visit the Barn?

THE SINKER STORY DISCREDITED BY A WITNESS

To Whom She Said She Wanted a Piece of Iron

WITH WHICH TO REPAIR THE SCREEN DOOR.

Inquiring About Miss Sullivan In Newport.

Wherever anybody went Sunday he was invited to give his latest theory concerning the Borden case. Theories have been so unsettled that a new one may be looked for every hour or two. A person who follows a line of reasoning today which is different from that which he started out on yesterday finds himself face to face with conclusions directly opposed to one another, and on reviewing his own arguments he cannot detect any flaws in them.

The testimony of Bridget Sullivan furnished new material to the talk, and there were points from which debaters on both sides of the case found comfort. On the government side it was pointed out that Miss Sullivan had not been asked many vital questions concerning Lizzie Borden's actions. They did not ask the servant to tell anything about the family relations and they did not make it clear how many handerkerchiefs she had ironed that morning; they did show, however, that Lizzie Borden was on the second floor where Mrs. Borden lay dead, that she was close to the top of the stairs when her father came in, and that she laughed at an innocent exclamation of the servant as a person might whose nerves were highly strung at earlier experiences. Then she took her place beside the dining room table at an ironing board where she could see the movements of the servant. All morning she had watched the servant with unusual interest. She was at the screen door when Bridget went by with the pail to wash the windows. She knew that the girl would not finish for awhile, and when the servant went in for a dipper, Lizzie was not ironing. She was upstairs probably, and she was upstairs a little while later when Andrew Borden went into the house. What she had seen and what she had done on that second floor that morning left her in a state of mind that she laughed aloud when Bridget tugged in vain at the door bolt and said "Oh, pshaw!" Lizzie Borden knew when Bridget Sullivan

LEFT HER ALONE

on that first floor with her father later. She probably saw the servant go upstairs, and it was the servant's custom to go to her room at that time and remain until she was needed to prepare dinner.

About 13 minutes then elapse during which somebody kills Andrew Borden. At the end of that time, Lizzie Borden shrieks for the servant to go and get help.

Following the evidence thus far offered, the friends declare that Lizzie Borden's actions when she discovered the body of her murdered father were no more demonstrative than one would expect who knew her well. Always accustomed to suppress any outbreak of emotion, she did not manifest the whole force of her feeling to others, but missed the supreme anguish at the sight of the terrible thing within her own soul.

These are the two views that are taken of the case, and a person is free to take his choice of them. There is more yet to be heard, and again the suggestion is offered to wait until all has been heard before one makes up his mind unalterably.

A QUIET DAY.

Nothing of Interest Transpired to Make the Sabbath Exciting.

Sunday was a quiet day around the police station. The attorneys spent the day in making preparations for the labors of the coming week, and in studying the little details of the testimony thus far submitted. Presumably their work must have been of a satisfactory nature to them, for, according to their own statements, they are all gratified at the developments thus far—the district attorney because he thinks that nearly sufficient evidence has been adduced upon which to hold Lizzie Borden for the grand jury, and Lawyers Jennings and Adams for the reason that they profess to believe that Judge Blaisdell will require the presentation of much more testimony, and that of a more direct nature, before he declares that in his opinion Lizzie Borden is probably guilty of the murder of her father and stepmother.

Lizzie Borden passed the Sunday as she has passed other days, in the quiet seclusion of the matron's limited chamber. Outside the door a stalwart officer kept guard, and prevented any one from even ascending the stairs. People passed by the place all day, and stopped to gaze at the cheerless stone structure, their reflections being assisted apparently by glancing at the gloomy building.

At the Central Congregational church, there was another large gathering yesterday. Since his prayer that the truth might be ascertained, Mr. Jubb, the pastor, has studiously avoided any reference to the tragedy while in the pulpit. He was absent Sunday on his annual vacation, and his place was filled by Rev. Mr. De Forrest, a western clergyman, who formerly resided in Warren. There was no mention in his discourse or prayer of the affair, and those who expected a reference to the tragedy were disappointed.

The prisoner spent the greater part of the day reading the religious journals and books, which have been her constant companions during the hours of her confinement. It might naturally be supposed that the officer on guard near the door was placed there for the purpose of effectually removing the possibility of escape were such an improbable thing thought of by the young woman. But this does not appear to be the case, and judging from the action of the police, the guard is not so much for the purpose of preventing Lizzie Borden from getting at anybody as to prevent anybody from getting at Lizzie Borden. Emma Borden was at the station for some time during the morning. Mr. and Mrs. Holmes also called after church.

TODAY'S EVIDENCE.

A Neighbor of the Bordens Opens the Evidence for the Week.

This morning the crowd waiting for admission to the trial was nearly as large as on the first day. There was quite as many women as on any day of the trial, and they jumped upon their feet to see everything that went forward. A photographer had invaded the sacred precincts of the court and had spread his tripod in the corner of the free seats ready to do deadly execution.

Promptly at the hour stated for opening the case all the prominent people interested were in their places. The prisoner entered as usual with Mr. Buck. Mrs. Brigham was on hand early. The Borden girls wore heavy sacks, but Emma removed hers directly after she was seated. The prisoner acknowledged the greeting of Lawyer Adams with a forced smile and at first did not see the hand he extended in greeting.

Without any delay the proceedings were opened. District Attorney Knowlton called Mrs. Churchill, who proceeded to give her testimony. She was nervous at first, but gathered control of herself as the examination proceeded. She testified as follows: The first I knew of the tragedy was seeing Bridget going over to Dr. Bowen's. I was coming home from the direction of the city hall. When I saw Bridget she looked frightened. I then went into my house and entered the kitchen, which is toward the Borden residence. When I looked out I saw Lizzie leaning against the screen door, looking distressed. I opened my window and asked her what was the matter. She said: 'Oh, Mrs. Churchill, come over; some one has killed my father." I went over and found her sitting on the second step of the stairs; I helped her to arise, and she said her father was in the sitting room. I asked her where she was when it happened, and she said she was in the barn getting a piece of iron. It was about 11 o'clock when I started for Hudner's market for meat. She asked that a doctor be sent for, and as Dr. Bowen was not in I went down to Hall's stable to ask them to telephone for one. When I came back Dr. Bowen had arrived, and afterwards I went upstairs with Bridget to get some sheets. Miss Russell arrived shortly after, and Lizzie wanted Bridget to go upstairs and look for her stepmother. She did not want to go alone, and I accompanied her half way up the stairs. I saw the prostrate form of Mrs. Borden near the bed. I then went downstairs. Miss Russell asked me if I had found another, and I answered yes.

Officer Allen arrived at the house after Dr. Bowen went out the first time. Charles Sawyer was the next person to arrive. I had seen Mr. Borden in the yard about 9 o'clock that morning, at the east side of the back steps, and shortly after saw him heading toward Second street as though to go down street. I cannot tell how long after Mr. Borden went off before I saw Bridget washing the windows. At that time I was washing dishes in the kitchen; but I do not remember how long I remained there before I went to the market, to which place I went and returned directly.

The first time Dr. Bowen came Lizzie asked him to send a telegram to Emma, but not to tell the worst, as the lady whom she she was visiting was old and it might shock her.

When the witness looked through the window Lizzie looked very distressed as she leaned against the screen door. In going to the house Mrs. Churchill noticed no one else, and Lizzie was all alone."The first question I asked was: 'Where is your father?' She had said nothing before to me,but then replied 'In the sitting room.' When I asked her where she was when it happened, she answered that she had been in the barn getting a piece of iron. I asked her where her mother was, and the answer received was that she had gone to attend a sick call. When Lizzie asked the second time to see if any one would find her mother, Miss Russell, Bridget and myself were present. The time I went up after the sheet was from the rear of the house, but the second time when Mrs. Borden's body was discovered it was from the front of the house. When I went up the stairs and saw the body the door of the room in which it lay was open. When I came back Lizzie was in the chair in the kitchen. When Miss Russell asked if there was another I said yes. When the officer asked about a Portuguese having committed the deed Lizzie said that she did not think it was he as he had worked for them a number of years. At the time I arrived in the house there was no sign of blood on her hands or clothes. She did not wear any covering oh her head and her hair was done up as usual. It was not disarranged, and there was no sign of blood on it. When she lay on the lounge in the dining room I did not notice whether her shoes showed or not. Lizzie was present when Bridget told about the note, and she told the story voluntarily.

I did not go into the house that day again, and that is substantially all I know about the case. There were present at the inquest Judge Blaisdell, Marshal Hilliard, Mr. Seaver, Dr. Dolan and District Attorney Knowlton. The latter asked the questions, and while I was present the gentlemen did not stop the proceedings and converse together.

This ended her examination, Mr. Jennings remarking that the inquest was "not very private," in a sarcastic manner.

EVIDENCE OF MISS RUSSELL.

What is your name? Alice E. Russell.

Where do you live? I live on Borden street about 300 yards from South Main street.

Are you acquainted with the Bordens? Yes, sir.

How long have you known Lizzie? About eleven years.

What time was it when you heard of the murder? About 15 minutes to 11.

What did you do then? I changed my dress and went over there.

Whom did you see there? I saw Lizzie.

Where was Lizzie? She was leaning against the frame of the door.

Did you see anything on Lizzie dress? I don't remember.

Did you ask Lizzie where she was when her father was killed? I don't remember asking her.

Do you remember her say anything of her father? Yes, sir.

What did she say? She said she came in from the barn and saw him lying on the sofa. She went out to get a piece of iron or tin to fix her screen or windows.

Did she say anything more? No, sir; I don't think she did.

Did she say what window she wanted to fix? I don't remember.

How many nights did you stay at the house after the murder? Four nights.

Mr. Jennings then cross-examined Miss Russell.

Where did you say Lizzie was when you went in? Leaning against the frame of the door.

How long did she stay there? Until I asked her to sit down.

Where did she sit? In an arm chair in the kitchen.

Did you notice whether there was any blood on her dress? No, sir; I didn't see any.

Did you see her hands? Yes, sir; I didn't see any blood on them.

Did you see her face? I bathed her face and saw no blood on it.

Did you notice her shoes? I don't remember about her shoes.

Was she panting? She was not panting.

Do you recollect whether she went upstairs before the officers came or not? She did not.

How do you know? Because I remember her talking and asking questions.

Do you remember whether the first search was made before Lizzie went upstairs? I do not.

Lucy Collet then took the stand. She said she lived on Borden street, but on the day of the murder was on the piazza of Dr. Chagnon's house about 15 minutes to 11 and stayed there until 11 o'clock. Her testimony was short and of no importance. When cross-examined by Mr. Jennings, she admitted that a man could have gone through the Chagnon yard without her seeing him. During the morning she had seen two men. One was a Mr. Robinson of Somerset, who called at Dr. Chagnon's for medicine and another was a man whom she did not know. The hearing closed at 12:25.

THE POISON STORY.

Eli Bence Insists That Lizzie Borden Called at Smith's Store.

The demand for seats at the afternoon session was more than large, and the number of disappointed nearly equalled those who were admitted. For the first time since the hearing opened a colored person occupied a seat, being probably the only new face of the regular attendants that greeted the eye. A large number of out of town persons are in attendance, and they seem to look on the affair as a scene not to be missed.

The defendant retains the same cool manner which has characterized her from the start. When Eli Bence was called, the druggist who is said to have recognized her as the party who called at Smith's store and asked for prussic acid the day previous to the tragedy, she listened and looked intently at the witness. When he stated that she wanted the poison the day previous and for what use not a tremor passed her face.

Mr. Bence said: I am a drug clerk at the corner of South Main and Columbia streets. I remember the day of the tragedy. I knew the defendant as Miss Borden.

When did you see her in your store? I saw her the day before the murder.

Was she alone? Yes, sir; she asked me for ten cents' worth of prussic acid. I informed her we didn't sell prussic acid. She said she wanted it to put on a sealskin sack or cape, I am not sure which. I told her we didn't sell it without a prescription. I believe she said she had bought prussic acid before.

Are you sure this (pointing to Lizzie Borden) is the woman? Yes, sir.

Are you sure? Yes, sir.

By Knowlton—Is prussic acid a thing often called for in your store?

Adams—I object.

Knowlton—I only ask to show that as it is not often called for it would strengthen his evidence.

Court--He may answer the question.

Bence—It was the first time I was ever asked for prussic acid in that manner.

How long before the authorities came to you did you talk with this man? About an hour.

Who was the person? Dr. Dutra.

Did you recognize Lizzie's voice? Yes.

Do you make any pretensions to vocal culture? Never.

Do you claim to have an educated ear? I do not.

What was there peculiar in her voice that you could recognize? asked Mr. Adams. She spoke in a tremulous voice.

Did she speak in the same manner when you called at the house with Officer Harrington? Yes, sir.

Bridget's Character All Right.

The defence in the Borden case has been actively engaged in Newport, learning something about Bridget Sullivan's career in that city. Detective Richards and Attorney Philips looked up her record there, but found nothing of importance, except a rumor that she had a very hot temper.

The purpose of the inquiry is to determine how reliable her evidence is, also to learn if she would become so much provoked that she would quarrel seriously with Mr. and Mrs. Borden. It is believed here that Miss Sullivan's character is above reproach. Her past employers speak very kindly of her, and say she was always a devoted church member. Her unshaken testimony has done much to establish the strength of the case of the government.

The defence proposes to call a witness who will show that much of Dr. Dolan's testimony is unreliable. Ex-Medical Examiner Dwelley has been a close listener to the trial, and it is understood that he will be called as an expert on the part of the defence to rebut much of the testimony that has been given. The defence claims that there are large holes in the government's expert testimony and some unlooked-for denials are expected.

A REMINISCENCE.

A Famous Trial for Murder Recalled by the Present Case.

One of the most famous murder cases which ever interested Fall River was likewise one of the most famous murder trials of the county. Many of the older residents of Bristol county recall it, and the difficulty of reconciling the christian reputation of the prisoner with the awful brutality of the crime was a feature, as it is in the case of the Borden tragedy.

In March, 1833, Rev. Ephraim K. Avery of Bristol was indicted for the murder of Sarah M. Cornell. Avery was a clergyman in regular standing in the Methodist Episcopal church, and his champions included almost every member of that respectable and numerous religious society in which he had been a teacher, and whose confidence was entirely his until the period of the alleged commission of this crime. His arrest was bitterly criticised by the leaders of his denomination hereabouts. On the 21st of December, 1832, Sarah Maria Cornell of Fall River was found suspended at a stake near a stack of hay on the estate of John Durfee, which was then in Tiverton. The previous night at 6 o'clock she left her boarding house in health and in usual spirits.

The evidence of the government was calculated to show that the circumstances attending the fixing of the cord, the adjustment of the dress, the position of her limbs, the condition of the body, the entire transaction, in fact, were such as to show conclusively that the act by which she lost her life could not have been committed by herself without assistance. From the appearances of the neck, the fastening of the cord and the manner in which it was drawn around the neck, her death was produced by strangulation, and the body subsequently taken to the stake and fastened there to give an impression that she had committed suicide. Her cloak was fastened from her neck down, with a slight opening below the breast. There were marks and bruises upon her body and her comb was found broken 20 rods from the body, indicating a struggle. Evidence was introduced to show between the prisoner and the deceased a correspondence and intimacy of long standing, and her situation was such previous to her death as to render her removal necessary to the prisoner.

On a cold blustering day—so cold that the body of the deceased was frozen—the prisoner left his home in Bristol. A ferryman testified to sailing him across the ferry to Portsmouth, in a gale of wind. From there a man answering his description was traced across a bridge to Lawton's tavern, on the Tiverton side, and thence to a lonely spot in a meadow, a few rods from the location where the deceased was found. Then he was traced to Fall River and back, and at 10 o'clock at night he was again at the ferry-house, where he implored the ferry-man to take him across, despite the wildness of the night, explaining his anxiety to the fact that there was sickness in his family at home.

The ground of the defence was that Miss Cornell committed suicide. The trial was commenced on May 7, when Avery pleaded "not guilty."

"How will you be tried?" asked the clerk.

"By God and my country," said the prisoner.

"God send you good deliverance," pronounced the clerk, solemnly.

There was very great difficulty in selecting the jury and several days were occupied in the empanelling. In addition to witnesses upon the points referred to above, the prosecution introduced letters found in the girl's trunk, alleged to be from Avery, with relation to her condition and making an appointment to meet him on the 20th, in Somerset, just over the ferry. The physicians testified to bruises and marks of strangulation upon the body.

Many clergymen and prominent church people were witnesses for Avery. The defence sought to show that the girl had been expelled from Avery's church in Lowell for fornication, and that she confessed her guilt and declared that she would be revenged on Avery if it cost her her life. This was the explanation of her charges that Avery was responsible for her condition. It was claimed that she had made repeated threats at suicide and had attempted to effect it; that her conduct was strange, and for 14 years she was traced in her lewdness, strangeness of conduct and tendency to suicide. There was evidence of her seduction long before the campmeeting at Thompson, where she met Mr. Avery. The defence pleaded that the fair character of the prisoner and the previous absence of disposition to vice should be some protection against the charge of murder.

After a trial which continued 27½ days, Avery was adjudged not guilty and was taken away as the guest of the fellow clergymen in Newport. While the verdict was regarded as a satisfactory vindication by the church people of Fall River and vicinity, there was much bitter feeling throughout the country against Avery on the part of others.

VIEWS FROM OTHER NEWSPAPERS

Holyoke Democrat

The murderer of the Bordens of Fall River hacked the bodies of his victims badly enough, but his cold-bloodedness is far excelled by that of the commonwealth's officers. They have had a dozen doctors hacking away at the remains. The bodies have been made sausage meat of. To crown these slashing exploits, the government officers have cut off the heads of the victims, and got the skulls ready for exhibition. There is no necessity for this mutilation of the bodies of the Bordens. The parties who have been conducting the postmortem examinations and finally severed the heads acted more from a sickening love of the loathsome and ghastly than from a sense of scientific duty.

Pawtucket Times

The idea of forming any intelligent and conclusive conclusion as to the Borden case at this early day is idle. One may, of course, from what has been shown and what appears day by day, be morally convinced as to where the crimes should be charged, but even this conclusion may be set aside by the evidence to be presented. The proper mental attitude is one of passive reception, not of the hundred and one rumors, but of the testimony as given in court. And the time for the summing up of that has not arrived.

The Boston Globe

Everybody in Boston has heard of Col. Adams, and to thousands his face is as familiar as that of Gen. Butler. For years he was assistant district attorney in the criminal courts of Suffolk county, and his record of unvarying success as a prosecutor has been since his retirement from that office only equalled by his success as a defender of persons accused.

Col. Adams has brought into the Borden case talent and experience sufficient to do battle with even so distinguished an advocate as Attorney-General A. E. Pillsbury, who, in the event of retaining his present office, will probably prosecute Lizzie. In appearance Col. Adams is over medium height, with a good form and face possessing great character and intelligence. He is fastidious in dress, of dark complexion, with brown hair and heavy mustache. Genial in disposition, of pleasing voice and fine conversational powers. he attracts people by his manifest good nature and cordial bearing. His treatment of witnesses is fair. He asks questions with great rapidity and with distinctness. His inquiries are direct and always intelligible, and he makes no attempt to "throw a witness down" by long, rambling interrogations.

The New York Times

NO TRACE OF POISON FOUND

PROF. WOOD'S TESTIMONY AT THE BORDEN HEARING.

THE CAMBRIDGE EXPERT GIVES HIS ANALYSIS AND SAYS THE STAINS FOUND ON THE AXE WERE NOT BLOOD, NOR WAS THE HAIR THAT OF A HUMAN BEING.

FALL RIVER, Mass., Aug. 30.-This has been a day of sensations in the Lizzie Borden hearing. To-night, with the Government story concluded, people are saying that unlesss the testimony presented by District Attorney Knowlton receives decided addition before it is given to the consideration of a jury as the evidence upon the strength of which conviction of murder is sought, the young woman may rest safe from any fear that her life will pay the penalty for the murder of Andrew J. Borden and wife, and that the crime has been committed by some person as yet unknown. That there is more evidence held by the prosecution than has been disclosed is certain, and is shown by the fact that neither City Marshal Hilliard nor State Detective Seaver, the two men under whose charge the case against Lizzie Borden was worked up, was called to the stand, and it is believed that, stopping where he did, the District Attorney must be confident that Judge Blaisdell will adjudge the prisoner probably guilty and hold her to await action by the Grand Jury. Perhaps the greatest surprise of the day was the testimony of Prof. Wood, the eminent Harvard chemist. After all the talk about prussic acid, the long stories of the police officers about finding hatchets and axes and their careful preservation, the demand of the stomachs of the murdered couple, and the forwarding of Lizzie Borden's clothing to Boston, it was expected by the large gathering in the courtroom and by everybody outside that the testimony of Prof. Wood would be the last nail needed by the Government to clinch its case. The clothing was to be bloody, the stomachs were to contain poison, and the hair on the hatchet was to correspond with that upon the head of Mrs. Borden. So everybody agreed, and everybody was mistaken, for even the wildest flight of imagination on the part of the attorneys for the defense could hardly result in an idea that the Cambridge expert would prove one of the strongest witnesses that they could desire or could possibly secure. But so it proved, and when after his story the noon recess was taken, Lizzie Borden's friends were jubilant. They said the prosecution had been completely routed, and the local newspaper which has espoused the cause of the young woman from the outset, announced its opinion that the Government had failed utterly in its attempt to fasten complicity in the crime upon Lizzie Borden.

OPINIONS FROM OTHER NEWSPAPERS

The Woonsocket Call

SAYS SHE IS INNOCENT.

A Former Teacher of Lizzie Borden Speaks About Her Case.

Mr. Horace Benson, a former Woonsocket boy, and at one time a successful teacher here, who has for some 12 years or more been making his mark in one of the best schools in Fall River, was in this city Saturday and visited his old friends, one of whom was a former teacher, Mr. L. L. Chilson. In speaking of the Borden case to a friend Mr. Benson said that he knew the family very well and that Lizzie was one of his former pupils. He said that as a pupil she was an average scholar, neither beingexceptionally smart nor noticeably dull. She was subject to varying moods, and was never fond of her stepmother. She had no hesitation in talking about her, and in many ways showed her dislike of her father's second wife.

Mr. Benson boarded at the next house but one to the Borden house, and as was his duty, he became acquainted with Mrs. Borden, whom he grew to know as a kindly hearted,lovable woman, who tried, but ineffectually, to win the love of the stepdaughters. Still the household was far from being an unhappy one.

When asked if he believed that Lizzie committed the murder, he replied quickly and emphatically, "No, I do not. It is impossible, and I know the girl and have known her for years. I believe that she is innocent and that her innocence will soon be established."

Mr. Benson in his capacity as a teacher and with his wide experience understands, as every successful instructor must, the study of human nature, and the relations that subsist between teacher and pupil are such as to give the former a deeper insight into the character of a child, as it unfolds day by day, than is given to any save the parents, and even in many cases a deeper knowledge than the parents possess. His belief is shared by hundreds of the other citizens of Fall River, who cannot bring themselves to believe her guilty. Mr. Benson was warmly greeted by his many friends in this city, who rejoice at his success in his chosen profession.

The Fall River Herald

FULL OF INTEREST.

Prof. Wood Found a Single Blood Spot

ON ALL OF THE ARTICLES SUBMITTED TO HIM.

No Trace of Prussic Acid in the Stomachs.

EXCITING COLLOQUY BETWEEN THE LAWYERS

Over the Custody of a Piece of Plastering.

Matters progressed rapidly in the Borden hearing Monday. The stand was occupied all day by people who were in the house directly after the crime had been done, and they told some very interesting things.

The proceedings of the day were of a nature to satisfy the crowd of spectators, not because of highly sensational disclosures, but because the story was being told with a fullness of detail that they had not heard before. There was much in the day's doings that gave further food for debate wherever the case was being talked over Monday night, and it was hard to find a place where it was not talked over more or less.

THE GROSS UNFAIRNESS

that is characterizing certain reports printed in and sent out from this city is receiving general condemnation of the friends of fair play. Having accepted the theory that Lizzie Borden is guilty of the crime of which she is charged, every bit of evidence offered against her is being seized upon and underscored to attract attention of readers. Time and time again when testimony can be interpreted with equal reason for or against the prisoner, the unfavorable one is emphasized by special comment, while the statement itself is buried in a mass of printed matter. Two interpretations are not placed side by side so that readers can make their own choice, but the unfavorable is thrust into prominence. Public opinion is outspoken in condemning this unfairness.

It is customary in criminal courts to hear the plaintiff's side first, and therefore a review of Monday's testimony may be made from the government's standpoint first. Mrs. Churchill says that Lizzie Borden, herself, was the first person to suggest that Mrs. Borden had been killed. This the government interprets as strange indeed.

Why should she imagine such a thing, and why did the fancy lay so strong a hold on her that she urged Bridget to go upstairs to look for her stepmother? Another point brought out emphatically was that the door of the spare chamber was open when Mrs. Churchill went up the front stairs because she had only gone half way up when she saw Mrs. Borden's dead body lying behind the bed. Lizzie Borden was near this open door, when her father entered the house. She stood near it when Bridget heard her laugh. Then she walked down that same staircase from which Mrs. Churchill had discovered Mrs. Borden's body. Churchill and Miss Russell

DID NOT NOTICE ANY BLOOD

on the girl's hands or dress. They were close to her, bending over her, and Officer Doherty says the dress was a light blue challie. Neither the women nor the officers detected blood, and today, more important than all, Prof. Wood says the microscope fails to reveal any.

As to the poison story, the friends of Miss Borden declare that thus far nobody has testified that she said she never went to Smith's drugstore. If it can be established that she did say so and the defence fail to prove an alibi for the time Aug. 3, when the druggists say they saw Lizzie, the friends admit that they will be disappointed. Still taken as evidence, the prussic acid story has not yet amounted to anything, and its importance as reflecting upon the truthfulness of the prisoner remains for the future to reveal.

The time Lizzie Borden told Assistant Marshal Fleet that she spent in the barn is not considered important, because everybody has had experience in estimating time spent at a particular occupation and knows how hard it is to tell what time has been spent if there are no events to fix it. Then the officers found no serious objections to a search of the house. The girls aided and appeared to have nothing to conceal. Then the axes in the cellar were covered with dust except one which looked as if it had been rubbed and carried down cellar to be laid in the box behind the furnace; it took a good deal of time, and the state has much to crowd into a rapidly narrowing quarter of an hour. The day's testimony, therefore, was not so discouraging to the defence.

OFFICER MICHAEL MULLALY.

I went to the house at 23 minutes of 12; Lizzie Borden was on the dining room sofa. I had some talk with Mrs. Churchill, and then talked with Lizzie. I told her I had been sent out to get a report, and asked her where she had found her father. She said she had found her father dead on the sofa when she came in from the yard. I asked her to tell me what kind of property her father had on him. She told me he had on a silver watch and chain, a pocketbook and a gold ring on his little finger. Did not go with Doherty to look. He reported that the watch and chain were on Mr. Borden, but did not say anything about the pocketbook.

Mr. Knowlton—Was the pocketbook there? I don't know.

Did you search the house? Yes, I went up stairs and saw Mrs. Borden in a pool of blood. We came down from up there and then went up to the attic. We searched all the rooms.

What do you mean by searching? Tell us if you opened the bureau drawers. No, but we went in and looked around. I was after two things: the person who committed the murders and the weapon. We looked into each room and then came down. We went into the cellar, or, I should say, we met Bridget and she led the way to the place. She searched and found a small box of tools.

and passed them to me. We then went into an apartment south of the furnace and I took down two axes. I noticed that one was larger than the other and had a small rust spot on it. Then, while in the wash cellar, I think they call it, Mr. Doherty called my attention to some things in a pail. He looked at them and then put them back.

Mr. Adams, to Mr. Knowlton—You disclaim any connection of that matter with this case, I thought? For this hearing.

Well, we had better understand. I thought you said this was disclaimed. I don't bind myself; but if I don't have any reasons, I never shall. I don't wish to run against anything accidental. As far as the present goes I admit that they are of no use.

Witness continued—We left the axes in the washroom. The cellar door was shut. Officer Doherty tried to get out. We found it locked. We didn't search Lizzie's room that day; not till afterwards.

Mr. Knowlton—Who was the searching party? First, Officer Doherty, afterwards Officer Hyde, I think.

Did you have any further talk with Miss Borden? I saw Miss Lizzie after that and inquired if she had seen anybody about the house. She said there had been a man there that morning. This man had dark clothes, she said, and was about the size of Officer Hyde. I don't think she said where she saw him. She was then in her own room. I searched the barn for the two things spoken of, the man and the weapon, and looked back of the fence. There was a pile of wood in the yard. I didn't disturb the pile that day.

This house has a number of trees in front of it, asked Mr. Adams in cross-examination. I think there are trees on the street.

Didn't Miss Lizzie tell you she saw a man out under the trees? I don't remember just what she did say.

You won't deny she said that? No, sir.

You went into a large closet at the head of the stairs in your search? Yes, sir.

Did this closet have a window in it? I can't remember.

What was the floor of the cellar? I can't say.

Isn't that portion of the cellar still earth? Yes.

How did you know there was a dull spot? By looking at it.

Were they sharp? The larger one was. I could not see any blood upon the handles. I saw no hair upon them, though I just looked at them, not giving a careful examination. I was looking for blood on them.

How did Dr. Dolan get possession of them? He came down the cellar, and I gave him the large hatchet.

Officer Doherty was recalled and said he took nothing from the body of Mr. Borden.

ASSISTANT MARSHAL FLEET.

The assistant marshal testified as follows: First heard of the affair at a quarter of 12 Thursday. I was home when the news came from the marshal, who had sent word to me by a man in a team. I drove down to the Borden house and arrived about 10 minutes of 12. I saw Officer Allen and Mr. Manning at the front door. Mr. Sawyer was at the rear door. Inside I found Bridget, Mr. Morse, Dr. Dolan, Dr. Bowen and Lizzie. I went into the sitting room and saw Dr. Dolan standing over Mr. Borden. Then I went upstairs and saw Mrs. Borden. Soon after I went into Lizzie's room and had a conversation with her. She was sitting in the room with the Rev. Mr. Buck. I asked her if she knew anything about the man who killed her father and mother. She said it was not her mother, but her stepmother.

"I asked her if Bridget was in the house during the morning, and she said she had been washing windows and came in after her father came, and then went upstairs. She said she didn't think Bridget had anything to do with it. Lizzie said that when Bridget went upstairs she went up in the barn. 'Up in the barn?' I said, and she said 'Yes.' 'What do you mean by up?' I asked. 'Upstairs,' she said. I asked her how long she remained in the barn and she said half an hour.

At this point some confusion was created by the fainting of Mrs. Bowen, wife of the physician. Mrs. Bowen has been a regular visitor at the court room during the hearing, and is credited with being a firm believer in the innocence of Lizzie Borden. The heat in the room, combined with the nervous strain of the affair, caused her momentary weakness Monday afternoon. She was carried into an adjoining room and the hearing proceeded.

The scene at this time was very dramatic. Every eye was directed towards the assistant marshal, and every person was bending eagerly forward to catch every word of the slowly uttered sentences. Lizzie herself bit her lips constantly, and her sister's hands were nervously moving up and down a fan which lay in her lap. At this time the gas was lighted, and this brightened the effect of the situation.

"What did you find down in the cellar?"

"Found Mr. Mullaly, with a number of axes on the floor of the washroom. We reached the cellar, and found nothing other than the two axes and two hatchets. The two axes were dusty, or covered with ashes, and so was the little hatchet. The large hatchet was clean with the exception of a small rust spot. It was about four inches long from the head, to the edge six inches, and it had a claw handle.

It was then a claw hammer? Yes. We looked at the hatchets a little more, and then left them there, the edges on the floor. I took one of them, the big hatchet, away, and put it in the adjoining cellar.

Was anybody near the hatchets when you first saw them in the cellar? They were on the cellar floor and others present were examining them.

Mr. Knowlton—What then?

Witness—I tried the cellar door, and then went out to the barn. I satisfied myself there was nobody there to do this deed. Then I went into the house again and consulted with two of my officers and State Officer Dexter. I made another search and saw Lizzie again in the presence of two officers, and Dr. Bowen was holding the door. I told him I wanted to search the room.

Miss Borden said: "How long will it take you?" I said that I didn't know, but that I had to search the room. She said: "I do hope you will get through soon; this is making me sick." I searched the room.

Did you say anything more to Miss Borden? Yes. I said: "You say, Miss Borden, that you went out to the barn, and that you were out there half an hour, while your father and mother were killed. You still say that?" She said: "I do not. I say I was in the barn 20 minutes to half an hour." Said I: "You told me this morning that you were out there half an hour." "I don't say so now," she said: "It was 20 minutes to half an hour." "What makes you say 20 minutes to half an hour?" I asked her. "Which is it now, 20 minutes or half an hour?" She said: "It was 20 minutes to half an hour."

Did you search the premises then? Did you have any more talk with her then? I searched the room and bureau and then

Were you looking to see if you could find any bloody clothing? Yes, I was. I was not looking very closely.

You went through this closet and looked at each garment? Yes, I did.

That was after you had seen the axes and hatchet? Yes, sir.

Who took the hatchet you laid aside? Officer Edson.

When? The following morning. He went there by order of the marshal.

What were the other axes brought in? I don't know.

Have you heard anything about a sack or bag? No, sir.

Now, this particular hatchet you laid aside, was it damp? Yes. It looked to me as if it had been wiped with a damp cloth.

See any hairs on it? On no part of it.

You examined all those hatchets to see if there was any indication of blood upon them? Yes, I did.

You made the search on Saturday? Yes.

Was it after the funeral? Yes, after the procession left the house. Mr. Seaver, Marshal Hilliard, Dr. Dolan, Mr. Jennings and myself were present.

You were given every facility to go through the house, were you not? Yes, sir.

And you searched this closet again? Yes, sir.

You went through band-boxes and barrels on Saturday, did you not? Yes, sir, we went through everything.

That's all, sir, concluded Mr. Adams, and the session was then adjourned for the day.

A DAY OF EXCITEMENT

Prof. Wood Says there was no Blood on the Axes.

The morning proceedings were opened with the promptness which has characterized all the sessions of Judge Blaisdell's court. There was the usual crowding for seats, and "standing room only" might have been hung out at the box office early if there were any box office to the court.

Senator Mitchell of Oregon appeared with the council for the defence and was an interested listener. Tony Pastor was there Monday, and no stranger feels his visit to this city at the present time quite complete without dropping into the second district court room. It is a continuous show, so to speak, and a little nerve is all that is needed to get past the ticket takers. Lizzie was accompanied by the usual friends. She begins to manifest a keen interest in the proceedings. "People wonder why she does not appear more distressed," said a womanly sympathizer Monday. "Do you think if anybody was watching me to see if I would cry that I would break down? Well, I guess not. It is a trying experience, and Lizzie Borden feels it more keenly than the public imagine. But for all that, she isn't shedding tears for show, and does not want the maudlin sympathy that such a show of emotion might gain for her."

PROF. EDWARD S. WOOD OF HARVARD was the first witness called and testified as follows: I am a professor of chemistry, and on Aug. 5 I received a box containing four jars. One jar was labelled "milk of Aug. 4," another "milk of Aug. 5," another the "stomach of Andrew J. Borden," and the last that of Mrs. Borden. On examining the stomachs I found their condition to be perfectly natural. Mrs. Borden's stomach contained 11 ounces of solid food. One-fifth of the contents of the stomach was liquid. There was a large amount of vegetable matter in the stomach. I should judge that digestion was going on about two hours. There was no indication of prussic acid. Mr. Borden's stomach contained six ounces, mostly water. About one-tenth of the contents was solid, the principal part of which was vegetable. His digestion had advanced three and a half to four hours. I tested his stomach also for prussic acid, but could find no sign of any.

I also received a package containing an axe, two hatchets, a blue dress waist, an under skirt, a package containing hair of Mr. Borden, another hair of Mrs. Borden, and another hair on the hatchet. The hatchet containing a number of suspicious looking spots was examined, but there was no indication of blood. The smirch on the dress which looked like blood was not so. The white skirt had a spot of blood about six inches from the bottom. There was no other spot on the garment. The carpet had two stains of blood, which I took to be the sitting room carpet. The carpet from the spare room was thick with blood. The lounge cover was not marked with blood. The hair taken from the hatchet was about an inch long and was not a human hair. The pair of shoes that I examined was all right. The only indication that one gave of blood would come from not being tanned properly. One of the marks on the hatchet would have been caused by a drop of water falling and remaining there. The red stains on the handle were not blood, but probably varnish.

There have been cases when food eaten at night has remained there until morning. I could answer to within a half hour as to digestion. I was in the house Aug. 10 with Dr. Dolan and looked at the different rooms. If one was struck with a sharp instrument as Mr. Borden was, there would be a spurt of blood. The direction of the blood would depend on the way the artery pointed. Blood never spurts over three feet. I have seen similar spatterings from a club as that shown on the wall. A photograph of the blood on the wall of Mr. Borden's room was then shown to the witness, and he believed that it could have come from the wound in the head. "If a person stood behind his victim and hit him, the spots would be elongated, and the heaviest spots would be at the farthest end."

The hatchet is 14 inches long, and in the examination I have done a little scraping of the handle. Blood coagulates most rapidly on exposure to the air. I do not feel confident to answer that by the coagulation of the blood how long a person has been dead. I have not examined any of the wood work or paper taken from the house. On the door from the kitchen to the sitting room I noticed the spot of blood.

Was there anything which would make you believe where the person stood when the blows were struck?

Only one thing. It was a long stain of blood, from an inch and a quarter to two inches long on the dining room side of the door frame. It appeared to me that a person standing in the dining room when the blow was given would have made the spot by blood dropping from the instrument.

Mr. Wood was then given a piece of the door frame to see if the stain upon it was blood. He examined it under a microscope near a window and then brought it back, saying: It doesn't look like blood stains.

Might it not be tobacco or other stains? It might be tobacco stains.

Knowlton—I supposed Mr. Wood had all of the hatchets. He is going to take the fourth hatchet now. He has only taken three. Another hatchet, smaller in size was then brought out and examined by Prof. Wood.

Adams—Do you see any appearance of

blood on that? I could hardly tell that after a five or ten minutes' examination.

Knowlton—There was no claim made on any hatchet. I had supposed that Mr. Wood had been given all the hatchets.

Wood—I don't see anything now upon this hatchet except something near the handle. Rust generally gathers in that place.

Jennings—Were there any stains of blood upon the parlor door? Yes, sir.

Did you examine these spots? Yes, sir; I looked at them.

Is there anything to conflict with the theory that the person stood behind the victim? No, sir; the assailant could not go through Mr. Borden's body.

From your knowledge of flowing blood would you say it was natural that the assassin should receive a large amount of blood on his clothes? I should say that it was impossible for him not to get considerable blood on him.

What part of the assassin would you think it would cover? I should think the upper part of the body.

The face, hair and head? Yes, sir.

A photograph of Mrs. Borden's room and body was then shown to Prof. Wood. You observe, said Mr. Adams, that the wounds were on the back of the head, on the right side of the back of the head. Now how do you think the person would stand to deliver such blows? Over the body.

Standing over the body would it have been possible for the assassin to deliver these blows without getting covered with blood? I should say not.

What part of the assasin would the blood stain? The blood-stains would have been on the lower part of the assassin. Anywhere above the feet.

At this juncture the district attorney wanted to give the piece of plastering to the expert, Mr. Jennings was willing to admit that it was blood and did not want it effaced. If they would assure him that it would be safe he would give up the piece of plastering; otherwise he would put it in his pocket.

Knowlton—I think that this is the most impertinent piece of business I have ever heard of or witnessed in the course of my professional career. This is only a preliminary examination. If it should happen, in the course of human events, that Miss Borden is bound over to a higher court, this piece of plastering would be of the utmost importance. I ask you, (addressing Jennings,) to give it up.

Jennings (rising with the piece of plastering covered)—I am willing to leave it in the custody of the court; but I want to know whether or not it is going to stay there.

Knowlton to the city marshal—Take those pieces of wood on the desk quickly and put them away before some one else takes them.

Marshal Hilliard jumped from his seat, sprang past the counsel of the defence without a sign or word, and grabbed the pieces of wood that were laid on the desk near Miss White, the court stenographer.

Judge Blaisdell (addressing Jennings) I cannot give you that permission.

Mr. Jennings then sat down. Blaisdell (continuing)—You may leave that parcel, Mr. Jennings, in the custody of the court.

Jennings—If I have the assurance of the court as to its safety I will.

Blaisdell—That (meaning the parcel) is to be left in the custody of the court. The court will give no assurance on the matter.

Mr. Adams then poured oil on the troubled waters by addressing a question to Prof. Wood. Would it have been easy to wash blood from that hatchet? It would not have been easy to wash the blood out of the cracks, and I have been over the hatchet very carefully.

Knowlton—Prof. Wood, I place this hatchet (the fourth hatchet brought upstairs by Marshal Hilliard) in your custody.

Prof. Wood then put the weapon into his satchel for future examination. This last weapon was nicked on the edge and had a handle about a foot and a half in length.

After a short conference with Mr. Adams, Mr. Jennings arose and said: We have agreed to surrender this with the custody of the court, but I would like to have it retained in the custody of the court until I can file a motion.

Knowlton—I have no objection to that. I only objected to the use of physical force in the handling of such an important piece of evidence.

Judge Blaisdell then took possession of the plastering wrapped in paper.

JAMES WINWARD, THE UNDERTAKER,

testified as follows: I removed the articles from Andrew J. Borden's clothes and gave them to Dr. Dolan. There were $78 in bills in the inside pocket of his coat; in a book there was a number of papers; a watch and chain; in the pants pockets keys and a small amount of change. I did not examine Mrs. Borden's clothes.

In answer to Mr. Jennings the witness stated that Dr. Dolan gave him charge of the bodies at 5:30 p. m. on the day of the murder. On Saturday about 9 o'clock the undertaker was notified not to bury the bodies.

John Dinnie, a stone cutter, stated that he was employed in Mr. Crowe's yard from 7 in the morning until 5 in the evening. He could not see the Borden or Chagnon yard from where he worked, but could the entire distance of the Crowe yard. He did not see a person pass through the yard other than had business there.

OFFICER PHILIP HARRINGTON

testified: My attention was first called to the matter at noon of Aug. 4. I was at dinner at the time. When I arrived at the place there was a large crowd. I asked a question on going into the house, and in consequence went into the sitting room. A body horribly mutilated was lying there. I then went upstairs and saw the body of Mrs. Borden. On coming down stairs I saw Lizzie and asked her if she could tell anything about the matter, to which she replied that she could not. The last time she saw her father was when he returned from the postoffice. She said that she was in the barn at the time of the murder. When I asked her if she had suspicion of any person she said no. In reply to how long she had been in the barn, she positively stated 20 minutes. When I told her to be careful what she said, as she could answer better the next day, Lizzie answered that she could tell the truth then as well as the next day. While the murder was being committed she said she was in the barn. As to whom she suspected she told of a party who called on her father and wanted to hire a store from him. They had angry words and then parted. From the conversation she thought the man was from out of town. When I looked in the stove there was the remains of what appeared to be burned paper.

I went into the barn about 3 o'clock in the afternoon. The window on the west of the barn was open, and one of the men opened the east window to allow a draught upstairs. I saw the hatchet lying on the floor directly in front of the door that leads to the back yard. There were two axes and a hatchet. The other hatchet was found in the west end of the cellar of the house. It was lying on a large block of wood.

THIS AFTERNOON.

The Court Room Crowded with Deeply Interested Spectators.

The court room was more than crowded this afternoon, it being expected that the government would place some stronger testimony before the court than it has yet offered. The testimony of Prof. Wood in the morning was a surprise to all not acquainted with the inside facts of the case. It is claimed by the government that they knew how Wood would testify, and the explaining that the spots on the axe are not blood does not seem to disconcert them.

"What was the deed committed with?" is the question that is now asked by everybody. The warrant claims that the murder was perpetrated with a hatchet in the hands of Lizzie Borden. Where is that hatchet? Nothing of a confirming nature has been found on the hatchet in the care of the chemist, and if the police have another hatchet when did they find it? Nothing has been said in court as yet to indicate that they have, and it may be that the government will not be able to prove the charge they have so specifically stated.

It was more than pleasing to the friends of Dr. Dolan who were present during the time Prof. Wood was giving his testimony to see how the latter corroborated all the statements made by the examiner. The causes as to the coagulation of blood, the time Mrs. Borden was dead and several other minor details were explained by the expert in nearly the same language as that used by Dr. Dolan, and this coinciding will probably prevent the defence from putting another expert on the stand to try and weaken Dr. Dolan's statements.

THE COURT STENOGRAPHER.

Miss White, court stenographer, was the first sworn. I was present at the inquest. I was present during the examination of Lizzie Borden. I took notes and have transcribed them. Mr. Knowlton then offered the notes as testimony.

On cross-examination Miss White said: I saw the different people during the inquest. Mr. Seaver, the marshal and Dr. Dolan were present. The statements Lizzie made were taken down by me when the people I have named were present. I made more than one copy of the testimony; I made two. I gave them both to Mr. Knowlton. That is the last I saw of them. The examination was suspended once during the inquest. Other witnesses were examined between the first time she was on the stand and the second. I and Officer Harrington were in the room, and the rest left and went into the judge's room. Mr. Knowlton was one. I can't remember the others. Miss Borden was in this room two different days. Her examination continued. I think all the afternoon one time and the next time about an hour. The date of her last examination was Aug. 11. On looking at my notes I find that Miss Borden was before the inquest on Aug. 9, 10 and 11. The examination of Wednesday lasted half a day and less than an hour, on Thursday. It lasted an hour and a half on Tuesday. No other inquiries were put, save by the district attorney.

Mr Jennings Talks.

Monday A. J. Jennings was interviewed by a Boston Post reporter, who asked him: "How about the identification of Lizzie as the girl who attempted to buy prussic acid at Smith's the day before the murder? If she bought poison for the purpose alleged, why don't you admit it and be done with it?"

"We don't admit it. I don't think she did it."

"The identification seems pretty strong. You certainly know whether she did it or not. You must have asked her."

"If I did and she told me it would be a confidence between counsel and client, which I would not tell in any case. But I don't believe she was in the store or tried to buy poison. Further, however, it is irrelevant. She is not being tried for poisoning. But there is not an absolute identification. All the witnesses differ somewhat. We will positively take pains to show that it was a case of mistaken identity."

"Will you put Lizzie on the stand?"

"We have not yet decided on that. We probably will."

LIKE ROBINSKY'S MAN.

A Brockton Pawnbroker's Suspicions Aroused by the Actions of a Stranger.

"What do 'Thomas' and 'Huldah' Smith know about the Borden murders?" asks the Boston Globe. There is at least one Brockton man who thought they might know a great deal about it, and he was so much impressed with this idea that he took a trip to Fall River to lay his facts and suspicions before Detective Hanscom. He did not see the detective, but he told Marshal Hilliard his suspicions, and has heard nothing from that official since.

The story told to a Brockton Enterprise reporter by this gentleman, who is a well-known and thoroughly respectable pawnbroker, is as follows: "I have followed the Globe's reports of the Borden murder very closely, and as I take an interest in such matters I had formed an opinion that Lizzie Borden was not the guilty one. On the Saturday following the Borden murder I had a very peculiar and suspicious customer in my place. I saw him go by with a woman; then he came back alone and came in to ask whose place it was. He had a couple of coats and a pair of gray pants over his arm, and he wore a pair of light pants. When I told him whose place he was in he went out and came back with the woman. They wanted to sell some of this extra clothing. I declined to buy the coats or pants. He had a couple of white shirts and I bought them for almost nothing. I asked him where he was from and he evaded the question. When I asked him to sign his name he said he did not know as he could very well, as he was so nervous. He did sign it, however, very plainly as 'Thomas Smith.'

"The woman had a pair of canvas rubber-soled sneaker shoes that she said she wanted to sell, as she did not care to carry them any farther. I looked at them carefully, saw they were nearly new, and that there was a dark spot on each shoe. I judged from their appearance that they had been worn by the seashore or in the sand rather than in gravel or clay. I asked them if the spots on the shoes were not blood and they said no. I bought the shoes and she signed 'Huldah Smith' to the receipt. They went out and up the street together.

"Pretty soon he came down the other side of the street and went into the barber shop. I had the curiosity to go over there and find out what he said or did there, for I knew that it would take about all he got for the shirts to pay for any barbering. The barber told me that the fellow got shaved and said he did not care for a very close shave; just close enough to make him look clean was all he cared for. All attempts to get him into a conversation there failed as they did at my place. He was looking for work and didn't know but he might find it in Brockton.

"This whole proceeding looked so suspicious to me that I took the things to Fall River and gave the description of the man to Marshal Hilliard. When I read the letter from Robinsky, as printed in Thursday's Globe, I declared that his description of the man he met tallied with my suspicious stranger. I thought from his appearance that he was or had been a sailor, and am of the impression, although I could not swear to it, that he had an india ink star pricked into his wrist. He did not belong in this vicinity, and it struck me at the time that he might be the one who committed the crime now charged upon Lizzie Borden.

"I don't know as all this has any connection with the Fall River tragedy, but this man, and his masculine appearing female companion were acting very curiously for honest people. There is another point I have seen raised in the Borden case, and that is that the axes and hatchets found in the Borden house were all dull. Now, if you ever tried to cut a hair with a dull tool you know it can't be done and leave a clean cut. Hairs were cut off and cut with a clean cut in thi case, so I fail to see how the Borden tools could have done it. I might add that it struck me as strange that a rather untidy and dirty man should spend about all the money he presumably had for a shave, as my customer did that Saturday morning."

THAT "QUARREL."

An Authorized Version of the Scene Described by Mrs. Reagan.

A HERALD reporter has been authorized to give the only authentic story of that celebrated "quarrel" between Emma and Lizzie Borden. It occurred on the afternoon of the day upon which the story was told. Emma had been a little late in arriving to see her sister. A caller had been at the house who came over from New Bedford, and while Emma was talking to him Mr. Jennings arrived. Emma explained that it was a friend of Lizzie's. When Mr. Jennings saw Lizzie that afternoon he told her about the caller and spoke lightly about the episode to cheer her. When Emma went in, Lizzie said: "I am glad you have come. Mr. Jennings has been here and told me about my caller." Then followed a short conversation, and during that some such conversation as has been reported. During all the time the best of feeling prevailed, and the remark about "giving me away" and "not speaking to you again" had reference to the friend's visit. It had no significance in the case, and when the sisters parted they did so most affectionately.

This story is told on the authority of one of the closest friends Lizzie Borden has today, who has sacrificed her own interests nobly to sustain her in this hour of trial.

OPINIONS FROM OTHER NEWSPAPERS

The Pawtucket Times

Lizzie Borden is a study in psychology. From the day of the death of her parents to the present time she has been impassive, unmoved and unfeeling in so far as has been discoverable when she has been before the authorities. Does this betoken guilt or innocence? The firmness is remarkable and evidences a constitutional power and "gift" which is of no feminine type. What is it which sustains her? Is it conscious innocence and indignation at her humiliation? Is it the determination to thwart the force of circumstances as evidence against her? The strain has been long and severe, and few could have so long, so fully withstood the pressure. The problem will be solved some day.

The Taunton Gazette

Some people have worked themselves up into considerable indignation because the heads of the murdered Bordens were removed for use as evidence. It is a question how much worse it is to cut off a head than to cut out a stomach, which is done so often that people do not shiver when it is mentioned. Any such act seems horrible, but a tragedy is usually packed with horrors.

The Boston Post

One of the most unseemly exhibitions of feeling is that which was exploited in a dispatch to a morning paper regarding the Borden case, in which it was represented that the comforts afforded Lizzie Borden in jail were improper as marking a distinction in the treatment of prisoners. Such a spirit as this criticism betrays has its place in the dark ages; not in this era of civilization. It goes with the system which held that an accused person was guilty until proved to be innocent, and which starved and tortured prisoners to extort confession. In these days, and under the system of law now prevailing among the people of our race, punishment follows conviction; it does not precede it. A person under arrest is merely held securely to answer to the charge brought against him. This is all that society asks; it is all that the law requires.

The Lewiston Journal

That individual who, under the name of Samuel Robinsky, wrote to Emma Borden describing an alleged interview with a man wearing blood spattered boots, did not fully sustain the role of an ignorant foreigner. A few fatal blunders betrayed the secret of the concoction.

In the first place the handwriting shows evidence of education in that one particular, and in the second the postscript is proof that the ignorance of our language was simulated.

A more plausible tale would have described the alleged farm hand as having blood spots on his clothing. The hero of the Waltham canard could hardly have passed from Second street to the New Bedford road, showing so unmistakable evidences of crime, without being noticed and apprehended.

Mr. Jennings wasted twenty-five cents in telegraphing for information about the author of the letter, which bore the stamp of fiction on its face. Of course he could not be found. If he pays attention to all the "smart" people and cranks who have ideas, he will have his hands very full.

The Fall River Herald

THE OTHER SIDE.

Opening of the Case for the Defence.

NOTHING OF MUCH IMPORTANCE ELICITED.

A Suffolk County Physician Talks at Length.

MISS BORDEN'S LAWYERS ARE HIGHLY GRATIFIED

At the Expert's Statement's Concerning the Blood.

The close of the fifth day of the trial of Lizzie Andrew Borden found the prisoner's friends triumphant. All morning they had sat in the court room and heard blow after blow delivered to the government's theory, shattering it piece for piece until only a ragged framework remained. The builders must begin their work anew, but where were they to get materials? While there was in sight a weapon upon which spots were to be seen and a hair or two fastened to its surface; while there were a gown and a shoe which may have been stained, and while there was evidence of poisoning unfathomed by medical experts, people found no difficulty in accepting the theory of the police as a theory, however they may have questioned the probability of it.

When Prof. Wood, who was chosen by the government for his pre-eminence in his profession, comes forward to testify as an expert who has looked into all these important matters in the light of scientific methods, it is natural that everybody in the court room should bend forward with open mouth to drink in every word he uttered. "I have examined the stomachs and there was no trace of poison in them. That was the first statement of the witness, and everybody looked at his neighbor. That disposes of the poison theory, they said, but there are the hatchet and the hairs and the spotted gown." There were no blood spots on the hatchets or axes," continued the professor. The announcement

SENT A TREMOR

throughout the court room. The dignified precincts of the court would permit of no outbreak of emotion such as characterized this same announcement as it appeared a few moments later on the bulletin boards of the newspapers in Boston, where the crowd paused to read and cheered the words which they firmly believed established beyond a doubt that an innocent woman had been unjustly accused. Newspaper men within hearing of the professor's words dropped their pencils for an instant and lost unimportant words. They did not, however, lose two very significant sentences which followed: "There are no bloodstains on the dress or shoes. The hair is not a human hair."

TODAY'S PROCEEDINGS

The Court Room Uncomfortably Filled, and Many Were Disappointed-

Inside the court room every seat was occupied early. The women who have been attending regularly have caught on to the fact that seats in the prisoners' pen are the best. There is no danger that the court officer will oust them to make room for witnesses, because witnesses do not like to sit in the pen. The free seats are too crowded for comfort, and only the backs of the heads of the important people can be seen. So there is a rush for the seats on the east side, and some of the faces to be seen there are proof against the deadliest execution any of the newspaper "artists" can do. There were many new faces in the room of people who do not lay claim to any other motive of going than of curiosity, just as they go to see the largest church, the biggest circus, the fattest man; for in the second district court room are gathered daily the principal charecters of the greatest sensation of the age.

Court opened three minutes late, and another minute or two delay preceded the appearance of the prisoner. Mr. Buck and Mr. Holmes escorted the sisters, and Mrs. Brigham was there before them. All seemed to be in better spirits than at any time during the trial. Dr. and Mrs. Bowen sat further along on the same bench. Lizzie Borden showed no marked change in her condition except that she seemed to feel more at ease. Her sister was brighter, and her face was more nearly its normal color. Contrary to his usual composure, Dist. Atty. Knowlton seemed to be not quite at ease. During the first lull in the proceedings which was necessary when Marshal Hilliard went downstairs, the prosecuting attorney paced up and down a narrow space in front of the witness seats, with his hands in his pockets and with eyes fixed on the floor. Everybody in the room seemed to feel that the proceedings would not last very much longer, and unless the counsel decide to make pleas the case might be finished before Thursday night.

CITY MARSHAL HILLIARD

was the first witness called: The first that I know of the matter was 11:15 Aug. 4. I then sent Officer Allen. I did not get to the house until about 3 o'clock in the afternoon. The next officers sent were Doherty, Medley, Gillan and Wilson. When I went there it was to search the barn and yards adjoining. In the search of the barn a thorough examination was made and all the hay overturned. I also looked the pile of lumber over that was against the fence adjoining the Chagnon property. I then went to what was the well. Then I went into the barn again and helped in the search of the lower part in which the carriages are kept; all the lower floor was thoroughly searched.

I then went into the house. At the time I went in there were no officers in the house. It was about 3:45; Drs. Coughlin, Dolan, Peckham and Tourtellott were in the house at the time. I am not positive that Dr. Abbott was present. They had brought the body of Mrs. Borden downstairs at the time. I did not examine the sofa on which Mr. Borden was found enough to know whether the cloth was cut or not. I saw blood spots on the door leading from the dining room to the sitting room.

The marshal then went down stairs to produce the pillow shams that were on the bed in the room in which Mrs. Borden was killed. He was also told to bring up the piece of marble that was taken from the bureau. In resuming the marshal said that the goods were delivered to him Aug. 10. The sham on which the blood spots are lay next to the bureau. That afternoon I made no personal search of the house, but sent men to do it, and they gave it a through search. There was nothing delivered to me that day as a result of that search. The piece of marble on the bureau lay north and south. There are one blood spot on its middle and two on the edge. I know from the reports of the officers that the upper part of the building was searched.

On Friday morning I received two axes and two hatchets as a result of a previous search. I did not make an immediate examination of the hatchets at the time. It was on Sunday morning that Dr. Dolan made a thorough examination of the axes. I am not sure, but think that it was Officer Edson, who brought the hatchet down, who discovered the hair on the hatchet. It was not Mayor Coughlin who called attention to it. The mayor did call attention to what looked like blood on an axe. Going back to the house on Saturday I made a search of three rooms, one of which was Miss Lizzie's.

At this point Mr. Jennings asked that Dr. Learned be allowed to take the stand, as his business called him elsewhere. The district attorney agreed, and he took the stand.

I was at the Borden house on the day of the tragedy at 3:15. I saw Mrs. Borden in the spare room. Her arms were under the body. They were not up over her head. There were several present at that time. That was just before she was taken downstairs for the autopsy. I remained during the autopsy.

Monday I did not go, but sent other officers. As far as I know a thorough search was made, including the cellar and barn. It was on Wednesday, Aug. 10, when I took the shoes and stockings. I asked Lizzie for them, and she raised no objections. They were brought down to me. I got the shams at the same day and time. I delivered the shoes and stockings to Dr. Dolan. The shams and pillow cases have been in my possession ever since.

I examined all the trunks and found no dress pattern there. Mr. Fleet went there to get the dress pattern since and was not able to get it. Mr. Medley first went there after it, and then I sent the assistant marshal.

STATE DETECTIVE SEAVER.

I took part in the investigation of the murder of Mr. Borden. I was first informed of the fact at 3:40 on the day of the murder. I went to the house between 5 and 5:30, that afternoon with Marshal Hilliard. I saw blood on the kitchen door leading to the sitting room. I noticed blood on the parlor door. I went into the front hall, but didn't go upstairs at that time. I went around the yard and looked over the fences. I did not see the axes at that time.

I went up there the next morning, and went down cellar and around the barn. I first saw the hatchet in the police station. I made no further search in the house that day. I had a talk with Bridget two or three times. Saturday I went there several times. I had a talk with Bridget about the murder. I made a memorandum of the conversation. I went into three rooms at 12:30 Saturday. We entered Lizzie's room first. We also went into Emma's and the spare room. We made a partial search and made an examination of the beds in all three rooms. The washing arrangement in Lizzie's room I think was a wash bowl. There were a pitcher and bowl in the spare room, We made another search later in the afternoon. I examined the clothes press at the top of the front stairs. There were no clothes hung in front of the window. The blinds were closed and the light came into the room very little. I opened the shutters and examined all the boxes. There was one trunk there. We examined about all the dresses. There were two silk dresses I didn't examine. I examined them for blood and found none. Mr. Fleet was in there with me. I took the dresses to the window to look at them. I found no blood. I took no part in Monday's search. I have been in the barn and cellar since. I looked through the cellar quite thoroughly.

There is a water closet downstairs run by city water. There is a faucet and sink downstairs. There was no other water in the house. Friday morning I looked in the cellar for bloody clothing. I saw nothing of a dress pattern in the trunks I looked into. I found no dress pattern at all. I think there were three or four trunks upstairs.

JOHN DONNELLY, THE HACKMAN.

It was about 12 o'clock when I went to the Borden homestead. When I went there I did not see Officer Medley. In the barn I noticed that the hay in the northwest part of the barn looked as though it had been lain on. The impression of a man's form was apparent. The impression was a foot wide and six inches deep.

"Do you think a man could lie in that space?" asked the district attorney.

The witness made no reply, as the whole court room, Lizzie included, joined in a light laugh.

The district attorney then put Mr. Donnelly through a severe cross-examination, but nothing of interest was drawn forth.

A SUFFOLK COUNTY PHYSICIAN.

My name is Frank Winthrop Draper, I have been medical examiner of Suffolk county for 15 years and two months. The Thursday following the autopsy I came to Fall River at the request of the attorney general. I was present at the autopsy in Oak Grove cemetery. I had no conference with Mr. Adams until today.

Who were present at the autopsy besides yourself? Medical Examiner Dolan, Dr. Cone, Dr. Leary, Undertaker Morrill and two policemen whose names I do not know.

You took notes then? Yes, sir, I took notes then and made other notes afterwards.

Beginning with the body of Mr. Borden what did you find and what was the character of the injuries to him? Answering the first question first, I found all the injuries in a group on the left side of the head between the left side of the nose and front of the ear, between the margin of the lower jaw and extending upward. Answering the other question, I should say the wounds were made by some edged instrument or weapon of considerable weight.

What instrument or weapon in your opinion would be adequate to produce those injuries you saw? I believe a hatchet would be adequate to cause the injuries.

Are you willing to name any other instrument that would have furnished an adequate cause for such injuries? I don't think of any other instrument. A chisel might have done so, but a hatchet would be the most probable weapon.

Why do you make a distinction between a hatchet and an axe? I say a hatchet because of the length of the wounds. I don't think a broad axe would have caused them.

Would an ordinary woodchopper's axe have furnished adequate means? I think it would, assuming the edge to have been at right angles and not rounded.

What do you mean in your answer by not rounded? I cannot describe in words; I will make a picture of it. Witness then drew a picture of a broad axe on a paper.

You mentioned as one of the reasons for preferring the hatchet was the length of the injuries; now, have you notes to the extent of those injuries? If you have, will you please to read them. I can tell you from memory. The first wound began above the left nostril; it was four inches in length and went through the upper portion of the upper lip, through the outer portion of the lower lip and came down near the angle of the outer jaw.

Was that injury in your opinion necessarily fatal? It was not necessarily fatal.

Now as to injury number two? It was four and one-half inches in length; it went parallel with number one and entered the mouth about the edge of the jaw.

Was that injury necessarily fatal? No, sir, it was not.

The next wound, if you please? The third was two inches in length, and just over the cheek bone, and went through the bone.

And its extent was what? Two inches in length.

Was that injury necessarily fatal? It was not.

Take the next one. Number four began in the forehead, by a secondary cut, went towards the left one-half an inch, and then down.

Laterally or upwards? Very nearly laterally.

The fourth wound? The fourth wound went into the jaw.

The length of that? Altogether three and three-quarters inches.

Was that necessarily fatal? No, sir, it was not. Number five was a wound in the forehead, two inches in length, parallel with the outer portion or number four.

Did that fracture the skull? I think not.

Was that necessarily fatal? No, sir.

How about wound number six? Wound number six was through the temporal bone above and in front of the left ear, parallel with the others.

Did that fracture the skull? Yes, sir.

Was it necessarily fatal? No, sir.

Describe the seventh wound. Number seven was an extension upward and two inches in length, running clear to the top of the head. It was a scalp wound and didn't fracture the skull. It was not necessarily fatal. The eighth was an extension upward to number five. It went along one-quarter of an inch.

This was not necessarily fatal? It was a superficial wound.

What about wound number nine? That extended from the one in front of the ear upward through the left temple, a distance of four inches, directly outward. Its edges were parted two inches. The bone was crushed into the brain.

Was that necessarily fatal? No, sir.

Was it probably fatal? Yes, sir.

How about the tenth wound? The tenth was behind, under number nine, and two inches long; at the lower portion it caused a fracture of the skull.

Speaking in general of the injuries you have described they were up in front of the opening of the left ear and proceeding around the left nostril, were they not? Yes, sir.

Was this last wound probably a fatal injury? I should say the wound at the left temple was the cause of death.

Taking the injury you have described coming out through the temple and cutting through the eye and coming down through the cheek; what was the character of that injury as to its direction with reference to the today itself? It was bevelled. Instead of entering at right angles it entered from the left towards the right.

That would be towards the nose? Yes, sir.

Were any of these other injuries bevelled in a similar direction? Yes, sir, the one in front of the left ear was bevelled in the same way.

Have you made any experiments with blood so as to give an opinion as to the direction it would come? I have made experiments. I pricked my finger with a pin and let the blood fall on a paper from above.

Have you the paper here? Yes, sir.

Knowlton—I object to having that paper produced as evidence.

Adams—Assuming then that blood is thrown up in force from an instrument what would be the shape of the spot of blood? The shape of a pear.

Where would the stem end of the pear be? Outward.

Assuming that blood was thrown from a small instrument and struck upward upon a light parallel surface, what would be the shape of the blood in this circumstance? Same as before.

Have you ever been to the Borden house? No, sir. I have never seen it.

Mr. Adams showed Mr. Draper a photograph of Mr. Borden as he lay on the sofa and asked him if he could, by that and the wounds as he had seen them at the autopsy, form an opinion as to where the assassin stood. I would prefer not to give an opinion. I have not studied the problem enough.

I suppose you have expressed no opinion upon it?

I expressed an opinion to you this morning.

Could the injury have been made by a person standing behind Mr. Borden with a hatchet? I should prefer not to answer the question.

I suppose these wounds were inflicted with a weapon very sharp? Not as sharp as a razor.

Nor as dull as a hoe? No, sir; the weapon was an edged instrument.

Did you observe the hair? Yes, sir.

Did you see any signs of cutting? I saw no evidence of cutting of the hair. I don't say it was not. I am not prepared to say it was not cut.

Can you give me an opinion as to the force of the blow that would have caused the injuries? I am unable to tell you, sir.

Could you tell by your experience if the blow was struck by a left-handed or right-handed person with a hatchet? No, sir, I cannot tell.

The coagulation of blood is caused by what? I do not know.

Have you an opinion about it? Yes, sir, but most physiologists are not certain about it.

Can you form an opinion from the coagulation of blood as to the time of death? Within about 15 minutes.

How near, by an examination of the stomach, can you give an opinion as to the time? It would be approximate only.

How soon? I am unable to give it in minutes.

Sixty of them? It might be an hour; different causes at different times alter the conditions.

Are there any arteries in the head? The principal artery is the temporal artery. I saw no evidence of any artery having been cut. I think the temporal artery was in the way.

And if cut what would be the effect? If cut through and through with a sharp instrument, the blood would spurt upwards.

How far would it go? It varies in different cases. The average is two feet. I have seen the spurting of an artery as much as five feet in a surgical operation, from an artery about the same size as the temporal artery.

I will ask one more question. From the appearance at the autopsy were there there any injuries on Mrs. Borden's head or person that were not caused by a blow? I saw some.

What was your opinion of the blow in the back? It was with the same weapon that caused the scalp wounds.

Was it a miss blow? I think it was. I don't think that blow was intended to go there.

This finished Mr. Draper's testimony.

This Afternoon's Session.

When Dr. Draper was placed on the stand in the morning it was expected by friends of the defence that he would explode all the statements made by Dr. Dolan, but in this instance they were very much disappointed. The expert from Boston agreed with the medical examiner in every particular, and Dr. Draper's testimony really strengthened the words of Dr. Dolan.

It is stated by a government official high in the case that any stories or incidents that are 48 hours old in this matter are not considered by the government, although anything that would tend to prove the innocence of the accused is being thoroughly examined. The story of Morgan W. Davidson of hearing a conversation in the Pennsylvania railroad depot at Jersey City is being looked into. An officer is now in that place examining the plausibility of the story. While the police do not expect to strengthen their case by any discovery made in Jersey City, they have adopted the principle of giving the defence every advantage.

When Officer Wyatt stated that all were full behind the rail previous to the opening of court, he forgot his prerogative as an officer and did not send them to the cell room. How some of the ladies present would resent the imputation!

Dr. Handy was the first witness called, and his testimony in substance was as follows: I remember the day of the tragedy and passed the house twice. The first time it was about 9 o'clock and the second between 10:20 and 10:40 o'clock. The last time I saw a pale, exceedingly pale, individual passing up the street. He was just south of Dr. Kelly's house. The man was of medium height, and dressed in a grayish suit of clothes. He was moving very slowly south. I could not state that I had seen the man before, but it is my opinion that I had seen him on Second street before.

In cross-examination by Mr. Knowlton, the witness said: It was to my cottage at Marion that Lizzie was going I could not say whether it was the man's agitation that drew my attention to him. When I first saw him it was in the space between Dr. Kelly's house and the grocery store adjoining. I was in my carriage at the time. I believe that the police have made every effort to find the man.

RECORD OF THE BUTCHERY.

Official Report of the Autopsy on the Bodies of Mr. and Mrs. Borden.

FALL RIVER, Aug. 11, 1892.

Record of autopsy held at Oak Grove cemetery on the body of Andrew J. Borden. Autopsy performed by W. A. Dolan, medical examiner, assisted by Dr. F. W. Draper. Witnesses, F. W. Draper of Boston and John H. Leary of Fall River; clerk, D. E. Cone of Fall River. Time of autopsy, 11:15 a. m., Aug. 11, 1892, one week after death.

Body that of a man well nourished, aged 70 years; five feet, 11 inches in height. No stiffness of death on account of decomposition, which was far advanced. Inguinal hernia on right side abdomen had already been opened. Artificial teeth in upper jaw. There were no marks of violence on the body, but on left side of head and face there were numerous incised wounds and one contused wound penetrating into brain. The wounds beginning at the nose and to the left were as follows:

1. Incised wound four inches long, beginning at lower border of left nasal bone, and reaching to lower edge of lower jaw, cutting through nose, upper lip, lower lip and slightly into bone of upper and lower jaw.

2. Began at internal angle of eye and extended to one and three-eight inches of lower edge of jaw, being four and a half inches in length, cutting through tissues and into the bone.

3. Began at lower border of lower eyelid, cutting through tissues and into cheek bone, two inches long and one three-eight inches deep.

4. Began two inches above upper eyelid, one-half external to wound No. 3, thence downward and outward through middle of left eyebrow through the eyeball, cutting it completely in halves and excising a piece of skull one and a half inches in length by one-half in width; length of wound four and a half inches.

5. Began on level of same wound. Superficial scalp wound downward and outward two inches in length.

6. Parallel with one above, inch long, downward and outward.

7. Began one-half inch below No. 5; three inches in length, downward and outward, penetrating cavity of skull; on top of skull transverse fracture four and one-half in length.

8. Began directly above No. 7 and one inch in length, downward and outward.

9. Directly posterial to No. 8, beginning at ear and extending four inches long and two in width, crushing bone and carrying bone into brain; also crushng from without in.

10. Directly behind this and above it, a wound running downward to backward, two inches long superficially:

The general direction of all these wounds is parallel to each other.

Head—Right half of top of skull removed. Brain found to be completely demoralized and in fluid condition.

Chest—Chest and abdomen opened by incision extended from neck to pubes; right lung glued to ribs in front; left lung normal; heart normal.

Abdomen—Spleen normal, kidney normal, liver and bladder normal. Stomach and portion of bladder has been removed. Lower part of large bowel filled with solid normal fœces. Fœces also in lower part of small bowel.

W. A. DOLAN, Medical Examiner.
D. E. CONE, Clerk.

FALL RIVER, Aug. 11, 1892.

Record of autopsy on the body of Abbie D. Borden, aged 64 years, held Thursday, Aug. 11, 1892, at 12:35 p. m., one week after death. The autopsy was performed by W. A. Dolan, medical examiner, assisted by Dr. F. W. Draper, and was witnessed by F. W. Draper of Boston and J. H. Leary of Fall River.

Body—That of female, very well nourished and very fleshy, 64 years old, five feet, six inches in height; no stiffness of death, owing to decomposition, which was far advanced. Abdomen had already been opened. Artificial teeth in the upper jaw; no marks of violence on the front of body. On back of body was:

1. An incised wound two and one-half inches in length and two and one-half inches in depth. The lower angle of the wound was over the spine and four inches below the juncture of neck with body, and extending thence upward and outward to the left. On the forehead and bridge of nose were three contused wounds, those on the forehead being oval, lengthwise with body.

2. The contusion on bridge of nose was one inch in length by one-half in width.

3. On the forehead was one, one inch above left eyebrow, one and one-half inches long by three-eighths of an inch in width, and the other one and one-fourth inches above eyebrow and one and one-half inches long by one-quarter of an inch wide. On the head were 18 distinct wounds, incising and crushing, and all but four were on the right side, counting from left to right with the face downward. The wounds were as follows:

No. 1 was a glance scalp wound two inches in length by one and one-fourth inches in width, situated three inches above left ear hole, cut from above downward, and did not penetrate the skull.

No. 2 was exactly on the top of the skull, one inch long, penetrating into, but not through the skull.

No. 3 was parallel to No. 2. one and one-half inches long, and penetrating through the skull.

No. 4 was two and one-fourth inches above occipital protuberance and one and one-half inches long.

No. 5 was parallel to No. 4 and one and one-half inches long.

No. 6 was just above and parallel to No. 5 and four and one-fourth inches long. (On the top of skull was transverse fracture two inches in length, the combination of a penetrating wound.)

No. 7 was two inches long, two inches behind ear hole, crushing and carrying bone into brain. All the wounds of the head following No. 7, though incised, crushed through into brain.

No. eight was one and one-half inches long, nine was two and three-fourths inches, ten was one and three-fourths inches, eleven was one-half inch, twelve was two and one-fourth inches, thirteen was one and three-fourths inches, fourteen was two and one-half inches, fifteen reached from middle bone of the head toward the ear, five inches; sixteen was one inch, seventeen was one-half inch, eighteen was four and one-half inches.

Those wounds on the right side were parallel, the direction being mostly from the front backward.

Head—There was a hole in the right side of the skull four and one-half by five and three-fourths, and through which the vein was evacuated in a fluid condition, being entirely decomposed.

Chest—The chest and abdomen were opened by one incision from chin to pubes.

Lungs—Bound down behind, but normal.

Heart—Normal.

Abdomen—Stomach and part of bowels had been removed.

Spleen, pancreas, kidneys, liver and bladder, intestines were normal. The womb was the seat of a small febroid tumor on anterior surface. The fallopian tubes and ovaries were normal. The lower bowel was empty and the upper portion of the small bowel contained a small portion of undigested food.

(Signed)
W. A. DOLAN, Medical Examiner,
D. E. CONE, Clerk.

ANOTHER YARN.

Davidson Adds a Spice of Variety to the Stories of Assassins.

M. W. Davidson, a new feature in the case, was in town Tuesday. He was an engineer of the San Antonio and Arkansas railroad and had a new story to tell about the real Borden murderer. Davidson said that he arrived in New York Sunday, and after walking about the city for several hours returned to the Pennsylvania railroad station in Jersey City. He says he had been there but a few minutes when two men entered the car, and without seeing him, began to talk about the Borden case.

One of the men asked the other if he knew "John" committed the Borden murders. "Yes, I know he did it," Davidson said the other man responded, and after some talk about the departure of "John" from Fall River the first man remarked that "John" was the luckiest man he had ever seen, and that if he had committed the crimes "John" had he would have been hanged 20 years ago. Davidson says the men caught sight of him at this point and that he tried to catch them by asking some switchmen to try to arrest them, but the yardmen were afraid to act with him.

Davidson arrived by the New York boat Tuesday morning. He went to City Marshal Hilliard first and told his story. He was referred to Mr. Jennings, and Messrs. Jennings and Adams saw him at noon. He told a very honest story and appears to be an honest fellow. Mr. Jennings saws he knows nothing about him, save what Davidson told him, but that he answered questions naturally. He told his story to newspaper men last night. Mr. Jennings says he is convinced the man is telling a straight story.

NEVER USE PRUSSIC ACID.

Furriers State That Its Use on Furs is Unknown to the Trade.

In the testimony introduced Monday in the Borden hearing at Fall River, Drug Clerk Bence testified that Miss Lizzie Borden asked him to sell her 10 cents' worth of prussic acid, stating that she wanted to use it on her sealskin cap or cape. "Is prussic acid ever used on furs in any way, shape or manner?" was the question asked several of the best known and most experienced Boston furriers yesterday by a Globe reporter.

The first one said that he had never heard of its use in his life on fur, and expressed the opinion that it was so powerful that it would destroy the fur rather than cleanse it.

Another dealer said: "I have been in the business since I was a boy, and I have never known of its being used on fur, or, for that matter, on aything else. I have never seen any of it, and I do not believe that you have either. When we receive a piece of fur that is in need of cleansing we use pure turpentine or benzine. We use it very gently, of course, and we know how to manipulate it so that the fur is not injured. If it is grease that needs to be taken out we use some fine absorbant, such as fine sawdust or sand. This we heat and rub into the fur. The heat absorbs the grease. But we never think of using any acid.

The Boston Advertiser

THE TIDE TURNS

LIZZIE BORDEN'S HOPES MUCH BRIGHTER

PROF. WOOD'S SENSATIONAL TESTIMONY IN HER FAVOR.

NO BLOOD AND NO HUMAN HAIR ON THE HATCHET.

Prof. Wood Also Demolishes the Prussic Acid Theory—The Hatchet Not the Terrible Weapon Generally Imagined, But an Almost Inoffensive Looking Instrument, With a Handle Only a Foot Long—Two Links in the Government's Chain of Circumstantial Evidence Broken—Defence Now Opens Its Case—Miss Borden's Deposition at the Inquest Read—Spats Between Counsel.

FALL RIVER, Aug. 30.—The government has presented all the evidence that it intends to the Borden hearing, and belief in the innocence of the accused woman is stronger than ever before, despite the severe setback which her chances were believed to have received yesterday. The surprises of the day were many, but the tide of public opinion was chiefly directed by Prof. E. S. Wood's testimony. It was the popular belief that he would show some traces of poison in the stomachs of the murdered people, and would produce a murderous-looking shipcarpenters' axe having a blade from five to seven inches in length.

On the contrary, he pulled out an innocent looking hatchet from a medium sized valise, and quietly but firmly told the court he could not find the slightest trace of blood on it; nor was it allowed that such an instrument in the hands of a woman could inflict ghastly wounds. He also demolished the prussic acid and other poison theories, and the crowds in the court room wondered what was coming next.

Of the hatchet episode, the News says tonight: "It needed no testimony to make it apparent that the hatchet was not the terrible weapon used in the murders. The wonder now is that the police attached such importance to it, except from the supposition that it was the only weapon to be found that approached even a possibility of having been used.

"Mayor Coughlin was the first to call special attention to it. He discovered the alleged blood spots and the innocent appearing hatchet at once became a terrible instrument of death. The hatchet is not an old fashioned affair after all. Similar hatchets, may now be purchased at any hardware store. It is a light hatchet, about two pounds weight, to be used in general work about a house or store. The head runs out into a claw for removing nails. The handle from the end to the hatchet is just 12 inches in length."

Prof. Wood looked for traces of all kinds of common poisons. His failure to find them added much weight to Miss Lizzie's strong denials that she was ever in Smith's drug store; but although popular opinion ran in these channels, it is well to remember that the government officials did not depend especially upon the poison theory. It was given out semi-officially some days ago that all the district attorney hoped to prove by Prof. Wood's testimony, was that Mrs. Borden was killed sometime before her husband. This fact was well established.

Prof. Wood said the materials in her stomach showed that they had been undergoing the process of digestion, in his opinion, about 2½ hours. This proved that Mrs. Borden died between 9 and 10 o'clock, probably about 9:30. The government had already established that Lizzie was in the hallway leading into Mrs. Borden's room at 10:35 o'clock, and she has not been able yet to prove that she was not in the house between 9:15 and 11:15 o'clock, when both murders occurred.

The government does not disguise its pleasure at positive statements about the time made by Prof. Wood, which was unshaken when his cross-examination was concluded. The unfortunate quarrel between District-Attorney Knowlton and Mr. Jennings at the morning session, caused much comment in intelligent circles this afternoon and evening. It evinced the intense strain under which Attorney Jennings has been laboring the past three weeks, and brought out clearly the strong determination of the state's attorney. Both men were pale for some minutes and hardly exchanged words during the day.

The only other legal spat which attracted attention occurred this afternoon, when Mr. Adams made a light remark during Mr. Knowlton's cross-examination of Dr. S. W. Bowen. It worried Mr. Knowlton some, and turning shortly he said: "I don't care, sir, to return pleasantries in this case." The expression caused general comment among the listeners and again fixed the attention of the public on the prosecuting attorney's determination. During Undertaker Winyard's cross-examination Attorney Jennings dwelt at length on the position of some keys on the key ring taken from Mr. Borden's pocket. The same matter was referred to in Dr. Dolan's cross-examination. The purport of it has not yet appeared.

John Dinnie's testimony regarding the impossibility of a man going over the back fence, after having committed the murders, without being seen, drives another contradictory nail into the defendant's theory that some one had escaped undetected that way. Officer Philip Harrington's description of Miss Borden's cool and collected manner was strangely at variance with the agitation spoken of by others. He also emphasized a well recognized fact when he said that Miss Lizzie heard her father say he would not let his property for any such purpose, meaning the keeping of a liquor store.

The most interesting testimony of the day to the general public was that given by District-Attorney Knowlton, when he read Miss Borden's testimony at the inquest. Her answers to District-Attorney Knowlton at that time were oftentimes sharp and of a secretive character. Tonight there is a great deal of talk about the intentions of the defence. Mr. Adams and Mr. Jennings assert that the government's presentation of its case was incomplete, and have decided to call many witnesses who were supposed to have been summoned by the State. Dr. Bowen and many others will be called on.

IT WAS NOT BLOOD.

Prof. Wood's Testimony Causes a Sensation—Miss Borden's Deposition at the Inquest Read.

FALL RIVER, Aug. 30.—The first witness called in the Borden case today was Prof. E. S. Wood, the man for whom everybody has been looking for days. He said he had received a package containing two stomachs on Aug. 5, and two jars containing milk used on the 4th and 5th of August. Mrs. Borden's stomach contained about 11 ounces of solid food; the food was partially digested and showed wheat, starch and meat. The contents contained chiefly meat, and there were vegetable pulp cells which might be bread or apples. The digestion seemed to be advanced in the neighborhood of 2½ hours, more or less. The stomach was tested for prussic acid, but with a negative result. The stomach of Mr. Borden contained only six ounces, chiefly water.

In Mr. Borden's stomach there was only a small portion of starch; the digestion in his case, the contents being nearly all water, was much further advanced than in the case of Mrs. Borden. There were a few threads of vegetable tissue in his stomach which might have been apple.

"Could they have been pears?"

"Yes."

Witness had not yet analyzed the milk and could not report on that.

"On the 10th of August," witness continued, "I received from Dr. Dolan a hatchet, two axes, a blue dress-skirt, dress-waist, white starched skirt, lounge cover and three small envelopes in which were hair taken from Mr. and Mrs. Borden and hair taken from the hatchet. On Aug. 16 I received a pair of shoes and a pair of black stockings. The hatchet contained a number of suspicious looking spots, but careful examination showed no traces of blood; every spot which looked like blood was examined, but no traces of blood were seen.

"A big smooch on the blue skirt looked like blood, but was found not to be blood. The white skirt had one spot which looked like blood. It was directly in front, about six inches from the bottom. The carpet was blood-stained (this was the sitting-room carpet), and there was blood, of course, on that. There was no blood on the lounge cover.

"The envelope marked 'Hair from A. J. Borden,' was simply white hair; Mrs. Borden's was dark. The hair on hatchet was not human hair [sensation]; more like that taken from an animal.

"The spot on the right shoe was not blood and there was no blood on either shoes or stockings. There was nothing on the two axes.

"Near the edge of the hatchet were spots which seemed to be blood, but were found not to be.

"There was a spatter on the blade, but it was not blood. There was a spot on the side of the head of the hatchet which looked to me like blood, and I thought it was, but it was not."

The hatchet was produced, and Lizzie examined it with as much interest as did her counsel. One paper was produced by witness on which was written "hair" placed there at (time mentioned), but no hair was there.

In cross-examination, Prof. Wood said the spot looked larger on the outside of the skirt than on the inside.

The size of the spot was about the size of a pinhead.

Q.—This you say was human blood?

A.—I don't know; I didn't say so. I haven't examined it."

Q.—Could you tell in what direction this blood came when it struck the skirt?

A.—I could not.

Witness said it was difficult to tell the difference in blood, its source, etc.; the grade was not so great as before science had progressed. He said that he knew of no difference in digestion in a stout person or a lean one. The amount of gastric juice assists digestion always. The stomach showed no appearance of irritation. The witness said he had been in the Borden house and made a cursory examination, taking notes.

"If one were struck by some sharp instrument would there be any spurting of blood?"

A.—Yes, if an artery was cut.

Q.—And there was an artery cut?

A.—There was one in the line.

Q.—In what direction would the blood spurt?

A.—I don't think the cutting of an artery would make any great difference. An artery never spurts over three feet.

Q.—What artery could be cut by such a blow—one from the top of the head down?

A.—I couldn't say; my anatomy is rather old.

Q.—You mean your knowledge of anatomy, professor; as your anatomy appears to be all right.

A.—Yes (with a laugh) that's what I mean.

Those spots seen at a distance must have come from a spattering and not from an artery; came the same as from throwing a stone into a mud puddle.

Prof. Wood said that if a person stood behind the person assaulted, the blood striking the wall paper would be more or less elongated and away from the wound or the point which it had left, and the heaviest part of the stain would be farthest away; it might be the little end of the spot, but it would contain the largest amount of blood.

Witness measured the hatchet and found the handle measured 14 inches; he was uncertain in regard to the exact time a person could be said to have been killed from the appearance of the blood. In regard to the position of the murderer, witness said that it appeared to him that the person stood in the dining-room when the first blow was given; this because of the spot found on the frame of the dining-room door.

Here witness was allowed to look at the stain on the door frame under his glass, and resuming the stand said it was not blood.

Another Hatchet.

A smaller hatchet was handed to the witness, but he said he could not examine it on so short a time as was allowed him; he had spent six or eight hours on the other one, but he said there was rust on it and rust spots might always be taken for blood until examined. The hatchet was put in his care for full examination.

Witness said it would be impossible for the assailant of the murdered ones to escape getting blood on his body in some way. The stains on the sitting-room door might have gone over the head of the assailant as the instrument was lifted. The blood would hit the assailant from the knees up, and the blood on the assailant in the case of Mrs. Borden would be shown anywhere above the feet.

Some controversy arose over a piece of plaster on which a spot of blood was. The plaster was handed over to Prof. Wood for examination, but Mr. Jennings objected, saying that he would not allow it to go out of his possession unless he could be assured that the blood stain would be left where it was. He was willing to admit it was human blood and to leave the plaster in the possession of the court.

The district attorney said this was the most absurdly impudent proceeding he ever heard of in his professional career; here was a man who said he was determined to take possession of his own evidence, and he requested Marshal Hilliard, since it appeared to have come to a matter of physical force, to remove the pieces of wood shown on which were blood stains before they were taken away, and the marshal removed them.

Then Mr. Jennings asked the court if he could have the assurance that it would be retained in the custody of the court, and the court refused to give that assurance. Then Mr. Jennings quietly put the plaster in his pocket and said he proposed to keep it there.

The court ordered him to produce it, and after a while he did so, but said he should file a motion for a hearing on the matter, and was told that it would be kept by the court until the motion was heard.

James Winyard, undertaker, testified that in searching the body of Mr. Borden he found $78 in bills, watch and chain, keys and some loose change.

In cross-examination witness said all the keys were on the ring; none of them were loose. When asked about the wounds on Mr. Borden's face, witness said he thought they had been given from behind, and began on the left side of the nose and extended down through the chin.

John Dennie, stone-cutter, testified that he was employed in the yard of Mr. Crowe on the day of the tragedy all day; was in the east end of the yard on the Third st. side of it; was nearest the south fence and could not see the Chagnon yard nor the Borden yard without stepping out; could see all of the Crowe yard, but saw nothing but the people who worked there.

On cross-examination, witness said there was a barn in the way of seeing the back part of the Crowe yard and the Borden yard; saw Wixon there, but didn't know how he got into the Crowe yard.

Officer Philip Harrington testified that in one room he found Miss Lizzie and Miss Alice Russell; Lizzie was cool and collected, but would not or could not tell witness anything at all about the matter. Said she was in the barn 20 minutes at the time the murder was committed; witness asked her if it might not be half an hour. "No," she said, "it was 20 minutes." Then witness said: "Perhaps it was but 15 minutes." "No," said Lizzie, "it was just 20 minutes."

Witness was interrogated particularly as to what Lizzie had told him about the man who had come to see her father about the store which he wanted to hire; he was sure that Lizzie told him that her father, although refusing the man, had told him to call again, and that she did not say he said he would come again.

Adjourned to 2 P.M.

The first witness was Annie M. White, official stenographer, who said she was present at the inquest and took notes of the whole examination. Her notes, as written out, were offered in evidence.

Cross-examined: She said that when Miss Borden was examined there were others present, but she could not tell who were there then especially; there was then there one stranger whom she did not know. The statements of Miss Borden were taken down by her when all the people were present; those present whom she knew were the judge, district attorney, Mr. Seaver, Marshal Hilliard and Dr. Dolan.

Witness corrected herself and said Miss Lizzie was before the court at the inquest on three days; the district attorney conducted the examination.

At this point Mr. Adams said he was willing to have this testimony admitted, but if statements were made which were unimportant or to which he would have objected, had he been present he would object to its admission.

The district-attorney asked if witness recalled the fact that when the examination was suspended it was because he had been called to consult with the attorney-general, but witness, while she heard that the attorney-general had been present and had gone away, could not connect the going away with this fact.

The examination of Lizzie Borden at the inquest was then read. Lizzie stated substantially that she was 32 years old; that her father had been married to her stepmother about 27 years; she had no idea of what her father was worth.

Here Mr. Adams objected to the reading of the testimony on the ground that it was immaterial, but the court overruled the objection and the reading proceeded. Miss Borden said her father gave the girls the house on Ferry st., and a few weeks ago he bought it back again, paying Emma and herself separately.

Lizzie has heard Mr. Morse say several years ago that her father had made a will. Her father never said anything to her about a will. "Father once about two weeks ago, she said, had trouble with a man whom I didn't know. They had some talk, and I heard the man say, 'I thought a man with a reputation for getting money like you would accept my offer.' My father said he had stayed long enough, and requested him to get out, and he went away saying he would consult with his partner."

Lizzie had had some trouble with her stepmother a number of times, but it was trivial. Emma had stood as a mother to her. Lizzie stated she had worn a navy blue dress on the morning of the murder. She made two statements about her whereabouts on the day of the murder when her father came home; at first she said she was upstairs; then she said she was in the kitchen, and to this last story she stuck.

Lizzie said she saw her stepmother down stairs, and that the latter said she had the guest chamber all ready except to put on some shams, for she expected company. On Monday Lizzie could not state whether her mother came down stairs again after she went up stairs with the shams; she might have come down when Lizzie was down cellar for a few moments, but she could not have come down without Lizzie seeing her, and she had no recollection of it.

After her father went out Lizzie never went up stairs, and, so far as she knew, she was alone in the lower part of the house for a large portion of the time when her father was away. The front door was locked and nobody could have got in there. When her father came in she was in the kitchen eating a pear. She did not see Maggie after her father came in. Lizzie said she went to the barn to get lead for a sinker. Lizzie said all the fishlines she had were at the "farm," and she had not seen them for five years and thought there were no sinkers there on her lines.

Several pages of the stenographer's copy were devoted to a tilt between the district attorney and Lizzie caused by his trying to find out just what Lizzie was doing in the barn to occupy 20 minutes; she ate three pears and looked out of the window and overhauled a box for the lead. When she got back she found that the kitchen fire had about gone out and she gave up ironing.

Then she discovered the condition of her father, that is, that he was bleeding, but she could tell nothing about the nature of the wounds. Could not remember whether she had on an apron that morning or not; knew nothing about any axe. When she found her father she ran at once to call her servant, never thinking of calling her stepmother, because she supposed she was out, and she said to Mrs. Churchill that she wished somebody would see if she was in the house. She thought it was not more than five minutes after her father came in when she went to the barn.

Lizzie could not tell how the blood came to be on her skirt unless it came from a flea bite; if the blood came from the outside she could not tell where it came from. Lizzie said she never went into any drug store in New Bedford or elsewhere at any time to inquire for prussic acid. About two weeks before the tragedy she heard or saw somebody run down the steps and away; she saw something similar about the house last winter. When she first saw the form recently, it was on the back steps, and ran towards the barn. Last winter she saw a person run away on a Sunday night when she was coming home from church. She told her father of the occurrence, but said nothing to him about the second affair.

This closed the govern ent's case. After the reading of the statement Dr. Dolan was called by the defence and said he had filed the record of the Oak Grove autopsy with the court. The records of the autopsies on the two bodies were separate. Both were put in by the defence as evidence and ordered put into the records.

Mrs. Churchill was recalled, and said that Bridget did not say who told her about the note.

Mr. Adams asked as a special ruling that the court strike out all of that portion of the evidence relating to prussic acid but the court declined for the present.

The first witness for the defence was Dr. S. W. Bowen, who had been in practice 25 years; was the neighbor and family physician of the Bordens. On the day of the tragedy, when informed of it, he went directly to the side door of the Borden house where he met Miss Lizzie; witness was excited because the message had been given him in such a manner as to excite him; Lizzie had said: "Father has been killed—been stabbed."

She had said she had seen nobody and she heard nothing. Mrs. Churchill and Miss Russel were then there. The witness described the position of Mr. Borden's body. One of the photographs was shown and witness said he thought the body appeared to have settled down more towards the foot of the sofa; witness then went out and telegraphed to Miss Emma; went to Baker's drug store and then went back to the Borden house.

In consequence of something told him when he got back he went up stairs and found the prostrate form of Mrs. Borden. She was lying about midway between the dressing-case and the bed. He thought he moved the bed to get to it. The body was lying squarely on its face, and the arms were folded across the breast underneath. Her hands were not over her head, and witness did not know how the arms came above the head, as it has been shown that they were later on. When Dr. Dolan came witness went up stairs with him. When Lizzie went to her room it was because of advice of witness.

When he went up with Dr. Dolan he did not examine the wounds particularly. At that time he had not formed any opinion as to the time of the death of the parties. Mrs. Borden called on witness early on Wednesday morning and said she was afraid she had been poisoned and that she was frightened. She said that Mr. Borden, herself and Lizzie had been sick the night before.

The witness contradicted himself somewhat from what was said at the inquest, and the district attorney remarked that undoubtedly the doctor was somewhat misled because of the excitement of the moment, and this was a sort of "secondary revivifying" of his recollections.

This closed the investigation for the day and an adjournment was made until 10 o'clock tomorrow morning, the defence desiring to have a conference before going any further at present.

CONTEMPORARY ADVERTISEMENTS

May seem a high price to pay for a pair of shoes, but is it? If you estimate COMFORT, the prime requisite in every pair of shoes, as worth anything; if you think that style, perfect fitting and wear-resisting qualities are essential in the make-up of your footwear, wouldn't you pay to have them all combined in one? We've got all these points in our $5 shoes.

SULLIVAN,

40 SO. MAIN ST.

MEDICAL ECONOMY.

Save time and expense by consulting

DR. LEWIS, SPECIALIST

on diseases of the nervous system, brain and spinal cord, spermaterrhœa, seminal weaknesses, fluid escapes, impotency, urinary complaints, acute or chronic discharges, stricture, retention of urine, gravel, kidney or bladder disease, syphilis, secondary symptoms, eruption, diseases of the nose, throat, lungs, stomach. No restriction in diet or hindrance from business. Recent cases cured in three or four days. Patients whose cases have been neglected, badly treated or pronounced incurable are particularly invited to visit Dr. Lewis. A written guarantee of cures given in all cases arranged and undertaken. Country patients corresdonded with until cured. Female complaints skillfully treated. Rheumatism effectually cured. Consultation free. Medicine, $5. **DR. LEWIS** is permanently located at 129 Friendship St., Providence, R. I. Office hours all the year round from 9 to 2 and 5 to 9. Sundays 10 to 2 and 5 to 7.

The New York Times

BORDEN TESTIMONY ENDED

THE DEFENSE RESTS AND THE ARGUMENTS WILL PROCEED.

AN ATTEMPT MADE TO SHOW THAT AN UNKNOWN MAN MIGHT HAVE COMMITTED THE MURDER—WHAT THE LACK OF RUNNING WATER MIGHT SHOW—DEMEANOR OF LIZZIE.

FALL RIVER, Massachusetts, Aug.31.-The preliminary trial of the great Borden case is practically at an end. There yet remains the arguments of the attorneys, and to-morrow morning District Attorney Knowlton will sum up the evidence advanced by the prosecution and will endeavor to show that the evidence is of a nature that will warrant the return of Lizzie Borden to the Bristol County Jail, there to remain at least until November, when the Grand Jury will be convened. The argument for the defense will be advanced by Col. Melvin O. Adams of Boston, who, though nominally the associate counsel for Lizzie Borden, has by reason of his wide experience in cases of homicide and his ability in the conduct of his portion of the young woman's defense, taken naturally the position of leading counsel in the opposition to the Government's case.

The District Attorney is confident that at the conclusion of the addresses the decision of Judge Blaisdell will be that in his opinion the case requires action by the Grand Jury. Perhaps Col. Adams is not confident of the release of his client to-morrow, but he assuredly believes that no jury of twelve men would convict Lizzie Borden of the murder of her father and stepmother upon even the line of evidence presented by the prosecuition. To the great mass of people in this section it would not come as a surprise if the prisoner is adjudged probably guilty and is returned to the prison walls at Taunton; but assuredly, even among those who believe her innocent-and there are many such-her discharge from custody would create as much astonishment as has any feaure of the case since the discovery of the bodies of the murdered couple.

It took just four hours for the defense to put in their case to-day. Nobody pretended that the testimony presented was of such a nature that the attorneys for the prisoner would care to go before a jury upon it as their complete answer to all the allegations of the defense. What they did endeavor to show was that it was possible for some unknown man to have committed this murder; that the actions of Lizzie Borden after her discovery of the body of her father was natural, and that there were no tell-tale blood stains visible upon her garments. They endeavored to make clear the fact that the failure of the Government to find the weapon was virtually an acquittal of the prisoner, for there was ample proof that she did not leave her yard upon the morning of the murder, and that search after serarch of the premises failed to reveal any weapon of a suspicious nature with the exception of the hatchets and axes.

"What has become of that weapon if Lizzie Borden is guilty?" said Mr. Adams in a private conversation. "Did it vanish into mid-air? No. The natural presumption must be that the murderer carried the instrument away with him."

The defense attempted to show that suspicious noises were heard in the vicinity the night before the affair occurred and that they sounded like the scraping which would naturally result from a man climbing over a fence. One of the witnesses saw a white-faced man near the house on the morning of the affair, and to-morrow Col. Adams will ask why suspicion should not be more honestly directed toward this alleged individual than toward the daughter of the murdered people. Some of the witnesses called by the defense were those summoned and not called by the Government, but the information extracted from these was meagre, and all through the day there was nothing that could approach in interest the stories related by the witnesses for the prosecution on the preceeding day.

Lizzie Borden maintained her calm demeanor throughout, but showed some interest in the testimony of Dr. Draper and that of her intimate friends. Apparently she is far from breaking down, and those who anticipate a scene to-morrow in the event of her being adjudged probably guilty will in all likelihood find themselves disappointed. The excitement of the hearing is commencing to tell upon Miss Emma Borden, however, and all day she seemed to be in what might be termed a fitful doze, rousing herself now and then with a start. Not withstanding the uneventful proceedings hundreds of people crowded themselves into the court room, while other hundreds stood outside in the rain endeavoring to induce the officers to admit them to the chamber.

The first witness of the day was the head of thelocal police, City Marshal Rufus B. Hilliard. There was nothing of importance brought out in his testimony, which related almost wholly to the details of the searches which had been made under his instructions. He said there was no running water upstairs, a fact which the attorneys for the defense desired to establish in order to show that if Lizzie Borden washed herself after the murder she must have used water in a bowl, and if such was the fact it would have been evident from the condition of the water.

Dr. Learned testified that when he saw Mrs. Borden's body the arms were placed upon the breast and were not over her head as sworn to by the Medical Examiner.

John Donnelly, a hack driver, tried to assist the defense by showing that when he went up to the barn the imprint of a man's form was in the hay. The District Attorney tore his story to pieces, and before the cross-examination concluded Donnelly said the imprint was a foot long, a foot wide and six inches deep.

The testimony of Frank W. Draper, Medical

DISTRICT ATTORNEY KNOWLTON.

Examiner of Boston, was interesting. He assisted in the autopsy at the cemetery, and the principal part of his story was in contradiction to the statement advanced by Dr. Dolan that the time of death of Mrs. Borden could be determined by the condition of her bloood.

Mrs. Dr. Chagnon and her daughter told of suspicious sounds they heard coming from the Borden fence upon the night preceeding the murder, and, with the testimony of Dr. Handy, who saw a frightened-looking person outside the Borden yard, and the stories of Miss Lizzie's intimate friends that she fainted after discovering her father's body, the defense rested.

OPINIONS FROM OTHER NEWSPAPERS

The New York World

In brief, the public knows absolutely nothing to justify the belief that this woman murdered her father. What proof the prosecuting officers may have we must wait to see. In the meantime the only just and right attitude for the public to assume is one of complete suspension of judgment. Upon that the doing of justice itself may ultimately depend.

Boston Enterprise

Lizzie Borden has friends, according to the newspaper reports from Fall River. Strange, passing strange! We supposed that the verdict of guilty passed by the Fall River police would enstrange them all from her and leave her an outcast among men. What right has she to have friends, we'd like to know?

Taunton News

Did some daylight ghost kill the Bordens? Look out for an attempt to cast suspicion on Miss Sullivan. Being a mere work girl and not nicely educated or socially "well connected," the Lizzie Borden admirers will insinuate that she, not the daughter, did the deed. In fact they have already "worked" this. Miss Borden may be innocent, but every shred of evidence thus far elicited bears irresistibly the other way. It is impossible to administer justice where officers are abused for performing their duty and where a portion of the community is determined to belittle facts that with honest, rational men and women exclude every reasonable probability of innocence.

New Bedford Mercury

The interest in the Borden murder trial at Fall River increases ratner than diminishes as the evidence in possession of the government is slowly unfolded. The public will now insist upon a complete clearing up of tne mystery which surrounded the humble household and its occupants on the fatal day.

"Lizzie Borden is too well treated," comes the cry from Fall River busybodies. "She is as comfortabie as any prisoner could be." This is a grave charge. Lizzie ought to be suspended by the thumbs, a la Private Iams, or placed in an especially dirty room, or housed up with rats, or otherwise maltreated. She has a little money and an example ought to be made of her for daring to possess it. Hale her to the deepest dungeon beneath the castle moat and apply the torture.

The New York Times

PROBABLE GUILT JUDGED

LIZZIE BORDEN HELD FOR HER PARENTS' MURDER.

REMARKABLE SCENES IN THE FALL RIVER COURT ROOM—THE PRISONER CALM BEFORE A WEEPING JUDGE—APPLAUSE FOR HER COUNSEL'S ARGUMENT.

FALL RIVER, Mass., Sept. 1.-With half the people in the court in tears and with the faces of the others white with nervous excitement, Lizzie Borden stood in the Second District Court room to-day and listened to her father's old friend as, in his judicial capacity, he adjudged her probably guilty of the brutal murders of her parents. Calm and collected, as though the matter was of the most uninteresting character to her, she faced the bar, while the presiding Justice was forced to pause in his brief remarks to wipe away his tears.

Remarkable as has been the demeanor of this woman throughout, her manner at this time was stranger than ever, and the excitement of the occasion died away in surprise at the remarkable self-possession she displayed. Twice only in the course of the day did she give away to emotion. The first time was when her attorney characterized the murderer as a person with a heart "blacker than hell itself," and again when he touched upon her babyhood and pictured her as the youngest daughter of the old man, twining herself lovingly around the heart of her father. Then sobs shook her frame, and her eyes were filled with tears. But the display of emotion was over in a minute, and from that time on she was a veritable iceberg in manner.

The presentation of the case by Mr. Jennings, her senior counsel, was a masterly effort. He charged that the absence of motive, the failure of the Government to find the weapon, and its inability to discover any blood upon the prisoner's clothing were practically an avowal of the weakness of its case. His peroration exceeded in eloquence anything ever before heard in a Fall River court room, and the scene as he concluded was remarkable. The associate counsel, Col. Melvin O. Adams, a man of great experience in murder cases, was weeping, and every woman and a majority of the men in the court room were in tears. As Mayor Coughlin, Ex-Congressman Adams, and other prominent persons pressed forward to grasp Mr. Jennings's hand there was a ripple of applause which rapidly swelled into a loud expression of admiration. There was no attempt whatever to check the noise.

The afternoon was devoted to the presentation of the Government's case by the District Attorney. Attorney General Pillsbury was present, and all the leading members of the Bristol County bar were on hand. The District Attorney said that he would rather resign his position than press this case, but the stern finger of duty pointed and he would not shirk. Lizzie Borden's was the opportunity, and it was possible for no one else to have committed the deed. He dwelt at length on the estrangement between the prisoner and her stepmother, and argued that there was but one course for the Judge to pursue.

Judge Blsaisdell said that it was a most painful duty to perform, and he would have been pleaseed to release the prisoner. The testimony was such, however, that he was forced to hold Miss Borden for the Grand Jury.

The session will be held upon the first Monday in November, and the prisoner will be taken to Taunton Jail to-morrow.

OPINIONS FROM OTHER NEWSPAPERS

The Brockton Enterprise

It did begin to look as if Brockton was going to be left entirely out of Fall River's celebrated case, and she hates to be ignored that way when anything big is going on. Now that it is suspected that a man who may have been the murderer has been seen here we can hold up our heads again. It is a pretty poor pie that this village doesn't manage to get a finger in. This community, in common with others throughout New England, is just now divided into two factions, and a good many hours are devoted to combative argument. One faction believes Lizzie Borden is guilty and the other that she is innocent, and each interprets the evidence from day to day in accordance with his own belief.

The Boston Daily Globe

"I think, if character is ever to count for anything, it should in a case like this," said ex-Mayor Green of Boston about the Borden murders. "I do not believe she would kill a tramp, and as for killing her own father and stepmother, the idea is too monstrous. If it is proved that Lizzie Borden is a murderess then she is a maniac, and she will develop a clear case of insanity and die a raving maniac."

"Provided they do not hang her first?"

"Provided that, of course, but it is not likely it will come to that. If she is a murderess and insane, the mania will develop unmistakably before that time. I do not believe yet she is either. She is entitled to be considered innocent until her guilt is shown."

The Fall River Herald

SHE WILL BE HELD

General Opinion That a Decision Unfavorable

TO THE DEFENDANT WILL BE RENDERED BY THE JUDGE.

Her Lawyers May Contest Inquest Proceedings.

ELOQUENT PLEA MADE BY ATTORNEY JENNINGS.

Moved Many to Tears by the Power of his Eloquence.

Wednesday night, after it was known that all the evidence in the Borden case had been submitted, people said that they had a right now to an opinion whether or not Lizzie Borden was guilty of the crime of which she was charged. All along they have been cautioned to wait and see the entire case as spread before them and to withhold judgment until then. When Mrs. Bowen stepped down from the stand and the defence announced that it had no more witnesses to call, people began to air their opinions and will continue to do so at intervals of a minute or two for many weeks to come.

Upon one thing nearly all seemed to agree, and that was that Judge Blaisdell would probably bind the prisoner over to the grand jury. It must be borne in mind that the judge is called upon to give judgment according to the facts that are presented to him in court. The privilege which belongs to the judicial public of interpreting little discrepancies and misstatements with broad liberality does not belong to the presiding justice in so important a criminal procedure. Lizzie Borden's case stands before him with apparent inconsistencies which everybody believed were sufficient to justify him in ordering her to be committed for the grand jury. Many of these inconsistencies were proved by means of doubtful evidence, but the counsel for defence raised no strenuous objections to the reading of the proceedings of the inquest, and the prisoner's testimony there became evidence in court which was to guide Judge Blaisdell in his decision.

By means of this evidence it was shown that the prisoner had told different stories as to the purpose of her visit to the barn, and as to her whereabouts during the morning of the murder. She had shown a suspicious interest in the servant girl's movements that day. Evidence has been introduced to show that she was alone on the second floor while Mrs. Borden lay dead, and could possibly have been there when that unfortunate woman was struck down by the murderer's blow. There are minor inconsistencies in the story that may raise a doubt in an unprejudiced mind.

A HEAVY TASK.

When it comes to a conviction on the evidence it has on hand, everybody agrees that the government has undertaken a very heavy task. Two things are positively certain, whatever else the prosecution may have held in reserve for a higher court. The weapon with which the terrible slaughter was committed has not been found. The government, by its warrant for arrest, has undertaken to prove that Lizzie Borden killed her father with a hatchet. This must be proved to a jury beyond a reasonable doubt.

On the seat reserved for the prisoner and her friends sat Mrs. Brigham, Mrs. Churchill, Mrs. Bowen, Mary Holmes and Mrs. Andrew Borden, wife of Treasurer Borden of the Merchants mill. Mr. Buck escorted Lizzie to her place. Her eyes bore the sign of weeping, and she was evidently filled with emotion hardly to be suppressed. Every eye in the court room was fixed upon her. People appreciated that this day was big with fate for her. Either she would go out from the room free of the terrible charge of murdering her father, or she would return again to confinement, in the eyes of the world probably guilty of the horrible charge. Many a throat felt a strange fullness and many an eye grew dim as the woman sank into her seat and fixed her eyes on the carpeted floor.

There was no unnecessary delay. Mr. Adams cleared a space around him of chairs, removed everything from the table in front of him and sought a place beside the prisoner. Mr. Jennings arose and the stillness was oppressive. "May it please your honor," he said, and eyes that had wandered to the prisoner darted back again and riveted themselves upon the speaker. If eyes were removed from his face after that it was to dry the welling of tears that stole down cheeks. At 10:40 o'clock, just four weeks from the hour that Andrew Jackson Borden met his death at the hand of a foul assassin, Andrew Jackson Jennings arose in the district court room to plead for the freedom of the murdered man's daughter upon whom had rested the heavy arm of the law. Piece by piece did he examine the evidence against the prisoner: the time the murdered man entered his home, the moment the alarm was given and then he shouted: "Lizzie Borden did not do this crime. It was the work of an insane man or of a person whose heart was black as hell itself."

The wounds were described and the pleader said: "The wounds speak for themselves." In this case he claimed the circumstances ought to be interpreted a thousand fold in favor of one whose guilt had not been proved. "The commonwealth has made up its mind that this deed has been done by an inmate of the house, and it has built up its case with that object in view." A little later he approached the judge's desk and, holding his right arm extended toward the district attorney and the marshal, shouted: "Why have not the police found these suspicious looking characters outside that house? Why, because they made up their minds the murderer was inside, and they are not looking outside."

Up and down the narrow space in which

he was penned did the lawyer go, driving argument after argument with the energetic force that characterizes him, growing eloquent as he proceeded. If Lizzie Borden has not shed tears before during this ordeal, she did today when she listened to her lawyer's earnest plea in her defence.

MR. JENNINGS' PLEA.

May it please your honor, this complaint upon which you have to pass your judgment today in substance charges that on August 4 Andrew J. Borden was murdered by his daughter, Lizzie. I must say that I do not approach the discussion of this question without feelings different from any other in my personal experience in the arguments of this case. This man was not merely my client; he was my friend. I had known him for many years and worked in his behalf, and if anyone had said to me three short weeks ago that I would stand here before your honor today defending his youngest daughter from the charge of murder I should have pronounced it beyond the bounds of human credibility or belief.

Your honor has heard of the horrible wounds inflicted on the heads of the bodies; the length of them has been described in their atrocious details. I will venture to say that no man would say that that was not the work of an insane man or the work of a man whose heart is as black as hell itself. Never in the history of crime was so horrible a butchery committed. Blow after blow was rained upon those heads, through the hair, through the flesh, into the very brain. Not one, not two, but in the women's case 18 and one in the back, making 19, were struck. Upon Mr. Borden a dozen, at least, were inflicted, showing that the person wanted to make sure of his work. After he had sunk his hatchet he must have known that each one went into the skull, but he wanted to make sure. There is a brutality about this thing which shows insanity or brutal revenge. Every blow shows that the person who wielded that hatchet wielded it with an experienced hand. Any man who has experience with hatchets could testify to that. Dr. Draper told you that all over the head every wound could be traced in a distinct line. All these wounds were in parallel lines. What does that show? It shows that the hand that struck those blows was a powerful one; he had a powerful wrist. It also shows that the eye that guided them was an eye of experience.

This case as it presents itself to you is a case of circumstances. If there are circumstances that weigh against the defendant, there are circumstances that weigh for her. It is better, it has been said, that 99 guilty men should escape than that one innocent should be convicted. The benefit of every doubt should be given to the one accused of the crime, to the one suspected of a crime like this. There is no chance of mistake about those wounds. They speak for themselves. They don't rest upon the recollection of officers or anybody else. Prof. Wood says it would have been impossible for anyone to have committed those murders without having been covered with human blood. He would have been covered about the feet while standing before Mrs. Borden, and about the face and hair while standing in front of Mr Borden.

The theory of the government seems to be directed against the inmates of that house. Now who are the inmates of the house, and what have the authorities to fasten the crime upon them? The isolation of that house shows that anyone could neither enter nor leave it at the time of the tragedy without being seen. The government has Mrs. Kelly on the south side, Mrs. Collet on the east side, Mrs. Churchill on the north side and Mrs. Bowen on the west side. Is it shown by them that there was no person about the house at that time? They know that the house has been burglarized twice within two years, and they know that the barn was broken into within two months. An unprejudiced person would say if that house and barn had been entered and burglarized there must be someone trying to do something to the inmates of that house. Where were the police that they didn't discover Mrs. Manley, who saw a young man near the gate at 11 minutes to 10 on the morning of the murder? The police have ransacked this house from top to bottom, from attic to cellar, I don't know how many times, but they didn't find the woman who saw this man at the gate that morning. There is but one explanation. They were not looking for anybody else outside of the family. There was Dr. Handy riding past at 20 minutes of 11, who sees a strange man, and the extraordinary part of it is that the police didn't find that man. They can find axes in the cellar with which Lizzie Borden killed her father, which almost fit into the wounds, but they cannot find the least trace of that man. It seems to look as if they had let other things go to prove their theory correct. So far as being limited to the inmates of this house, Mrs. Churchill and others never saw this man. Does it not follow that somebody else could have gone out and they not have seen him? Frank Wixon gets over the back fence from the lumber pile and jumps into the next yard, and yet Miss Collet didn't see him; neither did the woodchoppers until he was close upon them.

Miss Lizzie, in her testimony, has told about the man dodging around that house at night. Mrs. Chagnon tells you she heard a sound like a man getting over the fence. That sound didn't come from the ice house; it came from behind. Now as to the situation of this house on the morning of the murder. Two strange people have been seen near the house at the time. I claim the government has excluded anybody else from committing this crime except the inmates of the house. Assuming that it was done by inmates of the house. Who were in the house? John Morse, Bridget Sullivan and Lizzie. John Morse seems to have accounted for his time to the commonwealth and is left out of the case. That brings it down to Lizzie and Bridget. Now who would be the party liable to be suspected? Who would be the party whose clothes would be examined? Would it be natural to suppose that it was the stranger, one unconnected by ties of blood, or would it be natural to suppose that it was the youngest daughter, and that term youngest means something? It means that it was the last little head that leaned against her father's breast and called him father. If it starts up the theory that it was either of the two what then? Understand me, I don't believe that Bridget Sullivan did that deed any more than I believe Lizzie Borden did it. I don't believe either of them did it. I am showing the line of the government's theory. Was Bridget Sullivan compelled to tell how many dishes she washed, where she put them and how she laid them away? Has she been subjected to any such course of examination as this defendant has been subjected to? I would like to know if there is not something just as suspicious in her actions as there are in Lizzie Borden's? She was from 20 minutes past 10 to 15 minutes to 11 washing the upper half of one window. Did my learned friend over there try to show anything suspicious about that?

There is nothing in the evidence to

warrant the government in binding her over. If Lizzie Borden had opportunity to commit the crime, so did Bridet Sullivan. Bridget says she was out doors, she says so and yet who saw her out doors? Mrs. Churchill, I believe, saw her once. I am not arguing that Bridget did this crime. I say she did not. I am simply showing the line the government is following in the case of Lizzie Borden and Bridget Sullivan. Now if Lizzie did this when did she do it, your honor? It is almost impossible to tell with any degree of certainty the temperature of the bodies by mere contact of the fingers. There might be various things to affect the temperature. Prof. Wood testified that Mrs. Borden might have been dead an hour or an hour and a half before Mr. Borden, but he afterwards added "provided the digestion had been normal." If she was killed half an hour after the departure of Mr. Borden that would bring her death about 9:30. Mr. Borden arrives at the savings bank shortly after. Nobody will claim that Lizzie killed her mother before her father left the house. If Lizzie killed her at all she must have killed her from the time Mr. Borden left the house and before he returned. She tells the story of where she was that time. Your honor has heard it; your honor probably heard it at the inquest. I want to submit that on account of the circumstances in which that story was taken my astonishment is that her answers were not more inconsistent than they were. I say the course taken by the district attorney in regard to Lizzie Borden is an outrage. They had all the evidence that they presented at the inquest, and in to get a sort of a confession they did what they had aright to do. That inquest was taken for no other reason than to put Lizzie Borden on the rack. Is there anybody here who heard that testimony of the inquest read that didn't think she was on the rack? Just as they used to pinch the arms and legs of victims in olden times, just so much was she in the rack. Over and over again she was asked the same questions in order to get her to contradict herself. The minutest details were gone into, and she was obliged to state the exact order of her movements on that morning.

Look at the testimony of Mrs. Churchill. She was asked if Bridget Sullivan went upstairs or came downstairs or did this or did that and she said: "I don't know, I don't know, I don't know." Now Bridget Sullivan is not so small a body that she could be lost in thin air. Here is Lizzie Borden, who has been taking prescriptions to cause her to sleep, and because she cannot tell the minutest details she is supposed to be the guilty party. I asked Lizzie Borden what she did that morning and she couldn't recollect. But if Lizzie Borden cannot recollect anything that is a sign of guilt.

In conclusion Mr. Jennings said: I ask, I demand, the woman's release. She will still be here and will not flee. Don't put the stigma of probable guilt on this woman which will go out as the impartial decision of an impartial magistrate. Heaven grant your honor will do his duty as the laws tell you to do it and give the benefit of the doubt to the accused.

When Mr. Jennings reached his peroration the interest was intense. "I demand her release," he cried. Then turning to the judge, he implored God to grant him wisdom in this crisis.

The crowd hung upon those final words with an intensity that found relief in boisterous applause, forgetful of the dignity of the court. Tears flowed down the cheeks of Col. Adams and the friends of the prisoner. There was scarcely a dry eye in the room.

3:45—Lizzie was adjudged probably guilty and will be sent to Taunton jail.

LIZZIE'S FRIENDS.

Mrs. Lindsey and Mrs. Brigham Talk Freely of Her.

Small wonder that Lizzie Borden's friends are gratified with the result of the examination. Not that they would have doubted her in the face of circumstantial evidence that pointed to her guilt, but they are gratified for her sake. "For," said Mrs. William Lindsey, one of her close friends, "suppose Lizzie had, as many a woman would have dared, thrown herself upon the body of her father when she saw him lying there, she would have been found covered with blood and nothing could have saved her—they would have hung her."

It is in this spirit that her friends rejoice, for though they are anxious concerning the judgment to be passed by Judge Blaisdell, still they are confident in the unbiased judgment of the grand jury.

"Suppose I am compelled to go back to Taunton to remain there in jail until November," exclaimed Lizzie to Mrs. Brigham. "Isn't it too awful to speak of?"

"Yes," was the reply; "but you are not the brave woman you have always shown yourself if you do not bear up under it well."

"Oh," said the prisoner, "I suppose if I must, I must, but if Mr. Knowlton only knew the weight I am carrying here [pressing her hand to her heart], he would understand this matter better."

"If you could only hear the straight story she tells as she tells it to me, unembarrassed, by the cross-questioning of lawyers, you certainly would be sure of her innocence," said Mrs. Lindsey in further conversation. "They talk of her shedding no tears. She is amazed at the tears of her few friends who can shed them. The horror of these murders is too much for tears, and this added horror of being charged with committing them had swallowed even that. Emma, when she went away to New Bedford says she had not a care in the world; her mother was an excellent housekeeper, and took the whole care of it on her shoulders, relieving the girls of that, and their father always provided for their every want. When she got the telegram summoning her home she had no thought of a greater calamity than that her father was sick. When she arrived within sight of her house and saw the crowd about the door she wondered what it could mean. So you can understand what she must have felt when she realized what had taken place, and that not enough, to have this added. To Lizzie's friends this is so preposterous—they were such good girls, never told a lie. They have no idea what they are worth, but Lizzie says she would give it all to discover the perpetrator of the crime if she had to go to work tomorrow. Lizzie told me that on the morning of the murder she was very happy, filled with anticipations of her vacation trip.

The Rev. E. A. Buck speaking of the result of the hearing, said: "I have been this girl's spiritual counsellor for 20 years, and have always esteemed her highly, and I have to say that my intercourse with her since this affair has tended to raise her infinitely in that esteem. She is as innocent as the day she was born.

OPINIONS FROM OTHER NEWSPAPERS

New York Journal

Now comes the scientific evidence, to leave the prosecution in worse case than ever. No blood on her clothes; none on any of the numerous axes produced. So far as we can judge, there is no evidence that she committed the crime. What then ? It was most probably the work of a man, who concealed on his person and carried off the weapon. Neither Lizzie Borden nor the servant, Bridget Sullivan, may have had any complicity in the deed, but still there may have been complicity. The old detective motto was, "look for the women." As this is a case where two women are involved, we say, look for the man.

The Lowell Times

The government case fails at too many points to establish guilt beyond reasonable doubt or even beyond insuperable doubt. There was no blood and no human hair on the axes and hatchets found on the premises, and the prosecution breaks down utterly on this point. The weapon with which the murder was committed could not, therefore, have been left on the premises. The ugliest looking thing for the prisoner seems to be the story about Mrs. Borden's note from a sick friend. How the defence may be able to answer this is as yet unknown. On the whole, the indications are that the accused may be held for the grand jury. But it remains that she can never be convicted by a jury on any evidence which has yet appeared.

Providence Journal

It will be time enough to blame the authorities at Fall River when it is shown that they have made a serious blunder. The Borden case is a difficult one, despite the jaunty way in which the newspaper counsel for the defence talk about it, and whether Miss Borden be innocent or not, it was inevitable that she should fall under suspicion—a result for which a curious combination of circumstances was alone responsible. Nothing will be lost, at any rate, by waiting for her acquittal by due process of law.

New London Telegraph

There are certainly enough sensational features about the Fall River murder case to satisfy any morbid mind without adding an iota of manufactured stuff. It stands without parallel in many respects, and the developments made do not remove any of its gruesome features. That the state ordered the heads of the murdered pair cut off may be justifiable and perfectly proper, but it will never reconcile public sentiment to the perpetration of what will be thought needless brutality. Whatever the purpose in view, it could have been achieved by some other means.

Boston Record

The famous Harvard expert did not agree with Dr. Dolan, who, conscientious as he may have sought to be, bungled things. That the murderer who hacked and hacked at the bodies of the two victims could have escaped bloodless and speckless would seem to be almost miraculous. The strongest circumstantial evidence which has been developed at all injuring the case of the accused girl is that which locates her as very near the two people at the very hour of their death. No one else has been located anywhere in their vicinity. There arises and rests the awful suspicion.

The Baltimore Sun

If there was ever a case on earth that called for a kind and considerate suspension of judgment, it is this unrivaled mystery. If the sex and character of the accused do not (as many believe) absolutely preclude the possibility of her guilt, they surely put her guilt so far beyond the pale of probability that it is to be accepted only on the most overwhelming accumulation of circumstantial evidence. The law itself holds Lizzie Borden innocent, she has been most pitiably enmeshed by circumstances, and does not her case call for the kindest consideration on the part of everybody ? Has not the girl enough to endure in the unfortunate facts that have served to envelop her with suspicion ? Such a case as this is no case for the faker, and the creature who will invent fictions that are calculated to involve her at points where the facts do not involve her is to our thinking more worthy of hanging than the person who killed the Bordens, whoever that may be.

The Taunton Gazette

A citizen who has made a study of the Borden case contrasts the method of the Fall River police authorities with that of France. In Fall River, after the tragedy was discovered, Tom, Dick and Harry had full run of the premises and there was ample chances to carry off any compromising clothes or weapons. In France the house would have been at once sealed by the police, the family sent off and things kept just as they were at the time of the murder until the authorities had made a minute search and were satisfied that they had all the evidence that could be secured.

Providence News

If, as stated, Lizzie Borden was held for examination chiefly on her own contradictory testimony at the inquest, the prosecution showed very little knowledge of human nature. From any rational view point uncertain statements on minor points of time and place before the murder should incline the hearer rather to the presumption of innocence than of guilt.

The Boston Advertiser

HELD FOR TRIAL.

LIZZIE BORDEN JUDGED PROBABLY GUILTY

BY JUDGE BLAISDELL OF THE MURDER OF HER FATHER.

BUT THE PUBLIC THINKS SHE CAN NEVER BE CONVICTED.

Miss Borden Will be Taken to Taunton Jail This Morning—The Closing of the Hearing a Tremendous Relief to All—Belief in Her Innocence Stronger Today in Spite of Judge Blaisdell's Decision Than at Any Time Before—Attorney Jenning's Splendid Argument—The Police Still Active—The Old Hoax.

FALL RIVER, Sept. 1.—A huge sigh of relief was heard by all this afternoon when Judge Blaisdell's decision that Lizzie Borden must be held for the grand jury to stand trial for the murder of her father. Any decision was welcome after the painful suspense of the three weeks just passed and the terrible agony and anxiety of the last few days. While there are a number of Miss Borden's dearest friends who are indignant at the court's declaration, it cannot be said that the public at large condemns or criticises Judge Blaisdell's judgment. It had been foreseen what the end must be, and while the general public, again, does not by any means agree that the girl is "probably guilty," it feels that some broader knowledge of the case is due it and justice than the hasty, unsubstantial hearing could afford.

Upon the whole, then, according to the belief of the citizens of Fall River, all has turned out just as it must. There have been side issues and terrible doubts that have turned a flood of suspicion against the accused woman, and there have been, too, happenings that have re-established her innocence in the eyes of all. It has taught the credulous public that it must leave everything to the slow methods of justice, as typified by our laws, and that its quick sympathy and as ready condemnations only delay and complicate matters, if not actually distort them.

Naturally, her friends are indignant over the verdict rendered today, but if the truth were told, they have expected it from the moment Judge Blaisdell determined to preside at the hearing. Tonight Marshal Hilliard has commenced to outline the plan for the government to pursue. In this matter he has been directed by Attorney-General Pillsbury and District-Attorney Knowlton. Miss Borden will be taken to Taunton tomorrow morning. According to the statements of the police, her actions tonight do not differ from those of the first night she spent in their custody, three weeks ago.

It is said at police headquarters that there is much yet to be done before the case is fit for successful presentation to the grand jury. Perhaps the greatest relief felt in the city tonight is here in the station. Though he has not been ready to admit it, of course, there is good reason to believe that Marshal Hilliard has not been altogether sure of the result of the hearing and that the positively slack and stupid work of his force would not place him before the public in a wrong position, for the marshal is by no means a stupid man himself. It goes without saying that every stone will be turned to serve the ends of justice whether to establish the innocence of Miss Borden or to convict her of what even the government dreads to recall.

No habeas corpus plea will be made by the defendant's lawyers. They will devote their time to hunting down the mysterious people seen around the Borden house the day of the murder. A. J. Jennings believes firmly in Miss Lizzie's innocence. His great plea is the principal topic of conversation tonight. It appeals to the popular ear, and it will be many days before the citizens begin to look upon the prisoner as a criminal.

MISS BORDEN WEPT

At the Affecting Plea of the Counsel for Her Life and Liberty.

FALL RIVER, Sept. 1.—Court came in at 10:30. Mr. Jennings opened for the defence: That A. J. Borden was murdered there is no doubt, and that the time of the murder has been established there is no doubt. Clegg, Shortsleeves, and Bridget Sullivan have fixed the time by the city hall clock. Mrs. Kelley's time is wrong. The others are to be relied upon.

The alarm was given at 11:13 to 11:15, and we know, so far as we can know from the evidence, that between Mr. Borden's last entrance to the house and the alarm from 25 minutes to half an hour covers the time fully. What took place after he got there? Bridget Sullivan told her story. She left him in the sitting-room reading a paper. Within half an hour A. J. Borden had to go into the house, have his talk with Lizzie, if he had one, go up stairs and down stairs, and lie down.

Blow After Blow.

All this unless he was killed and placed on the sofa afterwards. The time must be reduced to from 10 to 15 minutes for the commission of the deed. It is found that after the alarm had been given the bodies were where they have been so often described as being, and any man of common sense would have said at once on seeing them that this was the work of an insane man, or of one whose heart was as black as black could be. Blow after blow cutting, through the hair into the brain, were rained on these persons. There was an unnecessary brutality about it that suggests infernal hatred and revenge or insanity. Every blow delivered shows its deep line of demarkation from the other, showing that the hand that struck those blows was powerful, and that the hand had experience in handling a hatchet. This case is one of circumstances, and if there are those which weigh against the defendant, you are bound to observe those which are for her equally as well.

The theory of the government seems to have been that the crime was committed by inmates of that house; all their work seems to have been directed by that one idea. The isolation of that house has been shown, it is claimed, because nobody could get out since there were people all around to see who passed and repassed, if any there were, and the attempt is made to show that no persons were seen. What is the fact, however? They know the house has been burglarized within two years and the barn broken into within two months, and the facts are not disputed; we show something the police ought to have discovered, the stranger within the gate, as told by Mrs. Manly. They have spent night and day following up clews to convict Lizzie Borden, but know nothing about Mrs. Manly and the man she saw. Why? Because they are not looking for anybody outside. The extraordinary thing is that the police cannot find the man Dr. Handy saw, but they can find the axe or axes Lizzie Borden killed her father with.

There's the fact that strange men were there who have not been found; these men got there and the neighbors did not see them, and doesn't it follow that others might have gone in and yet not have been seen by the neighbors? Miss Collett did not see Frank Wixon, but he went over the fence while she was right there. Neither Crowe's man nor the Frenchman saw him until he got down into the yard. Lizzie has told about seeing a man dodging about the house, and it hasn't been contradicted. Isn't it entitled to some weight?

So far as we know Morse, Lizzie and Bridget Sullivan were the only persons in the house at the time, with the murdered persons. Mr. Morse having accounted for his time, leaves the others alone, the youngest daughter and the servant—and right here counsel called attention to the words "youngest daughter." She is the pet of the family, the one whose fingers were last clasped by the dead father and the one whose head last rested against his breast. (Lizzie here burst into tears, and Mr. Jennings was himself almost in tears.) Continuing, he said he did not believe that either Bridget Sullivan or Lizzie committed the deed.

Now A. J. Borden could not have got into the house before 10:45, and there are 20 minutes of Bridget's time unaccounted for and nobody has asked her, on the side of the prosecution, what she was doing all that time. If she could do three windows in 15 minutes, did it take her three-quarters of an hour to wash the other four? The point is this, that if Lizzie doesn't explain everything as she goes along, if she trips in her testimony, then she must be the guilty party, think the government.

If Lizzie had an opportunity to commit this murder, Bridget Sullivan had an opportunity. Bridget says she was out doors, but who else saw her out there but Mrs. Churchill? Counsel did not desire to show that Bridget was guilty, but was only trying to show the extraordinary course of the government towards Lizzie. Now if Lizzie did this, when did she do it? The government have put in evidence to show that, from the appearance of the digestion, these persons had been dead so long, but that is a very uncertain thing to build on; it is only approximate, for digestion varies.

Following Mr. Borden from his house at 9:30, counsel brought him back at the time testified to, and said that if Lizzie killed her mother she must have done it while her father was out of the house, but she has told her story about her movements at that time and the telling of that story, counsel said, was in the line of an outrage, as he had told the district attorney at the time; that inquest was taken for no other purpose but to put Lizzie on the rack, and there is nobody who heard that testimony read the other day but said so. Over and over again she was asked the same question to see if she could be made to change her story.

Take the testimony of Mrs. Churchill, an intelligent woman, who couldn't tell where Bridget Sullivan went when they went to the upper room. And yet Bridget isn't so thin she couldn't be seen, nor could she vanish into thin air. Mrs. Churchill couldn't recollect what became of her, but here is Lizzie Borden, who had been subjected to a most severe strain, condemned simply because she could not remember some of the slightest, details in connection with her movements that morning. It was stated that Lizzie laughed at Bridget when she made that exclamation at the door, but it is beyond the bounds of human belief that any person could stand there and laugh over a simple thing like that when she had just come from killing her mother; only an insane person could do that, and Lizzie Borden is not insane.

There wasn't anything inconsistent in the fact that Lizzie, although she had been sick, was eating pears that morning; her father and mother had been doing the same thing, and the government's own witness said so, for they were found in their stomachs. When Mrs. Churchill first saw Lizzie she was agitated because she had just found her father; if she had seen her mother before that would'nt she have been likely to have shown some excitement and agitation then? Bridget says she was calm and it has gone all over this land that she showed no agitation. But Bridget and Lizzie do not agree in other things; Bridget does not know when Mr. Borden went out of that house, but why should her word be taken in place of Lizzie's?

Now no crime is ever committed without a motive, and the government is bound to show that Lizzie had a motive and without that they have got to fall. It has been published that this girl was on the most bitter terms with her father and mother and that was the motive given by the government, but the evidence does not back that up. There is only one little item, that five years ago Lizzie ceased to call her stepmother "mother," but Lizzie says her relations were friendly with her mother in every way and that her parents were on good terms. You hear of murders committed by those who are spendthrifts, who are pressed by their creditors or by their mistresses, but never in the case of a person who has $2500 recently paid her, who had no want of money and where there was never anything but the kindliest feelings between the persons. And yet, without a single thing to suggest the cause, the government holds to it that Lizzie Borden is a murderess. In regard to the prussic acid, counsel said it was clearly a case of mistaken identity.

This girl had just 15 minutes to clear herself of all traces of the crime; why did she not take more time in giving the alarm? What was her object in calling in the neighbors after so short a time? Was there anything to indicate she had taken part in such a tragedy as this? Oh, but they say she cleaned up after doing it. Yes, but how did she do it? If she had an apron on, where is it? It is for them to find and show. What did she do with the hatchet, for it seems to be claimed by the government that the deeds were done by such a weapon. Did she clean it, and where did she clean it?

The hatchet was shown up as a terrible instrument, sharp as a razor, could cut the hair easily, and counsel did not know what was coming from Prof. Wood until he took the stand and swept all of these dreadful things out of this case.

The government knew there was no poison long before Prof. Wood testified here, and they knew there were no hairs or blood stains on that hatchet or the clothes, but they never opened their mouths all the time, keeping

Lizzie Borden and her friends in agony; they shut Lizzie Borden up in her house at first with that "bloody" hatchet and waited events.

Prof. Wood's testimony was a song of deliverance for Lizzie Borden, but if that hatchet had been lost she would have been a convicted woman, because Dr. Dolan's story of the wound would not have been contradicted. Lizzie Borden's life rested in the hollow of Dr. Dolan's hand, but Prof. Wood came and lifted the load from sad hearts. He brought the hatchet and we saw it could not have made such a wound as Dr. Dolan saw or thought he saw.

Counsel demanded the woman's release; there is nothing to hold her on; this court is going to pass a judgment here that would stand, and if the grand jury has any evidence to hold her they can easily find her at any time; she is not going to run away. They cannot find any motive, any blood, any poison, and a woman brought up as she had been should not be sent to prison.

At the conclusion of Mr. Jennings' argument the crowd broke into applause. A recess until 2 o'clock was taken.

SHE IS BOUND OVER.

Judge Blaisdell Thinks Her Probably Guilty—District-Attorney Knowlton's Arguments.

FALL RIVER, Sept. 1.—It was precisely 2 o'clock when Judge Blaisdell took his seat and looked out on a sea of interested appearing faces. Mr. Knowlton said: "This murder was so causeless, so wicked, so unnecessary; the people who were killed, were so free from the active bickerings of many around them, that it is a case which presents the strangest features."

Attorney Knowlton's argument dealt with the fact that the blows were struck by an irresolute, probably a feminine hand. He also enlarged on the family difficulties as a possible motive.

The district attorney said: Both Mr. and Mrs. Borden were murdered, the woman at least an hour and a half before the man, for I am going to assume that your honor is going to take the testimony of Prof. Wood in regard to those stomachs rather than that of a medical examiner who never saw the stomachs. As to the motive of the murder, there was no motive: there never is a motive, but there is a cause, always.

How was the hatchet used? By some one who was a physical if not a moral coward; by one who didn't want the person to see who did it. It was from behind. Those blows were not even evidences of malice, because they were all weak, irresolute blows. I have found some singular things in connection with those two women, the older taking the younger almost a babe and taking care of her as she would a daughter, and yet the fact came out that within five years she had refused to address her stepmother as her mother. It isn't a woman who comes into the family after she has grown up, but she comes as a mother and whom she calls mother until the change comes. Do you suppose there was a well of affection and sympathy flowing between those two? There wasn't any adequate motive for killing this woman, however.

Now, what can be seen in this matter? Now, my brother never touched upon the fact that nobody could have gone into the house, done that work and got away without being seen. That house was the most uniquely locked up house in all Fall River. You could not even go from any one part of the house to another without a key. It was found that every person about there was seen, the man at the gate, the man on the street, but nothing was seen of a person going into or out of that house.

Tell me not about the appearance of the hay; that barn was locked by Mr. Borden at night and unlocked in the morning. And in the house when they got in, where could they hide? No possible hiding place; no way to get anywhere, and that sets us to thinking. I cannot conceive of a villain who is also a fool. All the movements of that family must have been known by anybody who would do that.

And so all the inmates of that house have been subjects of suspicion the moment the fact appeared that the murder was committed from within. Lizzie Borden was examined as closely as anybody, but what was there to grumble about? Why should the innocent object to that? When Lizzie Borden testified she told different stories; she contradicted herself. Where were Mrs. Borden and Lizzie when Bridget came into the house that morning after she had gone into the yard? They were upstairs alone. Mr. Borden had gone away, and when Bridget came to the screen door Lizzie appeared and was told by Bridget that she need not lock the door; that she would be in the yard and could see anybody going or coming.

Then Lizzie takes out her things to begin to iron: Bridget went up stairs, leaving Lizzie ironing at 10:57, nearer to her father than I am to your honor. In five minutes her father was dead. She could not have been down stairs, because she would have heard the noise; not up stairs, because she was ironing.

It is now more difficult than it was, to imagine the probability of the story she told about that barn where the man, whom Lizzie thinks did the deed, was all this time we do not know. Where was Lizzie between 9 and 10, when her stepmother was killed? "Where were you when your father returned?" I asked her, and she said: "I was down in the kitchen." No situation at all. Again I asked her, and she said she "was on the stairs when Bridget let him in."

I asked her which statement I should accept as true. Then I asked her to account for the time her father was away, nearly 1½ hours, and "What were you doing, Lizzie?" and she tells me she was "waiting for her flats to heat!" Waiting 1½ hours for her flats to heat! That is only one thing, but I have not heard any adequate explanation from her as to how she spent that time. Then she said she brought the slippers for her father and he put them on, but the picture shows the boots on her father's feet; they were never taken off.

She first says, and it is her own voluntary statement to Officer Fleet when he asked her if she could give him any idea of how her mother was killed: "She is not my mother; she is my stepmother." Take the statement of her bosom friend, Miss Russell, that she went out to get some iron or lead to fix a window, when she had told others she went to get some irons, and again lead sinkers.

And she stayed in that barn 20 minutes, where no woman would have stayed five minutes. I gave her all the chance in the world and asked her to account for that time, and she said she went up there and ate pears; there of all places in the world, and "she did not feel well and could not eat any breakfast."

About that note. When did it come? How did it come? It could not have come by the front door because that was fastened, nor by the back door because Bridget was on guard, and Bridget never had heard of it. There never was any note, for don't you believe that whoever wrote that note would have come forward in the interests of humanity? This note business was all a part of the scheme.

The Commonwealth has never said these people were not poisoned by prussic acid, but it does say that was the first proposition, because there was a suggestion of a motive in Lizzie going to the drug store; prussic acid could not be had, laws are strictly against it, and she gave it up, but not until she was recognized, not by her tremulous voice, but by her presence and her voice. Prussic acid out of the way, how was the scheme to be carried out? By pistol? No; because that would make too much noise, and so the steel was used. The fact is apparent that this woman was attempting to buy another means to do this deed.

The Fall River Herald

TAKEN BACK TO JAIL

The Alleged Murderess Returned to Taunton.

NO OUTWARD SIGNS OF DISAPPOINTMENT.

It is not likely that the Borden murder will be forgotten because there happens to be no court sitting on the case; people do not forget such crimes. For the past four weeks, with an interval of a few moments, there has been nothing at all upon which the mind could rest continuously for any length of time without beholding the grim scenes of that terrible slaughter creeping above and around the thought and finally taking full possession of the mind. Friends talked of nothing else; there was no relief to be found in the newspapers; at night a person dropped into a troubled sleep with the incidents of the murder before his eyes; he awoke in the morning to be confronted again by a vision of a maniac waving a blood-red axe which had penetrated the skulls of two aged people.

It cannot be wondered then that the final proceedings of the trial Thursday were heard with a keen sense of relief. Whatever was to be the outcome of the earnest pleading of two eloquent lawyers, there was to be a season of rest afterwards that was welcome. It did not follow that when Judge Blaisdell arose to order Lizzie Borden sent to jail to await the meeting of the grand jury that people would stop discussing the case upon the instant. It took a few hours to wind the matter up for the time being in one's own mind.

A CHANCE TO TALK.

Now that there is no more evidence to be given out for the present at least, people who have formed an opinion may consider themselves fully equipped to defend the same without danger that the next day's proceedings of the judicial hearing were going to put weapons into the hands of their adversaries with which to knock the underpinning out of an otherwise able-bodied argument.

Thursday night people talked much as they have talked from the start. The friends of Lizzie Borden were keenly disappointed.

THE DRESS AND AXE..

One very significant statement in the argument of the district attorney was that in which he stated that the axe with which the killing was done and the dress which Lizzie Borden wore that morning have not been shown in court. The prosecution needs these things, and needs them very much, and no effort will be spared to find them.

The Question of Priority.

The examination before Judge Blaisdell has furnished evidence on one important point, and upon this all the experts agree. It relates to the question of the priority of death and was a matter of the greatest importance to the relatives of Mrs. Andrew J. Borden. If she was left a widow for only a moment, she would be entitled to a widow's interest in a large property. If she was killed before her husband died, it has been pointed out that her heirs would have no interest in the husband's estate. These heirs are Mrs. George Whitehead and Mrs. George Fish of Hartford. Their counsel, James F. Jackson, Esq., was in consultation with Mr. Jennings this morning. The latter maintains that unless the woman died first the entire theory of the government upon which was based Lizzie Borden's arrest will fall through. Mr. Jackson did not state whether or not he would contest the question in the courts. There are about $5000 to go to Mrs. Borden's heirs of property in her name at the time of death.

Lizzie Used Opiates.

Lizzie Borden passed a night similar to those she has passed during the trial. Not being able to sleep, she has been taking opiates, and in this way has been able to maintain her strength. When she returned to the matron's room after the pronouncement of the judgment she gave way to a single outbreak of grief at the prospect of continued imprisonment, but her friends assured her that she would be free at the end of that time and the thought comforted her.

It was given out early this morning that the prisoner had already been spirited to Taunton; then that arrangements were made to take her away at 11 o'clock. Finally it became known that the hour fixed for her departure was 1:29 o'clock.

During the morning her friends called upon her. The Rev. Mr. Buck was down early and had a few moments' private conversation with her. He left very soon to attend to certain wants she had expressed, and Emma came down. Mrs. Brigham called, and the morning passed as pleasantly as the trying surroundings would permit.

As yet no steps looking to an application for a writ of habeas corpus have been taken by the attorneys for the defence. Mr. Jennings said this morning that he was not certain as to the grounds upon which such an application would be made if it was made at all.

Taken to the County Jail.

At 12:45 o'clock a carriage was driven around to the north entrance of the station house, and the crowd that was on the watch rushed to see what was going on. In a few minutes the prisoner appeared escorted by Mr. Buck. She wore the blue flannel gown she has worn during the trial. She was handed into the carriage, and Marshal Hilliard and Detective Seaver followed closely after her, the former bearing the necessary papers issued by the court to warrant her committal. The crowd made way, and the carriage was driven rapidly to the station. The party boarded the 1:29 train for Taunton. Lizzie's appearance had not changed materially, except perhaps that care had deepened the facial lines a little.

INDICTMENT.

COMMONWEALTH
VS.
LIZZIE ANDREW BORDEN.

MURDER.

Commonwealth of Massachusetts.

BRISTOL SS. At the Superior Court begun and holden at Taunton within and for said County of Bristol, on the first Monday of November, in the year of our Lord one thousand eight hundred and ninety-two.

The Jurors for the said Commonwealth, on their oath present,—That Lizzie Andrew Borden of Fall River in the County of Bristol, at Fall River in the County of Bristol, on the fourth day of August in the year eighteen hundred and ninety-two, in and upon one Andrew Jackson Borden, feloniously, wilfully and of her malice aforethought, an assault did make, and with a certain weapon, to wit, a sharp cutting instrument, the name and a more particular description of which is to the Jurors unknown, him, the said Andrew Jackson Borden feloniously, wilfully and of her malice aforethought, did strike, cut, beat and bruise, in and upon the head of him, the said Andrew Jackson Borden, giving to him, the said Andrew Jackson Borden, by the said striking, cutting, beating and bruising, in and upon the head of him, the said Andrew Jackson Borden, divers, to wit, ten mortal wounds, of which said mortal wounds the said Andrew Jackson Borden then and there instantly died.

And so the Jurors aforesaid, upon their oath aforesaid, do say, that the said Lizzie Andrew Borden, the said Andrew Jackson Borden, in manner and form aforesaid, then and there feloniously, wilfully and of her malice aforethought did kill and murder; against the peace of said Commonwealth and contrary to the form of the statute in such case made and provided.

A true bill.

HENRY A. BODMAN,
Foreman of the Grand Jury.

HOSEA M. KNOWLTON,
District Attorney.

Bristol ss. On this second day of December, in the year eighteen hundred and ninety-two, this indictment was returned and presented to said Superior Court by the Grand Jury, ordered to be filed, and filed; and it was further ordered by the Court that notice be given to said Lizzie Andrew Borden that said indictment will be entered forthwith upon the docket of the Superior Court in said County.

Attest:—
SIMEON BORDEN, Jr.,
Asst. Clerk.

A true copy.
Attest: Simeon Borden Clerk.

The New York Times

IS LIZZIE BORDEN INSANE

REPORT THAT THE GRAND JURY WILL SO FIND.

NO SUCH IDEA HAS PREVAILED UP TO THIS DATE—HER COUNSEL HAS DENIED THAT SUCH A DEFENSE WAS INTENDED—THE STORY RIDICULED AT TAUNTON.

BOSTON, Nov.30.-The "Journal" says: "while the report that the Grand Jury suspended its finding against Lizzie A. Borden in order that she might be examined by experts as to her sanity may prove incorrect, still such a thing is within the range ofpossibility. The law says:

" 'When a person held in prison on a charge of having committed an indictable offense is not indicted by the Grand Jury by reason of insanity, the Grand Jury shall certify that fact to the court, and thereupon the Court, if satisfied that he is insane, may order him to be committed to a State lunatic hospital under such limitations as may seem proper.'

"The Court must be satisfied that the certification of the Grand Jury is correct--that Lizzie Borden is insane, and therefore not legally responsible for her acts, and upon this issue all her friends have a right to take up her cause and show, if they can, to the satisfaction of the court that Miss Borden was a rational being, possessed of the entire mental balance and control on the 4th of August last, when her father and stepmother were so horribly murdered.

"The Grand Jury will come in at Taunton tomorrow morning, and, if then agreed upon any such certification as has been surmised, will report such to be the fact to Judge Thompson, who thus may be called upon to pass upon the question of Miss Borden's sanity. But it must be remembered that the Grand Jurors in such case declare that they find no indictment because, in their judgment, the prisoner is insane.

"On this point in a recent very interesting interview with Mrs. A. Livermore, that lady stated that from a long and intimate acquaintance with Lizzie Borden's mother, dating from her marriage with Andrew J. Borden, the girl's father, she had never known of the slightest indication of insanity on her part nor of anything of the kind in her family.

"It is also definitely established that there never was the slightest trace of insanity in Mr. Borden's family other than the single case of the old gentleman's brother's wife, between whom and Lizzie there were no ties of blood. Mrs. Livermore knew both the Borden sisters from their childhood and has never seen, she said, any indications of any lack of mental balance."

A special to the "Herald" from Taunton says: "A physician who has had considerable experience as an insanity expert said to-day that if the issue was brought by the defense, it would be a very difficult matter for the Government to prove that Lizzie Borden was not insane.

"With the boot on the other leg, however, he said it would be a most difficult thing for the Government to prove that she was mentally unbalanced when she and her counsel both declared otherwise, and offered evidence in the young woman herself to prove that they were right.

"So, as Messrs. Jennings and Adams (her counsel) are both of the opinion that it would be a decidedly poor move to admit guilt and plead insanity, and as they refuse point blank to do any such things, and as the doctors will not positively declare that she is wrong in her mind, it is very probable that the case will come before the jurors tomorrow forenoon with exactly the same status as that with which it left them a week before last Monday, and they will be called upon to ballot for or against an indictment.

"Lawyer Jennings, in his argument at the hearing in Fall River before Judge Blaisdell, when it was ordered that Lizzie Borden be held for the Grand Jury, declared that no matter who committed the brutal murder it was the deed of a maniac. At the same time with great force he declared that it was not Lizzie A. Borden. So he certainly did not commit himself to any theory of Lizzie's insanity, unless in the course of events it happened that overwhelming proof of the young woman's guilt was brought forth. Then he could go back to his original argument, and declare again that the murder was committed by the hand of a maniac.

"But this overwhelming proof of her guilt has not been offered to the public yet, and it is thought that it has not been offered before the Grand Jury."

PARTICULAR FOUR

THE TRIAL

THE CROWDS GATHER AT THE NEW BEDFORD COURT HOUSE

The Grand Jury met on November 15, 1892 to consider two indictments, that of Lizzie Borden and, it would later be revealed, that of Henry G. Trickey, author of the spurious Boston Globe story, herein covered in Particular Five. The Jury deliberated the Borden case for six days while District Attorney Knowlton presented the Commonwealth's evidence. On November 21, the Jury adjourned without reaching a decision.

Sometime after the adjournment, Alice Russell, lifelong friend of Emma and Lizzie, became convinced Lizzie was guilty of the murders. Knowlton summoned the Jury back into session and Miss Russell's testimony concerning the dress that was burned on the Sunday following the murders, tipped the scale and Lizzie was indicted for both murders on December 2.

In spite of repeated appeals by Attorney Jennings---appeals directed to Knowlton and to Massachusetts Attorney General Albert Pillsbury---the Government took no steps to schedule a trial. It would be later claimed that both men held the hope that extended imprisonment of the accused might bring about a physical or mental breakdown and make a trial unnecessary.

Finally, a trial date was set: June 5, 1893, ten months after the murders. Site: New Bedford, county seat of Bristol County.

Public interest in the sensational event had abated not at all since the first cry of "Murder!" Every hotel in the cameo town of New Bedford was booked in advance by a horde of newspaper reporters from around the nation, accompanied by artists, runners, telegraphers and photographers. August members of the bar, politicians, celebrities, the curious and the morbid had come to see the carnival of justice. New Bedford, the bucolic epitome of New England charm, gave way to the demands of a new industry, catering to the throngs attending the trial.

At exactly 11:28 on the morning of June 5th, the High Sheriff of Bristol County, Andrew Wright, now serving as bailiff, rapped the excited, chattering assembly to order. With pomposity that would be remarked upon throughout the trial and after, he swung open the door to the judge's chamber and ushered the three robed jurists to the bench. Massachusetts law stipulated there be three judges for such a crime as this.

The oppressively hot court room was crowded with 145 prospective jurors. Today there was no room for gawkers, celebrated or not. There was serious business at hand, the selection of the 12 good men and true who would decide the fate of Lizzie Borden. Of course there would be no women on the jury since this was 1893 and only bearded, middle-aged or elderly men would occupy the hard jury seats.

Notable among the "celebrities" was journalist Joe Howard, whose mein and demeanor attracted as much attention as the defendant herself. He styled himself as the first syndicated columnist, and his reports---ebullient and fanciful at times---were read by the thousands of subscribers of a dozen big-city newspapers. He acquired, by a means he never revealed, a front-row seat and this is his report of Day One:

SELECTED.

Jury to Try Miss Lizzie Borden.

C. I. Richards is the Foreman.

He Deals in Real Estate at North Attleboro.

Six Men of the Twelve Chosen are Farmers.

Two Manufacturers Are of the Number.

Three Mechanics Make Up the List.

Accused Was Impassive During the Day.

Spectators Were Not Admitted to the Court Room.

NEW BEDFORD, June 5—It has been a hot day for Lizzie Borden in more senses than one and an experience for every one else in the court room, a repetition of which is far from desirable.

As a matter of fact, in his palmiest days, general humidity never succeeded in causing discomfort more intense or conditions less endurable than those which prevailed in this section in general, and in court particularly today.

It will be impossible to exaggerate the interest felt and manifested by intelligent readers throughout the country in the outcome of this trial of a comparatively young woman for the murder of her father and stepmother. The best evidence of this interest is seen in the presence here of special correspondents and reporters from all sections of the country, necessitating the placing of a largely increased force of telegraphers by the telegraph companies.

Every hotel is taxed to its utmost limit and private hospitality is taken by individuals.

Locally, if we may use that term in reference to New England, and Massachusetts in particular, the Borden case is of interest in other directions than in that of baycolony. It may not be entirely fair to say that politics enter into it, but it is obvious that politicians are engaged on either side. Mr Knowlton, the district attorney and senior prosecutor, is ambitious to succeed the present attorney general, Mr Pillsbury, who declined to conduct the case on the ground of ill health. Mr Knowlton's friends laughingly insist that Mr Pillsbury did not care to put himself in such conspicuous comparison with the distinguished man of this city.

Mr Knowlton's associate, Mr Moody, the district attorney for an adjacent county, is also spoken of in connection with the attorney generalship. The senior counsel for the defense, Ex Gov Robinson, is potent in republican councils, and oddly enough will have considerable to say as to which of his two opponents shall figure in the list next fall.

To an observer from New York the solemn ceremonials of a Massachusetts superior court are odd enough, and were it not for the respect for legal tribunals, which dominates all Americans, the oddity would verge far over into the realm of comedy.

The chief justice, Mr Mason, is a dignified old gentleman, with a benignant expression of countenance, silvered hair and beard, so cut as to emphasize his square built and significant under jaw. His side partners, Messrs Blodgett and Dewey, apparently have nothing to do but to nod acquiescence when the chief justice speaks, fan their heated brows and bemoan the wretchedness of their condition.

When they entered the court room, this morning, they were preceded by a bustling little man with buttons, High Sheriff Wright, whose sense of the importance of his own position was commensurate with the dignity of their high mightinesses on the bench. Outside of this state, where one judge holds the trial term, such all-embracing discipline as that exercised by Sheriff Wright would not be tolerated.

If any one attempts to enter or depart, save at the general place of exit, he impressively turns them the other way. He dictates to the members of the bar where and how they shall sit and conducts himself precisely as a watchful and censorious schoolmaster might be expected to do in a room full of caloricized and impatient pupils. Such are the duties of his office unquestionably, and it must be conceded that if there ever was an official who deserved to be called the high sheriff, sitting aside from his fellow-mortals, directing their footsteps and positions, brother Wright completely fills the bill.

The chief interest pertains to Lizzie Borden, her appearance, her demeanor under the trying circumstances and such indices of character as she may unconsciously display.

After Sheriff Wright had drawn up in real New Bedford state with the judges, a modest little carryall stopped at the door, from which alighted the heroine of the day. Heretofore, from the morning of the murder until her last appearance, Miss Borden has worn a blue serge dress, Her costume today was becoming and of fashionable cut. Her hat was a model for theatergoers, flat built, of lace, ornamented with blue rosettes, a tiny blue feather. Her frock was of black merino, fastened at the neck with a modest brooch. She wore dark undressed kid gloves and very neatly-fitting shoes. Her self-possession was remarkable, and she ascended the long flight of stairs leading to the court room quickly, briskly in fact, and took her place in what is called the "dock," which in reality is nothing but a space between two rails, where two chairs are placed, one of which is occupied by the deputy sheriff, the other by herself.

Life here has a face. Her dark brown hair was modestly coiled behind. Her full forehead was very pale, her wide-apart eyes had an unpleasant stare. Her cheeks, which are over full, hang down below the line of the chin making a pronounced mark on either side of the face, carrying the line

JUDGE JUSTIN DEWEY

from the lower part of the ear a long distance down to the point of an obstinate and stubborn chin.

Later on, when jurors were catechised by the judge, a novel feature by the way, for everywhere else the judge is expected to hold his tongue while the lawyers fight over the qualifications and disqualifications of the candidates, something like 12 or 15 men, who would have made admirable jurors, were excused from serving because they don't believe in the penalty of death. This sentiment is spreading with noticeable strength throughout New England, and it wouldn't amaze either judges or politicians if Massachusetts were ere many years to join the antideath penalty procession. It was interesting to know that all sorts of men in every condition of life, young as well as old, entered that objection as a plea for excuse from jury duty.

But to return to Lizzie. Outside in a neighboring field was a most demonstrative cow, whose mooing was almost continuous, frequently interrupting the learned judge, often drowning the responses of mild-mannered witnesses, and causing as far as eye could see the one and only smile that changed the impassiveness of the Borden countenance from morning until night. Precisely why Sheriff Wright did not order the cow removed or rapped her bellowing into silence are matters for his own conscience to determine.

A most remarkable woman, a most interesting study is this young lady from Fall River. When the judges made their entrance she looked at them, but with no apparent interest. During all the little preliminaries, the fussings and the fumings, the arrangement of papers, and the seating of guests, she gave no heed. When in obedience to a nod from the chief justice, everybody in the court room rose in order that brother Julien, a local preacher of intense vitality and great aplomb, might have free course to address the throne of grace, Lizzie stood up with all the rest, and I don't doubt was quite as fervent in her petition as any of them. Brother Julien was rather emphatic in his suggestion that he would be especially pleased if the Lord would see to it that innocence was revealed and guilt exposed, but the entire delivery was so short and so devoid of mental imbecility and perfunctory indoctrination, that we all sat down with a sigh of gratitude and rest. So did Lizzie.

When she was arraigned to plead she obeyed the mandate with a frigidity which ought to have cooled the entire atmosphere.

JUDGE ALBERT MASON

You must consider that Miss Borden was the only woman in the room with the exception of two actively engaged reporters and one other, who was called as a witness. Hundreds of women have applied for passes, but thus far no one has been given any. It looks strange to see the defendant without her sister or other female relatives, but even that is another link in the chain of incident which goes to prove her isolation from her kind, and to disclose her a unique and peculiar personality.

It was the duty of Deputy Sheriff Thomas S. Butman, who sits near the press seats, to open court with a long rigmarole formula, the old "Hear ye!" business, to count the jurors and make other formal announcements, which he did in a peculiar and perfunctory manner, which one would suppose would attract the attention of a quick-witted girl, but Lizzie gave no heed to him or his sayings, more than to the impressiveness of the chief justice, whose well-modulated voice was utilized in so low a tone that much of what was said was inaudible 20 feet away. In fact, the slowest and dryest and least animated old-fashioned prayer meeting would be a wild and cyclonic demonstration in comparison with the quiet deliberation, the soft whisperings, the gentle utterances of everybody in that calm and solemn jurisdiction.

The examination of jurors in a Massachusetts court is no joke. Instead of occupying a comfortable chair on the witness stand at the side of the bench, the juror stands in an open space in front of the jury box exposed to the view of all concerned. The lawyers are not in it. They ask no questions whatever. The judge does all the talking. If the juror is to be excused the judge does it. If in his opinion the juror is all right the judge says so, announcing that he finds him indifferent. The lawyers then have a right to challenge 22 men peremptorily with or without cause.

In some instances today the scene was most embarrassing. The jurors, or nearly all of them, were from farming sections, and as this is a very busy time in the realm of agriculture they were naturally not anxious to serve. Judge Mason evidently appreciated the point, and was inclined to think that some of the death penalty scruples were a little strained. He treated them all, however, with impartial courtesy, and the result was after nine hours' weary talking a typical jury was secured. Every one of them wears a mustache, a majority of them are very tall, with sunburned necks and not over intelligent in expression.

The counsel for the people used their right to challenge sparingly, but Mr Jennings, in behalf of the defense, suggested something like 15, and each time upon his suggestion Miss Borden, who sat 10 or 12 feet in the rear of her counsel, rose, looked the wouldbe jurors squarely in the eye and softly uttered "challenged." That is also a queer feature in this part of the world.

JUDGE CALEB BLODGETT

The jurors occupy a room at the other end of a short corridor upon which my door opens. They are not a jolly looking set of men, and it is not unlikely their arguments will be stormy, so that unlistening ears will be compelled to digest their discussions. I must speak to the high sheriff about that, for sleep in this latitude and in this temperature is a great desideratum.

I have been studying them somewhat. Three of them are noticeably tall, above 6 feet, with very heavy mustaches and retreating chins; unaccustomed, I should say, to metropolitan experiences of any nature. There are three Wilburs, one with an "U." and two with an "A."

Juror Cole is so startlingly like Dave Wombald that I had to take a second look at him ere I could be rid of the idea of the resurrection. Juror Finn has a mustache which he twists all the time, and, all told, there isn't one who would be taken at first sight as a man of the world; but, for all that, it is a jury virtually selected by Chief Justice Mason and approved by the pugnacious counsel of the prosecution and the suave and courteous lawyer for the defence, so that any adverse suggestion from an outsider must of necessity be simply hyper critical.

Several gentlemen offered excuses today which brought them within the law of exclusion. For instance, two said that they had served as jurors within three years, but not being familiar with the technicalities of courts and records they had not provided themselves with an affidavit excuse. This led to a sort of search-warrant cross-examination, which must have made their blood boil with indignation.

The larger part of the court room was filled with men who had been summoned as jurors. They were crowded, hot, uncomfortable and impatient to be about their work. Yet at every move, at every whisper, at every shuffle of feet, they were rapped into silence as though they were so many children. The sheriff would be very careful not to intimate to the judges that they talked too much, or whispered over loud, or did this or that or the other thing to attract attention in the court room. He calls for them at the hotel in a coach, he personally escorts them to their seats, he puts the chief justice in a high chair and the associates in little low chairs, one on either side of the high, and then from his own lofty eminence complacently regards them as a kind of legal trinity to be worshiped and admired.

Now that is all right, but how about the jurors? They are just as much part and parcel of the court as the judges themselves, and if any one of them were to report to Chief Justice Mason that he was annoyed by the disciplinarian methods of the sheriff he would not only immediately be set right, but the sheriff would be instructed that a juror is of as much importance as a judge and a great deal more about the time the verdict is to be decided.

It is obviously the intention of the authorities to push this case as speedily as possible. Some feared it would take a week to impanel the jury, and the fact that the unfortunates are now cribbed, cabined and confined in a hotel bedroom, one day alone having been used, is most gratifying evidence that there will be no unnecessary delay.

The court adjourned at 6 o'clock, and will reassemble at 9 o'clock tomorrow, at which time brother Knowlton, who does not know whether he will speak two hours or four, will present the case for the people. He is a strong-built, massive-framed, pleasant-mannered individual, but if I am a judge of character at close range he is a fighter, and means to win this case if it is a possibility. He is in consultation tonight with his colleagne, Mr Moody, and both are confident that a conviction is a certainty.

The prisoner was removed from court by the deputy sheriff with urbane courtesy, and after a refreshing bath partook of a hearty dinner. The judges are quartered in quite nearby rooms, where they entertained numerous social callers. The jurors are the only unhappy parties, for they are securely locked up by themselves, unfamiliar with each other's habits, tastes or pursuits, debarred from all refreshments, save such as may be permitted by the charitable order of the court, and allowed to communicate with no one under any pretext whatever.

Thus ends the first chapter.

Howard

Boston Daily Globe

BORDEN JURY FOUND

Miss Lizzie Sat Calmly Through It All

NEW BEDFORD, June 5.—Before a stern and grim-looking bench of Judges as ever sat in Puritan New England of old, Miss Lizzie Andrew Borden was put on trial for her life, in the Court House in New Bedford, this morning. She had been occupying the large and rather comfortable room of the matron in the House of Correction. She was taken along the two short blocks to the Court House in a closed carriage at about a quarter to 11 o'clock. A little crowd had gathered to see her. It was a crowd mainly composed of well-dressed women and young girls, a crowd that added picturesqueness to the beautiful neighborhood of grand residences and park like gardens. The prisoner hurried into the Court House, closely attended by Deputy Sheriff Kirby, who is detailed as her escort. Those who saw Miss Borden for the first time were very much astonished. Her newspaper portraits have done her no justice at all. Some have made her out a hard and hideous fright, and others have flattered her. She is, in truth, a very plain-looking old maid. She may be likened to a typical school marm, plain, practical, and with a face that shows the deep lines of either care or habitual low spirits, and the transitory marks of a recent illness.

Beside her on her right sits her custodian. She was dressed in black, excepting for a blue plume of feathers, two blue velvet rosettes in her hat, and a large enamelled pansy pin at her throat. Her dress was of black brocade, with two rows of narrow velvet ribbon round her cuffs and around the bottom of her basque, and three rows of the same ribbon above the edge of her skirt.

A common sense, broad-toed, brand new shoe peeped out from under her dress, and she wore black cotton gloves. Her dress fitted her as perfectly as if she had been measured for it in Paris, but it was of a very old fashion, having the front of the basque puffed with great fulness. Excepting her rather loud pin she wore no jewelry. Her black straw hat was poke shaped, and of no existing fashion. Her beautiful, fine, nut-brown hair, soft and glossy to a degree, was pulled back into a long roll behind her head.

And now the difficult thing is to describe her face. Like her dress, it was that of a lady. She has large, brown eyes, and a fine high forehead, but her nose is a tilting one, and her cheek bones are so prominent that the lower part of her countenance is greatly overweighted. Her head is broadest at the ears. Her cheeks are very plump, and her jaws are strong and conspicuous. Her thick, protruding lips are pallid from sickness, and her mouth is drawn down into two very deep creases that denote either a melancholy or an irritable disposition. She is no Medusa or Gorgon. There is nothing wicked, criminal, or hard in her features. Her manner in public has often been described as if she were callous, or brazen. It was not so to-day. She behaved like a self-possessed girl, with all the grit that comes of American blood, which has flowed pure in her family during centuries. She was modest, calm, and quiet, and it was plain to see that she had complete mastery of herself, and could make her sensations and emotions invisible to an impertinent public. The Massachusetts law makes a prisoner very conspicuous and gives her a trying part to play. Further along we shall see how she played it.

The spick and span little court room is divided in halves, the rear for the public and the fore part for the actors in its legal dramas and tragedies. This division is made by a rail. One yard in front of that railing is a lighter rail, enclosing a space for the counsel. Between the two railings sits this wretched prisoner. Next to her is THE SUN correspondent, and the correspondents of the other New York papers sit all along on the same line.

The little fifty-year-old court house, like a toy building in its setting of greenery and blossoms is neat and clean, with the assertive cleanliness of everything in New Bedford. Its one court room on the second floor is also kept "shipshape and Bristol fashion," as the sailors would say. Its drab-colored walls are framed with white woodwork, and fluted white columns sustain its arched ceiling, and its ten windows look out upon as much foliage as if it were in the woods.

Through those embrasures comes the mingled perfume of wistaria and magnolia blossoms. Occasionally, too, the lowing of a cow sounds louder in the court room than the proceedings of the lawyers. A picture of a dead District Attorney tries hard to relieve the severe plainness of the room. The floor is all carpeted, and yawning spittoons are set about it.

When the proceedings began this morning it was seen that the Judges, the lawyers, the Sheriff, and most of the attendants were in the main a white-haired, aged lot of citizens. On one side of the room sat six rows of reporters, bending over their pads and looking like a writing class in school. The schoolmaster was well impersonated by the High Sheriff, soldierly looking Andrew Wright, who sat on the other side of the room in a box by himself, and every now and again startled everybody by rapping sharply for order with a lead pencil.

The square-headed, eagle-eyed Chief Justice then addressed the lawyers and the 150 talesmen of the jury panel. These talesmen, by the way, practically made up the audience of the court room. This was what the Chief Justice said should guide the talesmen in taking or rejecting places on the jury:

"It will be the duty of the Court to put to each person summoned as a juror questions as to whether he has formed or expressed any opinion in relation to the cause or is sensible of any bias or prejudice. It is also the duty of the Court to ask each juror, if he has any opinions which will prevent him from finding a verdict of guilty in a cause where the crime is punishable by death. It has been said by Chief Justice Shaw, and it has never been questioned as law, that the statute intends to exclude any person who has made up his mind, or formed a judgment in advance, no matter in favor of which side. Still the opinion or judgment must be something more than a vague impression formed from casual conversation with others, or from reading imperfect and abbreviated newspaper reports. It must be such an opinion upon the merits of the question as would be likely to bias or prevent a candidate's judgment upon a full hearing of the testimony. I desire to call the attention of all those persons who are summoned as jurors to this statement in reference to the opinions to which the statute refers, and I also wish to remind every juror that he will be called to answer these questions under oath, that he must answer them truly, and accept what may follow. Also with reference to the question as to whether opinions which would preclude one from finding defendent guilty of an offence punishable by death. It is not at all what opinions are entertained with reference to capital punishment, but there are some persons so constituted mentally that they could not sustain a law of the land which they deemed wrong. There are some persons so mentally constituted that they could not declare the simpliest axiom of mathematics if it were to follow that death was to be inflicted in consequence of the declaration. If any person thinks and is satisfied that he is so mentally constructed that he cannot find upon evidence that the defendant is guilty of an offense punishable with death, then in response to that question he will so answer. But in answering that question as the others each juror will keep in mind that he is answering upon oath."

The Chief Justice was narrowly watched and listened to while he delivered this address, for a great many persons were making his acquaintance. They noted that he spoke very carefully, firmly, and distinctly, enunciating each syllable separately, and rolling his r's a little. Nothing was more apparent than the kindliness of his tones.

It was evident that grim as he looks Miss Borden will find in him all the sympathy and gentleness that is compatible with justice.

The old clerk, Simeon Borden, called his namesake, the prisoner, to the bar. He is as neat and sleek as a typical Sunday school superintendent. This was how he prepared the first cruel ordeal for the imprisoned woman. "Lizzie Andrew Borden," said he, "You will now step to the bar to be tried by twelve good men of the commonwealth. If you object to any you have the right to do so as they are called. You have the right to challenge twenty-two of them, and as many more as you can show good cause for."

At the calling of her name, the pallid, pink-lipped old maid reached the railing in front of her, and thus helped herself to her feet with very visible effort. In that way she got up most of the many times that she had to stand. She listened to what the clerk had to say, and when he had finished she bowed very slightly, and sat down. Then with a break for dinner the examination of the jurors went on until 101 of them had been called, and yet it was an astonishingly rapid progress that was made, for instead of its taking a week to get a jury the twelve good men and true filled their box in the first day.

In Massachusetts the Chief Justice puts all the questions, and these are the ones he put over and over again a hundred times to-day: "Are you related to the prisoner at the bar or to Andrew J. Borden or Abbie D. Borden, deceased?" "Have you any interest in this cause; have you formed an opinion with relation to it?" "Have you any prejudice or bias in it?" "Such opinions as you have formed or expressed, would they prevent your giving a candid judgment upon a full hearing of the evidence?" "Have you any opinion that will preclude you from finding the defendant guilty of an offence punishable with death?"

Now and then one side or the other would ask Mr. Justice Mason to add this question: "Are you at present a client of counsel on either side in this case?" If all the questions were answered satisfactorily the Chief Justice then pronounced these words: "The juror stands indifferent." At that each little knot of lawyers would get its heads together and a mighty whispering would ensue. If Mr. Knowlton did not want the man he said: "The Commonwealth challenges." If Mr. Jennings did not want the man he had to tell Miss Borden to say so. At first he walked over to where she sat and whispered to her. But that got tedious, because he objected to sixteen men in all. So, after a little time, he only walked half way to her, and made believe say the word "challenge" with his lips. Even that got tiresome, and after a little more time he merely wriggled round in his seat and made a little mouth at Miss Borden, as if he and she were schoolgirls holding a pantomimic conversation.

At first it seemed that she was to challenge all Irishmen and Catholics, on account of Bridget Sullivan's connection with the case, and certainly the first few of that description that came along were challenged by the defence. But, on the other hand, one who was said to be Irish and a Catholic was chosen. Then, again, it seemed at first as though only men at or beyond the middle age were satisfactory, but this same Irishman was also exceptional in being young. Only three or four foreign names were called. The rest were all Wilburs, Palmers, and Folgers, and Parkers, and Lincolns, and Howlands, and that sort of Americans carrying such given names as Reuben and Eben and Gideon and Ezra and Elihu. The reason the jury filled up so quickly was that everybody seemed to want to get on it.

District Attorney Knowlton is a veritable Cromwell, a round-headed, powerful, and bustling big man, built like a bull, with a thick neck, bristling hair, a red beard, heavy jaws, and plump cheeks. His Assistant District Attorney, Moody of Essex county, is the youngest and handsomest of the lawyers. He is a pure blue-eyed blond, not much above 30, dressed like a New Yorker, and with a quick, intelligent face. He is as bright and alert as he is handsome.

These two lawyers for the commonwealth sat at a table in front of Miss Borden, and also in front of the jury box almost. Close to the clerk's desk, before the bench, was the table for the three lawyers for the defence. Of these the Hon. George D. Robinson, three times Governor of Massachusetts, is easily the most impressive and distinguished looking; indeed, he is the most notable man in the court room. He is of an old-fashioned type, such as Daniel Webster was familiar with. He is tall and stately, with a fine head and an intelligent face. His build shows that he loves the good things of life, and his face shows that he thinks and works hard. His hair is still black but very thin, and he combs it so as to make it cover as much baldness as possible. Mr. Melvin O. Adams, famous in Boston as an eloquent pleader, is typical of a large class of the young men of the Hub. He evidently pays attention to his looks, and they are worth it. He has the generous full mouth of an orator and the strong nose that usually goes with it. He has great, handsome brown eyes, and the part, that is exactly in the middle of his hair, terminates in two pretty little curls. Yet he is a very masculine and forceful looking man.

But the most interesting of its group is its leader, Mr. Andrew J. Jennings, who serves Miss Borden as a friend as well as a lawyer. He is very much such a man as Col. Lamont, the Secretary of War. He is a miniature of Lamont. He has the same round head, the same aggressive moustache, the same quick eyes and nervous manner, and the same ability to be everywhere and see everything at once. His eyes fairly snap when he is in motion, and he has got more energy than all the rest of the people in the court room except the reporters.

The court room is so small, and the population so large, that a free ticket to the trial, and board and pay besides, was a thing to be looked after. The lawyers had their pick of the county till about the eleventh man was reached, and then everybody seemed to dread being the twelfth, who, in case of the worst, would have to be the final person to say the awful word "Guilty."

The jury when it was chosen was formed of the following men: George Potter of Westport, William F. Dean of Taunton, John Wilbur of Somerset, Fred C. Wilbur of Raynham, Lemuel K. Wilbur of Easton, William Wescott of Seeconk, A. B. Hodge of Taunton, Augustus Swift of New Bedford, Frank G. Cole of Attleboro, John C. Finn of Taunton, Charles I. Richards of Taunton, and Allen H. Wordell of Dartmouth. They are a very solid lot of citizens.

Richards, the foreman, is a rich land owner; Swift is the manager of iron works, and the rest are farmers and master mechanics and such like. To get a dozen of them 101 were called. Fifty-two were excused for scruples or prejudices, sixteen were challenged by Miss Borden, and fourteen by the Commonwealth.

After the jury was formed it went off into a little room by itself, and the members sent telegrams to their families saying that they were shut up and might not get home for a month. In the mean time the Judges were inquiring into their characters and determining which one should be foreman. The wealthy Richards was chosen, and the court adjourned.

After this proceedings will begin at 9 o'clock in the morning and last till 5 in the evening. To-morrow morning Miss Borden will be called upon to stand up and hear the reading of the indictment charging her with the commission of a double crime such as only a fiend could conceive and a monster execute.

After that the talking of the spokesman for each side will open this the greatest of all criminal cases in the history of New England. Then the taking of testimony will begin, probably with that of Dr. Dolan, whom we would call the Coroner, but who is called here the Medical Examiner of Fall River.

He was in the court room this afternoon. So was Congressman Randall of this district and ex-Judge Bennett, the dean of the Boston University Law School. Three particular friends of Miss Borden sat not far from her beyond the high rail behind which she sat.

They were her former pastor, the Rev. Mr. Jubb of the Central Congregational Church of Fall River; City Missionary Buck of that town, and the President of the Five Cents' Savings Bank in the same place. All three were permitted to talk with her very freely without any supervision after the selection of the jury.

But that isn't half as amazing as the fact that Bridget goes shopping and knocks about the streets of New Bedford alone, or in any company she pleases, whenever she likes. It seems that after the preliminary examination three months ago, when she was to be sent to the House of Detention, Marshal Hilliard and State Detective Seaver went her bail, and got her a job as a servant in the House of Correction. Bridget was the grand lady of the Borden household, and she has been in luck ever since the tragedy. It must be remembered that she is the only one who is known to have been in the house at the time of the murder, and that some of the theories made her a conspirator or an accomplice. Yet she goes about telling her story to the servant girls of New Bedford before the court or the public is allowed to hear it.

Miss Emma, the elder sister called upon the prisoner to-day and spent some time afterward in one of the rooms under the court room. The prisoner had a sort of semi-visit from another member of the family in a very peculiar way.

The seventieth or eightieth talesman stood up to be examined, and was asked the first question, "Are you related to the prisoner at the bar?" "I am," said the man, to the astonishment of everybody, including the prisoner. "Then you are excused," said the Chief Justice.

Miss Lizzie Borden leaned over to Deputy Sheriff Kirby and said: "Who on earth is he?"

Mr. Kirby told her he was Mr. Oliver E. Gifford, and her uncle by marriage. Miss Lizzie put up her fan in front of her face and laughed quite heartily. Gifford saw her action, and he, too, laughed as he sought his seat.

After the noon recess to-morrow, and probably before any evidence is taken the jury and the lawyers will go to Fall River, and make a thorough examination of the scene of the murder—the Borden house and its surroundings.

In that way they will spend the whole afternoon, so that the probability is that the only court proceedings will be the reading of the indictment and the opening addresses of the counsel.

SHERIFF ANDREW WRIGHT

Sheriff of Bristol County and Bailiff of the court, Wright attracted considerable notice for the rigid discipline he imposed on those attending the trial.

The New York Times

BORDEN MURDER TRIAL BEGUN

JURORS IMPANELED TO TRY THE CELEBRATED CASE.

They Are to Decide the Fate of a Young Woman Accused of Murdering Her Father and Stepmother—Crowds Surround the Court House—No Spectators Admitted to the Trial Chamber—The Jury to View the Premises at Fall River Where the Crime Was Committed.

NEW BEDFORD, Mass., June 5.- The trial of Lizzie Andrew Borden for the murder of her father and stepmother began here to-day. At an early hour crowds gathered about the Court House on County Street, and many remained there all day in the hope of securing a sight of the accused young woman. Hundreds attempted to gain entrance to the building, but the rule that there should be no spectators was rigidly enforced.

The selection of the jury was all that was done to-day. This work was completed before 5 o'clock. The ease with which the jury was secured was a surprise to everybody, particularly as almost every man examined had formed an opinion about the case, and many of the candidates were opposed to capital punishment. The majority of the jury are farmers. All are advanced at least to middle age, both sides having objected to the presence of young men in the box.

The prosecution is represented by District Attorneys H. M. Knowlton and H. W. Moody. The attorneys for the defense are Andrew J. Jennings of Fall River, Col. Melvin O. Adams of Boston, and ex-Gov. George D. Robinson.

Each side has twenty-two challenges. When the jury was finally selected the prosecution had exhausted fourteen and the defense twenty-two. The Jury is made up as follows:

Augustus Swift, New-Bedford.
John C. Flynn, Taunton.
Louis D. Hodges, Taunton.
William F. Dean, Taunton.
George Potter, Westport.
Frederick C. Wilbar, Raynham.
John Wilbur, Somerset.
Frank G. Cole, Attleborough.
Charles I. Richards, North Attleborough.
Lemuel K. Wilber, Easton.
William Westcott, Seekonk.
Allen H. Wordell, Dartmouth.

The prisoner reached the courtroom at 11 o'clock. She entered the chamber from the jury room. She paused for a moment in the doorway and glanced over the room, apparently as self-possessed as ever. She looked unusually well. She wore a black brocade dress and a black lace hat.

Presently, as she stood there, the pink flush, which those who have watched her have learned to know denotes excitement, came to her cheeks.

She stepped forward as her attorneys, Mr. Jennings and Col. Adams, advanced to meet her. She gave her hand to each and smiled as she greeted them.

The three judges who are to preside at the trial came in soon after. Those in the chamber rose as the Judges entered. Proceedings began with prayer by the Rev. M. C. Julien of the New-Bedford Congregational Church. He prayed that the innocent might be protected and the guilty exposed.

Then District Attorney Knowlton opened the trial. After announcing that, on account of the illness of the Attorney General, William H. Moody of Haverhill, State's Attorney of the Eastern District, had been assigned to assist him, he moved that the jury be selected.

After a few words related to qualifications of jurors from Chief Justice Mason, the clerk, Simeon Borden, who by the way, is not a relative of the accused, called the prisoner and informed her of her right of challenge, adding that all challenges must be made before a jury is sworn. Edward G. Baker was called. Mr. Baker is an elderly man with a gray beard and pleasant features. He stood before the court and the following interrogations were propounded by the Chief Justice, this being the form in each instance:

"Are you related to the prisoner, or to Andrew J. or Abby D. Borden?

"Have you formed or expressed an opinion in relation to this case?

"Are you sensible of any bias or prejudice in it?

"Have you formed any opinion that would preclude you from finding the defendant guilty of an offense punishable by death?"

Mr. Baker had an opinion, he said, that could not be changed, and he was interrogated no further.

George Winslow was the next name called, and against him the first peremptory challenge of the defense was made. He is a man with a fierce black mustache. He had expressed an opinion, and appeared perfectly willing to serve.

"Juror, look on the prisoner," commanded the Chief Justice.

Winslow rolled his eyes toward the dock.

"Prisoner, look upon the juror."

As this sentence was spoken, Attorney Jennings hurried from his seat to that of his client and whispered to her.

She arose and, addressing the court, uttered the word, "Challenge."

Mr. Winslow retired.

The next juror called, George Potter, was accepted as a juror. William F. Dean was accepted as the second juror. After this, proceedings took on a routine nature and the afternoon was a dull one.

ON TRIAL.

Moody Opens the Borden Case.

Points Presented to the Jury.

Accused Woman Faints in Court.

First Sensation Caused by Gruesome Exhibits.

Opportunity a Text for the Plea.

What Miss Russell is Expected to Say.

Burned Dress to Figure in Evidence Presented.

Lawyers and Jury at Scene of the Tragedy.

NEW BEDFORD, June 6—Confronted with the skulls, she fainted.

This has been a tough day for Lizzie Borden.

Not alone because a red hot sun mercilessly superheated the New Bedford air, not because her confinement in the court room was unusually long, quite the contrary; not alone because for the third time she heard the harrowing story of the terrible tragedy, although each of these entered as a factor into the conditions of the day, but because her already overwrought nervous system touched its limit, and when, with adroit commonplaceness, Dist Atty Moody carelessly threw her blue frock on the table, her quick eye caught sight of the tissue paper covered skulls of her father and mother.

That settled her, and without fuss or demonstration of any sort or kind, she fell into a faint which lasted several minutes, sending a thrill of excitement through the awe-struck spectators, and causing unfeigned embarrassment and discomfiture to penetrate the ranks of the counsel.

It is a difficult matter to make the opening speech in a murder case, because so much time must necessarily be occupied in the dry details of plan and scope and diagramic exhibit.

MISS BORDEN LISTENING TO THE OPENING PLEA

Mr Moody spoke about two hours in a purely conversational tone.

The chief justice listened with undiverted attention, but the others were visibly affected by the weather and overcome by very natural drowsiness, which by the way affected everybody in the court room with the exception of Dist Atty Knowlton and High Sheriff Wright, upon whom rested the responsibility of upholding the dignity of the superior court of Massachusetts.

It must be borne in mind that Mr Knowlton and his associate, Mr Moody, share the conviction of Marshal Hilliard of Fall River that Lizzie Borden alone had the opportunity, alone had a motive to commit this murder.

Conscientiously they have worked upon

the case for nearly a year, until they are satiated with Bordenism and permeated with what seems to them incontrovertible proof.

He began with a terribly turgid and uninteresting description of the Borden house, grounds and barn, and then passed minutely into every detail of the incidents in that house on the morning of the murder.

Incidentally he touched upon what in my judgment will prove the strongest link in the chain of evidence against the little woman.

Little woman? Yes, for the descriptions which have been sent broadcast as to the amazonic proportions, the masculinity of Miss Borden's physique, are very far from the truth.

She is of medium height, has grown somewhat stouter by confinement and possesses muscular strength in her arms alone.

For the first time the matter to which I allude as having been suggested in the opening of Mr. Moody, namely, a conversation held by Miss Borden with her friend, Miss Russell, was made a prominent feature today.

According to the prosecution's theory, Miss Borden had determined to kill her father and mother, and deliberately prepared to do the deed.

The night preceding she called upon her friend, and in the course of her conversation said that she felt as though something terrible was going to happen, and that she had seen a strange man looking about the house.

After the discovery of the bodies Miss Russell found Miss Borden burning something in the stove, and in reply to a question as to what she was doing Lizzie said she "was trying to burn it, as it was all covered with paint."

Whereupon Miss Russell remarked: "Well I would not do it where all these people can see you, if I were you."

To which the sole recognition given by Miss Borden was a movement of a foot or more out of the range of observation.

Some time after that Miss Russell said: "What made you burn that dress?" and Lizzie ejaculated: "O, what made you let me do it."

According to the story of the prosecution, although Miss Russell felt that much that she saw was suspicious at the time of the discovery, she had such confidence in her friend, and was so anxious to shield her from unjust criticism, that she held her tongue.

Later her conscience troubled her, and she is now prepared to give all the information in her power.

Mr Moody, with considerable dramatic effect, had brought into the court room, first, two hatchets, and second, two axes, the only implements of the kind known to have been in the house on the morning of the murder.

The axes are so large and unwieldy as to establish their non-participation in the tragedy at the first glance.

The hatchets were devoid of any external substance which could rightfully cause suspicion.

In the haft hole was a small fragment of broken handle which fits perfectly with the broken handle in one of the other ax heads.

Moody made his grand coup after the tossing of the frock and the analysis of the axes and hatchets, by opening very quietly an ordinary hand bag in which reposed side by side the skulls of the late Mr and Mrs Borden.

All this time, in fact since the incident of the frock, Miss Borden's face was concealed by her fan, her eyes closed and her face flushed with heightening color.

Once she had been roused by an attendant who handed her a glass of water, which she drank, and without wiping her lips resumed her position behind the fan.

But although she could shut out the horrid paraphernalia by closing her eyes she could not shut out the words of the earnest attorney from her unwilling ears.

The sight of those skulls was pregnant with meaning to the most indifferent spectator in that court, and Mr Moody's minute description of their gashed and hacked mutilations must have intensified the vividness of the scene to the inner consciousness of the prisoner, who then, without sigh or gasp or convulsive movement of any kind, dropped her head and gently slid from her upright position far over toward her official companion, her face blue-red with congestive symptoms, an inert, consciousless mass of inanimate flesh.

It was quite half a minute after her condition was clearly seen from my seat ere the not over-bright deputy sheriff appreciated the gravity of the situation, and sat her up that he might vigorously fan her.

MR. MOODY: "ON THIS THIRD HATCHET IS A NEW BREAK"

It was some little time before she came to, and then her face was as pale as marble.

It is no joke for any one to sit in that court room, although the sheriff limits sitters by the number of the seats, keeps all the windows open and allows no crowding at the doors.

Nevertheless the heat is terrible, the

humidity unendurable and the atmosphere sultriness embodied.

If to an indifferent spectator the situation is trying, what must it be to a woman garbed to her very neck in heavy black, her temperature heightened by at least 10 percent by the wearing of her hat and gloves!

If she were to remove her hat and uncover her hands her comfort would be materially enhanced.

Superuncomfortable, then, as she would be were she an ordinary woman, a spectator and listener only, what must she not endure as Lizzie Borden, the target for every eye, conscious that her old friends and neighbors regard her with suspicion, and knowing that before her very eyes, were she to open them, could be seen the mute evidences of the horrible crime which somebody committed, and of which she is accused.

No wonder she fainted. The only wonder is that she ever recovered.

The interest in this case grows daily. Its purely circumstantial character makes it the chief puzzle of the age.

Carlyle Harris was not in it in comparison, for in the pills he gave his wife there was morphine, a something on which to build.

Here there is nothing, for although neither Lizzie nor her sister were ever permitted to spend any of the parental fortune and although they knew or had reason to believe that their father's will would put them at the mercy of their stepmother, both father and mother were aged people, and in the course of a not over-long time the inheritance must of necessity be theirs.

There was no lover in the case, no marriage dreamed of in which a portion of this world's goods might help along, no possible motive save that which may be surmised as an outgrowth from the not-at-all-concealed dislike between Lizzie and her stepmother.

In view of this unquestioned condition, the confidence of the prosecution seems odd enough, in view of Miss Russell's disclosures of the conversation of the night before, her remarks concerning the paint-covered dress and the finding of the little hatchet and tell-tale broken handle.

The cow, whose mooing was a conspicuous, not to say a continuous interruption of the proceedings on Monday, was noticeable by reason of her absence, and we were compelled to rely solely upon the high sheriff's pencil rappings and the inharmonious snores of weary yokels for enliventment of the court's proceedings.

At the close of Mr Moody's very well received opening, the first witness, Mr Thomas Kiernan, a civil engineer from Fall River, very tall, very straight, with a little tuft of coal black hair in the middle of his forehead, took the stand.

His testimony was purely professional, identifying diagrams of the premises and sundry streets in Fall River, mapped with distances from point to point, that the jury might be able later on to understand how far it was from the house to the police station, and so on.

The examination of Mr Kiernan occupied considerable time and afforded outsiders opportunity to contrast the discomforts of a witness in a Massachusetts court with the conveniences enjoyed in courts held elsewhere.

For instance, it is the custom in New York for witnesses to sit in a chair placed on a dais at the side of the judge's bench, where, at his ease, he can listen to, ponder and answer questions slung at him by the lawyers.

Here he is compelled to stand behind a two-foot rail, with no possibility of a seat even if he were kept literally, as well as technically, on the stand for hours or days.

The testimony of the witness was suspended about noon in order that the jury might go in a body to Fall River to view the premises, they first being, in the language of the learned chief justice, "suffered to partake of luncheon."

Through the red-hot streets, beneath the rays of a boiling, blistering sun, the 12 unfortunates were marched to the hotel, where they were served with good New England provender first, and then, attended by Mr Moody on behalf the commonwealth, and Mr Jennings, in behalf of the prisoner, they started for Fall River by train.

It was Miss Borden's right to go with them had she so chosen; but, by the advice of her counsel, she waived the right, preferring to seek the comfort of her pleasant room in jail, and partake of the substantial physique sustainers invariably provided for her by her attentive host.

With great form and ceremony the party were met by the Fall River police and escorted through the streets trod by Mr Borden the morning of his murder, and thence taken to the house, the sole inmates of which are Miss Emma Borden, who might much better have been with her sister when she fainted in court this afternoon, and her servant.

No person save the party and a few of us were permitted to enter either yard or house, which, by the way, was as cheerful and as homelike a place as can be found in many a mile.

It was a kind of holiday in Fall River to the population, to which were added many hundreds from adjacent towns who teamed it in hope to have a look at Lizzie, or, at all events, to enjoy a guying glance at their fellow-citizens, the unfortunate jurors.

From her own point of view Miss Borden was doubtless wise in not accompanying this scrutinizing party, but one can readily imagine the constraint which her presence would have put upon every man with a head on his shoulders and a heart in his breast.

Howard

The New York Times

LIZZIE BORDEN IN A FAINT

OVERCOME BY THE PROSECUTION'S STORY OF THE MURDER.

Second Day of the Great Trial at New-Bedford—The State Opens Its Case and Examines One Witness—Great Crowds About the Court House—Jury Goes to Fall River and Takes a Careful View of the Borden House and Its Surroundings.

NEW-BEDFORD, Mass., June 6.-The trial of Lizzie Borden for the murder of her father and stepmother was continued to-day. A few spectators were admitted into the court chamber, but hundreds sought admission in vain. Today, as yesterday, when the trial opened, great crowds surrounded the Court House and gazed at the brick wall of the building, as though by so doing they might gain some slight information of the celebrated trial in progress within. There were no empty seats in the courtroom, though there was by no means a crowd.

The majority of the spectators were men, but a score or more of women were in attendance.

After the reading of the indictment the outline of the Government's case was given by District Attorney William H. Moody, a young man with an earnest and impressive air.

The prisoner sat behind the Deputy Sheriff and listened to Mr. Moody's careful address with the closest attention, as calm and unmoved as ever. Her eyes looked straight toward the speaker. Indeed, the spectators seemed as much interested in the prosecutor's words as did Miss Borden, and but for the uniformed Sheriff sitting beside her she might have been taken by a stranger for one of those who had come to the courtroom with no greater interest than that of curiosity.

It was a great surprise, therefore, to everybody when just as Mr. Moody finished speaking Miss Borden fell back in her chair in a faint.

Mr. Moody's exposition of the circumstances attending the murder of the Bordens was clear and succinct, and he evidently left a favorable impression on the minds of the jury.

In reference to the cause of the murder, Mr. Moody said:

"There was or came to be between prisoner and stepmother an unkindly feeling. From the nature of the case it will be impossible for us to get anything more than suggestive glimpses of this feeling from outsiders. The daughters thought that something should be done for them by way of dividing the property after they had learned that the stepmother had been amply provided for. Then came a division and ill-feeling, and the title of "mother" was dropped."

The prosecution would show, Mr. Moody said, that when a dressmaker of the family had spoken of the stepmother as "mother", Lizzie had chided her and said:

"Don't call her mother; we hate her; she's a mean spiteful thing."

"When," said Mr. Moody, "an officer was seeking information from the prisoner, right in sight of the woman who had sunken under the assassin's blows, and asked, "When did you last see your mother?" the reply came from Lizzie:

" 'She isn't my mother; my mother died when I was an infant.' "

It would be shown, continued Mr. Moody, that there was an impassable barrier built up between the daughters and the stepmother, socially and by locks and bars.

For two hours the attorney spoke, calling attention to the constant presence of the prisoner in the house that morning, of her careless and indifferent demeanor after the crime, and of the various incriminating incidents which marked her conduct.

Then calmly and deliberately he delivered his peroration:

"The time for hasty and inexact reasoning is past. We are to be guided from this time forth by the law and the evidence only. I adjure you gentlemen to keep your minds in the same open attitude which you have maintained to-day to the end. When that end comes, after you have heard the evidence on both sides, the arguments of the counsel and the instruction of the court, God forbid that you should step one step against the law or beyond the evidence.

"But if your minds, considering all these circumstances, are irresistibly brought to the conclusion of the guilt of the prisoner, we ask you in your verdict to declare her guilty. By so doing, shall you make true deliverance of the great issue which has been submitted to you."

As the District Attorney ceased speaking the prisoner, who, with her face covered by the fan, had sat motionless for the last hour, suddenly succumbed to the strain that had been put upon her nervous system and lost consciousness. The Rev. Mr. Jubb, sitting directly in front of her and separated only by the dock rail, turned to her assistance, and Mr. Jennings, the attorney, hurried to the place from his position. Smelling salts and water were brought into immediate requisition, and soon entire consciousness returned.

Boston Daily Globe

LIZZIE BORDEN SWOONED

Sensational Incident in the New Bedford Court Room Yesterday.

Dist.-Atty. Moody's Opening Address for the Government - Intimation That Nobody Outside the Household Committed the Murders - Particular Stress Upon the Dress Burning Charge - Skulls of the Murdered Couple Exhibited Three Axes Shown - Blade of One Fits the Wound - Jury's Trip to the Scene of the Tragedy.

NEW BEDFORD, June 6.—Miss Lizzie Borden fainted in court to-day, and thus brought into clearer view the singular and awful misery of her position. There she sat and is to sit for weeks, alone in the open middle of the court room, as nearly like a pilloried criminal as it is possible for a woman to be, now that there are no actual pillories. Whatever she may have done she is a woman, a being who for thirty-two of the thirty-three years of her life pursued the quiet and sheltered routine of a maiden of good family and comfortable circumstances in a little town. She was wholly respectable all her life, with respectable surroundings, family, and friends, and with the gentle but invulnerable guardianship that comes to such a daughter in such circumstances. Her rounds are even narrower and quieter than those of most girls of her degree. If she is guilty, she must now be suffering the torture of dreadful anxiety, as well as remorse, for remorse is certainly the portion of such a creature. If she is innocent, fancy the horror of her plight, seated there as the most public and notorious character in New England, and listening to the minutest details and the most complete description of the crime that she was the first to discover and that bereft her of her father.

The strain which her situation produces on intelligent minds is felt by all who are connected with the court. They admit it. They talk of Hester Prynne and Jeannie Deans and of other women whose fearful experiences are suggested by this girl's misery.

But though Miss Borden fainted to-day her nerve is questioned by no one. Of a phlegmatic nature she sits like a graven image by the hour, except for the motion of the hand which plies her fan. In two days she has not been seen to alter the position she has first assumed when taking her chair each day. Occasionally she rests her head upon the rail above the back of the chair, but in the main it is only her eyes that she moves.

These reveal her intelligence and the activity of her mind. With them she sees every person and movement around her, and with them she shows how intently she is listening to all that is said. There came a time to-day, when the horrors of the butcheries of her people were being described, when she would put her fan before her face. She kept it there a long time. It seemed that she had fallen asleep, for her eyes were closed. It was found that she was unconscious. She had fainted, but with no theatricalism. With the same undemonstrativeness that is her peculiarity she had yielded to more than she could endure. One thing is certain, she has no art. Another is that her conduct is as consistent with innocence as with guilt.

The court room was not above two-thirds full and yet the imitation New York policeman at the gate seemed to have no crowd to battle with. The community is evidently used to this practical, business-like court, which refuses to recognize the wishes or even the existence of those not concerned in the trial. "The people must read the papers," says the Sheriff, and down in the town the people resignedly echo the remark and say: "We will have to read the papers." Thus it came that the tiny little court room only sheltered 120 persons this morning. The same dark red and light pink carnations were on the desk. The three grim and grizzled Judges sat behind them. The blue cloth and brass buttons of the swallow-tail coats of the sheriffs were again conspicuous, and the two groups of lawyers reassembled around their separate tables. Miss Lizzie Borden took her accustomed seat in the middle of the room, where fifty-eight persons could look into her face and sixty others could only see her hat and her glossy black hair. She wore the same black dress in which she appeared on the first day of the trial. Her heavy plain face, distinctly maidenly and younger than her years warrant, was lighted by a brighter sparkle in her eyes than on the first day.

The proceedings took on a funereal tone from the first and kept it to the end. Three men did nearly all the talking, and all adopted

DIST. ATTY. MOODY SHOWS LIZZIE BORDEN'S SKIRT TO THE JURY

subdued, sad voices. The first lugubrious tones were those of Mr. Borden, the aged Clerk of the court, who arose to put Miss Borden to the bar in technical language and to read the bill of her indictment for the crimes with which she is charged. It was a solemn and old-fashioned document, that kept on saying to Miss Borden that she "feloniously, wilfully, and with malice aforethought did do murder." It ended by the Clerk addressing to the jury this statement: "She has before pleaded not guilty, and put herself upon her country, which country you are."

Then William H. Moody, the Essex county District Attorney, who is assisting the local attorney, arose to open the case for the Commonwealth. He walked over to the railing close in front of the jurors, and addressed them in a low and confidential manner, and a melancholy tone. In most other States he would have sought to have impressed the court room audience, but in Massachusetts the people are little considered. They must read the newspapers. Mr. Moody did not cover himself with forensic glory. He seemed very much constrained and ill at ease. He attempted to explain the complicated arrangement of the Borden house, and was very clumsy and confusing. He made no pretence of eloquence, but talked as one man might to another. Perhaps it was that he was sensitive to the delicacy of his task and did not want to be cruel or too plain with respect to the prisoner. For that he deserved great credit. He was most considerate. He ascribed all the villainy of the murder to the person he always called "the assailant." At the very end he said that the Government believes Miss Borden to be that assailant.

The general opinion here is that Mr. Moody made a stronger case against Miss Borden than the public had any knowledge of. He brought out some notable new points. He promised to prove that Miss Borden did not wear the dress at the time the neighbors arrived that she is said to have had on at the time of the murder, and he told a dramatic story of an occasion two or three days after the murder when Miss Borden tore up and put in the stove one of her best dresses. She said it was covered with paint and when her friend, Miss Russell, told her that she wouldn't tear up the dress where people might see her Miss Borden only moved back a little way out of sight from the door.

Then, again, Mr. Moody promised to prove that no person outside the family could have entered the Borden house between the night before the murder and its occurrence. Not even Mr. Borden could get into it when he came there to his death, and when his wife was already butchered up stairs.

There was a little dramatic quality to the scene when the axes and hatchets were brought in and rattled together and shown to the jury. They were the old, historic implements of the case, and, being exhibited, were set aside as of no importance. Then Mr. Moody brought out another one, the mere blade of a hatchet without a handle, and sought to impress the jury that with this the bloody deed was done.

For more than half an hour Miss Borden listened to the theories of the Government without taking her eyes off Mr. Moody, and yet without looking at him in any marked way. Her attitude and manner were those of a person at a lecture or a sermon. For a still longer time she sat with the edge of a Japanese fan in her mouth, looking now at the floor and again at the speaker. She was experiencing emotions which were not revealed in her face, for her third position was taken by putting her fan against her face and leaving it there during that part of his address in which he described the bloody deeds and drove the crime home to her. It was after he had finished that she fainted.

On the table in front of Mr. Moody was a strange collection of exhibits in the case. There were two blue dresses, a white petticoat, a valise, some parcels, a pile of large photographs, and a number of diagrams, and plans of houses and streets drawn on oiled paper, and printed in white on blue backgrounds. Mr. Moody began by saying that before the jury to-day a woman of good society, possessing a heretofore unquestioned good character, a member of a Christian church, and the own daughter of one of the victims was at that bar accused of murder. He said that Mr. Andrew Jackson Borden, the father, was worth somewhere between $250,000 and $300,000. He had been retired from business for a number of years. He had got his property by earning and saving, and he retained the habit of saving to the close of his life. His home establishment was on what might be called a narrow scale. By his first wife he had two daughters. She died, and he married again twenty-five years before his death. Of this second marriage there was no issue. He was seventy and the second wife was about six years younger. He was a spare, thin man, somewhat tall, and Mrs. Borden was fat and short, weighing in the neighborhood of 200 pounds.

"The house in which these homicides occurred," said Mr. Moody, "had been occupied by the family for some twenty years. There came between the prisoner and her stepmother an unkindly feeling. Those who know most about that feeling, except the prisoner at the bar, are dead, and it is only possible to get glimpses of the cause and extent of that feeling. Mr. Borden had seen fit to do some benefaction for a relative of Mrs. Borden, and in consequence the daughters thought something should be done for them as an offset. The details are unimportant.

"It is significant that enough feeling arose to cause a change of feeling between the prisoner and Mrs. Borden. Up to that time she had addressed her as mother.' After that she ceased to do so. We shall show that some time before the murder a cloak maker at work for the family spoke of Mrs. Borden to the prisoner as her mother. 'Don't call her my mother,' said the prisoner. She is a mean thing, and we hate her.'

"'Don't you go to meals with her?' she was asked.

"Yes, but we have as little to do with her as possible and stay in our own rooms as much as possible."

Mr. Moody said that he knew nothing more significant than another little incident. When one of the officers spoke to the prisoner while her father and mother lay where they had been felled by the blows of an assassin, the officer asked:

"When did you last see your mother?"

"She isn't my mother," said the prisoner, "she is my stepmother—my mother is dead."

Mr. Moody thought the jury would be impressed with the method of living in the Borden household. "It will appear," he said, "that though the family occupied the same house there was built up between certain members by locks, bolts, and bars almost an impassable wall. In the early part of the autumn, the elder sister was away at Fair Haven. The household that was left consisted of Mr. and Mrs. Borden and a servant who had been in the service of the family for nearly three years, Bridget Sullivan, and the prisoner. On Tuesday night an illness occurred in the household. Mr. and Mrs. Borden were taken suddenly ill with a violent retching and vomiting illness, and to a less degree the prisoner was affected. Bridget, the servant, was not. On Wednesday morning Mr. and Mrs. Borden arose feeling as they might after such an illness, and Mrs. Borden consulted a physician. On the morning of Wednesday, the day before the homicides, the prisoner went to a drug store and asked the clerk for 10 cents worth of prussic acid for the purpose of cleaning a seal skin cape. She was told that it could not be sold without a prescription, and after some little talk she went away.

"I think you will be satisfied," said Mr. Moody, "that the person who made application for this deadly poison was the prisoner. Three persons recognized her. Two of them knew her by sight, and the third recognized her at once when he saw her. On the evening of Wednesday the prisoner made a call on a friend, Miss Alice E. Russell, and we shall commend to your careful attention what occurred that evening. The prisoner had been intending to spend her vacation with a party of friends at Marion. The talk between the two started on that topic. The prisoner said that she had made up her mind to go to Marion, and had written that day that she would go. 'But,' she said, I can't help feeling depressed. I can't help thinking that something is going to happen. I can't shake it off. Last night we were all sick. Mr. and Mrs. Borden were quite sick and vomiting, and we were afraid we had been poisoned. The girl did not eat baker's bread, and we did, and we think it might be that.' 'No,' said Miss Russell, 'if it had been that other people would have been sick.' 'Well,' said the prisoner, 'it might have been the milk.' 'What time do you get the milk?' 'Four o'clock in the morning,' said the prisoner. 'It is light then,' said Miss Russell, 'and no one would dare to touch it.' 'Well, that's so,' said the prisoner, 'but father has been having so much trouble with the people he deals with, I am afraid something is going to happen. I expect nothing but that the house will be burned over our heads. The barn has been broken into twice.' 'Well, that was the boys after the pigeons,' said Miss Russell. 'Well,' said the prisoner, 'the house has been broken into when only Maggie (the Bordens called Bridget Sullivan Maggie) and Emma and I were there. The other day I saw a man lurking around the house and when he saw me he ran away. Father had trouble with a man about a store the other day, and they had words and father turned him out.'"

Mr. Moody seemed to be very much impressed with this story, and tried to make it as impressive as possible. Then he said he had come to the most difficult duty he had to perform. It was to describe the Borden house. It was a double tenement, intended for two families. The Bordens have occupied it all. It was on Second street, Fall River, one of the most frequented streets in the city, a street of shops and homes, and the Borden house was but a short distance from the City Hall. There was a rear yard, with a barn in it; and back of that was a high board fence, with a barbed wire stretched across the top. There were three entrances, a front door, a side door on the north side facing Mrs. Churchill's house and leading by a small entry to the kitchen, and a third door exactly in the rear leading to the cellar. The front door hall has doors out of it into the parlor and the sitting room back of the parlor. In the hall is a stairway leading up stairs. From the upper hall open three doors. The first leads to a large closet for dresses, almost large enough for a bedroom. Another leads to the guest chamber, over the parlor. In that chamber Mrs. Borden was murdered. "It is a matter to be carefully considered," said Mr. Moody, "that as you turn upon the stairs going to the second story and as you begin to face into the hall you can look into the door of the guest chamber. The third door leads into the bedroom that was occupied by the prisoner.

"When you have got into this part of the house," said Mr. Moody, "you cannot go anywhere except into the clothes closet, into the guest chamber, or into the room occupied by the prisoner. All access to the other part of the house is closed—not by the natural construction of the house, but by the way in which the house was kept."

To make Mr. Moody's long story very short: Miss Lizzie slept over the sitting room, in which her father was murdered. Miss Emma had to go through Miss Lizzie's room to get to her room. The room in which Mr. and Mrs. Borden slept also adjoined Miss Lizzie's room. There was a door between the two, but Miss Lizzie hooked it on one side and her stepmother belted it on the other. The room of the old couple was over the kitchen, and they had to go through the kitchen and up the back stairs to get to it. The daughters went up the front stairs.

Thus what was practically a wall separated the two generations. The bolts and bars and hooks were fastened always, before, during, and after the murders. Both the old people were murdered in the front of the house, he in the sitting room, under Lizzie's bedroom, and she in the guest chamber, in front of Lizzie's bedroom.

"Who occupied the house on the night before the murder?" Mr. Moody asked. "The person who came in last was the prisoner, and she locked the front door. There are three fastenings on that door. These three fastenings were drawn by the last person in the night before. The door leading to the cellar had been closed by Mrs. Borden, and by the evidence it will be shown that that door was locked during the day of the murder. Bridget came in by the back door and locked it. So when the prisoner and Bridget came in every exit was closed. Now, in the front part of the house that night the prisoner slept in her own room. Mr. Morse, a passing visitor, slept in the guest chamber. Mr. and Mrs. Borden slept in their own room. Bridget slept in her own room in the third story. In the morning Bridget was up first. She went down stairs and into the cellar to get her fuel for building a fire. Then she went to the door and took in the milk. The rear door, I may explain, was a double door, the inside or screen door being kept fastened, while the outside door was open. When opened by Bridget the outside door was opened for the day.

Then Mr. Borden came down stairs. He went out into the yard to empty some slops and then went to the barn. Bridget saw him do that. Bridget did not see Morse until after Mr. and Mrs. Borden had taken breakfast. After breakfast Mr. Morse was first to depart. He went out at 7:45 o'clock, and Mr. Borden let him out and bolted the door behind him. Soon after Morse went away the prisoner came down stairs and began eating what passed for her breakfast in the kitchen. While she was there Mrs. Borden went up stairs, and while up stairs Bridget went out into the yard because she was sick. When she came back Mr. Borden had apparently gone down town. Mrs. Borden was dusting the dining room, while the prisoner was in the kitchen. There was some conversation, we believe, between Mrs. Borden and Bridget about washing windows, and Bridget received her directions. Mrs. Borden disappeared at about that time. It will appear that she thought the prisoner had made the bed in the spare room. She was going up to put two pillow cases on two pillows up there. On the evidence you will be satisfied she never left the room alive, and was killed a few minutes after she went up.

Mr. Moody thought it regrettable that Dr. Bowen was the family physician and was so naturally affected with horror and sympathy that his trained powers of observation failed when he thought Mrs. Borden had died of fright. Miss Borden went through the sitting room, where her father was lying, went up to her room, changed her dress, put on a loose wrapper, and lay down. She told Dr. Bowen she had gone out to get a piece of iron. She told Miss Russell she went to get iron or wire. She told Officer Medley she heard a peculiar noise, something like a scraping noise, and came in and found her father dead. She told Mrs. Churchill she heard a distressing noise.

"As inquiries began to multiply as to her whereabouts, another story comes into view. It is that she went out to the barn and into the loft of the barn to get lead to make sinkers. When she tells one person that she went into the barn to get the lead and to another person she says she came back and looked at the stove to see if the fire was hot enough for her to iron, and then put down her hat and accidentally discovered the homicide, gentlemen, it isn't a difference of words. In one case she tells that she discovers the murders while about her regular duties, and in another case that she heard groans. We will ask you to remember that the 4th of August was one of the hottest days of the last summer in this locality and that the loft of the barn was stifling. Officer Medley was among the first to enter the barn after the tragedy. He had heard the story and went up stairs to the loft. He found when he had touched the floor with his hands that it was thickly covered with dust. Afterward he walked there and found that every footprint was plainly to be seen.

"It is our duty to offer proof to you that Mrs. Borden died before her husband. We have evidence that when Lizzie discovered Mr. Borden's body it showed freshly running blood, and was warm. The blood of Mrs. Borden was coagulated, and the body was stiffened in death. The judgment of professional men who examined the bodies will be presented to you. The stomachs were sent to Prof. Wood and examined and prepared with exactness. Mrs. Borden's stomach contained eleven ounces of food in the process of digestion, one-fifth of which was water and four-fifths solid matter, partly digested. Mr. Borden's stomach contained six ounces, nine-tenths water and one-tenth of solids. The upper intestines of Mrs. Borden contained partly digested food, while Mr. Borden's were empty. Mrs. Borden's lower intestines were empty, while those of Mr. Borden's contained the matter which had been digested long before noon. Upon these facts the experts have determined that Mrs. Borden died at least an hour before her husband."

When Mr. Moody reached this point the impassive prisoner, who had been holding the edge of a fan between her lips for half an hour, motioned for a glass of water. It was brought to her by a deputy sheriff, and she lowered the fan and drank lightly.

"There was blood spattered in every direction," said Mr. Moody, "and it is probable spatters would be impressed on the clothing of the assassin. The clothing has been produced for the inspection of the Commonwealth. It was produced a great many days after the homicides. The clothing said to have been worn by the prisoner on the morning of the murder, shoes, stockings, dress, and skirt, was subjected to the most rigid examination, and it failed to disclose any marks of blood on the dress, but on the skirt that

ATTORNEY JENNINGS AND DIST. ATTY. KNOWLTON VISIT THE BORDEN HOME

THE JURY GOES TO FALL RIVER TO VIEW THE BORDEN PREMISES

examination revealed one spot of blood which I don't think it worth while to call your attention to at the present time.

On the morning of Sunday Miss Russell came into the kitchen. The officers were about, but none was in the house, and there Miss Russell saw the prisoner with the skirt of a dress on her arm and what appeared to be its waist on a shelf near her side."

At this point all in the court room listened with new interest. It was suspected that Miss Borden's close friend had been assisting the Government against her, but no one was prepared for the startling information she had given the law officers. Miss Borden seemed unmindful of the importance of the news. She looked on as calmly and imperturbably as before.

"It was a cotton dress and not a silk dress," said Mr. Moody, to distinguish it from the silk the family doctor thinks she wore. "It was a light blue dress, with fixed navy blue spots in it. You will recall Mrs. Churchill's description of it. As she saw the prisoner standing by the stove Miss Emma turned and said: 'What are you going to do?' 'I'm going to burn this dress. It is all covered with paint.' Miss Russell turned away.

"She came again into the room and found the prisoner standing with the waist of the dress, and apparently tearing it apart. She said: 'Lizzie, I would not do that where people can see me.' The only consequence of that was that the prisoner stepped a little back and went on tearing her dress."

This was brand-new evidence, and apparently much the most damaging to the prisoner of all that has been brought forward. It fell upon the ears of the people in court like a lightning flash. "On another day," said Mr. Moody, "Miss Russell said: 'Lizzie, I am afraid that burning that dress was the worst thing you could have done.' 'Oh, why did you let me do it?' the prisoner replied. A considerable search was made by the officers for weapons, and they say no clothing unconcealed and covered with paint could have escaped observation."

From that point the District Attorney took up the subject of the weapons, and announced that the Government meant to lay open all the evidence it possessed at that time. An attendant brought in two axes and two hatchets and they were shown to the jury and disposed of with an explanation showing that they could not have been the weapons with which the bloody deeds were committed. Then Mr. Moody produced his second sensational disclosure. He began by saying: "On the day of the homicide another weapon or part of a weapon was found and attracted little attention."

As he spoke the young attorney held up the handleless blade of a little hatchet of precisely the sort that is kept in almost every dwelling for chopping kindling wood. "It was covered with an adhesion of dust—not the fine but the coarse dust of ashes. This adhered to all sides of it more or less. Both sides were rusty."

It was at this point that the prisoner ceased fanning herself and put her fan to her face, hiding it from nearly all in the room. Behind her fan she closed her eyes as if she was wearied with so much monotony which she found in the proceedings. "Prof. Wood will say," the young lawyer went on, "that while the fragments of the wood of the newly broken handle would render traces of blood, that on a smooth weapon blood could be easily and effectually and completely removed." Just then Mr. Jennings, of counsel of the accused, got up, and, taking the hatchet blade in his hands, examined it carefully. "The fact," continued Mr. Moody, "unquestionably as told by the skulls of the victims is, that the weapons were sharp. Another fact is unmistakably told by Mr. Borden's skull. It is that the weapon was just exactly three and a half inches on the blade—no more and no less. That is exactly the measure of that weapon. The Government does not insist that the homicide was done with this handleless weapon. It may have been. It may well have been.

The bloody weapon was not found on or beside the victims. "You will consider whether these were the acts of a bloody villian fleeing through the streets at noonday or of an inmate of the house, familiar with its means of obliteration and concealment. Nothing was disturbed, no property was taken, no drawers were ransacked.

"Mr. Borden had on his person a considerable sum of money, as well as a watch and chain. There was nothing to indicate an assault on the woman for lustful purposes. There was not a sign of a struggle. The assailant had been able to approach each victim by daylight, and, without struggle or outcry, to lay them low. Mrs. Borden was prostrate, her face on the floor and her head hacked to pieces. Some of the blows were delivered with great force, some with vacillating weakness. Mr. Borden was reclining on a sofa in the sitting room. Apparently he passed away from life into death without a struggle, and his head, too, bore the same marks."

In his peroration Mr. Moody went hastily over the main points in his argument, and then said: "There was no other human being there except the prisoner. The acts were those of a human being, the acts of a person who must have had a familiar knowledge of the premises and whereabouts and habits of those persons in occupation of the house at that time. I ask if any other reasonable hypothesis except that of the guilt of this prisoner can account for these murders on that morning."

It was 11 o'clock when he ended his presentation of the Commonwealth's case. The black figure of the prisoner had not attracted attention during the preceding half hour. She had been sitting with the great Japanese fan close against her face. Only the correspondent of THE SUN and the deputy sheriff beside her could see behind the fan.

Two or three minutes passed and the fan and the arm that held it up dropped upon the prisoner's lap. Her head was back against the rail, her eyes were shut, her mouth was open, and her breast heaved with very long breaths.

"Lizzie Borden's asleep," was the whisper that galloped through the court room. Deputy Sheriff Kirby, who sat beside her, took friendly alarm at such disrespectful behavior, and tried to awaken her before the Court should see her. He shook her arm. He might as well have shaken a pump handle. Her head rolled over so that her cheek rested on the rail at right angles to the line of her body. A purple cast came over her face. Kindly Mr. Kirby looked alarmed and helpless. City Missionary Jubb of Fall River was sitting near by, and sprang to his feet and began to fan her.

A Deputy Sheriff came quickly with a glass of water. After a little she regained partial consciousness. Mr. Jubb ordered her somewhat sharply to find her smelling salts. Her hand went into her pocket mechanically and came out with a little cut glass bottle in it.

Then she put both hands on the arms of the chair and fell back against the railing, not half over her faint. Mr. Jubb was applying the smelling salts, and was so much in earnest that her breath went from her, and she put up her hand to push the bottle away. In another minute her eyes opened, and she heard Mr. Jubb advising her to drink some water, which she did. Sheriff Wright, in the mean time, began rapping on his desk for order. The people crept back into their seats, and the episode ended with Miss Borden leaning her head against the rail, with her eyes shut, while every one wondered whether she was going to faint again.

This was at 7 minutes past 11. The jury came back, and Mr. Moody called the first witness. He was a young Fall River civil engineer named Thomas Kieran. He was questioned about the distances between various points in Fall River, as, for instance, how far it was from the Borden house to the city hall and to the police station, and from that station to another.

It turned out that he had drawn the diagrams and house plans which were to be entered as exhibits in the case. His work now was to verify and swear to them. He was the servant of the Commonwealth, but Miss Borden's lawyers took a great deal of interest in his testimony.

When he left the stand District Attorney Knowlton moved that the jury be directed to go to Fall River and take a view, not only of the interior and exterior of the Borden house, but of such other points as it might be of value for them to see.

Gov. Robinson arose and said something to the Court about its being the right and privilege of Miss Borden to accompany the Jury to Fall River. He walked over to where the prisoner sat, and talked to her for a minute.

Then he said out loud that while she was, of course, entitled to accompany the jury, she did not desire to do so. She did not feel able, and would waive all her rights. "I state this in her presence," said the ex-Governor.

He ordered the Sheriff to designate four officers to go with the jury. The Sheriff stood up in his little box and named four men with good old Yankee names.

These four, in their blue shad-bellied coats, formed a line before the jury box and held up their hands in the way that an oath is administered in Massachusetts where the Bible is not used in court. Clerk Borden swore them upon the oath that they were to allow no persons except Mr. Moody for the Commonwealth and Mr. Jennings for the defence to speak to them while they were away.

They were going to trot out with the twelve jurors when the Chief Justice made them pause.

"I desire to say," said he, "that this view is not at all for the purpose of taking testimony. You will only observe the physical objects of the view. Counsel will only direct your attention to such objects. It will not be proper for you to ask questions, or for the counsel to make any statements. You are to keep all together, and all are to see what any of you see."

The last words of the proceedings in the second day of the trial were added by the Chief Justice: "The officers will now suffer the jury to partake of luncheon." Suffering the poor chaps to eat was a new way to put it.

Miss Borden was taken back to the jail, and there sat and chatted with the Master of the House of Correction while the noonday change of guards was being made.

Mr. Josiah Hunt, the Master, is a notable man in this place, and deserves to be for he is a true gentleman, dignified, courteous, kindly, and able. He had no idea Lizzie had swooned, and nothing in her behavior suggested it. She chose for a topic in their talk to-day the fact that she was fond of books. He offered to lend her some, but she said she had plenty and was then engaged in reading one of Charles Dickens's novels. She is very fond of Dickens, she said. She spoke heartily, and there seemed nothing the matter with her. Mr. Hunt finds her an every-day, sensible woman, not gay or lively, but calm and yet of good spirits.

Certainly not one has shown her a kindness in the court room, not one has sat by her or spoken to her, and to-day, when she swooned, though there were twenty-one women in the room, not one went to her or showed any concern or sympathy during the excitement.

FALL RIVER, Mass., June 6.—About 1:30 o'clock the Borden jury walked to the Borden house and were admitted with the four men who had charge of them. Also accompanying them into the house were District Attorneys Knowlton and Moody, Gov. Robinson, and Mr. Jennings.

Assistant Marshal Fleet and Lieut. Edson controlled a posse of men who had been about the house since the morning keeping back the crowds of curiosity seekers.

After the jury had examined carefully the inner part of the Borden house, a survey of the outside adjoining yard was made, the distance from the house to the fence, and the location of the lumber pile were noted, and the barn loft was visited.

The jury filed out from the yard and walked up Second street to Dr. Bowen's house and other points figuring in the trial were shown and looked over. Passing to Third street considerable time was spent in Crowe's stone yard, where masons were at work at the time the murder is alleged to have been committed, and the position and distance of the porch in Dr. Chagnon's house, where the Doctor's daughter was seated at the time of the murder, was also noted. Every place mentioned in the story of the crime, including the Union Bank, were visited. The tour was finished at 4 P. M., and the jury went to a hotel here for the night.

A FANCIFUL ILLUSTRATION TITLED, "*LIZZIE FAINTS AWAY*", USED IN A STORY APPEARING IN "*THE POLICE GAZETTE*", THE MAN'S MAGAZINE OF THE 1890'S.

The New York Times

BRIDGET SULLIVAN A WITNESS

THE BORDENS' SERVANT TELLS HER STORY OF THE MURDERS.

Her Testimony Establishes the Presence of Lizzie in the House at the Time the Crime Was Committed—She Weakens the State's Case, However, by Declaring that Lizzie and Her Stepmother Lived Together Peaceably—The Prisoner's Uncle Also Testifies.

NEW-BEDFORD, Mass., June 7.-Properly speaking, this was the first day of the Borden trial, for, while the two previous days had been occupied in the preparation of preliminaries, this day was marked by the rapid presentation of testimony. The progress made was marked, and was entirely in keeping with the course presaged by the prompt selection of the jury.

Judges and attorneys are alike interested in securing celerity, and the trial will now proceed as rapidly as possible to its conclusion.

The witnesses of the day comprised a number of persons who testified in relation to Andrew Borden's presence in the business portion of the city half an hour before his murder. John V. Morse, uncle of the prisoner, and Bridget Sullivan also testified.

Bridget Sullivan was the strongest witness of the day, but while her testimony placed Lizzie Borden, the accused, in the home at the hour of the murders, the effect of it was weakened by the statement, reiterated with emphasis, that between the accused and her stepmother there had never been, to witness's knowledge, an unkind word.

The Government needs a motive and must have one in its presentation of its side of the case. Bridget Sullivan helped the District Attorney out a bit on that point.

When she told of the food served at the Borden homestead she laughed, and there was a smile on the lips of the prisoner. Others have been amused at the parsimony of the man whose possessions were more than a quarter of a million, and who fed his family on a diet of mutton and cold mutton and mutton broth.

Again the prisoner laughed when John V. Morse, her uncle, went through some mathematical calculations, the deduction of which was the the prisoner was thirty-three years of age. The latter shook her head vigorously at the assertion, and there spoke the woman.

The weakness of yesterday had vanished, and to-day her strong will was again in evidence. She appeared highly interested in the proceedings, and watched the developments closely. To-morrow it is expected that Medical Examiner Bowen will be a witness and the skulls will be produced.

Proceedings opened with the recall of Mr. Kiernan, the civil engineer, whose examination stopped yesterday when the jury started for Fall River to view the scene of the murder. Mr. Kiernan's testimony was devoted to locating various points upon the Borden place, describing the fences, barns, and outbuildings, explaining the arrangement of the rooms, stairs, and closets. He also gave the results of certain experiments that he had made to determine from what points of view the bodies of Mr. and Mrs. Borden could have been seen.

After Mr. Kiernan came a photographer, who exhibited pictures which he had made of the premises and of the bodies of the murdered man and his wife.

John V. Morse, uncle of the prisoner and brother of Mr. Borden's first wife, was the next witness. Mr. Morse is sixty years old. He lives at South Dartmouth. He said Mr. Borden was first married about forty-seven years ago and had three children by his first wife, one of whom was dead. He said that Lizzie was thirty-three years old and Emma forty-one.

On Wednesday, Aug. 3, last, he went to the Borden house. He had been a visitor there several weeks before. The last time he saw Lizzie before that visit he could not place. He arrived at the Borden house about 1:30 o'clock. He did not see anybody that day except Mr. and Mrs. Borden and Bridget. He ate dinner there that day, but ate it alone. He left the house between 3 and 4 P.M. and got back about 8:30. He entered the front door, having been let in by Mrs. Borden. The door was shut after he went in.

He saw nobody there but the family. He went first into the sitting room and went to bed about 10:30. Mrs. Borden went to bed first, going out of the rear door to the back stairs.

"While we were sitting there," said Mr. Morse, "somebody entered the front door and went up stairs to Lizzie's room. Mr. Borden and I went to bed at the same time, I going into the guest room. The prisoner's room door was closed when I went into my room, but I do not know whether it was locked or not."

The next morning witness was up at 6 o'clock and breakfasted about 7 o'clock with Mr. and Mrs. Borden on mutton, bread, coffee, sugar cakes, and bananas. He didn't recall that there was fried johnny cakes on the table. At 8:40, he left the house and did not return until after the murder. Reaching the back yard he ate part of a pear before going into the house. It was not until after he had seen the bodies of Mr. and Mrs. Borden that he caught sight of Lizzie Borden.

On cross-examination witness said that on reaching the Borden house after the murder he saw no officers in the yard, that the barn door was closed, and he heard no one inside. This contradicted the Government's allegation that officers, by immediate examination of the barn, ascertained that the prisoner could not have been there at the time of the murder.

Witness said that at the first meal Mrs. Borden brought in the food, and he saw nothing of Bridget Sullivan. On the evening previous to the murder both Mr. and Mrs. Borden were sick. Of his own knowledge he did not know whether Bridget was in the house that day or not. He first saw her at breakfast the day of the murder.

Abraham G. Hart, Treasurer of the Union Savings Bank of Fall River, of which Mr. Borden was President, and others were called to show what time Mr. Borden was about town the morning of the murders. Their testimony established that he went toward his home soon after 10:30 o'clock.

Counsel Robinson stated that it was agreed, to save time, that Mr. Borden died intestate, and that his property was estimated between $200,000 and $300,000.

A buzz of excitement went around the room at 12:30, when Mr. Moody called "Bridget Sullivan." She was dressed on a maroon colored, fashionably-made dress, and wore a large hat, with large feather, and black kid gloves. She leaned on the left side against the rail, looked straight at Mr. Moody, and spoke so low that he had to tell her to speak louder. The prisoner changed posture so as to see witness plainly, and watched her steadily with her large eyes wide open.

Bridget said that she had worked for the Bordens for two yuears and ten months doing general housework, but having no care of any sleeping rooms except her own. She remembered Mr. Morse's visit the night before the murder. She remembered, too, that Mr. and Mrs. Borden were ill Wednesday night. She herself felt well until Thursday morning, when she waked up with a headache. She was out Wednesday night until 10:30 o'clock. She entered the house by the back door, and locked and bolted it.

Thursday, the day of the murder, she was up at 6:15 o'clock. She found all doors down stairs just as she had left them the night before. Witness then went on to detail minutely what happened in the house from the time of her getting up until the discovery of the murders.

At 1 o'clock the court took a recess until 2:15.

Resuming her testimony, Bridget Sullivan said that after Mr. and Mrs. Borden and Mr. Morse had finished their breakfast Lizzie Borden came to the kitchen and said that she would have coffee and cookies for her breakfast. Bridget left Lizzie in the kitchen and went outdoors feeling ill. When she came back there was nobody in the kitchen. She fastened the screen door on the inside as she came in.

About 9 o'clock Mrs. Borden told her to wash the windows, and she went to work at once obeying the order. Her work took her first to the front of the house, where she spent some time washing the outside of the parlor windows. She passed from the front of the house to the barn several times, and also entered the kitchen. At no time did she see any stranger about the premises.

She opened the door for Mr. Borden when he came in from down town. There were several locks on the door.

"I was so bothered with those locks," said Bridget, "that I said: 'Oh, pshaw!' and Lizzie, who was either at the head of the stairs or in her room, laughed at me."

"When I let Mr. Borden in," continued the witness, "he did speak to me. He had a parcel in his hand. When he came into the dining room he sat in a chair at the head of the lounge and I went on washing my windows. Miss Lizzie came down stairs about five minutes after, and went into the dining room. I heard her ask her father if he had any mail, and she told him Mrs. Borden had received a note and had gone out. Then Mr. Borden took the key of his bedroom door and went up the back stairs. When he came down soon after he took a rocking chair in the sitting room, and I went on washing my windows, this time in the dining room.

"When I was doing this Lizzie came into the room, took an ironing board from the kitchen and placed it in position. She asked me if I was going out that afternoon and I said I did not think I was. She says, 'Well, if you do, be sure and lock the doors, for Mrs. Borden has gone out on a sick call, and I may go out myself.'

"Then I went up to my room and lay down. The first notice I took of any time was when I heard the City Hall clock strike 11. I think I had been there three or four minutes. Don't think I went to sleep. Heard no noise. Am able to hear the opening and closing of the screen door if it is done by a careless person.

"The next thing I heard was when Lizzie called me to come down, as her father was dead; that was at least fifteen minutes after."

Counsel asked witness to describe the dress Lizzie had on that morning, but objections stopped an answer. She remembered a light-blue dress with a sprig on it of darker blue, bought the previous Spring.

Continuing her narrative, witness said:

"When I heard the outcry from Lizzie I went down stairs and first saw Lizzie; I cannot tell what dress she had on that morning. When

A view of Pleasant Street in Lizzie Borden's Fall River

I came down the back way the wooden door was open, and she was leaning against the door. The screen door was shut, but I could not tell whether it was hooked or not. I went to go into the sitting room, and she said:

" 'Oh, Maggie'--I was sometimes called by that name--'I've got to have a doctor right away. I was out in the back yard, and when I came in the screen door was open and I found father dead. Do you know where Miss Russell lives?'

"I did not, and she told me. I didn't find Dr. Bowen. Then I went to the corner of Borden and Second Streets for Miss Russell and she was not there. Then I found where she did live and tald her what Lizzie wanted. I guess I ran to Dr. Bowen's but I don't know. When I came back I found Mrs. Churchill. I said, when I came back, that if I knew where Mrs. Whitehead lived I would go and tell Mrs. Borden, if she was there, that Mr. Borden was very sick, and Lizzie said:

" 'Oh, Maggie! I am almost sure I heard her come in; go upstairs and see if she is there.'

"I said, 'I will not go up stairs alone,' and Mrs. Churchill went up with me.

"When I got far enough on the stairs to see into the room I saw the body on the floor and ran in and stood by the foot of the bed. The door was wide open.

On cross-examination Bridget said:

"I never saw or heard anything out of the way in the family relations, and during my nearly three years of service everything was pleasant. There were times when the girls did not eat at the same table with their parents most of the time. They rarely arose when the old people got up. There were times when they ate alone, or separately. Lizzie and her mother always spoke to each other.

"I heard them all talking in the sitting room that morning, and Mrs. Borden asked Lizzie some questions and she answered them civilly and properly. So far as I could see, they lived congenially and pleasantly. I waited on the table when all were there, and they conversed usually in a pleasant manner.

Speaking of the intercourse between Mr. Borden and his daughter just before the murder witness asked her what was the matter and Lizzie said, "Come down quickly, Maggie; father is killed."

Asked if she had stated this the same way before, if she had not used the word "dead", the witness replied she could not remember; it was all the same, anyhow; he was dead.

"When I got back," witness said, "from going after the people, I found Mrs. Churchill there and Dr. Bowen. Lizzie was on the lounge. Her dress was free from spots of blood and her hair was not disarranged."

At the close of Bridget Sullivan's examination, at 4:55, the court adjourned.

UNDER FIRE.

Bridget Sullivan on Witness Stand.

Her Story Occupies Several Hours.

She Tells of the Finding of the Bodies.

Lizzie Borden Calmly Hears Rehearsal of Facts.

Uncle Morse Also Goes Into Details.

Bank Officers Help to Fix the Time.

NEW BEDFORD, June 7—"Come down, Bridget, run for the doctor; father is killed," was the first intimation, according to Bridget Sullivan, given by the woman accused of the terrible crime, an investigation of which now interests the civilized world.

As is always the case, the chief interest in these celebrated cases attaches itself to the personalities involved—some as accessories, others as witnesses. The reading public throughout the land are as familiar with the name Bridget Sullivan as with that of Lizzie Borden. Save to a very few, her disappearance from the Borden premises two days after the tragedy, and her whereabouts since that day, have been a mystery. She was seen at the inquest, but her residence and occupation have until today been a closed book to the general public.

As a matter of fact, she was brought to New Bedford and turned over to the custody of the local jailer, in whose family she has been detained as a witness for the commonwealth. I studied her carefully for an hour or so. She is a woman of strong characteristics. Enamored as she was of Lizzie Borden, and pleased with her place in the Borden household, it would have been no easy matter to induce her to testify against the interests of the accused.

I inferred from her manner and speech upon the witness stand, first, that she is firmly resolved to say nothing which in her judgment can injure her younger mistress; second, that she has been so frightened, not alone by the developments in the house by her examinations, that she will keep within the hither verge of exact truth as she remembers it, and save herself embarrassment by getting behind the phrase, "I don't remember," and third, that during her long stay and virtually confinement in the family of jailer Hunt she has become so permeated with the ideas of the prosecution that she really doesn't know whether she stands on her head or her heels.

With customary pomp the high sheriff, who in private life is one of the most genial of men, conducted the three judges to the court house, rapped the audience into silence with a wave of his hand, announced the court, at which every one in the room rose and bowed to the three judges, who, standing in the bench, bowed, exchanged commonwealth recognitions with the venerable clerk, Mr Borden, and suffered the proceedings to begin.

Chief Justice Mason tells me that in other days capital cases were tried before a full bench only, but the growth of population necessitated such tremendous dockets that the supreme court was permitted to try such cases with two judges only. Recently the superior court was authorized to try this class of cases, but three judges were deemed desirable.

In reply to a question as to the necessity of the associate justices, it being the practice in New York and elsewhere to try capital cases before a single judge, he said the associates had much more to do than ordinary observers would imagine. They are consulted on all points of law and as a general thing it is the practice for one or the other of them to deliver the charge to the jury.

It is evident that neither the chief justice, Mr Mason, nor his associates, Judge Blodgett or Judge Dewey, are enamored of the capital crime. I judge them to be quick witted men of keen sensibilities. Their intellectuality of New England type, their personal characters, tastes and preferable pursuits, such as would naturally incline them from investigations of this nature. They are precisely the kind of a trio an innocent man would like to be tried by, and if I were guilty I should hope after careful study of their benignant countenances for merciful consideration and humanitarian judgment.

JOHN VINNICUM MORSE

Surveyor Kieran was recalled today and examined at some length with the aid of diagrams, and cross-examined, also, for the purpose of showing that Lizzie could not have seen her mother's body, which was lying under the bed in the guest chamber when she went upstairs.

From the examination it was evident that immediately after the homicides both the prosecution and the defense were alert in procuring measurements, distances, diagrams, plans, photographs and models. The examination of this witness was long and tedious, so much so that the learned justices appeared bored, as did the audience.

Lizzie alone maintained an unflagging interest, her hacking cough serving to stimulate curiosity as to her condition. It seemed odd enough to see this little woman unattended by one of her sex to support her while she endured the merciless scrutiny of the old women and maidens who stared and stared as though she was a petrification or a mummy from the pyramids of Egypt.

In the audience at this time were Congressman Randall of this district and Rising Sun Morse, also a congressman. Brother Morse is very bald, but he brushes his hair a la Talmage, and comforts himself in life by perpetually stroking his long side-whiskers with a well-shaped hand, on the little finger of which sparkles an enormous diamond.

A number of colored brothers, mostly in spectacles, representing the local bar, sat within the inclosure, imparting a decidedly interesting feature to the occasion.

The second witness was a photographer from Fall River, who exhibited some disgusting pictures, or rather horrid photographs of the Borden bodies; some as they were first discovered, others as mutilated and distorted they lay upon the dissecting table, and others which I don't care to describe. These were not only exhibited, but dwelt upon with what appeared unnecessary detailment, pregnant suggestions of what may be expected when the skulls from the beheaded bodies are exhibited in all their ghastliness as evidences of the brutality of the assassinations.

The first genuine stir of the morning was caused by the appearance of uncle Morse, a tall, farmer looking individual, 60 years of age, full bearded, but without mustache. He, it will be remembered, is a brother of the first Mrs Borden, and therefore own uncle to the Borden girls.

He slept in the guest chamber the night before the murder, and it was under his bed that the hacked and bloody body of his sister's successor was discovered. He was asked a multitudinosity of questions about the marriages, first and second, the ages of everybody in any way connected with the household, and a tediosity of apparently irrelevant questions as to what they had for breakfast, who cooked it, whether the door which was shut was locked, where the servants whom he didn't see at all slept, and where he passed the day preceding and subsequent to the murder. He was asked and replied at least a half dozen times as to the breakfast table, what kind of ware was on it, whether they had knives and forks, and whether the servant was called by bell or voice.

Bridget was asked the same questions, and it puzzles a mere layman who heard them both to testify three or four times that they had mutton, cakes, fruit, bread and coffee, to understand why they should be compelled to tell that all over again.

But he did, and so did Bridget.

According to uncle Morse, Mr and Mrs Borden and he breakfasted alone, after which he went out about some chores in town, and on returning to the house was informed of the tragedy. He saw Mr Borden first in the sitting room, and then as he went up the stairs he distinctly saw Mrs Borden lying under the bed on which he had slept the night before. This is considered a point by the prosecution, who claim that if Mr Morse could see the body Lizzie could, and therefore should have seen it when she went up the stairs.

Gov Robinson made his first practical appearance in the case today in cross-examination of some of the witnesses. He has a mild, pleasant countenance, a small but kindly eye, a kind of a mustache, a confidential manner and a rotund stomach which he emphasizes as he stands by throwing it out into unnecessary prominence. As a seducer into unwitting admissions, the governor is a charm, and would appear from his happy, go-lucky manner, a most taking manner by the way, that he has done well in switching from civil to criminal practice. It has been all along the cue of the prosecution to claim that the Borden household was run on miserliness, and the girls were annoyed and dissatisfied and half starved, constantly interfered with, scolded, until determined to be rid of it all Lizzie committed the frightful deed.

Gov Robinson developed in his confidential way from Mr Morse that the breakfast was particularly good, that there was nothing mean or stingy about it, that he and his host ate all they wanted and plenty of it, that when the servant was needed she was called by the bell, and so far as witness knew everything was as it should be in a well-regulated New England home.

In accordance with custom the chief justice gave the jurors a recess for a few minutes, during which nearly every one read the papers and Lizzie chatted pleasantly with her counsel, with Rev Mr Judd and with other friends. Perfect order was maintained during the recess, as it was conspicuously from the opening to the close of the court.

It would be impossible to conceive a more absolute picture of urbanity and dignity than that presented by the judges on the bench, leading up to a revelation of the same characteristics in sheriff Wright, clerk Borden and their respective subordinates. The deputy sheriffs wear a uniform blue dress coat, vest and trousers, the coat elegantized by velvet collar and brass buttons. They are not only respectful but respectable, and the old bay state has no cause to blush for its superior court as held and disciplined in New Bedford city.

Bridget Sullivan was a sensation. All manner of stories have been told concerning her peculiar intimacy and friendship for Lizzie Borden and her regard for the family in general. So it was interesting to note the curiosity of the New Bedfordites and the Fall Riverites as to the bent her mind would take under the promptings of the district attorney and cross-examination of Gov Robinson.

Bridget is very tall and spare, with an intelligent but not refined face, a good eye, a prominent nose, and a mouth indicating a love for the good things of life. She wore a black hat and gloves and a brown dress, fastened, as is the custom in this part of the world, with a brooch at the neck.

She is 26 years old, and seven years here. Somewhat unnecessarily she testified that she is Irish. Her residence with the Bordens of two years and nine months familiarized her with their affairs, and she gave a very interesting story and verbal photograph of the life of that household.

They kept no man, but had an occasional choreworker in and about the barn, which of late years, however, since the horse was sold, was not much used. Bridget did no chamber work, but confined her efforts to the washing, ironing and cooking lines. She had no knowledge of who attended to

BRIDGET "MAGGIE" SULLIVAN

the chamber work in rooms beyond that she did not herself. According to her story, every man and woman was his or her own chambermaid, and it will be recalled that on the morning of the murder, when Mr Borden went down to his breakfast, he carried what is graphically told as his slop pail with him.

It appears that Bridget had a clock in her room, and on both direct and cross-examination she was questioned as to the age, the kind, the whereabouts, the habits and the usefulness of that clock until the situation became grotesque and embarrassing and the subject ran down to nothingness.

The clock had nothing whatever to do with her going to bed at night, nor with her getting up in the morning, nor with the murder of the Bordens, but it served the learned brothers as a peg on which to hang a very wardrobe of verbia gistic nonsense.

An immensity of detail was drawn from Bridget as to Mr Borden's movements on the morning of the murder; when he came down, what he brought with him, what he had for breakfast, repeated and repeated who cooked the breakfast, when he went into the yard, what he went for, how long he remained and other revelations which had nothing whatever to do with the fact that after he returned from his morning routine some one as yet undiscovered killed him as he lay asleep in the sitting room.

She was pushed by both the learned brothers into a wide horizoned story of her kitchen duties, what day she washed, what day ironed; where she washed, where she got the water; how many pails full; whether when she washed the windows she used a rag or dipper, until the poor girl obtained an entirely novel view of her importance in the social realm and wondered what would happen next.

One point was made emphatic, and that is that during her nearly three years residence in that house she heard no quarrelling, saw no bickering and knew of nothing to show more than ordinary disagreements between the members of the family.

LAWYER ADAMS QUESTIONING BRIDGET SULLIVAN

It seems that the young ladies were not in the habit of taking the meals with Mr and Mrs Borden. So far as eating is concerned it was a sort of a go-as-you-please household, not only every man his own chambermaid but every woman her own provider.

After these trivialities were ended, however, Bridget's testimony became of a grave and serious import. She told of Mr Borden's return after his morning tramp, and that when he asked for Mrs Borden Lizzie told him she had received a note some little time before and had gone out, whereupon after some little time he sat down by the window in a rocking chair and presumably later went to sleep on the lounge in the sitting room.

Lizzie remained with him some time and then went into the dining-room and ironed her handkerchiefs. She asked Bridget if she were going out, and upon being answered in the negative advised her to go to a store where some cheap ginghams were for sale on that day only. Not feeling very well, Bridget preferred to go to sleep and went up to her room by the back stairs, hoping to be able to take a nap. Not long after that she was startled by Lizzie's calling to her: "Come down, Bridget; run for the doctor. Father is killed!"

She obeyed immediately and went at once on several errands to doctors, this friend and that one, returning as soon as she could, making all possible speed. It then occurred to her to go for Mrs Borden and asked Lizzie the address of the friend to whom Mrs Borden had gone. Lizzie replied, "I am almost positive I heard Mrs Borden come in. I think she is upstairs. Go and find her." Bridget said she would not go upstairs all alone for all the world, whereupon a neighbor went with her, and as she, Bridget, went up she saw the body of her mistress dead upon the floor. She went into the room, took one hurried look, rushed down the stairs and into the yard, where she relieved her nauseatic stomach by vomiting.

She told her story as straight as a string, but on cross-examination Gov Robinson tangled her up as to the precise words used by Lizzie when she called her to come down, she having said at one time that Lizzie called out "father is dead," and at another that she said "father is killed."

So far as ordinary mortals can discern a man who is killed is tolerably dead, but there may be some as yet undisclosed reason for the governor's insistence upon the exact phrase of logic.

The cross-examination of Gov Robinson was merciless and exhaustive, but as Bridget unquestionably told the truth so far as she told at all, nothing was made against her, nor could it be said that her testimony was especially damaging to the cause of the defense.

Howard

The Providence Journal

If the government's case against Miss Borden is to break down, then the question as to the identity of the murderer will become a more pressing one than ever. Who, under such circumstances, could have had either the inclination or the opportunity to commit such a crime? A double murder, and one of a woman against whom no outside enemy of Mr. Borden could have any grudge whatever. That is the most mysterious feature of the case, especially if Miss Borden's innocence should be demonstrated, as it hardly seems likely to be, absence of convincing proof being all that those who have followed the trial with a presumption in her favor appear to expect.

EVEN FIGHT.

Lizzie Borden Is Not Cast Down

MISS RUSSELL TELLS ABOUT THE DRESS

Saw It Burned Sunday After the Murder

HER TESTIMONY ON THE WHOLE A DISAPPOINTMENT

Mrs. Churchill Relates Prisoner's Story

MARSHAL FLEET AND HIS TALE OF A HATCHET

Found in Tool Chest in Cellar of Borden House

Dr. Bowen's Version of the Crime's Discovery

NEW BEDFORD, June 8—"Is there another?" asked Miss Russell. "Yes," replied Mrs Churchill. "She's up there."

Human nature with all its trimmings of vanity, superstition, self-conceit and itch for notoriety, has been admirably illustrated today in the presence of a tremendous audience, which was rapped into silence by jolly-hearted, stern-visaged, virile-fisted sheriff Wright at the cheerless hour of 9 o'clock this morning.

The country roads were alive with farmers' teams from early dawn, hurrying toward the court house, each occupant bearing an expectant look of curious hope to be sightseers. I was glad to find that the sheriff, in imitation of the final distribution of the peoples of the earth, like the shepherds of the olden time, who divided the sheep form the goats, had the men on one side and the women on the other.

There were two or three very pretty girls and an especially attractive bride from Boston, but a large majority were vinegar faced, sharp-nosed, lean-visaged and extremely spare. It was a totally different audience from any that has gathered before.

Some apprehension has been felt as to the health of the accused, which was emphasized by her fainting spell on Tuesday, but I think with a mild change of temperature and the unquestionable favorable look of affairs as at present standing she will pull through without collapse.

She ate an excellent supper last night, a substantial breakfast, a good dinner, and a light supper today. She never has color in her face save flushments which come and go, but her eyes though are bright and her nerves appear to be of steel. The only indication of agitation I have detected since the fainting described is a frequent tapping with her fingers either on the rail or her smelling bottle.

She is to all appearances as self-possessed as an iceberg, and to an ordinary spectator would

Appear as Unconcerned

as to the issue of this tremendous strain as himself. After the usual ceremonial, and no one who has ever seen it can forget it, court and counsel bestirred themselves for serious work.

The first man put upon the stand today by the prosecution was Dr. Bowen, the family physician, a most unwilling but obviously essential witness. It will be remembered that this gentleman was sent for by Lizzie when she discovered the dead body of her father. He was not at home, but was soon found and speedily attended. He is tall, with a ministerial look, grave, courteous, self-reliant and evidently biased in favor of the friend and patient.

When he took the stand he smiled upon Lizzie who, wrapped in an outer jacket, seemed tired and presently hid her face behind the fan as her quick eye detected Mr Moody's reaching for the faded dress concerning which so much has been said. So far as the direct examination went the doctor told the well known story of his being told by Miss Lizzie that her father was killed, that she found the body on the sofa, felt of the pulse, and noticed that nothing was disarranged in the room. He recalled that when he asked Lizzie where she was and where she had been she said she had been in the barn to get a piece of lead, and she feared that her father had had trouble with his tenants as she had heard angry words, and that when she returned she found her father dead.

Bridget Sullivan,

who, pale and apparently nervous, took the stand just as the cow of day before yesterday gave vigorous evidence of her reappearance by a series of loud and melodious moos.

It was the purpose of the defence, on the cross-examination of the famous Bridget, to show that she was quite officious in assisting the officers in their cellar search for axes and hatchets, and they admirably succeeded, for Bridget told that she went into the cellar with three officers and showed them where the implements were.

She was quite sure that she did not touch any of them and equally certain that she knew all about them.

The impression produced by Bridget was that she was a little oversmart today, and time and again the thought occurred that if she were on trial for this murder or transaction, precisely the same line of testimony could be produced against her as down to that point had been offered against Lizzie. When Gov Robinson insisted in reply to her assertion that Lizzie did not cry, that she had previously sworn that she did cry, she vehemently rejoined:

"I didn't say so. I did not say anything about my memory; I swear I did not say so; that's not correct."

In other words she protested too much.

After Bridget retired the audience had a picnic. The next witness was Mrs Churchill, who testified that she was a widow who rented rooms and did her own work, enjoying life as she passed through it, and she looked it.

When Gov Robinson questioned her as to the dress worn by Lizzie, she was inclined to be very positive as to Lizzie's dress, which she described as a light blue and white mixed groundwork woven together as it were, with a dark navy-blue diamond figure on which there was no spot of blood or anything else.

By the side of the court house runs one of the busiest thoroughfares of the city, along which ramshackle mill teams and rattletebang wagons incessantly do roll. Crowds stand there all day long, birds sing, the cow moos, and a regular monkey-and-parrot time is perpetually on the go. No wonder the court declined to sit all day. No wonder that at this point a recess was taken and all hands rushed pell-mell for the dining rooms, where, in spite of the crowds, an appetizing and satisfying lunch was neatly and correctly served.

The judges were rolled down

In the State Carriage,

guided and guarded by high sheriff Wright, but the unhappy jury marched two by two through the throng lined streets, preceded by a venerable deputy sheriff some 20 feet in advance, flanked on either side and guarded in the rear by associate officers.

I tell you this is an object lesson of rare entertainment and instruction for men with eyes and ears. Vivid is the word. The interest all along has been intense, but the intensity was made vivid by the report that Miss Alice Russell, for many years the, so to speak, bosom friend of Lizzie Borden, who had testified and sworn to tell the truth, the whole truth and nothing else at the inquest, had had her conscience gnawed some months ago, and had made up her mind to moult the wing of friendship and literally obey the mandate implied by the phraseology of her oath.

To men and women ordinarily constituted such an experience as Miss Russell had today would be tolerably tough, but candor compels the record that in the most unmartingaled manner she threw up her head with lofty disdain and told all her story again and again.

Miss Russell, who is very tall, angular and thin, with a lofty forehead and pale blue eyes, is extremely trim in her manner and holds her mouth as though prisms and prunes were its most frequent utterances.

ASST MARSHAL FLEET EXAMINES AN AXE

As she took the oath, Lizzie hitched up her chair close to brother Adams,

Removed Her Top Coat

and gave her a look. Inspired by the persuasive questioning of Mr Moody she told a story, which, condensed somewhat, I will give, retaining all its sense.

Mr Moody had considerately allowed her to say that she had lived in Fall River for a great many years without insisting upon the precise number, after which the story goes.

According to her, "Lizzie called at my house the night before the murder and seemed troubled and worried. She said:

"'I am going to Marion for a vacation,' to which I replied:

"'I am glad you are going,' as I had previously urged her, but did not know that she had decided. After some other talk, she said:

"'I feel that something is hanging over me. I cannot tell what it is; it comes over me at different times, wherever I may be. The other day at the table the girls were all laughing and talking and having a good time, but this feeling came over me and I could not join in. One of them said: "Lizzie, why don't you laugh?" but I could not.'

Just then the old cow outside gave three tremendous blasts on her accustomed trombone, which made everybody in the room snicker, all but the high sheriff, whose face was flushed as he recognized the impotency of the unquestioned importance. I think Miss Russell did not laugh, possibly she did not hear the cow. Continuing, she said:

"Lizzie told me that Mr and Mrs Borden had been very sick the night before, and that they were all sick except Maggie. 'It was something we had eaten,' she said, and I don't know but what it was the baker's bread.'

"'That can't be, because other families would be sick, too,' said I.

"Then she suggested that possibly it was the milk, but that at all events they were awfully sick; that she had heard Mr and Mrs Borden vomiting and stepped to the door to ask if she could do anything. They said 'No,' and she went back to bed.

"Lizzie also said: 'I feel afraid something is going to happen.'"

Continuing, with every little

Prompting Miss Russell

went on to tell further conversation and remarks made by Lizzie as to burglaries in the house and her feeling as though she wanted to sleep with one eye open half the time for fear somebody might burn the house down or hurt her father, because he was so discourteous to people, giving as an instance the rough manner in which he had treated Dr Bowen in the presence of herself and Mrs Borden.

Other matter relevant, but not absolutely essential to repeat, followed, concerning the transactions the night of the murder, when she remained at the Borden house, where, by the way, she stayed until the following Sunday night. On Sunday a little before noon, while the police officers were in the yard, she went into the kitchen, where she found Lizzie at the stove, with a skirt in her hand and the sister about the kitchen work. Emma said:

"What are you going to do?"

Lizzie replied, as she held out the skirt: "I am going to burn this old thing up, it is covered with paint."

"I left the room, returned in a few moments, and saw Lizzie tearing a part of the garment. I said: 'I wouldn't be seen doing that, Lizzie,' to which she made no reply, but stepped forward one step. Afterwards I said: 'I am afraid, Lizzie, that is the worst thing you could have done,' to which she replied: 'What made you, let me do it.'

Some talk having been made about the note Mrs Borden was reported to have received, a general search was made for it and when Dr Bowen asked Lizzie if she knew anything about it she hesitated and said: "Perhaps it is in the waste-basket, or perhaps she burned it."

ATTORNEY MOODY STANDS STRAIGHT AND ERECT

"One thing is certain there was no blood on the dress but it was soiled. I

Didn't See Her Burn It.

It was made of bedford cord, which is neither calico nor gingham."

As Miss Russell was one of the attentive friends, the devoted sympathizers who sat with Lizzie on the sofa and stayed in the house for several days, she of course would know as to her dress and general condition of the day of the murder.

In response to questions she testified that when Lizzie lay on the lounge in the dining room there was no blood on her clothes or person, that her hair was arranged neatly and everything was right, that she was excited and appeared to be faint, as she had talked to many persons, including police officers, newspaper reporters, friends and neighbors.

A newsdealer testified that he carefully examined the grass about the Borden house immediately after the tragedy, but could not discover any footprints, which is unfortunate for the reputation of his eyesight, as both Bridget and Mr Morse had been out there in the morning.

A police official testified that when he saw Lizzie on Wednesday she was cool and gave no evidence of crying; he also exhibited a handkerchief stained with blood which he found near Mrs Borden's body.

A cheeky deputy sheriff told of the frightful wounds on the bodies and contrasted the thinness of the blood on Mr Borden with that of Mrs Borden.

His idea was to prove that the woman was killed long before the man. This inference he was asked to give as an opinion, and after a long argument between the learned brothers the chief justice, the brothers, having come to a conclusion that they would hear it, directed the witness to give it, whereupon he promptly replied, "That he had none."

Then they all laughed, the boy outside whistled, the bird carroled, the cow mooed, the sheriff rapped, order was restored and the witness went on.

The Fall River assistant marshal, John Fleet, retold the story of the morning of the murder, and recalled in professional phrase the startling incidents of the day, together with a recapitulation of conversations with Lizzie as to the length of time she stayed in the barn, when she last saw Mrs Borden, the searchings of the room, the finding of the axes, and particularly the small one without the handle, which was covered with dust or ashes.

So long as Brother Moody had the marshal in hand it was plain sailing enough, but Gov. Robinson cross-examined him and then it was different. Fleet was confronted with his testimony given at the inquest, which in several instances was either radically wrong or what was said to-day was correct, or noticeably incomplete. When contrasted with the testimony of this afternoon, there was a particularly clean-cut knockout in his conflicting descriptions of his search in Lizzie Borden's closet.

At the inquest he said the dresses were covered with a cloth; this he lifted and turned the dresses, one by one, looking for blood and so on. To-day he said he did not think there was any cloth over the dresses; that he spent no time at all in the closet, and was looking for a man.

Gov. Robinson completely twisted the poor fellow, who, I dare say, meant to do the correct thing, but who unfortunately substituted smartness for frankness, and thereby missed his cue.

The court adjourned pending this cross-examination, which will be resumed at an interesting point at 9 o'clock to-morrow morning.

It was not a red letter day from the prosecution's point of view.

HOWARD

COLUMNIST JOSEPH HOWARD

The New London Day

Although the Lizzie Borden case is yet in its early stages, it is already apparent that the prisoner stands in no danger of conviction. The web of circumstantial evidence which the state has been weaving for 10 months, has been rent in various places by the skillful cross-examination of ex-Governor Robinson. That Miss Borden appreciates the hopeful change in her condition is shown by her altered demeanor. When the trial began she assumed an air of stoical endurance, but now her apathy has disappeared and she watches the proceedings with alert interest, and seems to share the confidence of her counsel that the prosecution has done its best and failed. But as the situation of the prisoner improves, the mystery that surrounds the case deepens. If Miss Borden, who had the opportunity and a possible motive, is acquitted there is no likelihood of fastening the guilt on any one else. The state's case begins and ends with the accused in this trial, and there is no clew or suggestion to any other line of investigation than that which the authorities have already followed up and exhausted.

The Brockton Enterprise

The Borden trial has been much talked of this week. Brockton has the same interest in the case that has been shown in other towns, and the newspapers have been eagerly scanned for the latest intelligence from New Bedford. We should say, from what is heard on the street and in public places, that the weight of local public opinion was in favor of the accused woman. Certainly her discharge would be received by thousands of people in this city with the liveliest satisfaction.

The Boston Globe

"Justice is all we want," the counsel on both sides in the Borden case agree. Justice is what the people want, and all the indications so far are that absolute justice will be done.

The New York Tribune

But it is a strange case. The wildest intellect among the French romantists never produced a stranger. If she is guilty, she is a monster of surpassing malignity and surpassing genius for evil. If she is innocent, she is the most cruelly used of unhappy women. Guilty or innocent she is marked for life. She has nothing now at stake but existence; and what will that be? The crier of the court, as he opens it in the morning and adjourns it at night, pronounces in solemn accents: "God save the commonwealth of Massachusetts!" So may we all now pray, God save it from an act of irremediable wrong.

OLD TIME CRIMINAL PRACTICE.

Borden Murder Trial in Some Respects a Striking Example.

(New York Tribune.)

The Borden murder trial is in some respects a striking example of old-fashioned criminal practice. There are no bickerings between opposing counsel; each side is allowed great latitude in examining witnesses; there are few objections and technical arguments; and the court is seldom asked for a ruling. The trial offers a marked contrast to criminal proceedings in this town, in which the lawyers on each side are constantly in conflict over trivialties of procedure and splitting hairs over technical objections. Each side exhausts its energies in embarrassing the opposing counsel and in badgering and confusing witnesses. While a foundation may be laid in this way for an appeal to higher courts and motions for a new trial, there is seldom any direct benefit so far as influence with the jury is concerned; and not infrequently the client's cause is prejudiced by these legal tactics. In Massachusetts these matters are managed in accordance with the older and better traditions of the bar.

It is for the interest of the defense in the Borden trial to impress the jury with the fact that it has a strong case, and has little to fear from the evidence for the state. At the outset it had few misgivings respecting the character and fair-mindedness of jurors. As the evidence for the state was produced, it allowed the witnesses to tell their stories naturally on the direct examination. Opposing counsel were not warned when they openly coached witnesses by their leading questions. Few exceptions were taken; no anxiety was displayed over trivial points; witnesses were seldom interrupted. The general effect of this method of procedure would naturally be to inspire confidence. It tended to minimize the importance of the evidence for the state and to create in the minds of the jurymen an impression that the defense had nothing to keep back or to distort, and that it stood in no dread of revelations from that quarter. No New York criminal lawyer would have conducted the defense in that way. It would have been considered unprofessional to allow the state so much latitude, or to make so little effort to confuse the witnesses, or to offer so few objections. But it was shrewd, common sense, nevertheless, and better art than many of the criminal lawyers hereabouts display, with all their aggressiveness and sharp practice.

Then as for cross-examination, ex-Governor Robinson has given as fine an exhibition of talent as has been witnessed for many a day. It is the same art of concealing art which Charles O'Conor once displayed at the New York bar; and let it not be forgotten that when he reappeared in his old age in the Walworth case, it was a revelation of the superiority of old-time methods, so marked was the contrast with the newer pettifogging and legal blustering. Ex-Governor Robinson proceeds upon the assumption that something is to be made out of nearly all witnesses, if their suspicions can be allayed and their confidence gained. So well does he conceal his motive that witness after witness, under his manipulation, has said precisely what he wanted, and has either damaged the theory of the prosecution or aided in establishing grounds of defense. This is old-time practice of the first order. The new-fangled idea is that witnesses in cross-examination are to be ridiculed, confused, worried, tortured and discredited in every way. The older and better practice is to use rather than to abuse them.

Remarkable discernment was displayed in the cross-examination of Miss Russell and Fleet, the officer who searched the Borden house and found the hatchets. Here were two witnesses who were hostile from different motives. The well-established rule of criminal practice is not to provoke such witnesses. The wily lawyer followed the rule in one instance and disregarded it in the other. Miss Russell, the former intimate friend of the prisoner, had evidently formed a private judgment of the case from having her suspicions excited by the destruction of the dress. She had pondered the matter in silence and finally revealed it to the prosecution, doubtless from a high sense of public duty. The cross-examiner's method was to deal gently with her and to feign an indifference to her story which would tend to minimize its importance. This was good art, for if irritated she would have been likely to harm rather than to help his case. With Fleet, the officer who had prejudged the case from professional motives, the method was reversed. The lawyer changed his manner and deliberately exasperated the witness, whose hostility to his client he was anxious to reveal to the jury. The Borden trial offers many opportunities for study of old-school practice of the best kind.

REVEREND JUBB AND LIZZIE LISTENING ATTENTIVELY TO THE TESTIMONY.

BURNING OF A DRESS

The Facts Told by Lizzie Borden's Friend.

Miss Russell Saw No Blood on the Gown When the Accused Was Holding It Near the Stove - Dr. Bowen Says Morphine Might Have Clouded the Prisoner's Memory During the Inquest - First Exceptions Taken.

NEW BEDFORD, June 8.—It was a bad day for Lizzie Borden—a day full of suggestion of her guilt. As usual her physical condition seemed to foreshadow what was to come. She was all but motionless most of the day. All of her stoicism seemed to have returned to her. It is the general belief that the Government brought out its worst to-day and reached the summit of its little hillock of circumstantial evidence against the unhappy woman. And yet, after all, the principal testimony was as to the burning of her dress, which had been foreshadowed by the Government. That and the facts connected with her singular action made up the measure of the injury done to her case.

Queer and unaccountable as it was for a young woman so placed to burn a dress, especially in so frugal a New England household, it was yet an easy thing for her counsel to show much that was in her favor with regard to it. For instance, she made no effort to hide her act. She did it in broad daylight, in the presence of her sister and a friend, when policemen were just outside the unlocked door. All day the Government kept bringing out its most important and, as it thought, its most damaging points, and just as steadily ex-Gov. Robinson, on behalf of Miss Borden, either riddled them or tried to do so.

In this most expeditious court a swollen tide of witnesses seems ever pouring in the court-room door. Swearing them, ridding them of their testimony, and sending them away again goes on as a lot of cooks might squeeze a basketful of lemons. To-day, as nearly all of the witnesses were very important, the tone and temper of the proceedings were feverish and strained most of the time. The witnesses and the counsel on both sides were, like pugilists, steadily sparring each to get advantage of the other.

The operation could almost be likened to a pigeon-shooting match, in which District Attorney Moody kept flinging up the birds and defying his antagonist to hit them, while the ex-Governor as constantly fired, and often, but by no means always, wounded or brought them down.

Ex-Gov. Robinson is certainly without an equal in New York city as a cross-examiner. Hamlet, in the play, is no more necessary or conspicuous than this gifted lawyer is in this case.

He has not yet found a Government witness whom he has not been able to turn more or less to his own account. His ability is very like that of an actor.

To-day he seemed determined to anger one of the witnesses. Then he showed his consummate art by simulating irritability, sternness, and impatience. That witness was a police officer named Fleet, and was the coolest, clearest-headed, shrewdest man the wily lawyer has yet had to deal with. In the other duels the ex-Governor has matched his big brains against far smaller ones, but John Fleet's brains were as good in their way as the lawyer's.

Fleet is assistant marshal in Fall River, and is evidently a believer in Lizzie Borden's guilt. Like a typical policeman having some one in custody, he finds it simpler to construe all the evidence against that one than to take up a new clue and hunt out another prisoner. He gave a great deal of testimony which the Government evidently thinks is very hurtful to Miss Borden, and some of it the Government had not outlined. Then, again, Fleet is the man who found the handleless hatchet, which they are going to show to have borne traces of blood.

Mr. Robinson set out to discredit all this testimony, and his plan was to get the witness angry and rattled. He succeeded in five minutes, and had the policeman glaring at him and answering him impudently. He also made the witness contradict himself, and in a measure disparage his own evidence. But just then it was time to close the court, so the wonderful wizard of a lawyer will have to work the witness up all over again to-morrow.

The Government kept on weaving its web all day, and the woman's counsel kept breaking through it at every vulnerable point, so that, while the web was there at the close of the day, it was all tatters. The steady effort that the Government made was to show that the doors of the Borden house were all locked on the morning of the murders, that many men and two women went through the house soon after the murder, that the officers saw workmen calmly at work on the other side of the fences around the Borden place, and that it was next to impossible that any one except an inmate committed the crimes. Then, too, they showed that other policemen were quickly sent to scour the woods and watch the depots.

THE PRESS AND SPECTATORS HEAR THE QUESTIONING OF MISS RUSSELL

Testimony of this sort was incessant. How cleverly Mr. Robinson dealt with all of it will be seen in what follows.

Miss Lizzie Borden attracted general attention all day, of course, but she did nothing to deserve it. She might be said to have done nothing at all but sit still, well back in her chair, and leaning her chin on one hand, her right hand in the morning and her left one in the afternoon. Once she attracted adverse attention. It was when the first blood in this terribly bloody case was shown in the form of a saturated handkerchief carried about like a British flag by District Attorney Moody. She turned her head as she had never done before so that her chin was over her shoulder and she cast her eyes down. And yet any woman might have done the same thing.

That last reflection brings to mind the fact that unless the Government has got more than it has shown, the Borden case will pass into history as one of the most mysterious of the celebrated cases of the century. Most fair-minded persons here are of the opinion, that there has been nothing yet brought forward that does not tend to prove the woman innocent quite as much as to suggest her guilty.

The Commonwealth to-day continued its efforts to exactly fix the time of the murder of Mr. Borden. It has at least narrowed things down so that if Lizzie Borden is the murderess she could have had only from 8 to 13 minutes in which to conceal all traces of the murder of her father after she did the bloody deed. In that period of from 8 to 13 minutes she must have either changed her dress or put another one over it, she must have broken the hickory handle of a hatchet, and she must have taken the bloody blade of the weapon down into the cellar and rubbed it a long while and thoroughly with ashes to remove the blood. Of course, she had to wash her face and hands and to attend to her hair and clean her shoes all in the little space of time which Bridget Sullivan says she spent up stairs, and which accords with the testimony of other witnesses.

The first witness of the day was Seabury W. Bowen, the family physician of the Bordens, who was the first person summoned by Miss Borden after the murder. He is also the first person to testify that nothing in the rooms where the murdered persons were found was disturbed by the murderer. "I asked Lizzie several times," he said. "'Have you seen anybody?' and her reply was, 'I have not.'"

"Where have you been?" the doctor asked. She said, "I have been to the barn looking for iron." She then said she was afraid her father had had trouble with his tenants, as she had overheard unfriendly conversations with them several times.

The doctor was another person to whom Lizzie said that Mrs. Borden had got a note asking her to call and see a sick person. The doctor went up and saw Mrs. Borden's body, and noted that she had been killed, probably by the same instrument that despatched Mr. Borden. When he came down he told Lizzie it was fortunate she was out of the way at the time. He denied that he had ever said that Miss Lizzie had on a drab dress at that time. All that he could say now was that the color of the dress was indefinite. Shown the blue dress which the Government keeps on the table in court, the Doctor said he did not call it drab, and that he could not tell whether that was the dress she had on or not.

Returning to his visit to the house, he told of seeing Lizzie in the kitchen, with the others leaning over her and fanning her. He told her to go to her room, and he prescribed something for her.

Mr. Melvin O. Adams took Mr. Robinson's place as crossexaminer of this witness. He had sufficient success to have satisfied even his brilliant colleague. He brought out from the Doctor the fact that Miss Borden was under the influence of morphine for several days after the murder.

On the day of the murder he gave her bromo caffeine. For Friday and Saturday he prescribed morphine. On Friday he gave her an eighth of a grain and on Saturday double as much. She had it again on Sunday and Monday

"How long did she take it?" said Mr. Adams.

"She had it all the time she was at the police station."

"Up to the time of her arrest and when she was at the station?" Mr. Adams asked.

"Yes, sir."

"After her arrest, when she was at the station, had she taken this double dose of morphine daily for several days?"

"Yes, sir."

"I suppose physicians understand that when morphine is given it affects the memory, changes the views of things, and gives people hallucinations?"

"Yes, sir."

"There is no doubt about it, is there?"

"No, sir."

Of course the reader will understand the very great importance of this testimony for the prisoner. She has been accused of many contradictions in her stories, of peculiar behavior after the murder in her home and when under examination. The defence can now ascribe to the morphine as much of this as it pleases.

Bridget Sullivan was put on the stand again for ex-Gov. Robinson to ply with questions in the continuation of his cross-examination of her. He made her describe the dress she had on during the morning of the day of the murders, and as it proved to be a blue dress, it was clear that he means to argue that hers was the dress that Mrs. Churchill saw and afterward thought was worn by Miss Borden. However, the dress was little like the one Mrs. Churchill describes. The ex-Governor next took up the subject of the robberies of the Borden house and barn prior to the murders. His questions were objected to.

The Governor paused and contemplated the Judges reflectively. Then he said: "I do not want to state anything before the jury which I ought not to, but I want to bring out the fact that some time, not long before the murders, the house was entered by burglars in broad day while this witness and the prisoner were in the house."

"I think it is not competent," said the Chief Justice. "It was too long before the commission of the crime about which she is to testify."

Mrs. Adelaide Churchill, the next-door neighbor of the Bordens to the northward, was the next witness. She is the neighbor who was the first person not of the household who entered the Borden house after the commission of the crime. She is a middle-aged matron of comfortable build and genteel, placid face. She told of seeing Andrew Jackson Borden as he started from his house on that round of business calls from which he came back to be killed. She went down town, and, in an uncertain measure of time, came back. She saw Bridget coming back from Dr. Bowen's rapidly. From her house she saw Miss Lizzie leaning against her kitchen door. The prisoner looked excited or agitated and the witness stepped to the window and said: "Lizzie, what's the matter?"

"Oh, Mrs. Churchill," said the prisoner, "do come over: some one has killed father."

The witness went over to the Borden house. As soon as she reached the door she stepped in, and there was Miss Lizzie sitting on the second stair to the right of the door. The witness put her right hand on the prisoner's arm and said:

"Oh, Lizzie, where is your father?"

"He is in the sitting room."

The witness then asked where Mrs. Borden was. The prisoner said: "I don't know. She got a note and went out. I sent for Dr. Bowen. I must have a doctor. Father must have an enemy, for we have all been sick. I think it must be the milk. I think we were poisoned."

The witness ran over into the street, and, seeing a man, said that a doctor must be had. Soon Bridget came and Dr. Bowen. Some one told the Doctor Mr. Borden was in the sitting room. Bridget, Lizzie, and witness followed the Doctor as far as the dining room door. The Doctor then came out and said: "Come in and see him." "Oh, no," said the witness. "I don't want to see him. I saw him this morning."

The Doctor wanted a sheet to cover up the body. Bridget got the key to the bedroom of the old couple, and she and Mrs. Churchill went up. Bridget found the door locked, went in, and got the sheet. Miss Lizzie asked the Doctor if he would send a telegram to Emma, her sister. "Tell it to her as gently as you can," said the prisoner, "for there is an old person there." Miss Russell (the prisoner's closest friend and companion) soon came. After that Miss Lizzie asked would some one try to find Mrs. Borden, for she thought she heard her come in. The witness and Bridget went up the front stairs. They went up so that witness's eyes were on a level with the front hall, and saw across the hall and the spare room on the far side of the bed what looked like the form of a person. The witness went back and Miss Russell asked: "Is there another?" The witness said, "Yes, she is up there." Miss Lizzie said she should have to go to the cemetery, but the witness told her the undertaker would attend to everything.

"Was her excitement manifested by tears?"

"No, sir."

"Did you suggest any change of dress?"

"No."

"Did any one suggest it in your hearing?"

"No."

Asked what dress the prisoner wore, she said it looked like a light blue with white groundwork. It was of calico or cambric, with a dark navy blue diamond pattern printed on it. This, of course, is the dress that the Government will seek to prove was burned by the prisoner two or three days afterward. District Attorney Moody took from his table a dark blue dress and asked:

"Is that the dress?"

"No, sir. Oh, no, sir," said the witness quite emphatically.

Then it was that ex-Gov. Robinson took the witness in his charge on behalf of the prisoner, and gave another exhibition of his marvellous power as a cross-examir[illegible]. He got from the witness the fact that there was no peculiarity about Miss Lizzie's dress that attracted her to call across the yards and ask what was the matter. It was the prisoner's looks, not her acts.

"Of course," said this magic-like juggler with words and vocal tones, "you did not examine that dress? You were too much excited?"

"Yes, sir."

"Of course you did not talk about dresses, then, when you heard about the murder?"

"No, sir."

"You did not notice Bridget's dress?"

"No."

"If we were to make particular inquiry, you couldn't tell?"

"No, sir."

"Mrs. Bowen came that morning. What sort of a dress did she have on?"

"I think she had on a whitish dress."

"Do you know what you had on?"

"Yes, sir."

"But beyond that you can't tell much about dresses?"

"No, sir."

"What dress did Miss Russell have on?"

"I don't remember."

Having thus weakened the Government theory about the missing dress worn during the perpetration of the murders, the ex-Governor took up another branch of the same subject in a most ingenious way. He asked the witness such questions as to produce testimony that Mrs. Churchill fancied Lizzie Borden had had a newspaper. Afterward, Miss Russell fanned Lizzie. Some one gave her something to drink, and the witness thought Miss Russell cooled the prisoner's face and hands with water. "You remained with her all the time up to noon?" the ex-Governor asked. "Did you see any blood on her dress?"

The witness did not.

When the witness went to the Borden house on the summons of the prisoner on the morning of the double murder, Lizzie said she had

ROBINSON AND LIZZIE LISTEN TO MRS. CHURCHILL'S TESTIMONY

been to the barn to get some tin or iron to fix a screen. When she came into the house she saw her father and that he was killed. The witness started to loosen Lizzie's dress, but the prisoner said: "I won't faint." The point in bringing this out was that perhaps she had on another gown under the outer one, and to open her clothing would have disclosed the fact.

"Are you able to give a description of the dress she had on?" Miss Russell was asked.

"None whatever," she replied. Witness went to Lizzie's bedroom with her before the prisoner changed her dress. Asked in what way it was suggested that she leave the room, she answered that the prisoner remarked that when it was necessary for her to have an undertaker she should want Winwood. Witness then went down to tell this to the family physician, Dr. Bowen, and, after waiting some time, went up stairs again. The prisoner was coming out of her sister Emma's room tying the ribbon of a wrapper which she had put on.

Then came the thunderclap of the alleged proof against the wretched prisoner—the chief stroke of the Government. The witness had been led up to Sunday morning, the day following the funeral and the third day after the murder. She had gone down into the kitchen. Miss Lizzie was at the stove and held a skirt of a dress in her hand. Her sister Emma said: "What are you going to do?"

"I am going to burn the old thing up," said Lizzie, "It's all covered with paint."

The witness turned and left the room. She spoke to neither sister. She came back into the kitchen and saw Miss Lizzie, who stood by the cupboard, and was either ripping something or tearing something apart in the garment. "I said to her," the witness went on, "'I wouldn't let any one see me do that, Lizzie.' She did not make any answer. She stepped one step further back. I don't know that it was the waist, but I saw the portion of the dress on the cupboard shelf. No officers were then in the house, but there were officers about the premises."

Witness afterward talked with officer Hanscom, and later saw Miss Lizzie. She said to her: "I am afraid, Lizzie, that the worst thing you could have done was to burn that dress. They have been talking to me about it." Lizzie said: "Oh, why did you let me do it? Why did't you tell me?"

District Attorney Moody paused a moment and then said: "Miss Russell, you testified at the inquest, at the preliminary examination, and before the Grand Jury. At any of those hearings did you say anything about that incident?"

"No, sir," said the witness.

"Stop one moment," said the magical cross-examiner for the defence, and he so strenuously objected to that question and answer that both were excluded. The witness finished for the Commonwealth by saying that the dress in question was a light blue dress with a small dark blue figure in it—a dress the prisoner had bought no longer ago than the early spring. This tallied with the description Mrs. Churchill gave of the dress the prisoner wore on the morning of the murder, a dress unlike any now in the possession of the Government.

The ex-Governor then took the witness, but it was not his purpose to make her seem of much account. He got her to tell how she had urged the prisoner to sit down, and had found her at the time of the discovery of the murders.

"Did she seem to have on more than one dress?"

"I did not notice," the witness replied.

"Did you see any blood upon her?"

"No, not a particle," said Miss Russell.

"Didn't see any on her dress or hair or hands or shoes?"

"No," said the witness.

"Everything looked all right?"

"Yes, sir."

"Did they go to Miss Lizzie's room?"

"Yes."

"What did you see them do up there?"

"After they took up all the things on the bureau and opened one or two drawers they did not do any more." They opened what was called the toilet room. They went into Emma's room, and she saw them pressing against a spare pillow in a closet, and the bed was next taken to pieces. There was no objection or resistance. The public had full sway, and this was the case with regard to all the searchers.

"I never heard of any resistance," the Governor got Miss Russell to say.

To all appearances the prisoner was much less interested in the testimony than the most unconcerned among the persons in the court. She spent her time in examining her fan and putting the handle of it in her mouth and out again mechanically. District Attorney Moody, for the Government, had the witness returned to him, and, after a little contention and strong objection on the part of the prisoner's lawyers, he got Miss Russell to say that Bedford cord is a cloth made of cotton and that it is a cheap material. That confirmed Mrs. Churchill's statement that when she reached the Borden house on the day of the murders the prisoner wore a cheap cotton dress.

"You saw no paint upon it?"

"No, sir."

"Couldn't it have been soiled with other things without your seeing it?"

"It could," said the witness.

The Government lays stress on the point that Lizzie Borden told a deliberate lie when she told several persons on the day of the crimes that her step-mother had received a note and gone out in consequence. The Government holds that she invented this lie to prevent an early discovery of the murder of the step-mother. Miss Russell had a story to tell about that. She testified that on the day of the murders Dr. Bowen made a search for that note, and declared to her and Miss Lizzie that he could not find it.

"May be she burned it," the witness suggested.

"Yes," said Miss Lizzie, "she must have."

"Now, then," said the District Attorney, "for what was that closet used, the cupboard in which part of Lizzie's dress lay, while she tore up the other part?"

"It was a closet for coal and wood," said the witness, "and I remember seeing some flatirons there."

That was the strongest part of the Government's case. It showed the full extent of the backbone of the theory that makes her the murderess of the old people.

John Cunningham, a Fall River newsdealer, who was the first man to whom Mrs. Churchill gave the alarm on the street, was next sworn. He was called by the commonwealth to swear that he and two reporters examined the grass and soil around the Borden house to see if they could discover the footprints of the assassin. He saw no tracks or footprints anywhere. This was part of the Government's proof that no one but an inmate of the house could have committed the crime.

Ex-Gov. Robinson turned that witness into a cipher by making him swear that he did not even see the footprints made by Mr. Borden that morning when he went under the pear tree and picked up half a dozen pears, nor did he see the tracks of Bridget where she had gone over the grass to the Kelly fence, where she had stood while chatting with the Kelly servant.

George W. Allen, a Fall River policeman, who was the first officer at the scene of the crime, testified to the fact that Miss Lizzie was not crying, and did not show a sign of tears. Up stairs he saw no person except Mrs. Borden—that is to say, no living person, for she was murdered. He went in the cellar also. He was led to say that only three feet away from where Mrs. Borden lay dead there stood a table bearing two books. There was no blood on it or the books. It will be remembered that there was other testimony yesterday showing that in other directions the man's blood had spattered more than eight feet away. The assumption is this testimony will be asked to show that the murderer need not have been bloody because this table was not. The Government holds that line of argument in check.

DEPUTY NICKERSON KEEPS WATCH OVER THE JURY

This witness was the means of bringing into the room the most horrible of exhibits yet seen. It is believed the progress of the case is to be punctuated with ghastly and horrible relics of the crime. The axes and hatchets shown on the first day were modest and common-place beside this exhibit of to-day. It was a blood saturated handkerchief found near Mrs. Borden's body. It is believed to have been worn by Mrs. Borden on her head while at her housework and when she was murdered. The old policeman went through the house and noticed that the front door was doubly or trebly locked. Up stairs in the guest chamber he saw a handkerchief close to Mrs. Borden's body. It lay near her feet and reaching out toward the door.

District Attorney Moody took up a paper parcel and opened it before the witness. Out of the paper he took a large bandana handkerchief that was all but cut or torn in shreds, and that was all but stiff and wholly discolored with dried blood. In carrying this exhibit about the Essex District Attorney held it widely opened so that it hung like a scarlet banner before the general gaze. Then it was that the prisoner turned her head directly away from the horrible object. She cast her eyes down to the floor.

Francis H. Wickson, a deputy sheriff, who has been in the army and seen dead bodies on the battlefields, also saw the corpses of the murdered Bordens. It was his observation that the wounds on Mr. Borden on the morning of the murder were fresh.

Officer Wickson testified to looking over the fences around the Borden yard right after the discovery of the crime. He saw one man sawing wood on the other side of one fence and two men at work in working clothes in another direction. They asked him what was the matter. This was part of the Government's effort to prove that no one but an inmate of the house committed the murders, that no one got away afterward, and that no one could have gotten away. What ex-Gov. Robinson did to weaken the force of that testimony was to make the witness admit that he did not go to the barn, or see any one else go to it, suggesting, of course, that the murderer might have been hidden in there.

A very important witness was John Fleet, the Assistant Marshal of Fall River, who made ex-Gov. Robinson very wroth at him by his apparent assumption that Miss Borden is guilty. He is a handsome and very shrewd man, but a typical dyed-in-the-wool policeman. On the day of the murder, to give his testimony, he saw Miss Lizzie and asked her if she knew anything about the murder. She said she did not. All she knew was that her father came home at about half past 10 or quarter to 11 o'clock, went to the sitting room, sat down, took out some papers and was looking at them. She was ironing some hankerchiefs in the dining room. She saw that her father was feeble, and went in to him, and advised and assisted him to lie down on the sofa. Then she went back to her ironing, and presently she went into the yard and up in the barn. She said she remained up in the barn about half an hour. She was up stairs over the first floor of the barn. She came down and went in the house, and found her father on the lounge in the position she had left him, but killed—or dead. Asked what she did, she said she went to the back stairs and called the servant girl. She was asked if Mr. Morse did the murders. She said she thought not, as he was away since early morning. Asked if the servant did it, she said no; that Bridget had gone up stairs before her father lay down and had not come down till after the murder. Asked if she had any idea who could kill her father and mother she replied: "She was not my mother, sir; she was my stepmother. My mother died when I was a child." She told the marshal about Mr. Clegg's calls upon her father about renting a store, and about her father's quarrel with a man who wanted to rent one of his houses for an improper purpose.

The hatchets and axes were brought in at this point. They were accompanied by the clanking and dashing that seems inseparable from being handled and that sounds terrible to those who sympathize with the prisoner and try to put themselves in her place. Miss Borden had been inattentive and drowsy up to that time, but now she raised her head and looked at the weapons with some show of interest. The other day she lowered her eyes when they were in the room. The assistant marshal went on to describe how, as soon as he could do so, he sent men to cover the roads and to visit the depots so as to intercept any fleeing criminal if possible. After that he went up to search Lizzie's room. Dr. Bowen was in there with the prisoner. The door was shut and locked. The marshal knocked, and Dr. Bowen opened the door. He was told that the officers wished to search the room. The Doctor closed the door and locked it, then opened it again and said Miss Borden wished to know if it was absolutely necessary to search that room at that time. The marshal replied that it was. The Doctor closed the door, said something to the prisoner, and then opened the door and let in the officers.

The search then began. The witness asked Miss Lizzie if she had said she was in the barn half an hour. She replied she had said twenty minutes to half an hour. When asked what was the last time she saw her stepmother she replied, "At about 9 o'clock." Mrs. Borden was then in the room where she was found dead, and was making the bed.

At this point the prisoner leaned over to her counsel, Mr. Adams, and whispered to him.

"She then said," continued the witness, "that some one had brought a letter or note to Mrs. Borden, and she thought she had gone out. She had not noticed her return. She said she hoped we would get through with this search quick, that it was making her tired, and we told her we would get through as soon as we could. We did not make a thorough search.

Then came what was meant to be sensational testimony about the finding of the hatchet with which the Government argues that the crime was committed. The two axes and the two perfect hatchets which are thrown aside as innocent by the Government were first found by the marshal's men, and it was not till later in the day that he came upon the handleless one in a box on a jog in the chimney. It was in the box with several tools. It was covered with a heavy layer of thick ashes while the other objects in the box were coated very differently with fine dust. Moreover, the handleless hatchet was covered with ashes on all sides; all over. The marshal did not notice all this at the time or think much of it. He put it back in the box, but afterward he went and got it, and the Government made it the star exhibit in the cause. District Attorney Moody led the marshal back to the dresses of Miss Lizzie, after he had examined the little hatchet blade and had testified that the handle was newly broken off from within the blade. On Saturday the marshal and his men searched the Borden house again.

"Did you see any dress with paint on it?"

"No, sir."

"How critically did you examine the dresses?"

"Very closely."

A hum ran through the court as the minds of the people grasped the fact that if he did not see the paint-soiled dress it must have been because it was skilfully hidden. Miss Lizzie Borden leaned over to Mr. Adams of her counsel and whispered to him again.

"Did you see any blood on any garment?" Mr. Moody asked.

"No, sir," said the assistant marshal.

When ex-Gov. Robinson took hold of Assistant Marshal Fleet he did so as a terrier takes hold of a rat. He flew at him at least as if he meant to shake him. Fleet was cool and not easily angered, yet such was the manner of the formerly oily lawyer that Job himself could not have endured his tone and words with patience. The ex-Governor was short, stern, and sharp.

"You've testified before several times in this case. This time you have added to your former testimony. Don't you know you have? Don't you know how you have done it? Do you mean to deny it?"

Thus he tried to rustle the witness all over. He first charged that the witness did not name the same persons as being at the Borden house on the morning of the murder as he had named before. But that was not what the lawyer was after. He was angry at the man for introducing testimony against his client to the effect that she actually led her father to the lounge on which he was battered out of human semblance. The talk to and fro is not important enough to report, but it was hot. Finally the ex-Governor got the assistant marshal to admit that he had not made a very thorough search of Lizzie's room. "Not as thorough as it should have been," said the marshal. He asked the witness to characterize Dr. Bowen's manner of holding Lizzie's door when he went there to search the room.

"He seemed to be holding the fort," said the witness.

Then the Governor was, indeed, angry.

"Do you call that a proper way to answer my question?" he shouted.

"It's the proper way to reply to your way of doing business," said the witness.

"You asked him to characterize it," said District Attorney Knowlton. The Chief Justice seemed by his manner to think that witness was not beyond his province and the battle went on. Next the Governor began to succeed in his purpose of muddling the officer.

EX-GOVERNOR ROBINSON
QUIZZES MISS RUSSELL

The witness had described his examination of Lizzie's dresses, and had said in the closet they hung behind a long white curtain, a covering like a sheet. Now he could not recall whether there was such a covering or not. He thought there was no such covering. Ex-Gov. Robinson made the most of this contradiction and uncertainty, because it tended to show that a man who was so uncertain about a chief fixture in the room could not be trusted as to whether or not he had examined the dresses carefully or had seen a paint-stained dress or not. Unfortunately for the plans of the vastly clever lawyer, it was then time for the night's adjournment, and the witness had to go away and cool down so that he will have to be brushed the wrong way all over again to-morrow. The white-haired jury keepers were summoned and sworn and charged to take the jury to a convenient place for the night. Then the old crier rose in his box and shouted: "Hear ye! hear ye! hear ye!" and told all persons having business with the court to depart and give their attendance at place at 9 o'clock next day. "God bless the Commonwealth of Massachusetts!" said the old man in conclusion.

SHERIFF WRIGHT SPOTS A MAN
WITH HIS HAT ON

The New York Times

BREAK IN THE STATE'S CASE

POLICE WITNESSES IN THE BORDEN CASE DISAGREE.

One of Them Swears that He Saw the Piece of Hatchet Handle Alleged to be Missing in the Very Box Where The Hatchet Was Found---If He Did the Prosecution's Theory of the Murders Fails in an Important Respect---A Momentous Question to be Decided.

NEW BEDFORD, MASS., June 9. - The police of Fall River told their story of the Borden tragedy to-day. All the details of the affair were rehearsed with a painful exactness; all the scenes in and about that ill-fated house were presented in clear, and almost startling colors.

But while these witnesses told stories damaging to the defense, in the same breath they nearly destroyed the Government's hope of producing the instrument with which the deed was done and nearly, if not completely, disposed of the last hatchet which has been brought forward as the instrument which took the lives of Andrew Borden and his wife.

Each witness by his evidence assisted to place the prisoner in the house at the hour and almost the moment when the homicides were committed. So far all went well for the prosecution, but then came an open discrepancy in the Government's testimony.

Assistant Marshal Fleet told his story of the finding of a hatchet without a handle. It was discovered in the cellar of the Borden house on the very day of the tragedy. Its blade was covered with ashes as if some one might have been trying to remove blood stains from it, and the fact that the handle was broken close to the steel looked suspicious.

Marshal Fleet said that the break was a fresh one, and that the broken handle was not to be found.

Then came Officer Mullaly to tell the story of the finding of the hatchet. He said that there was a broken piece of wood beside the hatchet when it was found which seemed to belong to the hatchet. He further testified that Fleet took this supposed handle and examined it.

Assistant Marshal Fleet, when he was recalled, flatly denied the statement of Mullaly.

Here was a break in the prosecution's case, and the attorneys for the defense were greatly elated.

One of the witnesses to-day testified that the blood from Mr. Borden's body when first examined was clear, while Mrs. Borden's was dark and thick. The purpose of this testimony was to show that Mrs. Borden was killed some time before her husband.

An interesting question is to be discussed to-morrow morning by counsel. It is whether or not the evidence given by Lizzie Borden at the inquest shall be read to the jury.

The attorneys for the defense will take the negative on the question. They will set up, in the first place, that Miss Borden was practically forced to testify at that inquest, and will urge that anything she may have said at that time should not be brought out in this trial, inasmuch as her statements were not freely made.

Further than this, they will assert that, even if Miss Borden had testified at the inquest without coercion, she was in such a condition that she hardly knew what she was about. In support of this proposition the testimony of Dr. Bowen given yesterday will be cited.

The doctor said that from the day of the murders up to the time of the inquest he was giving Miss Borden doses of morphine, doses of one-eighth grain at first and double that much later.

Yesterday, Mr. Adams, while examining the doctor, asked him if the continual use of opium to allay nervous irritation did not affect the patient's mind and produce hallucinations. The doctor answered this question in the affirmative and Mr. Adams seemed well pleased.

As soon as court opened, Assistant Marshal Fleet was called for cross-examination. Ex.-Gov. Robinson questioned him. He said that he arrived at the Borden house before 12 o'clock and at once visited all the rooms down stairs and up stairs.

"Then," said he, "I went to the cellar and found Officers Mullaly and Devine in the cellar. The former had some axes on the floor of the washroom-two of them and two hatchets. I was told by Mullaly that the hatchets were taken from the middle cellar on the south side. The hatchets were found near the chimney, in the same box where the broken-handled hatchet was found.

"I put the claw-headed hatchet in the cellar room under the stairs. Officer Harrington saw me put it there."

"Oh, he was there, was he? You haven't told me about that," said Mr. Robinson.

"There's a good many things I haven't told you about," answered the officer.

"I afterward searched the clothes closet. Then I went into the attic. I searched all the rooms, but did not open a trunk; we just looked in, but did not disturb anything. We looked into everything we could look into, but not very closely. We were not there long. There was some clothing in one of the rooms, but we did not take it down. I didn't discover any blood on Bridget's dresses; I did not look closely, and I wouldn't say to-day there was or there was not blood on them."

"What did you really look at those dresses for?"

"For blood or anything else."

"And yet you didn't see anything at all or make a very thorough examination?"

"Not very."

"The doors in all parts of the house," continued the witness, "were generously supplied with locks. There was nothing extraordinary that Lizzie's room should have a lock or that the door leading to the father's room should be locked, or that the guest chamber should be provided with a lock. Wherever we went the doors were all provided with locks. Even in the attic the same conditions existed."

"When did you find this hatchet with the broken handle?"

"On the second visit."

"Why didn't you tell me so?"

"You didn't ask me."

"Don't you know I am asking for all the information I can get about this case?"

"Yes; but you didn't ask me about this. I found it in the box where other tools were. It was in the box by the chimney."

"There was ash dust," said the witness, "however, all over everything, just like any other cellar where ashes are kept. It was natural ashes should be on these things. The clawhead, apparently, had been cleaned. There was a spot on the handle, but I don't see it now. It was a small spot, but I couldn't say what it was. It was red, and might be red paint or blood.

"Miss Lizzie had no chance to clean that hatchet. I am sure of that.

"When I first saw that clawhead there was one red spot on the blade."

Counsel showed the clawhead hatchet to the jury, calling attention to the location of a mark on the blade.

"There was dust on the broken-handled hatchet," continued witness, "as though it might have got into the ashpile. There were ashes on the head, on the handle, but none on the broken end, I think."

It was shown to witness that yesterday he had said there was ash dust on the broken part. He said that he must have misunderstood the question, and he could explain in no other way why he had made different statements. He was asked to take his pick of the two statements and said he would say he did not discover any ashes there, although there might have been some there. He would leave the matter by saying that he did not know whether there were any ashes on the broken part or not.

On his redirect examination witness said that the reason why he kept the clawhead hatchet was because it looked as though it had been washed and had a spot on it which looked like blood.

Officer Harrington of the Fall River police was the next witness. He said that soon after he reached the Borden house he had a talk with Lizzie Borden.

"I asked her," said the officer, "to tell me all she knew, but she said:

"'I can tell you nothing at all. Father came home from the Post Office with a small package in his hand. I asked him if he had any mail for me; then I went away in the yard and into the barn. I heard nobody in the meantime.'

"She said she was up in the loft. I asked her if the motive was robbery and she said no-everything was all right, even to the watch in her father's pocket and the ring on his finger. I asked her if she had any reason to suspect anybody and she said 'No' hesitatingly.

"I asked her why she hesitated, and then she told me about the man with whom her father had quarreled before that date."

Witness said in answer to a question as to Lizzie's condition at the time she was being questioned by him that she was cool, and at no time was she in tears. At no time was there any breaking of the voice.

"I asked her," continued witness, "how she fixed the time of her stay in the barn so accurately, and she said she was sure she was there twenty minutes and not half an hour.

Witness gave such a detailed description of Lizzie Borden's dress that she smiled and others laughed.

"When I was in the kitchen" said witness, "I saw Dr. Bowen with some scraps of paper in his hand. I asked him what they were, and he answered that he guessed they were nothing, and he started to arrange them so as to show me what they were. I saw the word 'Ellen' written in lead pencil. The doctor then lifted the lid from the stove, and I noticed the fire was nearly extinguished. There had been some paper burned, which still held a cylindrical form about a foot long and perhaps two inches in diameter. I can't tell what sort of paper it was.

"About that time," witness went on, "Dr. Dolan came in with three hatchets, I think, in his hand, and two or three cans. I stood guard over them until I was sent away by the City Marshal."

On cross-examination, Officer Harrington contradicted Assistant Marshal Fleet as to the place where the clawheaded hatchet was found. He said the hatchet was found on the chopping block.

Captain Patrick Doherty of the Fall River police, who was the next to testify, said that he reached the Borden house just before noon the day of the murders. He described his about. He was asked to state what Dr. Bowen had said about the body, but the court ruled the question out as being incompetent.

"Mrs. Borden," said witness, "when I saw her, was lying face down, with her hands up over her head; the head was close to the wall, six or seven inches away. I lifted the head and looked at it. The furniture in the room was not disturbed that I remember. On the floor was a bunch of hair as big as my fist, which appeared to have been cut off. The first time I went there, I did not see Miss Borden, Miss Russell, or Mrs. Churchill.

"During the afternoon I saw Miss Borden in the kitchen. I asked her where she was when this was done. She said it must have been while she was in the barn. She heard no outcries or screams, but she did hear some noise like scraping. Then I had some talk with Bridget and Mr. Mullaly and I went about the house and looked it over pretty thoroughly.

"I saw Miss Borden in her room that day before I went away. I went to her room and she came to the door and said, 'One minute, and went in and shut the door. It was a minute before she opened it. We looked about the room. When she was down stairs I thought she had on a light blue dress, with a small spot, and there was a bosom to the dress."

Dress shown with light sprigs on a dark blue ground. Witness said he did not think this was the one.

Cross-examined, witness said:

"I don't know as I ever saw that broken-handled hatchet before to-day. Lieut. Edson brought away the two axes and two hatchets. This was on Friday morning about 6:30."

Officer Michael Mullaly of the Fall River police, who followed Doherty on the witness stand, said he was sent to the Borden house and arrived there at 11:37 o'clock. He looked at his watch when he got there.

"I saw Miss Borden for a moment," said witness, "and she told me she was in the yard, and when she came in her father was dead on the sofa. She told me what property her father had on his person and she told me what it was.

"I asked her if there were any hatchets or axes on the premises, and she said Bridget Sullivan would show me where they were.

"Officer Doherty searched the body and found things as Lizzie had said they were. Then I went to where Mrs. Borden was lying and found much blood of a thicker nature. Then I went into the attic. Bridget was with us, opened all the doors for us, and we searched them.

"Then we looked into the cellar, looking for the hatchets. Bridget accompanied us. She took from a box two hatchets. This was in the wood cellar, near the chimney. The box was on a shelf, which she reached up for, taking them out and handing them to me."

Witness described his going to the barn, and told how he went about the house again and to the cellar the second time, searching about there again.

"In the afternoon," said he, "I was down there with Fleet when he took from a box a hatchet like this (pointing to the broken-handled one) and then he put it back again. The break in the wood was a fresh one."

Resuming his testimony after the recess, Mullaly spoke of the little hatchet and described its appearance about as did the other witnesses. He examined the cellar thoroughly, but found nothing. Went through the attic again and outside on the premises, but found nothing of a suspicious nature, nor did he find any appearance of blood anywhere. Miss Borden told him about seeing a man about the house a short time before who was dressed in dark clothes and was about the size of Officer Hyde.

On cross-examination Mullaly said he had made, so far as he knew, a thorough search of the premises, but had found nothing of moment. He went into Bridget's room and looked about, but did not remove the clothing on the bed. He was not sure there was a trunk in her room, and did not think there was a closet there. He did not examine any dresses there. He had no recollection of visiting Mr. Borden's room. Officer Doherty was with him most of the time. At the time he went into the cellar Officers Allen and Doherty and Bridget Sullivan were with him.

Mullaly said Bridget showed him where the hatchets were because Miss Borden told him she would show where they were. She made no search, but went directly where they were. She did not hesitate in the slightest.

Mullaly said he thought that the smaller of the two hatchets with handles had about the same appearance when found that it had now. It was clean and clear of dust. The two axes he found, and they were dusty.

In speaking of the broken-handled hatchet, witness said at the time Fleet found the hatchet in the box the handle had been broken, and he saw a piece of handle corresponding to the long part of the one broken off the light hatchet.

District Attorney Knowlton, on being asked for this extra piece of handle, said he did not have it, and this was the first time he had ever heard of it.

Mr. Fleet was recalled and asked about the

broken-handled hatchet, where he found it and what else he found. He said he found nothing in the nature of a piece of wood with a new break in it. There was a decided sensation as Fleet stepped from the stand.

Charles H. Wilson, police officer of Fall River says he went to the Borden house about 1 o'clock in the afternoon. Witness said he heard the talk of Miss Borden and Mr. Fleet. Mr. Fleet asked her where her mother was and she answered that she saw her last in the guest chamber about 9 o'clock, and that she had received a note and gone out.

District Attorney Knowlton here called attention to his desire to have somebody sent to Fall River to the Borden house to see if that piece of wood referred to above was in the box; all he wanted was justice.

"I want justice, too," said ex-Gov. Robinson, "but not in that way!"

"Well, you haven't any objection to our sending an officer over there to see about it, have you?" asked Mr. Knowlton.

"No such question has arisen yet," said Mr. Robinson, "and we will pass it now unless the court rules against it."

The court decided it was not necessary to proceed any further just now.

Annie B. White, the court stenographer of Bristol County, was called to tell her story of what took place at the inquest in Fall River. Asked if there was some conversation between the District Attorney and Miss Borden, Mr. Robinson asked that the further examination of this witness be dispensed with until a full explanation could be made of the important question which this testimony, proposed to be submitted, brought up.

A lengthy conversation took place between the Chief Justice and senior counsel, while the junior counsel for the defense put their heads together to see when they could get to Fall River and examine the box referred to by Mullaly.

The result of the consultation was that Miss White got no further in her testimony, and George A. Pettee was called. On the 4th of August last he passed the Borden house between 9 and 10 A. M., but saw no one when he was going down. When he came back he saw Bridget nearly at the front door. She had a pail and brush.

"I was in Wade's store about 11 or after," continued witness, "when I heard of the trouble at the Borden house. When I got there I saw Mrs. Churchill and Bridget, Frank Wixon, and Dr. Bowen. I went into the room where Mr. Borden was. The blood was quite fresh, and I think I could detect a movement of the blood."

The witness described the position of Mrs. Borden about as the others did. He went to her head to raise it up or to see what condition it was in. He found the hair was dry and matted, and as he passed his hand over it no moisture came away on it. The blood on the floor was dry and shiny and he saw no fresh blood anywhere there.

Witness said he had formed an opinion as to the priority of death, but the defense objected to using the witness as an expert.

MRS. CHURCHILL

Witness was not used as an expert, the court ruling against it.

After some relatively unimportant testimony had been given by Andrew J. Gorman and Mrs. Churchill, the court adjourned until 9 o'clock to-morrow. The first business to-morrow will be the presentation of the arguments concerning the admissibility of Miss White's testimony.

Before dismissing the jurors Chief Justice Mason cautioned them against discussing the case and reminded them that, as they could hear but one part at a time, they must be careful about making up their minds as to the value of any of the evidence until it was all in and carefully weighed.

The Boston Daily Globe

The tattered web which the legal spiders for the Commonwealth have been weaving around her had one of its strongest threads snapped by a sudden and totally unexpected blow that left it sagging at one side. The Government's witnesses did not agree. One stuck to the outlined programme in his testimony and another followed him with a startling disclosure. Then the first witness was brought back and made to confirm his apparent insincerity.

NEW LIGHT.

Big Sensation in Borden Case.

Officer Fleet Gets Sadly Twisted.

Did Not Mention All He Found at First.

Prisoner Laughs When Her Dress is Described.

Mullaly Contradicts Fleet's Story.

Says Hatchet Handle Was in Box.

Government Unable to Produce It in Court.

Bridget Sullivan Proves a Stubborn Witness.

NEW BEDFORD, June 9.—"I did not take the hatchets from the box. I did not put my hands at all on them. I couldn't tell you who took them out. Bridget Sullivan took us to the cellar and led the way to a box to which she pointed and from which she took two hatchets and handed them to me."—Officer Mullaly.

The foregoing is a mild illustration of the sensation of the day. You will remember I suggested that Bridget Sullivan was not so satisfactory a witness for the prosecution as the government expected her to be.

In her cleancut, pugnacious, dogged manner, when confronted with contradictions in her testimony given at the inquest and before this present time, she reiterated her insistance that she cared nothing for what appeared in the previous record, and swore with marked emphasis that, whatever she may have said before, she now testified to the truth.

I was quite convinced that she meant to tell the truth so far as she had to tell anything, but I must say it is difficult, after the explicit testimony of officer Mullaly, which diametrically contradicts her on a most significant point, the finding and first handling of the hatchets, to attach much importance to any assertion made by her unless it be confirmed by the testimony of others.

I see by the reports sent from Fall River all over the country that Deputy Marshal Fleet is universally respected for his official probity and his personal honesty. It is fortunate for him that he has a local background to lean against, for his experience today after yesterday is not exactly that which a man would care to stand under any great length of time.

On the cross-examination of Gov Robinson, Marshal Fleet contradicted the testimony given by him at the inquest

Time and Time Again.

It will be remembered that much has been said concerning the handleless hatchet, and it was generally supposed that that hatchet head, in the eye of which was a piece of wood, the breaking of which was comparatively fresh, had been found some time after the murder.

It turned out, however, during the cross-examination of Fleet this morning that on the very day of the murder when he made what he calls a very light search he went into the cellar with Mullaly and another, guided by Bridget, and found at that same time of finding the other hatchets, this handleless implement.

The sensation caused by that announcement equaled that caused by Mullaly's testimony that Bridget herself not only knew enough to take them directly to the box in which the hatchets were, but in spite of her sworn declaration that she never laid hands on them, she herself took them from the box and handed them to the officers.

The day was much pleasanter than its predecessors from a temperaturative point. As early as 7 o'clock dozens of farmers' wagons and all styles of vehicles surrounded the court house, and a noticeable crowd assembled in front of a high picket fence temporarily erected at the foot of the avenue leading to the main door.

Precisely what that small structure is expected to accomplish in the way of keeping off a crowd from the entire greensward which is something like 150 feet wide, the New Bedford supervisor may know, but the rest of mankind can't imagine.

The sheriff had given orders that persons should be admitted after 8 o'clock so long as there were any vacant seats. The women, far outnumbered the men, and students of human nature would have been delighted at the opportunity afforded for their favorite investigation. I never saw in any country town such an extraordinary collection of women as, thanks to the courtesy of the authorities, were on view today.

There were a few who looked like ordinary human beings, intelligent, well-informed, nicely garbed and there for an obvious purpose, but a large majority are unkempt looking, unintelligent and exceedingly unattractive.

The men in the audience proper are largely of the order of court sitters, with which magistrates in large cities are quite familiar. I see the same faces day in and day out.

Inside the bar the attendance today was noticeable, for in addition to the counsellors, white and black, who are to be seen there daily, there was a large number of experts from New York and Boston, headed by the veteran Prof Draper, near whom sat Albert Ross, the author, Prof Wood of Harvard college and other less known.

Lizzie Looked Pale.

She not only looked pale, but felt pale. The strain upon her nerves has been steadily uninterrupted now for nearly a year, and that combined with a lack of customary and needed exercise, while not interfering in any sense with her physical strength, has unquestionably produced an effect upon her nervous system, the outcome from which her friends and physicians regard with unfeigned apprehension.

Refreshed by a good night's sleep and a hearty breakfast, Chief Justice Mason, Judge Blodgett and Judge Dewey greatly enjoyed their drive furnished by the courtesy of Sheriff Wright through the shaded streets of this classic township, and I wish I could say as much for the jury.

The poor fellows are locked in their rooms immediately after supper, where without man, woman or child to look at, man, woman or child to speak to, without refreshment of any sort or kind, except three square meals a day, they chew the cud of reflection and endeavor to find consolation in their $3 a day, board and lodgings thrown in.

I was interested, as the readers will be, in a suggestion born of Chief Justice Mason's instructions to the jury, when the court adjourned today.

He said in grave and measured tones and with an expression of paternal solicitude on his intelligently handsome face:

"I wish the jurors to remember that they have as yet heard but very little testimony in this case and to caution them, therefore, against discussing among themselves to form any opinion as to the result."

The cross-examination of Marshal Fleet, which was continued from yesterday, showed very clearly that the search made by him and other officers was done with the single object of

Implicating Lizzie Borden in the Crime.

According to Mr Fleet, when he went into Mrs Borden's room, for instance, attended by two associates, they looked upon the bed and under the bed, but he could not recall whether there was a bureau in the

FLEET SAYS HE DIDN'T FIND AN AXE HANDLE

room, and flippantly replied, when asked if he examined the drawers of the bureau, he supposed if there was a bureau there he did; if there was not he did not.

Bridget Sullivan's conspicuosity was again shown. She preceded them during the entire search, carrying the keys, opened the doors when they went in and locking them when they went out.

The door locking in the household was a notable feature in their domestic economy. After taking Fleet and his companions through the attic down, Gov Robinson located them in the cellar and in discussing the handleless hatchet, it inadvertently appeared that Fleet had found it at the time he found the others. Quick as lightning the counsel pounced upon him and asked; "Why didn't you tell me that before?"

"Because you didn't ask me," was the response, surly and defiant.

Yet it appeared that at that very time he not only found the two hatchets constantly before the court, but this particular one covered with dust or ashes, from which the prosecution expects to prove so much.

In describing this Fleet said: "It had a spot which looked as if it might be blood or paint."

There is no such spot there now, and the counsel for the defense took care to emphasize the fact that Lizzie Borden can in no way be connected with any change there is, as all the implements have been in the hands of the court.

The next witness has missed his vocation. He ought to be a dressmaker, instead of which he is a police captain in Fall River, with the gliberty-glibbest tongue that ever ran.

His memory for details is marvellous. He told intelligently and with remarkable fluency the well-known story of the morning of August, described the condition of things of the Borden house, pictured the dark blood and other blood so fresh that it trickled on Mr Borden's face, drew an intelligible photograph of affairs in the guest chamber, the body under the bed, the blood on the spreads and the pillow sham and narrated a conversation that he had with Miss Lizzie at the time. He asked her to tell him all she knew

About the Murder.

Capt. Harrington was then asked to describe her dress, which he did in a way which would be creditable to a first-class dressmaker who had studied the garment for an hour and a half and taken voluminous notes.

JUDGES MASON AND BLODGETT CONFER

He gave the colors, the stripes, the cut-bias biz. the flutings of the bosom, the fittings to the figure, the trimming about the bottom, and continued in a blaze of glory about the entire circumference of what he called a bell skirt.

The court looked at him in amazement. The men wondered whether he was a woman in disguise, and the ladies lifted their hands in undisguised amazement, while no one would have been surprised if he had drawn a mouchoir from a dainty satchel and deftly dusted the powder from his nose.

It was now 11.15, a point of time made noteworthy by the first mooing of the cow, a gentle creature, stalled in a stable in the rear, and a five minutes' recess ordered by the court for the benefit of the jury, Mr. Barleycorn and other interested parties.

After recess, on cross examination, Capt Harrington related his routine search and movements all day.

Gov Robinson led him to swear that he particularly noticed that the shoes on Mr Borden's feet were laced, and then confronted him with a photograph which shows that they were not laced, but were congress gaiters. This did not upset the gentleman, however, who complacently remarked that

The Photograph Was Wrong.

According to his story, he was not excited in the least by the horrible sights he saw and was entirely competent to describe the dress he saw from memory, and he did it, winning fresh laurels and meriting bouquets.

Miss Lizzie looked like a wilted flower. Noisy teams outside frequently drowned the words of the witness, the birds sang merrily, the old cow gave her punctuating moomgs with great deliberation, some stone cutters in an adjacent building chipped in, and a general condition of feverish restlessness dominated the place.

After some testimony, given in a direct, straightforward manner by officer Dougherty, confirming the evidence previously given as to Bridget Sullivan's activity in showing the searchers about the house, under it and penetrating the closets, and owning up like a man that he didn't remember and could not tell anything about Lizzie Borden' dress, the sensations fairly occurred.

Officer Mullaly was called to offer further confirmatory evidence and testified the same old story which we have heard. He also told of a conversation he had with Lizzie while she was lying on the sofa, in which she substantially rehearsed her version of her visit to the barn, and so on.

He described Mrs Borden as lying in a pool of blood, which was the first intimation that the jury had been favored with as to any great outpouring of the vital fluid.

Having asked Lizzie if there was an ax in the house and received the reply:

"Yes, Bridget will tell you," Mr Mullaly immediately went to Bridget, who with the keys in her hand took him into the attic and then through the entire house, locking the doors as they went, until she led them to the cellar, himself, Fleet and I think another.

Without looking about, in any sense, she went straight across the cellar to a shelf on which there was a box about two feet long. She reached, standing as she was upon the cellar floor, up to the box, took out the hatchets and

Handed Them to Him.

Well, if a bomb had fallen in the court room more astonishment could not have been caused.

Continuing his story officer Mullaly told of the small hatchet that Fleet took from the box, described the little broken part of the handle covered with dust or ashes, and then on cross-examination by Gov Robinson inadvertently spoke of a second piece of handle found by Fleet in the box, from which he took it, examined it and then returned it.

This was the first intimation that anything was known of the handle of that hatchet, a handle which conformed in breakage to the little piece in the eye of the implement.

At once Gov Robinson, who, like every one in the court room, judges, sheriff, lawyers and audience, recognized the extraordinary conduct of the police officer who, making a search in the house of two murdered individuals, found so important a link and kept it to himself, turned to the prosecuting officers and asked that that handle be produced.

Mr. Knowlton said that they did not have a handle and didn't know anything about it.

Gov Robinson desired that the marshal be sent for, officer Mullaly meantime being ordered to take a seat in an adjacent room, a precaution taken so that the two would not have opportunity to communicate with each other.

When Fleet appeared Gov Robinson began a long way off, and asked him a series of questions about the hatchet and what else was found in the box.

Fleet replied that he found some other tools, iron, etc, and nothing else.

"Did you find a handle?" "No, sir; I did not see any."

"Was officer Mullaly there?"

"He was."

"If there had been a handle you would have seen it, wouldn't you?"

"I would."

"That is all, you may go," and he went.

I wonder how he felt? Officer Wilson repeated the story of the day and then Dist Atty Knowlton suggested that an officer be sent to the Borden house to see if the handle was still in the box.

Gov Robinson said he would make no response to the suggestion unless the court required it.

Chief Justice Mason looked down over his glasses a second and said: "The court

Declines to Interfere."

The event of the day, from a legal point of view, made its appearance in the comely presence of Miss White, who is short, stout, good natured, and the official stenographer of the court.

It was the purpose of the prosecution to put in through her the testimony given by Lizzie Borden at the inquest, which in the belief of the government is very damaging, by reason of its inconsistencies and contradictions.

The jury were ordered to retire, Gov Robinson having objected to the introduction of the testimony. Then after consultation adjournment was made until tomorrow, when the regular procedure will be taken up, the argument as to Lizzie's testimony being deferred until Monday morning next.

Howard

The New York Tribune

There is no question of deportment with the audience. It is the audience of a New England country town, an audience of factory hands, fishermen, sea-going lads, lawyers, business men and all kinds of women, good and bad, homely and beautiful, vulgar and gentle, that are born to gladden and trouble the earth. They keep very quiet. They sit very still. They feel themselves not only under the subduing spell of this tragic cause, but under the eagle, arching glance of one with whom, among all these, there is a question of deportment. This is the high sheriff of Bristol county, the highest sheriff that ever was; so high that he has to bob when he walks under the moon. Except when occupied in stately procession precedent to the movements of their honors the court, and when engaged in glancing around the court room to see that no unhappy wretch is daring to breathe without having previously consulted him, the high sheriff of Bristol county is engaged in introspection. He is happy when with stately tread, with his high silk hat fixed firmly on his head, and his swallow-tail coat of Websterian blue flapping its tails like a streamer from a flagpole, he precedes the honorable, the justices of the superior court of the state of Massachusetts as they enter the room and take their places behind the bench. He is happy when, with darkening frown, he glances around and indicates to some unhappy deputy his august displeasure. But the golden moments of his life come when he is introspective; when, seated behind his desk, in the full gaze of the multitude, he thinks real thoughts, all about himself. Then is the high sheriff of Bristol county in a condition of positive, supreme peace and satisfaction.

The Boston Record

If Officer Phil Harrington of the Fall River police ever loses his job he ought to have no difficulty in getting a situation in a millinery store or as a reporter on a society journal. His description of the dress that Lizzie Borden wore the day of the murder was so elaborate in detail as to arouse the suspicion that it was carefully prepared beforehand. It is a pity, in the interests of justice, that he and his brother officers of the Fall River police were not so observant of other details on that fatal morning as he was of Lizzie Borden's apparel. His knowledge of the details of a woman's costume is painfully accurate even for a policeman.

BROKEN HATCHET

It Plays Pranks with the State's Witnesses.

Police Officers Testify in the Borden Case and Contradict Each Other as to Who Wrapped Up the Hatchet Head, and the Kind of Paper Used—Government Scores a Point in Regard to Dust on Floor of Barn Loft.

SPECIAL DISPATCH TO THE SUNDAY BOSTON HERALD

NEW BEDFORD, June 10, 1893. The handleless hatchet, now generally known as "the hoodoo hatchet," continued its demoniish pranks in the trial of Lizzie Borden for her life today. It chopped another great hole in the case of which it is the most important feature.

Since the only theory of the murder that has been advanced is that Lizzie Borden butchered both her parents at the end of 32 years of an upright life, whatever damages that theory simply increases the mystery that shrouds the murders. It is as if the cause were a deep and pitch dark well, and the commonwealth had said, "We will rig up a Siemen's search light and throw its glare into the well and light up the bottom of it." They took 10 months to build the lamp, and on the first day in court set it up with a great flourish in New Bedford. They turned on the blaze, and it seemed very powerful, but the light only deepens the darkness.

The commonwealth's lawyers pretend to point out objects in the inky space, but these vanish like phantoms at a second glance. They fished up the hatchet with a triumphant blaze of boasting, but it is bewitched. It turned on them, and they have been dodging its blows ever since. They began to try to deal with it.

That hatchet is the most sensational exhibit in this most sensational case. It played the mischief with the government all Friday, and, instead of

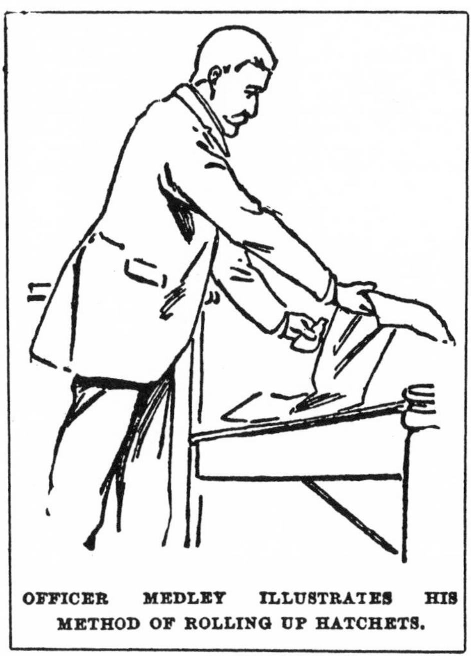

OFFICER MEDLEY ILLUSTRATES HIS METHOD OF ROLLING UP HATCHETS.

resting today, the court was no sooner opened than it flew at its own guardians, and began chopping and hacking their case pretty nearly as badly as the bodies of Mr. and Mrs. Borden were chopped.

The commonwealth's lawyers

Had Been Guarding It

as they would guard Aladdin's lamp if they could get hold of it, but today, after it had sent their witnesses all away, and shivered their testimony so it could be seen through, these lawyers tossed the unholy thing on the table at which Lizzie Borden's lawyers always sit, and there they left it lying, as if they wished to disown it.

The HERALD has told of the excitement in court when a policeman stepped beyond the stereotypen story that all the police of

MR. DESMOND SHOWS HOW HE ROLLED THE HATCHET UP.

Fall River tell on behalf of the government, and said he had seen the missing handle in he same box where the hatchet blade was ound. The lawyers for Miss Borde n saw to it that no one should speak to the assistant marshal, who had said he refound the blade, but had said nothing about the handle, that being understood to have been burned or stuck in the stove wrapped up in paper by the prisoner. Then the marshal came back and said flatly that he saw and found no handle, flatly contradicting the man who was with him, and says the handle was found after that.

There was another exciting contest outside the court room between the two sets of lawyers. The district attorney, Mr. Knowlton, sent two officers to the Borden home to get the box in which the blade was found, and the handle if it was in it. Miss Borden's sister Emma lives in that house, and her lawyer saw to it that their antagonists were kept out. That was what happened. Miss Lizzie's chief counsellor, A. J. Jennings, had better luck, he got the box, but lo! the highly important handle was missing. Who took it can only be guessed at. Had it been found it would have played hob with the theory that Miss Borden burned it. However, the policeman who saw it proves

As Good a Witness

for Miss Borden as the handle itself.

The famous box, marked "Muscatel grapes" in blue—the dominant color in this case—was on the table before the jury this morning. A new glass of flowers was before the judges—a bunch of heliotrope, along with the glasses of carnations that have lasted all the week. It stood between the deep red carnations that typify bloody guilt and the gentle pink ones that stand for maidenly sufferings. A change in the carnations was noticed. The guilty ones were dropping, and their heads hung down arounnd their vase. The others, emblematic of distressed maidenhood, were rigid and erect. Miss Lizzie Borden had been likened to a barometer, because heretofore her spirits at early morning have corresponded with what the day was to bring forth for or against her. It was not so today. She was limp and inert this morning. She seemed depressed. To be sure, the event of the day stimulated her so that she left the court room a bright and vigorous woman, but that does not mend the fact that her spirits belied her good fortune earlier in the day.

By the way, the strangers who are here begin to notice that Lizzie Borden's face is of a type quite common here in New Bedford. They meet Lizzie Borden's every day and everywhere about town. Some have even come into the court room. Some are fairer, some are younger, some are coarser, but all have the same general cast of features, heavy in the lower face, high in the cheek bones, wide at the eyes, and with heavy lips and a deep line on each side of the mouth.

for the ladies to know that all the reporters, even the one who writes this, have been mistaken about the material of which is made

The Dress Which She Wears

in court every day. It is simply black crepe.

It will interest both sexes to hear that Bridget Sullivan, as she visits he friends in the kitchens on the hill, is fond of saying that she scarcely knew Lizzie Borden when she saw her in court the first day, she has grown so fat. Evidently, as the district attorney would say, prison fare is better than the routine of mutton, cold soup, cookies and green peas she used to get in her cheerless hole in Fall River.

These reports during the last few days have seemed to take the part of the imprisoned woman. The reason why the reports have seemed to favor Miss Borden is very interesting It is that the case made out against her by the government has been steadily melting like a cake of ice in the sunshine. The presentation by Dist.-Atty. Moody on Monday has now been nearly all met by the evidence of the commonwealth's witnesses. Trey have little left that they outlined, and have not repeated through their witnesses.

Today the hatchet laid out more policemen. First one of them told when he found it he showed it to his captain, and then wrapped it up in a piece of brown paper and took it to the city Marshall. Then his captain took the stand, all unconscious of what had been testified to, und said that he did it up in a whole newspaper, and let the officer take it away. Mr. Robinson, who stumbled on this by his usual hard work that leaves nothing undone, actually made the two policemen show the jury how each one wrapped it up. The two officers went through the performace, each one swearing positively to his details. One made a brown bundle the size of a five-cent cut of pie, and the other made a great newspaper bundle big enough to conceal a pair of lonshoreman's shoes.

Worse still, for the commonwealth, that handle has been at last traced to the place, and they must account for its disappearance or suffer the consequences by resting under the fairly grounded suspicion that it was hidden or destroyed for a purpose involving a human life.

DEFENSE IN GOOD HUMOR.

Contradictions by Officers Brighten Miss Lizzie Borden's Chances

NEW BEDFORD, June 10--The sixth day of mortal tension and physical discomfort for Miss Lizzie Borden, and for that interesting body known as many others, was most interesting in developments.

As my eye fell upon the jaunty figure of Mayor Coughlin of Fall River, I recalled the testimony of the police officers from his district and was struck by the fact that nearly every one who has taken an active part in the endeavor to fasten this awful crime upon Miss Borden has within the year been promoted, until now captains in Fall River must be a thick as flies in a cow pasture.

Speaking of cows reminds me that the ingenuity of New Bedford's authorities must have been taxed in their selection of a site for Bristol county's court house, where the greatest possible annoyance in the line of extraneous soundings could be secured. It is not at all disagreeable to have the dull, monotonous level of official stupidity interrupted now and then by the sweet singing of birds, nor can I honestly say I object to the homely but nevertheless suggestive mooing of the cow, but there is a processional continuity of stone wagons, farmers' carts, coal wagons, mill wagons, loaded with all kinds of material, stone cutters, whistling boys and vociferating crowds, whose combined outputs furnish a bedlamistic hurrahdom, vexatious to the ear and exasperating to the understanding.

It is the endeavor of all good people in the commonwealth of Massachusetts to finish their work if possible by I o'clock in the afternoon, so that section of Saturday which immediately

Precedes the Lord's Day

may be not tinctured to any degree with worldly affairs. If that be so in ordinary walks of life you can imagine how it is regarded within the sacred precincts of a solemn court, which is opened with three "hear yes" and closed with invocation, "God save the commonwealth of Massachusetts."

As on all other days of this investigation the crowd desiring admittance was far in excess of the seating capacity of the court room, and as has been the case for two or three days past, a much larger number of women than men secured accomodations. There are some curious feminine developments in the court room.

One to which particular attention has been drawn is that of two ladies, one tall, one short, one thin, one fat, one dark, one blond, who have attended since the first hour of the trial, sitting with clasped hands, following with intense interest every phase of developoment, pausing now and then to exchange looks of pleasure, disapproval or whatnot, according to the testimony. They are from abroad, that is, out of Bristol County, and their names, business or interest in the case are unknown to any person.

I was somewhat surprised today to see a large number of young and rather pretty girls, apparently school girls, whose sole interest centered upon the artists who drew their pictures, the photographer who took snap shots at their countenances and their summer straws. The sheriff and his deputies are very gallant and polite to the women, old or young, but neither gallantry nor politeness could induce any of them to permit a single spectator to enter the court room unless there was a seat prepared for her occupation. Outside the door sat Bridget, sullen and morose in spite of all she could do or say she is painfully aware that her testimony, uncorroborated, fell powerless to the ground, and even if as Brother Moody believes the prosecution will be able to largely indorse her story, the flat and emphatic contradiction given her evidence as to the finding of the hatchets by officer Mullaly would warrant a disregard of all she might have to say.

The artists hoped Miss Alice Russell, the turn-coat friend, who injured her case by her obvious animus, would favor the court house with her appearance today, and had she done so would have given her such a showing in the Sunday papers as would furnish that extraordinary individual something to think of for many moons to conme.

When Lizzie was driven from the court house yesterday, she looked tired and wilted, today when she came into the court room she smiled and bowed to her counsel, to the Fall River missionary and another clergyman that sat within the enclosure.

Having adjusted her skirts she looked inquiringly at the bench where sat the learned justices, made more than usually attractive by vases of pinks.

It was a Curious Look

and one could not help querying whether it was a mute appeal from the heart of an innocent girl, or a curious inquisition from the keen eye of an assassin.

In spite of Judge Mason's warning to the jury against forming at this stage of the investigation any opinion as to the guilt or innocencce of the accused, it is of necessity impossible to avoid forming some judgment when it is remembered that the strongest part of the prosecution evidence is now before the jury and the public.

It must be conceded that Lizzie Borden had a splendid opportunity to do the deed.

REV. BUCK FINDS HEARING DIFFICULT

On the other hand so had Bridget Sullivan, and so when Lizzie was in the barn and Bridget was talking with a friend servant over the fence, had any stranger who so desired, and who had wit enough to get in and out as easily as the burglar who robbed them two or three years ago in broad daylight, or the other thief who robbed the barn.

It must be conceded that $300,000 might furnish a motive to Lizzie, but a desire for revenge might do the same kindly act for a tenant, who conceived himself a wronged and defrauded individual. The prosecution makes a great point of the fact that blood was found upon the doors, the bureaus and the looking glass, indicating a fiercely murderous assault, but that does not affect Lizzie any more than any other person. They point to the fact that she shed no tears and exhibited no emotion. The reply to that is that she is not that kind of a girl, that she has not cried a tear since this court opened, that she is a self-contained entity who has learned the folly of trusting friends and knows by bitter experience how flimsy a support a turncoat intimate proves in time of sorrow.

Much stress is laid upon the fact that

She Burned a Dress

This fact the defense cheerily admits and explains that it was done in broad daylight in a kitchen, by whose open doors passed and repassed numbers of police officers, done in the kitchen where her sister was, to whom in reply to a question as to what she was about, she said,"I am going to burn the old thing, it is covered with paint," and, further than that had Miss Russell seen fit to remain in the room it would have been burned in her presence also.

It will be remembered that quite a sensation was caused in the court room, yesterday, by an officer who testified that he saw Marshal Fleet take the handle of the handleless hatchet from a box in the cellar, wherein he found the hatchet referred to. At the opening of the court this morning, officer Edson, and, subsequently, officer Mahoney, a tall fellow from Fall River, testified that at 3:45 yessterday afternoon, he went to the Borden house in Fall River, and, although a servant came to the door, he could not get in.

It is evident that the prosecution felt the blow of that handle and endeavored by this attempt to produce it, to counteract somewhat the impression of unfair dealing on the part of Marshal Fleet which was unquestionably produced in the court room.

Mr. Moody who, by the way, no longer gives undue prominence to the "ho" in homicide, obtained from this officer an identification of the blue dress in court and testimony as to its whereabouts since it was first handed to Prof. Wood.

W. H. Medley, a typical police officer, ready to tell all he knew to the prosecution and equally ready to wait for cross-examination to bring out the rest, gave some very interesting recollections as to his

Talk With Lizzie Borden

immediately after the discovery of the murders, by which he confirmed the unvarying evidence of his predecessors to the affect that she was in the barn at the time of the homicide, and hadn't the remotest idea as to the person of the assassin.

He experimented with the barn floor and

the steps leading to the loft, and could find no other impressions than those he made himself, the details of the visit to the cellar not being given beyond the fact that they noticeably agreed with the testimony of his predecessors.

Medley with great particularity swore that he took the hatchet head from the box, showed it to Capt. Desmond, wrapped it in a piece of brown paper, and so on as above.

This testimony Capt. Desmond had not heard as, according to the wise direction, witnesses are not allowed to be in the room save when they are on the stand.

Desmond's attention being called to the search of the cellar, he said distinctly, "We searched everything in the cellar and carefully examined the box in which was the hatchet head, some iron stuff and no handle whatever."

"No handle there?" asked Gov. Robinson.

"No handle whatever," replied the witness. "There was nothing of any importance except a hatchet head, and that was covered with dirt rather than ashes."

It will be recalled that other witnesses have testified that this head was covered with ashes, others that it was dust, while the captain says it was dirt pure and simnple and nothing else. Continuing his story, he said:

"I wrapped the hatchet head up in a newspaper."

This flat contradiction of officer Medley's oath, that he wrapped it up in a piece of brown paper, was immediately taken advantage of by Gov. Robinson, who asked him if he was certain about it. Of course he was certain about it; they all are. There hasn't been an officer on the stand who has not been absolutely confident, nor has there been one who has not been

Flatly Contradicted

by one of his associates.

"Well," said Gov. Robinson, "let's see about it," handing him a large eight-page paper, "Was it like this?"

"Yes."

"Well, now show us how you wrapped it up." Whereupon the captain made a bundle about a foot long and proportionately large and exhibited it, reiterating that he was positive that he so wrapped the bundle up, thereby putting the prosecution to the cheerful condition of discrediting either him or officer Medley.

George F. Seaver, a state detective, after telling the story of the hatchet head and contradicting the officer who swore that its handle was found, Seaver testifying that he looked for one and there was none, and swearing also that the head was covered with ashes and not with dust, went on to tell about his examination of all the dresses in Miss Lizzie's closet. When asked to tell about them in detail, in a manly way he said he knew very little about dresses, but the first one he took down he said was a black silk, whereat Miss Borden shook her head and quietly informed her counsel that she had no black silk, not that that can be expected to in any way modify the officer's knowledge that he found one.

STATE OFFICER SEAVER

Continuing, he said that he made memoranda at the time of his examination of the blood spots in the sitting room, behind the lounge on which was found the prostrate form of Mr. Borden. Briefly put, he said he found five blood spots behind the lounge, and on the wall at the head of the lounge, in a space of 18 inches long by 10 wide, he found 86 small blood stains, and on the frame and glass of a picture and the cover of the lounge

There Were Forty Spots.

The highest spot on the wall was six feet and one inch from the floor, and the blood which he found on the door of the sitting room was nine feet seven and a half inches from the head of the lounge.

Under cross-examionation by Gov. Robinson Mr. Seaver testified that although he had been a carpenter, he could not decide of what kind of wood the hatchet handle was made. He thought it looked as if it had been a long time in the water, but he could not tell anything about it. Neither could he tell whether there was a blue dress in Lizzie's clothes closet or a bedford cord or an alpaca or a muslin.

He testified, however, that she had a blue dress on, but when told that was the day of the funeral, he "guessed" he was mistaken and would change his mind.

He contradicted Fleet, who insisted that the search was slight, saying that Fleet examined much more carefully than he, and that none of them found either blood or paint on anything. When asked if he testified to the spots from memoranda made at the time, he replied that he had made the memoranda later from recollection, and when asked why he didn't tell about the largest spot that was found, the one inside the door,

He Confusedly Explained

that he had lost the memorandum.

It appeared however, after much pushing, that although it was the biggest spot he made no mention of it, even on the last memorandum, but insisted that the omission was not due to the fact that he subsequently learned the spot was not of blood.

So you see these police officers, upon whose testimony Mr. Knowlton had a right to lean unreservedly, contradicted each other on many essential points, almost as significantly as in the cases of Miss Russell and Bridget Sullivan, and I marvel at the patience and dogged good nature manifested by the counsel for the prosecution from the opening of Monday last to the close of the session today.

In Mr. Moody's competent hands is placed the burden of direct examination so far, and he is as quick to notice these essential discrepancies as any one, but what can he do?

At the close of the session an agreement between council as to the facts with regard to Lizzie Borden's testimony was handed to the court. According to them, it appears that although Lizzie was not under arrest at the time of her testimony, she had been then three days notified by the marshal and the mayor of Fall River that she was suspected of committing the crime, and that the house and all its inmates, including herself were under the constant observation of the police who were stationed at the house.

If that is not equivalent to being under arrest, I don't understand the English language. She was, however, subpaened to attend, and when she requested that her counsel might be with her, she was refused the privilege, or right, as the case may be. It further appears, and is agreed to, as will be seen by counsel for the state, as well as those of the defense, that she was detained in the courthouse and arrested and further that

She Was Not Cautioned

by the court or the district attorney that she was not obliged to testify to anything which might criminate herself.

I don't know how the learned judges will decide, but I was struck by a remark made by Judge Blodgett last night to the effect that if wrong was done the prisoner she had the right to appeal to the supreme court, whereas if wrong were done to the prosecution there was no redress. That looked as though they might conclude to admit the inquest evidence.

Chief Justice Mason and Judge Blodgett left town this afternoon, but Judge Dewey, who will probably deliver the charge to the jury, will remain here, as it would be hard for him to ride over to Springfield and be back again by 9 o'clock Monday morning.

I asked him within bounds about the matter this afternoon, and he said that the people were jealous of their rights generally, and that in capital causes where in case of error the consequences might be very grave to the accused, the courts allowed very great latitude rather than have it said that they checked counsel for the defense too soon, for if they had been permitted to go on they might have scored a point, and so, adding that in cases of serious doubt where decisions were conflicting, it was a habit of the courts to favor the commonwealth as the defense had the right of appeal, which the prosecution did not.

So, that's the way it stands tonight.

After adjournment today, everybody who could hurried home. Lizzie was taken in a coupe, with the curtains drawn, to the jail, where she heartily relished a New England dinner, with the trimmings, apparently feeling 100 percent better than she did yesterday.

It would be folly to deny the exhilaration of the counsel and friends of Miss Borden. They know, of course, that the government intends to make an effort to prove that in the hour and a half as yet unaccounted for, Lizzie put in some heavy strokes, and they know that they will be expected to give some reasonable explanation of the burned dress business, but all this they are prepared to meet, and believe they can do so easily, so that unless brought face to face with the damaging stories, self-contradictory, told by Lizzie before the inquest their client will ere long be as free as the song birds in the air.

Howard

DAY OF DAYS

Mighty Question to Be Decided.

Result Means Much to Miss Borden.

Shall Inquest Testimony Be Admitted?

Howard Says that Some One Has Sworn Falsely.

Result--Government's Case Weakened.

Plea for Less Red Tape for the Jury.

One Member Sick Saturday Night and Sunday.

Points of Great Interest in the Case Thus Far.

NEW BEDFORD, June 11—What does Bridget Sullivan know about the burglary of the Borden house?

Where is detective McHenry?

What does uncle Morse know about the Borden murder which he keeps to himself?

Where is the handle found by marshal Fleet? The police had it last; how do they account for its disappearance?

This, according to the hymn book, is the day the Lord hath made and called it for his own, a sentiment, however, which does not, because it cannot, obtain in New Bedford during a session of a Massachusetts court.

We stand on the hither verge of a sensational week, having passed through one of exceeding trial to nerves and physiques, not to mention moral sensibilities. It is not too much to say that every one connected with the case, not even excepting the learned judges upon the bench, was heartily glad when the hour for adjournment came on Saturday, affording many an opportunity to go home and refresh their overtaxed energies by a day of rest.

I have my doubts of the jury, and would not be in the least surprised, assuming this week to be as hot and comfortless as the last, if they break down physically. One of them was quite ill all night, and is in very bad condition today.

According to the strict construction of the orders of the court the members of the jury are not permitted to use spirituous liquor of any kind. Men who are in the habit of drinking, even moderately, know what it means if they endeavor, even under ordinary circumstances and with their customary surroundings, to abstain literally and suddenly from their

Customary Stimulant.

What then must it be to men of similar habits, who are taken from the comforts of their homes, kept all day in the crampitudes of court room chairs, marched to and from the house, tired, hot, locked up at night, 12 of them in eight rooms, forbidden to discuss the one subject uppermost in their minds, shut out from the world about 6 o'clock in the evening, and not a drop to drink.

The jury is a coordinate branch of the court. Without it the procedure would be of no avail. It is just as important to this case as the judges on the bench, and the oath taken by each and every one of the 12 is just as solemn, just as binding, and in the presence of the same almighty God as that taken years ago by their honors who preside at the trial.

So far as the oath goes then, the 15 are on a dead level, otherwise it is different. For instance, yesterday afternoon Chief Justice Mason, with the gleam of domestic hope in his eye and his gripsack in his hand, accompanied by Judge Blodgett, whose intellectual face was fairly wreathed in smiles as he forecast a family welcome, sprang lightly into his coach and hurried to the Old Colony depot. Judge Dewey, who lives in Springfield, could have gone had he preferred, but he thought it wiser, inasmuch as he is to deliver the charge to the jury, to remain in town and block out, so far as is possible, the thoughts suggested by the evidence thus far educed, and also to study up the points involved in the important question to be decided tomorrow morning as to whether Miss Borden's testimony given at the inquest shall be admitted or excluded.

Later in the forenoon, literally used up in head and physique, I gladly accepted brotherBrownell's invitation to drive up on the point road, along the

Line of Buzzards Bay,

swept by breezes from the ocean so strong as to suggest the most vigorous boisterousness of a northeast gale. As we sped along just this side of Fort Tabor, which in its dismantled condition, neighbored by a score or more of costly guns and other paraphernalia of war, suggested thoughts of the waste of government, my eye was attracted by a picturesque figure, sitting on a rock a little this side of the rolling waters. As I drew near I recognized the classic contour of Judge Dewey's well-known face and felt a thrill of joy as I saw the refreshment he was getting while the wind toyed playfully with his whitening locks, cooling his fevered brow and toning him for the herculean labor yet before him.

And the jurors?

O! That's different. After their dinner they were bundled into an omnibus with their attentive undersheriffs, driven down to the Point and back again in less than an hour, given their suppers, and securely locked in theirs uperheated heated rooms not only without spirituous refreshments, but without any possible enlivenments or withdrawals from introspection. The officers are not permitted to speak to them. Queen Victoria might die, New York could burn up or Boston burn down, the whole Chicago exposition might fall into the lake or Mrs Palmer make another speech, but the jury would know nothing of it.

They don't even see Howard's letter nor are they permitted to glance at a daily newspaper, no matter how unsensational.

They must go and do together. For instance, the court had ordered that they were to be taken to the Unitarian church today, but as one of them was ill all were deprived of that

Intellectual Feast.

At the last session of the court the judge directed one of the officers to ascertain if there were any Roman Catholics on the jury. Had there been, none of the churches would have been honored by their presence.

It was my desire that the sick man should be furnished a little good whisky today, but the judge decided otherwise, wrongfully I think, so the poor fellow suffers. It is a fact, I dare say, that if this one were permitted a little liquid refreshment, other cases of illness would develop, demanding an equally considerate treatment; but as that is a matter so plainly within common sense and control of the sheriff, I don't consider the objection valid. If in consequence of this deprivation this particular juror breaks down the commonwealth will be put to great expense for naught, and I predict if we have equally hot weather this week and there is not some let-up in the discipline, some loosing of the red tape now irritating the jurors, there will come a collapse which will mean business in the jury.

In order that his companions need not suffer the pangs of hunger, the sick juror, Mr Swift, a merchant of this town, who sits next to the foreman, with much difficulty dressed and went down to dinner at 1 o'clock. They were gone, all told, about 40 minutes, and when they returned, filing in great shape past my door, I noticed that every one was vigorously using that hideous American implement known as the toothpick.

DISTRICT ATTORNEY MOODY

I think that in view of what is to come it might be well to look for a moment at the predicament in which the prosecution's witnesses have, in their effort to manifest zeal,

Led the Government Astray.

In the first place, either Bridget Sullivan or the police officer deliberately lied about the hatchets. She testified distinctly, reaffirming her evidence with great deliberation, that she did not touch the hatchets; that she did not lay her hands on them, while the officer, with equal distinctness and equal deliberation, swore and reswore that she led the officers directly to the box, put her hand into it, she standing on the cellar floor, took out the hatchets and handed them to him.

Both witnesses were called for the prosecution and one or the other government must discredit.

Second—Either the marshal or the police officer lied about the finding of the hatchet. The officer not only told of the handle found by marshal Fleet but described it, indicating by his two hands its length, showing by his thumb and finger its size, and when pushed by the pertinacity of Gov Robinson's admirable cross-examination he reaffirmed his original testimony and swore again that he saw Fleet take the handle from the box, fit its broken part to the little piece remaining in the eye and put it back again, thereby leaving in the control of the prosecution the box and the handle, which were just as much in the custody of the government as the house itself, because nothing could be taken from it without the knowledge of the officers of the law. But marshal Fleet distinctly, deliberately and repeatedly contradicted, with marked emphasis, this testimony of the officer, and within five minutes after evidence was given, showing that he took the handle from the box and examined it, while he swore that he not only did not touch the handle but he

Did Not See the Handle.

These witnesses were called by the prosecution, and one or the other of them must be discredited by the government.

Third, either the police captain or the police officer lied under oath about the wrapping of that hatchet head.

And, mind you, these lies are not mere inconsistencies. They are not minor discrepancies in a long story. They are deliberate statements under oath made conspicuously significant after reiteration. Nor are these lies told by ordinary witnesses. They are the positive utterances of public officials, familiar to scenes of blood, accustomed to excitements, knowing that they must of necessity testify before the court and jury.

The captain not only swore that he wrapped the hatchet in paper, but he took a great eight-page paper and wrapped it about the head, illustrating what, according to his oath, he did, when he took the head from the box for the purpose of having it given into the custody of the city marshal.

Tremulous with excitement internally, but sweet as a day in June externally, Gov Robinson gently led him on, until the unsuspecting captain had cut off all possibility of retreat from his position, and there he left him. He left an interesting figure, loaded to the guards with ammunition fatal to the government, because, immediately preceding him, the officer had testified, not alone that he wrapped the hatchet head in a piece of paper, but in order that there could be no doubt about it he described the wrapping as a bit of brown paper and kindly condescended to oblige the counsel by showing the court and jury precisely how he, not the captain with an eight-page paper, but he the simple officer, in a little bit of brown paper, which he subsequently tore open that his fellow officer might see that hatchet, wrapped it up.

These two are also witnesses for the prosecution, and one or the other of them must be discredited by the government.

Fourth, either marshal Fleet or Capt Desmond know nothing of the English language or else one of them deliberately lied about the

Search in the Household.

Marshal Fleet distinctly said over and over again that it was not a thorough search, while Capt Desmond was naturally indignant that he, a police officer, making a search for information as to the perpetrator of a brutal dual murder, should be so recreant to his trust, and so ignorant of his obvious duty, as to be satisfied with anything less than a most thorough, a literal search of everything, everywhere, in and about the house. The government tell us that Bridget Sullivan is not a prisoner, and she, too, testified that she was not in the jail, but the jailer's apartments. That is a distinction without a difference. She is and is not a prisoner. That is, she is not called a prisoner, but she is kept one all the same.

Why?

What does Bridget know about the burglary of the Borden house some time ago?

There are

All Sorts of Rumors

about Bridget's knowledge of the burglary, as there are, too, concerning detective McHenry and his extraordinary efforts, first, to weave a web about Lizzie Borden, and second, to keep himself in ungetable hiding.

And now where is the handle to that hatchet? Had Gov Robinson accepted Dist Atty Knowlton's suggestion that a man should be sent to examine the Borden cellar and the box it is quite likely the handle would have been found there, but Robinson is not falling into that sort of trap this year, and he declined to hunt for justice in that direction. Mr Knowlton was not to be baffled that way, however, and he ordered an officer to go to the Borden house and seek admission. He went, but was not allowed to come in. The agent for the defense had better luck, was admitted, went straight to the cellar and found the box, but it was empty, and now the defense triumphantly ask, where is that handle?

If the prosecution says "There was none" the defense will quote the prosecution's witness to the effect that there was one. If the government don't know where it is, the governor at once, by testimony given by the witnesses, finds the handle in the hands of marshal Fleet and insists he account for it.

So you see it is a very pretty muddle as it stands and in that muddled condition all parties will reassemble in the court room tomorrow morning, the prosecution embarrassed, but still hopeful, the defence exhilarated yet naturally still anxious.

I was not present at the inquest when Lizzie Borden testified, and I am indebted to Charles Carroll Harold of the Evening Journal for information concerning it, and also as to the practise in this state.

It seems that although Lizzie, as the habit of calling her we have all fallen into, although not under arrest, was brought before Judge Blaisdell, the magistrate who held the inquest and there

Plied with Questions By

Dist Atty Knowlton, who has been characterized as the "sharpest and shrewdest" prosecuting officer in the commonwealth. At that time Lizzie Borden was suffering tortures incident to the grief engendered by the loss of her parents, so recently that there had been no time to recover from the shock. She was suffering with horror at the fact that she was under suspicion of being guilty of murder, double murder. From one victim came her own flesh and blood, while the other was the companion of his bosom, the sharer of his pleasures and sorrows, entiled to the holy name of wife. She was under a terrible weight of anxiety because her character, which never knew stain before, was at stake, and had already been damaged beyond complete repair.

She was sickened with horrors upon horrors at the sight of the victims. Even if she was guilty that horror was none the less, for after the outburst of frenzied passion, which in that case impelled her to the deed, there must have been a relapse into normal condition and in the moments of sane contemplation the spectre of death was surely never absent from her vision.

She had been dosed with drugs because of her physical and mental prostration.

She did not come before the tribunal voluntarily, but was compelled to do this under forms of law. She was helpless. If she had been arrested no person in the state could have forced her to speak unless she was willing.

Considering the position she occupied was it right to take her before a stern magistrate and have

Answers Wrung from Her

y a trained professional. astute, vigorous questioner? Was it a fair and equal contest, such as chivalry delights in?

Now, the court says, and it is the universal rule, that statements made by parties under duress or compulsion shall not be used as against the parties themselves in any criminal case. This is not controlled by statutes here, but it is the practice. It is held, surely and unequivocally, that there is no law by which a prisoner can be compelled to testify against himself except in civil cases. That rule is so strong in Massachusetts that not only can no prisoner charged with an offence be compelled to testify against himself, but it is so strong, so humane, so tender, even, that a person charged with an offense need not in his own behalf testify, and if he fails to do this the rule still is that no inference shall be drawn from his refusing to take the stand: Not only this. but the refusal shall not be made the bias of any argument prejudicial to the defendant.

If a person cannot be called to testify against himself in a case of assault and battery or when accused of stealing a sheep—and need not testify in his own behalf—where does the government get the right to summon into court and force to testify a prisoner suspected of dual murder?

But the government will claim and argue that the very object of an inquest is to find out the facts, and to get information concerning persons under suspicion. The testimony of the suspected may lead to other inquiries; and besides if a person is guilty there is no harm in finding it out, even by his own admissions, if they are obtained under legal and regular forms; and the supposed individual interests must give way to public weal.

The very object of an inquest is to detect the guilty party, and bring him to punishment. The officers of the government use a great deal of strategy in their work of punishing the guilty, It is necessary, for the crime is secret. It is better for one to suffer than for the public to be the sufferer, and this is exemplified by the fact that men are arrested on suspicion, and if it is proved that an error is made the officers apologize for the injustice and

Let the Prisoner Go.

The rule is clear that no one is required to say anything that will tend to convict himself. And notwithstanding this rule the defendant, who declines to testify, may, despite the caution of the court, create the impression that it is because the testimony would be damaging, and so the very declination will to some degree tend to convict him.

I must say I don't see any loophole for the court on the duress question, for Lizzie knew very well that she was suspected of the murder, that her house was under police guard, that she had been shadowed wherever she went, and that she was taken before the magistrate under circumstances which do not attend the invitation of an ordinary witness. After the inquest, instead of being allowed to go home, she was kept in a room adjoining the court for several hours, and then on a warrant committed, and from that moment to this she has been a prisoner.

That is the question which, as I wired last night, must be presented, argued and decided tomorrow. If the inquest testimony is admitted the trial will be prolonged; if it is not, I can see no reason why the evidence should not all be in and the arguments made by Saturday night.

There has never been a trial so full of surprises, with such marvelous contradictions, given by witnesses called for a common purpose. Indeed, there was never such a murder before, and there certainly never was an accused person who kept herself so thoroughly to herself, as the palefaced, dumpling-bodied little woman, who rose with the lark that she might enjoy her pork and beans this morning, and who stood for a moment at her window that the breezes from Buzzards bay might fan her troubled brow this afternoon, and who now, after a peaceful day, has folded her hands to rest.

Howard

The Providence Journal

If Lizzie Borden is acquitted, where is the fiend who did the foul deeds for which she has been tried? She should spend her life in hunting him down, so that she can be as free from suspicion as Bridget Sullivan is already.

THE GENIUS OF DICKENS

It Furnishes Solace for Lizzie Borden.

Prisoner Receives No Visitors During Sunday—Not Known Whether She Will Testify—Bloody Garments, Battered Skulls and Gory Handkerchiefs to Be Exhibited in Court This Week—Medical Experts to Testify.

SPECIAL DISPATCH TO THE BOSTON HERALD

NEW BEDFORD, June 11, 1893. New Bedford is not only one of the most ancient and romantic, but it is one of the most beautiful towns in New England. The heart of its residence district is a park of grand elms, gorgeous gardens and green lawns. Today the flowers were open to their fullest splendor, the arching elms met in gothic lines over the shaded streets and the robins, knowing it was Sunday, preempted the lawns before the great mansions of the retired whaler folk.

None of these alluring beauties were for the most talked of woman in the town, for that woman is Miss Lizzie Borden.

She was in her prison quarters, scenting the aroma of the magnolias, perhaps, but enjoying nothing but her hope of eventual freedom and the book that she was reading.

CONFERENCE IN THE JUDGES' PRIVATE ROOM

At the prison office the lonely prisoner was reported to be in good health, because her appetite is all right, it was said, for none but her keepers had seen her.

Had any friends called upon her. No, not one, except her counsel, the officials said, since she had come from Taunton.

Had any flowers been sent to her? Not until last night, it was reported, but then there came a package of them by post from a distance. And how about letters, for it was known that her lawyers were getting little bales of letters every day. Well, she had received a few every day, perhaps three or four a day.

Anything particular about them? No, except that they appeared to be from lady friends. The officials do not read missives to prisoners. They only open the envelope to make sure that nothing contraband is sent in that way.

The genius of Charles Dickens was her solace and under that generally cheery influence she may be said to have been better off than in talking with visitors about the murders which she did or did not do.

Moreover, the dignity of this old court and place is not conductive to those scenes of crowds of mawkish visitors and cells full of flowers such as are matters of course elsewhere.

Her sister Emma cannot be seen, to most persons, to have been in a position altogether enviable, for she spent the day in the old family house of horrors at Fall River. She has been notified by the court that she need not attend every day, but must come when she is called. Under the rule she cannot sit in court with the sister from whom she was all but inseparable all her life and it is understood that she would not be allowed to see her sister if she called at the jail.

The commonwealth has submitted a list of no less than 90 witnesses, upon any or all of whom it may call for evidence. It will not, in all likelikood, put more than 45 or 50 on the stand, but, in the meantime, the rest must keep away from the courtroom, and they include nearly every friend that Lizzie Borden had on earth.

Whether she will herself become a witness is not yet decided. It is publicly understood that she will not be called, but the truth is that the question is not decided, and will not be yet awhile. It depends on the

Best Judgment of Her Counsel,

after a great deal more consideration. It depends also on whether her previous testimony is admitted and upon its effect.

There lives today no man or woman who can say whether or no she will be a witness in her own behalf.

The testimony yet to come at the call of the government is, first of all, the expert testimony as to the nature of the murders, the relation of one murder to the other in point of time, the analysis of the various blood spots and the value of the deadly and the gruesome exhibits as accessories or accompaniments of the crime.

The Woonsocket Reporter

After a week's testimony on the part of the prosecution in the Borden murder trial, the indications are that the accused young woman will never be convicted. The defense, if the layman can judge, has much the best of the case thus far, for there has been no direct evidence fastening the atrocious crime upon the prisoner, and leading witnesses have, in several important particulars, been flatly contradictory. As the case now stands, a disagreement is the most that the government can expect, while public sentiment already clamors for an acquittal.

The Boston Advertiser

Lizzie Borden, if confronted by her evidence at the inquest, would apparently have difficulty in reconciling it with facts now proven by undoubted veracity. In the light of what is now known, the worst phase in Lizzie Borden's defense was this testimony given before her arrest. If it could be introduced she must go on the stand and explain it. With it excluded, she may still confidently hope that not enough proof has been introduced by the government to justify her conviction, and she may easily relieve herself of the ordeal of the witness box. Yet few people who have watched this trial, or who know the respondent, apprehend that in August, when she gave this evidence, she was frightened out of her wits, or had lost mental control. Whatever she swore to then was in general the story she meant to tell, whether true or not. If it was false, she knew it perfectly at the time; if true, why not let it go in now as part of the case? Up to this point the government has distinctly failed to convict Lizzie Borden. The opinion deepens that it will not fasten the guilt upon her. No other person is now or in any reasonable way ever has been suspected. If she is not the one, then the mystery will remain unsolved, for about the only thing that the government has tried to demonstrate is to prove, beyond reasonable doubt, that the parents could not have been murdered by any one else. The duty of the government is to prove absolutely that Lizzie Borden committed these murders, or she ought to, and will, go free. She is entitled to every legal expedient to prevent her guilt being shown, but it is unfortunate for those who would be happiest at her complete exoneration that the exclusion of any sworn statement deliberately made by her should be advantageous to her defense.

THE PARALLEL VIEW

THE GOVERNMENT'S VIEW

92 Second Street was locked and could not be entered by anyone.

Men cutting wood and washing carriages saw no one escape.

The Government says Lizzie never went to the barn.

THE DEFENDANT'S VIEW

The back door was open when Bridget washed the windows.

Deputy Wixon climbed the fence unseen by the woodcutters.

Hyman Lubinsky saw a woman coming from the barn at 11:15.

HER TEARS FLOWED

A Vital Point gained for Lizzie Borden

Judges Refuse to Admit Her Testimony at the Inquest - Grewsome Relics of the Murders of Mr. and Mrs. Borden Introduced - Medical Examiner Dolan on the Stand - Prisoner Not Well, but Wore a New Dress.

GOV. ROBINSON: "IF THAT IS FREEDOM, GOD SAVE MASSACHUSETTS!"

(SPECIAL DESPATCH TO THE BOSTON HERALD)

NEW BEDFORD, June 12, 1893. The seventh day of the Borden trial did not discredit the reputation the case has earned as unique and crowded with sensations.

Gore and hatchets, axes, plaster casts that might have been borrowed from a bowery chamber of horrors, bloody garments, bits of bloody carpet and blood-spattered furniture and house fittings--these were the stage properties in this legal drama that is wending itself out to the length of a Chinese play.

The talk of the witnesses and lawyers went further, and dealt with autopsies and even with things that, though not unfit for publication, are yet much better out of print than in it.

In the hallway just outside the court room was the bloody sofa on which poor old Mr. Borden died so horribly. It was covered all over with gunny sacking, but whoever did not know what it was had it pointed out, so that all were prepared on the very threshold for the legal saturnalia that was to go on within.

Miss Borden is not well, and her face and manner showed it.

Out of court, in the hotel and the streets, it has been popularly believed that it would be a bad day for the prisoner when this testimony, given in her befogged condition during the day of badgering, should be read to the jury.

Some wanted her to have the worst that could befall her.

Others wanted her to have a fresh bill of health with which to meet this ordeal.

Thus is society here rent in twain upon the question of

Her Guilt or Innocence

As to the new point in law, the facts are these:

Plenty of persons in Massachusetts have borne witness at inquests and inquiries and then have been accused and confronted with their own previous testimony, but in every such case the first testimony has been given voluntarily.

The point raised in this case was that Miss Borden did not give voluntary testimony at the inquest after the murders in her home.

Her lawyers hold that she was not formally arrested, but that she was to all intents a prisoner and accused of committing the crimes. A warrant was, indeed, out for her; she was surrounded and watched by the police; she was told by the government that she had got to answer its questions "if she stood on the stand all day"; the benefit of counsel was denied to her, and she stood alone, a helpless woman who had never been in a court before, surrounded by this band of police and government officials, that now again gather at the court house door, and is seen to be the source of nine-tenths of the evidence in the case against her. This morning was set apart for the hearing of this argument.

The court room was crowded; even on the sidewalk thelawyers had to struggle to get through the perpetual and now swollen crowd of women idlers.

Great was the curiosity to hear the master lawyer, Ex-Gov. Robinson, as a speech maker.

Dist.-Atty. Moody, assistant to the local District Attorney, made the argument for the admission of the woman's previous testimony, and addressed himself solely to the court and to the legal precedents for what she demanded.

It was to be presumed that Gov. Robinson would follow the same course, but he had his client's cause too deeply at heart, and he departed so far from a merely legal argument that the audience enjoyed a sample of the eloquence and art that makes him so strong before a jury.

After Two Hours of Talking

pro and con, the three dignified judges left the room to consult and reach their decision. They were gone for a little more than an hour.

The judges found that Miss Borden had been, to all intents and purposes, a prisoner charged with two murders, and her testimony at the inquest was not voluntary,

The feeling of both sides in the contrsoversy over her guilt was that this was a grand piece of good fortune for her.

When the decision was reached by the chief justice, there was a man in front of the correspondent of the HERALD. Both spoke to him, and almost simultaneously:

"This is logic and good law" said one. "The commonwealth would have been disgraced by any other decision."

"Great God," said the other, "it is a crying shame that justice should be defeated and a murderer protected because of so slight a point as that decision is based upon."

Miss Borden had come into the room and was sitting behind Mr. Robinson. She burst into tears, hiding her face in her handkerchief, while her body shook with the force of her emotion.

The ex-Governor produced several copies in typewriting of points he had jotted down and meant to enlarge upon in his argument. He received permission to hand these copies to the Judges.

Taking a copy of his own in his hand he used it as a guide. The first point in the list was that the medical examiner is shown by the evidence to have taken charge of the bodies upon which the inquest was to have been held. Second, Miss Borden testified on Aug. 9, 10 and 11. From the second day after the crimes the woman was kept under constant observation of the police, all the time until the conclusion of her testimony. Her house was surrounded by the police, there was no time, day or night, when the eye of the police was not on her house and all the inmates of it. So far as any effect on the defendant was concerned she knew the police were around her and she was under uninterrupted surveillance. Before testifying the defendant made a request for counsel. This was denied, and no counsel was allowed to her, she stood alone, a woman, for three days, unguarded by counsel, confronted by the District Attorney, watched by the City Marshal, and at all times surrounded by the police.

The next point made by the shrewd and earnest ex-Governor was that Miss Borden was not properly cautioned.

"The complaint had been made against her and the warrant for her arrest was issued. That mandate was held by the Marshal when he escorted that woman to the inquest. Can any one say she had not been proceeded against? She had not been formally arrested, nay, but the Commonwealth had asserted its power and the City Marshal stood ready at any moment to make her his prisoner. We must assume in common sense that that was at the direction of the District Attorney. It was not at random that that was done. Some one in authority asked it. She was, in fact, a prisoner, never free. Then, later, she was arrested on another warrant. Perhaps this was done in order to say she was arrested subsequent to her testimony; so that, perhaps, without its being intended, it was, in fact an evasion of the law. It may appear, it might appear, to deprive this defendant of the rights guaranteed to her by the laws.

"She was a woman, she couldn't run, with the hand ever on her shoulder, under those circumstances she was taken to the inquest to testify, with no one authorized to tell her or who was bound to tell her that she had any rights at all. She stood alone, a defenceless woman, in that attitude. If that is freedom, God save the Commonwealth of Massachusetts. If anything that is done by a woman under such circumstances is voluntary, then "compulsory" must hereafter be known as "voluntary".

"The crimes had been committed, and knowledge of the fact was in the possession of the law. That inquiry was only used to extort from this woman something to be used against her in her trial.

"It is not to be lost sight of," the Governor continued, "that at the time she was examined she had been formally charged with the commission of the murders. She was not summoned in order to find out who had done the deed, for

MOODY ARGUES FOR THE ADMISSION OF THE INQUEST TESTIMONY

the Government had already sworn that she did it. Instead of serving that warrant they hid it away and said to themselves that perhaps they could get something out of her before they served it. Then they issued another warrant, and said that they would consider her testimony as previous to that warrant. I hope I have not said more than I ought to. If I do so I hope the court will consider that it is the defendant who is speaking to you out of her knowledge of her experience in Fall River and out of a jealous regard for her rights, into which she was born.

"It makes no difference that our statutes say a defendant so placed may testify, if he or she so desires, for they say, further, that no inference is to be drawn against her from the fact that he or she refuses to testify. We hear the constitution of Massachusetts read, and it passes glibly over the tongue, and in and out, and that until some one plants his feet upon it, and fails to recognize its declarations. Miss Borden stands on that ancient document to-day. It says that no person shall be forced to testify against herself. It was written when Massachusetts was born. It was the instinct of that hour. It has been the bulwark of our liberties ever since. When the Constitution of the United States was drawn it said in simple phrase: 'No person shall be compelled in any criminal cause to be a witness against himself.' The shield of the State and the shield of the nation are her protection in this hour."

Miss Borden, in her chair in front of the dock and close behind the line of chairs in which her lawyers sat, leaned forward and drank in every word of the decision. For a moment after the reading and during the veritable gush of relief that sounded in the court, she still sat thus stoical and heavy faced. Then, like lightning, a purple cast spread all over her face, her hand sought her handkerchief, and almost too quickly for her to get it to her face the tears shot into her eyes. A strange, strong convulsion wracked her body at the same moment. She pressed the handkerchief almost into her eyes, and again and again her body shook with the sobbing form that her over-strained emotions took. She was soon able to control herself, but when she showed her face again it was blue. She then had recourse to her smelling bottle.

The New York Times

A POINT IN THE BORDEN CASE.

A legal point of considerable importance was decided in the Borden case at New-Bedford yesterday. The prosecution desired to put in as evidence the statements of the accused made at the Coroner's inquest last August before she was placed under arrest charged with the murder. An agreed statement of facts was made up as a basis for argument and for the decision.

She had been summoned to testify at the inquest and had testified under oath. She was not allowed to have counsel present and was not warned that she was not obliged to testify to anything that might tend to incriminate herself. While she was not under arrest at the time, she had previously been notified that she was suspected of the crime and was under the constant observation of the police; a complaint had been made by the City Marshal charging her with the murder and a warrant of arrest had been issued, though it had not been served and she had not been informed of it; but she was arrested immediately upon the conclusion of her testimony under a warrant then issued upon a complaint then sworn to by the Marshal.

The admissibility of the evidence at the trial depended upon whether her testimony at the inquest was to be considered as voluntary. The court held that if the accused was under arrest at the time of the inquest her statements could not be considered as voluntary and could not be admitted as evidence, and it further held that "from the agreed facts it is plain that the prisoner was at the time of the inquest as much a prisoner as she ever has been." On that ground the evidence was excluded.

The Worcester Telegram

The exclusion of Lizzie Borden's testimony taken at the inquest, when she was without counsel, is another important point for the defense, and relieves her lawyers of placing Lizzie upon the witness stand. If the government can show that it was justified in arresting the girl, it had better be about it.

LIZZIE WEPT

But Her Tears Were Those of Joy

Signal Victory Won by the Defense.

Inquest Testimony Ruled Out by the Court.

Damaging Statements Are Thus Excluded.

Prisoner Breaks Down at Announcement.

Dr Dolan Tells About the Autopsies.

His Opinion of How the Wounds Were Inflicted.

Another Bombshell in Waiting for Prosecution.

NEW BEDFORD, June 12—And then she broke down and cried.

Who?

Miss Lizzie Borden, accused of the brutal murder of her father and stepmother—she's the one who broke down and cried.

What for?

For joy, pure, unadulterated joy, and I will tell you about it.

It will be remembered that when court adjourned on Saturday night last an agreement as to facts connected with Miss Borden's condition and the circumstances attending her testimony, at the time of the Fall River inquest, had been agreed and filed with the court, the understanding being that arguments should be held today pro and con the admissibility of the evidence given by her at the time of monumental distress, chagrin and mental suffering.

Although she had had two nights' rest

And Six Square Meals

since the adjournment and had devoured with zealous interest chapter after chapter from the facile pen of the poor man's novelist, Charles Dickens, she was not in good form. In the first place the wind had died away and the fierce burnings of a summer sun pierced the air with caloric spearings, prophetic of a day of intense discomfort. Her color was bad, her manner listless, and it seemed as though the demon of apprehension was dallying with her sensibilities.

The judges looked as fresh as daisies. Their bench was made fragrant by vases of flowers. Birds hopping from twig to twig on the branches of the great trees at the court house side seemed to suggest charity and good will to the judicial minds directed toward all men in general and the little woman in black in particular. There were no friendly hands outstretched to greet her save the perfunctory digits of her well-fed counsel. To be sure Rev Mr Jubb was on hand with his smile and his gloves and his posy, but he does not count, first, because he is her pastor, and second because he is from Fall River, and some of his friends--conspicuous, by the way, by their absence—would be quite as well satisfied if the reverend gentleman was not so much in evidence.

The jury, poor tired fellows, like so many wilted flowers, took their accustomed seats, with the exception of Juror Swift, who was allowed the rest and refreshment of a leather cushion, he being the invalid of the party.

The audience seats were filled to the uttermost, and extra camp chairs were placed in some of the aisles, while the enclosure

THE JUDGES DECIDE: THE INQUEST TESTIMONY WILL NOT BE ENTERED

ordinarily reserved for members of the bar was largely filled with experts of high and low degree.

Armed with a perfect library of law books, Dist Atty Knowlton, whose impassive countenance grows

More and More Sphinx-Like

as the days roll on, and Dist Atty Moody, who was evidently impressed with the responsibility placed upon him on this occasion, waited the pleasure of the court, while ex Gov Robinson, with his front locks as smooth as those of Jonathan Slick; counselor Jennings, nervously watching every motion, and counselor Adams, the best-groomed man of all the lot, alertly listened for the court's order concerning the jury.

This, mind you, was at 9 o'clock in the morning, eight hours before an adjournment for the day was possble, so it seemed rather unnecessary to have gone to the trouble of bringing the jury all the way to court, when it was seen that the sheriffs were directed to conduct them from the room during the argument which was then about to begin. However, like so many kings of France, they first marched up the steps and then marched down again, chewing the cud of reflection as, singly and concertedly, they wondered why, if they were really a coordinate branch of the court, they must be excluded at the very time when the excitement was expected to begin.

Order being restored, Mr Moody, upon whom down to this time the public burden of the prosecution has been laid, began his plea for the presentation, by the notes of the official stenographer, Miss White, of testimony given by Miss Lizzie Borden at the inquest in Fall River last August.

She was taken before the committing magistrate whose duty it was to hold the inquest, and denied counsel, although the state was represented by the brainy and experienced Dist Atty Knowlton. During three days of excessive heat, every moment watched by the police, her house sentineled by the police, herself escorted to and from the city hall by the city marshal, this girl, unattended by any of her own sex and unadvised by lawyers or the courts that she need not testify unless she wished to, may well be believed to have suffered the agonies of the damned.

Pushed, examined, cross-questioned, surrounded by hostile officials, she was badgered, confused and hetcheled to such an extent that during those long, tedious, three days of inquisition she contradicted herself time and time again.

It was in order that the state might benefit by these damaging contradictions that Mr Moody made his plea. He began by stating the statute law, and showing therefrom that all that was done by the police, the district attorney and the sitting magistrate was done in obedience to the explicit statutory direction. He argued that because Miss Borden responded to the subpena her testimony was voluntary, ignoring altogether the fact that she was taken by the city marshal, and that she had no adviser to warn her that she need not go unless she so chose, and ignoring the furthermost pregnant fact that the

Warrant for Her Arrest

was quietly reposing in the commonwealth's pocket ready for just that emergency.

Mr Moody made the ingenious plea that, as Miss Borden's testimony was in the nature of a denial, rather than confession, the law bearing upon the admission of confession was not applicable in this case. I was interested in following the peculiar bent of the young man's mind, shown not only in the argument immediately referred to, but in this, namely, that many rules in respect to criminal law were made at a time when the accused had not the right to testify in his own behalf. He insisted that if the present question were to arise in the state of New York the evidence offered would be admitted, and argued strenuously that the only question which occurred to his mind for the serious consideration was whether the testimony given by Miss Borden was voluntary or compulsory.

DR. WILLIAM A. DOLAN

Gov Robinson replied at considerable length, covering the precise ground so far as Miss Borden's condition is concerned, taken by me in my dispatches printed Sunday and today, proving beyond all possible question that although Miss Borden was not technically under arrest she was literally so, and that therefore in a matter so great as to affect not only the liberty but the life of the prisoner, the courts had no right to allow a palpable evasion, made for the purpose of trick, to affect the rights of one who, so far as that particular instance went, had no protection, save that afforded by the constitution of the commonwealth and the amended constitution of the United States itself.

"If this," said he, "is freedom, God save the commonwealth of Massachusetts. If this be freedom, compulsory must hereafter be known as voluntary."

It appears by the evidence that although the city marshal had a warrant for

Miss Borden's Arrest

in his pocket during the entire inquest procedure, the literal arrest was made by virtue of a subsequent warrant, on which Mr Robinson made a well directed thrust.

"They have," said he, "under oath sworn she had done the murders, but rather than serve it they said, 'We will hold the paper in our pockets and get what we can from her, and later if we decide to arrest her we will put away that paper,' worse than the burning of a dress, and literally arrest her on another warrant."

The profound sensation created by this characteristic point, admirably made by the counsel who bids fair to show himself as eloquent a pleader as he has already an adroit cross-examiner, was so marked that every one in the court room instinctively looked at his neighbor, and Miss Borden straightened herself in her chair in an adjoining room, where, although she could not see, she could hear all that was said.

The heat of the day and her condition had suggested to her thoughtful guardian early in the argument that she, like the jury, should have the privilege of retiring, and she did so.

It is no secret, nor was it after the adjournment on Saturday night, that public sentiment favored either a verdict of not guilty or a disagreement of the jury, and when the audience in the court room ascertained from the phrasing of Mr Moody's ingenious but untenable plea, that the government insisted that Miss Borden was not under arrest and, therefore, was a voluntary witness, it took the point at once, and, long before their honors decided, made up its mind that Lizzie's evidence would not be recalled during the present investigation.

The trend on the mind of the court is illustrated by the significant question of the chief justice, who, like the other learned judges on the bench, listened

With Solicitous Attention

to the argument from first to last to this effect:

"Was the defendant put on the stand by the government?"

To this Mr Moody replied:

"I don't know; the record is silent on that point."

Therefore it was that Gov Robinson made with marked emphasis his insistence that his client had been subpenaed by the government, had been conducted by an officer of the commonwealth, had been confronted by and examined by the district attorney for the commonwealth, and without the benefit of counsel was forced to answer, she being in no mental or physical condition to do so.

I must say I was surprised when Mr Moody alluded to Gov Robinson's well-put and courteously-delivered argument as a series of vocal gymnastics, as an argument surrounded by pyrotechnics, and as effusive rhetoric unsupported by a single case; was surprised because Mr Moody is a man of unusual natural cleverness, with an opportunity of distinguishing himself which is rarely given to so young a man, and because his own quick intuitions must have told him, as it did every one else in the court room, and many readers will do me the justice to recall I have predicted from the first that the learned judges must of necessity decide against him.

However, Mr Moody went on to argue that because Bridget Sullivan, a poor girl, was

Called to the Stand,

so Lizzie Borden, a rich woman, ought to be called to the stand; as the law makes no distinction between people of lofty and people of humble station, and, therefore, if it was proper to give Bridget Sullivan an opportunity to explain how and where she spent the hours of the morning it was an equal courtesy and kindness to extend a similar opportunity to Miss Borden.

I was glad for his own sake that brother Moody did not push that point and seek to draw a parallel between Bridget Sullivan, who was used to work up a case against a mistress who had always been kind to her and the woman against whom the police had directed their batteries when there was public opinion insisting that something should be done by the police for the city's protection.

Mr Moody intimated that Lizzie Borden had consulted with her counsel, and assumed that counsel had done his duty in informing her as to her rights and in cautioning her against criminating herself. I concede that Mr Moody did the best possible in an endeavor impossible of accomplishment, but it was weakness personified in comparison with the superbly ornate and charmingly delivered presentation of his opponent, concerning whom, however, it is but fair to say that his case was like that of an actor who did well with a good part, while Mr Moody was like that of an actor who was expected to do much with an extremely bad part.

Presently in a voice as clear as a bell, with enunciation as distinct as that of Edwin Booth, when he began his famous "To be or not to be," the chief justice delivered the decision of the court against the admission of the testimony.

And then she broke down and cried.

Who?

Miss Lizzie Borden, accused of the brutal murder of the father and stepmother, she's the one who broke down and cried.

What for?

For pure unadulterated joy, and hers were not the only wet eyes in the court room at that. She couldn't help it. She was nervous, upset, tired out, strained with a tension that no man need hope to understand, and when this great, wide horizon of relief was unfolded to her, human nature asserted itself, and of course she broke down and of course she cried.

Then the jury came in. They knew nothing about this. The agitation of the counsel, the nervous condition of Miss Borden, the cheery

Look of Popular Satisfaction

resting on everybody's face, was all Greek to that branch of the court.

Then began the work of the day. Dr Dedrick described the condition of the bodies when he saw them, and was permitted to give the reasons for his belief that Mrs Borden had died several hours before her husband, her blood being coagulated and her body colder and stiff, while her husband's blood was still trickling and the body was warm.

After recess, Dr Dolan, who is the medical examiner for the county of Bristol, a

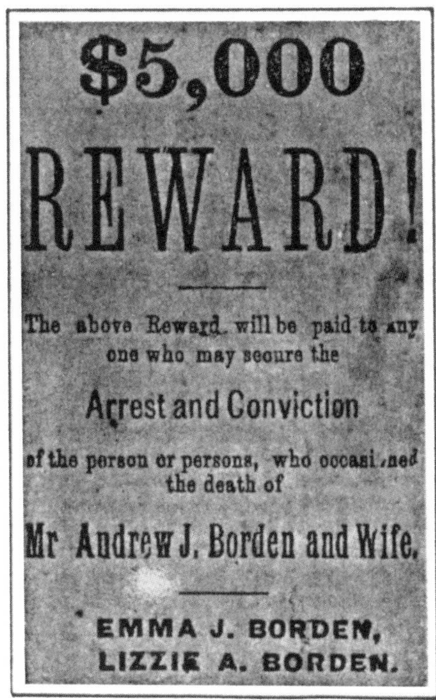

round-faced fat man, was examined by Dist Atty Knowlton, who, on this occasion, took his first part in the public proceedings with a strong, clear voice and an emphatic manner, indicative of business, and nothing but business, first, last and all the time.

Dr Dolan's testimony can be condensed in a few sentences. He simply told the condition in which he found the two bodies, the number of blood spots here and there and everywhere, and the number and location

Of the Hatchet Wounds

on the skulls and bodies of the victims.

The doctor evidently relished the story he told of a further examination of the bodies in the cemetery where they had been taken for burial, and where, it seems, he cut off the heads, leaving the mutilated bodies in the hands of the undertaker, and, as he turned to the jury to describe what was done in the way of cleansing and preparing the skulls for exhibition, a series of loud, shrill barkings, long and continued, bore vivid testimony as to a savage dog fight outside in the court yard, somewhat relieved by the connubial chirpings of two sparrows on the window sill, from which pleasant object the eye was quickly distracted, however, by the evident distress of Miss Borden, who sighed heavily, lowered her head far below the hand rail, vigorously blew her nose, swallowed a glass of water and sunk back in her chair as though she could bear no more.

Gov Robinson resolved himself into a solicitous care taker, whispered words of comfort as he fanned her while keeping an ear alert to the story of the medical examiner.

Dr Dolan continued his nauseating details by means of plaster casts, and made evident to the jury the number, location and

Character of the Cuts

in the skulls, which were crushed in before and behind the ear, some 5½ inches long, some 4 inches, and others smaller.

He inferred from the fact that he found nothing in Mrs Borden's lower intestines and some undigested food in the upper and that there were differing conditions in the intestines of Mr Borden, that the former's death preceded that of the latter by an hour or an hour and a half. In his opinion a woman of ordinary strength could have made all the cuts with a sharp instrument to which there was a handle, and closed by justifying his act of cutting off the heads of Mr and Mrs Borden without the permission of the family and of preparing them for the use of the government in the trial of this cause, without the knowledge of the family, in the jauntiest manner possible.

He desired to say that the hatchet had no blood upon it, although there was an appearance of blood, and asked permission to deny that he ever said the head of the hatchet was covered with blood.

MrAdams,who cross-examined the doctor, granted the request, but the district attorney objected to it, and the statement was excluded.

You can readily see that this has been a field day in the trial with one pronounced victory for the defence, with serious disaster, however, along the line of nervous organization, subjecting the prisoner to a mental strain for which her physical condition was not prepared. The excessive heat, combined with the revolting details given by Dr Dolan, in conjunction with the nervous strain consequent upon the exhilaration felt at the exclusion of the damaging testimony before the inquest, ran the prisoner to the very verge of collapse.

Howard

The Springfield Republican

The decision of the judges in the Borden murder case not to admit the defendant's testimony as given at the coroner's inquest seems under the circumstances not only good law but common sense. It also shows that the defendant is being given one of the fairest trials known in the history of criminal jurisprudence. The effect of the decision is, of course, to render it harder for the state to prove the defendant's guilt, but the people, whose cause the district attorney represents, will be content to have it so. The commonwealth of Massachusetts seeks only the murderer. Let not the guilty one escape; but let not the innocent be punished.

The Newport Herald

Lizzie Borden's chances for acquittal seem to grow brighter with every day of the trial. Her latest and probably greatest advantage was gained yesterday, when the judge decided that her evidence at the private hearing last summer is inadmissible at the trial. The responsibility resting on the jury in this case is weighty, but unless some much clearer evidence is brought forward than has yet been produced we do not believe that any twelve men of ordinary intelligence could bring in a verdict of guilty.

BLOWS FELL RIGHT AND LEFT

The Borden Murderer Swung the Axe Like a Woodchopper

Assassin Straddled His First Victim's Body While the Blows Were Dealt -- Features Suggest the Sex of the Slayer to Be Masculine Rather than Feminine. "Hoodoo Hatchet" Fixed Upon as the Implement - Blood-Spot on Lizzie's Skirt the Size of a Very Small Pin Head -- Testimony of Medical Experts.

NEW BEDFORD, Mass., June 13.—If Lizzie Borden is guilty the fact will be found out with a microscope and whatever instruments are used for measuring pin points. To-day the most important witnesses for the Government were sworn and then it was seen that a human hair is as thick as a club alongside of the proofs on which it is hoped she may be hanged. The medical experts reached their findings with microscopes and announced them as infinitesimal fractions. The blood spot on Lizzie Borden's white petticoat was declared to be equal in diameter to one three-thousandth part of an inch. The blood spot was the only physical thing that seemed to connect her with the crime, and it is sworn to as the size of the head of a very small pin. The Government has been describing it as on the front of her skirt, but their own chief expert to-day acknowledged this to be a mistake and said the spot was on the back of the skirt below its opening and six inches above the hem. The expert testimony all went to prove that no blood from the victims would be likely to reach the assailants from behind. Therefore that ought to be the last of that "damned spot."

Once beyond the reach of the microscope the points in the case against the prisoner to-day went into hypotheses, conjectures, and guesses at to the unproven circumstances. The main points in the testimony are reported in what follows, and the reader will see for himself whether it deals with facts or conjectures. The basis of all this speculation was a ground work of blood, skulls, and bowls. The blood and one skull were brought into court and handed about. Fortunately for her, Miss Lizzie Borden dodged this ghastly thing. It came in the afternoon session, just after she had complained of feeling poorly, and gone out. Her indisposition was due to the extreme heat and closeness following on a morning of sickening and horrible testimony. She had brought in a posy of bachelor's buttons, as an old maid might, and she seemed in fairly good spirits. There were no other notable flowers in the court room, but the pure white carnations were still in the centre of the Judge's desk.

A newcomer among the women spectators had Miss Lizzie Borden pointed out to her, and at the first glance exclaimed, "Why, she is a lady." That was an interesting exclamation. The prisoner is far from good looking, so heavy is the lower half of the face. Yet there is about her that indefinable quality which we call ladyhood. She is said to be generally thought of throughout the country as a brawny, big, muscular, hard-faced, coarse-looking girl. She is, in fact, neither large nor small, nor tall nor short, but is of the average build, and in demeanor is quiet, modest, and well bred—from a country rather than a city point of view.

When the great medical expert and chemist, Prof. Wood of Harvard, went on the stand, Lizzie Borden's interest in his testimony, bloody and hideous as it was, had no shadow of concealment. It amazed this semi-rustic girl to meet with a man who could extract eloquence from mute, insensate things. He had held converse with blood, had interviewed bones, had cross-examined half digested food in human stomachs, and was on speaking terms with infinitesmal specks of gore that had been spattered during the murders. She had seen the expert before at a previous trial, but it was evident that his species was strange and interesting to her, as it was to most persons in the room. The testimony might have seemed uncanny but that Prof. Wood was built like a heavy-weight pugilist and had an out-of-door, sun-tanned, vastly human countenance.

The handleless hatchet was conspicuous again to-day, and showed, as it did before, that the Government had first constructed its case with the clawhammer hatchet, and went into court with that theory. The examination freed the clawhammer hatchet from suspicion, and that hatchet was then abandoned, and the hoodoo hatchet was fixed upon as the guilty implement. This was shown yesterday by Dr. Dolan's evidence, and confirmed to-day by Prof. Wood. It was a shocking, feverish day for the prisoner, and her antagonists got some comfort out of it. Her lawyers scored some good points for her, and the honors were even.

The singular pranks that the hoodoo hatchet played to-day took the form of making the Government's own experts admit that certain features of the crimes suggested the sex of the murderer to be masculine rather than feminine; for instance, Mrs. Borden's murderer stood astride her body while he dealt the eighteen blows that were rained on her head. Then, again, on both bodies the blows were struck right and left, as a woodchopper swings an axe. It has all along been argued by many persons that only a maniac committed the murders, and now that theory is amended to make the maniac a woodchopper. The Government will conclude its case to-morrow evening. The trial is fast drawing to a close. It cannot last beyond the middle of next week.

All Dr. Dolan's testimony was to the effect that a sharp-edged hatchet had been used. He said he thought the handleless hatchet now has a sharp edge, so that in his opinion chopping two skulls to pieces did not dull the edge very much.

The woman's body was taken up next and its eighteen wounds were described. Foreman Richards of the jury was used as a pillow and had a sham spread over him while the counterpane was spread over the jury rail. The blood spots on these things were again testified to and these two important questions were asked and answered:

"Where, in your opinion, did the assailant stand when Mrs. Borden was attacked?"

"Astride her body," said Dr. Dolan.

"And the blows have a general left to right direction?"

"Yes."

"Though some were from right to left?"

"Yes."

The witness showed how the blows were dealt by taking a hatchet in his hand and whacking away at the head of the stenographer, who sat below him writing away for dear life and utterly unconscious of how the Doctor was swinging the hatchet around him. The cross-examination of the medical examiner went on as follows:

"Did you point out in the pocket of the prisoner's blue dress a place that had the appearance of blood?"

"Yes."

"Now you understand that it is not?"

"I haven't heard."

"Did you have her shoes and stockings?"

"Yes."

"Did you find blood on the soles?"

"Yes."

"You claim it was blood?"

"Not human blood."

"I don't ask you what kind."

"I don't know."

"Did you see a pinhead spot of blood on her white skirt."

"Yes."

"What about that?"

"It's blood, whether human or not I don't know."

Prof. Wood next took up the claw-hammer hatchet with which it was at first supposed that Miss Borden slew her parents. He had subjected this to chemical and microscopic tests, but was unable to detect any blood on the handle or blade. He had the same luck with the two axes and the second hatchet. That shows why the Government set out to find a new weapon, and came across the hoodoo hatchet.

The Doctor took up Lizzie Borden's blue dress skirt, and said that it had a brownish smutch near the pocket. It did not resemble blood, but to make sure he tested it, and found it not to be blood.

He examined the prisoner's low shoes and black stockings and found no blood on them. The hoodoo hatchet was his next text, and he repeated the time-worn evidence that both sides were uniformly rusty and covered with some fine dust like ashes. He found no blood. Think of it—no blood upon this hoodoo hatchet after all the fuss it has made!

Mr. Adams got back to that white skirt again with the pinhead spot of blood. He asked if the character of the blood was satisfactory for the determination that it was human blood, and the Professor's answer was peculiar.

"If it is satisfactory at all, it is," said he, an answer with which the prisoner's lawyers were well satisfied.

Mr. Adams next asked a question which left the Professor free to say that the spot might have been Miss Borden's blood, and he did say so. In all likelihood that is the last that will be heard of the only blood that was found upon anything belonging to the prisoner.

"Assuming that the assailant stood behind Mr. Borden," said Mr. Adams to Prof. Wood, "have you formed any opinion whether he would be spattered with blood?"

"I don't see how he could avoid being spattered from the waist up."

"Assuming that the assailant stood astride Mrs. Borden as she lay with her face down, and taking into account the spatters you saw, have you formed an opinion whether the assailant would be spattered?"

"I don't see how he could avoid being spattered from the lower portion of the body down."

Dr. Frank W. Draper was called.

He is the professor of medical jurisprudence in the Harvard Medical School.

He assisted in the autopsy upon the Borden bodies. He took up the plaster casts and began to verify the marks that showed the wounds upon them.

Mr. Knowlton said that he was sorry that he was obliged to send for one of the skulls of the murdered couple, but he must do so. It was brought in and handed to the witness, Prof. Draper. It was Mr. Borden's skull. It was done up in a white hankerchief, and looked like a bouquet, such as a man carries to his sweetheart.

The new expert said that the cutting edge of the weapon that made the wounds was 3½ inches long. Asked if such blows could have been dealt by a woman of ordinary strength, he said, "Yes," precisely as every Government witness has said, who has been asked the question. Like Prof. Wood, he thought Mrs. Borden's murderer stood astride and Mr. Borden's assailant stood in front of his victim. As standing astride a body is not a feminine trick, the defence likes to dwell upon it.

Mr. Adams brought out a brand new hatchet of the same kind as the hoodoo hatchet. He asked the expert to fit it in the big wound. If it had fitted it would have been a great point for the defense. But it had not been ground as much as the hoodoo hatchet, and it wouldn't go in. The hoodoo hatchet, by the way, fits the wound exactly.

The handle of the new hatchet is found to be twelve and a half inches long. It was taken for granted that the missing handle of the hoodoo hatchet was the same length. That would make the murderer stand close to his bloody work. The defence eagerly brought out that fact. Mr. Adams had the witness say that the murderer stood astride Mrs. Borden.

"Would not the assailant of necessity have been spattered with blood?"

"I should think so."

"What part of the body would have been spattered?"

"The front part of the dress."

"When you say dress," said Mr. Adams, "you mean the clothing worn by both sexes?"

"Yes."

With the prisoner poorly in health and one witness recovering from a fainting fit with the help of a fan and frequent draughts of ice water, the day's proceedings came to an end, none to soon.

NO BLOOD.

Experts Yield No Clew to Crime.

Spots on Axes Were from Rust.

Lizzie's Garments Pass the Ordeal.

One Suspicious Blot Found on Her Skirt.

Stains Were Not What They Seemed.

Theories as to How the Deed Was Done.

Surgeons Puzzled by the Thrusts of Counsel.

Danger That Trial May be Interrupted.

NEW BEDFORD, June 13—Three questions presented themselves during the morning session, after a hot session, a humidity ridden session, a miserable, poky, mind-wearying, physique-exhausting session.

First—In view of the extraordinary weakness manifested by Lizzie Borden when the skulls were first produced in court the other day, still covered, what may be expected from her in her present mentally anxious and physically weakened state, when the skulls in all their naked hideousness are not only produced but handled and described?

Second—In case she breaks down, as is not at all impossible, can the trial proceed? Proceed in her absence, even by mutual consent of the commonwealth and the prisoner?

Third—In view of an occurrence in the jury box today, will the case stand if 11 jurors continue in the box, and will it be possible for the trial to proceed without the full complement, even with the consent of the prisoner and the commonwealth?

This has been a most extraordinary trial in the development of special features, each day furnishing its full share of unexpected and sensational incidents.

Today broke with a suggestion of rain, but the spattering which fell in the early morning hours seemed only to intensify the discomfort and the irritation of all enveloped by the steaming atmosphere.

The judges, happily tempered individuals, having largely control of their own movements, literally so indeed, save and except their hours of confinement in the court room, were about the only ones who appeared bright, alert and ready for business.

The court room was early and easily filled, leaving enough people on the outside to crowd a dozen such edifices.

Miss Lizzie, escorted by an attentive deputy sheriff, clad a la mode, but very pale and nervously anticipating the horrors of the day, took her seat near Gov Robinson, where she was pleasantly greeted by her clerical friend and her counsel, but not by any one of the wild-eyed, haggard-featured, thick-skinned women who stared at her through their spectacles and opera glasses as though she were a beast.

Counsellor Adams continued the cross-examination of medical examiner Dolan, consuming much time and entering at great length into the edge of the hatchet, the condition of the blade, the direction from which the blood spots came, the state of Mrs Borden's hair, whether it was false or natural, the number and the character of the wounds, and his opinion as to the style of implement with which the

Killing Had Been Done.

No development in that jury box will cause surprise, although many will occasion excitement.

This morning while Dr Dolan was indulging in particularly revolting photographs, it was noticed that Mr Hodges was very faint.

The Irishman who sits by his side fanned him attentively, and he struggled with the fan himself.

A glass of water failed to revive him, and the chief justice, who is ever on the watch, appreciating the gravity of the situation, directed the jury to retire for five minutes.

JUROR HODGES ALMOST OVERCOME BY GRUESOME PHOTOGRAPHS

Dolan, who is a bright fellow, and an excellent arguer, seemed to have an idea that he must bother the defense as much as possible, and aid the prosecution as far as was possible, so he continually fenced with Mr Adams, who, adroit and unimpassioned, drew from him the admission that he knew nothing about the deaths of the Bordens or as to the relative points of when they occurred.

On the redirect he told with evident gusto how after the services, when the bodies were carried to the cemetery to be buried, they were first subjected to mutilation, their

Heads Being Cut Off,

their stomachs taken out and a general examination made, after which what was left of them, he believed, was buried.

Prof Wood of Boston, professor of chemistry in Harvard college, one of the most respected authorities, and the expert in chief for the commonwealth in this case, is a strikingly handsome man, with graying hair, very red face, a bright eye and a modest nature, in private conversation a typical gentleman.

Brother Knowlton, in his most gracious way, gently led the proffessor along a commendatory autobiography, eliciting the fact that he is an expert in medical chemistry, and is in every sense on the topmost twig of his branch of a dignified and honorable profession.

Prof Wood's testimony was of a negative nature, and might quite as well have been directed by the defence as by the prosecution.

He lifted the entire procedure up to a higher level, into a purer atmosphere, where not only truth, but the whole truth, seemed to be at home, and he gave his testimony with an honest vigor as though lecturing to a class, impressing every hearer with its factualness.

Holding the axes in his hand the learned professor explained to the jury that the spots looked like blood, but that on examination it was found

They Were Not Blood,

and he went through that entire list, with the exception of the skirt and the two pieces of carpet, with the same result.

On the white skirt he found a small blood spot much more minute than the head of the smallest pin, measuring, as near as he could get at it, one three-thousand-two-hundred and forty-thirds of an inch.

I may as well say here that the defense claim, for reasons not necessary to publish, and the proof does not interpose a negative, that this blood spot is natural.

The pieces of carpet were cut, one from beneath the lounge in the sitting room, where Mr Borden was murdered, and one from under the bed in the guest chamber where Mrs Borden was found.

Continuing his strange, and, to the lay mind, most unnecessary tale, from the prosecution's point of view, the professor said he also had been directed to examine what might have been blood on the soles of Lizzie's shoes; that he did as he was directed, and the spots were not of blood.

He testified also that the spots on the small hatchet which looked as though they might be blood, not only were not blood, but were most pronouncedly rust.

Apropos of the handleless hatchet, the handle of which deputy marshal Fleet, by the way, has not yet accounted for, he said it was sent or given to him by marshal Hilliard, that

Both Sides Were Rusty,

and the bright spots now seen upon it were the result of the scrapings.

When he first looked at it he saw, as the police had, several suspicious spots, where-

THE BORDEN JURORS LISTENING ATTENTIVELY TO THE EXPERTS

upon he soaked it and tested it for blood, but there was none.

This lame, impotent conclusion struck the funny bump of everybody in the audience, and when he went on to describe that the head was covered with a white film, like dirt or ashes, thereby contradicting one of his predecessors, who said it in no sense resembled ashes, and another who said it in no sense resembled dirt, everybody looked at everybody else, and a positive look of wonderment mantled the

Frank W. Draper was another distinguished professor whose specialty is medical jurisprudence.

This gentleman participated in the surgical ceremonies in the cemetery, and the general autopsy that was there indulged in.

Just then the skulls were brought in and Miss Lizzie went out.

The skulls don't look like the skulls we see in museums, dried and covered with parchment skin. They have been scraped, cleansed and whitened, the jaws being separated from the general skull.

Hideous indeed are they to casual observers, but what would they have been to Miss Lizzie Borden if she be innocent—the bandied about skulls of her father and her stepmother, with their eyeless sockets, their toothless gums, their fleshless bones, and what would they have been to Miss Lizzie Borden if she were guilty, with their gaping cuts, their cracks and splintered fragments, mute witnesses to the brutality of their assassin.

In his opinion two blows were given Mrs Borden by the assailant when they stood face to face, all the rest being given while she was prone upon the floor, face downward and the assailant

Astride of Her.

Mild, deliberate and gracious as Prof Cheever was when in the hands of Mr Knowlton, he developed antagonism when he was approached by the cross-examination of Mr Adams, who drew from him, however, some interesting details as to his habit of dress when performing operations upon patients, from whom blood spurted in volumes, spraying his face, dyeing his whiskers and covering with blood his all-enveloping ulster or apron.

According to him there are two arteries in the head, both of which were cut in Mr Borden's skull, which, when severed, eject blood in spurting sprays six feet—but why weary with these details?

Witness after witness goes over the same story, describes that with which the jury are nauseatingly familiar, proving again and again facts about which there is no dispute, that the Bordens are dead, that they were brutally murdered, that there was blood all over the place, that they had eaten a mild and moderate breakfast, all of which

was found in their several intestinal parts, some digested and some not—and that's all.

Thus far the learned brothers have not taken a step to establish the guilt of the accused, nor have they put in one scintilla of testimony which connects her with the case or which does not trend just as certainly in the direction of Bridget Sullivan as in that of Lizzie Borden.

Howard

The New York Herald

EDITORIAL

Yesterday was a field day in the Borden trial, and the result was a substantial victory for the prisoner.

The question was whether the testimony given by Lizzie Borden at the inquest last August should now be admitted against her or excluded. Each side realized the importance of a favorable ruling and earnestly argued for it. The decision of the court was against the admission of the testimony.

The point of contention was whether the evidence had been given voluntarily or involuntarily by Miss Borden at the inquest. If the latter it could not now be produced against her, for the reason that this would be compelling her to be a witness against herself, in violation of a right guaranteed by the constitution to every accused person.

Counsel for the government argued that when Miss Borden testified at the inquest she had not been arrested or formally charged with the crime; that she had been permitted to confer with her counsel before obeying the summons as a witness and that she was free to refuse to give her evidence.

On the other hand it was maintained in her behalf that, though not formally accused, she was openly suspected and under surveillance, and though not actually arrested a warrant for her arrest was in the hands of an officer, who took her into custody as soon as she had given her testimony. In the star chamber proceeding she was not permitted to be represented by counsel and was not cautioned by the magistrate or district attorney that she need not testify to anything that might tend to incriminate her.

It must be obvious to any one having a knowledge of the facts that when she testified at the inquest she was virtually accused, virtually a prisoner and virtually an involuntary witness against herself. This is the view which Chief Justice Mason and his two colleagues take, and accordingly they hold that the evidence cannot now be legally reproduced against her. We venture to say that this exposition of the rights of the prisoner will meet the general approval of lawyers as well as the community at large.

For Miss Borden the result must prove a twofold advantage. It will keep from the jury any contradictions or damaging admissions she may have made when in the hands of secret inquisitors, and it will save her from the necessity of taking the witness stand to break the force of such testimony—a step which would subject her to a searching cross-examination, which might perhaps hurt her case more than help it.

But broader than the fate or fortune of this unfortunate woman is the general principle involved and affirmed. This affects the criminal procedure of the entire commonwealth of Massachusetts on similar points, and must influence even that of other states. It is well known to those conversant with the subject that there has been a marked tendency in criminal courts to undermine the constitutional guaranty that no accused person shall be compelled to be a witness against himself. This is shown by the various pretexts which have been sanctioned or countenanced to extort testimony from persons accused of crime—in violation of the spirit, if not the strict letter, of the constitutional guaranty.

No more forcible or timely illustration of this tendency is needed than the array of authorities cited by the government counsel yesterday in support of their contention and the apt reply of ex-Governor Robinson that it was high time that the vital questions involved be determined on principle rather than precedent. The court did this, and its decision is well calculated to have a wholesome effect and become an oft cited authority.

The Worcester Spy

Lizzie Borden has not yet been acquitted, but it certainly looks as if the Fall River police were going to be disappointed in their hunger for a "pound of flesh." That warrant for arrest, sworn out before the inquest, but not served till after the girl had given her testimony, was a stroke of forehandedness that quite overreached itself.

The New York Tribune

One feature of the Borden trial cannot but impress all familiar with the prevailing custom in this state as strange and even cruel, namely, the requirement that the witness must stand while testifying—a rule which seems to be enforced impartially in the cases of both men and women, though undoubtedly a relaxation of it would be granted by the court in case of feeble persons. It is hard to see what can be gained by the course pursued, which must necessarily be exceedingly wearisome in cases where witnesses are kept under examination a long time. No lawyer in this state would say that the course of justice has ever been interfered with by allowing witnesses to sit when in the witness box. The Massachusetts practice has come down from an earlier generation. Considerations of humanity would lead to a change, and the ends of justice would be equally well subserved.

EVEN SO!

What if Lizzie Did Ask for Acid?

Defense Claims That Proves Nothing.

State Says It Shows Murderous Intent.

Admission of the Evidence In Hot Dispute.

Matron Reagan on the Witness Stand.

Swears the Prisoner Scored Her Sister.

"You've Given Me Away" Episode in Testimony.

Bridget Sullivan and Dr Dolan Recalled.

NEW BEDFORD, June 14—"I was standing in the closet not more than four feet away when Lizzie, who was lying on the sofa, said to her sister, 'So you have given me away, haven't you?' To which Emma replied, 'No, I haven't,' and Lizzie, measuring the end of her forefinger with her thumb, said, 'Well, I won't give in that much.' "—Matron Reagan.

Still more surprises, more contradictions, more arguments in the absence of the jury, more police stupidity, more illustration of the folly of zeal by witnesses, and more discomfort, heat and humidity combined, than I had supposed possible in a city so advantageously situated as this in the leafy month of June.

A heavy downfall of rain, lasting pretty much all night, gave us hope of a decent temperature today, but the red hot sun brushed every semblance of the temperate zone away, and before the slanting of an early line began its horizontaling course, umbrellas, palm leaf fans and iced drinks were in demand.

It has been a brutal day on the street and one utterly indescribable in the cramped quarters of this county court house.

How the jury endure the strain physical I cannot understand. When I reached the court this morning the jury were entering the lower door, the chief justice, with a new high white hat, the others in the customary black stove pipe tile. They were in excellent humor, laughing and chatting about a thousand and one things irrelevant to the situation.

Burly Dist Atty Knowlton rushed up the stairs two steps at a time, quickly and closely followed by his younger and smaller associate, Mr Moody, both anxious and with determination in every glance.

In the witness room sat Bridget Sullivan with a countenance as impassive as that of a graven image and a number of odd looking women clad in black. They subsequently made their appearance, one after another, on the witness stand.

Within the bar were the usual aggregation of local celebrities, Mr Davis, treasurer of the Massachusetts board of trade, the experts who testified yesterday, several freshly arrived ministers and the counsel for the defence, all looking with comparative cheerfulness, through which, however, was clearly distinct a very natural condition of anxiety.

That jury needs watching.

By that I mean they are wilting in this torridic atmosphere, subjected as they are to more unusual confinement and seclusion, not alone from their ordinary occupation but from out of door exercise and healthtul condition to which one and all are used.

Sheriff Wright, accompanied by his bright-eyed daughter, came into the court and as usual rapped on the desk immediately, and to the standing audience announced "the court." His deputy, my particular friend and neighbor, Mr Butman, with due solemnity counted the jury from 1 to 12 and announced in the name of the creator and the commonwealth of Massachusetts that a full dozen of the men and true were present then and there.

The jurors looked upon the prisoner and prisoner upon the jurors. She saw 12 jaded, tired men, and they a very pale, swollen-faced, dreamy-eyed, expressionless-featured woman.

Resembling a Hunted Fox.

The proceedings of the day might very well be divided into three parts, first, the police effort; second, the matron's testimony; and, third, the prussic-acid argument.

Marshal Hilliard, the deus ex machina of the whole business, who made up his mind in the earliest stage of the game that the Fall River police must have a theory, and having one substantiate it, was the first witness. He is a fine, orderly looking man, what the women call a nice-looking man, and I should judge self-reliance to be his chief characteristic.

He testified as to the search made on the morning of the murder and recounted the sensational conversation he had, or rather listened to, between the mayor, "uncle" Morse and Lizzie and Emma Borden. The marshal testified at considerable length as to property belonging to the Bordens which he, in his official capacity, took from the house and has since retained.

Under cross-examination of Gov Robinson he described his search, which in no sense differed from that given by the other policemen, every one swearing that they not only encountered no opposition in their search but received all possible help and much material assistance from the people in the house, Miss Emma saying to him that she wanted them to make as thorough an examination as possible, and if there was a box or trunk which could not be opened to send for her and it would be opened.

"Our whole search," said the marshal, smilingly, "as the doctors call it, was with a negative result."

The murder, it will be remembered, occurred on Thursday, and the marshal advised the mayor he suspected Lizzie of the murder, that the ladies had better stay in the house as there was so

Much Excitement,

and it was at that time the mayor said, "I regret very much, Miss Borden, that you are suspected," and in reply to Emma's remark that they had tried to keep it from Lizzie as long as they could, Lizzie said openly, earnestly and frankly, "I am ready to go at any time, or go now."

Fall River is fortunate in having a mayor who is not only a pleasant faced, courteous-mannered individual, but a square politician and a surgeon of repute. Mayors, like other dignitaries, amount to something in this part of the world, and are literally, as they are called, the chief magistrates in their several localities.

He testified that he ordered the crowd removed from the house, the sidewalk and the premises, and that calling the family together he requested them to remain in the house for a few days, and also to the conversation he had with the young woman when he told Miss Lizzie that she was suspected of the murder. They had such conversation as would naturally occur under the circumstances between a somewhat embarrassed official and two agitated young women, and when he left Miss Emma said, "I want you to do everything you can to find out this murder."

From the mayor's manner and words the inference is fairly drawn that nothing occurred at the time of his visit which could in any way

Reflect Against Them,

the marshal or himself.

A curious looking individual by the name of Gifford swore that at one time when she was talking with Lizzie about a garment she had made for her mother Lizzie said, "Oh, don't say that. She's a mean thing, and I don't have much to do with her.

A number of minor characters, a hostler, a mason, a laborer and a little French wood sawyer gave some unimportant testimony to the effect that they were working in sundry adjacencies to the Borden house, and saw no one pass on the morning of the murder.

Then came a sensation in the testimony as well as the manner and the presence of Hannah Reagan, matron of a Fall River police station, where she has charge of the women who are detained for whatever purpose. She is a very zealous witness for the prosecution, with a bulky encyclopedia easily and readily tapped by the counsel for the government, but which is drier than a bone and as hard to penetrate when assaulted by the counsel for the defense.

Divested of the verbiage of the learned brother who examined her and of herself as well, she testified a most interesting memorization of the date inasmuch as she could remember no other date, that on the 24th of last August, about two minutes of 9 in the morning, Miss Lizzie Borden being detained a prisoner in the matron's room, her sister, Emma Borden, called to see her. Lizzie was lying on a lounge. The witness was tidying up the room. As Emma entered the witness stepped into a closet some four feet from the lounge.

Accosting her sister, Lizzie said: "So you have given me away, haven't you?" to which Emma replied, "No, I haven't," and Lizzie, measuring the end of her forefinger with her thumb, said, "Well, I won't give in that much."

"I was standing in the doorway at the time," said the witness, "and Lizzie spoke as loud as I now speak, so I heard distinctly every word that was said. Emma took a chair and sat down by the settee, but Lizzie turned her back to her and didn't speak a word more during her visit, nor did she say goodby when she went away."

Under cross-examination of Mr Jennings, whose manner is particularly clean-cut, emphatic and understandable, the witness was very much confused, and imitated Dr Dolan in his famous sentence of "I don't remember" reply.

To Mr Jennings, she said:

"You passed me and Emma as she started to go home, and you said to her, Have you told all to Lizzie?' You remained till half-past 12, and Lizzie was very

Much More Excited

after you went than before you came in."

THE JURY ROOM WHERE LIZZIE BORDEN'S FATE WILL BE DECIDED

As to the second visit in the afternoon by Emma to her sister, the witness was greatly embarrassed by the cross-questioning, which was cool, concise and confusing. She couldn't remember about the time of Emma's second visit, nor could she recall who was present in the matron's room, if any one was, and testified that she was so excited and worked up by the quarrel of the morning that to all intents and purposes her mind was a blank as to what occurred thereafter.

In some way or other on the day on which Lizzie is alleged to have accused Emma of having given her away a report of it reached the newspaper and as there was no one present with the exception of the two sisters and the eavesdropping matron the reporters naturally hunted Mrs Reagan up and wanted to know all about it.

In reply to Mr Jennings' close questioning she denied having told the reporters that the story was a lie and also that she told Rev Mr Buck that it was a lie.

A typewritten statement was shown her, which Mr Jennings says was handed to her by Rev Mr Buck, it being a denial that there had been any quarrel between the sisters, with the request that she should sign it. She denied ever having seen the paper, with a knowledge of its contents, but swore that Mr Buck flourished the paper before her and a large number of others in the court room, asking her to sign it, to which she replied that if the marshal would permit her she would do so; that the story was a lie; that she and the minister then went to the marshal, who said, "What this woman has to say she will say to the court. Go to your room and mind your prisoner."

She denied that the marshal

Forbid Her to Sign It,

denied seeing counsellor Jennings in the marshal's office and emphatically repudiated as false and without a shadow of foundation a matter which was supposed to be in dispute and as to which she will be directly and promptly contradicted by Rev Mr Buck, several ladies who were in the matron's room when she returned and possibly by counsellor Jennings himself, who knows the story from start to finish, all of which he saw and much of which he was.

Mr Jennings is authority for the assertion that he went in person to the marshal and asked him why he objected to the matron's signing what he knew to be the truth, and that when he further refused to allow the woman to sign it and ordered her back to her room, he, Jennings, threatened to publish him to the world, and he has done it.

The prosecution has been cursed by the over-zeal of its witnesses, and the good lady who nervously spoke her piece today, remembering too much for one side and not enough for another, is a fair type of the silly pride which goes before a fatal fall.

You remember, I have called attention once or twice to the aims of the prosecution, which are to show, first, premeditation, and second, exclusive opportunity. The claim that premeditation was shown by Lizzie's attempt to purchase prussic acid on Tuesday and by her conversation with old lady Russell as to her apprehensions lest something might happen to her father on Wednesday. The latter the prosecution put in evidence when Lizzie's former friend, Alice Russell of Fall River, turned against her on the stand the other day and told with great gusto about the burning of the dress, about the conversations between her and Lizzie as to the troubles at home, the quarrels with the tenants and so on, and they sought to strengthen that today by the introduction of testimony to the effect that Lizzie went to a Fall River drug store some time before the murder and asked for 10 cents' worth of prussic acid with which to clean a sealskin sack.

When the witness, a drug clerk, Eli Bense by name, began his testimony Miss Borden fairly glared at him, leaned forward and stared him squarely in the eye. It was a new departure and possibly he may not have been prepared for it. However, that may be, the clerk, a good natured fellow, blushed and stammered as he hurriedly replied, "I do," before clerk Borden had finished the phraseology of the oath.

At this time there were two matters of interest before the court, Miss Borden's agitation and the collapse of the matron in an outside room. Gov Robinson calmed his client by a few reassuring remarks. The matron having left the stand, staggered rather than walked through the adjacent room, where the

Blood-Stained Lounge

stood, challenging attention into the next apartment, where deputy sheriff Falvey gave her a glass of water, which she swallowed at a gulp, and then sat upon a lounge in the retiring room, where the treasurer of the Fall River bank for savings fanned her, leaned over her and comforted her with words of consolation.

It was evident that a fight was on hand between the learned brothers, and Mr Moody in his blandly courteous way informed the court that, as the question would have to be decided sooner or later he thought it would be well to direct the jury to retire in order that the question as to the admission offered by the prosecution might be presented to the court. The chief justice, with the concurrence of his associates, ordered the coordinate branch of the court to retire, whereupon the jury, in custody of the deputy sheriff, left the room and know no more concerning the developments of the rest of the day than the pigeons on the roof, the bootblacks on the sidewalk, or the old cow ruminating in her stall. Yet it was a very important matter, for Mr Moody in behalf of the prosecution offered to prove that Lizzie not only tried once, but twice, to buy prussic acid, which is not an article of general commerce or one ordinarily purchased by young women of innocent intents.

Gov Robinson fortified his objection by the evidence of the experts, who testified that there wasn't a trace of poison in either of the bodies, and argues that he really didn't see how the prosecution could prove

POLICE MATRON HANNAH REAGAN

that Lizzie Borden did the murders with an ax or hatchet, as charged in the indictment, because two days before she tried to buy some prussic acid.

To this Mr Moody rejoined that it was evidence of premeditation and it was certainly one link in a chain of

Suspicious Circumstances.

It was known that she tried to get the poison and it was also known that the next night the entire family were so ill that Mrs Borden sent for the doctor, saying that she had been poisoned. That evening the conversation with old lady Russell occurred and the following morning the murders were committed by some one.

These incidents, Mr Moody claimed, were proof of a murderous state of mind, and he cited a large number of cases to substantiate his insistence that the introduction of this line of proof was entirely proper and in line with authorities.

Gov Robinson replied, following out his argument based on the evidence of experts, and insisting that the prussic acid business had nothing whatever to do with the case

After consultation the chief justice announced that the court was disposed to admit the testimony under certain conditions, and with that suggestion they would hold the matter in abeyance until tomorrow morning.

If, therefore, tomorrow the prosecution is permitted to utilize the prussic acid incident as corroborative proof of premeditation, a new element will have been added which in all candor it must be conceded by the warmest friends of the prisoner tends somewhat to becloud the defense, which down to date, very decidedly had the best of the investigation.

The heat tonight is something fearful, and if the court proceedings begin at 9 and continue until 5 I don't see but what a charge of premeditated manslaughter might be suggested against them in case the jurors melt in their seats or the prisoner goes mad.

Howard

WAS HER WORST DAY

Visible Shadow Cast on Lizzie Borden

Prisoner's Lawyers Sought to Shut Out Testimony Without Succeeding - Clockmaker Said Accused Called Her Stepmother "A Good-for-Nothing Thing" - Police Matron Told of the Quarrel of the Two Sisters.

SPECIAL DISPATCH TO THE BOSTON HERALD

NEW BEDFORD, June 14, 1893. Lizzie Borden, the girl whose life is the stake the lawyers are pleading for, was not at her best today.

Her face looked swollen below the eyes, as if she had been crying, and she was again limp and without energy.

There was excuse enough in the horrors of the charnel house performances of yesterday for almost any degree of poor health today, and it turned out that she had been so racked the day before that both sets of lawyers had agreed to allow her to leave the room, as she did in the afternoon.

Under the Massachusetts law a prisoner must hear the testimony at his trial, and she was seated in an ante-room behind the witness stand, where she could hear the witnesses, but could not see the gaping, battered skulls and the blood-saturated paraphernalia of the government side of the case.

Today she again had to pass the sofa on which her father was butchered, and the trunks and bags and boxes of ghastly and sickening exhibits were again before her on the floor when she took her seat.

Taken altogether, this was Lizzie Borden's worst day; in fact, the only one that has cast a visible shadow on her. There was nothing in any part of the testimony that was of great weight for or against either side unless it be the prussic acid incident. But the damage was done before that came along. The jurors were hustled out of court so as not to hear the talk of the lawyers. Then they came back, and soon were marched out again, each time hearing and seeing enough to know that the Government had testimony about which they had all read, and that Miss Borden's lawyers were extremely anxious to keep that testimony away from them. The lonely woman's lawyers tried also to keep out other matters, without succeeding, so that the marked peculiarity of the day may have seemed to the jury to be that the prisoner's friends were timid and nervous, while the Government was businesslike, without any absence of candor or show of too great earnestness.

First, the prisoner's lawyers sought to shut off the family cloak maker of the Bordens, who was to testify that months before the murder Lizzie Borden called her stepmother "A mean good-for-nothing thing." It would hardly have been supposed that gossip of that sort would be seriously considered by either side. After all, when it was allowed to be heard, it did not prove to be even the firecracker that the District Attorney had promised, for the witness failed to say that the prisoner used the expression, "We hate her," as has been said.

The next protest of the defence was against the admission of the testimony of a young woman who went to Europe with the prisoner and came back with her. She was to swear that Miss Lizzie Borden told her she was sorry to be going home after such a pleasant time, for hers was "an unhappy home." The jury was put out of the room before it had heard any more than that the witness was the prisoner's stateroom companion going to Europe and coming back. There was an argument, and the testimony was excluded by the Court. A little time after this out went the jury for the second time. On this occasion it was because the Government brought forward the drug clerk who proposed to swear that Miss Borden had attempted to buy prussic acid to clear a fur cape with on the day before the murders in her home. His story is to be let in to-morrow.

These occurrences may not prove important in their effect on the jurors, but they have had the result of changing many of Miss Borden's friends from enthusiasm to thoughtfulness. Only last night there was a great deal of talk of the chance the prisoner's lawyers had to put in no testimony for the prisoner, simply letting the case for the Government go to the jury just as the Government left it. A considerable fraction of the community believed that the woman's lawyers could safely adopt that course. It was even said that the Fall River police had given up all hope that the girl would be convicted. To-day's proceedings have not strengthened these conditions. It seemed to many persons that the sum of the testimony that was objected to had very little value except for the fact that it was objected to. A full account of the day's work will show how nearly the Commonwealth has ended its case. To-day's contributions were all fag ends and loose pieces, and to-morrow's will end the job-lot assortment.

The first witness was the chief of the Fall River police, Marshal Hilliard. He swore that he did not go to the house of the Bordens until the afternoon of the day of the murder. Then he looked around the yard and the pile of lumber and the barn. He found the loft of the barn where the prisoner says she was when the butcheries were committed was extremely hot and almost stifling. He said that when he asked for the dress that Miss Lizzie Borden wore on the morning of the murder, Lawyer Jennings brought it and handed it to him. It was the blue dress that is always exhibited by the Government, and that had what Prof. Wood calls a smutch near the pocket. Miss Borden's friends say, by the way, that she then had fourteen dresses in her wardrobe, and that the great majority were blue, or mainly blue. As showing how loose the memory of ordinary persons is, and how poor their powers of observation are, it will be remembered that the Government witnesses either remembered no blue dresses at all, or at the most recalled only one or two.

The Chief of Police told of an interesting visit he paid to the Borden house on Saturday, two days after the murders. This is how he described that visit, which, with the Mayor and the prisoner as central figures, sounds like something out of a French novel or a French criminal trial:

"The Mayor, Mr. Morse, Miss Lizzie and Miss Emma were there. The Mayor said that he had a request to make of the family, and that was that they remain in the house for a few days. There was a great deal of excitement, he said, and he thought it would be better all around if they remained indoors and did not go on the streets. He told them if they were annoyed by the people to send word to the City Marshal, or to himself, and he would see that they were dispersed.

"Miss Lizzie said: 'What, is there anybody suspected in this house?'

"The Mayor said: 'Well, perhaps Mr. Morse can answer that question, after what occurred last night.'

"At that Miss Lizzie spoke up and said: "I want to know the truth.'

"The Mayor said: 'I regret to say so, but I think you are suspected, Miss Lizzie.'

"At that Miss Emma said: 'We have tried to keep it from her as long as we could.'

"Prior to that evening did you tell Mr. Jennings that you suspected the defendant?" Mr. Robinson asked.

The question was objected to, but the objection was overruled. Witness then said he did not say that he suspected any one.

"Did you tell him that some did?"

"Yes."

Mrs. Hannah Regan, a police matron, was next called to tell of a mysterious quarrel which she saw take place between the Borden sisters. This was her testimony:

Q.—Are you a married or a single woman? A.—Married.

Q.—You are the matron of the police station at Fall River? A.—Yes sir.

Q.—And have occupied the position some time? A.—Yes sir.

Q.—What are the duties of the position? Do you have charge of the women taken into custody? A.—Yes, sir.

Q.—The prisoner was at one time in your custody? A.—Yes, sir.

Q.—What room did she occupy at that time? A.—The matron's room.

Q.—Your room? A.—Yes, sir.

Q.—Were you with her during the day time? A.—Yes, sir.

Q.—All day? A.—Yes, sir.

Q.—On the 24th of August did Emma Borden come into that room? A.—Yes, sir.

Q.—At what time? A.—At 20 minutes of 9 in the forenoon.

Q.—Were you in the same room with them? A.—Yes, sir, in a closet opening into the room.

Q.—Tell what occurred in your own way? A.—Emma came into the room at 20 minutes of 9 on the 24th of August and spoke to Lizzie, and I heard them talking together. I was standing in the doorway. Their talk was loud. Lizzie was lying on the lounge, and Emma was talking to her. I heard Lizzie say, "You gave me away, Emma." Emma said: "No, Lizzie, I did not give you away." Lizzie replied. "You did give me away, but I won't give in an inch."

Q.—Were they talking in loud tones? A.—Yes, sir.

Q.—And Lizzie's voice was louder than Emma's? A.—Yes, sir.

Q.—Where were they? A.—Lizzie lay on her left side and Emma was sitting in a chair beside her.

Q.—How long did Emma stay there? A.—She sat there until 11 o'clock.

Q.—During this time did they speak again. A.—No, sir; I gave Emma a chair and she sank down beside the settee. They sat there all that forenoon until about 11 o'clock. Lizzie never spoke to Emma again that forenoon. She did not turn her face to her sister again that forenoon. Mr. Jennings came in after 11 o'clock. After he came I did not remain in the room. I stood right in the door of the closet when I heard the conversation.

Q.—Then Mr. Jennings came? A.—He came at 11 o'clock.

Q.—After he came you didn't remain in the room? A.—No, sir.

Q.—Where were you standing when the conversation between Emma and Lizzie commenced? A.—I was right at the door.

Q.—Where did you see them; in what position? A.—Emma was bendidg over Lizzie.

Q.—Did you see them, that is, Lizzie and Emma, when they parted? A.—Yes, sir.

Q.—Was there any good-by on either side? A.—No, sir.

Q.—Did you see either of them looking at you when this conversation took place? A.—Yes, sir, they saw me.

Mr. Jennings, the chief of Miss Borden's counsel, seemed to know all about the witness and to have had a good deal to do with her personally. He got her to tell what a jolly time she and Lizzie Borden had that day. She bet a dollar that she could tell Lizzie something she couldn't do, and that was how to break an egg in a certain way. Lizzie said she bet a quarter she could do it. Emma was sitting near by and the witness told her to move out of the way, for if Lizzie succeeded the egg would spoil Emma's dress. She got an egg and handed it to Lizzie, who failed to perform the trick.

"There," said Lizzie, "that is the first thing that I ever triedto do that I could not do."

Mr. Jennings wanted the witness to say that instead of a quarrel between the sisters, the whole truth was that all three had a pleasant time laughing and joking together. The cross-examination indicated that Mr. Jennings had personally studied this branch of the testimony months ago, but whatever he said the witness denied. He asked her if she hadn't said to several reporters that there was no truth in the story she told on the stand. She denied that, though two of those reporters were then in the court room.

Q.—Didn't you tell them it was all a lie, and that there was no truth in it?

A.—No, sir.

Q.—Didn't you tell Mr. Buck it wasn't true?

A.—No, sir.

Q.—Didn't you tell Mrs. Holmes that it wasn't true?

A.—No, sir.

Q.—Was a paper drawn up for you to sign about that story?

A.—Yes.

Q.—Was it read to you before you signed it?

A.—I don't remember.

"Now," said Mr. Jennings, "wasn't this the substance of that paper: 'This is to certify that my attention has been called to a report

THE DEFENSE OBJECTS TO TESTIMONY BY ELI BENCE

relative to a quarrel in which Miss Lizzie Borden said to her sister, "Emma, you gave me away." I positively deny that there is any truth in it, and that any such quarrel took place.' Now, wasn't that the substance of it?"

"I can't tell you."

Q.—Did you express a willingness to sign that paper if Marshal Hilliard was willing for you to sign it? A.—No.

Q.—Then why did you go with the paper and with Mr. Buck to see the Marshal? A.—To see what the paper was.

Q.—What did the Marshal say to you about it? A.—I don't remember his saying anything.

Q.—Not a word? A.—No, sir.

Q.—Sure? A.—Yes.

Q.—Didn't he say that if you signed that you would do so against his express orders? A.—I don't remember. He ordered me to go to my room.

Mr. Jennings's next question showed that he was in the Marshal's office at the time and that he said to the Marshal: "If she is willing to sign the paper are you unwilling to let her?"

It transpired also that the Marshal said that if Mrs. Regan had a story to tell she would tell it in court, and Mr. Jennings said to him that if he didn't let her sign that paper that he would publish him to the whole world. The witness's memory was questioned on all these points and she remembered nothing at all about any of them.

Then came Eli Bence, the drug clerk, who was to open the most important question of the day—whether the prisoner's effort to buy prussic acid was to be admitted or not. He gave his name, and said he had been in the drug business thirteen or fourteen years, and had been with his present employer, E. R. Smith, about four years. At this point the lawyers expressed their determination to argue for and against the admission of this testimony. The witness was sent away, and the jury was directed to retire.

Mr. Moody, assisting District Attorney Knowlton, said that the Government offers to show that prussic acid is not in commercial use, and is sold only at the direction of a physician. This drug clerk never had a call for prussic acid except from Lizzie Borden. The Commonwealth offers to show that she asked for ten cents' worth of prussic acid, and said she wanted it for cleaning capes. The Commonwealth will show that it is not used to clean sealskin capes or other kind of capes, and has no value for such a purpose.

Ex-Gov. Robinson, arguing for the prisoner, said that such an action by the defendant does not connect itself with the act she is charged with. Her's was an attempt to buy an article that is used for many purposes. It is an article a person may legitimately buy, and it is not to be said because it can be used wrongfully that therefore its purchase tends to show that a person has committed some other crime. This evidence had no tendency to show that this defendant killed these two persons, which is what they were inquiring into.

Mr. Moody, taking the ground that Lizzie's

MR. JENNINGS CROSS-EXAMINES HANNAH REAGAN

act indicated premeditation, cited half a dozen precedents and authorities some of which were strikingly similar to the case in hand. His argument was entirely upon the law.

Mr. Robinson followed him with an argument having slight reference to anything but the logic of this particular case.

"At a time prior to the murder," said he, "in March, she spoke unkindly to Miss Gifford of her stepmother. No one can argue that an attempt to injure or harm her. Subsequent to the murder the defendant, being talked to by the police, said: 'She is not my mother, but my stepmother.' That was a statement of a truth in either case. Now, can either of these statements be raised into the force of a declaration tending toward violence? Nothing other than this has been shown against the defendant in this case.

"The sickness in the family previous to the homicides has been alluded to, but the evidence clearly shows that the defendant was himself ill, and nothing in the testimony of the expert who examined the stomachs of the deceased gives any force to this matter. In this offer of testimony from the drug clerk, there is no effort to prove an intent to do an injury to any specific person. There is a world wide difference between the instances cited here and the case in hand. If a person does an innocent act we cannot presume to say, you did an innocent act but it was for an evil purpose. The Government admits that it doesn't claim to show the least tendency in this evidence alone to indicate for whom this purchase was intended."

At the close of the arguments the Court retired and remained away nearly an hour. When the Judges returned the Chief Justice said that he desired to have restated the limits purposed by the Commonwealth in its use of this testimony.

Mr. Moody replied: "We have no purpose of offering it for any other use than as bearing on the state of mind of the defendant prior to the homicides—the intent, preparation, and deliberation."

"The Court are of the opinion that the evidence is competent," said Chief Justice Mason. "The jury may be brought in."

It being time for adjournment, nothing more was done.

The Boston Record

The fame G. Washington's little hatchet is being temporarily eclipsed by the one that was found down in the Borden cellar, without a handle.

The Boston Herald

A peculiar feature in the Borden case crops out in the statement that District Attorney Knowlton, who is trying Lizzie Borden, did not at first suspect her of any part in the murder. He conducted the preliminary hearing and called her as a witness in order to simply get at the facts, believing himself that some man did the work. It is said that the evidence given by her at that time, and excluded from the present trial, shows conclusively in its internal development that the interrogator had no idea of connecting her with the crime, and that she was unconsciously involved by her contradictions, which Mr. Knowlton endeavored to have her harmonize, so intent was he in trying to get a connected and consecutive story from her. That day's evidence convinced him for the first time.

ONE SIDE.

State Rests Upon Its Case.

Last Evidence for Prosecution.

Jennings in Defense of Lizzie Borden.

Her Life History an Answer to the Charge.

Mysterious Strangers Now Recalled.

Exclusive Opportunity Idea Is Rudely Disturbed.

Lemay's Man in the Woods Causes Contention.

NEW BEDFORD, June 15—Apropos of the effort to prove that Lizzie Borden endeavored to buy some prussic acid two days before the murder, Chief Justice Mason, in behalf of himself and Judges Blodgett and Dewey, said: "It is the opinion of the court that the preliminary proceedings have not been sufficient; the evidence is excluded."

This has been a hot day for the defense, but might have been a greater, as I shall endeavor to show.

It could not have been hotter and even now, when the shades of night prevail, water dries instantly when thrown upon the pavements. The atmosphere is supercharged with humidity, and there is not a comfortable individual in town.

For the first time since the beginning of these proceedings the prisoner's face has lighted up at the sight of a friendly female eye.

In the morning, accompanying banker Holmes of Fall River were several well-appearing ladies, nicely dressed, with New England's choicest cut and bearing, who accosted Lizzie during the recess, forming a semicircle about her, laughing and chatting for several minutes in conversation cheerily participated in by Lizzie herself.

Perhaps the most startling rumor of the day was that which attributed a full-orbed degree of wisdom to the counsel for the prisoner, in that they intended to go to the jury without producing a particle of evidence, pro or con.

That was too sensible to be true.

Had they done so, in my judgment, before this time tomorrow night Miss Lizzie Borden

Would be a Free Woman.

On Wednesday, when court adjourned, the bench had consented that certain agreed upon preliminary evidence should be presented, for the purpose of informing the mind of the court as to the rightful introduction of the prussic acid testimony.

At the beginning today, an immense crowd being outside, the city filled with Grand Army men, the hotels and boarding houses packed to their uttermost capacity, the vicinity of the quaint old court house filled as roads are during the holding of the county fair, every seat in the court room was occupied, and a day of extreme discomfort was anticipated.

Mr Knowlton called a series of witnesses, druggists, furriers, chemists and the government medical witness, Dolan, to testify as to the qualities, properties and uses to which prussic acid, in particular, and other poisons, such as arsenic, and chloroform are put.

The jury, each armed with a palm leaf fan, and as full of iced water as human corporosities can be, airing themselves in blissful ignorance in the outer room, waited patiently for the decision.

A brief recess was taken by the court, at the close of which the jury returned, and the prosecution reoffered the testimony of the druggist from Fall River, in whose store Lizzie is said to have tried to purchase 10 cents' worth of prussic acid.

Whereupon the chief justice said: "It is the opinion of the court that the preliminary proceedings have not been sufficient; the evidence is excluded."

Mr Knowlton then put in evidence all the exhibits in the case, and at 10.30

The Commonwealth Rested.

Rested?

Yes, rested, without connecting the prisoner with ax, hatchet, blood, or anything whatever, save an unmotived opportunity to kill her stepmother, with whom, according to the evidence of the prosecution, she had no quarrel or disagreement discernable to the quick eyes of Bridget Sullivan, during her service of nearly three years, and also of brutally assassinating her father, with whom she had ever been on terms of affectionate intimacy.

Mayor Coughlin of Fall River, Mrs S. S. Fessenden, president of the Woman's temperance union, Mrs Washburn, who has been an attentive student of the case from its beginning, now nearly a year ago, and the flower of New Bedford's yachting crew, were honored with particularly good seats and shared the general interest.

Mr Jennings, who is so literally like Secretary of War Lamont as to be a constant text of provocation, has an admirable voice, which he uses

With Great Effect.

He began by explaining that he had been counsel to the late Mr Borden many years, and that the intimacy engendered by that connection brought him in contact since her young girlhood with the defendant, as he styled the prisoner, concerning whom man or envious woman had been unable to coin even a suspicion of anything beyond the pale of upright, honest, Christian life down to the date of suspicion that she murdered not only her stepmother but her good old father, with whom she had always been on terms of affection and regard.

After continuing at some length in this way, Mr Jennings suggested that while it was undoubtedly the proper thing for the commonwealth to find out, if possible, who killed the Bordens, it was equally its duty to protect the innocent, and scored a specially good point when he insisted that the jury were empanelled so to answer the question, "Did Elizabeth A. Borden kill her father and stepmother in a certain way, at a certain time," and were not to be switched off into an investigation of a mysterious murder, in the hope that they might determine by whom it was done.

He defined a reasonable doubt as one for which you can give a reason.

Running rapidly along the line of the testimony, he insisted, with a vigor that was all the more noticeable for its candor, that there was no direct testimony in the case which even pretended to connect his client with any blood or weapon or anything joined to the murderous act, and insisted that the entire horizon of the investigation was covered by a consideration, first of motive, second of weapon, third of exclusive opportunity, and fourth the appearance

Of the Defendant.

As to the motive, he argued that the prosecution's evidence showed distinctly that there was none, but that, even if inferentially there was one in the case of Mrs Borden it was an enormity to suggest that there was a shadow of motive that could induce this affectionate daughter in blood to murder her considerate father.

URIAH KIRBY TALKS TO THE JURY

He ridiculed, with neat sarcasm, the futile efforts of the police, who have been compelled by stress of circumstances to put the axes out of the case, the clawheaded hatchet out of the case, all the blood stains, so far as Lizzie Borden is concerned, out of the case, and, strange to relate, to find, after Prof Wood testified that there was no blood anywhere on anything, this headless hatchet, so that the defense defiantly challenged them to produce the weapon with which the murder was committed, and in any way to connect the defendant with it.

As to the opportunity, he put it to one side with the remark, most significant, that by a very multitude of witnesses the testimony of the police in general, and of officer Medley in particular, would be flatly contradicted, showing that there was ample verge and scope for dozens of individuals to come and go unmolested and unobserved.

Everything, he insisted, that his client had said, from the moment the murders were discovered down to the present time, her visit to the barn and her general doings, especially the burning of the dress, which was done in broad daylight, with police officers near her and in the presence of witnesses, was fully sustained and absolutely indorsed.

Mrs Chagnon, a typical French woman of the better class, corroborated her daughter's story.

A painter said that when he was hired to paint Mr Borden's house he was directed by the old gentleman to take his orders from Miss Lizzie, who told him to put his paint pots in the barn, she going herself, at the cheerful hour of 6 in the morning, to consult with him as to colors, and, to a certain extent, superintend the mixing of the paints for the

Experiments on the Walls.

Mrs Mary Durfee, a familiar Fall River name, a nice looking old lady, in black, rather short, with enormous high bows in her hat, wanted to tell that she saw a man on the steps of Mr Borden's house one morning, but brother Mason thought the time was too remote, and the little lady retired with a graceful bow embracing the court, the jury and the learned brothers.

Mr Charles Gifford and Mr Uriah Kirby told of a strange man whom they found sitting on Mr Kirby's doorsteps, quite near the Borden house, at 11 o'clock the night before the murder, and when Mr Kirby, who is a venerable, white-haired old gentleman of the frontier type, was asked to point out his house and steps to the jury, he stepped down to the rail in front of the jurymen, photograph in hand, and, much to the amusement of everyone in the room, entered into an animated conversation, punctuated with pointings and explanations, from which he was with difficulty drawn by the laughter-convulsed counsel of both sides.

At this point the dinner hour was announced, the supreme being was invoked to save the commonwealth of Massachusetts, the deputies were sworn to keep the jurors in some convenient place and give them nothing to eat or drink without the order of the court.

It is pretty hard work to eat dinner at 1 o'clock under any circumstances, but to enjoy it at that hour, with a red hot sun broiling outside and hundreds of strangers sizzling inside, is something beyond my capacity, but evidently as an eater I am not in it with the judges, the learned brothers or the jurors, for every one of them partook with zealous relish of their hearty noonday meal, and washed it down with coffee.

The afternoon session was bright, cheery and helpful.

Dr Handy, a pleasant-faced physician from Fall River, testified that on the morning of the murder, at 10.30, a medium-sized young man, unnaturally pale, with his eyes fixed on the sidewalk, attracted his attention in front of the Borden house to such an extent that he turned in his buggy to get a second look at him.

Mrs Manly also saw a young man about the same time, dressed like the one described by Dr Handy.

This and other evidence which the defense seeks to introduce may be very well from their point of view, when coupled with their proof of ample opportunity for others to do the murder.

A reporter by the name of Stevens was

JENNINGS: "There is not one particle of evidence against Lizzie Andrew Borden!"

called to testify that he looked over the Borden fence the morning of the murder and went into the barn, but was quite sure he could remember nothing that he did of any moment, whereupon he was allowed to retire, and did so.

A plumber and gasfitter, appropriately garbed, testified that he went into the barn where

There Were Four Others,

an interesting contradiction of the police officers, corroborating other witnesses for the defense, all testifying that they were in the barn, the dust on the floor of which the officer swore had not been touched by any foot save his own on the morning of that day.

A pedler gave some unimportant testimony at great length, the grain of wheat in the immensity of chaff being that that morning when he was on his ice cream route he saw Miss Lizzie Borden coming from the barn toward the house.

A cheeky but quick-witted lad by the name of Brown testified that shortly after 11 o'clock that day he and a party named Barnes went down to the Borden house, round the yard to the barn, and entered; that he went to the loft first, the party with him being afraid, lest some one might drop an ax on him. They were in search of the murderer.

At the time they got out of the barn, which, by the way, was quite cool, marshal Fleet had arrived and ordered them away, and after that they were obliged to be content with such observation as was afforded by the sidewalk.

Tom Barnes, a typical Fall River boy, was the party referred to by the previous witness, and corroborated with great circumstantiality of detail the

Testimony of His Pal.

Cross-examination, very adroitly conducted by Mr Knowlton, developed that in the barn and household they had breakfast at 7, dinner at 10.30, and supper at 5; that "Me" and "Brown" went into the barn, thinking that the murderer might be in the hay loft, and that they were looking for him, and were not afraid of him.

Mark Chase, now a hostler and formerly a policeman, stands somewhere in the neighborhood of 6 feet 6 inches high, and when he took the oath he elevated his arm and hand to their extreme length, as though he would touch the ceiling, sending another ripple of merriment through the audience.

In fact, I must chronicle that the entire day has been one of cheer, laughter, good-looking witnesses, bright sayings and general upliftment along the line of defense.

Several times the spontaneous outburst of snicker and a number of literal laughing roars stimulated brother Wright, the sheriff, into a condition of intensest activity, sending

The Red Hot Blood

of indignation to the roots of his more or less auburn hair.

Court adjourned promptly at 5 o'clock, when, as the throng dispersed, Miss Emma Borden made her first appearance, and immediately the young women entered into sisterly confidences, over which the veil of record, so far as I am concerned, is hereby drawn.

I wish the defense had gone to the jury without evidence.

There is no reasonable expectancy of any verdict save one of "not guilty," and a disagreement would mean disappointment to both sides, and a duplication of the enormous expense already fastened upon this God-saved commonwealth of Massachusetts.

Howard

The New York Tribune

The sessions are attended by as many people as are permitted to enter by the extremely magnificent high sheriff of Bristol county, who goes around in a Websterian blue swallow-tailed coat, with enough gilt buttons on it to fit out a regiment of Haytian generals, and a high silk hat, the sight of which would fill Mr. Evarts with admiration and envy. All the sheriffs of Bristol county are not as high as the high sheriff. The silk hat is his peculiar distinction, and with an irate temper and a stout figure, it renders him formidable to look upon. But all the sheriffs have sky-blue swallow-tailed coats and a gross or two of gilt buttons, and when they all stand up to salute the Court, and the Court stands up to salute them, one is profoundly impressed with the majesty of the commonwealth of Massachusetts. It is a part of the high sheriff's function to precede the Court as it enters, and to call out in a feeling way, "The Court!" whereupon the Court, standing before the bench, is greeted by the public, who stand also. The prisoner at the bar is taken from the dock and placed where she half confronts the Court and half the jury.

The Springfield Union

The prosecution certainly didn't go out with any crushing forcible evidence; it quietly dropped, and there was almost a dull thud.

The Worcester Spy

Now that the evidence against Lizzie Borden is all in one of the densest mysteries of this mysterious case appears to be why in the world was the girl ever brought to trial?

LIZZIE BORDEN'S TURN NOW

For an Hour Lawyer Jennings Pleads the Prisoner's Cause

Accused Has Her Second Good Cry Before the Public - Witnesses for the Defense Hurried Along with His or Her Little Story - Pedler Saw a Woman Coming from the Barn on the Fatal Morning - Two Boys in the Loft Before Officer Medley Who Swore That He Failed to Find Footprints in the Dust.

SPECIAL DISPATCH TO THE BOSTON HERALD

NEW BEDFORD, June 15, 1893. The trial of Lizzie Borden for her life is practically ended.

It may not be formally closed until Monday, or it may come to a verdict on Saturday, but as far as the backbone of it goes, it came to an end when the "wizard lawyer," ex-Gov. Robinson, flung the government's tales about poison out of the window and cut off the case of the prosecution before it had developed substance.

In New York her lawyers would have asked the court to throw the whole case out of court on top of the discredited poison testimony. But the practice is different here. Ex-Gov. Robinson said to a HERALD correspondent that such a dramatic course is not approved in criminal trials and would not be regarded as prudent.

To take the chance and then have the court hold that there was sufficient evidence to go before the jury would magnify the importance of the commonwealth's evidence in the minds of the jurors.

The case is ended, because the only story to be unfolded was that of the government, which has now been told. The defence has nothing of importance to put forward.

The theory of the prisoner's lawyers is that they do not know who committed the murders and that the commonwealth has not brought out a scintilla of evidence that their client did it.

The case has ended in a burst of sunshine for the imprisoned woman.

What was left of suspicious circumstances against her is now to be attacked by her lawyers, and already, in one afternoon, great gaps and holes were made.

A pedler was put on the stand to testify that he saw a woman coming from the barn to the Borden house at the very time the prisoner claims to have made the journey, and two boys were sworn to give evidence that they were in the loft of the barn before the arrival of the police officer who testified to visiting the loft and finding none of Miss Borden's footprints in the thick dust that covered the floor.

It would be interesting to know just what was the usual demeanor of the Puritan maidens in Endicott's time when they were on trial before the witch burners, knowing the hopelessness of their plight, feeling the implacable sternness of their judges, stripped of sympathy and companionship, badgered, and having every word and look tortured into evidence against them.

The Puritan maiden now on trial has seemed to behave like a girl with nothing to hope for-hardened to unkindness and suspicion.

How her position operated upon her could not be understood until today. Today her friends came to the front, and her side of the case had its first hearing. Instantly her demeanor underwent a change. A hint of this same thing was noticed the other day when the judges decided to exclude her testimony given at the inquest when she was surrounded by the unbroken circle of her captors, the police.

At that decision she burst into tears-into a convulsion of pleasure, gratitude and sudden relief wracked her whole body.

She had learned to brace herself against adversity and unkindness, but mercy and active friendliness were so new to her that she broke down before them.

Today the new current of testimony and eloquence on her behalf set in strongly, and she was lifted up like a parched plant after a shower.

She was overcome and wept when her old friend and the leader among her lawyers arose and talked of her home life and her yet unspotted good name in opening the case on her behalf.

He was eloqueant, but he was still more earnest, and his belief in her innocence shone in his words like a loving light in a forest.

For an hour he championed her cause with an ancient knight's consideration for her sex and herself. It must have been a strange sensation to that girl to hear, for the first time in 10 months of agony, a bold and defiant voice ringing out in her defence. She wiped her eyes furtively a few times, but the tears came so fast that she had to put up her handkerchief. Her face being hidden, she yielded to nature and had her second good cry before the public.

Mr. Jennings called the attention of the jury to the singular haste of the government in selecting this woman as the one person subject to suspicion. From the very outset they believed her guilty, and from that moment tried to prove her so. Yet she is one of the daughters of the old man who was murdered.

That Man Was Her Father

whom she tenderly loved, and in regard to whom the government has not even hinted that he was not the subject of her tender filial regard. For 32 years up to that morning she had led a spotless life, and for 21 years had moved in and out of that old house in happy relations with him and with her sister.

Mr. Jennings adopted the low, measured, funereal tone of voice, with its subdued tone and touch of melancholy, which is the stereotyped voice of all who speak at this trial. Only the crier calling for God to save the commonwealth is an exception to the rule.

Mr. Jennings put a little shading of triumph in his voice when he summed up the commonwealth's failure.

At the end he promised to show the jury that her relations with her father were such as they should have been, that Miss Borden did go to the barn on the morning of the murder, as she said she did; that she did get paint on the dress she burned, and that around the Borden house on the morning of the murder were strange characters not yet identified or placed.

LAWYER JENNINGS OPENS FOR THE DEFENSE

"Mr. Foreman and gentlemen of the jury, one of the victims of the murder charged in this indictment was for many years my client and my personal friend. I had known him since my boyhood. I had known his eldest daughter for the same length of time, and I want to say right here and now, if I manifest more feeling than perhaps you may think necessary in making an opening for the defence in this case, you will ascribe it to that cause.

"I want to say right here, and I do not think that the Commonwealth will question the statement when I make it, that there is not one particle of direct evidence in this case from the beginning to end against Lizzie A. Borden. There is not a spot of blood, there is not a weapon that they have connected with her in any way, shape or fashion. They have not had her hand touch it, or her eye see it, nor her ear hear of it. There is not, I say, a particle of testimony in this case, direct testimony, connecting her with this crime. It is wholly and absolutely circumstantial."

ALL THE EVIDENCE

Now Before the Jury in the Borden Case

Matron Reagan's "You Have Given Me Away" Tale Demolished by Several Witnesses—Miss Russell Told of Paint-Grimed Dress Only When Begged to by Sisters—Emma Borden's Story—Arguments Monday.

SPECIAL DISPATCH TO THE BOSTON HERALD

NEW BEDFORD, June 16.—All the evidence of the trial of Lizzie Borden for her life is now before the jury except that of a little boy, who is to contradict the two young shavers who went up in the Borden barn ahead of the policeman who swore he was the first person there, and that Lizzie had not been there. Those lads trouble the Commonwealth's lawyers, who are clutching at straws now that all their important evidence has slipped out or been chopped out of the case.

To-day the lawyers for Lizzie Borden had a gala day. They put on many important witnesses, and the District Attorney had such bad luck cross-examining them that it seemed as though he strengthened every point for the defence. The court room was crowded, and special passes by the lawyers were of no avail, because not a seat was empty in the place. The sable-garbed prisoner was at her very best in looks and spirits, and sat wedged in among her lawyers, a bright faced, bright eyed, wideawake old maid. In the morning she carried no posy, and there was nothing new in the floral line upon the bench before the Judges, who came back to the court after having decided that they could not admit the French woodchopper's testimony about seeing a wild-eyed lunatic in the woods, with his bloody shirt, his axe, and his monotonous wail about "Poor Mrs. Borden!" As the girl's lawyers do not feel the need of fastening the murder on any one, but are only concerned in clearing Lizzie's skirts of suspicion, they manifested utter indifference when their offer of this rambling yarn was declined.

In the afternoon, when the case was soon to go beyond its witness-stand stage, there was a burst of floral ornaments. Miss Lizzie Borden had received a box of tea roses and other gentle-hued blossoms by express from some gallant stranger named McLean in Connecticut. She came in with three or four of these pale but fresh blossoms in her hand to be read by the people as a sign of her rapid progress from the deep-red flowers of earlier days toward the pure, white bloom of vindicated maidenly rectitude. Indeed, already one white wild flower nestled among the roses in her hand. But on the bench before the Chief Justices there appeared a veritable floral glory—a brilliant bit of bloom the size of a pillow. It was as much as a bushel of great golden lilies shining amid a wealth of small white flowers. It looked like a fragment broken from a cloud and illuminated by a brilliant sunset.

The day was short, busy, and very important. The defence has no story or explanation to offer. Its only aim has been to weaken or contradict the Government's charges. The topics treated to-day were the alleged stolidity of the prisoner at the time the murder was discovered, the story of the paint-stained dress that she burned up, and the veracity of Mrs. Reagan, the police matron, who says she heard Lizzie Borden say to her sister, "You have given me away." The defence enjoyed perfect and overwhelming success in disposing of all these matters. Too much time was spent over Mrs. Reagan's tale of the quarrel of the sisters. It was utterly demolished by a little New England miss named Lizzie Brigham, yet other women, reporters, and citizens generally were called to bury the story deeper than Kidd's treasure is hidden. As to the paint-grimed dress, there was equally ample proof of it, and proof, too, that Miss Russell, the close friend of Lizzie Borden, had told the police of it only when begged to do so by the Borden sisters after she had neglected to betray their secret. As the poor woman has been roughly handled for the part she appeared to play in betraying her friend, this statement should lift from her the load of anguish that is said to weigh her down. Finally there was evidence that Miss Lizzie Borden wept in the presence of the mutilated remains of her father. Her lawyers not only proved this by their own witnesses, but they dug up Bridget Sullivan's testimony to that effect as she gave it at the inquest.

The sensation of the day was the appearance of Miss Emma Borden on the witness stand. She was subjected to a long examination by her sister's lawyers, and then was handed over to the mercy of District Attorney Knowlton.

Emma Borden is the aged double of her sister. She is like her in everything except her chin—Lizzie's chin is strong and firm and obtrusive, Emma's is weak and retreating. Otherwise they are very much alike. Both were dressed in plain black, and this was relieved for each only by a touch of blue in the plume of the hat. From that plume to their black gloves and the patent leather boot tips that peered from under their skirts they were clad alike. Emma is blest with big brown eyes, and a high forehead and a strong, large, coarsely modelled mouth, just as her sister is, and, like her sister, has a face that is abnormally wide at the top of the cheek bones in front of the ears. She is not as tall or as big boned as Lizzie, and she looks every bit of eight years older. Both suggest the typical old maid schoolmarm. As Miss Emma gave testimony on every point in the case, it is not possible to digest it in this part of the report.

Among the lawyers District Attorney Knowlton cut the supreme figure to-day. He has had charge of this case from the date of the inquest on the bodies, when he excluded the girl's lawyer and had already decided her to be a murderess. He knows his own side of it as Paderewski knows a piano, and he appears not to be able to find a flaw in it or to comprehend that there is any other side to the matter. If he were a witch burner, or possessed the spirit of one unimpaired since early colonial times in Massachusetts, he could not be more firm and unyielding than he is in this regard, and he has behind him the strong pressure of his big and forceful personality. He is a very large and powerful man, with a head as hard as iron set on a neck that is a tower for strength. His shoulders are a yard apart. His legs are like the foundations of a bridge. He is by nature combative, and he snorts like a war horse whenever he lunges or receives.

It was worth a great deal to a lover of the sports of the legal arena to see this colossus pitted against the slender sister of the prisoner. He could not shake her testimony on any main point, so he took to prodding her on the shadings and edgings and lace work of the meanings of words and of the smallest details of what she told about. He advanced toward her with something like the impetus of a locomotive, and he shook her bits of testimony as a bull terrier would shake a rat. She was as interesting in her way. She had been smiling and agreeable toward her sister's lawyers, but upon Mr. Knowlton she turned a cold, steely eye, a set mouth, and a proudly held head. She nerved herself for him at the start, and she never relaxed her cold, calm demeanor for an instant. He made nothing of her, and the shadow he threw on her testimony fell on his own cause and not on her sister's.

The first disturbance of the even tenor of the police testimony instantly made a turning point in the trial. It was when a patrolman stepped beyond the line of what had been said by his associates, who testified about the handleless hatchet, and swore that he and another one found the missing handle of that hatchet. Three terrible charges were made against the prisoner. First, she had not been to the barn during the murders; second, she had burned up a dress; third, she had burned the handle of the hatchet with which the crime was committed. This jarring policeman blew away the tale of the hatchet handle with a breath, and from that time on the hoodoo hatchet began those mad and devilish pranks which rattled the Commonwealth's lawyers and set in motion that retreat which has not yet been interrupted.

It was after this that public attention was called to the police.

It then came out that at the very time of the discovery of the murders they suspected Miss Lizzie Borden, and had got out a warrant for her within a few days. That warrant served to throw out of court the girl's testimony at the inquest, which was the most important matter the Government boasted, because it made the prisoner appear to be a liar. Then came the combined assertions of all the policemen that in all their searches they had not seen the blue dress of Bedford cord that Lizzie burned up, with its peculiar color and pattern and paint stains. On top of that came the ridiculous mess about a quarrel between Emma and Lizzie in which Lizzie said in the presence of a police matron thet her sister had given her away. Naturally did this seem to be a case of lying, but it was accompanied by testimony that the Chief of Police had forbidden the matron to deny it in writing while she was verbally denying it to all who spoke to her about it.

Next came the showing that the peddler who saw a woman coming from the Borden barn on the morning of the murder had told his story to the police, and they had made no public mention or use of it. There was also the accumulated testimony of several witnesses that they had tramped around the barn loft before it was visited by the policeman who clinched Lizzie Borden's account of her movements by swearing there was not a footprint in the dust on the floor of that loft. Finally, on top of the Government evidence that Lizzie's physician "held the fort" at her door and tried to hinder a search of her room, there came a plenty of evidence that the Borden sisters flung everything wide open to the police and even assisted them in their searches. Perhaps the most remarkable development by the defence was that the medical examiner had made one hatchet fit the crime at one trial, and now was giving the same testimony with quite a different sort of a weapon for its basis.

The gap in the police testimony which was started by the hoodoo hatchet kept on widening, and has not yet ceased to spread, so that it looks to an impartial observer as if it was a waste of time and animal heat to visit the police with any worse consequences than have attended their own adventures upon the witness stand. Whether individuals who have testified in the trial can and should be made to account for the discrepancies between their stories and the well-attested evidence for the defence is another matter. But certainly nothing more is necessary to procure fairness in Lizzie Borden's trial than the opportunity the jury has already got to detect the unfairness of the police, if in their judgment any unfairness has been shown by them.

John D. Manning, a reporter of the Fall River *Herald*, was very early at the house on that day and noticed that there were two or three persons in the loft of the barn, of course long before the arrival of Policeman Medley, who found no footsteps up there to corroborate Lizzie Borden's explanation of her whereabouts during the murder. This clever reporter and bright witness said that Mrs. Reagan, the police matron who told the story about Lizzie accusing her sister of giving her away, swore that Mrs. Reagan told him there was no truth in that story.

Thomas Hickey, another reporter connected with the Fall River *Globe*, asked Mrs. Reagan about her rigmarole, and she said, "I have got to take that all back."

He said to her, "Then, Mrs. Reagan, there is absolutely no truth in the story," and she said, "No, sir, no truth at all."

When Mr. Jennings called the name of Emma Borden the women who crowded the court room made such a stir to see this most important witness that the sound of their dresses was like a whiff of wind in an open forest. They were surprised when they saw the elder of the distressed sisters and noted how much older she was than Lizzie, how much slighter of frame, and how much plainer in appearance. Miss Emma walked and looked like a self-reliant woman, and spoke with a firm, clear voice. It was a kindly voice, and was often accompanied by a very pleasant smile. Her appearance suggested that she might be of a lighter heart than Lizzie, but she took pains to tell the court that she was more prejudiced and narrow minded.

According to the cruel Massachusetts custom, she stood for nearly two hours, though at one time, while the lawyers were disputing, some one gave her a chair for a few minutes.

In view of the fact that a whole force of policemen could not find any blue dresses or any dresses with paint on them in Lizzie Borden's clothes closet, Miss Emma was asked to state what dresses were in Lizzie's closet during the search on the Saturday after the murder. She said there were about eighteen or nineteen dresses there.

The witness said that she and Lizzie assisted the officers as much as was in their power. They did not raise the slightest objection or obstacle, but told them to search as thoroughly as they could. The witness was asked to tell what she knew about the notorious Bedford cord dress which the Government believes that Lizzie had on at the time of the murder and burned to get it out of the way.

"It was a very light-blue gown," she said, "with a darker figure about an inch long and, I think, about three-quarters of an inch wide. It was made during the first week of the previous May by Mrs. Raymond, the family dressmaker, who made it at the Borden house. It was very cheap. It cost either 12½ or 15 cents a yard, and contained not above eight or nine yards. It was almost plain, with just a ruffle round the bottom.

"Lizzie and I assisted the dressmaker, as was our habit, and the dress was done in two days. We worked in the guest chamber. That work was always done there. Mrs. Borden had her work done at the same time in the same way. We always had it all done together. Lizzie got the dress soiled with paint. I should say the paint was along the front and along the side toward the bottom."

Mr. Jennings tried in six or seven ways to show that the Borden girls always burned up their old dresses, but, no matter how he put his questions, the Court excluded them.

Q.—What did you do with your rags and pieces of cloth? Did you or your sister keep any rag bag? A.—We did not.

The answer was excluded. "What was the custom of your sister in disposing of her old dresses?" "Did you know your sister's habit of burning old dresses?" These were some of the questions that Mr. Jennings tried, but none would do. Then Miss Emma continued: "Miss Russell came in the dining room and said that Mr. Hanscom, a policeman, wanted to know all the dresses that were in the house at the time of the murder, and whether they were all there. Miss Russell said she had answered 'Yes,' and told a falsehood. I asked her what falsehood, and she spoke of the Bedford cord dress. I can't remember all that happened then, for that frightened me so thoroughly. Miss Russell took courage and went and told Mr. Hanscom it was a falsehood. My sister and I told her to do so. We decided that she must tell him it was a falsehood and that we wanted him to know it. I do remember Miss Russell saying to my sister that burning the dress was the worst thing that she could have done, and Lizzie said: 'Oh, why did you let me do it?'"

EMMA BORDEN ON THE STAND

Miss Lizzie Borden had been more than wide awake all the time her sister was on the stand. She never once took her eyes off her lifelong companion. She drank in every syllable that Emma uttered. It was plain that this was the brightest day in the term of Lizzie's connection with criminal proceedings.

That was the end of the proceedings and will be until Monday morning. The court foresaw that it could in no event keep the case from going into next week because even if the lawyers summed up on Saturday, there would be no time for the judge's charge until Monday. So both sides agreeing, all of what is to come went over until that day. It is perfectly easy to see what arguments the lawyers on both sides will use.

The only unknown quantity in the case now is what the jury will do. As twelve men are pretty nearly as uncertain as one woman, none of the lawyers venture to prophesy further than that the jurors will not find the rich maiden of Fall River guilty of the butcheries.

HOPEFUL.

Lizzie's Counsel Sustained.

Emma Borden Tells About Burning the Dress.

Mrs. Raymond Swears to Paint On It.

Strange Man Story Barred Out.

Hilliard Contradicts Matron Reagan.

Gov Robinson's Trousers Prove a Mascot.

The Arguments Will Probably be Heard Monday.

All the Testimony Has Now Been Heard.

NEW BEDFORD, June 16—The defense is closed, the rebuttal is ended, and court is adjourned until Monday morning at 9 o'clock.

The judges and the counsel have gone to their respective homes, but the jury, poor fellows, are securely locked in their hotel quarters, utterly uninformed as to the why and wherefore, hungry for information and thirsty for something else.

We had a very interesting day, the first act of the chief justice being a knock-out for the defense, the court having concluded that the man in the woods, seen by the good lady who was on the stand at the last adjournment, was so remote an object of interest as to be unworthy of an exhibit in this case.

This has been an odd trial in respect to the raiment novelties being sprung upon the spectators day after day. The Chief Justice, for instance, favored us yesterday with the sight of a new white stovepipe. To-day Judge Blodgett for the first time wore a white necktie, aiding his always pale visage in further resemblance to a clean cut cameo. Gov. Robinson sported a new pair of trousers yesterday, which was a lucky day for the defense, and his associates insisted upon his keeping them on until the close of the trial, that the luck might not be changed.

Miss Lizzie told Gov. Robinson, as he greeted her this morning, that she had not passed a very restful night; and the intimation came, with a cheering smile, that she would feel better by and by.

The decision relative to the admission of the evidence of the Frenchman, who saw the man with the bloody hatchet, was in order the first thing. The Court decided that the evidence could not be admitted, and Mr. Jennings took an exception, stating that he would put in writing just what he had intended to show.

Sarah R. Hart of Tiverton said she passed the Borden house on the morning of the murder and saw the "pale young man" standing in the gateway.

It was current rumor in the courtroom that after the close of yesterday's session the Fall River police got hold of the two boys, Brown and Barnes, and endeavored to make the place rather warm for them because of their testimony as to their visit to the Borden barn. Therefore, the testimony of Painter Charles S. Sawyer, who stood guard at the Borden door the morning of the murder, to the effect that he saw the boys go to the barn, was interesting. Sawyer was one of the first persons to reach the house after the murder. He said Lizzie seemed much distressed. There was no blood on her clothes. He locked the cellar door after he was put on guard.

TOLD A PLAIN STORY.

Reporter Manning of the Fall River Globe proved one of the best witnesses thus far developed, for without hesitation or zeal, but in a straightforward, businesslike way, told his story of the day clearly and distinctly. He aided in upsetting the police barn theory that no one had been in that building with the exception of the policemen, and directly contradicted Matron Reagan, who, it will be remembered, testified that she had never said that there was no truth in the story of the quarrel, and also that she knew nothing whatever of the contents of the paper which the Rev. Mr. Buck desired her to sign.

Mr. Manning told in detail of his visit to the Borden house, where he saw all the other witnesses testified to, of his visit to the barn and of his conversation the very day of the publication of the Reagan story with Mrs. Reagan in her own house, to which, with a New York reporter, he made a visit.

At that time she distinctly said, he testified, that there was no truth whatever in the story as to the quarrel, and that she knew nothing whatever about it. Going further in her denials, she told another reporter that the story of the quarrel was absolutely false, and when he laughingly said: "You are getting into the papers," she replied: "But that has all got to be taken back. There was no quarrel, and I never said there was."

This evidence was, as far as it concerned Mrs. Reagan, corroborated by Reporter Hickey, who was with Mr. Manning.

Next to the interest felt in Lizzie Borden, with a possible exception in favor of well-meaning Bridget Sullivan, the popular desire has been greatest to see Miss Emma Borden, daughter of the murdered man and sister of the accused.

She is over 40 years of age, and looks it, a prim, little, old-fashioned New England maiden, dressed with an exceeding neatness in plain black with the impress of a Borden in every feature.

Self-reliance and personal dignity, I should say, are conspicuous factors in her composition. There was no swaying of her slender form, no drooping of her straight-out eye, no quivering of her tight-shut mouth.

Everybody looked at her, but she looked at the counsel only. She first gave an itemized list of Lizzie's property, amounting to deposits in sundry savings banks of about $2500, two shares in the Fall River national bank and nine shares in the Merchants' manufacturing company.

She said that the gold ring on Borden's finger was given to him by Lizzie 10 or 15 years ago, she having worn it a long time, and that he prized it highly and always kept it on his little finger, where it was when he was buried.

She produced an inventory of 18 or 19 dresses hanging in their clothes press, and swore, in response to marshal Fleet's assertion that the search didn't amount to much, that Dr Dolan told her they had searched from attic to cellar, Bridget taking the paper from the walls and the carpets from the floors.

The court would not allow Mr Jennings to prove by Miss Emma that it was the custom in the house to dispose of remnants and pieces of dresses by burning, although that would have been a tolerably good reply to adverse critics who insist that burning was a very odd way to get rid of an old dress.

However, according to Miss Borden, although Miss Russell said nothing to Lizzie about the burning of the dress where people could see it at the time, she did say to her later that she feared the burning of the dress was the worst thing Lizzie could have done, whereupon Lizzie exclaimed:

"Why did you let me do it?" Later Miss Russell said to the Borden girls that she had told Mr Hanscom a story in saying that all the dresses that were in the house at the time of the murder were there on the day of the search, and that it had troubled her conscience and that she had gone to him, confessed her falsehood and told of the burning of this dress.

The girls were thoroughly frightened and after consultation concluded that the only proper thing for them to do was to see Mr Hanscom and tell him the facts precisely as they occurred.

Her attention was then called to the Reagan yarn about the quarrel between Lizzie and herself. Sentence by sentence she denied the truth of every word, deliberately and emphatically setting at rest, so far as she was concerned,

The Whole Fabrication.

Mr Knowlton's ingenious cross-examination endeavored to prove a condition of ill-feeling in the Borden household, but succeeded only so far as the witness herself was concerned.

She said that some years ago her father gave Mrs Borden, her stepmother, one-half of a house, of which the other half was owned by her sister, the price being about $1500; that this angered Lizzie and herself, in consequence of which their father gave them what is known as their grandfather's house, and that after this the cordial feelings between Mrs Borden and Lizzie Borden were restored, but that such was not the case as between Mrs Borden and the witness.

The noonday recess was taken while Miss Emma was on the stand, and if ever a body of men thoroughly enjoyed a hearty meal our friends the jurors did, putting away great quantities of corned beef, roast beef, turkey, vegetables, ice cream, cake and fruits, all of which were washed down with that admirable fluid known as aqua pura.

It being noised about the town that Emma Borden was on the stand everybody made a rush for the court house, but they might as well have rushed to the spire of nearest church, for the good people already favored with seats knew a good thing when they had it, and not a soul stirred during the entire recess save such as knew they would have no difficulty in getting back.

The sisters were not allowed to be together, nor later at the conclusion of her testimony was Miss Emma permitted to join her sister at the bar.

The usual notice concerning exhibits having been given, Gov Robinson announced, to the surprise of everybody, that the defense rested.

Howard

WITH LIGHT HEART

Lizzie Borden Waits for the Arguments

Remarkable Court Room Scene Expected Monday,

When Attorneys Argue for and Against Her Life.

New Bedford Seems Very Dull After Exciting Week.

Jurymen Write Letters and Indulge in Games.

[SPECIAL DISPATCH TO THE SUNDAY HERALD.]

NEW BEDFORD, June 17, 1893. Two gentlemen well skilled in the law and with no mean reputation as lawyers will on Monday tell 12 men what they think of the murder of Andrew J. Borden and his wife Abby. They are George D. Robinson and Hosea M. Knowlton.

The former will contend the innocence of the accused party, Lizzie Borden; the latter will declare her guilt.

Probably never in the history of the commonwealth has there been such a struggle for mastery in a criminal case as will occur on that day. Probably never were two men more thoroughly convinced of the justice of the positions taken, although they are diametrically opposite. Probably neither has ever contended with more force or argued with greater brilliancy than they will. And last, but not least, never before have the people all over the country waited so anxiously to hear words fall from lawyers' lips as they are waiting now to hear from these men.

It will be a battle for a life—one demanding, the other pleading that it be saved, as the 12 men cannot be certain that the allegation and indictment stands proved.

And, as is not often the case when men of the legal profession argue, each is sure he is right, and will talk not only for the advantage to be gained and the money to be earned, but for principle as well.

So, in this battle of words on Monday will be combined with legal oratory and erudition a demand that justice neither overstep its bounds or fall short of its true position, and as the jurors see the matter they must decide on which side of the line justice stands.

Hundreds of persons want to hear Gov. Robinson utter the words which he trusts will set his client free; as many more wish to listen to the remarks of the popular district attorney, remarks which he hopes will make clear to the jury that his premises in the matter are correct and that she is a murderess.

So, while the city of New Bedford is comparatively deserted tonight by the men and women who have crowded its hotels and boarding houses for the past two weeks, they are all expected to rush back again tomorrow, and with them others, who will wait to take advantage to listen to the

Greatest Court Room Contest

of the time, at least in Massachusetts, and probably in New England.

The court house and its grounds looked like a different establishment today.

For the past two weeks its windows have been crowded with spectators; its halls and corridors filled with officers and waiting witnesses; its anterooms occupied by attorneys and stenographers; its back yard turned topsy turvy by telegraph operators and newspaper men and its sidewalks lined with unfortunate ones who did not get around in time to enter the portals of the charmed structure.

Today the windows were open to give exit to the clouds of dust; the halls and corridors were vacant; the anterooms deserted; the sidewalk frequented by pedestrians who hurried to and fro in attendance on their every day business, while the hive of industry in the back yard looked like a closed-up bar-room in a no-license town.

Mr. Jennings came down from Fall River this afternoon, but he did not have any opinion to offer beyond the declaration that he did not see how any man could hold forth that the prosecution had proved beyond a reasonable doubt the guilt of Lizzie A. Borden. Gov. Robinsson didn't care to talk at all.

Miss Borden passed a very comfortable day, according to all reports. She sat in her room and tried to keep warm while reading one of Dickens' works. There were several callers in the afternoon, among them Lawyer Jennings. She had two or three bouquets of June garden flowers sent in, which she enjoyed greatly. The prisoner appeared to have a good appetite, and seemed more encouraged and less depressed than at any time when she has been obliged to spend a whole day in a cell. During the past week of the trial Miss Borden has been more

Communicative to the Officers

whose duty it is to administer to her wants, and infrequently the conversation has led her to comment somewhat on the incidents of the trial. Her pleasantest days, as they have been called, have been prolific of the most interesting talk.

She is no mean conversationalist at any time, her friends say, and her enforced idleness of the past nine months has given her an opportunity to familiarize herself with English literature, which she has not been slow to take advantage of. Unquestionably the signs of the times have had their effect on her.

The opening argument of Atty. Moody, masterly, and, to many, convincing, was shock enough to her to cause a slight fainting fit. But as the skein has been untangled and her counsel have drawn forth many yarns which it was promised would weave the net about her, she has gradually dispelled the depression which seemed to bear her down, and since Dist. Atty. Knowlton's sudden announcement, "the commonwealth rests," she has been actually jolly—at times laughing heartily in the court room.

She seems to share the opinion of her counsel, which is apparently concurred in by many of the townspeople, that most of them expect a disagreement, while the chances favor an acquittal.

Of course the adherents of the government still maintain that the anticipated brilliancy of Mr. Knowlton's argument will result in a conviction.

People in this city had so much confidence in Hosea M. Knowlton that they expected him to wring water from stones, and now that they see the result of his nine months' of hard work they are inclined to condemn him for ever bringing the charge against the young woman. They neglect to consider what he had to contend with.

But "Horsey" has lots of grit and has announced that he has no doubt that he can satisfy the jury that the prisoner had exclusive opportunity to murder her stepmother, hinging less in his argument Tues-day on the killing of the father than was maintained in the opening argument. He believes that the murder of the stepmother is his strongest point to work a conviction on that would prove as much a victory for him as would a conviction for the slaying of both.

While he will not let the other count go by default, he will cling tightest to the theory of exclusive opportunity of killing Mrs. Borden. He is given an exceptional advantage in this, too, by the decision of the defence not to make any opposition to the claim that the murder of Lizzie's stepmother was some time prior to that of her father.

Tomorrow will be a dull day of anxious waiting. There is practically nothing for those detained in town to do but to

Go to Church or to Ride.

While Gov. Robinson did the lions share of the work for the defence during the trial and won golden enconiums by his skilful cross-examinations and sharp lookout for the points of advantage, the inside work on the case performed before the presentation of evidence in all probability did more to weaken the government's position than even the efforts of the ex-Governor.

The "steering" of this was done by the only Boston man in the case, Lawyer Melvin O. Adams, a colonel who utterly discards his title. He prepared the case, took up the law and precedents, made a special anatomy of the head and the weight and sharpness of hatchets and generally kept the wheels within wheels, of which an immense number has been shown in this case.

His voice has not been heard so frequently as some of his Boston friends would like, but his ability has, nevertheless, been most intensely manifested to Messrs. Knowlton and Moody and other government workers.

Mrs. Mary A. Livermore is still a strong friend to Lizzie Borden. Here is something she said to a reporter today which expresses her views of the case.

"Why, they talk about that dress burning. It is always our practice at home to burn up everything that is of no value, so as to get the useless things out of the house.

"It is not an uncommon thing, and Emma tells me that it was always the practice in her family. Lizzie and herself always burned their old dresses. They were people who did not want clutter around. That was the best way to get rid of it.

"I hear from Fall River, from one of my old Sunday school boys, that there has been since the presentation of the government a complete overturn in public sentiment, and that the feeling now is that if this is all the government has against Lizzie Borden, she should be acquitted."

People in New Bedford tonight generally look for a disagreement. There are many who anticipate an acquittal; hardly any one expects a conviction.

The New York Press

After the three New Bedford gentlemen had testified the court retired, and when it came back Chief Justice Mason said: "The preliminary proof not agreeing with the proffer, the testimony is excluded." The capstone of the edifice on which Hosea Knowlton had been building for nigh a year, the cornerstone being Lizzie Borden's own extorted "contradictions," had fallen, but Hosea Knowlton made no sign. He is of as pure a grit, that district attorney, as Lizzie Borden herself.

However the prosecution may have felt at the ruling, there was no sound of grief or sign of it in the "meetin' house" court room but the snappy furling of a fan in the "amen corner." The "amen corner" is right across the bar from the jury box. It holds just twelve women, the elite of the deputy sheriff's entirely respectable friends, and every one of them has hanged, drawn and quartered Lizzie Borden long ago, because she looks "wild" and spiteful. The owner of the furled fan leaned over to a correspondent, asked "Is it shut out?" and said, "Oh, that makes me mad!"

The New York Times

EDITORIAL - JUNE 17, 1893

WILL IT REMAIN A MYSTERY?

It is many a year since a criminal case in this country has excited such universal interest and been the subject of so much discussion as that of the Borden murder. It has all the fascination of a mystery about which there may be a thousand theories and upon which opinions may differ as variously as the idiosyncrasies of those who form them. There is so little absolute evidence that everybody can interpret the probabilities and the circumstantial indications to suit himself, and much will depend upon his general view of human nature and its capabilities. There seems to be little prospect that the mystery will be cleared up by the trial that is going on at New-Bedford. The verdict, if there shall be a verdict, will make little difference unless there is to be some disclosure of which there is yet no sign.

The whole case is a tangle of probabilities and improbabilities, with little that is certain except that a man and wife were murdered in their own home on a frequented city street in the middle of an August forenoon, with nobody about the premises, so far as has been shown, but the daughter and a servant girl. It was improbable enough that such a crime should be committed at such a time and place at all. That any one should enter the house from the outside and commit it and get away without being observed or leaving any trace behind was most improbable. But the officers of the law were unable to find any evidence that the crime was perpetrated by any one outside of the family, and the testimony brought by the defense to show that it might have happened in that way has proved nothing as to the crime.

The utter absence of any other explanation was the sole support of the suspicion against the daughter. In spite of the circumstances that made it look dark for her, there was as complete a lack of direct evidence against her as of any kind of evidence against anybody else. If circumstantial evidence is a chain only as strong as its weakest link, we have presented here an attempt to make a chain out of wholly disconnected links, which has no continuity or binding strength at all. Almost as strong a case could be made out against anybody who had the misfortune to be in a house where murder was committed and not on the happiest terms with the victim. The utter absence of proof of anything except the fact of murder, and the lack of real evidence against anybody, is likely to leave this as a baffling mystery, unless a revelation should be made of which there is as yet no premonition.

GUILTY OR NOT?

Fate of Lizzie Borden in the Balance.

Arguments and the Charge Next.

Resume of Evidence for and Against.

Wherein Case Against Her is Weak.

Howard Predicts that Prisoner Will be Acquitted.

What Others Think Will be the Result.

Case Will be Continued at New Bedford Monday.

NEW BEDFORD, June 18—Tomorrow morning the superior court will convene in New Bedford for the purpose of listening to the arguments in the case of the commonwealth against Lizzie A. Borden, and the charge of the court, which is, I understand, to be delivered by Mr Justice Dewey of Springfield, a college professor in appearance, a clear-headed logician, a tender-hearted man.

The Bordens were murdered in Fall River, which, like New Bedford and Taunton, is a shiretown, but it was deemed best to try the cause in New Bedford, and to exclude from the jury all residents of Fall River, because of the intense prejudice for and against the prisoner in that place, and because of the almost superhuman activity of the police in their endeavor to convict one of the occupants of the Borden household of the assassinations.

Therefore it is that all parties concerned, with the majestic court itself, have been here during the past two weeks, and will come again tomorrow morning. Their coming tomorrow morning will, however, find them occupying

Very Materially Altered

relative positions, the one to the other, from those we found them in two weeks ago.

The judges are not changed a whit. Chief Justice Mason, who approximates as nearly as possible to one's idea of an old-fashioned gentleman, will be tomorrow, as he has been from the first, receptive, impassive, quick to appreciate and prompt to decide. He went home last night delighted and charmed beyond adequate description with the calm and peaceful conduct of the trial and delighted beyond measure at the courtesy manifested from first to last by the belligerent counsel on the one side and the impassioned counsel on the other.

In speaking of it he said that in all his experience he had never before encountered such a degree of considerate courtesy as had attracted his attention and merited his approval on this occasion. That it is as it should be the chief justice fully recognized, as also that it is as it usually is not.

On the judge's left side his associate, Judge Dewey of Springfield, Mass, a scholarly looking man with a large head, thickly covered with silver gray hair, which falls upon a massive face, lighted by kindly eyes and shaded by a carefully kept beard. While the chief justice is deliberate in his movements, brother Dewey might properly be described as logy in his. However, unless I am greatly in error, there is nothing slow about his gray matter and nothing turgid in the movements of his brain.

Judge Blodgett, who sits at the right hand of the supreme judge, is younger and of a more modern type of individual, scrupulously careful as to the cut of his hair and beard, with an intellectual forehead, a piercing eye, a noticeably neat habit of attire, clad indeed a la mode from his white necktie to his well-polished boots.

The three men have been a triple target for 1000 curious eyes, an attractive subject for scores of artists' pencils, a study pregnant with suggestion to dozens of men accustomed to read, divine and portray character, thought and probability. All this they have borne with perfect composure, maintaining an unruffled dignity, delighting common sense, satisfying every cavilier and showing themselves, in the full glare of unaccustomed publicity, the very embodiment of discretion and the personification of manner in its best estate.

To outsiders the dignity of the court, the solemnness of the scene, the unwhispering presence of spectators, the marked deference shown by counsel to the bench, the urbanity of the court and the form and ceremony strictly observed by the people, and rigidly enforced by the sheriff, present a picture at once unique and suggestive.

The judges believe in it, the counsel have been brought up in it, the sheriff finds it a pleasurable duty, and the people stand it because they have to.

Doubtless on Tuesday night a verdict will be reached. The evidence is all in. Let's see for a moment where we stand. The Bordens are dead; there's no doubt about that to begin with. On the 4th of August last the two were assassinated, one up stairs and one down, by a hatchet wielded by the well-disciplined hand of some frenzied individual, name and occupation as yet unknown. Not content with two savage blows in the face, either of which would have caused instant death, according to the testimony of the experts, the assassin must have straddled the body of Mrs Borden and rained upon her prostrate form 18 blows, one after the other in quick succession, the blood spurting in all-defiling sprays upon the bed clothes, the furniture, the carpet and presumably the murderer.

The police being notified took possession of the house and all there was in it. They occupied the premises, and drove all strangers even from the sidewalk in front of the house. They put under surveillance the daughters of the murdered, their uncle and their servants. They carefully examined these individuals and searched the house from attic to cellar, not forgetting the premises of the barn, until, as one of them said, they had not only gone through everything, but had taken the plaster from the ceiling and the carpet from the floor.

Public Excitement Ran High.

An excitement in New England is analogous to frenzy in other sections in the land, where crime is of more frequent occurrence. Recognizing the universal demand for the detection and punishment of the assassin, conscious of the lack of evidence against any one, the police appear, in their wild-eyed way, to have made up their minds that a victim must be found, and found, too, near the scene of the infamy. As Miss Emma Borden, the elder of the sisters, was out of town at the time, it was evident she had nothing to do with it. As Mr Morse, uncle of the young ladies, could establish an alibi from early in the morning until after the murder, it was equally clear that he had nothing to do with it, so the matter narrowed itself down to Miss Lizzie Borden and Bridget Sullivan, the servant.

For reasons satisfactory to themselves, the police selected Miss Borden as their game and from that moment to the present time have done nothing but seek to fasten the guilt upon her. Armed with police testimony Dist Atty Knowlton and Dist Atty Moody called Lizzie Borden to the bar two weeks ago tomorrow morning and confronted her with the commonwealth which charged her with murdering on the morning of the 4th of August 1892, with an axe or hatchet, her father and her stepmother. The charge you see is clean cut, straightforward, concise and understandable.

Did they prove and how?

They pretend that they did and this is the way they did it.

They showed by unimpeachable testimony that the brutally butchered remains of Mrs Borden were found lying under the bed near the wall of the guest's chamber, and that any quantity of blood was spattered about the room. Having cut off her head and bleached the skull, they showed that she had received many serious wounds with a hatchet. Having taken out her stomach, they showed that part of her breakfast had been digested and the remainder had not.

By equally incontrovertible testimony they proved that Mr Borden's body was found lying upon the sofa in the sitting room, also mutilated in a frightful manner. Having taken out his stomach, strange to relate, they ascertained that some of his food had been digested and that the remainder had not; and also that any quantity of blood was spattered on the wall and saturated in the carpet.

They searched the house, not only permitted, but aided and

Begged So to Do

by Miss Emma and Miss Lizzie. They went through it thoroughly, but found absolutely nothing which could in any way connect anybody—Lizzie, Bridget or uncle Morse—with the bodies or the blood. In the cellar they found sundry axes and hatchets, rusted, but not with blood, but even with these had they been covered with blood and steeped in gore they found no connection leading to any individual in the house.

The prosecution, fully aware of their inability to bring any direct evidence, resorted by police methods to circumstantiate proof and argued that because of certain financial transactions Lizzie hated her stepmother, thereby showing a motive; that she was alone in the upper part of the house with her mother, thereby showing opportunity and that she had attempted a short time previous, unavailingly, however, to purchase prussic acid, thereby arguing premeditation.

The police, in their anxiety to serve their chiefs, swore with abundant and amazing recklessness at the inquest held a year ago, and strange enough every one of them has since been promoted, presumably for his zeal.

The matron of the station house, where Miss Lizzie was held a prisoner, swore that she had heard Lizzie charge her sister with having given her away, and in order that there might be no doubt as to her having heard it, with extraordinary lack of thought she testified that she stood in the open doorway some four feetl only from the sisters, where she could be seen and was seen by them both.

A Miss Russell swore that Lizzie on the Sunday following the murder burned one of the dresses. Then the prosecution rested and the counsel for defense looked up in unfeigned amazement, astonished at the weakness of the assault.

O what a chance was there.

O for a moment of courage, confidence and skill.

Not a thing had been shown which by the wildest presumption could lead Lizzie Borden anywhere near a weapon as yet undiscovered with which those murders were committed. Not a scintilla of proof connected her in any way with any incident having the faintest bearing upon the tragedies of the eventful morning.

The defense should instantly have moved the dismissal of the case. I dare say the chief justice and his learned associates, in view of the

Enormity of the Crime,

would have hesitated and very likely refused to grant the motion.

And then.

Go to the jury. And how about that jury? We who have studied them for two weeks past agree with an estimate formed by Dr T. S. Robertson of this city, who looked at them with the eye of an expert, that they are a fairminded, honest-appearing, well-meaning set of men, not intellectually great, but morally substantial. They know this story by heart. They saw Dist Atty Knowlton, as vigorous in mind as he is in body, as adroit in cross-examination as he is in seducement, pale, as witness after witness contradicted each other standing under oath in the presence of Almighty God and the jury in the box. There has been no communication between the jury and the public since they were impaneled two weeks ago, save that indefinable communion of saints and sinners which proceeds from contemporaneous human nature, all-embracing like the atmosphere itself, sending on wings of electric communication the subtlest impression an all-convincing argument.

Tell me they don't know what popular sentiment is and public feeling? That's nonsense, for they are part of the populace themselves, and in this particular instance the conceit essence of the public.

Then came the defense, standing off against a cordon of self-contradicting policemen a band of New England ladies and gentlemen, giving evidence of birth and breeding, as they stood in a God-fearing, oath-respecting attitude before the court and jury.

Dead, of course they were. Blood, certainly, quantities of it. Agitation, why not? Undigested food, who cares? Where is the weapon? Where's the handle to the hatchet found by Marshal Fleet and since mysteriously disappeared? Any quantity of blood, but not on Lizzie's garments. Considerable ill-feeling toward the stepmother, but in Emma's breast it rested, according to her own testimony. Dislike of Mrs Borden, I dare say, but the affectionate father was killed that morning as well as the irritating stepmother.

Mystery by the cord, but what has the jury to do with the mystery? Mysteries are for the police. The charge is for the jury. So it all narrows down to this, that the police charged Lizzie Borden with the murder of her father and step-mother, have sworn falsely to that end according to their own testimony, have allowed the matron to become hopelessly involved in a series of extraordinary statements, explanations, contradictions and denials, and all to what end?

That's where we are today.

That's where the commonwealth and the prisoners will be tomorrow when the crier will announce the presence of the court, and the jury, sitting in the presence of a multitude of fellow-citizens, will be addressed by the facile tongued ex governor of the commonwealth, argumentatively bombarded by the brainy headed district attorney for the county of Bristol and elaborately charged as to the law in the case by one of the accomplished jurists on the bench.

Howard

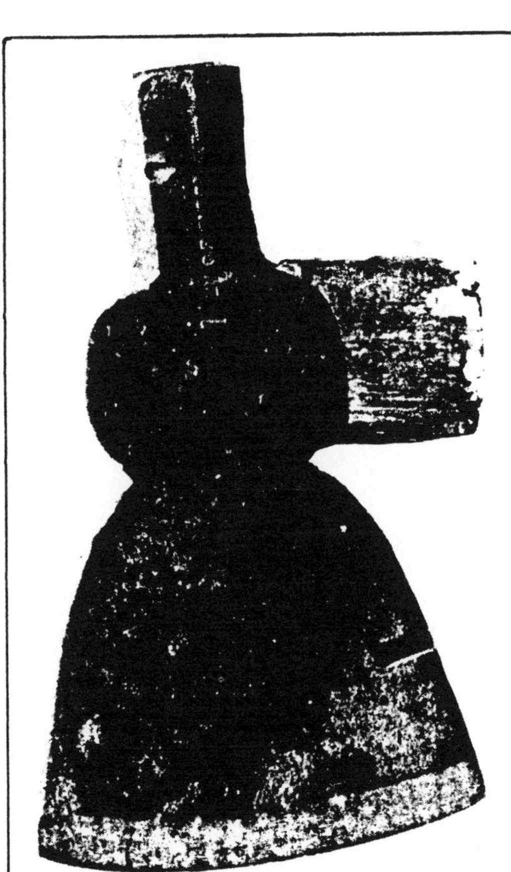

THE CONTROVERSIAL "HOODOO" HATCHET CLAIMED TO BE THE MURDER WEAPON

The New York Times

EDITORIAL

CONDUCT OF THE BORDEN TRIAL

Whatever may be the result of the BORDEN trial, there can hardly be two opinions as to the superiority of the manner in which it has been conducted over that which is apt to characterize "sensational" murder cases in this State. It is, in fact, a credit alike to the bench and the bar of Massachusetts. It has been prompt and orderly, without any sign of the laxness or the scandalous incidents with which we are too familiar here. This appeared conspicuously on the first day in the selection of a jury. The examination of the talesmen was conducted wholly from the bench, and was confined almost entirely to certain statutory questions touching the qualifications of jurors. It is doubtful if there could have been found in Bristol County twelve men of mature age and sound mind who had not read about the case, discusseed it more or less, and formed some kind of opinion about it, but the crucial question was whether they were in a state of mind to render a verdict upon the legal evidence to be submitted. If it was shown that they had no personal interest or prejudice in the case, that is considered by the Massachusetts law sufficient, and, with the statutory right of challenge, affords an ample guarantee of fairness. The result was that a jury was obtained in a single day in a community in which the case had been a matter of discussion for months.

The court and counsel have alike been disposed to observe the legitimate rights of evidence and of argument, and there have been no unseemly wrangles or unnecessary delays. Important questions as to the admission of evidence have come up and have been argued pertinently and incisively and decided promptly. There has been expert medical and chemical testimony, but it has not been biased or conflicting. It so happens that it was submitted by the prosecution, but proved to be wholly favorable to the defense. There was no attempt to twist or distort it or to make it prove anything but what might appear as the result of an expert examination of the facts.

Whatever there may be that is discreditable in this case must appear in the efforts of the police authorities of Fall River to unravel a mystery which baffled their moderate skill and in the preliminary examination, which seems to have been directed to fixing the crime upon the only person whom those authorities could subject to suspicion. The trial itself has been conducted ably and expeditiously and kept within the limits of the proper dignity of a judicial proceeding. There has been a dearth of evidence for the prosecution and, consequently, little for the defense to do in meeting it, but in such a case under lax methods there is apt to be all the more straining for sensational effect and greater efforts to overstep the bounds of regulated procedure. The BORDEN trial, considering the sensational aspects of the case, has been a model proceeding from the opening day and can now only be marred by the conduct of the jury.

LAST WORDS IN THE GREAT TRIAL

Ex-Gov Robinson's Denial of Lizzie's Guilt Answered by Dist Atty Knowlton's able Argument

NEW BEDFORD, June 19—

This has been a peculiar day in many respects.

Instead of concluding, so that the judges could charge the jury the first thing in the morning and the verdict be reached early in the afternoon, Mr Knowlton had made so little progress as to render a late session an intolerable burden in this day of excessive heat, so an adjournment was taken at 5 o'clock until tomorrow morning at 9, when he will proceed and occupy the entire morning session.

The judges are in no hurry; they are on the bench for life, and don't mean to make any mistakes if they can avoid it.

So, while it is possible a verdict may be reached by tomorrow afternoon it is quite as probable it will be night before that end is obtained.

The actors in the scene appeared early upon the stage, so that when in his most majestic tones sheriff Wright announced "The court," three judges bowed to a reciprocating assemblage of heroic proportions, every one in his best bib and tucker, with flowers and feathers galore, the aisles filled, the outer rooms packed, the stairs and lower passages in the same condition, leading to the roped off multitude outside.

New Bedford has had two or three days of chill, but the temperature today made up for it, nearly equaling the excessive discomfort of the first fortnight of this truly celebrated case.

I was pleased to see that the judges appeared refreshed after their two days' rest, and even the jury looked as though there might be a suggestion of a backbone among some of them.

The prisoner seemed brighter and cheerier, in spite of her dignified reserve, as she was taken to the dock, the privilege of sitting within the bar, by the side of her counsel, being no longer deemed a necessity.

Miss Emma Borden and uncle Morse sat near the counsel and immediately in front of the dock, where at a second's notice they could give personal attention in case

Miss Lizzie Should Faint,

collapse, break down, or do any of the hysterical acts freely predicted of her by sensational correspondents, who ought to know better, and probably do.

Gov Robinson was dressed, as he has been since the beginning of the trial, in a plain suit of black, with an alpaca coat and spectacles provided with glasses of the half-moon type, so that he can read his notes and at the same time have his eyesight unimpeded when he looks at the jury.

I noticed that he invariably spoke to the jury, while Mr Knowlton, later on, always spoke to the foreman or to some individual member of the panel.

He began in a low, earnest tone of voice, telling the story of what he termed one of the most dastardly and diabolical crimes known to the history of Massachusetts, and, having in a few concrete sentences told the story, answered his own question, "Who did it?" by insisting that it must have been a maniac, an abnormal production of the Deity, a maniac frenzied beyond the possession of reason, or else a devil.

His insistence that the blows were given by a hand practised in the use of weapons was obviously to counteract the assertion that the blows were dealt by a nerveless hand and by one, too, who struck and struck after the necessity for violence was ended.

He made a strong point by not only admitting, but arguing in favor of the necessity of a most rigid investigation, which led to a well-directed series of sarcasms at the expense of

The Fall River Police,

the first attempt to depart from the simple, beaten track of ordinary narrative, and then made marked the contrast between the value of direct and circumstantial evidence.

He insisted that the commonwealth was bound by the opening assertions of Dist Atty Moody and that he had lamentably failed as a representative of the commonwealth in numerous instances, one of which was the assertion that Lizzie Borden was preparing a dangerous weapon the day before the murder, carrying the war into Africa also by a very neat ridiculing analysis of the prussic acid business.

Having to the best of his ability disposed of the debris, as it were, in the front yard, he went into the house and told the story of the murder, prefacing it with a record of Mr Borden's day, as agreed upon, and also that of Mrs Borden, as far as it is known, admitting that while Mrs Borden probably died between 9.45 and 10.15, Mr Borden was doubtless killed between 10.55 and 11.10.

This he claimed to be a physical impossibility, so far as the defendant was concerned, unless she had a confederate, and there is no evidence connecting an accomplice with the case.

As to the opportunity, he admitted that Lizzie was in the house in the morning and justified her being there on common sense ground, proved to his entire satisfaction the impossibility of her seeing a body lying under the bed, save while standing on one of the stairs, and that, too, with the face turned upward, it being a physical impossibility to see a body placed where Mrs Borden was, while a person going down the stairs could not see from any one of them.

There was no reason for her to look under the bed going up or coming down; she knew of no trouble, she

She was Not a Detective

searching for anything or anybody; she was simply attending to her business about her father's house.

Then came the note.

I was surprised until later, when I heard Mr Knowlton's reply, that Gov Robinson should dwell so long and carefully upon the matter of the note, there being absolutely no testimony save that of hearsay concerning it, yet at great length he discussed its reception and possible fate, and insisted that Mrs Churchill learned from Bridget Sullivan, as well as from Lizzie Borden, that Mrs Borden had received a note from a sick friend and had gone to attend her, the fact being, Mr Knowlton very cleverly put it, that all Bridget knew of the note was what Miss Lizzie had told her.

I think he rather emphasized the weakness of his point when he said that there may be people in this country who don't know of this trial and some one of them may have written this note.

It is evident that if there was any note received by Mrs Borden it came from some friend, and if in response to the note she visited that friend, it is entirely unreasonable to presume that such an individual would remain quiet, when the simple assertion that she wrote the note would relieve the daughter of her friend, presumably her friend as well, from this which the prosecution evidently considers one of its material weapons against the accused.

As for the barn episode, the governor made a very happy use of the extraordinary contradictions of the government.

He showed that it was Lizzie's habit to go to the barn, and she, being about to start on a fishing expedition, and wanting lead for sinkers, probably made two errands at the same time, one for iron for the door, one for the lead for sinkers.

Fortunately they had a witness who was unimpeached,

The Ice Cream Pedler,

who although not a great lawyer, a doctor nor a minister, had eyes, and using them he saw Miss Borden coming from the barn.

He ridiculed the idea that because Lizzie's hands were white, and not covered with dirt and rust from the barn, it was proof positive that she had not been in the barn.

The governor had been talking two hours, the mercury had risen perceptibly, the crowd inside was one vast fan, the multitude outside one great blister, and it occurred to the learned brothers on the bench that the jury might like a rest, a change of position, so the talk was suspended for five minutes, during which everybody stood up and talked, buzzed his or her neighbor, and were having such a thoroughly enjoyable time that the sheriff deemed it best to put an end to it by three short decisive raps with his pencil on the table.

I think it was a relief to Miss Borden, who had listened intently to every word, and who had evidently settled herself to endure whatever must be heard.

While not in the remotest degree intimating or allowing the inference that Bridget Sullivan knew anything about the murders, the governor made an admirable point by showing that if Lizzie Borden had said what Bridget had said about her unwillingness to go up stairs, although the death of Mrs Borden was not yet known, when they wanted a sheet to throw over Mr Borden's body, it would have told against her, yet when Bridget said it nothing was thought of it.

A point which is clear enough to sensitive natures was made in reply to the criticism that Lizzie did not look at her father, and cry and take on, by showing that she behaved in the most natural and self-contained manner, the way in which she always bore herself, never giving way to waves of hilarity

Or Bursts of Grief.

He thought it did not look much as though she was stinted for money, or could have found in her desire for money any motive for the killing of her father, as she had in bank and in personal property between $4000 and $5000 on which she could realize any time.

She had money enough, so the motive could not have been a desire to kill her stepmother first, and then her father, so as to get half of his property, and it seems odd to say that she killed Mrs Borden because she did not like her, then killed her father, although she did like him, because she wanted his money.

He denied that the government had made any point at all as to the ill feeling between Lizzie and her stepmother.

Especially had it failed to show what the district attorney said he would prove, that she hated her stepmother.

As for her saying "She is not my mother, she is my stepmother," the governor thought that that was a mere incidental remark, very natural.

He did not expect to find heaven in the Borden house, he said, any more than in his own or that of any other man.

EX-GOVERNOR ROBINSON ADDRESSING THE JURY ON BEHALF OF LIZZIE BORDEN

He would not contend that Lizzie was a saint, but he declined to agree with the theory that because she and her sister Emma were not always at the breakfast table with Mr and Mrs Borden she had murdered them in cold blood.

All this time Lizzie looked intently upon him, now and then fanning herself, occasionally tapping her rather pretty foot on the lower portion of the rail, now and then putting a boquet to her nose, never taking her eyes from the face of the man upon whom much of her fate, she thinks, depends.

The first emotion she showed was when the governor told the story of the gold ring she gave her father many years ago, and which was buried with what is left of him in the family plot in the adjacent cemetery.

It was, however, but a transient flood; her perfect composure was soon recovered, and, without a glance at any other individual, she continued her attention to her counsel.

Her conduct at the time of the discovery of the bodies was photographed by the governor as perfectly in keeping, not only with her own character, but with that of any young woman who had received a shock so sudden and so severe.

The government one minute insisted that she had not been out of the house at all, and yet they claim that she rushed in and discovered her father, having

Pre-Knowledge of the Death.

Mrs Churchill saw her standing at the screen. She had shrunk from her father's dead body,not knowing but that the assassin might yet be there, and leaned against the screen for support, calling to Bridget, and looking, according to Mrs Churchill, who saw her, pale and agitated to such an extent that she called out and asked her what was the matter, and Bridget Sullivan swore that she looked whiter than she ever saw her before, and that she was crying.

She was frightened; she was alarmed the night before, and told Miss Russell so.

That night the family were all ill, an additional cause for alarm, and then the discovery of the dead body of her father, superadded to her other disturbing conditions, came as a fatal climax.

It occurred to me, as an interested observer and listener, that the governor went into detail somewhat overmuch, but I found that Mr Knowlton followed him closely, and they doubtless know their fellow-citizens better than we from a distance.

It may be that the evidence is not soaked into the jury yet, and they need all this recapitulation, but I should have supposed it would have run clean through by this time.

He went at great length through the doings of the night of the murder, explaining what Miss Russell and Miss Borden did, and why, and then exhaustively treated of the burned dress; showed how it was customary in these days, when rags are no longer valuable to anybody, in many homes to burn them; held up to scorn Dr Dolan and his idiotic opinion that paint was blood, and contrasted what the Fall River examiner did not know with what the famous expert, Prof Wood of Harvard, does know.

He made much sport of the police, whose search was not a search, in spite of its thoroughness, insisting that among

The Eighteen or Twenty Dresses

which these povertystricken girls were permitted to have, in spite of their miserly father, the identical blue dress on which Dolan mistook paint for blood, was hanging there at the time; that when it was given to Dolan for the government on his opinion that the paint was blood, they framed their indictment, and did not want any other dress.

When it came to Prof Wood, who by his testimony compelled them to throw up the dress theory, they were forced to call for another dress, which was the reason of their damning the bedford cord, which they now claim was the dress Miss Lizzie burned.

It seems this burned dress was worth about $2 at the outside, and there is abundant evidence that it was soiled, stained and spotted with paint; so, in obedience to her sister's suggestion, on Sunday morning, three days after the murder, doors and windows wide open, Emma and Miss Russell in the room, Lizzie burned the dress.

The police had had charge of the house all that time.

If they made a search they would have discovered a blood-stained dress had there been one, and if they made no search the fault does not remain with the defendant.

He laughed at the idea suggested by the prosecution that Lizzie assaulted her stepmother, she being stark naked at the time, and, having given her two tremendous blows, stood astride her as she hacked her prostrate form.

He also retold the story of the axes and the suspicions that first attached to them, and subsequently the hatchets, and held aloft with enjoyable sarcasm the mentality of Dr Dolan, who not only found blood on hatchets, which was subsequently determined to be rust, but actually insisted that the hair of a cow came from a human head.

The governor put a hypothetical murderer in the house, and told how he might have done the deed and passed out of the house without detection, a very unnecessary procedure, it seems to me, because, as the government's case can only succeed by proving that Lizzie did the murder, so the defense's main hope ought to rest in the self-contradictions of the prosecution's testimony and the absence of the weapon, coupled with the non-connection of the defendant with the act itself.

Why should the defense seek to unravel the mystery?

However, he went on to show that it was no more absurd to argue that

No One Saw a Man

enter the house than it was to recall that no one saw Mr Borden go out of the house when he went downtown in the morning, and the first seen of him was in the bank.

Besides that, Mrs Hart and her companion did see a man at the gate, and others testified to having seen suspicious characters in and about the vicinity during the 24 hours preceding.

Again the barn theory of the police, that no one had been in the barn except Mr Medley, was gone over, with its numerous contradictions; again the story of what was necessary for Lizzie to do, assuming that she had done the murders, was gone over, and then, approaching a conclusion, he demanded an acquittal on the ground that the prosecution had not proved its case; that her conduct was that of an innocent woman, although she did not cry and wail and make an exhibition of herself, but that, on the contrary, like a well-disciplined New England woman, when confronted with this terrible affair in her own house, her common sense came to her relief, and she not only aided in but directed the search, doing all she could to facilitate the police officers and the authorities in general.

Then, after picturing in complimentary phrase her bearing before the court room fiends, male and female enemies, he begged a verdict that she might be Lizzie Borden of Fall River once more, and return to her home, that wrecked and blood stained home where she has already passed so many years of an exemplary christian life.

It was 3.05 when recess was ordered, after which, the audience being wedged together in the jamedest jam I ever saw, Dist Atty Knowlton, who looked very solemn and severe.

Began His Argument

with the assertion that this was a heart-rending case, an incredible crime, emphasized by the extraordinary charge that the murders were done, the impossible crime committed, by a christian woman, who is no ordinary criminal, but one of the rank of lady, the equal of his own wife, the wives of the jurors or of any other man, against whom down to the time of the commission of this deed nothing but good had ever been said.

He argued that as christian directors had robbed banks and women reputed to be good had done brutal murders, it was entirely proper to dismiss all consideration of previous conditions and all thought of sex, it being the government's insistence that the woman at the bar was the assassin of the victims of this terrible outrage and called upon the jurors to face the consideration as men, not as gallants.

He discussed at some length, and quite interestingly, the different kinds of evidence, direct and circumstantial, and when entering upon a justification of the course pursued by the police he said that while in his judgment of guilty the proof was such as must justify a verdict of guilty against her, he was quite sure that there was not a man in all the world so base as to hope that she did the deed.

Lizzie kept her eyes straight upon him.

She lost no word, no inflection, no gesture, but looked at him as though with a pitying amazement at the whole procedure.

That, however, produced no effect upon the district attorney, who warmed with his subject, and time and again left his place

Behind the Bar,

walked around to the jury, stood at their side or immediately in front of them, and spoke with marked earnestness, distinctness and emphasis.

He argued that youth was no protection against crime, and referred to the Pomeroy case, known as the most fiendish in the history of the commonwealth; that sex was no protection against crime, for within a very short space of time a woman murdered a whole cartload of relatives for the sake of a miserable pittance of a fortune.

In his opinion women, while lacking vigor, make up in cunning and although their loves may be stronger so, too, are their hates.

He admitted that, while he was impervious to ordinary criticism, it might be some gratification to those who said he was prosecuting this case for ambition, for hatred, to know that their shaft had struck home, but that he hoped to God if such were the case his right hand might be palsied and his tongue cleave to the roof of his mouth.

He ridiculed the idea that direct evidence could fairly be asked for in a case like this, especially in this case, and on the question of motive asked who would be benefited by the death of Mrs Borden, answering him: "One would, and she a woman, the prisoner at the bar."

Very ingeniously and with much force and logic Mr Knowlton arrayed incidents, facts, conversations and appearances against the prisoner, whom he spoke of as assassin, murderer and liar, warming up, as he proceeded, to a white heat of intense mental activity and physical development, walking to and fro, gesticulating with violence, and looking with comprehensive sweep, a carom of regard, as it were, from the bench to the jury, from the prisoner to the counsel, and thence about the audience, whom he greatly interested.

The court ordered a recess at 5 o'clock of five minutes, and it looked as though an evening session was inevitable.

Better counsels prevailed, however, and the proceedings were adjourned until tomorrow morning at 9 o'clock.

It looks now as if all Tuesday would be occupied by the conclusion of Mr Knowlton's argument and the charge of the court, in which event the case would go to the jury some time during the afternoon, the time of the rendering of their verdict being obviously simple guesswork so far as I am concerned.

It must be conceded that Mr Knowlton's plea is not only ingenious and forcible, but in a certain degree effective.

If the charge of the court is in any sense analagous to the district attorney's line of argument, a disagreement is by no manner of means an impossibility.

Down to the opening of Gov Robinson the bets were 2 to 1 in favor of an acquittal; now they are 2 to 1 in favor of a disagreement.

Howard

LAST SCENE IN THE GREAT BORDEN TRIAL.

CLERK: "What say you, Mr. Foreman?" FOREMAN: "NOT GUILTY!"

NOT GUILTY.

Miss Lizzie A. Borden is Acquitted.

Decision Reached on First Ballot.

Judge's Charge a Plea for the Innocent.

Knowlton Hurt Case by a Comparison.

Howard Pictures the Scene in the Court.

Spectacle When the Verdict Was Announced.

Bench, Bar, Press, Everybody Express Opinions.

NEW BEDFORD, June 20—"I want to go home: take me straight home tonight."

"Tonight?"

"Yes, tonight. I want to see the old place and settle down at once."

That Lizzie Borden should throw her hands upon the rail, her face upon her hands, and indulge in hearty sobs after the ordeal of facing, her hand uplifted above her head, the foreman of the jury as he pronounced the words, "Not guilty," was to have been expected.

Nothing else?

Well, yes. If she were an ordinary woman she would have cried and cried, perhaps fainted, then smiled, and in effective pose reasserted the habitudes of her sex.

The difficulty is she is not an ordinary woman; she is a puzzle psychologic.

Presumed by the law to be innocent, and as it now appears, judged by the law of the land so to be, she has lived in the broad glare of red-hot publicity nearly a year.

Every great newspaper in the land has had its reporters, its staff correspondents, its artists, and its pests, male and female, watching, searching, studying, analyzing, photographing, sketching, picturing, and if possible interviewing her.

They found texts for columns in her looks, her bearing, her method of speech, her personal habits, her ability to sleep, her fattening process, her approaching trial and everything connected with her.

The great Beecher used to say that a public man could not blow his nose on his own doorsteps without its report being echoed throughout the entire city, and so it has been with Lizzie Borden, whether she washed her face, wiped her eyes, blew her nose, puckered her mouth or raised her hand, whatever she did, wherever she went, she was an object of curiosity and unmitigated assault by the gossips of the time.

During all this period, to use a vulgarism, she has not given herself away once, by which means she has done nothing which might reasonably have been expected from an ordinary woman in her trying and embarrassing circumstances.

She is an abnormality, but she does not look it nor would one have the right to so judge her, were nothing known of her beyond the simple

Christian Life She Led

down to the moment of her arrest.

In works of good repute she passed her time. A member of the band of Christian Endeavor she visited those in prison and comforted her kind in trouble. A manager

JUSTICE DEWEY CHARGES THE JURY - "Gentlemen, the case is now in your hands."

of the Fall River hospital she visited the sick, and gave not only words of cheer and cups of cold water, but her presence and individual interest to her brothers and sisters of low degree.

The Bible class, the Sunday school and the prayer meeting were about the most exciting of her pleasures and she grew to woman's estate the favorite of a hard natured, close fisted, money saving, but daughter loving New England miser.

Womanly traits and christian qualities were the only developments of Miss Lizzie Borden's character, save such petulances and outbursts of temper as are natural enough in every household in the land and might well be looked for in a home where a father of the Borden type had taken to himself a second wife, thereby furnishing to his daughters a stepmother of the Mrs Borden type.

Who says all this? Not the police, not the state detectives, not madam rumor or dame gossip.

But who does tell it?

First the jury, her sister and her uncle. Next the pastor of her church and the city missionary, to whom she often went with contributions of money and that which sometimes costs us more than money, personal presence and individual interest. Then come the neighbors and the church folk.

Just here a point. It would have done you women who read this story, heart good to have seen the women of Fall River on the stand for the first time in their lives testifying to their love and confidence for and admiration of this young christian woman, flesh of their flesh in the church, bone of their bone in the good works which as one good old lady naively expressed it, "naturally interest our young people."

No one could have studied, as I did, the contrast afforded by the witnesses for the prosecution, and the men and women called by the defence, leaving out of consideration, obviously the experts whose testimony was negative, if not almost entirely substantiating the claims of the defence.

Police marshals, police captains who had been promoted from patrolmen through the year, police medical examiners, and policemen of every possible grade furnished the contradictory evidence for the prosecution, handicapping the climax with the matron of the station house.

In all my experience, which includes attendance upon the chief criminal trials since the famous Burdell murder, somewhere in the later 50's, I have never seen

A Prosecution so Handicapped,

first by the crime, abnormal and extraordinary in its character; second, by the absolute barrenness of direct proof; third, by the contradictions of its own witnesses, and fourth, by the utter impassiveness and stolid self-reliance of the accused party herself.

The opening of Dist Atty Moody was not only ingenious, but clean-cut, admirable in delivery and effective, while the closing plea of Dist Atty Hosea M. Knowlton entitles him to rank with the ablest advocates of the day.

It is fair to remember that it is much easier to assault than to defend and in forming an estimate of ex Gov Robinson's interesting and convincing plea for the defense, it must be remembered that after he had reexposed the police officers in their great act of tumbling one over the other, of riddling the matron because of her unnecessary and ridiculous story, there really was little left for him to do beyond those glittering generalities of which Rufus Choate, the master of pyrotechnic oratory, was so fond.

Now and then during the somewhat unnecessary details indulged in by her own counsel Lizzie Borden shed a furtive tear, and when Chief Justice Mason, to whom she looked almost hoping against hope for exclusion of the inquest testimony sustained the position taken by ex Gov Robinson, overcome by joy and recognizing the full horizoned significance of the aid her case had received, she broke down, and for two or three minutes indulged in the luxury of a first-class cry.

With these exceptions the defendant has sat as motionless, as expressionless and apparently as uninterested as a wooden Indian.

Therefore I say she is, as counsel on both sides have characterized, a woman of extraordinary mentality and unusual self-control.

In view of her life, as pictured by the solid men and women of the city of her residence, all this seems strange. Yet the fact is she was always peculiar in her ways, as was shown by her selection of old Mrs Russell, for instance, as an intimate, and the further fact that she never cared at all for the society of men, old or young.

Yesterday was a corker. Today knocks sun spots out of it.

I never suffered so much from literal heat as I did in the court room today, although appropriately clad and provided with all the creature comforts that a freely spent fortune could procure.

The jury were on their mettle. They had listened courteously to ex Gov Robinson and to Dist Atty Knowlton the day before, but by the exercise of a God-given intuition they felt in their bones that this day was their last, and bore themselves in their best bibs and tuckers like men and brethren conscious of the heavy responsibility resting upon them.

Lizzie was Very Pale,

but self-contained, as usual, and having riveted her eyes upon Dist Atty Knowlton accepted every blow without a flinch and endured to the very end like a woman of pluck and grit and tremendous self-reliance

Mr Knowlton has had a tough time in various ways the past month. He has had severe and dangerous sickness at home; he has held the laboring oar in this great case.

He has seen, little by little, how unstable and unsatisfactory were the men and women upon whom he depended.

He felt, right or wrong, that the dress handed to him from the Borden house was not the gown he wanted, and he knew that a great wave of popular disgust with a verdict obtained by circumstantial evidence in New York in the cases of Carlyle Harris and Dr Buchanan had swept so thoroughly over the entire country as to affect very seriously the chances for conviction.

I never in my life was so impressed with the outrageous point to which modern habit has brought the state's attorney in his desire for conviction as in this admirably managed trial.

In other days, when accused persons were not defended by paid counsel of their own choosing they were safe in the hands of the lawyers of the commonwealth, and his sole idea was to ascertain truth, and nothing but the truth.

The modern practice which enables wealthy people to hire lawyers for their defense and leave courts to assign lawyers to defend people too poor to hire them for themselves, is responsible for the feeling which district attorneys now invariably have, that a verdict against the prisoner is a victory for them, while a resultant not guilty is a defeat for the county or the commonwealth.

This was noticeably shown in the present instance, and with the same pride of bearing, the same earnestness of purpose, the same tremendous potentiality which we find displayed in the engine No. 999 on its 20-hour trip from New York to Chicago was superbly developed in that magnificent specimen of God's handiwork, Hosea M. Knowlton, today.

"I am innocent. I leave it to my counsel to speak for me."

Ordinary men like you and me can understand how nerve pure and unadulterated could enable a guilty man or even woman to bear up with defiance against any accusation.

Here, however, was a young woman, short and, although stouter than she was a year ago, fragile and delicate, who never flinched nor quailed, but looked her accuser and her assailant straight in his flashing eyes.

Mr Knowlton ridiculed the story of the barn and her being in the hay loft on a brutal day in August, and made unquestionably a good point when he asked:

"Where is the bit of iron with which to fix the door; where is the sinker with which to go a-fishing?"

I was not pleased with Mr Knowlton's frequent iterations of his desire to remember at all times that the defendant was a woman, his desire to be truthful and his appeal to heaven to do something dreadful to his arm and seriously embarrass his tongue if he were to be in any sense unfair or prejudiced in the conduct of this case. In other words, he protested too much, a fault most grievous when viewed in the light of his otherwise magnificent work.

He appeared chagrined and mortified to find that he had been fooled by the defense or misled by the police about the dress that Miss Lizzie wore on the fatal day.

He was evidently convinced that she wore the bedford cord and subsequently burned it, and in accounting for the fact that the police did not find the dress at the time of their thorough search, he said they were not especially careful, because they believed they had the dress they wanted in their possession.

He thought no one would hesitate a moment as between Lizzie Borden and Alice Russell, insisting with great show of earnestness that Miss Russell was a woman with a conscience, and when with great impressiveness he said, turning to the jury, "You saw her," a smile ran through the court room and one irreverent member of the bald-headed club remarked, "We did."

Mr. Knowlton hurt his case seriously by drawing very unnecessarily a contrast between Lizzie Borden and Bridget Sullivan, the rich and the poor, the mistress and the maid, the educated and the uninformed.

It was unnecessary, because Lizzie Borden has no better friend than Bridget Sullivan, and no witness on the stand did so much as Bridget to help the cause of the defense, who sought to persuade the jury that the house was not the home of hate and malice, when she testified that in all her term of service she heard no quarrels and witnessed no disagreement.

During the recess a large pile of letters were handed to Lizzie by sheriff Wright, some of which she read, smelling bottle and fan in hand.

It was uphill work for the able district attorney, and sweltering spectators regarded him with curious interest, such as is manifested when a strong man bursts chains that are bound about the muscles of his arm or a thousand-pound weight is lifted by the teeth by the woman of the iron jaw.

His contention that the story told by the matron was told in Lizzie's interest was so manifestly grotesque as to make even the police officers smile. Mrs Reagan did not care a rap for Lizzie or anybody else; what she was thinking of was her own bread and butter.

The ax and hatchet theory was then exploited, and he took them up one by one, literally, as he subsequently did the skulls metaphorically, protesting with a weakness of voice that it disturbed his sensitive nature to be compelled by the strict mandate of sternest duty to talk of such horrid things in the presence of a real born lady.

He made a strong analysis of the story of the note, its non-confirmation and importance to the case, and closed with an eloquent peroration praising the evidence produced by the prosecution as an array of impregnable facts.

It was an extraordinary spectacle.

That Lizzie Borden sat on the edge of her chair leaning forward and listening with breathless anxiety, you may well believe.

The judge's charge was remarkable; it was a plea for the innocent.

Had he been the senior counsel for the defense making the closing plea in behalf of the defendant, he could not have more absolutely pointed out the folly of depending upon circumstantial evidence alone.

With matchless clearness he set up the case of the prosecution point by point and in the gentlest and most ingenious manner possible knocked it down.

He started with a definition pronounced and emphatic of the defendant's position before the law, an innocent woman with every inference in her favor, showed the value of her exceptional christian character and unmasked the absurdity of her pretending that her stepmother had received a note if she had not received one, embarrassing herself with an unnecessary and burdensome lie.

He assumed that it was not impossible for some one other than Lizzie to have committed the murder, and then instructed them that they had no right to pronounce an accused prisoner guilty on circumstantial evidence unless they were convinced beyond a reasonable doubt that she did the deed and that no one else could have done it.

The dear old fellow went on in this strain for an hour, until I began to fear that there would be another side to it presently, which would put a very different face on the matter, but I was mistaken, for like the saints he continued to the end, throwing bombs of disheartenment into the ranks of the prosecution, and causing smiles of joy to play about the lips of Lizzie's friends.

And hers, too?

Not a smile. Not a tear.

Simply sat she there, giving every evidence of intelligent observation, but not a sign that indicated either joy or apprehension.

I doubt if ever there was such a charge before. On the other hand there was never such a case before. There was never a prosecution so handicapped before. There never was such a defendent, and so far as I know there never was such a day of brutal discomfort as this now verging on the midnight hour.

To make a long story short let's get at once to the end. The jury had been out one hour and a half, but so confident were the people of a verdict that very few of the spectators retired.

Word was brought to the sheriff that a verdict had been reached. The judges took their seats, the jury stood before them.

Clerk Borden—Lizzie Andrew Borden, stand up.

"Not Guilty!" - THE PRISONER CRIES WITH JOY

The little woman in black obeyed the mandate of the court and every eye was fastened upon her.

Clerk Borden—Hold up your right hand, look upon the foreman; foreman, look upon the prisoner. Have you found a verdict?

Foreman—We have.

The clerk then handed a document to the court and it was handed back to the clerk, who restored it to the foreman.

All this time Lizzie stood there a monument of patience, a pillar of self-reliance, her eye fastened upon the foreman.

Clerk Borden—What is your verdict?

Foreman—Not guilty.

At once there rose so wild a yell that every prisoner in his cell could hear it.

Lizzie sank into a chair, rested her hands upon the rail, her face upon them, and cried her second cry of joy.

She was no longer friendless. Her sister, her counsel, the women in the court room, all the men from everywhere rushed to greet her, and burying her head in her sister's arms, she said:

"Now take me home, I want to go to the old place and go at once tonight."

I had a brief conversation of congratulation and satisfaction, but it was such a talk as would only naturally pass between a woman relieved but a moment before from a terrific strain and one who felt it to be the privilege and duty of a man to congratulate her on the changed condition of affairs.

Howard

"Now take me home. I want to go to the old place and go at once tonight."

The Boston Advertiser

LIZZIE BORDEN GOES FREE.

THE JURY NOT LONG IN REACHING A VERDICT.

A Scene of Tremendous Excitement in the Court Room When the Verdict Was Announced—Cheers and Waving of Handkerchiefs—Tears Mingled With Joy.

United Press Dispatch to the REPORT.

NEW BEDFORD, June 20.—District Attorney Knowlton resumed his argument this morning in the Borden trial, and made rather a strong presentation of detailed circumstances to sustain his contention that Lizzie Borden first murdered her step-mother, as a result of hatred and jealousy, then murdered her father when he come home, because he knew too much about family relations, and she did not dare to let him live.

The prisoner watched Mr. Knowltan fixedly during his long argument. In concluding, Knowlton claimed the defence amounted to nothing. He closed at 12:05 with an eloquent appeal to the jury to decide as their consciences should decide.

Court then took a recess till 1.45.

LIZZIE SAYS "I AM INNOCENT."

At 1.45 the court resumed its session, and the defendant was given an opportunity to speak.

She said, "I am innocent, but I will leave my case in your hands and with my counsel."

Justice Dewey then charged the jury. He told them to disregard previous hearings and defined the different degrees of murder. He stated the presumption of innocence, which was increased by defendant's character. There must be a real and operative motive.

The judge concluded his charge at 3:09, and the jury retired.

NEW BEDFORD, Mass., June 21.—Lizzie Borden was yesterday afternoon at 5 o'clock acquitted of the murder of her father and step-mother.

The jury filed into their seats after being out about one hour and a half, and were polled on their return. Miss Borden was asked to stand up and the foreman was asked to return the verdict, upon which he announced "Not guilty."

After the verdict had been received, the district attorney moved that the other cases against Miss Borden be *nolle prossed*, and the order of the court was to that effect.

Justice Mason gracefully thanked the jurors in appreciation of their work and faithful service, and reminded them that the precautions taken with them, which may have seemed irksome at the time, were solely in the interest of justice, a fact which they undoubtedly realized now. The jury was then dismissed and court adjourned.

THE VERDICT RECEIVED WITH CHEERS.

The closing scene in the trial was in direct contrast with those which had preceded it. Heretofore all had been decorous and in keeping with the dignity of the most dignified court in the country. But when the verdict of not guilty was returned a cheer went up which might have been heard half a mile away, and no attempt made to check it. The stately judges looked straight ahead at the bare walls, Sheriff Wright was powerless, and not once during the tremendous excitement, which lasted fully a minute, did he make the slightest sign of having heard it. He never saw the people rising in their seats and waving their handkerchiefs in unison with their voices, because his eyes were full of tears and completely blinded for the time. Miss Borden's head went down upon the rail in front of her and tears came where they had refused to come for many a long day, as she heard the sweetest words ever poured into her willing ears, the words "not guilty."

"THANK GOD," SAID MR. JENNINGS.

Mr. Jennings was almost crying, and his voice broke as he put his hand out to Mr. Adams, who sat next to him, and said, "Thank God," while Mr. Adams returned the pressure of the hand and seemed incapable of speech. Governor Robinson turned to the rapidly dissolving jury as they filed out of their seats and glanced on them with a fatherly interest in his kindly eyes, and stood up as Mr. Knowlton and Mr. Moody came over to shake hands with counsel for the defense. When the spectators had finally gone, Miss Borden was taken to the room of the justices and allowed to recover her composure. At the expiration of an hour, she was placed in a carriage and driven to the station, where she took a train for Fall River, her home no longer probably, but still the only objective point for the immediate present.

The New York Times

EDITORIAL

THE ACQUITTAL OF MISS BORDEN

It will be a certain relief to every right-minded man or woman who has followed the case to learn that the jury at New Bedford has not only acquitted Miss LIZZIE BORDEN of the atrocious crime with which she was charged, but has done so with a promptness that was very significant. The acquittal of this most unfortunate and cruelly persecuted woman was, by its promptness, in effect, a condemnation of the police authorities of Fall River and of the legal officers who secured the indictment and have conducted the trial. It was a declaration, not only that the prisoner was guiltless, but that there never was any serious reason to suppose that she was guilty. She has escaped the awful fate with which she was threatened, but the long imprisonment she has undergone, the intolerable suspense and anguish inflicted upon her, the outrageous injury to her feelings as a woman and as a daughter, are chargeable directly to the police and legal authorities. That she should have been subjected to these is a shame to Massachusetts which the good sense of the jury in acquitting her only in part removes.

The theory of the prosecution seems to have been that, if it were possible that Miss BORDEN murdered her father and his wife, it must be inferred that she did murder them. It was held, practically, that if she could not be proved innocent, she must be taken to be guilty. We do not remember a case in a long time in which the prosecution has so completely broken down, or in which the evidence has shown so clearly, not merely that the prisoner should not be convicted, but that there never should have been an indictment.

We are not surprised that the Fall River police should have fastened their suspicions upon Miss BORDEN. The town is not a large one. The police is of the usual inept and stupid and muddle-headed sort that such towns manage to get for themselves. There is nothing more merciless than the vanity of ignorant and untrained men charged with the detection of crime, in the face of a mystery that they cannot solve, and for the solution of which they feel themselves responsible. The Fall River police needed a victim whose sacrifice should purge their force of the contempt that they felt they would incur if the murderer of the BORDENS was not discovered, and the daughter was the nearest and most helpless. They pounced upon her.

But the responsibility of the law officers was very different. They were men trained in the law, accustomed to analyze and weigh evidence. They knew what justice required in the way of proof of the crime of murder in the first degree. It is not easy to believe that they did not know that no such proof, and nothing like it, was in their possession. Indeed, they seem to have entered upon the trial without it, and to have groped along afterward in clumsy efforts to develop it. We cannot resist the feeling that their conduct in this matter was outrageous; that they were guilty of a barbarous wrong to an innocent woman and a gross injury to the community. And we hold it to be a misfortune that their victim has no legal recourse against them and no means of bringing them to account. Her acquittal is only a partial atonement for the wrong that she has suffered.

PARTICULAR FIVE

THE TRICKEY AFFAIR

TRICKEY BUSINESS

One of the most detailed and rococo hoaxes ever perpetrated on and by a major newspaper took place during the investigation of the Borden murders and subsequently became known as "The Trickey Affair".

On October 10, 1892, the august Boston Daily Globe devoted virtually the entire front page of that edition to a series of gaudy headlines trumpeting their single-handed expose of the evidence it said would be presented by the Commonwealth when Lizzie Borden was summoned into court. The Globe, in pharisaical detail, assured their readers that the story had been "corroborated in a most convincing manner". The headlines screamed:

LIZZIE BORDEN'S SECRET.

Mr. Borden Discovered It and Hot Words Followed

Startling Testimony from Twenty-five New Witnesses

Emma Was Kicked During that Quarrel Family Discord and Murder.

Continued on four pages were summaries of the testimony to which 25 previously unknown witnesses were prepared to swear.

At least three had been immediately in front of the Borden residence at the moment Abby had been slain. Each had heard screams and groans and had looked up at the window in the guest room. There, Lizzie, with a rubber hood covering her head, lurked behind the curtains. Lizzie, the Globe said, "must have been standing over the mutilated remains of her mother at the very time that her father was about to enter the house."

Three other witnesses professed to have visited the Bordens the evening before the murders and had overheard a quarrel between Lizzie and Andrew. The colloquy was straight out of one of the pulp magazines then called Penny-Dreadfuls.

All had heard Andrew say: "You can make your own choice and do it tonight. Either let us know what his name is or take the door on Saturday! "And when you go fishing, fish for some other place to live as I will never listen to you again! I will know the name of the man who got you into trouble!"

Lizzie supposedly responded in kind: "If I marry this man, will you be satisfied that everything will be kept from the entire world?"

One can almost visualize Andrew twirling the ends of his non-existent moustache as he replied, "I would rather see you dead than have it come out."

The visitors queried Andrew about the identity of Lizzie's careless lover, asking if he knew his name. He replied, "No, but I have my suspicions and have had all along. If I am right, I will never recognize this man in the world. She has made her own bed, so let her lie upon it."

A fourth witness, one who had not "visited" that evening, was prepared to verify Lizzie's un-maidenly condition, based on Andrew's having consulted him about it and had described the unsettling matter in detail. The witness had advised Andrew to cut her off without a cent if she refused to identify her swain.

A number of other witnesses had signed affidavits involving various conversations between Lizzie and Bridget supposedly overheard.

One was an exchange which took place at the funerals of Abby and Andrew. Lizzie had said to Bridget, "Are you a fool or a knave? Why don't you say how much money you want to keep quiet?" Bridget had replied, "I don't know what you mean, but you are not the girl I took you to be."

This imagined exchange was all the more interesting since it was known Bridget did not attend the funeral.

The question of a will would be answered by a witness who had sworn that less than a month before the murders, Andrew had told him he had prepared a will leaving Emma and Lizzie a token $25,000 and all else to Abby. Only Abby's importuning persuaded him to leave the sisters anything.

And on and on the bizarre stories went.

A witness had signed a sworn statement that Lizzie had offered to sell her for $10 the watch that had supposedly been stolen during the daylight robbery of the Borden home several months prior to the murders.

Bridget, the story continued, was prepared to add to the testimony she had given at the inquest and the preliminary hearing. Now, she would relate a conversation she had overheard the night before the murders during which Uncle John Morse had said to Andrew, "Quarreling will not fix the thing. Something else must be done and I will do all I can." Bridget would also testify that Lizzie had come down from upstairs and told her that Abby was dead. Lizzie, on the day of the murders had said to her, "Keep your tongue still and don't talk to these officers and you can have all the money you want." Bridget then began to be afraid of Lizzie and immediately left the house.

As fascinating as this concoction of stories was, the most outlandish was the tale woven by the "author" of all of them, Detective E. D. McHenry. In his contribution to the fantasy, he detailed how he had picked up a great portion of this new information by hiding himself under Lizzie's bed in her cell! From this coigne of vantage, he had tuned in to all Lizzie's conversations with the Rev. Buck, Emma and all other visitors to the prisoner. Conspicuously, he did not reveal how he had taken his meals, used the men's room or otherwise occupied his time while snuggled under Lizzie's cot.

He overheard, along with a number of interesting theological discussions with Rev. Buck, a quarrel between Lizzie and Emma during which Lizzie had kicked her sister three times, flung biscuits at her and called her a damn bitch. He had copious notes to confirm the tirade.

Fearing his hiding place might be noticed, McHenry claimed he had gone across the hall, dismantled part of the wall, replaced it with a muslin cloth and settled down in comfort to view and hear everything that took place in Lizzie's cell.

The thrust of the entire story was that the Fall River police had admitted they could not solve the murders and had called him in to find the miscreant. It had been the work of just a few days before he and his assistant wife had been able to round up these 25 witnesses and solve the puzzle. A piece of cake.

The difficulty was, of course, that none of the statements were true. The names of the witnesses had been invented and some of the addresses were either non-existent or were vacant lots.

How McHenry had imagined he could get away with this hoax cannot be imagined. When he had it all down on paper, he approached Henry Trickey, the Globe's star reporter assigned to the Borden case. For $1,000, McHenry would reveal all his findings...all there was to know about the prosecution's case against Lizzie.

Dizzy with anticipation over his "scoop", Trickey handed over all the money he had, $30, and took the next train to Boston to get the rest.

He returned to Fall River immediately and searched for his benefactor. McHenry dodged him for several days but finally produced all his "documents". Back to Boston went Trickey with, certainly, visions of the 1892 version of the Pulitzer prize dancing in his head.

Despite their unctuous claim to have corroborated every detail, the Globe obviously corroborated nothing. But, they did boast of their revelations on the front page of the afternoon edition:

LATEST!

ASTOUNDED.

All New England Read Story.

Globes Were Bought by Thousands.

Lizzie Borden Appears in New Light.

Belief in Her Innocence Sadly Shaken.

Excitement Runs High in Fall River.

Police Think the Scoop is a Corker.

Lawyer Jennings Says Lies Have Been Told.

Doesn't Believe There is Any Secret.

Opinions on That Spying by Detective McHenry.

Doubts about Lizzie's guilt, the Globe said, were shaken by these revelations; no shadow so profound had fallen on her before. People were running into the streets, it said, clutching Globe's and crying, "For Heaven's sake, have you seen The Globe?" Crowds had gathered at news kiosks to scoop up the copies, it continued, describing the scenes of near panic as copies were snatched from frantic dealers.

The scene in Fall River was one of pandemonium, the story went. Within 10 minutes, thousands were gathered on Main Street to read their "corker". No story in the history of journalism had caused such a furor.

"The Globe's story caused an awful cloud to settle over the influential part of the city," the newspaper said. "On the hill, among Lizzie Borden's friends, and around the Central Congregational Church, there was a gloom that was pathetic. In that part of the city, hopes in her innocence were centered; hopes that aroused to fervent prayer." There was poignant grief, it said, and many wept for Lizzie.

By afternoon, the Globe's printing of 200,143 copies had been sold out and an additional edition was rushed to the beleaguered newsboys. It, too, was jubilant:

LIZZIE HAD A SECRET.

Mr. Borden Discovered It. Then a Quarrel.

Startling Testimony of 25 New Witnesses.

Theft of a Watch---Money Offered to Bridget ---Story of a Will.

Seen in Mother's Room With a Hood on Her Head.

Accused Sister of Treachery and Kicked Her in Anger.

By morning, the story began to unravel. Telephone calls and telegrams began to come in from Attorney Jennings, Uncle Morse and some citizens who had supposedly made the statements Trickey had written about. Most denied they had ever been talked to and the few who had, denied making any of the statements which had appeared in the paper.

The Globe's attorneys gathered quickly in the editorial offices of the paper. Though they were well aware of the libel the paper had committed, the editors were reluctant to admit to their subscribers they had been "had". The next issue began to backtrack but half-heartedly.

Perhaps it was those worried attorneys who had visions of libel suits by Lizze and Emma for sums that would bankrupt the paper, who were at last heeded.

The following day, centered on page one was an "abject apology":

ABJECT APOLOGY

Globe Begs the Pardon of Lizzie Borden and Morse

"To err is human and as newspapers have to be run by men and not by angels, mistakes are inevitable. The Globe feels it a plain duty as an honest newspaper to state that it has been greiveously misled in the Lizzie Borden case. It published on Monday a communication that it believed to be true evidence. Among all the impositions which newspapers have suffered this was unparalleled in its astonishing completeness and irresistible plausibility. Judging from what we have heard, it impressed our readers as strongly as it did the Globe. Some of this remarkably ingenious and cunningly-contrived story is undoubtedly based on facts, as later developments will show. The Globe believes, however, that much of it is false, and never should have been published. The Globle, being thus misled, has innocently added to the terrible burdens of Miss Lizzie Borden.

"So far as lies in our power to repair the wrong we are anxious to do so, and hereby tender her our heartfelt apology for the inhuman reflection upon her honor as a woman and for any injustice the publication of Monday inflicted upon her.

"The same sincere apology is hereby tendered to John V. Morse and any other persons to whom the publication did an injustice.

"The Globe comes out in th[illegible] [illegible]anner because it believes that honesty is the best policy, and because it believes in doing what is right. We prefer to build up rather than to tear down, to help rather than to injure, to carry sunshine and not sorrow into the homes of New England. When we make a mistake, whether through our fault or not, we believe that justice to our readers demands that we should fairly and honestly and boldly proclaim the fact in the same conspicuous place in the Globe where the error was committed."

On September 1, the grand jury that indicted Lizzie also handed down a second indictment which was kept secret from the public. It was later revealed the man named was Henry G. Trickey, accused of tampering with a government witness. It seems Trickey had offered Bridget an undisclosed sum of money to leave the country. What additional hanky-panky this represented was never revealed. Trickey was never brought to trial, however. Two days later, supposedly on another assignment for the Globe but more likely fleeing prosecution, he was killed as he attempted to board a moving train in Hamilton, Ontario.

In 1971, the Belknap Press of Harvard University Press published a book commemorating the centennial of the Globe. The anecdote of how the paper had been gulled by McHenry and Trickey was recounted, tongue in cheek.

Ironically, it was obvious no one corroborated the writing of this story either. In it, Abby is called "Erma" and is referred to as Lizzie's "mother" rather than stepmother. Lizzie, 32, was said to be in her "mid-twenties" while Emma, also called "Erma", was said to be 12 years older than Lizzie, rather than ten. Lizzie was said to have burned the paint-stained dress on Thursday rather than Sunday and was arrested on September 1. In the next paragraph, it was stated she was arrested on September 14. The worst of the more than 20 factual errors in the story was that Lizzie had not only killed her "mother" and father, but had also killed her "sister, Erma" in a quarrel.

Obviously, the ghost of Henry G. Trickey still walks the halls of the Globe.

PARTICULAR SIX

THE REPORTERS

THE REPORTERS WHO COVERED THE TRIAL

The ten months between the time Lizzie was arrested and the time she was brought to New Bedford for trial whetted the appetites of newspapers from coast to coast and even from the European continent. The courtroom was packed each day to far beyond its normal capacity. At the outset, 25 additional chairs were provided for the press corps, then 25 more were added when it became obvious more were needed to accomodate the horde. Even then, another score stood along the walls, balancing their notepads on their knee and making their notes as best they could. Many newspapers sent artists with their reporters and their jockeying for an advantageous view of the accused and the other principals was a daily struggle.

The Fall River Herald was represented by John J. Manning, formerly of the Boston Globe. He had been among the first on the scene the day of the murders and was notably qualified to follow the story to its conclusion. His beat at the Herald had been, primarily, politics and city government.

The Fall River Globe sent two men to cover the trial, Thatcher Thurston, rated by his fellow workers as the ablest of the Fall River men and E. H. Porter who had his early training on the Louisville Courier-Journal and a stint in Providence. On the Globe he covered police news. Immediately after the trial he wrote the first "history" of the Borden murders. The Globe had been so outspoken in its suspicions of Lizzie that, when the book was published, it is said Lizzie bought up the entire printing and had it burned. There is no positive confirmation of this; the strongest evidence being that only about 25 subscription copies were known to exist before the book was reprinted in 1985 by Robert A. Flynn of King Philip Publishing Company, Providence, Maine. When historians later compared Porter's account with the trial transcript and with other newspaper accounts of the investigation and trial, it became obvious his "history" was flawed by his and the Globe's conviction that Lizzie was guilty of the murders no matter what the jury had said.

Walter P. Stevens, another reporter who had covered the story from the first day, represented the Fall River News. He, like Porter, was a police and court reporter.

The Providence Dispatch was represented by one of the youngest reporters in the cadre, 25-year-old John J. Rosenfeld who had begun his career at the Despatch, moved to the Providence Telegram and from there to a position as city editor of the Pawtucket Times. He had recently returned to the Despatch and was engaged there in special assignments.

H. K. Stokes wrote for the Providence News and provided some of the more colorful sidebars. He also acted as stringer for the Pawtucket Times, the Portland Argus the Woonsocket Call, Springfield News, Hartford Times and the New Haven Register. He was another of the reporters who covered the story from its first days.

The Providence Journal was served by S. S. Colvin, a Brown University graduate who had first written for the Telegram of that city.

The city editor of the Taunton Gazette, W. F. Greenough, covered for his paper as well as contributing to the Associated Press.

The New Bedford Evening Journal was represented by William Emery whose lasting contribution to "Lizzie Lore" was a giant scrapbook containing hundreds of contemporary newspaper accounts, many of which are reproduced in this book.

The Boston papers had the largest contingent in the courtroom.

The evening edition of the Boston Herald was fed by a veteran of homicide reporting, Warren T. Billings. He had previously reported on two other sensational murders, the Sawtelle murder in New Hampshire and the Almy case further north. He had arrived in Fall River within hours of the murders and was knowledgeable of all the early events.

George H. Brennan, a former attorney, covered for the morning edition of the Herald.

Charismatic veteran newsman, Charles F. W. Archer, of the Boston Journal, was a graduate of the Massachusetts Institute of Technology and had begun his career covering Essex County for the Boston Advertiser. He had signed on the Journal ten years earlier and followed the case from the first day.

The Boston Globe had replaced the discredited and now deceased Henry G. Trickey with John W. Carberry. Though the area's largest paper, the Globe was now gun-shy of the case and Carberry's work was undistinguished.

Mrs. M. A. Worswick, writing under the name, Amy Robsart, covered the opening of the trial in a breezy style and was replaced by Harry C. Smith who acted as a stringer for a number of New York papers, including the New York World, Herald, Recorder, Sun and Press.

One of the few reporters who covered the story for two papers in the same city was Henry L. May whose pieces appeared in both the Boston Record and Advertiser.

Undoubtedly the most widely read accounts of the trial and certainly the most entertaining, were those of Joe Howard whose daily despatches, signed "Howard", appeared on the front pages of the Boston Globe and other leading papers in New York and the east coast. His stories recounted the daily goings-on of the trial and were laced with his acerbic comments on everything from the pomposity of the bailiff to the mooing of what he called "the court cow". He openly chided the prosecution for its paucity of evidence and made no effort to conceal his belief that Lizzie was innocent of the crimes.

John R. Caldwell wrote for the New York Herald and Julian Ralph for the Sun.

Ralph was a noted magazine writer as well. New York's World was represented by H. C. Taylor.

A. E. Watrons reported the trial for the New York Press. More than a reporter, Watrons was a member of the editorial staff of that paper, contributing not only daily editorials but covering much of the political scene in Albany and in Washington, D. C.

No writer was more prolific than L. E. Quigg of the editorial staff of the New York Tribune. His average daily output was said to have averaged 10,000 words. Prior to the trial, Quigg had travelled to the midwest and written extensively about the states of Wyoming, the Dakotas, Montana, Idaho and Washington at the time of their admission to the United States.

The newspaper "of record", the New York Times, did not send a reporter to New Bedford even though their coverage was probably the most level, unbiased version of what took place there. The Times relied on the despatches of the Associated Press and what was rumored to be a dozen other sources among the reporters working for area and New York papers. By virtue of this variety of opinions and descriptions, the Times was able to distill the verbiage into an essence that no other paper was able to achieve.

The news gatherers compressed into that sweltering New Bedford court house may well have been the most talented coupling ever assembled.

The New Bedford Sunday Times
19 July 1943

Reporter at Famous Borden Trial Recalls Efficient Coverage by Newspapers of That Day

William M. Emery of 138 Main Street, Fairhaven, author of the following article, recalls the Lizzie Borden murder trial as one of the high spots in his long newspaper career. Mr. Emery covered the trial in New Bedford 50 years ago for the old New Bedford Evening Journal. His recollections provide an interesting description of the efficient manner newspapers of that day handled a "big" story.

By WILLIAM M. EMERY

Should anyone take the trouble to search the files of old newspapers for the reports of the trial of Lizzie Andrew Borden, charged with the murder of her father and stepmother, held in this city in 1893, he might be surprised to find the various accounts both full and satisfactory. The news coverage of this famous and sensational event was a marvel of the age, that has never been improved upon.

In its scope, its conception, and its efficiency it was fully as up-to-date as anything modern newspaper genius can devise—with the single exception of pictorial illustration. Scenes in the courtroom and outside were caught by accomplished sketch artists rather than by flashlight photographers, and newspapers of the period had not yet begun to use halftone cuts, though they were common in the magazines. It so happened that the artists from Boston did a far more effective job than the New York illustrators.

The highly dramatic happenings in the old Superior Court room on

County Street formed the chief news highlight everywhere during two weeks in June 1893. Herbert H. Fletcher, then New England chief of the Associated Press, planned to carry in his wire service the entire report of the official court stenographers, but found the idea too cumbersome and impracticable. However, as a private and profitable enterprise he organized a syndicate of three Boston newspapers to which he sold the official report, which in turn he purchased from the stenographers.

The four highly experienced court stenographers from Boston, all men, one of whom was the Rev. Charles E. Barnes, previously rector of St. James' Episcopal Church in this city, brought with them four women typists and a clerk. The men worked in relays, say of 10 or 15 minutes each, and on leaving the court room each would repair to a room on the lower floor, and dictate his notes to a typist.

Four copies of the report were made, with the use of carbons, one for the judges, one for the district attorney, one for counsel for defense, and one for Mr. Fletcher. The clerk assorted, arranged and numbered the pages. With such incredible rapidity were the typed sheets turned out that the judges and lawyers often were supplied with transcripts of the early testimony of a witness almost before his examination was completed. One set is now on file in the attorney general's office in Boston.

Press headquarters were established in the old carriage shed in the rear of the court (on the site of the present western addition to the original building), and were fully equipped with telegraph instruments, typewriters, and other necessary equipment. Private wires were strung to the offices of the New York, Boston and Providence newspapers, leading directly into the news rooms, and to A. P. headquarters. There was only one press association at the time.

Complete Reports Carried

Mr. Fletcher's sheets of the verbatim report were transcribed forthwith by swift typists to be ticked quickly into Boston, three copies of course being required. The Hub newspapers did a good job in handling the vast accumulation of "copy," and their evening editions which reached New Bedford carried the testimony complete up to 1 p. m., the hour of recess for lunch. Their evening city editions did even better, and next morning each of the three papers had the day's report in full. Naturally this was preceded by a running story turned out by one of the regular staff. None of the New York newspapers carried the full stenographic report. Newspapers in other large cities, as well as in the smaller ones, depended on the A. P.

Probably 50 or more reporters, from New Bedford, Fall River, Providence, Boston and New York, covered the trial. For press accommodations High Sheriff Andrew R. Wright ordered built half a dozen rows of what might be called desks, on the north side of the courtroom. These were really shelves, mounted on supports not especially substantial, which jostled easily. High stools were provided for seats. The writers were much cramped for space. Each writer had a ticket of admission, which must be shown at all times.

Before the trial Sheriff Wright, a stern martinet, declared he would allot allot no places for correspondents outside Massachusetts. The New York and Providence newspapers at once laid their plaint before Chief Justice Albert Mason of the Superior Court, head of the board of three presiding judges, and he promptly ordered Mr. Wright to prepare extra seats. These were located in the south half of the prisoners' dock. Joseph Howard, famous New York writer, somehow inveigled Sheriff Wright into assigning him more comfortable quarters at a deputy sheriff's desk, to the envy of all his colleagues.

The reporters, correspondents, artists and copy boys were a source of worry to the scowling sheriff through all the hot days of the trial. The press section disturbed him, as he sat glowering, far more than it did the judges, who never called anybody to account.

Wore High Silk Hat

Sheriff Wright wore the customtary swallow tailed coat of blue, with brass buttons. Out-of-doors he donned a high silk hat, with a cockade, which caused much merriment among the visiting pencil pushers.

Julian Ralph, representing the New York Sun, and syndicating to the Boston Herald, wrote, without question, the best running stories of the trial. He was a distinguished traveler, correspondent, and magazine writer, author of several books. Second to him in nationwide fame was Joseph Howard, nestor of the entire group of writers, and more picturesque than anybody there. He made his initial entree at court with a yellow linen coat, a "plug" hat, and an umbrella. His low-cut vest displayed a shirt front dazzling in whiteness, on which gleamed a large diamond. He was the type of an elderly Broadway boulevardier. His gray hair was closely cut, he was partially bald, and he wore a mustache and goatee. Some days he appeared in a long dark Prince Albert coat.

Thirty years before, in the Civil War, he had been a correspondent at the battle front. At the trial he represented the New York Recorder and the Boston Globe. Joe Howard was not an especial favorite with some of the out-of-town newspaper men. But I found he was always ready to do an act of kindness. On the first afternoon our office boy brought to me in the press box some copies of my paper, the New Bedford Evening Journal. Howard was all agog to see what the "country press" was doing with the trial. On looking over the sheet he voluntarily wrote me a note on his visiting card as follows:

"Please accept my hearty congratulations on the admirable and interesting story in the Journal of today."

Needless to say I was pleased with this manifestation of good will, and have always kept the souvenir. Ralph and Howard were cynosures of all eyes in the packed court room.

As I recall, there were no big-city "sob sisters" who remained throughout the trial. Mrs. M. A. Worswick (Amy Robsart) was here for several days for the Boston Post. Mildred Aldrich, an author of several books, now probably forgotten, came one day for the dignified old Boston Journal.

Friend of Lizzie's

Behind me sat Mrs. Kate Swan McGurk of the New York World, a former Fall River girl, who knew Lizzie Borden personally. She was a cousin of the late R. A. Swan, for many years city clerk of New Bedford. She and I had been long acquainted, as editors of High School papers in our respective cities. When the defendant was acquitted, as I turned to speak to Kate, tears were streaming down her cheeks in hysterical happiness over the outcome.

Probably the most celebrated woman journalist to put in a few hours in the courtroom was Elizabeth Jordan, also of the World, subsequently a well known writer of short stories and novels. In her reminiscences, "Three Rousing Cheers," published in 1938, she spoke of Lizzie Borden as follows:

"She was the neatest human being I have ever seen. She radiated cleanliness like an atmosphere."

We New Bedford reporters were quite overshadowed professionally, in the public eye, by the highly-paid out-of-town celebrities of our craft, with whom, however, we fraternized on terms of perfect fellowship evenings, when the day's work was done.

Had To Be Quick

We of the two evening papers certainly worked as hard as anybody, as we had to write co-incidentally with the giving of testimony. Only those who have attempted this can realize the difficulty of the task. A man must be able to judge instantly where the line of examination is going, and catch in a second the bearings of all the witness' answers.

I have always had a feeling of pride that I was privileged "to have my place reserved among the rest," as reporting this trial was one of the highlights of my long newspaper career, and is recalled with gratification. The touch of fascination still lingers. Edmund Pearson, student of criminology and writer about murder cases, has said that "the Borden case is without parallel in the criminal history of America."

Following Lizzie Borden's acquittal many of the correspondents crowded about to congratulate her and shake her hand, but her lawyers soon hustled her away.

And Julian Ralph, beginning one of his unrivalled pen pictures, apprised his readers as follows:

" 'The court orders that you be discharged and go.' These were the last words the old State of Massachusetts said to Lizzie Borden this afternoon."

PARTICULAR SEVEN

THE AFTERMATH

The Boston Herald

AN EDITORIAL

AN HISTORIC MYSTERY.

The verdict of the jury in the Lizzie Borden case is simply a confirmation of the opinions entertained by those who followed the evidence submitted by the prosecution and witnessed the effect upon it of a vigorous cross-examination. The government was obliged to prove guilt beyond a reasonable doubt, and this it failed to do. The case is likely to be referred to for a long time to come as one of the most singular and interesting episodes to be found in the range of criminal records, all the more singular and interesting to the student of human nature because the defence made not the least attempt to account for the double murder.

The prosecution rested its argument almost entirely on the ground that it was impossiblle for any one other than Lizzie Borden to have committed the murders, and, under the careful marshalling of facts by the district attorney, it was made evident that there were a number of incidents in her course of procedure at the time which can be described, with no approach toward exaggeration, as suspicious in their character. But the one material connection beween this list of suspicions and the guilty deed was wanting.

Circumstantial evidence is sometimes quite as strong in its character as direct evidence; but there must be, if it is to be used as a means of brushing away reasonable doubts in the minds of the jurors, certain points where the act committed and the presumable reasons for any circumstances of the act impinge closely one upon the other. In the case in question, no such obvious connection could be pointed out, and it was upon this fact that the defence chiefly rested, and the effective work of the counsel for the defense consisted in bringing out in strong relief the small amount of evidence, other than suspicion, that the prosecution had at its command.

There has not been a case of murder within our recollection in which the minds of the community have been so far divided as in this case.

It is clear that those who carried on the preliminary investigation arrived at conclusions in this respect with a celerity which prejudiced their case. So far as the effect upon the public opinion is concerned, it would have been vastly better if the police authorities at Fall River, and those connected with the district attorney's office, had made it evident that they were forced, after a hard struggle and after exhausting all other avenues of investigation, to come to the conclusion that the murders could have been committed by no other person than Lizzie Borden. But they jumped to this conclusion too readily. At least, that is the drift of public opinion on this subject, and, having so made up their mind, were not mentally receptive, as they otherwise might have been, to new impressions and the possibility of developing other incriminating clews.

Doubtless the insufficiency of the material at their disposal must more than once have impressed itself upon the minds of those representing the prosecution, and it was, no doubt, in the hope of a mental or physical breakdown on the part of the accused, or of new facts coming to light, that the trial was postponed month after month; for, so far as can be seen by what was brought out during the last two weeks, it might just as readily have been undertaken last winter. This would have been accounted clever policy provided it had attained its object; but it wholly failed of this, and, in consequence, produced a reaction which, popularly considered, was seriously detrimental to the prosecution. Many persons who were inclined last fall to believe in the guilt of Lizzie Borden were induced, by her long imprisonment and the obvious unwillingness of the government authorities to push forward the trial, to believe that she was innocent; and that the prosecuting officers and the police were endeavoring to force or draw her into some indirect admission of criminality.

The verdict has been given, and the accused is forever free from all possibility of further legal judgment. The tragedy remains quite as much a mystery as it was before. Nothing has been proved, except that no evidence was brought out at the trial that would justify the conviction of Lizzie Borden as the one guilty of the act.

The Associated Press

Ex-Governor George Robinson, Lizzie Borden's attorney at her recent trial, gave these answers in a June 22 interview:

"Contrary to the newspaper reports and the general impression which they convey, I have found Miss Borden in all my dealings with her, ladylike, quiet and pleasant. From the newspaper reports which I had previous to my first consultation with her, I might reasonably have expected to find a fiend incarnate who revels in thoughts of blood and crime, but I found no such person. The public has been led to believe her without feeling, but I have known her better than anyone else and if there are those who think she is unaccustomed to shedding tears, they are mistaken. She had to maintain a cool demeanor in court and it is a wonder to me she bore up as well as she did",

Crimes a Mystery to Everyone

"Has Lizzie Borden a theory as to the commission of the crimes?" he was asked.

His answer was: "The crimes are a mystery to her as they are to everyone else."

"Would you be willing to state what her theory is?"

"I could not, in all fairness, do that. There may be an investigation."

"Has Miss Borden formulated any plans?"

"I don't know that she has. Her present plans are, I think, to take an entire rest. She has gone to Fall River and will take up her residence in the old home. The house will be cleansed from the evidence of the crimes. The present condition, which is, of course, just as it was left on the morning of the murders, is far from pleasant. but Miss Borden considers that as her home, having spent 20 years of her life there."

"Was there at any period during the time from when you were first engaged as her counsel until the present when you had any doubt as to her innocence?"

"Not one moment. I have been her most confidential adviser and never has she by either word or act given me the first reason to believe that she was anything but perfectly innocent."

"What first led you to have this firm belief in her innocence?"

"Her appearance, and above all, her perfect fairness in considering others who were at first under suspicion. Instead of trying to cast suspicion on them, she seemed to fear lest some innocent person should be wrongly accused."

"Did she at any time in the trial lose faith in the favorable outcome of the trial?"

"She endeavored to hold herself in readiness for the result, whatever it might be, expecting, of course, that the verdict would be not guilty. There was always the uncertainty of how the jury would weigh the evidence. She thought that the trial was the best thing, for when once she had finished it she knew that no one could rightfully accuse her of the crime."

"Do you think that the findings in the preliminary trial was unjustified?"

"As a juror, I would not have voted to bind her over. But as a lawyer, I can find no fault with the process. Someone had to be held for the crime, but I don't think they were justified in holding Miss Borden. Remember, however, the object of that trial was not to determine guilt. That was reserved for the later proceedings when she was vindicated."

June 23, 1893

The Boston Sunday Herald

3 June 1905

LIZZIE BORDEN LEFT BY SISTER

Former Writing Play for Nance O'Neil —Emma Borden Objects to Actress, Entertainment of Theatrical People and to Coachman.

FALL RIVER SISTERS HAVE SELDOM AGREED

Lizzie Borden Said to Be Infatuated with Stage and Stage Folk— She and Nance O'Neil Warm Friends.

[Special Dispatch to the Sunday Herald.]

FALL RIVER, June 3, 1905. After repeated disagreements, Lizzie A. Borden and her sister, Emma Borden, have parted company. Several days ago Miss Emma packed up her belongings, called a moving wagon and shook the dust of the French street home, where they have lived together ever since the acquittal in the famous murder trial, from her feet. She is reported to have moved to Fairhaven. Ever since her departure the tongue of gossip has been wagging tremendously, even for Fall River, which is saying a great deal. All sorts of reasons for the quarrel between the sisters have been afloat, but the best founded ones involve the name of Miss Nance O'Neil, the actress, and also that of Miss Lizzie's coachman, Joseph Tetrault.

It is nothing new to learn that the sisters have not agreed; that has been known ever since the famous murder, and even during that cause delebre it came out that they had never agreed on many things. Miss Emma was sedate and retiring. Miss Lizzie was fond of good times and jolly company. When they moved from the Second street establishment, where the murder occurred, to the handsome residence on French street, rumors of disagreement continued to escape from the neighborhood, and when the moving van backed up, a few days ago, the gossip fairly poured out.

Some three or four years ago, it is said, there came near being a rupture of friendliness between the sisters because of Miss Emma's dislike of some of the doings and position of the coachman. That ended in the dismissal of the coachman and he returned to his former trade, a barber. After a time, the talk subsided and again Tetrault became the coachman in the Borden establishment. Miss Emma is said to have still found offence in his comfortable preferment. Tetrault was a fine looking young man and reported to be very popular among the ladies, although Miss Emma took a dislike to him.

Another reported cause of the disagreement was Miss Lizzie's recent infatuation for stage folk and dramatic matters. The stage was distasteful to Miss Emma's orthodox ideas and when Miss Lizzie came to entertain a whole dramatic company at midnight hours, it passed Miss Emma's limit. And right here comes in Miss Nance O'Neil, the well known actress. It appears that Miss Lizzie and Miss O'Neil are warm personal friends. The two women met at a summer resort near Lynn last year, while Miss Borden was passing the vacation period there. A mutual attraction led to the cementing of a close and hearty friendship.

When Miss O'Neil came to this city with her company early this season she was entertained by Miss Borden. Not only was Miss O'Neil most hospitably treated, but her whole company dined at Miss Borden's table. Later, when Miss O'Neil came here and gave an impersonation of "Queen Elizabeth," which startled most people, but pleased others, Miss Borden's carriage awaited her after the play, and together they went to Miss Borden's home. Miss O'Neil was entertained there, and it was not long after this entertainment that Miss Emma and her sister broke. The efforts of the gossips to tie these two things together have developed a story of the quarrel.

The entertainment afforded Miss O'Neil is said, however, to have been of the quietest character, such as one friend might give another, Miss O'Neil on the last visit being ill from overwork. Miss Borden has never seen her performance in Fall River, but the reviews of her acting published in the local papers have pleased her greatly. Miss Borden has seen Miss O'Neil act in Boston and New York, and has been entertained by the actress in Boston at the Hotel Touraine.

Among the stories that are current is one that has exceptional interest. It is said by rumor that Miss Borden is to write a play and that Miss O'Neil is to act it. Of course, Miss Borden makes no pretensions to stage knowledge, but it is known that she has literary ability, and has passed much of her time in reading, writing and travelling. No hint is given as to what the new play will be based on.

June 2, 1927

LIZZIE BORDEN DEAD

SISTER IS NEXT OF KIN; FORTUNE IS BELIEVED INTACT

Attorney Has No Knowledge that Woman Left Statement on Murder of Parents in Fall River

Miss Lizzie Andrew Borden, nationally known as the defendant in the famous Lizzie Borden murder trial of 1893, died at 8:30 last evening at her home, 306 French street, Fall River. Death was due to heart disease, her physician, Dr. Annie Campbell Macrae, stated this morning. She had been in poor health for some years. She was 68.

The parents of Miss Borden, Mr. and Mrs. Andrew J. Borden, were found dead in their home Aug. 4, 1892, hacked to death by an ax. The only person upon whom suspicion was ever directed was Miss Borden. Sufficient evidence could not be obtained to convict her. She was found not guilty in one of the most celebrated murder trials in New England history, and the mystery of the murder has remained unsolved to the present day.

A sister, Miss Emma Borden, is next of kin, and was joint heir with Miss Borden to their father's estate, estimated in 1893 to be worth about $350,000. It is assumed that it has increased in value since. There is no record that this estate was ever divided. According to last reports, Miss Emma Borden has been making her home in New Hampshire. She formerly resided in Providence, after breaking with her younger sister.

Knows of No Statement.

Charles L. Baker, Fall River attorney to whom Miss Borden entrusted her legal business, stated this morning that he had only just been notified of his client's death. He could make no statement as to her will, and if she had left any statement concerning the murder with which she was charged, he knew nothing of it, he said.

The Borden house was solely in charge of the servants today, there being apparently no friends or relatives who felt called upon to take charge. The housekeeper and others who had been in touch with Miss Borden refused to talk, and the only statement issued was that the funeral service would be private. Neither time nor place were revealed.

Although known as Lizzie Borden throughout the trial, Miss Borden chose to be known thereafter as Lizbeth A. Borden, and was so listed in the Fall River city and telephone directories

Suspicion on Her.

Lizzie A. Borden's history, as being different from the ordinary run of other people, began Aug. 4, 1892, when her father and stepmother were found dead in their home in Fall River, and no suspicion was directed toward any other hand than that of the younger of the two daughters of the house as having hacked them to death with an ax.

Lizzie Borden was about 32 then. In the succeeding nearly 11 months, she went through an experience, of examination, tedious waiting, and final trial, enough to test one's soul; without giving trace of any inner working of mind or heart.

Was Found Not Guilty.

She came out Not guilty, by the verdict of the jury, because, as one of them said afterwards, there was nothing offered to prove her guilty.

One wonders whether the experience of the years since has been much easier to bear, for they have been years of loneliness, most of them, so far as close relationships have been concerned. She was never accorded, apparently never sought, the confidence of the people she had known before suspicion attached itself to her name and life.

She continued to live in Fall River, in a nice home, well cared for by servants, with liberal means. She traveled and had long stays in a Boston hotel and at other places away from home. It is known that she was fond of the theater. In her own home in Fall River, she had the companionship of dog and cat, two horses at one time, canaries, and squirrels lived in houses on her grounds and she fed them, luring them to her shoulders.

It was said that when a young woman, she had been fond of social life. She had been active in a Fall River Congregational church, had sung in the choir, helped in the fruit and flower mission, had taught a Sunday school class, belonged to the Christian Endeavor; and had worked with the W. C. T. U.

It came out after the murder that her life had not been so serene under the surface as it had seemed in the public view—for her wealthy father had kept his home in the old business section of the city, in a house without conveniences, not even a bathtub; and Lizzie had been graduated from the high school and had had a summer trip to Europe. She had ambitions for more attractive living conditions.

Mother Was Dead.

Moreover, her mother had died when she was a child of two or three and her young life had grown up in the chief care of her older sister, variously stated to have been from five to nine years older than herself—until her father had married again, when Lizzie was between five and six, and Lizzie, according to items brought out at the trial, had not been on entirely friendly terms with the stepmother. In general, however, life had seemed to be a wholesome, normal affair for the Borden family, well-connected, advantaged, and highly respected people, until the day of the murderous end put to the lives of Andrew J. and Abbie D. Borden, the heads of the home.

Knowlton Made Statement.

By way of an aside, it is interesting to recall that upon the death, nine years afterwards, of the prosecuting district attorney in the case, Hosea M. Knowlton, later attorney general for the state, it was revealed that he had said, while waiting for the jury's verdict, and again a few weeks before his death, that if he could have known what Andrew J. Borden had said to John V. Morse, in the long conversation that the two men had had the night before the murder, in which Lizzie had come home and gone to her room, he believed he could have convicted somebody of the murder.

If Mr. Borden had talked of making a new will, it did not appear in the testimony at the trial.

Re-establishing a Home.

Andrew J. Borden was one of the wealthy business men of Fall River. He owned valuable real estate. He was president of the Union Savings bank, and a director of the Merchants Manufacturing company, a safe deposit company, and the Troy Cotton and Woolen manufactory, and had other sterling business connections in the city. He was owner of one of the finest business blocks of the place. He came of an old and representative New England family. "A venerable, law-abiding,

God-fearing man," is the way he was looked upon in Fall River.

Lizzie Borden was said to have her father's business acumen and temperament generally.

By the death of the father and stepmother, Emma L. Borden and Lizzie A. Borden were heirs to an estate valued at about $350,000. When things had settled down after the trial, they bought a good house at 306 French street, in the good part of Fall River, and entered upon what might seem to be the enjoyment of every comfort and nicety of living. Miss Borden had attended her sister through the trial, and had spoken in her defense, though she had had to agree to frictions in the home. Now they began life again at the new residence. They had a carriage with a span of horses. But the home did not become a center of social activity. It soon became apparent that Emma Borden's friends were not intending to admit Lizzie Borden within their circle. There was no evidence that she sought such entry. She went on living her life in the midst of the old home-town surrounding, asking no quarter and giving no explanations. There was no appearance of defying the conditions of suspicion. They were simply ignored by her.

She fell out of the old life apparently completely. She never took up her church connection again. She did not shop in the Fall River stores. She made trips away from home. The time came when Emma Borden withdrew from the home on French street and made a home apart from her sister.

Leaving Lizzie Alone.

After reports of dissension, or disagreement, Miss Borden in June of 1905 had her personal possessions taken away on a van, and she herself went to Providence to live. That was only for a while, however, and probably as a cover for the break, for after a while she returned to Fall River and took up her residence for several months with the Misses Buck, daughter of the late Rev. E. A. Buck, who as a family pastor had sat at Lizzie Borden's side throughout the trial. This home was within easy walking distance, but apparently there was no visiting between them. Later on Miss Emma Borden returned to Providence and made her permanent residence there.

The Borden estate was never settled for separate ownership between them. It continued for years to remain in the management of the real estate dealer who had done business for the father, Charles W. Cook.

Just how long Mr. Jennings continued to serve Lizzie Borden's personal interests can not be said.

Her Later Years.

Though Miss Lizzie Borden's home never became any center of social life, and though her life seemed lonely and devoid of satisfactions, it was not without its interests. She had a couple of women servants, a man of all work, and a chauffeur when the carriage had been given up for a motor car. And these were not without their loyalties in her behalf. When the coachman, or the chauffeur, had been allowed to go, because he was distasteful to the elder Miss Borden, he came back again when his absence was found not to smooth out the tangles, and Miss Lizzie asked him to.

She also had generous opportunities for travel and out-of-town living experiences; she traveled abroad; and she was fond of reading.

The Boston Globe

Lizzie Borden's Ambition

In the latter years of her life Lizzie Borden retained few of her old-time friends, and they often maintained that attitude at some cost in social standing. One of them, who continued to call, said to Miss Borden that since Fall River had turned against her, she ought to pull up stakes and go to a new community and there make her home and her career, with the abundant financial resources which were hers. Miss Borden replied that she would never do so. She had one great ambition in life, which she set forth as follows, according to this veracious informant: "When the truth comes out about this murder, I want to be living here so I can walk down town and meet those of my old friends who have been cutting me all these years."

One may make any of a great many inferences from this observation. The jury acquitted her. Public sentiment convicted her, and in that situation she lived her life. Incidentally, a search for the axe, with which those two aged people met their end, should seemingly have been carried far enough to include the demolition of the old house, if necessary. It was never found. Its finding at the time might have proved a big factor in the settlement of the question. But the mystery remains unsolved.

LIZZIE A. BORDEN WILL BE BURIED BESIDE PARENTS

Open Grave by Father, Mother and Stepmother Reveals Plan as Body Is Being Prepared

ELDER SISTER TOO ILL TO COME

If No Will Is Found, Property Will Go to Miss Emma Borden---Value Greatly Increased

An open grave in the family plot of Andrew J. Borden in Oak Grove cemetery, Fall River, this afternoon revealed the hitherto carefully guarded fact that Lizzie A. Borden is to be buried there, beside her mother, and the father and stepmother whom she was accused of having brutally murdered.

Body Being Prepared.

The body of Miss Borden, who was declared not guilty of the murder by a jury in 1893, but never cleared of the suspicion that rested upon her, was being made ready for burial this afternoon behind the locked doors of her home. That much the presence of an undertaker's automobile outside disclosed. But when the funeral was to take place not even the cemetery authorities knew.

Sister Confined to Bed.

The only near relative of Miss Borden, her elder sister, Emma, is confined to her bed at her home somewhere in New Hampshire and is too ill to come to the funeral, Charles L. Baker, for many years legal adviser to Lizzie Borden, said today. He does not know where in New Hampshire Miss Emma Borden lives.

The sisters, despite an estrangement of many years, held in common the large estate left by their father, which was never divided. If Miss Borden made a will, no lawyer consulted to date knows anything about it. If she left no will, her share of the property goes automatically to her sister.

A single item of the estate, the A. J. Borden block at Anawan and South Main streets, a visit to the Fall River assessors' office today revealed, is worth nearly as much today as the appraised value of the entire estate at the time Andrew J. Borden and his second wife were hacked to death by an ax wielded by an unknown murderer in 1892. This property is listed by the assessors at $341,900. The estate was valued in 1892 at $350,000. Miss Emma Borden disposed of her share in this property four years ago to Jacob Dondis, who has continued to hold it since then.

Another large piece of real estate, a block of dwelling houses and stores at South Main and Spring streets, listed in the names of Emma L. and Lizzie A. Borden, is assessed at $172,600. The dwelling house at 306 French street where Miss Borden died Wednesday night is assessed at $11,500, though obviously worth much more. She was also the owner of a handsome piece of residential property directly adjoining her house on the east, which she bought a few months ago and altered and improved extensively. It is now vacant.

Miss Borden's own house, a big slate colored wooden dwelling set in a tree shaded lawn, is meticulously well-kept and bears every earmark of affluence. Its name, Maplecroft, is painted on the side of the upper step of the stone flight that leads to the veranda.
ter how persistent, go unheeded by the servants who keep vigil within, as reserved about their mistress in death as she was about herself in life.

Praised for Charity.

Near neighbors of Miss Borden, among whom is John T. Swift, treasurer of the Citizen Savings bank, who occupies the house adjoining on the west, spoke only well of her. One had seen her but three times in the past 10 years.

The kindest words spoken of Miss Borden were those of Laughlin W. MacFarland, proprietor of Adams's bookstore, 165 North Main street, Fall River, who said she did a great deal of charitable work in a fine, quiet way and was a fine, cultured woman. She bought hundreds of books from him, he remarked, to give to poor people of the city, and displayed a taste for nothing but the very best.

Mr. Macfarland asserted that many poor people would sorely feel her loss.

A taciturn, "I have nothing to say," was the sole comment of one of the few other persons close to Miss Borden in the years since the murder, Charles C. Cook, real estate and insurance agent. A man of advanced years, Mr. Cook has been agent of the Borden property since 1889 and still has his office in the Borden block.

Had Decided Opinions.

Nurses who knew Miss Borden as a patient at Truesdale hospital two years ago mentioned to their friends, it is said, that she was a woman of decided opinions and will, more masculine in appearance and ways than feminine.

Mr. MacFarland, the bookseller, mentioned that he had been much commended for never having carried in stock in his store the book, Studies in Murder, by Edmund Lester Pearson, published in 1924, which devoted its first 120 pages to the Borden murder case. The book was excluded from the Fall River public library until April a year ago. Since then, it has been practically constantly in circulation until this April.

The New York Times

A Celebrated Murder Case

Lizzie Borden has died 35 years after she was acquitted of the charge of murdering her wealthy father and her stepmother in their Fall River nome. It was one of those broad daylight murders; a whole city was awake. The mystery is still a mystery.

It was a celebrated case, still stirring one's memory with a bare, bleak, gripping horror. It made reputations for at least two of the opposing lawyers—the chief prosecutor, Hosea Knowlton of New Bedford, later attorney-general of Massachusetts, and ex-Gov George D. Robinson of Chicopee and this city, who made the argument to the jury for the defense.

Lizzie Borden, innocent, could not have been glad she was alive these past 35 years. She was a tragic figure to the end. She not only shunned society; society shunned her. Her elder sister, who had stoutly supported her during the trial, separated from her. Miss Borden thereafter lived as a recluse, without friends and without seeking them. When shopping, she was a marked women. Unfriendly gossip ever pursued her. Such a life, for an innocent person, must have been a hell. The injustice of it is a record of a pitiless fate working to no good end.

What was the truth? The story must remain unfinished, so far as human knowledge goes. The last person who, presumably, actually knew the truth, the refinements and safeguards of the criminal law aside, is now dead. Yet no one can regret that Lizzie Borden was acquitted and that she was allowed freedom to the end.

Lonely Woman Rests in Family Lot

The Borden burial plot in Oak Grove cemetery, Fall River, just after the interment of Miss Lisbeth A. Borden yesterday. A workman is tamping down the sod over the new grave preparatory to putting the floral pieces into place.

OLD EMPLOYES ARE BEARERS

Seclusion Marks Burial of Lizzie Borden in Family Lot

Few Intimates at Grave --- Expensive Floral Pieces Abound

[By The Associated Press.]

The seclusion which characterized the last 34 years of her life yesterday marked the funeral of Lisbeth A. "Lizzie" Borden, central figure more than three decades ago in one of the nation's outstanding murder trials.

Funeral arrangements had been kept secret to prevent a gathering of morbidly curious and few who saw a small cortege entering Oak Grove cemetery, Fall River, realized that the woman who was acquitted 33 years ago of the murder of her father and mother was going to her grave.

Simple Service at Grave.

The Rev. Edmund J. Cleveland, pastor of the Church of the Assumption, officiated at simple services beside the grave and in the house where Miss Borden died last Wednesday. Fred Coggeshall, the coachman, Ernest Terry, her chauffeur, Norman Hall, gardener who served the dead woman in her later years, and Eseson Robinson acted as bearers. A little group of former intimates gathered at the grave.

There were many costly floral flifts, but nothing to indicate from whom they came. The names of those who attended the services were not revealed nor could it be learned if Miss Borden's sister, Emma, from whom she has been separated for many years, was present.

BURIAL LOT WELL KEPT.

Plot on Grassy Knoll in Keeping with Miss Borden's Taste.

The Borden burial lot in Oak Grove cemetery is on a grassy knoll, only a short distance from the Prospect street entrance to the cemetery.

The lot and its modest stone monument is in keeping with the appearance of good taste in everything that has concerned Miss Borden in all the years she was chosen to continue to make her home in Fall River. There are much more elaborate burial places in Oak Grove cemetery, but none is kept in more perfect order. The Borden monument is a stone of brownish shade with four smooth faces. The inscription on the side facing to the northwest records that this is the burial place of Andrew Jackson Borden, his two wives and a child who died young. The inscription on this reads:

Andrew Jackson Borden
1822 — 1892
His Wife
Sarah Anthony Borden
1823 — 1863
Abby Durfee Borden
1828 — 1892

On the face toward the west in the inscription:

Children of Andrew J. and Sarah A. Borden
Alice Esther
1856 — 1858

There is ample room below this inscription for the names of the two other children of Andrew J. and Sarah Anthony Borden.

Smaller markers on the lot show that Mr. Borden lies between his two wives, with the little child buried beside her mother.

MANY VISITORS AT BORDEN PLOT

Attracted to Grave of Daughter, Lisbeth A.— Estate Thought to Be Worth About Million.

Many of the visitors at Oak Grove cemetery yesterday were attracted to the Andrew J. Borden burial plot, in which the body of his daughter, Lisbeth A. Borden, was placed Saturday afternoon.

The funeral of Miss Borden took place at her late home, 306 French street, services having been conducted by Rev. Edmund J. Cleveland, rector of the Church of the Ascension. The body of the central figure in the most mysterious tragedies in the history of Massachusetts was laid beside those of her father and stepmother, Andrew J. and Abbie D. Borden, slain in their home on Second street the morning of Aug. 4, 1892. Only relatives and a few intimate friends of Miss Borden attended the services and followed the body to the cemetery.

The grave had been prepared and all was in readiness for burial last Friday, but almost at the last minute word was received that the funeral would not take place until Saturday. The hour of the services at the house was made known only to the immediate family and a few friends, who were asked to be present. At the service, Mrs. Alfred G. Turner sang "My Ain Countrie." The bearers were Ernest Perry, Miss Borden's chauffeur; Fred Coggeshall, coachman for Miss Borden for many years; Norman Hall, another former employe, and Edson Robinson. The floral tributes were numerous.

The estate of Lizzie A. and Emma Borden, daughters of Andrew J. Borden, is valued at nearly a million dollars, the property in Lizzie Borden's name including the A. J. Borden building on South Main street, at the corner of Anawan. Emma Borden sold her interest in this property several years ago. This is assessed for $311,000. Besides this valuable block, the estate comprises business and dwelling houses on South Main street in the vicinity of Spring, assessed for $172,600, in the names of Emma and Lizzie Borden.

The family home on French street, where Miss Borden spent the latter part of her life, is assessed for $11,500 and the estate in addition includes stock in Fall River mills with an estimated value of fully $100,000.

Whether Lizzie Borden left a will has not been made public, but the matter of her estate will likely be placed before the Probate court in a short time, as an inventory will have to be made and an executor appointed.

The New York Times

LIZZIE BORDEN DIES; HER TRIAL RECALLED

Acquitted Thirty-three Years Ago of Murdering Wealthy Father and Stepmother.

MYSTERY NEVER SOLVED

Stoutly Defended by Her Sister, Who Became Estranged From Her In Later Years.

FALL RIVER, Mass., June 2 (AP).—Miss Lisbeth A. Borden, better known as Lizzie Borden, who was acquitted of the murder of her father and stepmother in 1893 after one of the most celebrated murder trials in New England, died at her home here last night at the age of 68.

Miss Borden, who had lived quietly in this city since her acquittal, underwent an operation about a year ago and never had fully recovered.

During her later years she had lived virtually alone and had few if any close friends. So far as known she never discussed with any one the murder of her parents, and her lawyers said today that they knew of no will or statement which she might have left.

The country was shocked on Aug. 4, 1892, when the bodies of her father and stepmother were discovered in their home on Second Street, Fall River. They had been hacked to death.

Lizzie was arrested and charged with the crime. Some of the most famous lawyers of the day took part in the trial. The leading attorneys in the trial are now dead. Attorney General Hosea M. Knowlton represented the State and Andrew J. Jennings of Fall River was chief counsel for the defense.

Other persons connected with the trial also have died, except for a sister, Emma, and possibly Bridget Sullivan, a servant in the Borden home, who was a leading witness and returned to her home in Ireland later.

Andrew J. Borden was a retired cotton broker and owned much valuable real estate in this city. In the middle of the forenoon of Aug. 4, 1892, his daughter Lizzie rushed into the home of a woman neighbor and told her that she had found her father dead in the living room.

The neighbor returned with her and saw the body, then went upstairs and found the body of Mrs. Borden in a bedroom. The autopsy showed that both had been killed with either an axe or a cleaver.

Case Baffled Authorities.

For several days the case baffled the authorities. Finally, building up a case of circumstantial evidence, they arrested Lizzie and brought her to trial in New Bedford. The State sought to show that, in view of the fact that Mrs. Borden was her stepmother, Lizzie feared that she would not get a liberal share of her father's estate upon his death and decided to do away with both father and stepmother, that she and her sister Emma might get the estate at once.

Miss Borden testified that she was not in the house at the time of the murders. She said that Mr. and Mrs. Borden were alive when she went out to the barn to look for some fishing tackle, and when she returned she found them dead. Her sister, it was established, was away on an errand. Emma Borden stood by Lizzie, insisting that her sister could have had no possible motive for the crime.

There was testimony at the trial about a man, possibly a peddler, who had been seen in the vicinity of the house on the day of the murders, but his identity never was established.

Seeks Distribution of Property.

In May, 1923, Lizzie Borden appeared in the Probate Court at Taunton, Mass., in an effort to obtain an equal distribution of the property known as the A. J. Borden block, in Fall River, which she owned jointly with her sister. This was her first known appearance in a court room since her acquittal thirty years before.

In April, 1913, Emma Borden broke a silence of twenty years and declared her positive belief in the innocence of her sister, Lizzie. She said in part: "Often it has occurred to me how strange is the fact that no one save Lizzie was ever brought to trial for the killing of our father and his wife. Lizzie is queer, but as for her being guilty I say 'no' and decidedly 'no.' Here is the strongest thing that has impressed me of Lizzie's innocence: The authorities never found the axe or the implement or whatever it was that figured in the killing. If Lizzie had done that deed, she could never have hidden the instrument of death so the police could never find it."

In 1905 Emma Borden left her sister and made her home with friends, the action causing an estrangement between the sisters. Of this, Emma Borden said: "The happenings in the French Street house that caused me to leave I must refuse to talk about. I did not go until conditions became absolutely unbearable."

So far as known, Emma is the only surviving relative of Lizzie.

LIZZIE BORDEN LEAVES $30,000 TO ANIMAL RESCUE LEAGUE

Mentions Love for Animals in Her Will---Nothing for Sister, as She Is Supposed to Have Enough---$500 Set Aside for Care of Father's Burial Lot.

Taunton, June 7—The will of Lizzie Borden was filed in Probate court here this afternoon. The largest single bequest is one of $30,000 to the Animal Rescue league, Fall River, to which she also leaves the shares of stock that she owns in the Stevens Manufacturing company, Fall River.

In making this bequest she says in her will "I have been fond of animals and their need is great and there are so few who care for them."

To the city of Fall River, she leaves $500 for the perpetual care of her father's burial lot in Oak Grove cemetery, Fall River. To her housekeeper and to each of her servants who have been in her employ for five years at the time of her death she bequeaths $3.000.

In the latter part of her will, she states: "I have not given to my sister, Emma L. Borden, anything, as she has her share of her father's estate and is supposed to have enough to make her comfortable."

Charles C. Cook, Fall River and Tiverton, for his long and faithful service receives $10,000 and also the so-called Baker lot on French street, Fall River. To Miss Helen Leighton, she leaves three diamond rings, a diamond and sapphire brooch, inlaid mahogany desk and chairs in her library and also her library desk and reading lamp.

Miss Leighton is also given her first choice and may take any and all of the rugs, books, paintings, pictures and furniture that she may choose to take from Miss Borden's home on French street. The will also gives to Miss Leighton one half of Miss Borden's share in the A. J. Borden building on South Main street, Fall River. If Miss Leighton does not survive Miss Borden, her share is to be given to Mrs. Grace H. Howe.

To her cousin, Mrs. Grace H. Howe, she leaves her diamond and amethyest ring. She directs that Mrs. Howe shall have the second choice of any rugs, books, china, and furniture. She also gives her the privilege to use her Oak Grove cemetery lot for burial purposes. She also gives to Mrs. Howe one-half of her share in the A. J. Borden building, Fall River.

Other bequests are:

To Margaret L. Streeter, Washington, D. C., $5,000. Also her diamond and sapphire ring with five stones, "which she always liked."

To Mrs. Minnie E. A. Lacombe, Washington, D. C., $5,000.

To S. Howard Lacombe, son of Mrs. Minnie E. A. Lacombe, $2,000.

To Catherine M. MacFarland, Fall River, $5,000.

To Gertrude M. Baker, Fall River, $1,000.

To Mary L. Orters, Charon, $5,000. If she is not living at the time of Miss Borden's death, the sum is to go to her husband, Henry L. Orters.

To Winnifred F. French, Fall River, $5,000; if not living to her sister, Sara H. French.

To Alice Soderman, Fall River, $2,000, also her jeweled watch and chain.

To Elsie F. Carlisle, formerly of Fall River, now of California, $1,000.

To Dr. Annie C. Macrae, Fall River, $1,000.

To an old schoolmate, Adelaide B. Whipp, Fall River, $1,000.

To my housekeeper, Ellen B. Miller, always called Nellie, all of the contents of her room if she wants them.

To Ethel H. Engel, Los Angeles, Cal., $1,000.

To Cousin George E. Robinson, Swansea, $1,000.

To Cousin Edson M. Robinson, Swansea, $1,000.

To Cousin Percy V. Robinson, $2,000.

To Grace L. Perry, daughter of my chauffeur, $2,000.

To Ellen B. Perry, wife of my chauffeur, $2,000.

To Ernest Alden Perry Jr., $2,000, and the so-called Belmont lot west of my house lot.

The Animal Rescue league, Washington, D. C., $2,000.

All the rest and residue of the estate, in equal shares, goes to Helen Leighton, and to her cousin, Mrs. Grace H. Howe.

The will was executed Jan. 30, 1926, and Miss Borden signed it twice, first as Lisbeth A. Borden, and then as Lizzie A. Borden.

The Boston Daily Globe

LIZZIE BORDEN'S WILL PROBATED

Leaves $30,000 to Animal Rescue League—Many Small Bequests

ESTATE THOUGHT WORTH $1,000,000

The will of Miss Lisbeth (Lizzie) A. Borden of Fall River, disposing of an estate estimated to have a value of nearly $1,000,000, was filed for probate in Taunton yesterday.

In it she leaves $500 in perpetual trust for the care of the grave of her father, Andrew J. Borden, for whose murder, and that of her step-mother, Mrs. Abby Borden, she was tried and acquitted nearly 35 years ago.

SISTER IGNORED

The specified bequests total about $100,000, the largest of which, $30,000, is left to the animal Rescue League of Fall River. Amounts ranging from $1000 to $10,000 are bequeathed to cousins, servants, schoolday friends and others; and to a cousin, Mrs. Grace Howe, and Miss Helen Leighton of Boston, intimate friend and co-worker in relief of animal distress, is given not only Miss Borden's interest in the A. J. Borden building in the Fall River business district, but also the residue of the estate after the specific bequests are subtracted.

Lizzie leaves nothing to her sister, Emma L. Borden of New Hampshire and only next of kin, and the language of the will seems to substantiate the story that the sisters were estranged from each other. A notation in the document reads: "I have not given my sister anything, as she had her share of her father's estate and is supposed to have enough to make her comfortable."

No estimate of the value of the estate was filed with the petition for probate, but when the estate of her father, a banker, was entered in probate it amounted to more than $300,000, which was shared between Lizzie and her sister. There is no mention in Lizzie's will regarding the murder of her father and step-mother, in Fall River, in August, 1892.

Charles C. Cook of Fall River, who for years has been in charge of Miss Borden's estate, is bequeathed $10,000 and "my so-called Baker lot on French street," and is named executor of the will. The document was drawn on Jan. 13, 1926, just before Miss Borden was to undergo an operation, and she signed two names, first writing "Lisbeth A. Borden," the name she took after her acquittal of the murder of her father and her stepmother; and directly underneath, "Lizzie A. Borden."

"FOND OF ANIMALS"

In addition to the gift of $30,000 in cash to the Animal Rescue League of Fall River, she gives to the same organization her shares of stock in the Stevens Manufacturing Company of Fall River, and stated: "I have been fond of animals, and their need is great, and there are so few who care for them." The only other public bequest in the will was $2000 to the Animal Rescue League of Washington, D. C.

Miss Borden's housekeeper, Ellen B. Miller, and the servants who were in her employment for the last five years are to receive $3000 each, and to her chauffeur, Ernest Alden Terry, Jr., and his wife and their daughter, Grace L. Terry, Miss Borden bequeathes $2000 each.

Miss Borden's interest in the A. J. Borden building is divided equally between her cousin, Mrs. Grace H. Howe, and Miss Helen Leighton. In addition she left to Miss Leighton "my three diamond rings and diamond and sapphire brooch, my inlaid mahogany desk and chairs in my library, also my library desk with reading lamp; and I also direct that she shall have first choice and may take any and all of my rugs, books, china, pictures and furniture that she may choose."

(AUTHOR'S NOTE:)
On June 12, 1927, Miss Helen Leighton, founder of the Fall River Animal Rescue League, responded to an interview by the Fall River Herald concerning Lizzie's bequest of $30,000:

Miss Helen Leighton Feels Faith in Her Interest in Work Prompted Bequests

Head Says Unhappy Benefactor Not as Friendless as Sometimes Pictured

"Lizzie Borden was one of the first to contribute to the league's work and she was delighted by the splendid progress made by the organization. She personally inspected the new headquarters soon after they were opened and expressed great satisfaction that such comfortable shelter had been provided for friendless animals.

"Miss Borden was most sensitive to pain. She could not bear to see suffering. It distressed her most terribly to see a person or the humblest of animals in pain. It seemed a strange irony of fate that such a tender-hearted, kindly woman as Miss Borden should have been linked in the public mind with such an atrocious crime.

"Miss Borden was bitterly unhappy. Tragedy and sorrow ever overshadowed her. Only on rare occasions did she lay aside the sorrows. These happy and gay moments usually seem to come when she was away from Fall River. When with her in Boston or Washington, there were occasions when Miss Borden seemed really carefree.

"But these moments of happiness were fleeting. Much of the time she was desperately unhappy and she had days of most terrible depression. I know that in later years she questioned the wisdom of having remained in Fall River. She established her home here on the advice of friends, who told her it would appear as if she were running away if she went elsewhere to live. This seemed wise to her at first, but in after years she wondered if it would not have been better had she settled in another place. She felt that every time she stirred from her house that she was a marked woman and it cut her to the heart to be shunned by people.

"She never went into a store in Fall River; the bank was one of the few places she went and she avoided appearing in public. I understand that during her earlier years she used to go to Boston and stay at the Bellevue but during recent years she was more in the habit of making day trips to Boston. She came up frequently to attend the theatre and I often went with her. Her enjoyment of the theatre was one of the greatest pleasures which life afforded her. How she loved to see a good play!

"While Miss Borden led a most unhappy life, she did not lack for a number of warm, staunch friends. She was not as friendless as she has been described. She had at least a dozen devoted friends who did all they could to cheer and brighten her life. Miss Borden was most appreciative of the solicitude shown her and bestowed many, many kindnesses upon her friends. She disliked to accept gifts but could never do enough for her friends.

"Miss Borden had a number of callers and she occasionally entertained at dinner or luncheon. She rarely had house guests.

"She went to church but once after her acquittal, the Congregational church in which she had been an active worker for years. Women drew their skirts about them and turned away from her and men whom she had known for years passed her without a word of greeting. She never set foot in the church again and would not contribute to its support. It was an Episcopalian clergyman who pronounced the last words over her body as it was lowered into the grave at Oak Grove cemetery.

"Many people seemed unwilling to accept the verdict in the case. I often called to their attention that 12 men absolutely unbiased, with all the evidence before them, found Miss Borden not guilty and it seemed to me that this decision should have been generally accepted.

"She gave away thousands of dollars to aid needy cases which came to her attention. She also brought cheer to scores by sending them little luxuries their slender purses could not afford. She helped several young people to obtain a college education. Fond of good reading herself, she saw to it that many persons who enjoyed good books but could not afford them, were well supplied with reading matter. Very few people knew of the extent of her charities."

EMMA BORDEN FOLLOWS SISTER

Dies at Newmarket, N. H., Home Just Nine Days After Lizzie

REMAINS TAKEN TO WARREN, R. I.

NEWMARKET, N. H., June 10—Emma Borden, who shunned the girlhood home in which her father was murdered 35 years ago, returned to its vicinity early today.

She died shortly after 3 o'clock this morning. Nine days ago she learned that her only sister, Lizzie Borden, who was accused of the murder of her father, Andrew J. Borden, Fall River banker, and his wife, their step-mother, was dead. She evinced no added sorrow, nor has she made any further inquiries regarding her sister's later years of life, or her death, or the simple funeral services which were attended only by relatives.

LED SECLUDED LIFE

Emma Borden came here to live down the tragedy and sorrows of her girlhood.

She lived with only one companion. She had no interest in the townspeople, or in anything except the quiet life she was living, and on her infrequent appearances on Main street, she gave no heed to the proffered neighborliness of the townspeople.

Within a few hours of her death her body was prepared for burial, and, was proceeding to Warren, R. I., the nearest point to her old home she ever wished to go. Two undertakers' assistants rode with the body on the automobile hearse; a distant counsin rode alone a short distance behind in another car. The townspeople didn't know until some hours later that Emma Borden had died and had been taken away.

The body was taken to the undertaking rooms of George Wilbur, at Warren. Funeral services will be held Monday at the home of Henry A. Gardner, in Touisset, a part of Swansea. The time of the funeral was not given out. Burial will be in the Borden family lot in Oak Grove cemetery, Fall River, where Miss Borden's sister, Lizzie, was buried last week. The Rev. J. Wynne Jones of Christ Episcopal Church, Swansea, will conduct the services.

Emma Borden came to Newmarket first about seven years ago, seeking quiet and rest, and wishing to forget both the scene of her girlhood sorrows, and the few friends she retained after the tragedy of her father's murder and her sister's accusation and trial. Though she remained steadfastly loyal to her sister during the long ordeal of the trial, and proclaimed her belief in Lizzie's innocence, they became estranged a few years later, and remained apart until their deaths. Emma was too ill to have gone to her sister's funeral, if she had wished to.

She came to the summer boarding house of Miss Alice O'Connor on Main street, for the summer months. A season later she returned and took up her permanent abode in the home which Miss O'Connor had maintained for her. Miss O'Connor abandoned her summer boarding house business to become Emma Borden's constant companion in her own home.

IDENTIFIED BY FEW OF TOWNSPEOPLE

For a time the people of Newmarket didn't know who Emma Borden was. The Borden murder mystery of more than a generation ago was not remembered by most of them, and even when it became known that their new neighbor was Emma Borden, few were able to identify her and associate her with one of the greatest murder mysteries in New England.

Gradually she came to be known to the villagers, but she paid no heed to them. She was invariably accompanied on her walks through town by Miss O'Connor, who volunteered no information regarding her. Occasional visitors from Rhode Island and Massachusetts were accepted as "friends" and no other curiosity was roused.

For several years Miss Borden occupied the "front room downstairs" at the summer boarding house. When weather permitted, she took morning walks through the village and spent the remainder of the day in the big back yard, or in the house, away from the village and aloof from all except her companion.

Her advanced age (she was 76 years old last March) told against her when her health became impaired by reason of kidney trouble. Dr. George H. Towle, who had attended her on several occasions when she was ill, was called nearly two weeks ago.

When her father's estate was settled, Lizzie and Emma Borden divided it. They had real estate and securities valued at more than a third of a million dollars. It is believed that Emma's portion increased considerably throughout the years of her frugal living, but it has been disposed of through a will she made several years ago. Her sister, Lizzie, left her fortune to distant relatives—it is believed Emma named the same relatives. Her legal residence was Rhode Island, and her will is to be offered for probate there soon.

EMMA L. BORDEN IN FAMILY PLOT

Funeral at Home of Cousin in Swansea and Burial in Oak Grove Cemetery in This City.

The funeral of Miss Emma L. Borden, who died in Newmarket, N. H., Friday, at the home of her cousin, Henry A. Gardner, "Riverby," Touisset, at 1'30 this afternoon, with services conducted by Rev. J. Wynne Jones, rector of Christ church, Swansea. The services were attended only by relatives and immediate friends.

It was held at Mr. Gardner's home in accordance with a request which Miss Borden made to Mr. Gardner's wife many years ago. The bearers were colored, also in accord with Miss Borden's expressed wishes. Among the cousins present were Joseph Luther Morse and Jerome C. Borden and family and Mr. and Mrs. Everett N. Slade and Mr. and Mrs. William Blaisdell. Floral tributes from relatives and friends rested on and about the casket.

Requests, made by the Society for the Prevention of Cruelty to Children, Y. M. C. A., District Nursing association and the Boys' club, to be permitted to be represented at the funeral, were granted. The representatives were: District Nurses, Miss Mary A. Jones, R. N., superintendent; S. P. C. C., John F. Hallahan, agent; Boys' club, Thomas Chew, superintendent; Y. M. C. A., Lewis W. Crane, general secretary.

Interment was in the family lot in Oak Grove cemetery. The body was placed beside that of Miss Borden's sister, Miss Lisbeth (Lizzie) A., whose funeral was held a week ago, and at the foot of the grave of their mother.

Miss Emma L. Borden had been able to transact her own business affairs within three weeks before her death and was not seriously ill at the time of her sister's death, according to a relative. The day before her sister died, however, she fell in her home in Newmarket, N. H., and this combined with the shock of her sister's death, no doubt hastened her end, relatives said.

Twenty-two years ago Miss Emma Borden quit the mansion where she and her sister were living and made her home with friends. This move caused an estrangement and since that the two women have not met or communicated with each other.

"Often it has occurred to me how strange is the fact that no one save Lizzie was ever brought to trial for the killing of our father and his wife," Miss Borden said in April, 1913, when she broke a long silence in regard to the homicide.

"Some others have stated that for years they considered that Lizzie acted decidedly queer. But if she did act queerly, don't we all do something peculiar at some time or other?"

"Queer? Yes, Lizzie is queer, but as for her being guilty, I say 'no' and decidedly 'no.' Here is the strongest thing that has impressed me of Lizzie's innocence: The authorities never found the axe or the implement, or whatever it was taht figured in the killing. If Lizzie had done that deed she could never have hidden the instrument of death so the police could never find it.

"The happenings in the French street house that caused me to leave I must refuse to talk about. I did not go until conditions became absolutely unbearable."

NEGRO PALL BEARERS

Carry Emma Borden to Last Resting Place

Funeral services for Miss Emma Borden, whose death followed that of her sister, Miss Lizzie A. Borden by 10 days, took place this afternoon at 1:30 from the home of Henry A. Gardner at Touisett. Services were private and were teanded only by immediate friends and relatives. The services were conducted by the Rev. J. Wynne Jones, Christ church, Swansea. Interment was in the family plot, at Oak Grove cemetery.

Negro bearers were employed, a social custom which had almost been forgotten although formerly followed in many funerals of prominent persons. Miss Borden expressed a desire that this custom be used at her funeral. The services at the Gardner home were in accordance with arrangements made by Mrs. Gardner, now deceased, more than ten years ago.

BEQUESTS OF $100,000 FOR PHILANTHROPY

Will of Miss Emma L. Borden Filed in Probate Court at Fall River.

Taunton, June 30—The will of Miss Emma L. Borden, sister of the late Lizzie A. Borden, Fall River, filed in Probate Court here today, includes bequests of more than $100,000 for philanthropy. The larger part of these bequests goes to Fall River social service organizations.

To her sister Miss Borden willed, if she should survive her, all her interest in the French street residence, Fall River, in which Lizzie A. Borden died, provided she had not previously disposed of it, together with her interest in the property and furnishings. If she had disposed of it, and the sister survived, the sole bequest made to Lizzie A. Borden was the sum of $1,000. These provisos are the only mention of Lizzie Borden in the will. Lizzie in her will said Emma had enough and left her nothing.

One of the most notable bequests is a trust fund to comprise one-fifth of the residue of the estate, the income to be used for scholarships of not more than $300 each to be awarded equally among boys and girls of the Fall River high schools. The Fall River Animal Rescue league, which was a beneficiary under the will of Lizzie Borden, is to receive $20,000 and the income from one-fifth of the residue of the estate. The income of the other residual shares goes respectively to the Fall River Y. M. C. A. for general purposes, the Fall River Home for the Aged, and the Community Welfare association, Fall River.

Bequests of Emma Borden's Will

Josephine Ridlon, Somerset, $3.000 and wearing apparel.
Orrin A. Gardner, Touisset, $10,000, and all household furnishings.
Preston H. Gardner, Providence, $15,000.
Mary E. Gardner, Providence, $5,000 and jewelry.
Maude Preston Gardner, Providence, $5,000 and jewelry.
Charles C. Cook, Tiverton, $2,000.
Frank H. Gardner, Somerset, $1,000.
William W. Gardner, Swansea, $1,000.
Andrew J. Jennings, $1,000.

Trust Funds (beneficiaries all of Fall River unless otherwise noted).

Ninth Street Day Nursery, $4,000.
Rescue Mission, $2,000.
Children's Home, $4,000.
Women's Union, $2,000.
Home for Aged, $10,000 and one fifth of residue.
Community Welfare, $6,000 and one fifth of residue.
Animal Rescue League, $20,000 and one fifth of residue.
High School Scholarships, one fifth of residue.
Animal Rescue League, Providence, $20,000.
Deaconess Home, $3,000.
Y. M. C. A., $10,000 and one fifth of residue.
Salvation Army, $6,000.
Girl Scouts, $5,000.
District Nursing Association, $10,000.
Bishop Stang Day Nursery, $3,000.
St. Vincent's Home, $4,000.
Boys' Club, $5,000.
S. P. C. C., $5,000.
Boy Scouts, $5,000.
Joseph Luther Morse, an annual income of $200.

DEATH OF JOHN V. MORSE

Prominent Figure at the Borden Murder Trial 20 Years Ago.

John V. Morse, a native of Somerset, and a former resident of Fall River, died this morning in Hastings, Iowa, at the age of 79 years.

Mr. Morse was visiting in the home of Andrew J. Borden, on Second street, at the time Mr. Borden and his wife were murdered, Aug, 4, 1892, but was calling in another part of the city when the crime was committed. He was a brother of Sarah A. Morse, who was Mr. Borden's first wife, and he came into great prominence as a witness at the trial that followed the murder.

John Vinnicum Morse, who was the son of Anthony Morse, was born July 5, 1833, and spent his youth in this city. As a young man he was employed for two years by Charles and Isaac Davis, of South Dartmouth, who were engaged in the meat business, but at the age of 22 he went to Illinois, where he remained for 14 years, and then went to Iowa, where he had since lived. His business was the raising of horses and cattle.

Early in his career, Mr. Morse made a promise to himself that when he was able to retire, he would do so, and spend his last days in comfort. He kept this promise, and for more than 20 years came East each summer, to visit in this city and New Bedford. He used to spend much of his time while in New Bedford in the marble shop of ex-Mayor Thomas Thompson, where he and Mr. Thompson had many discussions on the possibilities of existence after death. He was also fond of fishing, and for some years had a boat in New Bedford. He was a familiar figure both in that city and in Fall River.

Mr. Morse was never married. In addition to his nieces, Miss Lizbeth A. Borden, of this city, and Miss Emma L. Borden, of Providence, he is survived by a brother, William Morse, of Excelsior, Minn., and a half-sister, Arabel Davidson, of Hastings, Iowa. Mrs. Louisa A. Morse, of this city, now deceased, was a sister.

In connection with the Borden murders, Mr. Morse used to relate a curious circumstance that came to him while in Hastings shortly before the double tragedy. Mr. Morse had a fancy for having his fortune told. He was in a store in Hastings one day when a gypsy was there telling fortunes. The woman had told a number of fortunes and when Mr. Morse came in he requested that she tell his fortune, offering her the money at the time. She refused to tell it, even though Mr. Morse and others urged her to do so. She finally replied that no money could tempt her to tell his fortune. "You don't want it told," she said, and that ended it; she refused absolutely to say anything. It was shortly after this that the murders were committed. Speaking of the circumstances subsequently, Mr. Morse said he would give $50 to have known what was in the woman's mind when she refused to tell his fortune. He always wondered if the woman had the dark tragedy in mind.

New Bedford Standard

ACTRESS SURE HER OLD FRIEND WAS GUILTLESS

Tall Tragedienne Remembers "Frail, Little Gentlewoman" Met in 1904

SPEAKS RETICENTLY OF SECLUDED WOMAN

Tells of Few Friends Who Were Golden Rift in Leaden Life

By MINNA LITTMANN.
(Standard Staff Correspondent)

New York, June 4.—From the time Lizzie Borden was accused in 1892 of the murder of her father and stepmother to the hour of her lonely death last week at her home in Fall River, few strangers came into her life as friends to replace those who had dropped away from her, chilled by the cloud of suspicion which the court verdict of not guilty could not dispel.

Friends in Memory.

But there were a few, among them Nance O'Neil, famous actress of tragic roles. When Miss O'Neil played in Boston in 1904 her personality and emotional power so gripped Miss Borden that she stepped out of the bonds of her habitual reserve and sought the acquaintance of the actress, then the idol of the city for her brilliant playing in Magda Leah the Forsaken, and other tragedies of her repertoire. They became friends and remained friends, though only in memory, for they never met again after Miss O'Neil finished her season in the East and went on a tour.

Miss O'Neil, the stately, eloquent-voiced woman New Bedford remembers from the three weeks she played with the Hathaway stock company in 1912, spoke, with sincere affection and admiration of Miss Borden when I brought up the subject during a brief call at the actress's luxurious apartment in 55th street this afternoon. She spoke also with reticence.

Actress Loath to Speak.

Miss Borden shrank so from publicity in her life, she said, that she could not feel free to speak in more than a general way of her after her death, despite the fact that her only recollections are favorable ones.

It was an unconscious tribute to the compelling power of Lizzie Borden's personality that after all these years a woman of the impressive caliber of Miss O'Neil should say "I don't believe Miss Borden would like it."

But Miss O'Neil did not hesitate to say warmly that Miss Borden was not the sort of person one could believe guilty of such a crime as that with which she was charged. It was not the unemotional, grim, stocky and stalwart Lizzie Borden of popular conception that Miss O'Neil knew and remembered, but a quiet, reserved, frail little old-fashioned gentlewoman.

Distinctly Attractive.

Miss O'Neil, benig unusually tall herself, is perhaps inclined to see persons smaller than others do. She found the reserved little gentlewoman, with her gray eyes and graying hair and her unmistakable air of refinement and intellect, distinctly attractive. She was exceedingly well read, conversant with the best literature, and spoke interestingly of her travels abroad, which Miss O'Neil recalled as extensive. With her intellectual qualities she combined kindness and thought for others and a great foundness for animals. She was a life member, Miss O'Neil recalled, of the Boston Animal Rescue league.

Th outstanding recollection, the actress mentioned, however, was that Miss Borden seemed utterly lonely. She was obviously always depressed by the shadow of some tragedy, the nature of which Miss O'Neil did not know until some time after their brief friendship began. A note from Miss Borden expresing admiration for the brilliant acting of the star and asking permission to call on her, was the beginning of their acquaintance. With it came a bouquet of flowers.

Circle of Warm Frienls.

Nance O'Neil received Miss Borden, as she did hundreds of others who sought her, in her dressing room at the Tremont theater. Thereafter, however, they met at each other's homes. Miss

Borden was accustomed to come frequently to Boston, to the Bellevue, to enjoy plays and concerts and the company of a few friends, among whom Miss O'Nell recalled Mrs. Mary A. Livermore, and a brilliant woman novelist and her husband, who were not merely friends, but warm companions of Lizzie Borden.

Not Slightest Difference.

The Borden murder trial had been history for 10 years, but it was still vivid in public memory, and some one soon told Miss O'Neil that her new friend whom she knew only as Lisbeth A. Borden, was the woman who figured in it.

"That made not the slightest difference to me," said the actress, looking out earnestly from the shadow of great black hat which shaded her face, cameo-like above a clinging black gown, illuminated by a single vivid scarlet tassel hanging from the waist.

"I want to make that clear. It did not alter our relations in the least. Of course, the tragedy itself was never mentioned between us; never was there even so much as an allusion to it. I simply felt a great sympathy for her, and a great deal of admiration for the way she carried on. She was always so alone."

Golden Rift in Leaden Years.

To have heard Miss O'Neil pronounce in her vibrant contralto, the words alone and lonely as they recurred in her almost reluctant reminiscence of her friend was to realize for the first time with any vividness the extent of the loneliness which must have engulfed Miss Borden, despite the distractions she could purchase with her wealth. The friendship of the actress must have been a golden rift in a stretch of leaden years, though that Miss O'Neil did not intimate. She mentioned that Miss Borden was once a guest for a few day at her country place at Tyngsboro, not far from Lowell. Reports that she had spent some time at the Borden home in Fall River, or that she had ever met Miss Emma Borden, she characterized as in error.

Asked point blank whether Miss Borden ever seemed to her a person who could possibly be associated with such a crime as the murder, with which she was charged, Miss O'Neil's face as well as words answered in the negative. Not in the least could she associate such a thought with the Miss Borden she knew.

Poor Correspondent.

No letters were exchanged in the nearly quarter of a century which has elapsed since Miss Borden and Miss O'Neil bade each other good-by.

"I am afraid I am a rather poor correspondent," said the actress, flicking an ash from her cigarette into a tray of a red Chinese lacquer stand—gorgeous Chinese lacquer and carvings, embroideries and jade dominated the whole room.

"We were like ships that pass in the night and speak each other in passing."

The Fall River Globe

Lizzie Borden's Ambition

In the latter years of her life Lizzie Borden retained few of her old-time friends, and they often maintained that attitude at some cost in social standing. One of them, who continued to call, said to Miss Borden that since Fall River had turned against her, she ought to pull up stakes and go to a new community and there make her home and her career, with the abundant financial resources which were hers. Miss Borden replied that she would never do so. She had one great ambition in life, which she set forth as follows, according to this veracious informant: "When the truth comes out about this murder, I want to be living here so I can walk down town and meet those of my old friends who have been cutting me all these years."

One may make any of a great many inferences from this observation. The jury acquitted her. Public sentiment convicted her, and in that situation she lived her life. Incidentally, a search for the axe, with which those two aged people met their end, should seemingly have been carried far enough to include the demolition of the old house, if necessary. It was never found. Its finding at the time might have proved a big factor in the settlement of the question. But the mystery remains unsolved.

Recalls Lizzie Borden Trial

Ban on Special Privileges to Press at Forthcoming New Jersey Trial Reminiscent of Clash Between Newspapermen and Sheriff Wright Here in 1893

Publication of a story that Sheriff Curtis and Judge Trenchard will not accord special privileges to the press at the coming trial of Hauptmann for the Lindbergh kidnaping, at Flemington, N. J., is reminiscent of some of the difficulties which newspapermen encountered at the trial of Lizzie Borden in this city in 1893. The case of this young woman, charged with the murders of her father and stepmother in their home in Fall River, attracted nation-wide attention, and while the number of applications for press seats fell far short of those already filed in connection with the Hauptmann trial, there was a good-sized contingent that desired to be accommodated.

Sheriff Andrew R. Wright consequently ordered a row of what by courtesy might be termed desks set up on the north side of the court room in the historic edifice on County Street, in a small enclosure devoted usually to deputy sheriffs and witnesses. These desks were merely long strips of wood, mounted on supports that were not especially substantial, and jostled easily when writing was being done. However, they served the purpose. They had accomodations for probably 25 reporters.

The sheriff's idea was to provide seats only for representatives of the newspapers in Bristol County and Boston. He did not propose to accomodate any newspaper men from outside of the Commonwealth, a whim that seems almost incredible. Each of the Massachusetts papers planned to have two men on duty all the time at the trial.

A fortnight before the date set for the momentous event, the sheriff summoned all the allotted writers to the court house to draw for seats. He placed numbers in a hat, and the drawing was held in two rounds, one seat to be drawn at a time. The result was that The Mercury, for example, might have drawn seat No. 3 on the first round, and No. 13 on the second round; and the same for all other papers. Thus the two seats allotted one paper would not be contiguous, and in fact were quite far apart.

This would never do, said the disgruntled newspaper men. Accordingly the suggestion was made that each paper draw for its choice of seats, and thereupon select two, side by side.

But the sheriff at once became suspicious. He frankly said he feared the boys were trying to put something over on him. It took some time to convince him such

SHERIFF ANDREW R. WRIGHT

was not the case. Eventually he was persuaded, and matters were adjusted to everybody's satisfaction.

Then one of those present stated he had been commissioned to draw two seats for the Providence Journal. Sheriff Wright instantly demurred, saying he would allot no seats to papers outside Massachusetts. Asked what the New York papers would do, the sheriff frowned, and firmly declared he would do nothing for the New York correspondents.

Sheriff Wright wore his customary scowl throughout the trial. The presence of copy boys who flitted quietly in and out, seemed to annoy him, although the judges on the bench did not mind a particle. If a paper transferred one of its admission tickets to another member of its staff, particularly a sketch artist, the sheriff's frown deepened, and he at once proceeded quickly to the press seats to engage in an argument with the new-comer, creating a greater disturbance in the court room than any of the press representatives did all through the trial.

All cameras are to be barred from the court room in the Hauptmann case. In the days of Lizzie Borden there were no press cameras, but some very accomplished sketch artists made excellent pictures of scenes in court. One of these, a New Yorker, had a ticket of admission. He was accustomed to range quietly around the room, sketching from various angles. This greatly enraged the august sheriff, though the bench made no complaint.

One afternoon the artist in question was occupying one of the press seats in the dock. For some unknown reason the sheriff ordered him out. The man refused to go. Two stout deputies were called to remove him by force. The artist resisted, clinging to the rail before him. The loud noise made by the tugging of the deputy sheriffs sounded like tearing a bunch of clapboards from the side of a house. It startled the judges, who were paying rapt attention to a witness. The artist had a bottle of India ink in a hip pocket, and in the scuffle this became uncorked, and a perfectly good pair of pants was ruined.

The incident created great indignation among the press fraternity, not a few of whom criticised the sheriff severely in the next edition.

A year and a half later Sheriff Wright again ran afoul of the newspaper men when he refused admission to the hanging of Robinson, a wife murderer, in New Bedford jail, to all but two press representatives, one being the correspondent of the Associated Press. This was the last hanging in Massachusetts, and it also was the sheriff's last coup. At the following election he was attacked by all the newspapers in Bristol County, and was defeated by a large margin by Edwin H. Evans, of pleasant memory.

PARTICULAR EIGHT

THE BALLET - THE OPERA - THE PLAYS

THE BALLET - "FALL RIVER LEGEND"

As eccentric as it may sound, it is possible that Agnes de Mille's 1948 ballet, "Fall River Legend", captured the dark, brooding ambience of the Borden murders and the oppressiveness of Victorian New England life better than any of the novels or factual accounts have ever been able to do.

Except for a single reading of the indictment against "The Accused" in the opening scene, there are no other spoken words.

Combining the sometimes chimerical arts of pantomime, the dance and music, the ballet, danced before stark, minimal sets, transmits a sense of the grimness of that time with a terrifying clarity that words alone have not been able to do. The ballet, with music by Morton Gould, was first staged by the Ballet Theatre at the Metropolitan Opera House in New York in 1948.

The Borden name does not appear on the program; Lizzie is simply The Accused, and, unlike real life, she is guilty of the murders. The story is of an overly sensitive girl, deprived as a child of an adoring mother, held in the bondage of Victorian mores by a tyrannical, tight-lipped stepmother. It is a bleak story of a life, as that of Lizzie might well have been.

The settings of the original production, done by Oliver Smith, were acclaimed as both stark and beautiful, contributing significantly to the aura of suppression. A special effect of a blood-red sky at the moment of the murders was particularly notable.

The Morton Gould score carries moments of singular quality when heard as an independent composition. As a ballet score, it pronounces and sustains the mood of the dance without intruding and dominating the presentation, certainly a challenge to the composer.

Louis Bromfield, writing in Theatre Arts Magazine, said: "The choreography is a singular happy blending of the classical and traditional with the "modern" free pantomimic style...a tense, emotional experience-so intense as to approach very closely the catharsis attained by any fine work of art.".

Miss de Mille's ballet enjoys frequent revivals in New York and around the country, one of the latest being by the American Ballet Theatre in New York in 1990.

Opening scene: Lizzie faces her accusers as she approaches the gallows. Center is her pastor who loves her.

The old stepmother whispers confidences, intent on breaking up the romance with the clergyman.

The murders are discovered by the townspeople and Lizzie swoons as she is confronted with the bloody axe.

THE OPERA - "LIZZIE BORDEN"

As well it should, the riddle and the robust drama of the Borden murders finally challenged the world of serious music in 1965, seven decades after the event it commemorates. In that year, the New York City Opera mounted Jack Beeson's impressive opera, "Lizzie Borden." It was a predestined event; the story demanding to be told in this flamboyant medium. Beeson's rendering of the story draws an intimate portrait of the Bordens, a roundness and a reality seldom found in the medium.

The scenario is credited to Richard Plant; the libretto to Kenward Elmslie. As in the Agnes de Mille ballet, "Fall River Tragedy", Lizzie is unquestionably guilty of delivering the mythical forty whacks and the subsequent forty-one. Abby is now 'Abigail', though Andrew remains 'Andrew'. Lizzie's mother, Sarah, is renamed 'Evangeline' and Emma becomes 'Margaret'. But these are minor things; they are the license of the poet.

There is love for Lizzie in the three-act, two-hour opera as there was in the ballet. In the ballet, she was loved by a minister; in the opera by a sea captain, wonderfully named Captain Jason McFarlane. One feels that Lizzie, aficionado of the romantic novel, would have approved of that.

On its opening, critics acclaimed Beeson's score as "striking", though he modestly said, "The whole focus is on the stage, not the orchestra pit." Irving Kolodin, the premiere reviewer of the day, wrote: 'His treatment of the libretto is...secure in workmanship... balanced in its interweaving of vocal and instrumental values. As suits an explosive story with a predestined blood bath, he writes explosively for the orchestra.'

Beeson, Professor of Music at Columbia University, attended the Eastman School of Music at the University of Rochester, where he earned B.M. and M.M. degrees. He later worked with composer Bela Bartok for a year and Bartok's influence can be heard in his music.

The opera begins quietly, with Lizzie rehearsing her children's Sunday school choir and steadily mounts in fury and intensity to the murder scene climax.

See also the Bibliography at the end of the Sourcebook.

THE PLAYS

The Lizzie Borden story has not been neglected by the theatre, but it has been ill-served.

The most often cited drama written about the events that took place at 92 Second Street on the fourth day of August, 1892, is "Nine Pine Street", written by John Colton and Carlton Miles, based on another play by William Miles and Donald Blackwell. It starred the eminent actress, Lillian Gish. It was produced in New York in 1934 to often scathing reviews and closed, deservedly, after a brief run.

It is part of the literature of the Fall River mystery only by a scant thread. The play touches on the basic facts of the event, but only barely. The Borden family is renamed Holden and the locale is inexplicably moved from Fall River to New Bedford. In the play there is a father, stepmother and two daughters but little attempt was made to conform the story to actual events. The stepmother is murdered by one of the daughters in revenge for her having previously murdered the natural mother. As in the ballet and the opera, there is an unrequited love interest for Lizzie, a minister. The play falls far short of the drama it lightly plagiarizes and is neither drama nor melodrama.

Another play, "Goodbye Miss Lizzie Borden: A Sinister Play in One Act" was written in 1947 by Lillian de la Torre and is remembered here only because Lizzie's name appears in the title. The amateurish skit portrays Emma as the murderer, though Lizzie accepts the blame for reasons not made clear.

In 1975, actress Elizabeth Montgomery, appeared in a television dramatization of the story. Like all other efforts on the musical or dramatic stage, Lizzie was presented as the unquestionable miscreant, portrayed by Miss Montgomery as a dull-witted zombie who tramped naked from room to room dragging a bloody axe she was miraculously able to flush away in a basement toilet. The made-for-TV movie is shown frequently on late-night television.

Other plays may be found in the Bibliography. Most only incidentally mimic the actual events or paraphrase parts of the Borden story.

The author offers no comment on his own play, "Slaughter on Second Street" written in 1991. It will be premiered by the Fall River Little Theatre during the Centennial observation of the Borden murders in 1992.

MARGARET HEWES

Presents

"NINE PINE STREET"

With

LILLIAN GISH

By JOHN COLTON *and* CARLTON MILES

Based on a Play by
William Miles and Donald Blackwell

Settings and Costumes Designed by
Robert Edmond Jones

Staged by A. H. Van Buren

CAST
(In order of their appearance)

CLARA HOLDEN .... *Helen Claire*
ANNIE .... *Barna Ostertag*
MRS. HOLDEN .... *Janet Young*
MRS. POWELL .... *Eleanor Hicks*
EDWARD HOLDEN .... *Robert Harrison*
EFFIE HOLDEN .... *Lillian Gish*
WARREN PITT .... *Raymond Hackett*
MRS. CARRIE RIGGS .... *Roberta Beatty*
CAPT. JAMES TATE .... *John H. Morrissey*
MISS LITTLEFIELD .... *Catherine Proctor*
MISS ROBERTS .... *Jessamine Newcombe*
DR. POWELL .... *William Ingersoll*
LIEUT. MIDDLETON .... *Joseph Hollicky*
REV. APPLETON .... *James P. Houston*
ERNESTINE .... *Andree Corday*
MARTIN LODGE .... *Clinton Sundberg*

SYNOPSIS OF SCENES

The action takes place in the Holden home, New Bedford, Mass., starting in 1886 and ending 1907.

SCENE I. *A September afternoon in 1886.*
SCENE II. *An early October afternoon in 1886.*
SCENE III. *A December afternoon in 1886.*

INTERMISSION

SCENE IV. *Late August morning in 1887.*
SCENE V. *An hour later.*

INTERMISSION

SCENE VI. *Three months later in 1887.*

(NO INTERMISSION)

EPILOGUE

Twenty years later in 1907

TOOK 35-YEAR HOPE TO GRAVE

Lizzie Borden Lived in Expectation of Proving to Sceptical World She Never Killed Kin

BY RUTH BODWELL

"I would give every cent I have in the world and beg in the streets, if it could only be proved while I live that I did not kill my father and my stepmother."

This was the prayer and the hope of Lizzie Borden who died the other day in Fall River after living for 35 years suspected, though acquitted, of having killed her father and her stepmother with an axe.

"BITTERLY UNHAPPY"

Lisbeth Borden, as she chose to call herself after the trial which doomed her to a living death even though it gave her freedom, was not as friendless as some would believe. One of the closest of these friends, perhaps the nearest and the dearest, lifted the veil a little bit on this woman's tragic life yesterday, in an exclusive interview with the Boston Post.

"She was one of the most unhappy women I ever knew. She was bitterly unhappy," the friend admitted.

"She lived always in the shadow of this crime. Naturally a very sensitive woman, the treatment she received from people made her super-sensitive, and she shut herself up in her big house and never went anywhere in Fall River for fear of the jibes and sneers of those who had known her in happier days.

"But it is not true that she was friendless. At least a dozen people were her very staunch friends and did what they could to relieve her life of its burden, for a burden life surely was to her.

"When she laid it down the other day, no one who knew her intimately was sorry. They were very glad that it had come to an end, and knew she was glad, too.

"Lisbeth A. Borden would have been 68 years old next July. She had been in poor health the last two years, having a heart affection, and in that time had lost considerable flesh and her hair had commenced to turn gray.

"Up to two years ago, she had been vigorous and healthy," said this friend whose knowledge of her has been very close and intimate for 10 years.

Probably this woman is one of the only two to sleep under the roof with Lizzie Borden in 35 years, as friend and equal, excepting her sister.

Sisters Never Congenial

"Very few people visited her. Occasionally some one of the friends who stuck by her to the last came there to dinner, but these visits were so few that it can truthfully be said that no one in Fall River of her old-time friends ever went to her home, which was a handsome one on French street, and beautifully furnished.

"Her sister, Miss Emma L. Borden, with whom she was never congenial, left her 20 years ago and the two never met again. Miss Emma Borden was 10 years older than Lizzie and never had they been happy together. The Borden family was not a very happy one anyway," declared this friend.

"Both girls detested their stepmother. Emma liked her even less than Lizzie. After trying to live together for 15 years after the tragic occurrence in their home, the sisters agreed to separate.

"Lizzie Borden managed her life as best she could and she filled it with many things. Not all of it was bitterness nor in any way related to grudges.

"She was a great theatregoer for one

thing. At least once in two weeks she came to Boston to attend the theatre. Sometimes she took in two shows, a matinee and an evening performance.

"She was a great spender also, and liked nothing better than shopping for herself and friends. She made many beautiful presents, but she never wanted anyone to give her anything. She always said that she had money to buy whatever she wanted herself.

Shopped in Boston

"Whenever she came to Boston she spent hours in the stores, though she never stepped into one in Fall River. When she wanted anything there she sent a maid or her chauffeur, so greatly did she fear meeting some one who would show by their actions that they despised her and suspected her of that dreadful deed.

"Her favorite eating place in Boston was the Adams House. She liked good food, but she was conservative and if she changed her dining place, it was to go to the Touraine, or a place of that type.

"Pickwick was the last play she saw in Boston before her death and she did enjoy it, being very fond of Dickens.

Put Pair Through College

"At least one boy and one birl were put through college by her, and in Fall River, where she lived out the dreadful years of her life, she did many acts of kindess and charity. She had a regular list of pensioners to whom she sent coffee, tea, butter, eggs, and other good things weekly. Whether those who partook of her bounty knew who their benefactor was, I do not know, but she did it year in and year out.

"At Christmas she gave regally to her friends. She paid for hundreds of boxes of candy for poor children at the holiday season. Another one of her kindnesses the year round was the loaning of her automobile to take invalids and shut-ins to ride.

Tried Church Just Once

"Just once after her release and acquittal she tried going to church. But never again. She said women drew their skirts away from her and men she knew turned their faces away from her and she could not endure it.

"Aside from visits to New York and Washington, which she made quite frequently and where she had some real friends, and her theatre and shopping trips to Boston, Lizzie Borden lived a quiet, home life.

"She was a splendid housekeeper and took pride in keeping her home. She had two maids all the time, but her house was large and she spent considerable time superintending its upkeep. It was always like wax and was filled with beautiful things. A very orderly person, the care of her home gave her much pleasure and interest.

Loved Dumb Animals

"Reading was another pleasure in which she lost herself. Dickens was a special favorite and good fiction generally commanded her attention.

"Next to her home, animals were her sincerest interest. She could not bear the thought or the sight of an animal in pain.

"The Animal Rescue League in Fall River and Washington are the only organized charities she ever gave any money to and she could always be depended on to give generously and often to the cause of animals.

"One day in Fall River her chauffeur ran over a dog," the friend related. "The animal's leg was broken. She used an expensive automobile robe to wrap the suffering creature in and had it taken to a veterinary. She emptied her purse into the hands of the dog's owner, a poor man driving a wood wagon, and paid all the expenses of his care until the dog recovered.

"She was upset for days over the incident, always was in the event of hearing of any suffering among animals.

Charm in Her Laugh

"While she was never a pretty woman, she had one great charm. This was her laugh. Even under the stress and strain of her life she would laugh when pleased like a child, a bubbling care-free laugh, that forced others to laugh out of joy with her."

Only once during the friendship of this woman for Lizzie Borden did they talk directly about the gruesome murder. One night the woman who was cleared of the murder but always suspected talked way into the night and early morning.

"She said she had a theory—but—'When I know how easy it is to be accused, it ill befits me to accuse in my turn, since I do not know.'

Never Told Theory

"What the theory of the murder was, she never divulged, but she constantly hoped that before she died she would be proven clean-handed in the matter."

Among those who were friends were the late Elizabeth Stuart Phelps, Mary J. Livermore and ex-Governor Robinson of Massachusetts who defended her.

At her funeral the other day there were some 40 people, all Lizzie Borden's friends through thick and thin. Each was invited to attend. There were many beautiful flowers and the service was the Episcopal one for burial, the rector of the Episcopal Church in Fall River officiating.

"Anyone who knew Lizzie Borden could not believe her guilty of any such deed." said the friend staunchly.

God rest you, Lizzie Borden.